THE ECONOMICS OF WOMEN, MEN, AND WORK

D1302674

Sixth Edition

THE ECONOMICS OF WOMEN, MEN, AND WORK

Francine D. Blau
Cornell University

Marianne A. Ferber
University of Illinois at Urbana—Champaign

Anne E. Winkler
University of Missouri—St. Louis

Boston   Columbus   Indianapolis   New York   San Francisco
Upper Saddle River   Amsterdam   Cape Town   Dubai   London
Madrid   Milan   Munich   Paris   Montreal   Toronto   Delhi   Mexico City
Sao Paulo   Sydney   Hong Kong   Seoul   Singapore   Taipei   Tokyo

Editorial Director: Sally Yagan
Editor in Chief: Donna Battista
Acquisitions Editor: Chris Rogers
Editorial Project Manager: Susie Abraham
Director of Marketing: Patrice Jones
Marketing Manager: Elizabeth Averbeck
Marketing Assistant: Ian Gold
Project Manager: Renata Butera
Creative Art Director: Jayne Conte

Cover Designer: Bruce Kenselaar
Manager, Rights and Permissions: Charles Morris
Cover Art: Getty Images, Inc.
Full-Service Project Management: Chitra Ganesan
Composition: GGS Higher Education Resources, A division of PreMedia Global Inc.
Printer/Binder: Bind-Rite Graphics
Cover Printer: Bind-Rite Graphics
Text Font: Palatino

Credits and acknowledgments borrowed from other sources and reproduced, with permission, in this textbook appear on appropriate page within text.

Prentice Hall
is an imprint of

10 9 8 7 6 5 4 3 2 1
ISBN 10:   0-13-702436-3
ISBN 13: 978-0-13-702436-0

BRIEF CONTENTS

CONTENTS

PREFACE

We wrote *The Economics of Women, Men, and Work* because we saw a need for a text that would acquaint students with the findings of research on women, men, and work in the labor market and the household. We are extremely gratified on the publication of the sixth edition to reflect that this belief was justified, and hope that this fully revised and updated edition will serve as effectively as the earlier editions.

OVERVIEW OF THE TEXT

The book is written at a level that should both utilize and enhance students' knowledge of economic concepts and analysis but do so in terms intelligible to those not versed in advanced theory. Even though we assume a knowledge of introductory economics on the part of the reader, an interested and determined individual wanting to learn more about the economic status of women as compared to men could benefit considerably from the material offered here. The book also draws upon research in the other social sciences. The text, used in its entirety, is primarily intended for courses specifically concerned with the economic status of women. However, this book could be used to good advantage in interdisciplinary women's studies courses, as well as courses in economic problems, general labor economics courses, and courses on the economics of the family. In addition, it would serve as a useful reference work for those not already familiar with the rapidly growing body of literature on the economics of gender or those seeking to supplement their knowledge from a comprehensive source, as well as for practicing economists looking for a single volume on this topic.

WHAT'S NEW IN THIS EDITION

The sixth edition reflects the numerous changes in the labor market and in the family that have occurred in recent years. All data and tables have been updated and discussions and references take into account the most recent research on each subject covered. As in the recent prior editions, questions are provided at the end of each chapter to review major concepts and to stimulate further discussion among students and instructors. Key features of the sixth edition include the following:

- As in the past, we thoroughly review trends in the labor supply of women and men to the market. In Chapter 4, we summarize these trends and provide some analysis of important recent developments including the large increase in labor force participation of single mothers since the mid-1990s. The leveling off of the participation rates of married women is also highlighted.
- To assist students' learning we have included several new features. Key terms have been added to the end of each chapter to help students identify and learn major concepts. We have also added internet-based data questions to Chapters 4, 5, and 10. These provide students with an opportunity to learn more about the sources of much of the data discussed in the text and to locate the most recent figures. In addition, Chapter 6 includes a new inset on how to calculate the net present value of an educational investment so that students can obtain a more concrete understanding of this concept.
- In examining human capital in Chapter 6, we present the latest research evidence on young women's performance on math exams in the United States and examine the extent to which their performance is affected by cultural

forces, drawing upon research findings on women's math performance in other nations.

- We present an analysis of the reasons for the gender wage gap in Chapters 6 and 7, as well as a summary of research on the sources of convergence in the gender-wage gap in recent decades in Chapter 8.

- We also highlight other important recent developments in the labor market and their consequences for women and men. These developments include the increasingly divergent outcomes for individuals and families by level of educational attainment, including the continuing employment problems of less-educated men, as well as growing wage inequality, and changes in welfare policy that moved greater numbers of welfare recipients, largely single mothers, into the labor force. Each chapter reflects these changes as relevant, and Chapter 8, "Recent Developments in Earnings," Chapter 9, "Recent Employment Trends," as well as Chapter 11, "Policies Affecting Paid Work and the Family," focus specifically on these developments.

- We devote considerable attention to changes within married-couple families as well as to changing family structure and the implications of these shifts for labor market outcomes. Chapter 3, which focuses on nonmarket work, includes new data on the allocation of housework between women and men and provides an expanded discussion of the usefulness and importance of collecting time use data on nonmarket activities. It also discusses trends in time spent with children, which is of interest, both in terms of its implications for time spent in nonmarket work and its potential implications for children's development. Further, as in earlier editions, this chapter considers alternatives to the standard economic approach, including the transaction cost approach and bargaining models, as well as a discussion of the Marxist and radical feminist views of decision making in the family.

- Chapter 10 examines trends in marriage, divorce, and overall fertility, along with trends in births to unmarried mothers, teen births, cohabitation, and same-sex relationships. The chapter also devotes considerable attention to the implications of the large increases in the number of dual-earner, married-couple families, and single-parent families for children's outcomes. This edition also discusses the state of marriage in the United States in the late 2000s, including the legal status of same-sex marriage.

- All discussions concerning policy have been thoroughly revised. In Chapter 7, we discuss recent developments concerning affirmative action and equal employment opportunity court decisions, as well as findings regarding the effectiveness of antidiscrimination legislation. Updated discussions of policies that affect paid work and the family in Chapter 11 focus on three broad policy areas: (1) policies to alleviate poverty, including the Temporary Assistance for Needy Families (TANF) program, the Earned Income Tax Credit (EITC), and child support enforcement; (2) government tax policies; and (3) policies designed to help workers and their families balance the dual demands of paid work and family responsibilities. The chapter includes evidence on the effects of welfare reform on labor market and family outcomes, as well as a discussion of recent government efforts to promote marriage. In addition, the text discusses U.S. income tax polices in the late 2000s and their effect on the marriage penalty and labor force participation.

- Finally, Chapter 12 offers extensive revisions of the discussion of gender differences from an international perspective. As in the earlier editions, it considers differences in women's status across broad regions of the world, then compares the United States with a number of other economically advanced nations, especially Sweden and Japan, with respect to labor force participation, the gender wage gap, occupations, sharing of housework, and demographic trends. This chapter also specifically looks at the situation of women in developing countries, highlighting the difficulties they face as well as the progress they have made, and briefly considers the problems of women living in the countries of the former Soviet bloc. New to this edition, we have added a section on women's economic status in the countries of the Middle East and North Africa.

ACKNOWLEDGMENTS

We each have considerable experience teaching courses on the economics of gender and we wish to acknowledge that this book has benefited from this experience and the insights we have gained from our students. In addition, over the years, a large and diverse group of colleagues, from a number of disciplines, have contributed material and provided valuable comments on the various editions. We would like to warmly acknowledge their contributions, including a few who have since passed away.

Deborah Anderson
Orley C. Ashenfelter, Princeton University
Nancy S. Barrett, Western Michigan University, Kalamazoo
Andrea H. Beller, University of Illinois, Urbana–Champaign
Lourdes Beneria, Cornell University
Gunseli Berik, University of Utah
Barbara R. Bergmann, American University
Sherrilyn Billger, Illinois State University
Judy Bowman, Baylor University
Charles Brown, University of Michigan
Clair Brown, University of California, Berkeley
Michael Brun, University of Illinois, Urbana–Champaign and Illinois State University
Mary Corcoran, University of Michigan
P. Mitchell Downey, University of Missouri–St. Louis
Greg J. Duncan, Northwestern University
Margaret C. Dunkle, American Association of University Women, Educational Foundation
Cristina Echevarria, University of Saskatchewan
Paula England, Stanford University
Robert Fairlie, University of California, Santa Cruz
Belton M. Fleisher, Ohio State University
David Gillette, Truman State University
Claudia D. Goldin, Harvard University
Janet Gornick, Baruch College, City University of New York
Ulla Grapard, Colgate University
Shoshana Grossbard–Schechtman, San Diego State University
Daniel S. Hamermesh, University of Texas, Austin
Francis Horvath, Bureau of Labor Statistics
Michele Hoyman, University of North Carolina–Chapel Hill
Joan A. Huber, Ohio State University
Randy Ilg, Bureau of Labor Statistics
Thomas R. Ireland, University of Missouri–St. Louis
Debra Israel, Indiana State University
John Johnson IV, University of Illinois, Urbana–Champaign
Heather Joshi, City University, London
Joan R. Kahn, University of Maryland
Lawrence M. Kahn, Cornell University
Lisa Blau Kahn, Yale University
Kristen Keith, University of Toledo
Mark R. Killingsworth, Rutgers University
Andrew Kohen, James Madison University

Marcia Brumit Kropf, Girls Incorporated
Fidan Kurtulus, University of Massachusetts, Amherst
Pareena Lawrence, University of Minnesota
Phil Levine, Wellesley College
Hilarie Lieb, Northwestern University
Shelly J. Lundberg, University of Washington, Seattle
Julie A. Matthaei, Wellesley College
Ann Davis, Marist College
Joan Moriarty, UNITE HERE
Janet Norwood, Urban Institute
Elizabeth Peters, Cornell University
Leila Pratt, University of Tennessee at Chattanooga
Harriet B. Presser, University of Maryland
Barbara B. Reagan, Southern Methodist University
Barbara F. Reskin, University of Washington, Seattle
Patricia A. Roos, State University of New York, Stony Brook
Elaina Rose, University of Washington, Seattle
Steven H. Sandell, U.S. Department of Health and Human Services
Lisa Saunders, University of Massachusetts, Amherst
Richard Stratton, University of Akron
Myra H. Strober, Stanford University
Louise A. Tilly, New School University
Donald J. Treiman, University of California, Los Angeles
Jane Waldfogel, Columbia University
Alison Wellington, The College of Wooster
Herbert D. Werner, University of Missouri–St. Louis
H. F. (Bill) Williamson, University of Illinois, Urbana–Champaign
Frances Woolley, Carleton University, Ottawa

Without their help, this book would have had many more deficiencies. For those that remain, as well as for all opinions expressed, we, of course, take complete responsibility.

This list of acknowledgments would be incomplete if we did not also thank Peter Brummond, P. Mitchell Downey, Albert Yung-Hsu Liu, Caralyn Olie, and Lauren Wein, the extremely able research assistants who helped us track down sources and references and prepare tables and graphs for this edition. Finally, we are very grateful to the team that worked with us on this edition at Pearson: Editor-in-Chief, Donna Battista; Executive Editor, Chris Rogers; Assistant Editor, Susie Abraham; and Project Manager, Renata Butera; as well as for the careful attention to our manuscript by Production Editor, Chitra Ganesan, and her colleagues at GGS Higher Education Resources.

F.D.B.

M.A.F.

A.E.W.

CHAPTER 1

Introduction

Chapter Highlights

- What Economics Is About
- Uses of Economic Theory
- The Scope of Economics
- Individuals, Families, and Households

- A Note on Terminology
- Outline of the Book
- Appendix: A Review of Supply and Demand in the Labor Market

---

Courses in economics abound at universities and colleges, along with an ample supply of texts focusing on the many facets of this discipline. These courses and books increasingly recognize that women play an important role in the economy as workers and consumers and that in many ways their behavior and their problems differ from those of men. However, male patterns often receive the major emphasis, just as patterns of the majority racial and ethnic groups do, while gender differences are, at best, just one of many topics covered. For example, workers are often assumed to enter the labor market after completing their education and to remain until their retirement. Similarly, institutions studied are mainly those involved in traditional labor markets, from businesses to labor unions and relevant government agencies. Although women in growing numbers are spending an increasing proportion of their time working for pay, their lives and their world continue to be significantly different from those of men, and more of their time continues to be spent in nonmarket activities.

Considerable attention has been focused on the increase in women's labor force participation rates and particularly on the changing economic roles of married women. Much has been made, especially in the popular media, of the growing representation of women in nontraditional occupations, not to mention the publicity received by "the first woman" in a given field, whether it be the first woman to win a major car race or to become a strong contender for presidential nominee of a major political party. All this focus tends to obscure both the continued responsibility of most women for the bulk of nonmarket work and the large occupational differences between men and women that remain, despite considerable progress. As long as this situation persists, there is a need to address these issues in depth, as is done in this book.

Although economic behavior is clearly not isolated from the remainder of human existence, the primary focus of this book is on the economic behavior of women and men, on economic institutions, and on economic outcomes. To refresh the memory of students who have some acquaintance with economics, and to provide a minimal background for those who do not, we begin with a brief introduction to the tools of economics. Neoclassical or mainstream economic theory provides the major emphasis of this book. However, students need to be aware that we endeavor to constantly stretch and challenge the existing theories to shed light on issues related to gender and work. So, in addition to presenting conventional analyses, we sometimes offer critiques of existing approaches. We discuss the importance and implications of gender inequities in the labor market and in the household, to the extent they exist, and we make every effort to take note of diversity by race and ethnicity where space permits. In addition, we point to the increasingly divergent outcomes for individuals and families by level of educational attainment. Finally, we attempt to take account of institutional factors, alternative perspectives, and the insights of other disciplines where relevant.[1]

Throughout this book, but especially in those segments where we deal with policy, we are confronted by a dilemma common to the social sciences. On the one hand, much of what we present is positive, rather than normative, in the sense that we present facts and research results as we find them. Furthermore, we try to avoid value judgments and prescriptive attitudes; personal values should not be permitted to intrude upon objective analysis. On the other hand, it is unrealistic to claim that the choice of topics, the emphasis in discussions, and the references provided are, or even can be, entirely value free. A reasonable solution is to try to present various sides of controversial questions, while making clear that different premises will lead to different conclusions and that the policies one should adopt depend on the goals one wants to reach. We attempt to follow this approach.

At the same time, the tenor of this book is undoubtedly colored to some extent by our feminist perspective. Thus, we recognize, for instance, the extent to which persons of the same sex may differ, and persons of the opposite sex may be similar. And, like other feminists, in considering gender differences, we are increasingly aware of how these differences vary by race and ethnicity. Our feminist perspective also means we believe that, as much as possible, individuals should have the opportunity to live up to their potential, rather than be forced to conform to stereotypical roles. Most of all, it means that, while recognizing differences between women and men, some possibly caused by biological factors and others by the way girls and boys are reared in our society, we are less inclined to emphasize the differences between them than the common humanity that unites them.

WHAT ECONOMICS IS ABOUT

Neoclassical economics is concerned with decision making under conditions of **scarcity**, which means not enough resources are available to satisfy everyone's wants, and choices have to be made about their use. Given this constraint, it is crucial to recognize that using labor, capital, and land to produce one good means that fewer of these inputs will be available for producing other goods. Hence, the real cost of having more of one good is forgoing the opportunity of having more of another.

This concept of **opportunity cost** is fundamental to an understanding of the central economic problem—how to allocate scarce resources so as to maximize well-being. In order to make a rational decision whether to spend money to buy a new coat or whether to spend time going for a hike, it is not sufficient to know how much **utility** (or satisfaction) will be derived from each. Because the amount of money and time is limited, and we cannot buy and do everything, it is also crucial to be aware of how much

---

[1] For a feminist critique of neoclassical economics, see Julie A. Nelson, *Feminism, Objectivity and Economics* (London: Routledge, 1996); see also Janice Peterson, and Margaret Lewis, *The Elgar Companion to Feminist Economics* (Cheltenham, UK and Northampton, MA: Edward Elgar, 1999).

satisfaction is lost by giving up desirable alternatives. **Rationality**, as economists use the term, involves some knowledge of available opportunities and the terms on which they are available. Only on the basis of such information it is possible to weigh the alternatives and choose those that provide more utility than any others.

One of the most fundamental assumptions in traditional economics is that people may be expected to behave rationally in this sense. It does not mean, as critics have occasionally suggested, that only monetary costs and benefits are considered. It is entirely rational to take into account nonpecuniary factors because it is *utility*, not, say, money income, that is to be maximized. This definition is so broad that almost everyone might be expected to behave this way. Nonetheless, rationality cannot be taken for granted. It is not satisfactory simply to argue that whatever a person does must provide more utility than any alternative course of action because he or she would otherwise have made a different choice. Such an argument amounts to a mere tautology. An individual who blindly follows the traditional course of action without considering costs and benefits, or who fails to consider long-run implications or indirect effects, is not necessarily rational. Nor is it uncommon to find persons who, with surprising regularity, make choices that they presently appear to regret. Most of us have probably known someone whose behavior fits one or more of these patterns.

These facts should be kept in mind, lest we accept too readily that whatever people do must be for the best. On the other hand, as a first approximation it is probably more realistic to assume that people tend to try to maximize their well-being rather than that they are indifferent to it. We shall, for the most part, accept this as a reasonable generalization, while recognizing that it is not necessarily appropriate in every instance. Specifically, one must keep in mind that the knowledge needed to make optimal decisions is often difficult and costly to obtain. When this cost is likely to exceed the gain derived, it is rational to *satisfice* rather than to insist on maximization.[2] By the same token, however, when additional information can be provided relatively cheaply and easily, it is likely to be useful in improving decision making.

USES OF ECONOMIC THEORY

Assuming that individuals are rational is only one of the many simplifying assumptions economists tend to make in formulating **theories** and building **models**. The justification for making such assumptions is that, much like laboratory experiments in the biological and physical sciences, these abstractions help to focus our attention on the particular issue we are attempting to clarify and on the main relationships we want to understand.

In many instances, the approach is to examine the effects of changes in a single variable, such as price or income, while assuming that all else remains the same. This approach does not suggest that economists believe the real world actually works in such a simple way. An aerospace engineer finds it useful to test a plane in a tunnel where everything except wind speed is artificially stabilized, even though the vehicle will later have to fly in an environment where temperature, atmospheric pressure, and humidity vary. Similarly, the social scientist finds it helpful to begin by abstracting from numerous complications.

A theory is not intended to be a full description of the underlying reality. A description is like a photograph, which shows reality in all its details. A theory may be likened to a modern painting, which at most shows the broad outlines of its subject but

---

[2] This concept was first proposed by Herbert Simon in *Models of Man* (New York: Wiley, 1957). He argued that when the knowledge needed to make optimal decisions is difficult and costly to obtain, an individual may be content with selecting a "satisfactory" alternative—one that meets a minimum standard of acceptability.

may provide deeper insight than a more realistic picture would. Hence, a theory or model should not be judged primarily on its detailed resemblance to reality, but rather in terms of the extent to which it enables us to grasp the salient features of that reality. Thus, economic theory, at its best, can help us understand the present and correctly predict the future.

Economists should not, therefore, be faulted for making simplifying assumptions or using abstractions, as long as they are aware of what they are doing and test their conclusions against empirical evidence, which is drawn from the real world with all its complexities. Unfortunately, such testing is not always easy to do. Computers now enable us to process vast amounts of information, and econometricians have made substantial progress in developing better methods for doing so. The availability, timeliness, and quality of the data, however, often still leave much to be desired.

Collecting data is a slow, expensive, and generally unglamorous undertaking. The U.S. government does more and better work in this respect than governments of many other countries. Even so, collecting, compiling, and making the information available may take quite some time. Some data are, in any case, collected only intermittently, other data not at all. For a variety of reasons, including the government's appropriate reluctance to invade certain areas, as well as lack of interest in pursuing topics with no strong political constituency, some substantial gaps occur in official data collection. Private research organizations endeavor to fill these gaps to a degree, but they are even more likely to be constrained by lack of necessary funds. The data from such special surveys are particularly likely to be collected sporadically or at lengthy intervals. Despite these difficulties, the possibilities for empirical work have improved beyond the wildest dreams of economists of even one or two generations ago.

When suitable data are available, evidence for some relationships can be obtained using such simple devices as averages and cross-tabulations. In other instances, however, sophisticated statistical methods are required to analyze the data. Such studies are time consuming, and rarely are conclusions from any one study regarded as final. At times ambiguities occur, with different sets of data or various approaches producing inconsistent results. Even so, such studies enhance the progress of science and help us to identify important areas for future research.

Because of these difficulties of data collection and analysis, timely and definitive answers are simply not available for every question. We have, however, done our best to summarize existing knowledge on each topic considered in this book.

THE SCOPE OF ECONOMICS

Traditionally, and for the most part even today, economics has focused on the market and on the government. In the market, goods and services are sold. Government is itself a major buyer and seller of goods and services and is also an agent that regulates and otherwise influences the economy. Only in recent decades have mainstream economists devoted any significant attention to the allocation of time within the household itself, and even now such material is not always included in general economics courses. Also, for the most part, the value of nonmarket household production is ignored when aggregate indicators of economic welfare, such as gross domestic product (GDP), are computed. This exclusion is a matter of concern, in part because women play the dominant role in the nonmarket sector. The U.S. government, following the lead of many other countries, initiated a national survey in 2003 that collects data annually on time spent in nonmarket activities. Such data could be used in the future to incorporate household production into some measures of aggregate economic welfare. It also promises to provide greater insight into a number of issues related to how people allocate their nonmarket time. We point to data from this survey in our discussion of the division of labor within the family in Chapter 3.

In its microeconomics section, the typical introductory economics course puts primary emphasis on the analysis of product market transactions with the firm as seller, concerned with maximizing profits, and the household as buyer, concerned with maximizing satisfaction or utility. Later it introduces markets for factors of production, specifically labor, in which the household is generally the supplier and the firm the purchaser. As a rule, however, this discussion is a brief portion in the section on factors of production, and most students may well come away with a view of the market as chiefly an institution where goods and services are supplied by businesses, and the demand for them comes from the household.

In this book, our interest is most specifically in women and men, their work in the labor market and in the household, and the interdependence among individuals within the household. Therefore, we briefly review supply and demand in this context in Appendix 1A at the end of this chapter.

In a market economy, the forces of **supply and demand for labor** determine both the jobs that will be available and how much workers will be paid for doing them. Much of our analysis throughout this book will be concerned with the determinants of the supply of labor. We shall examine how individuals and their families decide to allocate their time between housework and market work and how women's changing roles in this regard are affecting their own well-being and that of their families.

Demand is essentially determined by the behavior of employers, who are in turn influenced by the business climate in which they operate. In the simplest case, their goal is to maximize profits, and their demand for labor is related to its productivity in making the goods or producing the services sold by the firm. Thus, the firm's demand for labor is *derived* from the demand of consumers for its final product. It is, however, possible that employers depart from the dictates of profit maximization and consider aspects of workers that are not directly related to their productivity. Discrimination is one such aspect. In this text, discrimination against women in the labor market and its role in producing wage and occupational differences between women and men is another topic that we shall explore in some depth. In doing so, we also take note of the fact that differences exist within each of these groups, most notably by race and ethnicity.

On the supply side, workers may influence their productivity by attending school or getting training on the job. We shall also consider the determinants of such human capital investment decisions and their role in producing gender differences in labor market outcomes.

INDIVIDUALS, FAMILIES, AND HOUSEHOLDS

Throughout this book, we shall at times focus on the behavior of families and, at other times, on that of individuals. A **family** is officially defined as consisting of two or more persons, related by blood, marriage, or adoption, living in the same household.[3] It is, of course, the individual who, in the last analysis, consumes commodities and supplies labor. Nonetheless, it is often appropriate to treat the family as the relevant economic unit because decisions of various members within a family are interdependent, much of their consumption is joint, and it is common for them to pool income. At the same time, it is important not to lose sight of the fact that the composition of families changes as individuals move in and out and that the interests of family members may diverge to a

---

[3] This official definition is used in government statistics. The typical nuclear family is composed of married parents and children, but single-parent families are becoming increasingly common. An extended family, a type of unit more common in some other societies, may include grandparents, uncles, aunts, and other relatives. Cohabiting couples, who are also growing more prevalent, are not included in the official definition of a family. Also, same-sex couples are not permitted to be legally married in most states and hence are not recognized as a "family" in government statistics.

greater or lesser extent. We shall return to these issues throughout this book as we discuss the status of women and men within the family and in the labor market.

The broader concept of the **household** is also relevant to economic decision making and is becoming increasingly more so. A household consists of one or more persons living in one dwelling unit and sharing living expenses. Thus, all families are households, but one-person households, or those composed of unrelated individuals, are not families. The term *household* is more general than *family* and does greater justice to the increasing prevalence of alternative living arrangements; however, because families still constitute a substantial majority of households that include more than one person, and because the term *family* is more familiar and connotes a more uniform set of relationships, in this book we choose to use it primarily.

A NOTE ON TERMINOLOGY

Traditionally the terms *sex* and *gender* were used interchangeably to refer to the biological and social differences between women and men. More recently, it has become increasingly common to use the term *sex* to refer to the biological differences between males and females, and *gender* to encompass the distinctions society has erected on this biological base.[4] Thus, *gender* connotes a cultural or social construct, including distinctions in roles and behaviors as well as mental and emotional characteristics.[5] We see enough merit in this distinction between sex and gender that we have generally observed it in writing this book.

The question of appropriate language also arises with respect to racial and ethnic groups. Historically, people of African origin in the United States were generally called *Negroes*. Several decades ago the term *black* came into use, followed more recently by *African American*. For purposes of this book, we generally use *black*, mainly because *black* is the term that continues to be used in the official government statistics on which we frequently rely. For the same reason, and to keep terminology consistent in the text, we use the term *Hispanic* rather than other alternatives such as *Latino*. In government statistics, race and ethnicity are identified as separate categories. In recent years, the Census Bureau and the Department of Labor have, in some cases, made available data for the category "white, Non-Hispanic." Where feasible, we provide statistics on this group because it provides a sharper comparison group for examining how minority groups are faring. The broad category of "white," includes persons of Hispanic and non-Hispanic ethnicity. Since most Hispanics are white, the inclusion of this growing disadvantaged group among whites would artificially inflate the relative progress of minority groups. Also, starting with the 2000 Census, individuals are permitted to select more than one race group to describe themselves. Due to space considerations, however, it is not possible to fully reflect the rich variation in racial background of the U.S. population. Thus, the figures on specific race groups presented in the text continue to report data for the major race categories of white, black, and Asian (the vast majority of the population) and do not report data separately for those of mixed race.

OUTLINE OF THE BOOK

As suggested earlier, the primary focus of this book is on "economic behavior." It is not, however, treated in isolation from the remainder of human existence. To provide a more comprehensive picture, subsequent chapters will reflect insights from other social sciences, which enhance our understanding of a variety of factors. Such noneconomic

---

[4] Francine D. Blau, "Gender," in John Eatwell, Murray Milgate, and Peter Newman, eds., *The New Palgrave: A Dictionary of Economic Theory and Doctrine*, vol. 2 (London: MacMillan Press, 1987), p. 492.
[5] Helen Tierney, ed., *Women's Studies Encyclopedia* (New York: Greenwood Press, 1989), p. 153.

factors help determine economic behavior and how that behavior, in turn, shapes other aspects of life.

Chapter 2 deals with the historical evolution of the roles of women and men, focusing particularly on the United States. Chapter 3 considers the gender division of labor within the family, with special attention paid to the allocation of household tasks between men and women, as well as to alternative approaches to family decision making such as bargaining models. Chapter 4 analyzes the individual's decision about how to allocate his or her time between the household and the labor market, with emphasis placed on explaining the factors behind recent trends in women's and men's labor force participation.

The next five chapters deal specifically with women's position in the labor market as compared to that of men, beginning with an overview of gender differences in occupations and earnings in Chapter 5, followed by an in-depth examination of the various explanations of the existing situation. Specifically, Chapter 6 reviews the human capital approach, and Chapter 7 concentrates on discrimination as a possible cause of women's less favorable labor market outcomes. Chapter 8 examines trends in real wages by gender and the increasing payoff to education for both women and men. We especially focus on describing and explaining the substantial decrease in the gender pay gap that has occurred in recent years. Chapter 9 rounds out the picture by examining a number of recent employment trends and their effects on women and men, including the growth of the nonstandard workforce, the rising self-employment of women, and the declining rate of unionization.

In Chapters 10 and 11, we return to the economics of the family. Chapter 10 examines the impact of women's employment on family structure and on the well-being of family members, with special attention paid to the growing number of dual-earner and single-parent families. Chapter 11 looks at a variety of policies affecting paid work and families, including those designed to alleviate poverty, government tax policies, and the growing number of "family-friendly" policies designed to assist individuals in balancing paid work and family responsibilities.

Finally, in Chapter 12, we compare the economic status of women relative to men throughout the world, with special emphasis on similarities and differences between the United States and other economically advanced nations. We next examine issues concerning women and economic development and conclude by looking at the economic status of women in two parts of the world: the countries of the former Soviet bloc and the countries of the Middle East and North Africa. Substantial differences in the behaviors and economic status of men and women across countries suggest that particular outcomes are not inevitable but rather are subject to choice. In instances where a country appears to have impressive achievements in gender equality to its credit, we may be able to learn from the experiences there.

APPENDIX 1A

A Review of Supply and Demand in the Labor Market

As we explained in Chapter 1, supply and demand provide economists with a framework for analyzing labor markets. We briefly review these concepts here in the context of a particular type of labor, clerical workers.

Curve *DD* in Figure 1-1 shows the typical downward-sloping **demand curve**. Wage rate (price) is on the vertical axis, and quantity (number of workers) is on the horizontal axis. The demand curve represents the various amounts of labor that would be hired at various wages by firms in this labor market over a given period of time. If all else remains the same, including methods of production and prices of other inputs,

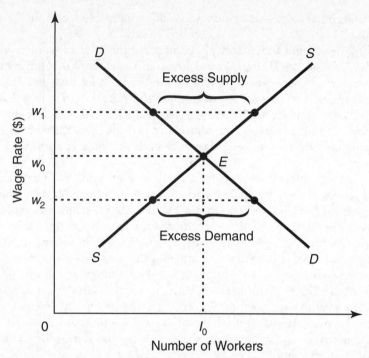

FIGURE 1-1   The Market for Clerical Workers

changes in the wage rate cause movements along this curve. In this case, a change occurs in the *quantity demanded*, but demand (i.e., the demand curve) remains the same. If, on the other hand, other factors do not remain the same, the entire demand curve may shift.

Demand curves are normally expected to slope downward to the right, which means that the firm will hire more workers at a lower wage rate and fewer at a higher wage rate. There are several reasons for this. The first is that in the short run there is **diminishing marginal productivity** of labor, meaning that additional units of labor provide progressively less additional output when combined with fixed amounts of capital (plant and equipment). Capital can only be expanded or contracted over a longer period of time, which means that the only way to immediately increase output is to hire additional workers or have workers put in longer hours. The second is the **substitution effect**. When the price of a particular input changes, while prices of potential substitutes remain the same, the tendency is for profit-maximizing employers to use more of the input that is now relatively cheaper and less of the input that is now relatively more expensive. In the short run, for example, less-skilled labor may be substituted for more-skilled workers. In the long run, it may be possible to substitute capital for labor. Last, the **scale effect** can operate in both the short and long run. As wages increase, the price of the product will go up, less of it will be purchased, and fewer workers will be employed. The scale effect is likely to be especially large when wages constitute a substantial part of the costs of production, as is usually the case for services. These factors cause the quantity of labor hired to decrease as the wage rate increases, but the movements are along the given demand curve and do not involve a shift of the demand curve.

The **supply curve**, shown by *SS* in Figure 1-1, slopes upward and to the right. It shows the number of workers who would be willing to do clerical work at all possible wages. The supply curve is upward sloping because, if rewards for one type of job increase while those for all others remain the same, additional workers will be attracted from related occupations. So, for example, an increase in the wages of clerical workers may induce individuals who are currently employed in other jobs to improve their clerical skills and compete for clerical positions. Similarly, if pay for clerical work declines relative to others, the quantity of labor supplied to clerical jobs is expected to decline as workers move to other sectors.

It is important to emphasize that the supply curve depicted in Figure 1-1 represents the number of individuals available for a particular line of work. As we shall see in greater detail in Chapter 4, the number of hours supplied to the market by any particular individual may not increase when wages rise. This situation may happen because, at a higher wage rate, an individual who participates in the labor market may choose to allocate more of his or her time to nonmarket activities and the satisfactions they bring.

The intersection of the supply and demand curves shown in Figure 1-1 represents a stable **equilibrium**. An equilibrium exists when all persons willing to work at the going rate are able to find employment and all employers willing to hire someone at the going rate are able to find workers. In other words, the quantity demanded and the quantity supplied are equal at E, and no forces are causing the wage to move from its present level as long as no external shocks take place. In this case, the equilibrium wage is w_0, and the equilibrium quantity of labor employed is l_0. To illustrate why point E represents a *stable* equilibrium, let us assume that, for whatever reason, the wage rate is initially set higher than w_0, say at w_1. At this point, the quantity of labor supplied would exceed the quantity of labor demanded and push wages down toward E. Conversely, if wages were initially set at w_2, the opposite would be true. In short, we have a stable equilibrium when there is no tendency to move away from E. If an external shock were to cause a deviation, the tendency would be to return to E.

External shocks may, of course, also cause shifts in demand, supply, or both, leading to a new equilibrium. Such shocks may come from changes in markets for goods, for nonlabor inputs, or for other types of labor, and they are extremely common. Therefore, a stable equilibrium is not necessarily one that remains fixed for any length of time. It merely means that at any given time the tendency is toward convergence at the point where the quantity of labor supplied equals the quantity of labor demanded, until conditions cause this point to shift.

It may be instructive to consider a couple of examples of shifts in the supply or demand curves. These sample situations can help clarify the difference between factors that cause a movement along an existing supply or demand curve and those that cause a shift in the entire curve. We shall also be able to see how the new equilibrium position is established.

Suppose that the government issues a report on the dangers of credit spending and that, as a result, there a reduction in the demand for such services provided by the banking industry. That is, at any given price of these services, consumers demand less of them. Because this industry employs a substantial number of clerical workers, such a change would cause an inward shift in the marketwide demand curve for clerical workers, from DD to $D'D'$ in Figure 1-2a. At any given wage rate, then, firms are willing to hire fewer clerical workers. This example illustrates that the demand for labor is a *derived* demand: It is derived from consumer demand for the goods and services that the workers produce. A new equilibrium will occur at E_1, where the quantity of labor supplied again equals the (new) quantity of labor demanded. At E_1, fewer individuals are employed as clerical workers and a lower wage rate is determined for that occupation.

Shifts in supply curves can also alter the market equilibrium, as shown in Figure 1-2b. For instance, suppose that the government's antidiscrimination policies increase opportunities for women in managerial jobs, raising their wages in these jobs and making it easier for them to obtain such employment. This change will result in a reduction in the

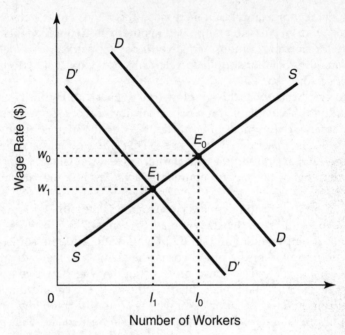

FIGURE 1-2A A Shift in Demand

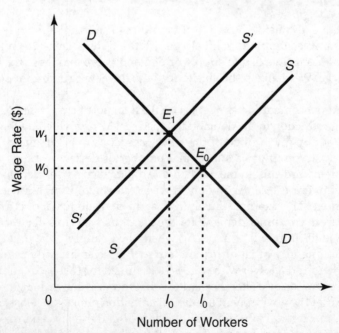

FIGURE 1-2B A Shift in Supply

supply (inward shift in the supply curve) of clerical workers, an occupation staffed primarily by women. At any given wage, fewer women would be available to work in clerical jobs than previously. At the new equilibrium (E_1), the wages are higher, and the number of workers employed is lower than in the initial situation (E_0). This example illustrates that improved opportunities for women in traditionally male jobs can potentially improve the economic welfare even of those women who remain in traditionally female pursuits.

Questions for Review and Discussion

1. Define *scarcity* and explain why the concept is so central to neoclassical economics.
2. In everyday language *cost* generally means the amount of money it takes to purchase a commodity. Can this meaning be tied to the concept of opportunity cost and, if so, how?
3. Discuss the uses and abuses of simplifying assumptions in economic models.
4. Using a graph, show how each of the following labor markets (assumed to be competitive and initially in equilibrium) is affected by the following changes. Clearly explain your reasoning.

   a. Labor market for math and science teachers.
      Wages available in private industries utilizing these skills rise.

   b. Labor market for university professors.
      College enrollments expand.

   c. Labor market for low-skilled workers.
      The 1996 federal welfare legislation requires that a much larger fraction of welfare recipients work than in the past.

   d. Labor market for workers who completed high school only.
      The workplace becomes more computerized and technically sophisticated.

   e. Labor market for workers who completed college or more.
      The workplace becomes more computerized and technically sophisticated.

Key Terms

scarcity *2*

utility *2*

opportunity cost *2*

rationality *3*

theories *3*

models *3*

supply and demand for labor *5*

family *5*

household *6*

demand curve *7*

diminishing marginal productivity *8*

substitution effect *8*

scale effect *8*

supply curve *8*

equilibrium *9*

CHAPTER 2

Women and Men: Changing Roles in a Changing Economy

Chapter Highlights

- The Nature of Males and Females
- The Role of Sociobiology in Explaining Gender Differences
- Factors Influencing Women's Relative Status

- Women's Roles and Economic Development
- The U.S. Experience

> *It seems to me that an economic interpretation of history is an indispensable element in the study of society, but it is only one element. In layers below it lie geography, biology and psychology, and in layers above it the investigation of social and political relationships and the history of culture, law and religion.*
>
> —Joan Robinson
> *Freedom and Necessity**

We are constantly told today that we live in an era of rapid change—change in economic conditions, in economic and social institutions, in mores and beliefs. And so we do. Changes in the roles of women and men, their relations to each other, and the nature of the families in which most of them continue to live take place at an unprecedented speed. This situation inevitably creates stresses and strains. Not surprisingly, people who feel insecure in a world of shifting boundaries and values are prone to look back with nostalgia to the "good old days" when women were women and men were men, and both "knew their proper place."

How realistic is this picture some hold of traditional gender roles, unchanging for all time and pervasive for all places, which is supposed to have existed before the recent era of turmoil and upheaval? The answer has substantial practical implications. If the same roles of women and men have existed always and everywhere, some may conclude that these roles are biologically determined and that they probably cannot, and perhaps should not, be changed. If, on the other hand, the roles of men

---

* Joan Robinson, *Freedom and Necessity: An Introduction to the Study of Society* (London: George Allen and Unwin, 1970), p. 5.

and women varied a good deal over time and space, it is likely that there is also room for flexibility now and in the future.

For this reason, gaining some insight into the nature of changing gender roles through the course of human development is very valuable. Further, awareness of the complexities of history is indispensable for an understanding of the present. It is also crucial if we are to make any progress toward correctly anticipating the future. The following brief historical review shows that, although the rate may have been a great deal slower in the past, change is the one constant. Furthermore, societies throughout time have been characterized by a diversity of economic and social institutions.

We begin by briefly considering the biological and anthropological evidence about the nature of males and females and the sociobiologist's explanation for gender differences. This discussion takes us away from traditional economics but provides valuable background for the historical analysis that follows. Next we consider the changing roles of men and women in the household and in the economy, and the evolution of the family, in the course of economic development through the period of industrialization that started in the nineteenth century. Although other factors are not ignored, economic causation is assigned the predominant role in shaping these changes. Also, the focus is primarily on the United States.

THE NATURE OF MALES AND FEMALES

As late as the 1970s, a common interpretation of the behavior of, and relation between, men and women emphasized the importance of "man the hunter" and of the biological maternal function of the female in determining the nature and content of her being.[1] In this view, a woman's early life is a preparation for becoming, and her later life is devoted to being, a successful wife and mother. Accordingly, her nature is compliant, not competitive; nurturant, not instrumental. Her activities, though not necessarily confined to the home, at least center around it, for her primary mission is to be a helpmate to her husband and to provide a warm and safe haven for her family. If she does work for pay, she will do best in jobs compatible with her household responsibilities and her "feminine" personality. Men, on the other hand, are not constrained by their paternal function from fully entering the world outside the home. On the contrary, their natural role as a provider and protector spurs them on to greater efforts.

Based on this early work, the popular perception was often that male and female roles among nonhuman species provided support for the view that biology is destiny.[2] However, more recent research suggests that no generalization holds for all species and that extrapolation from animal studies does not support the traditional view of male dominance and aggressiveness, or of female passivity and nurturance. Many of the new studies of various animal groups show evidence of "female dominance, autonomy, and power; of male nurturance and cooperation; and of monogamous behavior as well as promiscuity in both males and females."[3] This evidence signals that caution is warranted concerning the argument that any attribute or behavior is always male or female, even if generalizing from animals to humans were otherwise acceptable. Further, such generalization is itself debatable. An alternative

---

[1] See, for example, Lionel Tiger, *Men in Groups* (New York: Random House, 1969).
[2] Foremost among these were Robert Ardrey, *The Territorial Imperative* (New York: Atheneum Press, 1966); Desmond Morris, *The Human Zoo* (New York: McGraw-Hill, 1969); and Lionel Tiger and Robin Fox, *The Imperial Animal* (New York: Holt, Rinehart & Winston, 1971).
[3] Cynthia F. Epstein, *Deceptive Distinctions: Sex, Gender, and the Social Order* (New Haven, CT: Yale University Press, 1988), p. 59.

view is that what distinguishes homo sapiens from other species is that, for humans, it is primarily the norms and expectations of their societies, not blind animal instincts, that are important in shaping their actions and their relations. In this view, biology constrains, but does not determine, human behavior. Human gender roles are no more limited to those of animals than is human behavior otherwise limited to that of animals.[4]

There are, to be sure, physiological and psychological differences between men and women but, it is argued, they fail to adequately explain all existing variations in behavior or why female traits are so often viewed as inferior to male traits. Biological nature, which determines the difference between the sexes, is seen as a broad base upon which a variety of structures, with respect to socially determined gender differences, can be built. This hypothesis is consistent with the diverse male and female roles that sprang up under varying conditions in early societies, in spite of the fact that some differentiation of the work and roles of men and women appears to have been present in all known instances. Anthropologists of this school, such as Ernestine Friedl, point out that women vary in their social roles and powers, their public status, as well as their cultural definitions, and that the nature, quantity, and social significance of women's activities are far more varied and interesting than often assumed. At the same time, other scientists emphasize biology, and particularly the biological origin of differences between men and women, and nature as well as nurture. As a result, sociobiology is once again enjoying a great deal of attention.

THE ROLE OF SOCIOBIOLOGY IN EXPLAINING GENDER DIFFERENCES

Since the publication in 1975 of Edward O. Wilson's *Sociobiology: The New Synthesis*, sociobiologists have followed Darwin's theory of natural selection and have argued that genes determine human as well as animal traits.[5] Their views created a good deal of uneasiness among social scientists, because, in the past, social Darwinism had been used to justify such causes as colonialism, racism, sexism and, at its worst, mass murder.[6] Selective criteria were frequently employed to indicate superiority and inferiority in order to justify the exploitation and subjection of particular groups. For instance, it was after Africans were enslaved to further the economic well-being of their owners that criteria such as skull volume and brain size were constructed to rationalize and justify this practice, while criteria that did not favor white men were discarded.[7]

Recent decades saw much change in this way of thinking. On the one hand, sociobiology today differs from the social Darwinism of the nineteenth century. On the other hand, social scientists who have often been reluctant to incorporate biological variables in their models are now increasingly ready to embrace the notion that

---

[4] This view was first emphasized by anthropologists such as Ernestine Friedl, *Women and Men: An Anthropologist's View* (New York: Holt, Rinehart & Winston, 1975); and Michelle Z. Rosaldo and Louise Lamphere, eds., *Women, Culture and Society* (Stanford: Stanford University Press, 1974).

[5] Edward O. Wilson, *Sociobiology: The New Synthesis* (Cambridge, MA: Belknap Press of Harvard University Press, 1975). For a critique see, Betty Rosoff and Ethel Tobach, "Introduction," in *Challenging Racism and Sexism: Alternatives to Genetic Explanations,* edited by Ethel Tobach and Betty Rosoff (New York: Feminist Press of the City University of New York, 1994), pp. 1–30. Donald Cox provides a useful discussion of how biology may enhance our understanding of family decision making in "Biological Basics and the Economics of the Family," *Journal of Economic Perspectives* 21, no. 2 (Spring 2007): 91–108.

[6] Melwin Konner, "Darwin's Truth, Jefferson's Vision: Sociobiology and the Politics of Human Nature," *American Prospect* 45 (July 1999): 30–38.

[7] Ruth Hubbard, "Race and Sex as Biological Categories," in *Challenging Racism and Sexism: Alternatives to Genetic Explanations,* edited by Ethel Tobach and Betty Rosoff (New York: Feminist Press of the City University of New York, 1994), pp. 11–21.

many patterns of human behavior have a basis in evolution. Many also accept that male and female brains, although similar, may function differently.[8] Similarly, they recognize that although measured attributes of individual boys and girls reveal few consistent sex differences, children show a powerful tendency to seek out playmates of the same sex, and groups of boys and of girls behave very differently from each other, they accept that such differences greatly influence their development.[9] Nonetheless, significant unresolved questions remain. The sociobiological explanation of existing differences between women and men in preferences for mates provides a good example.

Research in prior decades showed that when searching for mates women placed considerable emphasis on finding good providers, while men were looking for relatively young women who would bear children and be good homemakers. Even in the 2000s women and men continue to consider these factors, according to evidence from a "speed dating" experiment conducted in 2004.[10] This behavior may be viewed, to some extent, as the result of different selection pressures experienced by ancestral humans. Women needed mates who were able and willing to support them and their children, while men wanted partners who would bear and nurture their children and also tend home and hearth. By virtue of their youth, women at the beginning of their childbearing age tended to possess physical characteristics that came to be accepted as standards of beauty. Those who conformed to these standards generally experienced greater reproductive success than those who did not and passed their genes on to their offspring. Similarly, intelligence, aggressiveness, and territoriality, "all characteristics of the stereotypical male,"[11] were qualities that enabled the men who possessed them to leave more offspring than others. Hence these attributes, inherited by sons from their fathers who were more successful at surviving and reproducing, increased in frequency in subsequent generations.

Thus, preferences that served their purpose well in the past presumably became part of men's and women's sexual natures and are maintained, to a greater or lesser extent, throughout the world to this day. Therefore, while fully recognizing the complex interaction between biology and voluntarily chosen behavior,[12] sociobiologists generally conclude that, in spite of some psychological differences among individuals, the basic characteristics of the sexes are extremely difficult to change. This view is, for instance, supported by the finding of one study that women who are financially independent are as likely as those who are not to have a preference for good providers.[13] This finding would clearly not be expected if women were merely motivated by rational economic concerns. At the same time, men particularly value physical appearance and prefer mates who are at least somewhat younger than they are.

This sociobiological view of differences between the sexes does shed a good deal of light on the behavior and social organization of animals—including humans. It is not

---

[8] Deborah Blum, *Sex on the Brain: The Biological Differences Between Men and Women* (New York: Viking Penguin, 1997); Melissa Hines, *Brain Gender* (New York: Oxford University Press, 2004); Doreen Kimura, "Sex Differences in the Brain," Scientific American.com (May 13, 2002); and Natalie Angier and Kenneth Chang, "Gray Matter and the Sexes: Still a Scientific Gray Area," *New York Times* (January 24, 2005).

[9] Eleanor Maccoby, *The Two Sexes: Growing Up Apart, Coming Together* (Cambridge, MA: Harvard University Press, 1998), p. 287.

[10] Raymond Fisman, Sheena S. Iyengar, Emir Kamenica, and Itamar Simonson found that men tend to more highly value appearance while women tend to focus on intelligence in "Gender Differences in Mate Selection: Evidence from a Speed Dating Experiment," *Quarterly Journal of Economics* 121, no. 2 (May 2006): 673–97.

[11] Gisela Kaplan and Lesley J. Rogers, "Race and Gender Fallacies: The Paucity of Biological Determinist Explanations of Difference," in *Challenging Racism and Sexism: Alternatives to Genetic Explanations*, edited by Ethel Tobach and Betty Rosoff (New York: Feminist Press of the City University of New York, 1994), p. 76.

[12] Maccoby, *Two Sexes*.

[13] Michael W. Wiederman and Elizabeth Rice Allgeier, "Mate Selection," in *Human Sexuality: An Encyclopedia*, edited by Vern L. Bullough and Bonnie Bullough (Buffalo, NY: Garland Publishing, 1994), pp. 386–90.

surprising, then, that it has been widely accepted not only among researchers in natural history and animal behavior but also among many psychologists and other social scientists. Even so, reservations about this interpretation deserve to be taken seriously, all the more so because neo-Darwinist theory, accepted by Wilson and his followers, often leads to oversimplifications. This is most likely a major reason why it has not replaced other behavioral sciences, but has rather become a small, albeit significant, part of the whole field.

One of the objections to this explanation of human behavior is that it views gene replication as the main or even sole purpose of life,[14] with reproduction taking precedence even over survival.[15] Moreover as a number of authors point out,[16] the tendency is to exaggerate biological differences between women and men, to emphasize distinctions rather than to recognize the many similarities, and to ignore the great diversities within each group. It is, for example, common to stress the difference in means of height, strength, math SAT scores, and so forth, rather than the fact that the range for each substantially overlaps and that the gender difference in math SAT scores has decreased over time. The same attitude is indicated by the use of the phrase "the opposite sex" rather than "the other sex."

An alternative to the uncritical acceptance or rejection of sociobiology is a middle course. This approach embraces many elements of evolutionary theory but no longer imposes rigid limits on social change as early theories did.[17] It accepts the importance of biology without ignoring the possibility that function may to some extent influence structure[18] and leaves room for adaptation in behavior to changing circumstances.[19]

For instance, in earlier days men looked for women who would make good mothers, while women generally looked for men who would make good providers. While as we have seen, these factors continue to play a role today, many men and women have broadened the characteristics they are looking for in a partner. Men are increasingly taking into account women's ability to share in supporting the family, and women are searching for men who are likely to become nurturing fathers and partners in homemaking. This view is supported by findings that male and female preferences for characteristics of mates are slowly becoming more similar.[20]

In sum, all differences in the roles of men and women are not likely to disappear. This conclusion is supported by, among other things, the evidence that women continue to spend a significantly larger share of their time and income on their children.[21] Importantly, however, differences need not mean that superiority and dominance is assigned to the characteristics of one sex, and inferiority and submissiveness to those of the other. It is, for instance, now acknowledged that in some species among primates,

---

[14] Kaplan and Rogers, "Race and Gender Fallacies."

[15] Konner, "Darwin's Truth."

[16] Hubbard, "Race and Sex"; and Blum, *Sex on the Brain.*

[17] This is discussed in Cynthia Russett, *Sexual Science: The Victorian Construction of Womanhood* (Cambridge, MA: Harvard University Press, 1989).

[18] For instance, evidence on the adult brain indicates that it is "remarkably responsive, even in terms of its structure, to experience, as well as to hormones." See Brines, p. 228. See also, Blum, *Sex on the Brain,* p. 41.

[19] See, for instance, Joan Huber, *On the Origins of Gender Inequality* (Boulder, CO and London: Paradigm Publishers 2007) who emphasizes the extent to which women's lives were constrained during the early days when women were pregnant or nursing virtually all their lives and infants were entirely dependent on mothers' milk for their survival. This situation changed considerably with the arrival of bottle feeding and bottle sterilization.

[20] Wiederman and Allgeier, "Mate Selection."

[21] Rae L. Blumberg, "Income Under Female Versus Male Control: Hypotheses from a Theory of Gender Stratification and Data from the Third World," *Journal of Family Issues* 9, no. 1 (March 1988): 51–84; Shelly J. Lundberg, Robert A. Pollak, and Terence J. Wales, "Do Husbands and Wives Pool Their Resources? Evidence from the U.K. Child Benefit," *Journal of Human Resources* 32, no. 3 (Summer 1997): 463–80; and Nancy Qian, "Missing Women and the Price of Tea in China: The Effect of Sex-Specific Earnings on Sex-Imbalance," *Quarterly Journal of Economics* 123, no. 3 (August 2008): 1251–85.

males are dominant by virtue of their strength and aggressiveness, but that in other species females dominate over individualistic males by forming strong group bonds.[22] Nor is there any reason to accept traits of males as the standard and the traits of women as deviant. For example, devoting time to care of the young and the old at the expense of maximizing earnings in the labor market need not be viewed as aberrant behavior. In other words, the most realistic and also the most constructive approach is likely to be one that recognizes the role of both biology and the environment, of limitations imposed by heredity and the opportunities for overcoming them, and of the importance of history as well as the possibility for progress.

FACTORS INFLUENCING WOMEN'S RELATIVE STATUS

In their studies of human societies, anthropologists, particularly women anthropologists who began to focus on this issue in the 1970s, agree that the relative status of women has varied over time and across societies. There is less agreement regarding the factors determining their relative position. Although it may not be possible to definitively answer this question at present, some important insights can be gained by considering existing theories.

Ernestine Friedl was one of the first anthropologists to emphasize the importance of environmental constraints in shaping human organization.[23] She argued that the technology employed by a society to produce the necessities of life has tended, in the past, to determine the division of labor on the basis of gender. In turn, the more important women's role is in production and in controlling distribution outside the family, the higher their status compared to men. Friedl and others espousing this viewpoint to the relatively egalitarian situation in primitive societies where men and women shared in providing food, clothing, and shelter for their families or, in modern days, when both earn an income. In contrast, the status of men and women was unequal in societies where men provided all the needed resources and women devoted themselves to transforming these resources into usable form and creating a pleasant atmosphere in which they could be used.

Others tend to disagree, at least with the emphasis on the importance of production roles in determining status. In past epochs, slaves did a great deal of productive work without achieving correspondingly high status, and members of the upper class derived their power and prestige from ownership of wealth rather than from any work they did. This is consistent with Friedl's argument that property, often inherited or acquired by conquest, gives owners power over distribution and this power helps to determine status.

We are inclined toward the view that the structure of social relationships and participation in productive work both play a role. Specifically, in the case of women, it appears that sharing in the acquisition of resources for the family's needs is a necessary, though not a sufficient, ingredient in achieving a greater degree of equality.[24] Clearly, the extent to which women's activities are confined to the home, while men monopolize the public sphere, also plays an important role.[25]

In the remainder of this chapter, we explore how changing technology and changing property relations affect the nature and perception of gender roles, focusing primarily on the United States. First, however, we briefly consider the issue of the relationship between women's roles and economic development in more general terms.

---

[22] Blum, *Sex on the Brain*, p. 73.
[23] Friedl, *Women and Men*. See also Joan Huber and Glenna Spitze, *Sex Stratification: Children, Housework, and Jobs* (New York: Academic Press, 1983).
[24] Joyce M. Nielsen, *Sex and Gender in Society: Perspectives and Stratification*, 2nd ed. (Prospect Heights, IL: Waveland Press, Inc., 1990).
[25] Michelle Z. Rosaldo, "Women, Culture, and Society: A Theoretical Overview," in *Women, Culture, and Society*, edited by Michelle Z. Rosaldo and Louise Lamphere (Stanford: Stanford University Press, 1974). See also Julie A. Matthaei, An *Economic History of Women in America* (New York: Schocken Books, 1982).

WOMEN'S ROLES AND ECONOMIC DEVELOPMENT

In technologically primitive **hunting and gathering societies**, men and women shared in providing food, clothing, and shelter for their families. Men hunted large animals and defended the tribe, whereas women gathered a variety of vegetable foods, occasionally hunted small animals,[26] and had the main responsibility for food preparation and care of children. Such a division of labor was undoubtedly expedient when women were pregnant or nursing most of their adult lives, and thus could not participate in activities that would have taken them far from home. The greater strength of men also gave them a considerable advantage for such activities as hunting large animals and fighting.

The extent to which men and women contributed to the necessities of life was determined by the availability of various resources, and women's status appeared to vary accordingly. In general, the fact that men provided for the safety of the tribe and furnished most of the meat, always regarded as the prestige food, gave them the advantage. Nonetheless, the common payment of a bride price suggests that women were also valued for their contributions.

In the somewhat more advanced **horticultural societies**, plants were cultivated in small plots located near the home. Men continued to conduct warfare and also prepared the ground by slashing and burning; women tended the plots, prepared the food, and cared for infants and others in need of assistance. Virtually all other activities were shared. Accordingly, men and women tended to be considerably more equal during this stage than in the agricultural societies that followed.

In **pastoral societies**, on the other hand, men tended to monopolize the herding of large animals, an activity that often took them far from home. Herding provided the bulk of what was needed for subsistence. Women's contributions were largely confined to tending the primitive equivalent of hearth and home, and females never reached more than a subservient status.

The situation changed radically when horticultural societies were superseded by **agricultural societies**, which arrived with the introduction of the plow. Although women "helped" in the fields,[27] looked after small animals and gardens, and worked in the now permanent homes taking care of large families, only men owned and worked the land, and the disparity in power and influence became great indeed. The **dowry**, paid by the father of the bride to the groom, who henceforth undertakes her support, and purdah, the practice of hiding women from the sight of men, came into use during that period in some of these societies. Both may be viewed as ways of subordinating women as well as signs of their subjugation.

One factor helped to offset this lowly position for at least a small minority of women. As ownership of land and other assets created an upper class of landed gentry, membership in that class entailed great wealth and power. Under these conditions, birth in the right family conferred status even on women. Property was generally owned and inherited by men, but in the absence of a male heir in a ruling family, a woman might even become head of state. For example, ruling queens included the well-known Elizabeth I of England. In general, however, while upper-class females enjoyed a rather luxurious lifestyle, they were mainly seen as producers of children, rarely had influence except as behind-the-scenes manipulators, and were typically used as pawns in political and economic alliances. Only in exceptional cases did women

---

[26] Some evidence suggests that women may have participated in hunting more than was acknowledged earlier, especially in tribes where group hunting was common. See, for instance, Agnes Estioko-Griffin and P. Bion Griffin, "Woman the Hunter: The Agta," in *Woman the Gatherer*, edited by Frances Dahlberg (New Haven, CT: Yale University Press, 1981), pp. 121–52.

[27] Very poor women also worked as hired laborers and domestic servants.

achieve important roles in the economy and in the development of culture, aided by achieving high rank in religious orders or by the extended absence of fighting men.[28]

Women were also more likely to be partners, though not equal ones, among the growing class of merchants and artisans in the urban centers that began to grow along with developing agriculture. They participated in what were, in those early days, truly family enterprises, generally took charge when the men traveled on business, and often took over after the husband died. Household and workplace were not rigidly separated, nor were consumption and production. Father, mother, children, perhaps other relatives, and often apprentices lived and worked together. Yet their tasks and responsibilities were determined by their age and sex. Whenever the father was present, he was the head of the family enterprise.

As we have seen, women tended to have a higher status in horticultural societies than in agricultural ones, where women's activities came to be increasingly centered within the home. Nonetheless, because much production was concentrated in the household, and because women were active participants, they continued to be perceived as productive members of the family in agricultural societies, albeit not equal partners.[29] There was a further decline in women's status during the early stages of **industrialization**, when much of the production previously concentrated in the household was shifted from the home to the factory and the office. This shift reduced the burden of housekeeping, but since women continued to center their activities around the home, the perceived importance of their productive role declined, as did their relative status. Before long, however, continued industrialization began to draw ever-increasing numbers of women into the paid labor force, paving the way for a "subtle revolution" in gender roles.[30] In the following sections, we review this process in greater detail, focusing upon the situation in the United States.

The case of the United States is in some respects unique, even in comparison to other economically advanced countries. In particular, the frontier experience was shared by only a few of these countries, such as Canada and Australia. Nonetheless, the broad contours of the shifts outlined here are to some extent applicable to many economically advanced countries. Indeed, the alteration of men's and women's work roles that continues in the United States today may be seen as part of a transformation taking place in much of the industrialized world. (Recent developments in other countries are discussed in greater detail in Chapter 12.)

THE U.S. EXPERIENCE

The Preindustrial Period

In **colonial America**, as in other preindustrial economies, the family enterprise was the dominant economic unit, and production was the major function of the family.[31] Most of the necessities for survival were produced in the household, though some goods were generally produced for sale, the proceeds of which were used to purchase some market goods and to accumulate wealth. Cooking; cleaning; care of the young, the old,

---

[28] For an interesting example of the latter, see Robert K. Fleck and F. Andrew Hanssen," 'Rulers Ruled by Women': An Economic Analysis of the Rise and Fall of Women's Rights in Ancient Sparta," Montana State University Working Paper (2007).

[29] Nancy Folbre, *Who Pays for the Kids?* (London: Routledge, 1994), p. 135.

[30] Ralph E. Smith, "The Movement of Women into the Labor Force," in *The Subtle Revolution: Women at Work*, edited by Ralph E. Smith (Washington, DC: Urban Institute, 1979), pp. 1–29; and Claudia Goldin, "The Quiet Revolution that Transformed Women's Employment, Education and Family," *American Economic Review* 96, no 2 (May 2006): 1–15.

[31] A more detailed account of the position of women during the colonial era and the early years of the Republic may be found in Alice Kessler-Harris, *Out to Work: A History of America's Wage Earning Women* (New York: Oxford University Press, 1982), pp. 3–45.

and the infirm; spinning; weaving; sewing; knitting; soap and candle making; and simple carpentry were carried on in the home. Much of the food and other raw materials were grown on the farm. All members of the family capable of making any contribution participated in production, but there was always considerable specialization and division of labor.

Among the nonslave population, men were primarily responsible for agriculture and occasionally trade, whereas women did much of the rest of the work, including what would today be characterized as "light manufacturing." But gender-role specialization was by no means complete. Slave women were used to work in the fields. Widows took over the family enterprise when the need arose, and in early days, single women were on occasion given "maidplots." Even though men and women often had different tasks, and men were more often involved in production for the market and generally owned all property, everyone participated in productive activity. Even aged grandparents would help with tasks that required little physical strength but considerable responsibility and judgment and would perhaps also supervise children in carrying out small chores they could adequately perform at an early age.

All family members, except for infants, had essentially the same economic role. They either produced goods and services for household use or earned money by selling some of these in the market. The important economic role of children, as well as the plentiful availability of land, encouraged large families. High infant mortality rates provided a further incentive to bear many children. In the eighteenth century, completed fertility may have averaged as many as 8 to 10 births per woman.[32]

Wealthy women were primarily managers, not workers, within the household. Their responsibilities were, no doubt, less arduous and possibly more rewarding, but no less absorbing. Most women, regardless of their affluence, experienced little role conflict. The ideal of the frugal, industrious housewife working alongside her family corresponded closely to reality. The only women for whom this picture was not true were the poorest women, who often became indentured servants, and, of course, black women, who were generally slaves. The former were, as a rule, not permitted to marry during their years of servitude; the latter might potentially have their family entirely disrupted by their owners' choice. Both had to work very hard, and slaves did not even have the modest legal protection of rights that indentured servants enjoyed.

The one thing all these diverse groups had in common was that they were productive members of nearly self-sufficient households. Government played a minimal role, and although some exchange of goods and services, chiefly barter, took place, it was not until well into the nineteenth century that production outside the home, for sale rather than for direct use, came to dominate the economy.

Industrialization

During the early period of industrialization in the late eighteenth and early nineteenth centuries, women (and children) in the United States, as elsewhere, worked in the textile mills and other industries that sprang up in the East. Initially, primarily young farm girls were employed in the factories, often contributing part of their pay to supplement family income and using some to accumulate a "dowry" that would make them more desirable marriage partners. The employment of these young women in factories may have appeared quite natural to observers at the time. They were doing much the same

---

[32] For a description of demographic trends during this period, see Karl E. Taeuber and James A. Sweet, "Family and Work: The Social Life Cycle of Women," in *Women and the American Economy: A Look to the 1980s*, edited by Juanita M. Kreps (Englewood Cliffs, NJ: Prentice Hall, 1976), pp. 31–60; and Larry E. Jones and Michele Tertilt, "An Economic History of Fertility in the U.S.:1826–1960" in *Frontiers of Family Economics* edited by Peter Rupert (Bingley, UK; [Cambridge, MA]: Emerald Group Publishing, 2008).

type of work they had done in the home, only in a new location and under the supervision of a foreman rather than the head of the household.[33] Once married, women generally left their jobs to look after their own households, which would soon include children.

Although early industries (these included millinery and cigars, as well as textiles) did employ women, mainly young single ones, the more sophisticated industries that subsequently developed relied almost entirely on male workers. The earliest available data show that at the end of the nineteenth century, when industrialization was well established, the labor force participation rate for men was 84 percent, but only 18 percent of all women were in the paid labor force, and the percentage of married women who worked outside the home was even smaller—only 5 percent.[34]

There were also important differences by race and ethnicity. Participation rates were higher for married black women than for all married women. About 23 percent of black wives were employed; most worked either as domestics or in agriculture in the rural South. In addition, among some immigrant groups, who in the course of the nineteenth century increasingly replaced American-born workers in factories, it was not uncommon for married women to be employed.[35] Most of these people came to the New World determined to improve their economic condition and particularly to make sure that their children would get a better start than they did. At times, the whole family worked. Often if a choice needed to be made between the children leaving school to supplement family income or the mother seeking employment, the latter choice was made even among groups traditionally reluctant to have women work outside the home. By the same token, maternal employment was associated with dire need and was viewed as a temporary expedient to give the family a better start. Few wives remained in the labor force once the husband earned enough for an adequate living. The immigrants' goal of achieving the desired standard of living included what by then was widely considered the American ideal of the family—the male breadwinner who supported his family and the female homemaker who cared for his domestic needs.

Industrialization and the Evolution of the Family

As an increasingly larger segment of the population began living in urban centers rather than on farms, and family shops were replaced by factories, women found that their household work increasingly came to be confined to the care of children, the nurturing of the husband, and the maintenance of the home. They no longer had responsibility for tending a garden, caring for farm animals, or providing seasonal help with the crops. Further, they less often had an opportunity to participate in a family business. As husbands left the home to earn the income needed to support their families, a more rigid division developed between the female domestic sphere and the male public sphere.

---

[33] This similarity was pointed out by Edith Abbott, *Women in Industry* (New York: Appleton and Company, 1910). For a recent discussion, see Dora L. Costa, "From Mill Town to Board Room: The Rise of Women's Paid Labor," *Journal of Economic Perspectives* 14, no. 4 (Fall 2000): 101–22.

[34] All labor force participation figures cited here are from Claudia Goldin, *Understanding the Gender Gap: An Economic History of American Women* (New York: Oxford University Press, 1990), with the exception of the overall male and female participation rates, which are from U.S. Census Bureau, *Historical Statistics of the United States: Colonial Times to 1970*, part 1 (1975), pp. 131–32. As discussed later, official figures undoubtedly underestimate the proportion of women who worked for pay. Not only was seasonal work frequently ignored, but work done in the home, such as taking in boarders and bringing home piecework, was often overlooked as well.

[35] Milton Cantor and Bruce Laurie, eds., *Class, Sex and the Woman Worker* (Westport, CT: Greenwood Press, 1977) contains a great deal of interesting information on immigrant women during the early years. For further indepth discussion of differences by race and ethnicity, see Teresa L. Amott and Julie A. Matthaei, *Race, Gender, and Work: A Multicultural Economic History of Women in the United States* (Boston: South End Press, 1996).

Thus, along with industrialization in the nineteenth century arose the concept of the **traditional family**, which lingered to a greater or lesser degree well into the twentieth century.[36] The family shifted from a production unit to a consumption unit, and the responsibility for earning a living came to rest squarely on the shoulders of the husband. Wives (and children) grew to be dependent on his income. Redistribution became an important function of the family, as it provided a mechanism for the transfer of income from the market-productive husband to his dependent wife and children. Not only did specific *tasks* differ between men and women, as was always the case, but men and women now had different *economic roles* as well. Many workers and social reformers explicitly advocated that a man should be paid a "family wage," adequate to support not only him but also his wife and children.

As we have seen, among the poor, particularly blacks and immigrants, it was often necessary for wives to enter the labor market. But for the middle-class white wife, and even for the working-class wife whose husband had a steady income, holding a job was frowned upon as inconsistent with her social status. If the wife entered the labor market, it was assumed that she was either compensating for her husband's inadequacy as a breadwinner or selfishly pursuing a career at the expense of her household responsibilities.

The status of children also changed. Only in very poor families would they be expected to help raise the family's standard of living, though some might work to earn spending money or because their parents thought it would be good for their moral fiber. Furthermore, the age when children came to be considered young adults and were supposed to become productive members of the family rose considerably. By the end of the nineteenth century, states passed child labor laws that prohibited employment of "minors," and in 1938, child labor was made illegal at the federal level.[37]

As a consequence of industrialization and urbanization, more and more goods and services used by households came to be produced outside the home. Nonetheless, much time and effort were still expended to purchase and maintain these commodities and to use them to attain the desired standard of living. With soap and bleach purchased at the store, and the washing machine doing the scrubbing, laundry became far less of a chore, but it was done far more frequently, and housewives came to take pride in making it "whiter than white." Groceries bought at the supermarket and a gas or electric range made cooking much easier, but homemakers would now serve elaborate meals rather than a pot of stew. To do otherwise would not be consistent with the role of dedicated mother and wife, whose every thought was for the well-being of her family. The husband might help her, but this assistance was never to interfere with his "work." The children, too, particularly girls, might be expected to assist their mothers, but the basic responsibility for the household rested with the wife.

The net result of these developments was that the number of hours that full-time homemakers devoted to housework, more than 50 per week, did not change from the beginning of the twentieth century to the 1960s.[38] Two additional trends contributed to

---

[36] Historian Carl N. Degler termed this shift the *first transformation*. In his view, the second transformation came in the 1940s, when married women began to enter the labor market in large numbers. See his *At Odds: Women and the Family in America from the Revolution to the Present* (New York: Oxford University Press, 1980). It was also during this period that women's work in the household came to be officially classified as unproductive, as pointed out by Nancy Folbre, "The Unproductive Housewife: Her Evolution in Nineteenth-Century Economic Thought," Signs: Journal of Women in Culture and Society 16, no. 3 (Spring 1991): 463–84.

[37] This legislation, the Fair Labor Standards Act, also established the federal minimum wage and rules regarding overtime pay.

[38] Joann Vanek found that even as late as 1966, full-time homemakers were devoting as much time to their work as their grandmothers had in the 1920s. See Vanek, "Time Spent in Housework," *Scientific American* 231, no. 5 (November 1974): 116–20. See also, Ruth Schwartz Cowan, *More Work for Mother: The Ironies of Household Technology from the Open Hearth to the Microwave* (Basic Books, 1983). It was not until the 1970s that this situation changed; see our discussion in Chapter 3.

this situation. One was the decline in the number of household servants, whose presence was not uncommon in middle-class households in the nineteenth and early twentieth centuries. Probably more important was the tendency to use the time no longer needed to produce essentials to raise the standard of cleanliness and comfort the family could enjoy, not to increase the wife's leisure time.[39]

Fertility declined with industrialization, in part because of the diminished economic value of children. With far less opportunity for children to participate in production in urban households and growing immigration, hired workers were more readily available as a source of farm labor.[40] Further, the number of years of schooling grew in both towns and rural areas, so that children remained dependent for a longer period of time. Hence it is not surprising that women born in the early nineteenth century averaged somewhat fewer than five births, considerably below the rate of their eighteenth-century predecessors, and those born toward the end of the nineteenth century averaged only about three births.[41] However, as the number of children declined, the amount of maternal care per child increased greatly, and the number of years of such care was extended substantially.

Responsibility for spending the family's money and for determining the amount to be saved was not as clear, but certain norms were generally accepted. The wife made most of the everyday purchases but was expected to comply with her husband's wishes and to try to please her family. Thus, to some extent, she might be viewed as the purchasing agent rather than an independent decision maker when she did the shopping. The husband generally determined where the family would live and what major items should be bought, such as larger durables and, particularly, the house.

The man's authority as "head of the household" was supposed to be absolute in all important matters, because he basically determined the family's lifestyle by providing the money income on which it depended.[42] Further, the husband's decisions defined the parameters within which the other family members operated. Thus, he was dominant within the household as well as in the outside world. It was, however, generally assumed that, within the family, he would determine how consumption and income were distributed among family members.

As the economic role of women changed within the family, so too did the image of the ideal wife. Whereas the colonial wife was valued for her industriousness, the growing **cult of true womanhood** that developed with industrialization in the nineteenth century equated piety, purity, domesticity, and submissiveness with the femininity to

---

[39] Newly available information has suggested the importance of cleanliness to raising a healthy family; see Joel Mokyr, "Why 'More Work for Mother?' Knowledge and Household Behavior, 1870–1945," *Journal of Economic History* 60, no. 1 (March 2000): 1–41. And, as Bonnie J. Fox points out, advertisements tended to emphasize improved housekeeping standards and better service to the family rather than liberation from household chores; see "Selling the Mechanized Household: 70 Years of Ads in the *Ladies Home Journal*," *Gender and Society* 4, no. 1 (March 1990): 25–40.

[40] Improved methods of birth control are often credited for the declining birth rate, but significant decreases occurred in much of the industrialized world before any major breakthroughs in contraceptive techniques. See Joan Huber, "Toward a Sociotechnological Theory of the Women's Movement," *Social Problems* 23, no. 4 (April 1976): 371–88.

[41] For analyses of these trends, see Jeremy Greenwood and Ananth Seshadri, "The U.S. Demographic Transition," *American Economic Review* 92, no. 2 (May 2002): 153–59; and Jones and Tertilt, "An Economic History of Fertility in the U.S."

[42] See, for instance, Janet R. Wilkie, "Marriage, Family Life, and Women's Employment," in *Women Working*, edited by Ann H. Stromberg and Shirley Harkess (Mountain View, CA: Mayfield Publishing Company, 1988), pp. 149–66. She suggests that "the husband's occupation affected where the family lived, whether they moved, how they spent disposable income, whether the wife worked, and so forth. In fact, the husband's primacy went well beyond this. Men enjoyed greater power in other non-job related spheres of the marital relationship" (p. 151).

which all women were expected to aspire.[43] Their role was in the now consumption-oriented home—as daughter, sister, but most of all as wife and mother. This ideal particularly extolled the lifestyle of affluent middle- and upper-class women, who were to a great extent freed even from their domestic chores by the servants their husbands' ample incomes could provide. Understandably, overburdened working-class women, who often contributed to family income, if not through wage labor then by taking in boarders or doing piecework at home, might come to look longingly at such a leisurely existence as something to hope for and strive toward. For men of all social classes, it came to be a mark of success to be the sole wage earner in the family.

This image of the family was fostered not only by the example of the middle and upper middle classes, which was the envy of the poor woman bearing the double burden of paid and unpaid work or toiling at home to make ends meet on a limited budget,[44] but also by male workers and their trade unions. Initially, the availability of women and children for work in industry was welcomed by national leaders because they provided cheap labor, while agricultural production could be maintained by men.[45] However, attitudes changed as workers became more plentiful with the growing influx of immigrants. Working men were particularly eager to get married women out of the labor force entirely and women out of all but the lowest-paid jobs. Their goals were to reserve the better positions for themselves, make sure they would not be underbid, and give greater force to the argument that a "living wage" for a man had to be sufficient to support a dependent wife and children. Thus, women received little, if any, support from organized labor in trying to improve their own working conditions and rewards.[46]

This was the genesis of the traditional family, once accepted as the backbone of American society. As we have seen, it is in fact comparatively recent in origin, dating back only to the mid-nineteenth and early twentieth centuries. Even in its heyday, it was never entirely universal. Many poor, black, and immigrant married women worked outside their homes; in addition, many others earned income at home, taking in boarders or doing piecework. Moreover, the historical record indicates that single-parent families were not all that uncommon; in 1900, 9 percent of children lived in such families, in most cases with a widowed parent. As a point of comparison, the same proportion of children lived with a single parent in 1960.[47]

Throughout this period, market work was quite common among single women, and a relatively small number of women, particularly college graduates, chose careers over marriage as a lifelong vocation. Nonetheless, exclusive dedication to the role of mother and wife was widely accepted as the only proper and fulfilling life for a woman. It was not long, however, before this orthodoxy was challenged. Progressive modernization brought about dramatic changes in conditions of production and in the economic roles of men and women, followed by changes in ideas and aspirations.

---

[43] Barbara Easton, "Industrialization and Femininity: A Case Study of Nineteenth Century New England," *Social Problems* 23, no. 4 (April 1976): 389–401; and Barbara Welter, "The Cult of True Womanhood, 1820–1860," in *The American Family in Social-Historical Perspective*, edited by Michael Gordon (New York: St. Martin's Press, 1978), pp. 313–33.

[44] As Louise Tilly and Joan Scott, *Women, Work and Family* (New York: Holt, Rinehart & Winston, 1978) forcefully point out, mothers found it very difficult to combine employment outside the home with housework and child care.

[45] George Washington is quoted as writing to Lafayette, "I conceive much might be done in the way of women, children and others [producing yarn and cloth] without taking one really necessary hand from tilling the earth." Cited in Alice Kessler-Harris, *Women Have Always Worked* (New York: McGraw-Hill, 1981), p. 8.

[46] Alice Kessler-Harris, "Organizing the Unorganizable: Three Jewish Women and Their Union," in *Class, Sex and the Woman Worker*, edited by Milton Cantor and Bruce Laurie (Westport, CT: Greenwood Press, 1977) is eloquent on this point.

[47] For an interesting historical perspective on the family, see Linda Gordon and Sara McLanahan, "Single Parenthood in 1900," *Journal of Family History* 16, no. 2 (April 1991): 97–116.

As family size continued to shrink, the amount of time and energy needed for childbearing and childrearing declined. At the same time, women were living longer. Although, as previously noted, full-time homemakers continued to work long hours, thus achieving ever higher standards of homemaking, women had the choice of devoting time to other activities, especially during the years after their children grew up. More and more of the goods and services that were previously provided within the household for its own use were now mass-produced and available for purchase. New appliances facilitated faster and easier production of many of the others. Increasingly, the market also provided many new goods and services desired by consumers that could not readily be produced at home. These developments likely help to explain why increasing numbers of women and men decided that a second paycheck would make a greater contribution to the family's standard of living than additional time devoted to upgrading the quality of homemaking. Other factors, to be discussed in Chapter 4, such as increased education and changes in the demand for labor, were important in facilitating the influx of women into the labor market. However, the shrinking household and household sphere were among the basic developments that made it possible.

ECONOMIC INCENTIVES: AN ENGINE OF CHANGE FOR WOMEN'S PROPERTY RIGHTS

In 1848, in the Declaration of Sentiments and Resolutions issued at the Seneca Falls Convention, Elizabeth Cady Stanton and other prominent women's rights activists set forth a list of demands.* One of the best known was a demand for the right to vote, which women ultimately gained in 1920 when the Nineteenth Amendment of the U.S. Constitution was passed. Another demand was for the right for women to own their own wages and property. For instance, as of 1840, in most of the then 27 U.S. states, wives were not permitted to buy, sell, or own property, nor did they did have ownership of their own labor market earnings. Once women were married, their husbands had legal claim to their earnings and property, under a system known as patriarchal property rights. Only starting in the middle of the 1890s did states begin to extend to married women property rights to their earnings and property holdings. By 1920 married women in all but three states had such rights. What precipitated these changes in state laws governing married women's property rights? This inset draws upon recent research by Rich Geddes and Deal Lueck that points to the pivotal role of economic incentives as the catalyst for change in women's property rights.**

Geddes and Lueck argue that prior to industrialization, economic incentives to change existing property laws for women were minimal because women had few opportunities to buy or sell goods or to get paid jobs. However, by the latter part of the nineteenth century, industrialization was in full swing, cities were growing, wealth was increasing, and a larger proportion of women had some education. As opportunities for women in the market economy expanded, the existing set of patriarchal property rights became, in the authors' words, a "relatively costly institution." That is, without legal ownership of their own earnings, married women had little economic incentive to participate in the growing economy, which in turn, constrained families' potential income. Hence, Geddes and Lueck argue, it was in the interests of both women and men to extend property rights to married women. Further, once married women were given the legal ownership of their wages, this further increased their incentive to get an education, invest in market skills, and participate in the market economy.***

Research by Claudia Goldin on marriage bars—rules implemented by firms that prohibited married women from employment in teaching and clerical jobs—provides another example of how economic incentives can serve as an engine of change for women. She points to the fact that marriage bars fell to the wayside in the 1940s when schools and firms faced a shortage of the young, single women they had traditionally employed in these positions. This shortage increased employers' demand for married women, thus providing an incentive for them to discard their marriage bars. In both cases, we are reminded that economic incentives can be an important force in changing long-standing, seemingly immutable institutional arrangements. Moreover, these examples illustrate that improvements in women's rights and opportunities can benefit society at large.

*Elizabeth Cady Stanton, "Declaration of Sentiments and Resolutions," Seneca Falls Convention, 1848.
**Rick Geddes and Dean Lueck, "The Gains from Self-Ownership and the Expansion of Women's Rights," *American Economic Review* 92, no. 4 (September 2002): 1079–92. This inset also draws on Elissa Braunstein and Nancy Folbre, "To Honor and Obey: Efficiency, Inequality, and Patriarchal Property Rights," *Feminist Economics* 7, no. 1 (March 2001): 25–44; and Claudia Goldin, *Understanding the Gender Gap: An Economic History of American Women* (New York: Oxford University Press, 1990).
***Matthias Doepke and Michelle Tertilt, "Women's Liberation: What's in It for Men?" Stanford University Working Paper (October 2008) provide an alternative explanation for this same change in women's property rights. They argue that men might have been willing to vote for these expansions not because of increased labor market opportunities for their wives but rather to improve the well-being and economic prospects of their daughters and grandaughters.

Women in the Labor Market

As suggested previously, some women were always economically active beyond taking care of family and home.[48] Official statistics cited earlier indicate that 84 percent of men, but only 18 percent of women and less than 5 percent of married women, were in the labor force in 1890. Even though the census did not severely undercount the paid work of married women outside the home in the early years of collecting separate data for men and women, it did considerably understate paid work in the home (such as taking in boarders or doing piecework) and on the farm. One estimate of women's labor force participation, more broadly defined to include paid work done within the household, is as high as 26 percent in 1890; but participation rates decreased thereafter with the decline in the family farm and in paid work done at home, not to reach the previous high again until around 1940.[49] Interestingly, these trends are consistent with the notion, discussed earlier in this chapter, that women's participation in productive activity is likely first to decline, but to rise once more as the economy moves from one dominated by agriculture through early, and then advanced, industrialization.

Each of the two definitions of labor force participation has merit, depending on whether one is primarily interested in the extent to which women are independent

[48] Much useful information on the economic status of women in the United States, and how it changed over time, is found in Goldin, *Understanding the Gender Gap*; Matthaei, *Economic History*; Costa, "From Mill Town to Board Room;" and Claudia Goldin, "The Quiet Revolution that Transformed Women's Employment, Education, and Family." *American Economic Review* 96, no. 2 (May 2006): 1–20.
[49] This figure reflects Goldin's estimate that including undercounted workers would lead to a 7 percentage point increase in her calculation of the overall labor force participation rate for women. For white married women, in particular, including such workers would raise their rate by as much as 10 percentage points, from 2.5 to 12.5 percent. See Goldin, Understanding the Gender Gap, pp. 44–45. See also Claudia Goldin, "The U-Shaped Female Labor Force Function in Economic Development and Economic History," in Investments in Women's Human Capital, edited by T. Paul Schultz (Chicago: University of Chicago, 1995), pp. 61–90.

TABLE 2-1   Distribution of Workers by Occupation, Race and Gender, 1890/1900

	Men	Women		
	Total (%)	Total (%)	White (%)	Nonwhite (%)
Professional	10.2	9.6	12.5	0.9
Clerical	2.8	4.0	5.2	0.4
Sales	4.6	4.3	5.7	0.1
Service*	3.1	35.5	31.3	48.2
Manufacturing	37.6	27.7	34.7	6.4
Agricultural	41.7	19.0	10.8	44.0
Total Employed	100.0	100.0	100.0	100.0

*For women, service primarily refers to domestic service.

Source: From *Understanding the Gender Gap: An Economic History of American Women*, by Claudia Dale Goldin, Tables 3.2 and 3.3. Copyright (c) 1990 by Claudia Dale Goldin. Used by permission of Oxford University Press, Inc.

wage earners or in their productive contributions to the household. The issue is mainly relevant for wives because, throughout the period for which data have been available, single women were considerably more likely to be gainfully employed outside the home. As late as 1940, the labor force participation of married women was only 14 percent, while it was 46 percent for single women. One reason for the low rates for married women were the previously mentioned *marriage bars* prohibiting the employment of married women, which were instituted in the late 1800s and lasted into the mid-1900s. Marriage bars were particularly prevalent in teaching and clerical work, two occupations that were to become among the most common for married women in later years. Another obstacle to married women's employment outside the home was the lack of availability of part-time work at a time when women's household responsibilities were quite demanding.[50]

Not only were relatively few women employed during the early years of the twentieth century, but they also tended to work in different occupations than men and were concentrated in relatively few jobs. As shown in Table 2-1, even at the turn of the century, a very large share of men—42 percent—still worked in agricultural jobs; women's concentration in this sector was substantially less, with only 19 percent of women in such jobs. Manufacturing accounted for a sizable share of both men and women workers, although here again the percentage of women in such jobs (28 percent) was considerably less than for men (38 percent), and, virtually all the women in manufacturing were in just three industries—textiles, clothing, and tobacco. Perhaps the sharpest contrast was for service jobs. Relatively few men, 3 percent, were in service jobs (e.g., waiter or barber), while nearly 36 percent of women were in the service sector, with the majority employed in domestic service. Table 2-1 further shows that more than 90 percent of black women worked either as domestic servants or as farm laborers, as compared with only 42 percent of white women. It was also the case that foreign-born white women were overrepresented in manufacturing and domestic service, as compared with native-born white women, though these figures are not shown separately here.

---

[50] Goldin, *Understanding the Gender Gap*, Chapter 6, pp. 159–84. For further discussion of obstacles faced by women, see Rosalind Chait Barnett, "Preface: Women and Work: Where Are We, Where Did We Come From and Where Are We Going?" *Journal of Social Issues* 60, no. 4 (December 2004), pp. 667–74.

A similar share of men and women, 18 percent, held white-collar jobs (professional, clerical, and sales combined). Just over one-half of white-collar workers of both sexes were in the professional category, but the jobs held by men and women differed considerably. Almost all the women were schoolteachers or nurses, whereas men were more likely to be managers and proprietors. While the "female" professions of school-teacher and nurse, like domestic service, might be regarded as extensions of women's domestic role, interestingly, initially almost all schoolteachers were men. The remainder of men and women white-collar workers were in clerical and sales occupations. Like teaching, clerical work was originally a primarily male occupation. Although Table 2-1 indicates that a somewhat higher share of female than male workers held clerical jobs, the number of men in clerical positions greatly exceeded that of women because women were such a small share of the labor force at that time. Thus, as late as the turn of the century, 85 percent of all clerical workers were men. It was not until after 1900 that women's employment in this sector began to increase markedly, absorbing a substantial proportion of employed women. By the early 1970s, when the share of employed women in clerical jobs peaked, nearly one-third of all women workers were in such occupations.

A wide variety of factors undoubtedly contributed to the rapid growth of female clerical employment. Among these was the growth of large corporations, which greatly increased the volume of paperwork and thus the demand for clerical workers. The large proportion of women with a high school education who needed little or no on-the-job training to perform such work provided an inexpensive labor pool to satisfy this expanding demand. Employers were willing to hire these women, even when they were not expected to stay for a long time; this practice became all the more common after these positions came to serve a purely clerical function rather than serving as a training ground for advancement. Women, in turn, were likely to find these jobs attractive because relevant skills did not tend to depreciate much during periods out of the labor force and reentry was relatively easy. It is also possible that many preferred clean white-collar jobs to the dirtier, noisier, and at times more physically demanding blue-collar jobs. In any case, they generally had few other alternatives.[51]

Women's labor force participation has increased dramatically since the 1890s, the first year for which official data are available. The increase was fairly slow over the 50-year period from 1890 to 1940, when it rose from 18 to just 28 percent. However, from 1940 through the mid-1990s, participation rose from 28 to nearly 60 percent, and rates remained at that level through 2007.[52] The causes of this increase are detailed in Chapter 4; however, the growth in the demand for clerical workers undoubtedly facilitated the rapid influx of women into the labor force, particularly in the initial decades after World War II.

In addition to differences in occupations between men and women, there were also substantial differences in relative earnings. Some evidence on earnings is available dating back to the early nineteenth century. In the early years, we have information only for the manufacturing and agricultural sectors, rather than for the economy as a whole. Around 1815, women in agricultural and domestic activities earned as little as

---

[51] For analyses of women's occupational choices and of their entry into clerical work, see Mary C. Brinton, "Gendered Offices: A Comparative-Historical Examination of Clerical Work in Japan and the United States," in *The Political Economy of Japan's Low Fertility*, edited by Frances McCall Rosenbluth (Stanford, CA: Stanford University Press, 2007), pp. 87–111; Claudia Goldin, "Historical Evolution of Female Earnings Functions and Occupations," *Explorations in Economic History* 21, no. 1 (January 1984): 1–27; and Margery Davies, "Woman's Place Is at the Typewriter: The Feminization of the Clerical Labor Force," in *Labor Market Segmentation*, edited by Richard C. Edwards, Michael Reich, and David M. Gordon (Lexington, MA: D.C. Health, 1975), pp. 279–96.

[52] For more detailed historical data, including differences by race and marital status, see Goldin, *Understanding the Gender Gap*, Chapter 2.

29 percent of what men earned. They did better in the early manufacturing establishments where the gender ratio was in the range of 30 to 37 percent in 1820. The gender gap in both sectors narrowed from this time, around the start of early industrialization, through the turn of the twentieth century. Later data, which are available for the economy as a whole, indicate that the gender wage ratio increased from 46 percent in 1890 to 56 percent by 1930. The rise over these 40 years was largely due to an increase in the relative wages of women within broad occupations, though it also reflects some movement of women into higher-paying sectors.[53] Subsequently, little change took place until about 1980, but since then the ratio has risen to 78 percent. We present recent trends in the gender earnings ratio in greater detail in Chapter 5.

Married women's access to nonwage benefits, on the other hand, were generally not affected by whether they were employed outside the home. Because the foundations of the modern welfare state were laid during the time when the traditional family was still accepted as the norm, these programs generally addressed the needs of such families rather than those of two-earner or one-adult households. The preferential treatment of the traditional family applied both to the benefits employers began to provide early in the twentieth century, including health insurance, disability coverage, and pensions, and to those introduced by government in the 1930s, most notably Social Security.

By 2008, substantial change in family structure and women's employment had occurred. Nearly three-fourths of all employed married men and more than 90 percent of employed married women had a spouse in the labor force. In addition, more than 13 percent of employed women maintained their families (with no husband present).[54] These figures reflect the long secular increase in women's labor force participation as well as the much higher divorce and nonmarital birth rates of recent decades. As a result of these changes, programs and policies are emerging to assist the growing number of employed single-parent and dual-earner families. These recent trends, as well as others, will be discussed in greater detail in subsequent chapters.

COLLEGE-EDUCATED WOMEN OVER THE LAST 100 YEARS: WORK, FAMILY, OR BOTH?

Research by economic historian Claudia Goldin points to dramatic changes over the twentieth century in the ability of women who are relatively career oriented—those who are college educated—to combine paid work and family.* Her work provides a useful historical context for understanding the challenges faced by career-oriented women today.

Goldin begins with a cohort of women who graduated from college about 1910. She finds that they experienced a stark choice between a career (most often teaching) and having a family. Indeed, fully 50 percent did not marry or, if married, did not have children compared to only 22 percent of their contemporaries who did not attend college. Their experience suggests that prevailing social norms strongly discouraged married women from working outside the home.

The cohort of women who graduated from college about 1955 was more demographically similar to other women in the general population. During a time when Americans were generally marrying younger and having more children, college women

---

[53] Goldin, *Understanding the Gender Gap*, pp. 58–63.
[54] U.S. Census Bureau, "Historical Income Tables–Families," www. census. gov; and Bureau of Labor Statistics, *The Employment Situation: January 2008.*

were part of the trend, with only 17.5 percent not married or, if married, childless. Moreover, in contrast to their predecessors, many were able to have both a family *and* a job, though for the most part they did these activities in stages. Like many other women at that time, they first had a family and took a job later. For this group, college provided an economic reward, not only because it increased their potential earnings, but also because college women were more likely to marry college men (who outnumbered them 2 to 1). Thus, they reaped the added benefit of a higher-earning husband. Even though the experience of this cohort suggests that it was becoming more acceptable for married women to work for pay, even the college-educated generally had "jobs" rather than "careers," which require substantial human capital investment and more continuous labor force participation.

Among the cohort of women graduating college about 1972, a larger share sought to have careers, rather than simply jobs. Because of the investment required to do this, many women in this cohort delayed childbearing and pursued the route of career first, family later. Still, Goldin's data suggest that the proportion of those who were able to "have it all," that is, family and career, is surprisingly small. Only 13 to 18 percent of women in this cohort achieved both goals by about age 40, when *family* is defined as having given birth to at least one child and *career* as having earnings over a certain amount during the two to three preceding years.** The latest cohort for which data are available are women who graduated college in the early 1980s and were followed to about age 40. Using the same definitions, Goldin finds that 21 to 27 percent of these women attained family and career, certainly an improvement over the earlier cohort.

Of course, career is a difficult concept to define and the proportion found to have careers varies with the definition. Moreover, the estimates of career may be low among the age group surveyed because of the presence of young children among a substantial proportion of the women who had families. Yet even this qualification suggests that women face the need to make decisions and trade-offs seldom confronted by their male counterparts. Goldin's findings regarding the difficulty of combining family and career are reinforced by considerable evidence suggesting that, among women as a group, children have a negative effect on earnings and employment.

Nonetheless, there is reason to be optimistic about prospects for future cohorts. Access to family leave, for instance, has been found to substantially mitigate the negative effect of children on women's wages. Thus, the difficulties that women face in achieving career and family are likely to continue to decrease as more firms adopt such policies. Moreover, as discrimination in the labor market continues to decline, marriages gradually become more egalitarian, and various other family-friendly policies are offered on a more widespread basis in the workplace, more women who want to "have it all" will be able to do so.

*Claudia Goldin, "Career and Family: College Women Look to the Past," in *Gender and Family Issues in the Workplace*, edited by Francine D. Blau and Ronald G. Ehrenberg (New York: Russell Sage Foundation, 1997), pp. 20–59; and Claudia Goldin, "The Long Road to the Fast Track: Career and Family," *The Annals of the American Academy of Political and Social Science* 596, no. 1 (2004): 20–35. Evidence on the impact of children and the availability of maternity leave on women's earnings is from Jane Waldfogel, "Understanding the 'Family Gap' in Pay for Women with Children," *Journal of Economic Perspectives* 12, no. 1 (Winter 1998): 157–70.

**Specifically, having income or average hourly earnings at least as high as a man at the 25th percentile of the college-educated male earnings distribution. When Goldin, instead, defines *career* as working full-time during the preceding three years, she obtains a somewhat higher estimate of 22 percent. In related work, Marianne A. Ferber and Carole Green examined a sample of women predominately in their fifties and found a larger share who meet the definition of career and family; see "Career or Family: What Choices Do College Women Have?" *Journal of Labor Research* 24, no. 1 (Winter 2003): 143–51.

Conclusion

The overview provided here, though general, permits us to draw some conclusions. The roles of men and women and the social rules that prescribe appropriate behavior for each are not shaped by biology alone. Rather, they are determined by the interaction of technology, the role of women in production, and a variety of social and political factors. The evidence provides reason to believe that women are less likely to be seen as dependents, defined solely in terms of their maternal and family role, when they participate in "prod uctive" work.

It is also likely that the roles of men and women, which developed initially as a rational response to conditions that existed at one time in the course of economic development, continued their hold even after they ceased to be functional.[55] Thus, the view that women should devote themselves to homemaking, once a full-time occupation when life was short, families were large, and housekeeping was laborious, lingered long after these conditions changed substantially. Jobs originally allocated to men because they required great physical strength often continued as male preserves when mechanization did away with the need for muscle power. Lags in adjustment are not uncommon, a fact that should be kept in mind when we come to analyze the current situation.

Our review also suggests that neither the role of housewife nor that of working woman is without significant problems for women. Men's work in the public sphere (i.e., outside the family) has usually enjoyed higher status than women's domestic work within the family circle. Even when women succeeded in entering the world beyond the household to a greater or lesser extent, men failed to show much inclination to share in household work. This situation, in turn, makes it difficult for women to achieve substantial equality in the public sphere. Many of those who tried found themselves confronted by the problem of "the double burden" of responsibility for home and market work, or felt forced to choose between a career and marriage. In modern times, machines eliminate much of the need for muscle, and physical strength is no longer required for the most highly valued work. At the same time, childbearing absorbs an increasingly smaller proportion of a woman's adult life and can, for the most part, be timed at will. It is entirely possible that, under these conditions, it is the unequal distribution of labor in the home rather than women's lesser ability to perform other types of work that increasingly poses the main obstacle to equality.

Questions for Review and Discussion

1. Explain how women's and men's roles in production changed between the colonial period and early industrialization.
2. From a historical perspective, how has the labor market experience of black and white women differed?
3. Compare and contrast the role of women in the following stages:

   a. hunting and gathering
   b. horticulture
   c. agriculture
   d. early industrialization
   e. today

4. In view of what we have learned from sociobiologists, to what extent can traditional roles of men and women be expected to change with changing economic conditions?
5. Discuss possible relationships between economic development and women's rights.

---

[55]"Although stereotypes are often initially based on fact, they are seldom revised as quickly as the facts change." Smith, "The Movement of Women," p. 3.

Suggested Readings

Amott, Teresa L., and Julie A. Matthaei. *Race, Gender, and Work: A Multicultural Economic History of Women in the United States*. Boston: South End Press, 1996.

Blum, Deborah. *Sex on the Brain: The Biological Differences Between Men and Women*. New York: Viking Penguin, 1997.

Brines, Melissa. *Brain Gender*. New York: Oxford University Press, 2004.

Costa, Dora L. "From Mill Town to Board Room: The Rise of Women's Paid Labor," *Journal of Economic Perspectives* 14, no. 4 (Fall 2000): 101–22.

Cox, Donald. "Biological Basics and the Economics of the Family." *Journal of Economic Perspectives* 21, no. 2 (Spring 2007): 91–108.

Friedl, Ernestine. *Women and Men: An Anthropological View*. New York: Holt, Rinehart & Winston, 1975.

Goldin, Claudia. "The Quiet Revolution that Transformed Women's Employment, Education and Family," *American Economic Review* 96, no. 2 (May 2006): 1–15.

Goldin, Claudia. *Understanding the Gender Gap: An Economic History of American Women*. New York: Oxford University Press, 1990.

Goldin, Claudia. "The U-Shaped Female Labor Force Function in Economic Development and Economic History." In *Investments in Women's Human Capital*, edited by T. Paul Schultz, pp. 61–90. Chicago: University of Chicago, 1995.

Huber, Joan. *On the Origins of Gender Inequality*. Boulder, CO and London: Paradigm Publishers, 2007.

Matthaei, Julie A. *An Economic History of Women in America*. New York: Schocken Books, 1982.

Nielsen, Joyce M. *Sex and Gender in Society: Perspectives and Stratification*, 2nd ed. Prospect Heights, IL: Waveland Press, Inc., 1990.

Rosaldo, Michelle Z., and Louise Lamphere, eds. *Women, Culture and Society*. Stanford: Stanford University Press, 1974.

Tilly, Louise, and Joan Scott. *Women, Work and Family*. New York: Holt, Rinehart & Winston, 1978.

Welter, Barbara. "The Cult of True Womanhood, 1820–1860." In *The American Family in Social-Historical Perspective*, edited by Michael Gordon, pp. 313–33. New York: St. Martin's Press, 1978.

Wilson, Edward O. *Sociobiology: The New Synthesis*. Cambridge, MA: Belknap Press of Harvard University Press, 1975.

Key Terms

hunting and gathering societies *18*

horticultural societies *18*

pastoral societies *18*

agricultural societies *18*

dowry *18*

colonial America *19*

industrialization *19*

traditional family *22*

CHAPTER **3**

The Family as an Economic Unit

Chapter Highlights

- The Simple Neoclassical Model: Specialization and Exchange
- Other Advantages of Families
- Disadvantages of Specialization
- Transaction Cost and Bargaining Approaches
- Marxist and Radical Feminist Views of the Family

- Nonmarket Work
- The American Family in the Twenty-First Century
- Appendix: Specialization and Exchange: A Graphical Analysis

For a long time, neoclassical economics, the dominant school of economics in the United States and most of the rest of the world today, and the approach we primarily draw on in this text, concerned itself largely with the behavior of "economic man." It was, of course, acknowledged that this man interacted with others, in competition or in cooperation, but it was his individual well-being that he would attempt to maximize. Consumer economics had long recognized the existence of the family and its importance as a unit of consumption. However, it was not until the 1960s, with the path-breaking work of Gary Becker and Jacob Mincer, that mainstream economists began to concern themselves with the issues confronted by men and women in allocating their time and wealth so as to maximize family well-being.[1] Since then, using sophisticated theory and advanced econometric methods, economists have developed and tested models that have produced important insights in this area. Yet, many of these models are not altogether satisfactory, because the tendency is still to treat even this multiperson family as a single-minded, indivisible, utility-maximizing unit.

---

[1] See Gary S. Becker, "A Theory of the Allocation of Time," *Economic Journal* 75, no. 299 (September 1965): 493–517; and Jacob Mincer, "Labor Force Participation of Married Women," in *Aspects of Labor Economics*, edited by H. Gregg Lewis, Universities National Bureau of Economic Research Conference Series, no. 14 (Princeton, NJ: Princeton University Press, 1962), pp. 63–97. An early pioneer was Margaret G. Reid, *Economics of Household Production* (New York: Wiley, 1934). A large number of authors contributed to the growing literature of the "New Home Economics" in recent decades, but much of this work has been conveniently summarized by Gary S. Becker in *A Treatise on the Family* (Cambridge, MA: Harvard University Press, 1981, enlarged edition, 1991). For theoretical critiques and extensions of Becker's work, see, for instance, Robert A. Pollak, "Gary Becker's Contributions to Family and Household Economics," *Review of Economics of the Household* 1, no. 1–2 (January/April 2002): 111–41; and Paula England, "Separate and Soluble Selves: Dichotomous Thinking in Economics," in *Feminist Economics Today*, edited by Marianne A. Ferber and Julie A. Nelson (Chicago: University of Chicago, 2003), pp. 61–80.

In this chapter, we draw heavily upon neoclassical economic analysis, with appropriate simplifying assumptions, to better understand the determinants of the division of labor in the family. Because a substantial majority of people continue to live in married-couple families, we focus largely on the division of labor between husbands and wives. At the same time, it would be a mistake to overlook the considerable increase in the number of cohabiting heterosexual couples, or the presence of gay and lesbian couples, some of them married since 2004 in the United States.[2] We shall examine both types of couples in Chapter 10.

Our focus on economic analysis does not mean that we believe families are established or dissolved entirely, or even primarily, for economic reasons. On the contrary, human need for companionship, sexual attraction, affection, and the desire to have children all play a substantial part in family formation. Human need for independence and privacy as well as incompatibilities and preference for a variety of partners all play a large part in family breakups. Nonetheless, it is our belief that economic factors are important and that focusing upon them considerably enhances our understanding of the determinants of the division of labor in the family.

After presenting the neoclassical model of the family, we provide an evaluation and critique of this approach and introduce a more complex reality. In particular, the simple neoclassical model points to potential efficiency gains arising from the traditional division of labor in which the husband specializes in market work and the wife specializes in home work. Nevertheless, such an arrangement is less and less prevalent. Moreover, individuals continue to form families despite this decrease in specialization. We shed light on the reasons for these developments by extending the simple model in two ways.[3]

- We point out other types of economic benefits to forming families besides specialization. Thus, couples may discard specialization and still reap economic gains from living in families.
- We examine the disadvantages of the traditional division of labor, particularly for women, which are not considered in the simple neoclassical model. These disadvantages help explain the decline of the traditional division of labor.

We then briefly discuss the alternative neoclassical approaches of transaction costs and bargaining models, as well as the radical feminist and Marxist feminist approaches.

Next, we examine available evidence on the allocation of time to market work, housework, and volunteer work by men and women, as well as changes in this allocation during recent decades. This discussion will provide some indication as to the extent that husbands and wives continue to specialize and to what extent we are moving toward egalitarian marriages, in which both spouses share the responsibility for earning a living and for homemaking. Here we focus on trends in nonmarket work, and in Chapter 4 we examine trends in female labor force participation.

Finally, we conclude by looking at the American family in the twenty-first century. As we shall see, married couples, the focus of this chapter, have been declining as a share of all households. We briefly summarize the changes that have occurred and point to the increasing complexity of families in the United States and elsewhere. More detailed analyses of these trends are provided in Chapter 10.

---

[2] The first country to recognize same-sex marriage was the Netherlands in 2001.

[3] Much of this material was first developed in Marianne A. Ferber and Bonnie G. Birnbaum, "The New Home Economics: Retrospect and Prospects," *Journal of Consumer Research* 4, no. 4 (June 1977): 19–28. For an updated discussion, see Marianne A. Ferber, "A Feminist Critique of the Neoclassical Theory of the Family," in *Women, Family, and Work: Writings on the Economics of Gender*, edited by Karine S. Moe (Oxford: Blackwell, 2003), Chapter 1.

THE SIMPLE NEOCLASSICAL MODEL: SPECIALIZATION AND EXCHANGE

The neoclassical analysis of the family relies on the following basic underlying assumption: The family is a unit whose adult members make informed and rational decisions that result in maximizing the utility or well-being of the unit. Beginning with this premise, economic analysis has been applied to understanding the division of labor within the family. Such economic models have also been used to explain women's rising labor force participation rates, trends in divorce rates and fertility, the greater emphasis on children's education, and a number of other aspects of people's behavior as members of families.

The simplest model assumes that the family's goal is to maximize its utility or satisfaction by selecting the combination of **commodities** from which its members derive the greatest possible amount of utility. These commodities are produced by combining the home time of family members with goods and services purchased in the market using labor market earnings.

Virtually all purchased goods and services require an infusion of home time to transform them into the commodities that provide utility—from food that needs to be bought and prepared and furniture that needs to be purchased, arranged in the home, and maintained, to day care centers, which must be carefully chosen and where children must be dropped off and picked up. Similarly, even time spent in leisure generally requires the input of market goods and services to be enjoyable—from television sets and DVD players to rock concerts and baseball games. Thus, time spent on paid work produces the income necessary to purchase market goods, which in turn are needed together with home time to produce commodities. A crucial question for the family is how the time of each individual should be allocated between home and market most efficiently in order to maximize satisfaction.

Comparative Advantage

Under certain conditions, commodity production is carried out most efficiently if one member of the family specializes, at least to some extent, in market production while the other specializes, at least to some extent, in home production. They may then exchange their output or pool the fruits of their labor to achieve their utility-maximizing combination of purchased goods and home-produced goods. For there to be gains from this arrangement, it is necessary for the **comparative advantage** in home and market production of the two individuals to differ. That is to say, the ratio of the value of time spent at home to the value of time spent in the market must be higher for one individual than the other.[4]

Is it generally the case that women are relatively more productive in the home and men are relatively more productive in the market? Whether or not one assumes that women are biologically better suited for housework because they bear children, it is frequently the case that women have a comparative advantage in household production and that men have a comparative advantage in market work. The reason is that men and women are traditionally raised with different expectations and receive different education and training. It may also be the case that women have been discriminated against in the labor market, lowering their market earnings. Moreover, the traditional

---

[4] The case for specialization as a way to maximize the well-being of the family is similar to that for international trade, where each country specializes in production for which it has a relative advantage. Among the important differences between the two situations, however, is that countries generally need not rely on a single trading partner, allowing somewhat less opportunity for the stronger partner to take advantage of the weaker one. Another difference is that couples, unlike countries, must also share a good deal of consumption.

division of labor itself is likely to magnify differences in the household and market skills of men and women because both types of skills tend to increase with experience "on the job." Thus, even a small initial gender difference in comparative advantage is likely to increase considerably over time.

Although each of the preceding factors tends to produce gender differences in comparative advantage for homemaking as compared to market work, it is not necessarily the case that the traditional division of labor is the optimal arrangement. Treating children according to gender rather than individual talents and discriminating against women workers in the labor market clearly introduce distortions. Even more obvious is the fact that circular reasoning is involved when women supposedly specialize in housework because they do it better, but, in fact, they do it better because they specialize in it. To the extent that women's relative advantage for homemaking is socially determined and reflects unequal access to market opportunities, the traditional division of labor is not always efficient, let alone desirable, particularly when, as we shall see, it entails many disadvantages for women.

In the following discussion we assume that women have a comparative advantage in housework relative to men because the reality that we seek to explain is one in which women generally assume primary responsibility for homemaking. We do not mean to imply, however, that the traditional division of labor is inevitable or that it will persist indefinitely into the future. Indeed, we are also concerned with better understanding the reasons why traditional patterns are changing.

Specialization and Exchange: Numerical Examples

Two simple examples will help clarify the notion of comparative advantage and illustrate the efficiency of specialization and exchange. The analysis is analogous to the standard proof of gains from international trade and is illustrated in Tables 3-1a and 3-1b.

ABSOLUTE ADVANTAGE   The simplest case is when one individual has an **absolute advantage** in market work while the other individual has an absolute advantage in household production. Suppose John could earn $10 for working one hour in the labor market or could produce a mediocre dinner worth about $5 at home during the same period of time. A second individual, Jane, would earn only $5 an hour in the labor market but is able to prepare an excellent dinner at home worth about $10 in one hour. In this case, it is clear that John and Jane's combined level of economic well-being will be greater if they each specialize. John, who has an absolute advantage in market work, can spend all his time in the labor market earning money while Jane, who has an absolute advantage in cooking, can prepare the dinners.

This scenario is illustrated in the top section of Table 3-1a. Initially, John and Jane are each self-sufficient and both allocate some time to market work and some time to the preparation of home-cooked meals. John devotes six hours to earning income and two hours to cooking. His total income (including the value of home-cooked meals) is $70. Jane spends seven hours in the market and one hour on cooking. Her total income is $45. The sum of their two incomes (although they are not necessarily sharing at this point) is $115. If they collaborate, they have the option of each specializing to a greater extent in the activity they do better and exchanging (or pooling) their output, as shown in the bottom section of Table 3-1a.

Through specialization and exchange, John and Jane can produce a higher value of both market goods and home-cooked meals and, thus, increase their total income. The concept of opportunity cost is useful in understanding the benefits of specialization. As we explained in Chapter 1, opportunity cost is the benefit forgone in the next best alternative. John's opportunity cost of obtaining $10 worth of market goods in terms of the value of meals forgone ($5) is lower than Jane's ($20). On the other hand, a

TABLE 3-1   An Illustration of the Gains from Specialization and Exchange

(a) Case 1: ABSOLUTE ADVANTAGE

Separate Production

	Value of Market Goods		Value of Home Cooking		Total Income
John	(6 hrs. × $10)		(2 hrs. × $5)		
	$60	+	$10	=	$70
Jane	(7 hrs. × $5)		(1 hr. × $10)		
	$35	+	$10	=	$45
Total (John and Jane)	$95		$20		$115

Specialization and Exchange

	Value of Market Goods		Value of Home Cooking		Total Income
John	(8 hrs. × $10)		(0 hrs. × $5)		
	$80	+	$0	=	$80
Jane	(5 hrs. × $5)		(3 hr. × $10)		
	$25	+	$30	=	$55
Total (John and Jane)	$105		$30		$135

(b) Case 2: COMPARATIVE ADVANTAGE

Separate Production

	Value of Market Goods		Value of Home Cooking		Total Income
Dave	(6 hrs. × $10)		(2 hrs. × $5)		
	$60	+	$10	=	$70
Diane	(7 hrs. × $15)		(1 hr. × $15)		
	$105	+	$15	=	$120
Total (Dave and Diane)	$165		$25		$190

Specialization and Exchange

	Value of Market Goods		Value of Home Cooking		Total Income
Dave	(8 hrs. × $10)		(0 hrs. × $5)		
	$80	+	$0	=	$80
Diane	(6 hrs. × $15)		(2 hr. × $15)		
	$90	+	$30	=	$120
Total (Dave and Diane)	$170		$30		$200

home-cooked meal valued at $10 is cheaper for Jane to produce in terms of the value of market goods forgone ($5) than it is for John ($20). Suppose John decides to devote all his time to the market, and Jane transfers two additional hours from market work to cooking. By reallocating their time, the couple is able to raise their total income from $115 to $135.

COMPARATIVE ADVANTAGE   Less obvious is the fact that specialization can also raise the income of the couple when one individual not only earns more in the labor market but is also a better cook. In other words, one individual has an absolute advantage in both types of work. In this situation, the crucial question is whether each has a *comparative advantage* for doing one type of work.

As illustrated in Table 3-1b, Dave earns $10 per hour for time spent in the labor market or can produce a meal worth, say, $5 for an hour spent cooking. Diane is more efficient than Dave in both activities. Her market wage is $15, while she can produce a meal worth $15 in an hour's time. The important point here is that, although Diane earns a bit more than Dave in the labor market, she is a far better cook than he is. The opportunity cost (in terms of market goods forgone) of a home-cooked meal worth $10 is lower when Diane produces it than when Dave does. It takes Dave two hours (valued at $20) to produce such a meal, and Diane can do so in 40 minutes (valued at $10). Table 3-1b shows that through specialization and exchange, the couple can increase their total output of both market goods and home-cooked meals and raise their total income from $190 to $200.

Gains to Specialization and Exchange

These examples illustrate the potential gain in output of specialization and exchange. They do not, however, tell us how much time John and Jane will spend on each type of work. The goal of the family is to maximize utility or satisfaction. Thus, the value attached to various commodities and the time allocation actually chosen by each couple will depend on their preferences for market- versus home-produced goods. Many outcomes are possible. For example, perhaps Jane and John have such a strong preference for market goods that their well-being would be maximized by both of them only working for pay and purchasing all the goods and services they consume rather than producing any at home. Or Diane and Dave might have such a strong preference for home production that she would entirely specialize in housework, and he would divide his time between market and home. In Appendix 3A, we present a fuller treatment of the decision making process that explicitly takes into account both the production possibilities available to the couple and their preferences for each type of good.

In any case, however, each couple will seek to produce their desired combination of market and home goods in the most efficient way. Thus, as long as they produce some of each type of good, if the wife has a comparative advantage in housework (relative to the husband) and the husband has a comparative advantage in market work (relative to the wife), the analysis suggests that they will choose to specialize, at least to some extent.

It would appear, then, that this analysis provides an explanation for the traditional family with a male breadwinner and a female homemaker. Each may help the other if demand is high for the production he or she is not particularly qualified for, but each has a clearly defined sphere of primary responsibility. For whenever such specialization does not take place, the couple will fail to maximize their output and, potentially, their well-being.

Yet, as we know, the traditional family has become much less common in recent years, as families in which both husband and wife work in the labor market have become the norm. Within the context of the model, this shift may be traced in part to trends that narrow differences in women's and men's comparative advantage. As discussed in greater detail in Chapters 6 and 7, women's educational attainment and labor market experience have substantially increased and it is likely that the extent of labor market discrimination against women has declined. As a result, women's wages have increased.[5] At the same time, the relative value of nonmarket time has fallen, with the rapid adoption of appliances such as the microwave oven and the increased consumption of fast food in place of home-cooked meals. In addition, more out-of-home child care is available than in the past, though issues of access, affordability, and quality remain, as discussed further in Chapter 11.

The direction of causality for such changes is difficult to establish and the effects are likely to be mutually reinforcing. For example, rising educational attainment of women may reduce their comparative advantage for household work, but, at the same time, women's reduced desire to adhere to the traditional division of labor in the family is likely a factor explaining their rising educational attainment. As another example, greater availability of fast food is expected to reduce women's comparative advantage in household work, but is no doubt also a result of the growing demand for prepared meals due to women's rising labor force participation. However, the important point from the perspective of the issues we are considering here is that such shifts in comparative advantage of women and men substantially reduce the gains to marriage. Thus, it

---

[5] If women' wages rise relative to men's (and nothing else changes), less specialization is expected.

is not surprising that marriage rates have fallen somewhat, as discussed in Chapter 10. Nevertheless, a substantial majority of people continue to marry.

Part of the reason for the continued prevalence of marriage is that gender differences in comparative advantages have not completely disappeared. Women continue to earn less than men in the labor market, and the data presented later in this chapter show that they continue to do the bulk of the housework, even when they are employed outside the home. Moreover, even if wives and husbands have identical comparative advantages, other economic gains can be realized in marriage, in addition to important noneconomic advantages. It is also important to recognize that even when there are substantial gains from the traditional division of labor, this arrangement has a number of disadvantages, particularly for the wife. In the following sections we extend the simple analysis by pointing to other economic advantages of marriage, as well as the disadvantages of complete specialization.

OTHER ADVANTAGES OF FAMILIES

When husbands and wives have very similar, or even precisely the same, relative abilities in the market and in the household, there are still other economic advantages to forming families. These reasons include economies of scale, public goods, externalities in consumption, the opportunity to make marriage-specific investments, risk pooling, and institutional advantages. Arguably, most of these benefits do not necessarily require a husband-wife family, but they are likely to be enhanced when individuals expect to have a long-term relationship with a strong degree of commitment.

Economies of Scale

Economies of scale exist when an increase in the scale of operation of a productive unit can result in increased output at decreasing incremental cost. To the extent that a couple is able to benefit from such economies of scale, both in the production of some home goods and in purchasing market goods and services, economic gains result from living together. For example, housing for two usually costs less than the combined amount each would pay for their housing separately. Meals for two generally take less than twice as much time to prepare as meals for one, and so forth.[6]

Public Goods

A **public good** has the unique characteristic that the consumption or enjoyment of the item by one person does not diminish the consumption or enjoyment of the same item by others.[7] Within the family, many goods are likely to have this characteristic. For example, one partner's enjoyment of a television program is unlikely to be reduced by the fact that the other partner is also watching. Similarly, the delight of a parent in his or her child's adorable antics is not apt to be diminished by the other parent's pleasure.[8] Many aspects of housing—the views from the windows and the decoration of the rooms—also have public goods aspects. In fact, the enjoyment of these goods by one

---

[6] Economies of scale also explain the advantages of larger groups living together. The fact that such arrangements are not common in affluent societies suggests that most people value additional privacy highly once they can afford it.

[7] A *pure* public good also has the characteristic that others cannot be excluded from using or enjoying it or that it is at any rate too difficult or costly to exclude them. For further discussion of public goods and the concept that follows, externalities, see Jonathan Gruber, *Public Finance and Public Policy*, 2nd edition (MIT: Worth Publishers, 2007).

[8] As Nancy Folbre points out, children not only provide benefits to their parents—in earlier days for their economic contribution to the family and today largely in the form of enjoyment—but they also provide benefits to the larger society; children are the innovators and taxpayers of tomorrow. See "Children as Public Goods," *American Economic Review* 84, no. 2 (May 1994): 86–90.

partner may even enhance that of the other. To the extent that public goods are important, the gains from joint consumption are increased because two individuals derive more total satisfaction from sharing a given stock of public goods and services by living together than they would by living separately.

Externalities in Consumption

Externalities in consumption occur when the consumption of a good or service by one of the partners affects the well-being of the other who does not consume it. When these externalities are positive—one person derives enjoyment from the other's consumption—gains will be greater than indicated by the simple model. For example, a husband's purchase of a new suit may increase his wife's utility as well as his own. Both members of a couple may enjoy their summer vacation more because they are traveling together than they would if each were traveling alone. When two people care for one another, one partner may even derive satisfaction simply from the enjoyment and happiness of the other.

Marriage-Specific Investments

Marriage-specific investments refer to skills and knowledge developed in marriage and other investments made during a marriage that are worth far more within the marriage than they would be if the marriage were terminated.[9] Examples of such investments include learning to cook each other's favorite meals or learning to do the same recreational activities, such as skiing or rock climbing. Perhaps the prime example of a marriage-specific investment is the rearing of children. Parents devote considerable time and energy to nurturing their children and fostering the values that they share. Thus, children generally provide considerable satisfaction to parents within the marriage. They may, however, not provide such satisfaction to a different partner, and their presence may even be an obstacle to forming and maintaining a new relationship.

Risk Pooling

Married-couple families, particularly those consisting of two earners, have the added advantage that if one of the spouses becomes unemployed, they may be able to rely on the earning power of the other partner to cover at least part of their family's expenses. In bad economic times, if the husband loses his job or his earnings decline, even a traditional homemaker may enter the labor market to maintain family income. This "added worker" effect is discussed in Chapter 4. In addition, couples have much greater flexibility to switch jobs, change careers, or pursue additional education or job training because they can rely on the other spouse's earning power, whether or not he or she is already in the labor market.

Institutional Advantages

Married couples also frequently enjoy institutional advantages. In the United States, these include coverage by a spouse's health insurance, pension rights, and Social Security benefits. Some employers extend benefits such as health insurance to the cohabiting partners of unmarried heterosexual workers, as well as gay and lesbian workers, but to date this practice is far from universal. Also, as of 2008, a handful of states permit civil unions, which extend a wide range of legal protections to gay and

---

[9] See Becker, *A Treatise on the Family*; and Robert A. Pollak, "A Transaction Cost Approach to Families and Households," *Journal of Economic Literature* 23, no. 2 (June 1985): 581–608.

lesbian partners, and a few states permit gay marriage.[10] Nevertheless, the vast majority of gay and lesbian couples do not live in states that provide opportunities for marriage or civil unions for same-sex couples. And, even in states where gay marriage is permitted, these married individuals are ineligible for spousal benefits in federal programs. These issues are discussed later in the chapter in an inset on the "State of Unions in the United States."

DISADVANTAGES OF SPECIALIZATION

Thus, as we have just seen, significant economic advantages derive from forming families, even in the case of couples whose comparative advantage in market work and home production is similar, so that they gain little from specialization and exchange. We now return to the issue of specialization and exchange itself, which the simple model suggests is the economic foundation of marriage. Here we consider the possibility that such specialization and a gender-based division of labor may not always be desirable, particularly for women, even when specialization and exchange does yield some economic gains to the family. The potential disadvantages of specialization are generally not discussed in the standard models but are nonetheless important.

Sharing of Housework

Even if a wife has a comparative advantage in doing housework as compared to her husband, a fuller consideration of the issues suggests a number of reasons why a couple might often find it desirable to share the housework rather than for each spouse to specialize completely. First, the sweeping assumption that women have a comparative advantage in all household tasks is unrealistic. The problem is that the simple model assumes only one type of home good. In our numerical example, it was home-cooked meals; more generally it is an aggregate category of home goods. In fact, tasks typically performed within the household include not only child care, house cleaning, cooking, and shopping, but also gardening, home repairs, car maintenance, and taking care of the family finances. It is not likely that the wife will have a comparative advantage in performing all of these tasks as compared to the husband; rather it is likely that he will have a comparative advantage in at least some of them, even taking his larger market earnings into account. Of course, once the wife is at home because she is better at some, or many, of the household tasks, it may be more efficient for her to do other related work as well. Nonetheless, the husband also spends a good bit of time in the home, and, in any case, not all household tasks are performed in or around the house (e.g., shopping, dropping off a child at day care, or going to the bank). Therefore, even a traditional family will generally find it efficient for the husband to do a bit more housework than suggested by the simple model.

Second, it is worthwhile to consider the utility or disutility that people derive from work itself. The simple model considers only the utility derived from the consumption of market-produced and home-produced goods. Yet most people spend much of their time working, and their well-being is influenced by the satisfaction or dissatisfaction directly associated with their work. If everyone always enjoyed more (or disliked less) the kind of work they do more efficiently, the gains from specialization would be even greater than indicated by the simple model; and that may to a degree be the case. However, this line of reasoning ignores the possibility that how we feel about doing particular tasks depends on how much time we have to spend on them. Persons who dislike a particular

---

[10] In 2000, Vermont became the first state to permit civil unions and, in 2004, Massachusetts became the first state to permit gay marriage.

type of work to begin with are likely to hate this activity even more as they do increasingly more of it. Even those individuals who like what they do are, nonetheless, likely to become less enthusiastic.[11] The stronger this effect, the less likely are the gains in utility from complete specialization suggested by the simple model.

A similar issue arises with respect to the utility each individual derives from leisure. The model fails to consider adequately that leisure is likely to be more highly valued by the partner who has less of it and that the one who has a great deal of leisure may even become bored or come to feel useless. Thus, the situation in which the wife works in the market and retains full responsibility for housework is not likely to be optimal if it results in considerably less leisure for her than for her husband; this situation is especially likely to occur during the childrearing years. Alternatively, when the husband holds a demanding full-time position, while the responsibilities of the full-time homemaker become rather modest because the children are growing up or may even have left home, he will be short of leisure, whereas the wife may have more of it than she finds desirable.

Life Cycle Changes

A serious shortcoming of the simple model is that it ignores the fact that the comparative advantage of an individual does not necessarily remain the same over the life cycle. The value of home production for women peaks during the childrearing years and then declines as children grow up and become more self-sufficient. At the same time, labor market earnings and career opportunities tend to increase with work experience and decline during years out of the labor force. If a woman withdraws from the labor force for a considerable period of time for childrearing, she is likely to pay a high price in terms of career advancement and earnings when she reenters the labor market. Hence, specializing for some time entirely in homemaking may not be advantageous to the wife or to her family in the long run, even if it maximizes family well-being in the short run. Couples who are aware of this trade-off may decide it is worthwhile for the family to give up some utility during the early years so that the wife can remain in the labor market in order to improve her long-run career prospects and enhance her lifetime earnings. As women increasingly value career achievement as an end in itself, the costs of work disruptions are apt to loom even larger. These issues are considered in greater detail in Chapter 6.

It might be argued that offsetting these disadvantages for the wife's career and the lifetime income of the family is the opportunity for a stay-at-home mother to spend more time with her children. However, as discussed later in this chapter, differences in the amount of time that employed and nonemployed mothers spend with children appear to be quite modest. Also, maternal care is only one factor, of many, that affects children's well-being and achievement, as discussed further in Chapter 10.

Costs of Interdependence

Whatever the probability that the well-being of husband and wife will be maximized by specialization under existing circumstances, they will be less well prepared to deal with unforeseen developments. When each spouse is able to manage the household and to earn a living if the need arises, the family will not be devastated if the husband is laid off or does not get a promotion or if the wife becomes ill and needs care instead of providing it for the rest of the family. Each will also be better equipped to manage alone in the event of divorce, separation, or death.

---

[11] The reasoning is analogous to diminishing marginal utility as additional units of the same good are consumed.

In the case of complete specialization, although both spouses likely gain from the greater proficiency each acquires in the area in which he or she specializes, their skills in the other area are likely to deteriorate or, at best, fail to improve. In the event that the couple's relationship ends, the full-time homemaker faces particularly serious negative consequences. The husband who has concentrated on market work may be considerably inconvenienced by a lack of household skills, but his market earnings can be used to purchase household services. The wife who has specialized in household production, on the other hand, is left with no earnings and market skills that are likely to have deteriorated or even become obsolete. The challenges faced by female-headed families are discussed more fully in Chapter 10.

Other potential difficulties exist for a full-time homemaker even if the partnership lasts until her death or until a time when she has an adequate pension, inheritance, or savings. As pointed out earlier, the value of the homemaker's contribution to the family is greatest when the children are young. Now that the average number of children is about two and female life expectancy is 80, this period is most often relatively early in a woman's life, and after that, the value of her contribution at home declines. Because her earning power (generally lower than her husband's to begin with) is also likely to decline during the time she was out of the labor market, her contribution during the latter part of her life will most often be considerably smaller than her partner's.

One way of looking at this scenario is that the husband's increasing earnings in the market may compensate for the wife's declining productivity in the home, so that she can now enjoy her share of the family's total income and a good deal of leisure. Yet, even if her partner is fond of her, is happy to share his largesse, and is grateful to her for the considerable contributions she made earlier, she may come to wonder about her present worth to the family. This is, no doubt, the reason we used to hear so much about the *empty-nest syndrome*. On the other hand, she may not be so lucky. Her spouse may ask what she has done for him lately; he may take advantage of his increasingly greater bargaining power and appropriate a larger share of family income for commodities only he uses or only he wants and, in general, by adopting a lifestyle that conforms to his, but not necessarily to her, preferences.

Tastes and Bargaining Power

In our development of the simple model, we did not consider how the couple determines the allocation of income and of time to various commodities the family would enjoy. The decision will be relatively simple if they both have the same tastes and preferences because they will each opt for the same combination of goods and services to be shared. If, however, their tastes differ significantly, the question arises as to how they will decide on the combination of commodities to be produced and consumed. Or, in other words, whose preferences (husband's or wife's) will receive greater weight? These issues are considered here in general terms and then, in the next section, are examined in light of alternative approaches to analyzing family decision making that have been developed more recently: transaction cost and bargaining models.

Sharing of joint production is easiest in the case of *private goods*, that is, goods that provide benefits to the individual user only. However, even in this case, if spouses have different tastes, there may be conflicts about what share each will receive. Disagreements are particularly likely regarding expenditures on large ticket items such as one partner's purchase of a new bike or the other partner's proposed ski vacation with friends. Even more difficult problems arise in the case of *public goods* or commodities that have significant externalities. As we saw earlier, for people with similar tastes, public goods and positive externalities increase the gains from joint consumption and collaboration. However, where one person's public good is another's public "bad" or where negative externalities in consumption exist, consumption of the commodity by one individual may reduce the well-being of the other. For example, one partner may derive enormous satisfaction from the presence of children, whereas the other may dislike having them around. Or one individual listening to loud music may reduce the enjoyment of the evening for the other.

These difficulties are relevant to the conclusions we derived from the simple model regarding the benefits of specialization. They suggest that conflicts of interest may arise between husband and wife and that relative bargaining power would likely play a role in resolving these conflicts. Because in the traditional family the husband earns the money, he may be viewed as having the "power of the purse" and, therefore, be accorded a greater say in spending decisions and quite possibly in other respects as well. Further, the wife's economic dependence on her husband means that she stands to lose more if the marriage breaks up. For this reason as well, she is likely to be under greater pressure to subordinate her wishes to her husband's than vice versa. As might be expected, women's earning power changes this dynamic. As their relative earnings increase, so does their control over how money is spent,[12] and they likely have greater say over a range of family decisions.

Domestic Violence

An additional disadvantage of specialization is that it will tend to limit opportunities for women to get out of an abusive, harmful situation.[13] That is, women who are not employed are less likely to have the financial means to leave an abusive relationship or to effectively persuade their husband that they will leave the marriage if the battering does not stop. Therefore it is not surprising that research identifies a link between improvements in women's economic status and reduced domestic violence. Similarly, changes in factors external to the family, such as states' adoption of unilateral divorce, have been found to be helpful, presumably because they improve women's bargaining power in the family.[14] The availability of services for victims of domestic violence such as shelters, counseling, and legal advice would be expected to have the same effect.

Dealing with spousal abuse, whether the aggressor be a husband or occasionally a wife, is often made more difficult by the ambivalent attitudes of society. Many believe that such battering is a family matter and that the legal system should not intrude, or may even suggest that the victim might have "asked for it." Another complication is that children in the household may further add to the emotional as well as the financial difficulty of leaving.

The consequences of domestic violence likely vary, depending on the length and severity of the abuse, and may include both psychological difficulties as well as

---

[12] For studies regarding the allocation of money and decision making within marriage, see Catherine T. Kenney, "The Power of the Purse: Allocative Systems and Inequality in Couple Households," *Gender and Society* 20, no. 3 (June 2006): 354–81; Philip Blumstein and Pepper Schwartz, *American Couples* (New York: William Morrow, 1983); and Edward P. Lazear and Robert T. Michael, *Allocation of Income within the Household* (Chicago: University of Chicago Press, 1988). See also Marianne A. Ferber, "Labor Market Participation of Young Married Women: Causes and Effects," *Journal of Marriage and Family* 44, no. 2 (May 1982): 457–68.

[13] For a discussion of how domestic violence is measured, see Francine D. Blau, "Trends in the Well-Being of American Women, 1970–1995," *Journal of Economic Literature* 36, no. 1 (March 1998): 112–65; recent statistics are available at the U.S. Department of Justice web site, www.ojp.usdoj.gov/bjs. Robert Pollak formalizes the notion of a cycle of domestic violence in "An Intergenerational Model of Domestic Violence," *Journal of Population Economics* 17, no. 2 (June 2004): 311–29.

[14] For evidence on the benefits of employment, see Amy Farmer and Jill Tiefenthaler, "An Economic Analysis of Domestic Violence," *Review of Social Economy* 55, no. 3 (Fall 1997): 337–58; and Audra J. Bowlus and Shannon Seitz, "Domestic Violence, Employment, and Divorce," *International Economic Review* 47, no. 4 (November 2006): 1113–49. Regarding the impact of changes in divorce laws, see Betsey Stevenson and Justin Wolfers, "Bargaining in the Shadow of the Law: Divorce Laws and Family Distress," *Quarterly Journal of Economics* 12, no. 121 (February 2006): 267–88.

physical injuries. Domestic violence may also affect employment and earnings. Interestingly, studies find that labor force participation rates of women who are victims of domestic violence are the same or even higher than of otherwise similar women who are not victims. This finding could be because battered women seek employment outside the home as a refuge or as a means of achieving economic independence (in preparation for leaving). On the other hand, some evidence indicates that battering negatively affects women's job performance and consequently may lower their wages.[15]

TRANSACTION COST AND BARGAINING APPROACHES

One of the shortcomings of the neoclassical model of the family highlighted by the preceding discussion of the disadvantages of specialization is that it ignores the internal decision making structure of the family. The model simply assumes that the family operates efficiently and without friction either because of a consensus on preferences within the family or because decisions are made by an altruistic family head and accepted by all other members.[16] In this view of the family, power is irrelevant.

More recently, however, alternative approaches have been developed that emphasize transaction costs and bargaining. These approaches endeavor to unlock the "black box" of the family and look more deeply into how families are organized and make decisions.[17] The transaction cost approach, for instance, focuses on the role of institutions in structuring complex, long-term relationships so as to minimize transaction costs. That is, just as a merger between firms eliminates the costs of negotiating repeated contracts and ensures that the initially separate firms will do business together for years to come, a marriage fosters a long-term relationship between partners. Marriage incorporates both rules about the nature of the ongoing relationship and about the rights of each individual should the union break up. Hence, it might be seen as a contractual affiliation that is "flexible enough to allow adaptive sequential decision making in the face of unfolding events."[18]

Marriage as an implicit contract provides incentives for couples to make substantial marriage-specific investments. Hence, couples are likely to invest more time and effort in activities that produce "commodities" more highly valued within the marriage than outside the marriage. Most importantly, they will be more willing to devote much time and effort to raising their children. Children are likely to be particularly valued by their own parents; they may not be valued by another partner and may even be a liability in their parents' search for a new spouse.[19] This is likely to be a particular problem for women since they generally retain custody of the children if the marriage breaks up. Moreover, women, especially traditional homemakers, are more likely than men to make such marriage-specific investments, which puts them at a greater disadvantage if the marriage should end.

---

[15] Amy Farmer and Jill Tiefenthaler, "The Employment Effects of Domestic Violence," *Research in Labor Economics* 23 (2004): 301–34.

[16] The consensus model was proposed by Paul Samuelson, "Social Indifference Curves," *Quarterly Journal of Economics* 70, no. 1 (February 1956): 1–22. The altruist model was introduced by Gary S. Becker, "A Theory of Marriage: Part II," *Journal of Political Economy* 82, no. 2 (March/April 1974): 11–26.

[17] Even though this section focuses on decision making among spouses, bargaining models have been applied to decisions made by a parent and an adult child as well. See, for instance, Lilliana E. Pezzin and Barbara Steinberg Schone, "Intergenerational Household Formation, Female Labor Supply and Informal Caregiving: A Bargaining Approach," *Journal of Human Resources* 34, no. 3 (Summer 1999): 475–503.

[18] For a discussion of the transaction cost approach, see Pollak, "A Transaction Cost Approach"; quote is from p. 595.

[19] See, for instance, Evelyn Lehrer, "On Marriage-Specific Human Capital: Its Role as a Determinant of Remarriage," *Journal of Population Economics* 3, no. 3 (October 1990): 193–213.

Because marriage is intended to be a long-term relationship, it is not realistic to specify everything in advance, that is, to provide for all possible contingencies.[20] At the same time, it is quite unlikely that husbands and wives share the same preferences regarding all consumption and production decisions. Thus, bargaining between the partners is likely very important. A class of **bargaining models** has been developed that allows for husbands and wives to have different preferences, with outcomes determined through a process of bargaining.[21]

In these models, the bargaining power of each spouse is determined by his or her *threat point*—the level of well-being that each would attain if they cannot reach agreement within the marriage. In the most common type of family bargaining model, termed *divorce-threat* bargaining models, the threat point depends on the amount of income each partner would control if the marriage were to terminate.[22] As in the case of negotiations between a vendor and a customer, the final solution is likely to more closely reflect the preferences of the party with the stronger threat effect, the one who is better able to "walk away" from the deal. Apart from each individual's control of resources outside the marriage, other factors external to the family may also affect one or both of the partners' threat points. These might include laws defining the division of marital property, the probability of remarriage, as well as eligibility rules for and benefit levels under welfare.[23]

To make the discussion concrete, let's reconsider the example of John and Jane, one of the married couples discussed earlier. They maximized total family income by specializing; Jane split her time between home production and market work while John did only market work, with no time spent in home production. Once total income is maximized, the next issue is to decide how to allocate this joint income among the different commodities the family might want. For instance, even if parents agree on the amount they want to spend on their children, they may differ on whether the money should be spent on children's clothing as opposed to, say, music lessons or gymnastics classes. As another example, one spouse may prefer to spend discretionary income on an expensive car, while the other may prefer travel. These situations differ from the simple model that assumes that John and Jane have the same preferences or that John is an altruistic head who assigns appropriate weights to the preferences of other family members.

In some instances one of these assumptions may be reasonable, but bargaining models are likely more realistic because they allow for the possibility that John's and Jane's preferences may differ and that both matter. In this view, the outcome will in large part depend on their relative bargaining power. Assuming a traditional division of

---

[20] For a discussion, see Paula England and George Farkas, *Households, Employment and Gender: A Social, Economic, and Demographic View* (New York: Aldine Publishing Co., 1986).

[21] For reviews of the literature, see Shelly J. Lundberg and Robert A. Pollak, "Family Decision Making," New Palgrave *Dictionary of Economics*, 2nd edition, edited by Steven N. Durlauf and Lawrence E. Blume (New York: Palgrave Macmillan, 2008), pp. 254–60; Bina Agarwal, "'Bargaining' and Gender Relations: Within and Beyond the Household," *Feminist Economics* 3, no. 1 (March 1997): 1–51; and Theodore Bergstrom, "Economics in a Family Way," *Journal of Economic Literature* 34, no. 4 (December 1996): 1903–34. For early work in this area, see Mary Jean Horney and Marjorie B. McElroy, "Nash-Bargained Household Decisions: Toward a Generalization of the Theory of Demand," *International Economic Review* 22, no. 2 (June 1981): 333–49; and Marilyn Manser and Murray Brown, "Marriage and Household Decision Making," *International Economic Review* 21, no. 1 (February 1980): 31–44.

[22] Shelly J. Lundberg and Robert A. Pollak suggest an alternative threat point within the marriage itself, in which the partners fully specialize in the provision of public goods according to traditional gender roles; for example, the wife provides all the child care, while the husband does all the outdoor work. In this "separate spheres" model, family behavior depends not on the incomes each spouse would receive after divorce but on the resources each spouse controls within marriage. See "Separate Spheres Bargaining and the Marriage Market," *Journal of Political Economy* 101, no. 6 (December 1993): 988–1010.

[23] Marjorie B. McElroy, "The Empirical Content of Nash-Bargained Household Behavior," *Journal of Human Resources* 25, no. 4 (Fall 1990): 559–83.

labor, Jane is expected to have less bargaining power because she has a weaker threat point. The reason is that if the couple were to divorce, she would probably not fare as well as John. Even if she were to receive child support and perhaps a small divorce settlement, she would likely have more difficulty supporting herself (and their children) because she has mainly invested in marriage-specific rather than market skills. Other factors that affect her relative bargaining power would be the level of welfare benefits and food stamps available to her if she were divorced, her labor market opportunities, and her chances for remarriage. John, on the other hand, is likely to be in a much stronger bargaining position because, during the marriage, he remained fully attached to the labor market. However, once divorced, John may need to pay alimony and child support, and may also have less contact with his children, depending on the provisions of the child custody agreement. In addition, he is likely to have to purchase some household services formerly produced by his wife.

One way of determining whether husbands' and wives' preferences differ significantly is to see if they spend their personal income in the same way. A good deal of research shows that they generally do not. Two studies specifically examined the effect of a policy change in the United Kingdom in the 1970s that transferred receipt of income, in the form of a child benefit, from the father to the mother. Both found that this change led to an *increase* in expenditures on children's consumption (as measured in one study by expenditures on children's clothing, and in the other, by expenditures on children's clothing, toys, and "pocket" money).[24] These studies, among others, suggest that the "common preference" assumption of the simple model does not hold up. Indeed, mounting evidence shows that, consistent with bargaining models, who controls family resources affects a wide array of outcomes beyond consumption expenditures, including decisions as to how couples allocate their time, as well as how much they give to charities and who should receive these donations.[25] In addition, as discussed earlier, women who have greater economic resources are less likely to experience domestic violence. These findings neither directly prove that bargaining takes place, nor do they indicate what specific form it might take, but they are more consistent with a bargaining framework than with either the consensus or altruist models.

In our preceding discussion, we focused on expenditures on children's clothing as an illustrative example of a case in which husbands and wives differ in their spending patterns. In fact, a growing body of research suggests that mothers generally allocate more resources and place greater emphasis on their children's well-being than do fathers. Notably, in developing countries where resources are scarce, children's health and survival probabilities have been found to improve when mothers have greater control over family resources.[26]

One implication of this research is that the government has the *potential* to promote certain outcomes, to the extent that its policies and laws affect the distribution of

---

[24] Shelly J. Lundberg, Robert. A. Pollak, and Terence J. Wales, "Do Husbands and Wives Pool Their Resources? Evidence from the U.K. Child Benefit," *Journal of Human Resources* 32, no. 3 (Summer 1997): 463–80; and Jennifer Ward-Batts, "Out of the Wallet and Into the Purse: Using Micro Data to Test Income Pooling," *Journal of Human Resources* 43, no. 2 (Spring 2008): 325–51.

[25] Regarding the labor supply of married couples, see Paul Schultz, "Testing the Neoclassical Model of Family Labor Supply and Fertility," *Journal of Human Resources* 25, no. 4 (Fall 1990): 599–634; and for cohabitors see Anne E. Winkler, "Economic Decision Making Among Cohabitors: Findings Regarding Income Pooling," *Applied Economics* 29, no. 8 (August 1997): 1079–90. Regarding charitable contributions, see James Andreoni, Eleanor Brown, and Isaac Rischall, "Charitable Giving by Married Couples: Who Decides and Why Does It Matter?" *Journal of Human Resources* 38, no. 1 (Winter 2003): 111–33.

[26] See, for instance, Duncan Thomas, "Intra-Household Resource Allocation: An Inferential Approach," *Journal of Human Resources* 25, no. 4 (Fall 1990): 635–64; Duncan Thomas, "Like Father, Like Son: Like Mother, Like Daughter: Parental Resources and Child Height," *Journal of Human Resources* 29, no. 4 (Fall 1994): 950–88; and Rae L. Blumberg, "Income Under Female Versus Male Control: Hypotheses from a Theory of Gender Stratification and Data from the Third World," *Journal of Family Issues* 9, no. 1 (March 1988): 51–84.

resources between men and women, both inside and outside marriage.[27] As we have seen, in the United Kingdom, when the government paid the child benefit to mothers rather than fathers, it was found to raise expenditures on children. Another way that government may affect families is through laws that govern the distribution of marital assets in case of divorce. For example, adopting community property law (which mandates equal division of property) would generally give the wife a larger share of marital assets and hence increase her bargaining power within marriage. Interestingly, one study found that marital property laws that favor women are associated with wives' increased labor supply and reduced time in housework.[28] Similarly, as discussed earlier, the adoption of unilateral divorce laws have been found to reduce domestic violence, again most likely by increasing women's bargaining power. It has been further suggested that changes in men's and women's relative bargaining power may affect not only decisions *within* existing marriages, but even the decisions of unmarried individuals, such as whether to get married, and if so, to whom.[29]

MARXIST AND RADICAL FEMINIST VIEWS OF THE FAMILY

Up to now we have focused on the neoclassical model of the family, first developed by Gary S. Becker, followed by a discussion of the transaction cost and bargaining variations of the neoclassical model. Now we turn to the so-called heterodox views of Marxists[30] and radical feminists,[31] who offer substantially different interpretations of the division of labor within the family and of its relation to the position of women and men in the family and in the labor market. Like proponents of bargaining models, adherents of both the Marxist and radical feminist schools of thought emphasize the role of power relationships. And, both emphasize the potential for exploitation of the weaker party. Beyond that, however, their views differ fundamentally from each other. Marxists focus on the role of class and capitalism, while radical feminists focus on the role of gender and patriarchy, a concept we shall return to later.[32]

Capitalism describes an economy where the preponderance of capital is privately owned and controlled, even though government may also play a large part, as is the case in all capitalist countries, including the United States. Marxists see such an economy as one in which capitalists, who own the means of production, wield power over workers

---

[27] Agarwal, "'Bargaining' and Gender Relations."

[28] Jeffrey S. Gray, "Divorce-Law Changes and Married Women's Labor Supply," *American Economic Review* 88, no. 3 (June 1998): 628–51.

[29] Lundberg and Pollak, "Family Decision Making."

[30] While only the first volume of *Das Kapital* (Karl Marx, *Das Kapital. Kritik der politschen Oekonomie* (Hamburg: Verlag von Otto Meissner, New York: L.W. Schmidt, 1867)) was published in his lifetime, while the others were completed by his long-time collaborator Friedrich Engels, Karl Marx is universally viewed as the founder of the school of thought that bears his name.

[31] See, for example, Heidi I. Hartmann, "Capitalism, Patriarchy, and Job Segregation by Sex," *Signs: Journal of Women in Culture and Society* 1, no. 3 (Spring 1976, pt. 2): 137–70; Heidi I. Hartmann, "The Family as the Locus of Gender, Class and Political Struggle: The Example of Housework," *Signs: Journal of Women in Culture and Society* 6, no. 3 (Spring 1981): 366–94; and Nancy Folbre, *Who Pays for the Kids? Gender and the Structures of Constraint* (London: Routledge, 1994); and contributions in Janice Peterson and Margaret Lewis, eds., *The Elgar Companion to Feminist Economics* (Cheltenham, UK and Northampton, MA: Elgar, 1999. For an institutional approach to the family, see Clair Brown, "Consumption Norms, Work Roles, and Economic Growth," in *Gender in the Workplace,* edited by Clair Brown and Joseph A. Pechman (Washington, DC: Brookings Institution, 1987); and Daphne Greenwood, "The Economic Significance of 'Women's Place' in Society: A New-Institutionalist View," *Journal of Economic Issues* 18, no. 3 (September 1984): 663–80.

[32] The following analysis draws on the explications of Nancy Folbre, "Socialism, Feminist and Scientific," in *Beyond Economic Man,* edited by Marianne A. Ferber and Julie A. Nelson (Chicago: University of Chicago Press, 1993), pp. 94–110; Julie A. Nelson, "The Study of Choice or the Study of Provisioning? Gender and the Definition of Economics," in *Beyond Economic Man,* edited by Marianne A. Ferber and Julie A. Nelson (Chicago: University of Chicago Press, 1993), pp. 23–36; and Therese Jefferson and John E. King, "Never Intended to be a Theory of Everything: Domestic Labor in Neoclassical and Marxian Economics" *Feminist Economics* 7, no. 3 (November 2001): 71–101.

who do not and are therefore forced to sell their labor for wages. Women, whether they are workers or not, supply unpaid labor, including reproductive services in the family, thereby reducing the wages capitalists have to pay. Hence they are presumably exploited by capitalists, indirectly as housewives, as well as directly if they are workers. In addition, Marxists recognize that women are often oppressed by their wage-earning husbands.

Engels,[33] Marx's collaborator and close friend, whose ideas about the family are part of Marxist dogma, argued that women's inferior position came about as a result of men gaining control over private property over long years of pre-industrial history. In this view, married women, who had been publicly recognized household administrators, became a kind of private servant. Later, with the rise of large-scale industry, employed women did regain some access to the public sphere—as workers— but also remained responsible for housework. Marxists promised that they would relieve women of this burden by "socializing housework," providing such services as day care for children, nursing home care for the elderly and infirm, and public dining rooms for workers. However, the former Soviet Union, for many years the premier example of the Communist state, was very slow to provide these facilities and gave priority to rapid industrialization. It was argued that the fall of capitalism, which was the cause of women's oppression, would bring about their liberation.[34] At the same time, leaders never questioned that the household was women's responsibility, nor were men hired to do jobs that were previously performed by women in the household.[35]

Socialists have often been more sympathetic to women's concerns, with views that are much closer to those of feminists than are those of doctrinaire Marxists. For instance, one of the best-known early British socialists, Robert Owen, wanted to eliminate the rigid boundary drawn by both neoclassical and Marxist economists between the dog-eat-dog economy where all people single-mindedly pursue their own self-interest, and the family, where everyone is dedicated to the common good. Owen further viewed allegiance to family as basically another version of self-interest.[36] Similarly, the early German socialist August Bebel provided an extensive account of legal injustices, with emphasis on women's lack of control over their own lives.[37] These authors, while sharing Marxists' concern with class, were clearly concerned with patriarchy as well.

Patriarchy refers to a system where men's dominance as a group over women as a group is the real source of gender inequality.[38] Radical feminists generally see the family as the true locus of women's oppression. In addition, although they recognize both the existence of emotional ties and the existence of some unified interests within the family,

---

[33] Friedrich Engels, *The Origin of the Family, Private Property, and the State* (New York: International Publishers, 1884 [1972]).

[34] In fact, however, their promises to socialize housework had been only partially fulfilled by the time of the dissolution of the Soviet Union.

[35] One of the exceptions to this way of thinking was Clara Zetkin, "Dialogue with Clarra Zetkin," reprinted in Robert C. Tucker, *The Lenin Anthology* (New York: W.W. Norton and Company, 1975). Another was one of the greatest Marxian economic theorists, Rosa Luxemburg, "Women's Suffrage and Class Struggle," in *Selected Political Writings of Rosa Luxemburg*, edited by Dick Howard (New York: Monthly Review Press, 1912 [1971]), pp. 216–22. Both women argued that the Soviet Union needed to make greater efforts to provide services that would take the place of household labor.

[36] Robert Owen, *Lectures on the Marriages of the Priesthood of the Old Immoral World ... with an Appendix Containing the Marriage System of the New Moral World* (Leeds: J. Hobson, 1840).

[37] August Bebel, *Women and Socialism* (New York: Schocken Books, 1971).

[38] Folbre, *Who Pay for the Kids"* suggests that it is also based on age and preference for heterosexual relationships. Other useful discussions of patriarchy are to be found in Nancy Holmstrom, ed., *The Socialist Feminist Project: A Contemporary Reader in Theory and Politics* (New York: Monthly Review, 2003); and Julie Matthaei, "Marxist-Feminist Contributions to Radical Economics," in *Radical Economics*, edited by Bruce Roberts and Susan Feiner (Boston: Kluwer, 1992), pp. 117–44.

they nonetheless see the family as the locus of struggle. Radical feminists were also the ones who originated the slogan "the personal is political." In this view, Jane's responsibility for taking care of the household and the children, while John perhaps "helps her" by clearing the table, taking out the garbage, and putting the children to bed, is not merely the result of a private decision of these individuals, but is, to a considerable extent, influenced by patriarchal tradition. Adherence to this tradition serves in turn to perpetuate it. Further, radical feminists assert that the patriarchal tradition existed long before capitalism and would, absent other changes, continue even if capitalism disappeared. In fact, they believe that the particular economic system is largely irrelevant to their concern with patriarchy, just as Marxists believe that patriarchy is irrelevant to their concern with the economic system.

The Marxist feminist interpretation of the situation is somewhat different from either of the other two. Adherents of this view believe that the present status of women is the result of a long process of interaction between patriarchy and capitalism. They argue that patriarchy preceded capitalism and helped to shape its present form, but that capitalism in turn has helped to shape patriarchy as it exists today. Specifically, they claim that the primary mechanism for maintaining male superiority in the capitalistic economy has been occupational segregation, the restriction of women in the labor market to a relatively small number of predominantly female jobs.[39] This job segregation, caused and perpetuated not only by capitalists but also by male workers and their unions, depresses wages for women and thus makes them economically dependent on men. At the same time, the traditional division of labor in the home reinforces occupational segregation in the labor market. Therefore, Marxist feminists argue that if women's subordination is to end, and if working men are to escape class oppression, occupational segregation and the traditional division of labor in the household will both have to end. In their view, in order to achieve freedom for everyone, men must be persuaded, or forced if need be, to join with women in the struggles against patriarchal capitalism, the embodiment of the stratified society par excellence.

NONMARKET WORK

Economists have traditionally focused their attention on market work although much work is performed outside the market, both in the household and in the voluntary sector. Such unpaid work substantially contributes to the well-being of individuals, their families, and society at large. In this section we consider both types of nonmarket work and how women's and men's involvement in these activities has changed with women's rising labor force participation. Available data provide some evidence regarding how much time husbands and wives spend on market work, home production, and volunteer work, and the extent to which changes have occurred in recent decades in the allocation of time to each of them. In addition, we consider the complex issues involved in estimating the value of unpaid nonmarket contributions.

Housework and Child Care

Estimates of hours spent in housework vary considerably for a number of reasons. They are based on different samples, drawn from different populations, the information was collected in different ways, and definitions of housework often differ as well.[40]

---

[39] Some Marxist feminists go so far as to analyze the household itself in class terms, seeing the husband as the capitalist who appropriates the surplus value of the worker-wife. See, for instance, Harriet Fraad, Stephen Resnick, and Richard Wolff, *Bringing It All Back Home: Class, Gender and Power in the Modern Household* (London: Pluto Press, 1994).

[40] For a discussion of methodological issues, see. F. Thomas Juster, Hiromi Ono, and Frank P. Stafford, "An Assessment of Alternative Measures of Time Use," *Sociological Methodology* 33 (2003): 19–54.

For instance, some studies collect information based on stylized questions about particular activities such as "How many hours did you spend doing laundry last week?" while other studies ask respondents to record in a "time diary" what they do during specific blocks of time. It turns out that estimates of hours spent in housework obtained from stylized questions tend to be quite a bit higher. In terms of definitions, some studies explicitly include child care, others do not; some include only work done around the house, while others include household-related activities performed elsewhere.[41]

It is only as recently as 2003 that the U.S. government launched its first-ever time use survey, the **American Time Use Survey** (ATUS), following the lead of many other countries, including Canada, Australia, and a number of countries in the European Union.[42] In the ATUS time diary, reports are collected from one respondent per household using a subsample of households who were interviewed for the Current Population Survey (CPS). (The CPS is the U.S. government survey used to collect data on unemployment and *paid* work and is the source of much of the data provided in this book.) We use the ATUS data to describe the current division of labor between women and men. Because these data have only become available recently, we rely on other surveys to provide information about trends in housework and child care.

Let us begin by looking at Table 3-2, which provides detailed information on the current division of labor between women and men based on data from the 2006 ATUS. A useful feature of these data is that they show patterns in paid work and housework disaggregated by marital status and by employment status of the wife. As seen in Table 3-2, wives spent 18 hours per week in core housework activities such as laundry, cleaning, cooking, and yard work as compared with just under 10 hours for husbands. When household activities are more broadly defined to include time spent on grocery shopping and caring for household members, principally children, wives spent 29 hours versus 16 hours for husbands. Using either definition, wives spent nearly twice as much time in household activities as husbands in 2006. Not surprisingly, time in unpaid housework is highest for nonemployed wives.

How does the current situation shown in Table 3-2 compare to previous years? Data from various sources indicate a similar set of trends regarding time spent in housework from the 1960s to 2000. They show that wives, both employed and nonemployed, did substantially less housework in the 1970s than was the case in the 1960s, while time spent by husbands in housework did not change much.[43] Subsequently, from the late 1970s to 2000, wives' time in housework decreased even further. In contrast, husbands' housework time increased modestly through the late 1980s, though it did not change appreciably thereafter, at least through 2000.[44] As a result of these changes, from the mid-1960s to

[41] See, for instance, Suzanne Bianchi, Melissa A. Milkie, Liana C. Sayer, and John P. Robinson, "Is Anyone Doing the Housework? Trends in the Gender Division of Household Labor," *Social Forces* 79, no. 1 (September 2000): 1–39; W. Keith Bryant, Hyojin Kang, Cathleen D. Zick, and Anna Y. Chan, "Measuring Housework in Time Use Surveys," *Review of Economics of the Household* 2, no. 1 (March 2004): 23–47; and Anne E. Winkler, "Measuring Time Use in Households with More Than One Person," *Monthly Labor Review* 125, no. 2 (February 2002): 45–52.

[42] A description of the ATUS can be found on the U.S. Bureau of Labor Statistics' web site, www.bls.gov; and in Michael Horrigan and Diane Herz, "Planning, Designing, and Executing the BLS American Time-Use Survey," *Monthly Labor Review* 127 no. 10 (October 2004): 3–19. Regarding international efforts, see National Research Council, *Time-Use Measurement and Research* (Washington, DC: National Academy Press, 2000).

[43] See Joseph H. Pleck, "Husband's Paid Work and Family Roles: Current Research Issues," *Research in the Interweave of Social Roles: Jobs and Families*, edited by Helena Lopata and Joseph H. Pleck (Greenwich, CT: JAI Press, 1983), pp. 251–333; and Francine D. Blau, Marianne A. Ferber and Anne E. Winkler *The Economics of Women, Men, and Work*, 3rd ed. (Upper Saddle River, NJ: Prentice Hall, 1998), Table 3.2, p. 52.

[44] Francine D. Blau, Marianne A. Ferber, and Anne E. Winkler, *The Economics of Women, Men, and Work*, 5th ed. (Upper Saddle River, NJ: Prentice Hall, 1998), Table 3-2, p. 57; and Bianchi et al., "Is Anyone Doing the Housework?"

TABLE 3-2   Average Weekly Hours in Paid and Unpaid Work, 2006

	Time in Paid Work		Time in Unpaid Work			
	Market Work	Commute to Work	House-work	Grocery Shopping	Care of Household Members	Total
Women	24.3	1.9	16.5	3.3	6.4	26.2
Nonmarried	26.1	2.1	13.1	3.1	3.7	19.9
Married	23.4	1.8	18.3	3.4	7.8	29.4
Employed	33.4	2.6	15.0	3.1	5.9	24.0
Not Employed	0.2	0.0	25.8	3.9	12.1	41.8
Men	36.0	3.2	9.5	2.3	2.9	14.7
Nonmarried	32.4	2.7	9.2	2.0	0.7	12.0
Married	37.8	3.4	9.7	2.5	4.0	16.2
Wife Employed	38.7	3.3	9.9	2.5	4.1	16.5
Wife Not Employed	35.8	3.7	9.2	2.5	3.9	15.6
Gender Ratio of Time Use						
Women-to-Men	0.7	0.6	1.7	1.4	2.2	1.8
Married Women-to-Married Men	0.6	0.5	1.9	1.4	1.9	1.8

Note: Figures are for respondents age 25–64.

Housework includes routine activities such as laundry, food preparation, and cleaning, as well as yard work, pet care, vehicle repair, interior and exterior up-keep, and household management.

Grocery shopping includes purchasing groceries, food, and gas.

Care of household members includes children and other adults.

Figures on housework, grocery shopping, and care of household members include travel time.

Wife's employment status is measured using information on usual hours worked.

Source: Authors' calculations from the 2006 American Time Use Survey.

2000, married women's housework time fell substantially—from seven times that of married men to around twice as much.[45] Women also increased their market hours considerably, largely as a result of the rise in the proportion of married women in the labor force but also because of an increase in hours of paid work among employed wives. (The rising labor force participation of married women will be discussed further in subsequent chapters.) As a result of both sets of changes, the difference in the allocation of time to market work and nonmarket work between wives and husbands narrowed considerably.[46]

There are a number of reasons why wives spent so much less time in housework in 2006 than in earlier years. The trend toward smaller families, changes in household technology, and the increasing availability of market substitutes provide at least part of

---

[45] The mid-1960s figure is from Bianchi et al. Is Anyone Doing the Housework?" The figure for the 2000s is from Table 3-2 of this text.

[46] There is also the question of whether the reallocation of wives' time between the home and the market came at the expense of a reduction in leisure time for them. A recent study by Mark Aguiar and Erik Hurst suggests that this is not a concern. Examining trends from 1965 to 2003, they found an *increase* in leisure time of about 5 to 6 hours for women as well as men; see "Measuring Trends in Leisure: Evidence from Five Decades of Time Use Surveys," *Quarterly Journal of Economics* 122, no. 3 (August 2007): 969–1006. One of the first to raise this issue was Victor R. Fuchs, *Women's Quest for Economic Equality* (Cambridge, MA: Harvard University Press, 1988).

the explanation.[47] For these same reasons, absent some reallocation between husbands and wives, we would have expected husbands' housework time to have also declined. The fact that husbands' housework time actually increased during the 1980s suggests some reallocation of tasks between husbands and wives during this period, though as noted earlier, the increase did not continue after that. The rise in real wages for women, which increased the opportunity cost of their time spent in nonmarket activities, is likely an additional factor that contributed to the decrease in the time they spend on housework. A dynamic process may be going on in which rising market wages induce women to allocate more time to market work and less time to housework. As they do so, they accumulate more labor market experience, further increasing their wages and resulting in further decreases in their housework time.

Research conducted using data from the mid-1970s to 2000 identified other notable trends. For one, in 2000, although nonemployed wives continued to do more housework than employed wives, the time they spent on it decreased somewhat more than for employed wives.[48] This trend is particularly notable in light of the fact that, during the first half of the twentieth century, the amount of time that full-time homemakers spent on housework remained virtually unchanged.[49] Further, during this same period, time spent on housework increased not only for husbands with employed wives but also for husbands whose wives were not employed. A possible explanation is that women's rising earnings potential may have altered the balance of bargaining power in the household, whether or not the wife was actually employed, and that wives may have used their increased bargaining power to obtain some reallocation of housework.

Recent research also suggests several other interesting patterns in the allocation of housework. For instance, based on Gary Becker's theory, we would expect to see husbands spend more time doing housework in families where the wife, rather than the husband, brings home most of the earnings. Available evidence, however, suggests that even in these families, wives still do the majority of the housework, though the division of labor is a bit more equal as compared with households in which the husband is the main earner. Available data also indicate that nonemployed husbands spend surprisingly little time on housework. These findings suggest that time spent in housework remains tied to traditional notions of women's and men's gender roles.[50]

In fact, the gender difference in time spent on housework starts long before young men and women first head their own households. Data from 2003 indicate that teenage girls spent 50 percent more time doing housework than teenage boys.[51] This gender difference is further compounded by the fact that girls are less likely to be paid for their efforts. A recent study, covering the same period, found that girls are 15 percent less likely than boys of the same age to receive an allowance for doing household chores.[52]

---

[47] Regarding the role of household technology, see Jeremey Greenwood, Ananth Seshadri, and Mehmet Yorukoglu, "Engines of Liberation," *Review of Economic Studies* 72, no.1 (January 2005): 109–33.

[48] Blau, Ferber, and Winkler, *The Economics of Women, Men and Work*, 5th edition, Table 3-2; and Bianchi et al., "Is Anyone Doing the Housework?"

[49] As noted in Chapter 2, until the mid-1960s housewives continued to spend as many hours on housework as their grandmothers had at around the turn of the century. See Joann Vanek, "Time Spent in Housework," *Scientific American* 231, no. 5 (November 1974): 116–20.

[50] Michael Bittman, Paula England, Nancy Folbre, Liana Sayer, and George Matheson, "When Does Gender Trump Money? Bargaining and Time in Household Work," *American Journal of Sociology* 109, no. 1 (July 2003): 186–214; and Julie Brines, "Economic Dependency, Gender, and the Division of Labor at Home," *American Journal of Sociology* 100, no. 3 (November 1994): 652–88.

[51] Shirley L. Porterfield and Anne E. Winkler, "Teen Time Use and Parental Education: Evidence from the CPS, MTF, and ATUS," *Monthly Labor Review* 130, no. 5 (May 2007): 37–56.

[52] "Time, Money and Who Does the Laundry," *Research Update*, University of Michigan Institute for Social Research 4 (January 2007), based on the research of Frank Stafford.

Interesting differences are also evident in the allocation of housework between married spouses and cohabiting men and women. In both types of living arrangements, men spend less time on housework than women, but cohabiting men spend a larger share of time on it than married men.[53] Evidence also shows less specialization among partners in gay and lesbian couples.[54] As discussed further in Chapter 10, these patterns prevail, at least in part, because same-sex and cohabiting opposite-sex couples have far fewer legal protections than married couples, thereby making investment in homemaking and other "relationship-specific" capital particularly costly in the event that the couple breaks up.

Given the considerable interest in how much time parents spend with their children, particularly in light of women's rising labor force participation, we now turn to these patterns. A challenging aspect of looking at this issue is that it is not clear what activities should be included.[55] For instance, is going for a walk with a child nonmarket work or leisure? Further, the nature and "quality" of time parents spend with children varies depending on what else is going on and who else is around. During some of the time parents spend with children, they are directly engaged with them, for instance playing a game, listening to them talk about their day, or feeding or bathing them. At other times, care consists of supervising the child while engaged in another primary activity such as cooking, cleaning, or reading the newspaper, or while the parent and child are together in the car running errands. In the latter examples, the children are not the focus of the activity, so one might be inclined to ignore this dimension of time together. Still, value may be derived from having a parent in close proximity, even when she or he is primarily focused on other activities.

Keeping in mind these measurement difficulties, Table 3-3 provides figures on how much time wives and husbands spend in child care in households that include children. The estimates presented are for time spent in "primary" child care activities, when the parent is actively engaged with the child, and do not include time when they are merely "available."[56] Looking at the table, it should come as no surprise that it shows that nonemployed mothers spend more time with their children than employed mothers do. However, the difference is not as great as might have been expected. For example, the data in the table indicate that employed wives with at least one preschool age child spent nearly three-fourths as much time directly engaged with their children as their nonemployed counterparts.[57]

Suzanne Bianchi, among others, offers a number of plausible explanations for why the difference between employed and nonemployed mothers in time spent with children is relatively modest. For one thing, a considerable fraction of employed women work less

---

[53] Scott J. South and Glenna Spitze, "Housework in Marital and Nonmarital Households," *American Sociological Review* 59 (June 1994): 327–47; and Leslie S. Stratton, "Specialization in Household Activities Within Cohabiting Versus Married Households," Working Paper, Virgina Commonwealth University (April 2004).

[54] Lisa A. Giddings, "But... Who Mows the Lawn?: The Division of Labor in Same-Sex Households," in *Women, Family, and Work: Writings on the Economics of Gender*, edited by Karine S. Moe (UK: Blackwell, 2003), pp. 85–102.

[55] For an excellent discussion of these issues, see Nancy Folbre and Jayoung Yoon, "What Is Child Care? Lessons from Time-Use Surveys of Major English-Speaking Countries," *Review of Economics of the Household* 5, no. 3 (September 2007): 223–48; "and Karrie Ann Snyder, "A Vocabulary of Motives: Understanding How Parents Define Quality Time," *Journal of Marriage and the Family* 69, no. 2 (May 2007): 320–340.

[56] Figures on time spent in primary child care differ somewhat across studies depending on what specific activities are included (e.g., basic care or more), the treatment of travel time, the age, marital status, and employment status of the respondent, and the age of the children. For details on the definition used here, see the note to Table 3-3.

[57] Suzanne M. Bianchi, John P. Robinson, and Melissa A. Milkie find that for all mothers this figure is closer to 63 percent, while other studies have found figures just over 80 percent, with the variation due to such factors as the time use survey used, whether time use is calculated based on a survey of adults' or childrens' time use, and the precise definition of child care time; see *Changing Rhythms of American Family Life* (New York: Russell Sage Foundation, 2006), pp. 74–78.

TABLE 3-3 Wives' and Husbands' Average Weekly Hours in Primary Child Care, by Presence of Household Children and Wives' Employment, 2006

	With at Least One Child	With at Least One Preschool-Age Child
Wives	10.1	18.1
Employed	8.0	15.5
Full Time	7.1	14.3
Not Employed	14.6	21.6
Husbands	5.0	8.5
Wife Employed	5.1	9.5
Full Time	5.0	10.1
Wife Not Employed	4.9	7.3

Note: Figures are for respondents age 25–64.

Child care time refers to primary time spent with children. Figures include routine activities, reading, playing, talking, organizing, attending events, looking after child as the principal activity, and associated travel time; figures exclude time spent in activities related to children's education and health.

Wife's employment status is measured using information on usual hours worked.

Source: Authors' calculations from the 2006 American Time Use Survey.

than full time, full year. In addition, even women who are employed full time may be able to juggle their schedules in order to pick their children up after school or occasionally take an afternoon off from work. Indeed, as shown in Table 3-3, time spent in child care by mothers who are employed full time, around 14 hours per week, is quite close to the figure for all employed mothers (including those who work part time) of 15.5 hours. In addition, school-age children spend a good part of their day in school and preschool has become quite common even for children with nonemployed mothers, reducing the amount of time for mothers and children to be together even when the mother is not employed. Employed mothers also take time from their own leisure activities and sleep to spend time with children. All these factors reduce the difference in the amount of primary time spent that employed mothers spend with their children as compared to their nonemployed counterparts.[58] Finally, it should be kept in mind that the figures reported in Table 3-3 are for primary time spent with children. When supervisory time is included, the gap is larger.[59]

Recent evidence also indicates that more highly educated mothers spend more time directly engaged with their children than less educated mothers and that this gap has increased over time.[60] This finding is perhaps a bit surprising in light of the fact that more highly educated mothers have higher employment rates and earn higher wages, so their opportunity cost of time spent with children is higher. One possible explanation is that time with children may be a luxury good, meaning that time with children increases with income. It may also be the case that highly educated mothers (and fathers, for that matter) view one-on-one time with children as a necessary "investment" in their children, alongside formal education and extracurricular activities.[61] A further

[58] This discussion, apart from the figures reported in Table 3-3, is drawn from Suzanne M. Bianchi, "Maternal Employment and Time with Children: Dramatic Change or Surprising Continuity?" *Demography* 37, no. 4 (November 2000): 401–14; and Bianchi et al., *Changing Rhythms of American Family Life*, Chapter 4.

[59] Bianchi et al., *Changing Rhythms of American Family Life*, Table 4.4.

[60] For evidence and discussion see Jonathan Guryan, Erik Hurst, and Melissa Kearney, "Parental Education and Parental Time with Children, *Journal of Economic Perspectives* 22, no. 3 (Summer 2008): 23–46; and Bianchi et al., *Changing Rhythms of American Family Life*.

[61] Guryan et al. "Parental Education and Parental Time with Children," suggest these possibilities among several others.

explanation for this pattern is that, even if less-educated mothers work the same number of hours and have similar preferences, they may have less flexible schedules, reducing the opportunity to take time off at will.

Recent research also indicates that, despite concerns about maternal employment, whether children live with two parents or only one is a more important determinant of time spent with their mother than whether their mother is employed. This finding is largely due to the fact that two parents can often coordinate their schedules so that one of them will be free to spend time with their children. In fact, the amount of time that mothers and fathers in two-parent families spend with their children, whether narrowly or broadly defined, increased between 1965 and 2000. Notably, married fathers particularly increased their participation in routine child care tasks, such as giving children a bath, further evidence of their changing family role. Single mothers also increased the amount of time they were directly engaged with their children, although there was no change in the total time they spend with them, reflecting the much greater constraints on their time. Although comparable data on trends are not available for noncustodial divorced and never-married fathers, the average level of their involvement with their children tends to be much lower.[62]

Thus, recent trends regarding the allocation of housework and market work between husbands and wives and of child care between parents in two-parent families are generally heartening. Still, many questions remain, including what is a fair share of housework for each partner and how are specific housework tasks to be allocated? This is made more difficult by the fact that many men were raised in traditional homes where boys only did "male chores" such as raking leaves or shoveling snow and were not expected to do the laundry, cook dinner, or mind their younger siblings. Beyond all that, spouses need to accept that the other individual may not perform specific tasks in precisely the same way that they do.[63]

As for the problems of women, it is important to note that the data reviewed here may tend to underestimate the difficulties of both nonemployed and employed women. Full-time homemakers may have more leisure than either employed women or men but for most of them it is unequally distributed over the life cycle. Equally important, they tend to have less bargaining power within the family and, most seriously, they will often be in dire straits if, for whatever reason, the need arises for them to manage on their own. As for employed women, the problems they face differ greatly depending on whether they are part-time or full-time workers. Those employed part-time, often because they have primary responsibility for their family, are likely to confront a smaller and less attractive choice of jobs, frequently lower earnings, scant fringe benefits, and fewer opportunities for promotion, while those who work full time must deal with a considerably heavier workload. Finally, employed women who are responsible for taking care of very young children or other family members needing personal care are likely to confront particular problems. The difficulties of mothers of infants and toddlers are especially serious because many of these women are also at the age when they need to prove themselves on the job if they are to make much progress. Their extra responsibilities at home are apt to make it more difficult for them to compete with their male counterparts. Thus, whatever route employed wives choose, the unequal division of labor in the home is likely to adversely affect their success in the labor market.[64]

---

[62] This paragraph draws from Sandberg and Hofferth, "Changes in Children's Time"; Bianchi et al., *Changing Rhythms*; and Joseph H. Pleck, "Balancing Work and Family," *Scientific American Presents* 10, no. 2 (Summer 1999): 38–43.

[63] Lisa Belkin, "Will Dad Ever Do His Share? *The New York Times Magazine* (June 15, 2008), pp. 44–51, 74, and 78.

[64] For further discussion, see Barbara R. Bergmann, *The Economic Emergence of Women* (New York: Basic Books, 1986).

On the other hand, it has been argued that the unequal division of household and market labor is in some ways less of a problem for women than the discussion suggests. First, many tasks women perform are no longer as physically exacting as those their grandmothers did. Second, as discussed earlier, such activities as shopping and, to a considerable extent, child care may be enjoyable enough to be regarded as quasi-leisure. However, much of paid work has also become less onerous, and time on the job spent interacting with coworkers and entertaining clients may also be quasi-leisure. In fact, an extensive study of people's preferences indicates that, on the whole, they enjoy child care more than any other activities included in a comprehensive list, but enjoy their jobs far more than any other kind of housework and considerably more than many leisure activities.[65]

The question also arises as to what has happened to all of the housework that used to be done in past years.[66] Part of the answer is that "norms" for what needs to be done have changed. For instance, one study finds that while women's overall satisfaction with the cleanliness of their homes has changed little during the past two decades, sales have declined for products like furniture polish and carpet cleaner, indicating that individuals are spending less time on "discretionary" cleaning.[67] Another part of the answer is that homemakers have increasingly taken advantage of household appliances such as washing machines and dishwashers, microwaves and food processors. These appliances considerably reduce the effort required for many basic housekeeping activities, as well as the time. Further, many items that were previously produced at home are now often purchased; these include not only clothing, but also prepeared meals and child care. Another strategy for families is to hire firms or individuals to come to their homes to do regular tasks such as house cleaning or mowing the lawn. As might be expected, the research evidence indicates that family income matters, especially the wife's earnings, in determining whether a family purchases these types of market substitutes. This strategy, however, is not simply an issue of affordability, because even with the same income, African Americans are less likely to use market substitutes than other groups.[68]

In spite of the changes that have taken place, it is likely that for the foreseeable future the ultimate locus of responsibility for homemaking in most instances will continue to rest with women. So, when unexpected problems and small emergencies come up, it is still women, rather than men, who will be expected to give family needs greater priority. Part of the explanation for the slow pace of change is that, as noted, the role of homemaker continues to be associated with femininity but is seen as in conflict with masculinity. To the extent that this persists, it is likely that even wives who are employed full time will continue to do a considerable amount of housework and that nonemployed men will likely continue to spend relatively little time on housework. Nevertheless, as men assume more homemaking responsibilities, these cultural definitions may be expected to erode and hasten the decline in the traditional gender division of labor.

Volunteer Work

In addition to market work and housework, many people also spend an appreciable amount of time on volunteer work. Volunteer activities are defined as tasks performed without direct reward in money or in kind that mainly benefit others rather than the individuals themselves or their immediate family.

---

[65] F. Thomas Juster, "Preferences for Work and Leisure," in *Time, Goods and Well-Being*, edited by F. Thomas Juster and Frank P. Stafford (Ann Arbor, MI: Institute for Social Research, University of Michigan, 1985).
[66] Bianchi et al., "Is Anyone Doing the Housework?"
[67] John P. Robinson and Melissa Milkie, "Dances with Dust Bunnies: Housecleaning in America," *American Demographics* 19, no. 1 (January 1997): 37–59; and John Fetto, "Off The Map: The White Glove Test," *American Demographics* 24, no. 7 (July/August 2002): 56.
[68] Philip N. Cohen, "Replacing Housework in the Service Economy: Gender, Class, Race-Ethnicity in Service Spending," *Gender and Society* 12, no. 2 (April 1998): 219–31.

Thus, volunteer work is neither a way of earning a living nor an integral part of homemaking. Nevertheless, much business is transacted and many profitable contacts are made by business owners at local Chamber of Commerce meetings. At least in part, people participate in labor unions to improve their own working conditions and join their symphony's volunteer association to take advantage of special benefits such as free or reduced-price concerts. They are also more likely to participate in the PTA or scouting when they have children who are involved in these activities. Further, anything that enhances life in the community influences the well-being of the individuals themselves and of their families, at least indirectly, and often the connection is fairly close. In principle, the distinction between volunteer work and other forms of work is made in terms of which is the dominant purpose, but in practice it is by no means easy to decide where the line should be drawn.

There is also the issue of distinguishing between volunteer work and leisure activities from which individuals derive gratification. Examples would be bringing meals to a sick neighbor or taking a Brownie troop to a museum. This problem is often solved by including only organized activities, but this tends to exclude some valid volunteer activities. Thus, it is not surprising that estimates of the amount of volunteer work done vary widely, depending on the definition used, the questions asked, and the respondent who answers the questions.

An alternative view of volunteer work is that it is mainly a "conscience good," an undertaking that is not intended to indirectly enhance either the income or the direct enjoyment of the participants. This interpretation is based on the finding that people most often do volunteer work in response to a request.[69] To the extent that this view is realistic, volunteer work is distinct from both paid work and recreation.

In any case, much valuable volunteer work is performed. As shown in Table 3-4, a national survey conducted in 2007 found that 26 percent of adults volunteered for some type of organization, ranging from stacking shelves at a food pantry to serving as a board member.[70]

A notable gender difference seen in Table 3-4 is that women volunteer at higher rates than men. In 2007, the rates were 29 percent for women and 23 percent for men. Part of the explanation for this difference is that women are more likely to be part-time workers, a group with a much higher volunteer rate, though notably, even women who are employed full time volunteer at a higher rate than their male counterparts. It is also worth noting that women and men who are out of the labor force spend less time in volunteer work than their employed counterparts. The reason for this difference is in part because they are considerably older, but also because volunteer work is frequently job related, as when people are active in a labor union or a local business association. For this group as well, women volunteer at higher rates than men.

Women and men also differ in the kinds of volunteer work they do. Women contribute more time to health organizations and educational institutions, while men do more voluntary work for civic and political, as well as sport and recreational organizations. There are, however, no substantial differences in the proportions of women and men involved in social welfare organizations and religious institutions.[71]

---

[69] Richard B. Freeman, "Working for Nothing: The Supply of Volunteer Labor," *Journal of Labor Economics* 15, no. 1, pt. 2 (January 1997): S140–66; and John Wilson, "Volunteering," *Annual Review of Sociology* 26 (2000): 215–40.

[70] Data on volunteering are now also available from the American Time Use Survey (ATUS) conducted by the Bureau of Labor Statistics and can be found on their web site, www.bls.gov.

[71] "A Vast Empirical Record Refutes the Idea of Civic Decline," Special issue of *Public Perspective* 7, no. 4 (June/July 1996); and Stephanie Borass, "Volunteerism in the United States," *Monthly Labor Review* 126 no. 8 (August 2003): 3–11.

TABLE 3-4   Participation Rates in Volunteer Work, 2007[a]

	Women (%)	Men (%)	Total (%)
Total	29.3	22.9	26.2
Race/Ethnicity[b]			
White	31.4	24.2	27.9
Black	20.2	15.7	18.2
Asian	18.5	16.7	17.7
Hispanic Origin	17.2	10.1	13.5
Educational Attainment[c]			
Less than HS Diploma	10.5	7.5	9.0
HS Graduate Only	21.4	15.6	18.6
Some College	34.3	26.3	30.7
College Graduate	45.8	37.7	41.8
Employment Status			
Employed Full Time	30.3	24.4	26.9
Employed Part Time	40.0	26.4	35.4
Unemployed	28.2	18.5	23.2
Not in Labor Force	24.5	18.8	22.3

Note: Figures are computed for individuals age 16 and over for period Sept. 1, 2006–Sept. 1, 2007.

[a]Figures on volunteers count those individuals who performed unpaid volunteer activities for an organization; figures exclude informal volunteer work such as helping a neighbor.

[b]The participation figures for race/ethnicity do not sum to 100% because the figures for "other races" are not included and because a person of Hispanic origin may be of any race.

[c]Data on educational attainment are computed for those age 25 and over.

Source: U.S. Bureau of Labor Statistics, "Volunteering in the United States, 2007", *News,* USDL 08-0090 (January 23, 2008), Table 1. Available at www.bls.gov/cps.

Rates of volunteerism also differ by race and ethnicity. In 2007, the participation rate for the population as a whole was 26 percent, while it was only 18 percent for African-Americans and just under 14 percent for Hispanics. The lower figures for these groups are likely explained by the fact that volunteerism is greater, on average, for more highly educated and for higher-income individuals.

Due to changes in the designs of the major surveys used to collect volunteer data, consistent evidence is not available on long-term trends in volunteerism. For the recent period 2003 through 2007, data based on the same source as those reported in Table 3-4 indicate a modest decline in the percentage of women and men volunteering, from 32 to 29 percent for women, and from 25 to 23 percent for men.[72] Over this same period, there was no change in median volunteer hours among women and men reporting information on time spent volunteering. More data are needed to assess whether the decline in the rate of volunteering portends a long-term trend.

[72] 2003 figures are from U.S. Bureau of Labor Statistics, "Volunteering in the United States, 2003" *News*, USDL 03-888 (December 17, 2003), Table 1.

In sum, many reasons explain why people do work that, by definition, brings few or no direct material rewards. True altruism (or conscience), contact with congenial people, dedication to a particular cause, desire for recognition, furthering business, and advancing one's own or a spouse's career or the well-being of one's loved ones all may play a part.[73] Research also suggests that volunteer activities may help women who are out of the labor force get better jobs when they reenter. Indeed, some recent research finds that volunteer work confers economic benefits in the form of higher earnings and greater occupational achievement, perhaps by providing the individual with valuable human capital or networking opportunities. Although experience gained in volunteer work is probably not as valuable, in general, as that acquired on the job, women with demanding family responsibilities, such as caring for young children or elderly relatives, may value the more flexible schedule, and others may enjoy the greater ability to choose the type of work they do.[74] Experience in volunteer work is also likely to be particularly useful for persons interested in running for political office, both because of the skills acquired and the valuable contacts often made.

From the point of view of society, voluntary organizations of course serve a number of useful functions. Beyond the benefits listed, volunteers provide free services. It is frequently argued that as increasing numbers of women enter the labor market and have less time for volunteer work, their contributions to worthy causes will be greatly missed. However, as already noted, even women who are employed full time appear to participate in volunteer activities more than men. Further, because an increasing number of women now earn an income, they are able to contribute more money to worthy causes in place of time. Finally, because employed women pay taxes, more money is available for government expenditures on public services which, at least in some instances, might substitute for the role of charities.

Estimating the Value of Nonmarket Production

No one doubts that unpaid activities like housework and at-home child care are valuable to households and to the community. At present, however, these contributions are not included in U.S. **gross domestic product (GDP)**. GDP is the total money value of all the goods and services produced by factors of production within a country over a one-year period. The consequences of the omission of nonmarket production from GDP are potentially serious. For instance, comparisons of GDP between countries are distorted to the extent that the relative sizes of household and market sectors differ. Further, within a country, the growth in GDP is overstated if women reduce home production as they work more in the labor market, as has been the case in the United States.[75]

---

[73] Notably, Richard Freeman finds that the opportunity cost of time, as reflected by the wage, explains only a minor part of the decision to volunteer in "Working for Nothing."

[74] See Franz Hackl, Martin Halla, and Gerald J. Pruckner, "Volunteering and Income—The Fallacy of the Good Samaritan?" *Kyklos* 60, no. 1 (February 2007): 77–104; John Wilson and Marc Musick, "Doing Well by Doing Good: Volunteering and Occupational Achievement Among American Women," *Sociological Quarterly* 44, no. 3 (August 2003): 433–50; Marnie W. Mueller, "Economic Determinants of Volunteer Work by Women," *Signs: Journal of Women in Culture and Society* 1, no. 2 (Winter 1975): 325–38; and Francine D. Blau, "How Voluntary Is Volunteer Work? Comment on 'Economic Determinants of Volunteer Work by Women,'" *Signs: Journal of Women in Culture and Society* 2 , no. 1 (Autumn 1976): 251–54.

[75] These distortions have been recognized for some time. For instance, in 1946, A. C. Pigou observed that "... the services rendered by women enter into the dividend [Britain's measure of GDP at the time] when they are rendered in exchange for wages ... but do not enter into it when they are rendered by mothers or wives.... Thus, if a man married his housekeeper or his cook, the national dividend is diminished." This quote is cited in Statistics Canada, "Households' Unpaid Work: Measurement and Valuation," *Studies in National Accounting* (December 1995), p. 3. For recent empirical evidence, see Christopher House, John Laitner, Dmitriy Stolyarov, "Valuing Lost Home Production of Dual Earner Couples," *International Economic Review* 49, no. 2 (May 2008): 701–36.

Estimating the value of nonmarket activities, and ultimately including this value in GDP, however, poses a number of challenges. Many of these difficulties are well known to forensic economists—economists called upon to estimate the value of lost household services in court cases involving wrongful death and permanent injury. Most recently, such estimates were needed in the aftermath of September 11, 2001, as discussed in a subsequent inset.

One problem, the lack of an ongoing national U.S. time use survey, has been surmounted with the initiation of the Bureau of Labor Statistics American Time Use Survey in 2003. The complex issue of what nonmarket activities should be included in an augmented measure of GDP, however, remains to be settled. As in the earlier example, should taking a walk with children be counted fully as nonmarket work, or is it partly leisure?

Perhaps the greatest challenge is the lack of agreement regarding the preferable method of placing a value on nonmarket activities.[76] There are two fundamentally different methods, each with its own advantages and drawbacks. Economists, for the most part, tend to use the **opportunity cost approach**, which sets the value of unpaid work equal to the income the person could have earned in the labor market. It meshes well with the theory of labor supply, which will be discussed in detail in Chapter 4, in which individuals who participate in the labor force equate the value of an hour of nonmarket time to the market wage rate. For individuals who do not participate in the labor market, the value of nonmarket time must be at least as great as their potential market wage.

However, despite its theoretical appeal, a number of difficulties arise with this approach. First, there is the nontrivial problem of estimating potential market earnings for those who are out of the labor force. Second, although the market wage is known for those who are employed, the presumption that it accurately represents the value of nonmarket time may not be correct. Many workers do not have the option of working precisely as long as they wish but must work a specified number of hours or forgo an otherwise desirable job. Hence, they may not be able to divide their time so that the value of the last hour spent at home is exactly equal to their wage rate.

In addition to these problems, although correct application of the opportunity cost approach may identify the value of the nonmarket production to individuals and their families, it results in a higher value being placed on the nonmarket production of those whose (potential) market productivity is higher. So, for example, an hour spent scrubbing floors by a college graduate is valued more highly than an hour spent by a high school graduate in the same activity, even when they both do the task equally well.

The main alternative to the opportunity cost approach is the **market cost approach**, which sets the value of nonmarket production equal to the cost of hiring someone to do it. One way to estimate market cost is to first determine how much time is spent on each specific activity and then to use the wages of specialists such as cooks, home decorators, chauffeurs, and even child psychologists to estimate the value of nonmarket time. This is often referred to as the *specialist method*. One concern about this method is that it is unlikely that the typical homemaker can perform all these skills as competently as a specialist. For this reason, a recent government report recommends using this approach with adjustments for quality differences.[77] A simpler alternative is to value unpaid home work at the wage of a housekeeper. Regardless of the specific

---

[76] See National Research Council, *Beyond the Market: Designing Nonmarket Accounts for the United States.* (Washington, DC: National Academies Press, 2005); and Nancy Folbre, *Valuing Children* (Cambridge, MA: Harvard University Press, 2008), Chapter 7.
[77] National Research Council, *Beyond the Market.*

market-based measure, a common criticism is that they fail to capture the value of "personal and emotional care" in much nonmarket work, such as caring for one's own children, thus yielding values of nonmarket work that are too low.[78]

Despite all these difficulties, some preliminary efforts have been made in the United States to adjust standard GDP for nonmarket work. One recent study found that by ignoring nonmarket output, U.S. GDP for 2004 was underestimated by as much as 58 percent using the opportunity cost method, and between 18 to 23 percent using a market-based approach. Estimates for earlier years are even higher because a larger fraction of women were full-time homemakers and household technology was less advanced.[79] Such estimates could be used to supplement existing data on GDP, or GDP could even be redefined to include the value of unpaid work, though this would raise comparability issues with past GDP data.

Another question that remains is whether including the value of nonmarket work in GDP would really affect the status of women as a group. Some argue that the exclusion of unpaid work from GDP brands it as "unproductive." In this view, assigning money value to housework would improve women's status because it would increase recognition for the activities of women in the home and validate their economic contributions.[80] Others dispute this contention and believe that the inclusion of housework in GDP would not fundamentally affect the status of women because it would not make housewives economically independent nor raise the wages of women who perform these services for pay.[81]

Looking to the future, given that other economically advanced countries are estimating adjusted measures of GDP (along with the standard measure), it is likely that the United States will continue to explore alternative approaches. In light of the many methodological challenges, however, it may be some time before a standard method is widely accepted.

THE SEPTEMBER 11TH VICTIM COMPENSATION FUND OF 2001: JUST COMPENSATION?

The terrorist attacks that occurred in the United States on September 11, 2001, took the lives of a diverse cross-section of individuals: U.S. citizens and noncitizens; males and females; old and young; spouses, significant others, parents, and children; food workers, investment bankers, flight crews, and nonemployed persons. In some instances, more than one family member was killed. In the wake of the attacks, Congress set up a special fund called the September 11th Victim Compensation Fund of 2001 to provide some measure of financial compensation for the families of the victims. Those who accepted awards from the Fund had to agree not to sue the airlines involved or the U.S. government. The U.S. government appointed a "Special Master" to be in charge of the disbursement of monies. He faced the difficult task of deciding how much compensation each family would receive within the guidelines specified by

---

[78] Nancy Folbre and Julie A. Nelson emphasize that some nonmarket work has a caring component. "For Love or Money—Or Both?" *Journal of Economic Perspectives* 14, no. 4 (Fall 2000): 123–40.

[79] Figures are from J. Steven Landefeld, Barbara M. Fraumeni, and Cindy M. Vojtech, "Accounting for Nonmarket Production: A Prototype Satellite Account Using the American Time Use Survey," BEA Working Paper (Washington, DC: Bureau of Economic Analysis, December 2005), Table 8.

[80] See Susan Himmelweit, "The Discovery of 'Unpaid Work': The Social Consequences of the Expansion of 'Work,'" *Feminist Economics* 1, no. 2 (Summer 1995): 1–19; and Nancy Folbre, *Who Pays for the Kids? Gender and the Structures of Constraint* (London: Routledge, 1994).

[81] Barbara R. Bergmann, "The Economic Risks of Being a Housewife," *American Economic Review* 71, no. 2 (May 1981): 81–86.

Congress. The final ruling by the Special Master could not be disputed. Families were eligible to receive monies for the loss of their loved ones, independent of economic considerations (to reflect the loss of enjoyment of life and to compensate for the pain and suffering their loved ones experienced during the attacks). They were also to be compensated for the "presumed economic loss" of their loved ones, which is the focus here. The Final Rules, promulgated March 13, 2002, reflect input from a wide array of groups, including the National Organization for Women (NOW) Legal Defense and Education Fund.[*]

In the Victim Compensation Fund, economic loss was computed as lost income and benefits less consumption expenditures. For those who were employed at the time of the attack, income loss was calculated as lost future earnings potential. That is, how much they *would have* earned, given their recent earnings stream, if they had been employed until the end of their projected worklife. Early on, when the Fund's rules were first set forth, the value of household work was not counted as lost income for *full-time* workers, while it was estimated at "replacement value" for homemakers and part-time workers. As noted in NOW's memo to the Special Master, excluding the value of household services for full-time workers seriously understates women's economic contribution because many women who work full time for pay also work a "second shift" when they get home: They make dinner and clean up, do laundry, and take care of their children's needs. Men who work full time also do some housework, but as we have seen, they spend far less time on it than women. The Final Rules gave the Special Master the discretion to include the value of lost household services for full-time workers as well. The replacement value of lost household services was calculated using information on average weekly hours for specific activities, valued at commercial wages.[**] This value is likely a lower bound of lost services because it does not adequately reward the "managerial" function that many wives and mothers provide.[***] Further, family members offer more than just household labor; as discussed in the text, their services include a "caring" component that cannot be readily quantified.

Another concern raised in the NOW memo was that the income loss for women workers was based on their lost earnings, which may be too low as a result of gender discrimination. The Final Rules did not make a specific adjustment for women's earnings in this regard, nor is this adjustment presently made in tort litigation involving wrongful death or permanent injury. However, in the Final Rules, estimates of men's average worklife were used in calculating women's as well as men's economic loss. Because men's average worklife estimates are longer than women's, this factor should work to many women's advantage. In addition, to the extent that women's lower earnings are the result of greater time and effort in household activities, the inclusion of household services in the economic loss estimate addresses this concern to some extent.

Apart from issues of gender equity, other equity concerns have been raised about the methodology used by the Victim Compensation Fund. For instance, the use of labor market earnings to estimate economic loss has made many uncomfortable because this method conferred substantially higher awards to families of high-level executives than to those working in lower-level positions (though both received identical compensation for noneconomic losses). Indeed, total awards varied from $250,000 to $6 million, principally as a result of differences in estimates of economic loss. However, it should be noted that the approach followed by the Fund in this regard is quite standard in other cases in which an economic value is placed on loss of life or injury.[****]

Some concern also focuses on the difficulties that long-term unmarried partners, whether opposite sex or same sex, faced in obtaining awards from the Fund. State law determined who could seek compensation for the loss of a loved one. In 2003, the lesbian partner of one September 11th victim received monies from the Fund, so at least some precedent was set, but other unmarried partners may have been deterred by the considerably lengthier hearings process required, or by the publicity.[*****]

This discussion of the compensation awarded to the families of the victims of September 11th points to the fact that issues related to valuing housework have important practical applications. It also highlights the considerable challenges faced by those charged with the task of estimating such values.

*This inset draws on Kenneth R. Feinberg, Camille S. Biros, Jordana Harris Feldman, Deborah E. Greenspan, and Jacqueline E. Zinns, *Final Report of the Special Master for the September 11th Victim Compensation Fund of 2001* (Washington, DC: United States Department of Justice, 2004); and Memo from NOW Legal Defense and Education Fund to Mr. Kenneth Feinberg (February 11, 2002).
**Feinberg et al. *Final Report*, footnote 123.
***Thomas R. Ireland, "Economic Loss in the Case of a Full-Time Mother and Homemaker: When Lost Services Are the Only Pecuniary Loss," *Assessing Family Loss in Wrongful Death Litigation: The Special Roles of Lost Services and Personal Consumption*, edited by Thomas R. Ireland and Thomas O. Depperschmidt (Tucson, AZ: Lawyers & Judges Publishing Co., 1999); and Anne E. Winkler and Thomas R. Ireland, "Time Spent in Household Management: Measurement and Implications," *Journal of Family and Economic Issues* (September 2009.)
****Figure is from "Judge Affirms 9/11 Fund; Finds Award Process Is Fair," *Newsday*, May 9, 2003. See also Steven Brill, "A Tragic Calculus," *Newsweek*, December 31, 2001, p. 28; and Thomas R. Ireland and John O. Ward, *Assessing Damages in Injuries and Deaths of Minor Children* (Tucson, AZ: Lawyers & Judges Publishing Co., 2001).
*****"U.S. Awards Lesbian 9/11 Compensation for Loss of Partner," *Washington Post*, January 23, 2003. See also, Jennifer Barrett, "Shut Out," *Newsweek*, February 15, 2002.

THE AMERICAN FAMILY IN THE TWENTY-FIRST CENTURY

Although this chapter focused on married-couple families, it is important to discuss to what extent this type of family is still dominant in the United States, to what extent even this type of family has changed in recent decades, and what the increasingly common alternatives are. The changes that occurred in the United States did not happen in isolation, but rather occurred as part of a wave of similar changes in other economically advanced nations. Here we provide an overview of the developments in the United States, with a more detailed examination reserved for Chapter 10, and some discussion of trends in other countries in Chapter 12. Demographic changes are both a cause and a consequence of changes in women's labor force activity. Chapter 4 considers the substantial impact of changes in the family on women's labor market activity and outcomes. Chapter 10 then "turns the tables" and explores the economic factors, including women's rising labor force participation, that have led to changes in the family.[82]

The most fundamental shift in the family in recent years relates to what has been termed a "retreat" from marriage.[83] Marriage rates have fallen considerably, from 10.6 marriages per 1,000 population in 1970 to 7.3 in 2006, alongside an increase in unmarried, opposite-sex couples, often termed *cohabitors*. As of 2002, 50 percent of women age 15 to 44 had cohabited with a person of the opposite sex at some time in their lives, and this figure was as high as 60 percent for women in their thirties. In addition, the once strong link between marriage and childbearing has become substantially weaker. The proportion of births to unmarried mothers increased from slightly more than 1 in 10

---

[82] Who should be defined as a family is increasingly complex. Teresa J. Rothausen argues that the current notion of "family" may be biased toward a "white middle-class" reality in "'Family' in Organizational Research: A Review and Comparison of Definitions and Measures," *Journal of Organizational Behavior* 20, no. 6 (November 1999): 817–36.

[83] For a recent discussion and evidence, see Lundberg and Pollak, "The American Family." See also, Andrew J. Cherlin, "The Deinstitutionalization of Marriage," *Journal of Marriage and the Family* 66, no. 4 (November 2004): 848–61.

births in 1970 to more than 1 in 3 by 2006. Another notable change is the considerable rise in the divorce rate from the 1970s through the 1980s, although it subsequently leveled off and has declined somewhat since then. [84]

These demographic patterns can be seen in children's living arrangements. In 2004, 70 percent of all children were living with two married parents. Most of the others were living with a single parent, and a small fraction were living in households with cohabiting parents, a grandparent, another relative, or a nonrelative. Even married, two-parent families have changed over time, with many more children today living in a blended family rather than in a traditional nuclear family.[85]

The definitions used by the U.S. Census Bureau to categorize family structure and children's living arrangements have failed to fully keep pace with these recent demographic changes. For instance, the government defines **family** as any two or more individuals living together who are related by blood, marriage, or adoption. Under this definition, a household consisting of an unmarried couple and their own children may be counted as a single-parent family. As rates of cohabitation have increased, government statistics have become increasingly misleading regarding the extent to which children live with one parent or both. Indeed, one recent study finds that nearly 40 percent of all children born to unmarried mothers in the early 1990s went home to households that included both parents. All told, it is estimated that 40 percent of all children will spend some time in a cohabiting family before they reach age 16.[86] How to classify opposite-sex cohabitors, whether to include them in the definition of family or as a distinct category, as well as the question of how to classify gay and lesbian couples remain highly charged issues (see the following inset on the state of unions).

Along with and related to changing family structure, the demographic mix of the U.S. population also continues to change. Changes in race and ethnicity are a consequence of shifts in immigration, both in terms of source countries and the number of new entrants, as well as of differences in birthrates among various groups in the U.S.-born population. The largest increase is projected among Hispanics, from 12.6 percent of the population in 2000 to 19.4 percent by 2020. The percent of the black population is also expected to increase over the same period, but only from 13.2 to 14 percent, while it is anticipated that the share of the non-Hispanic white population will decrease from 69.4 percent to 60.1 percent of the total population.[87]

Classifying individuals of mixed races and ethnicities is another issue receiving attention. Regarding race, prior to the 2000 Census, individuals had been limited to choosing a single category from a list of five: white, black or African American, Asian, American Indian or Alaska native, and Native Hawaiian or Other Pacific Islander. This survey design forced individuals of multiracial backgrounds to place themselves in "one box." With rising rates of interracial parents, increasing numbers of Americans were confronting this situation.[88] Starting with the 2000 Census, individuals

---

[84] Figures on marriage and divorce cited here are from Table 10-1 and figures on unmarried births are from Table 10-4. Figures on cohabitation are from U.S. Department of Health and Human Services, "Fertility, Family Planning, and Reproductive Health of U.S. Women: Data from the 2002 National Survey of Family Growth," *Vital and Health Statistics* Series 23, no. 25 (2005), Table 48.

[85] See U.S. Census Bureau, "Living Arrangements of Children: 2004," *Current Population Reports* P70–114 (February 2008).

[86] Larry Bumpass and H.-H. Lu, "Trends in Cohabitation and Implications for Children's Family Context in the United States," *Population Studies* 54, no. 1 (March 2000): 29–41.

[87] Figures for 2000 are from U.S. Census Bureau, "Annual Estimates of the Population by Sex, Race, and Hispanic Origin for the United States: April 1, 2000 to July 1, 2007," Table 3 (May 1, 2008) available at www.census.gov; and projections for 2020 are from U.S. Census Bureau, "Projections of the Population by Sex, Race, and Hispanic Origin for the United States: 2010 to 2050," Table 4 (August 14, 2008) available at www.census.gov.

[88] For recent trends, see Roland G. Fryer, Jr. "Guess Who's Been Coming to Dinner? Trends in Interracial Marriage Over the 20th Century," *Journal of Economic Perspectives* 21, no. 2 (Spring 2007): 71–90; and Sharon M. Lee and Barry Edmonston, "New Marriages, New Families: U.S. Racial and Hispanic Intermarriage," *Population Bulletin* 60, no. 2 (June 2005): 1–36.

may select as many of these categories as apply, rather than being restricted to choosing a single race. In that census, just under 2.5 percent of the population designated themselves as of more than one race group, a figure that is likely to rise in future surveys.[89]

The previous discussion suggests that the American family in the early twenty-first century is rather different from that of the 1950s' characterization of an invariably white family, comprised of a homemaker wife and breadwinner husband with two or three children and a dog as immortalized in television, movies, and American lore. A historical perspective indicates that this family was, to some extent, a demographic aberration. In fact, fertility rates were lower and the average age of marriage was higher in earlier times than in the 1950s, and divorce was, even then, by no means unheard of.[90] And, of course, considerable racial and ethnic diversity existed at that time as well. Nonetheless, without a doubt, there has also been substantial change in both how people live and how they make a living. These issues will be discussed further in subsequent chapters.

THE STATE OF UNIONS IN THE UNITED STATES

During the last few years, it has been hard to read a newspaper or a magazine that does not have at least one article on some aspect of marriage. Part of the reason for this is that strengthening marriage has come to be viewed by some as an important solution to many of America's ills.[*] For instance, as discussed in Chapter 10, a number of academic studies, though not all, show that children do better in married families with both biological parents present than in single-parent families. Some people advocate marriage as a potential antipoverty solution, as discussed further in Chapter 11. Finally, marriage continues to make headlines as gay and lesbian couples seek to have the same rights and privileges as opposite-sex couples, and especially since some localities began permitting same-sex marriages. In this inset, we discuss the state of marriage as of 2008.

The U.S. federal government and many state governments began actively promoting marriage starting in the mid-1990s. For instance, a goal of the 1996 federal welfare legislation was to "encourage the formation and maintenance of two-parent families." Most recently, in 2006, reauthorization of this legislation included $150 million per year to promote marriage and responsible fatherhood. State policies have run the gamut from reducing marriage penalties in their welfare programs to funding premarital education classes for couples. Several states, including Louisiana, Arizona, and Arkansas, enacted laws permitting an alternative, stricter form of marriage called "covenant marriage." Couples who choose to enter a covenant marriage must obtain marriage counseling prior to marrying, must seek counseling if their marriage is in trouble, and must provide a specific reason for divorce.[**] Because these programs are fairly new,

---

[89] Reynolds Farley, "Racial Identities in 2000," *The New Race Question: How the Census Counts Multiracial Individuals*, edited by Joel Perlmann and Mary C. Waters (New York: Russell Sage Foundation, 2002), pp. 33–61.

[90] Andrew J. Cherlin, "American Marriage in the Early Twenty-First Century," *The Future of Children* 15, no. 2 (Autumn 2005): 33–55; and Catherine A. Fitch and Steven Ruggles, "Historical Trends in Marriage Formation: The United States 1850–1990," in *The Ties That Bind: Perspectives on Marriage and Cohabitation*, edited by Linda Waite (New York: Aldine de Gruyter, 2000), pp. 59–90.

conclusive evidence is not yet available on their effectiveness. At the federal level, changes have been made in the individual income tax to somewhat alleviate marriage penalties faced by some two-earner couples as well as increase the marriage bonus received by single-earner couples. This topic receives further attention in Chapter 11.

Also, in 1996, the U.S. Congress passed the Defense of Marriage Act, which defines marriage as the "legal union between one man and one woman" and defines a spouse as a husband or wife of the opposite sex. The act also specifies that if a state were to permit same-sex marriage, other states do not have to provide legal recognition.

As of 2008, same-sex couples can marry in Massachusetts and Connecticut.[***] Recent opinion polls indicate that even though the majority of Americans remain opposed to marriage for same-sex couples, considerably more support can be found for civil unions. Starting in 2000, Vermont was the first state to permit civil unions, and since then a handful of other states have followed. In Vermont, a civil union grants the couple "all the same benefits, protections and responsibilities under Vermont law ... as are granted to spouses in a marriage."[****] Other states, including Oregon and Washington, recognize domestic partnerships, which is a move in the same direction. Without marriage or one of these provisions, an unmarried partner may not be permitted to make health decisions in the event that his or her partner is incapacitated. However, given the Defense of Marriage Act, same-sex couples who marry (not to mention those who enter civil unions or domestic partnerships) are not eligible for federal benefits as married couples or spouses under federal programs such as Social Security.

In the United States, permitting marriage among gay and lesbian couples continues to generate a firestorm of debate. There are those who argue that gay and lesbian couples should not only be legally entitled to precisely the same rights and protections as opposite-sex couples, but also enjoy the same status in society.[*****] Others argue that the extension of marriage to gay and lesbian couples is a harbinger of the demise of marriage. As of 2008, over half of states had passed constitutional amendments to ban same-sex marriage, though efforts to pass a similar amendment at the federal level had not been successful. Nevertheless, as we have seen, efforts are underway in a number of states to permit same-sex marriage, civil unions, or domestic partnerships, and legal recognition of same-sex arrangements is increasing elsewhere as well. Countries such as the Netherlands, Canada, Belgium, Norway, Spain, and South Africa permit same-sex marriage and quite a few other countries including France, Denmark, Germany, and the United Kingdom allow for legal partnerships for same-sex couples.

[*]See, for instance, Wade F. Horn, "Wedding Bell Blues: Marriage and Welfare Reform," *The Brookings Review* 19, no. 3 (Summer 2001), pp. 3–42.

[**]Karen N. Gardiner, Michael E. Fishman, Plamen Nikolov, Asaph Glosser, and Stephanie Laud, *State Policies to Promote Marriage,* Final Report (Washington, DC: U.S. Department of Health and Human Services, Assistant Secretary for Planning and Evaluation, September 2002). See also Robert A. Moffitt, Robert Reville, Anne E. Winkler, and Jane McClure Burstain, "Cohabitation and Marriage Rules in State TANF Programs," RAND Working Paper Series, WR-585-1 (February 2009).

[***]In Spring 2008 the California Supreme Court legalized gay marriage and subsequently many couples wed but a ballot initiative later that year overturned this decision. For details on U.S. state and federal policy, see National Conference of State Legislatures, "Same Sex Marriage, Civil Unions and Domestic Partnerships" (May 2008).

[****]"The Vermont Guide to Civil Unions," Vermont Secretary of State web site, www.sec.state .vt.us (2008).

[*****]Katharine B. Silbaugh, "After Goodridge: Will Civil Unions Do?" *Jurist* (February 11, 2004).

Conclusion

We saw in Chapter 2 how the concept of the traditional family evolved with the man as the breadwinner and the woman as the homemaker, combining her time and the goods and services purchased with her husband's earnings to satisfy the family's needs and wants. The simple neoclassical model explains how such a division of labor may be advantageous under appropriate conditions. However, it cannot be taken for granted that these conditions are satisfied at any given point in time, let alone that they will be for the rest of each person's life.

The traditional specialization began during a time when the family was large and life was short, cloth was spun, bread was baked, and soap was produced at home, and market wages in jobs available to women were low, so that women's relative advantage for home work was great. With many children and a shorter life expectancy, the problem of the decline in the value of housework after the children grew up was far less serious. Also, with severe social and religious sanctions against divorce, women were less likely to find themselves and their children on their own, without financial support from their husbands. However, as these conditions changed, the advantages of the traditional division of labor decreased and the costs associated with it, particularly for women, increased.

Growing recognition of the drawbacks of the traditional division of responsibilities between husband and wife is likely an important factor contributing to the increase in women's labor force participation and the decline of the traditional married-couple family comprised of a homemaker wife and breadwinner husband. Furthermore, these changes together with improvements in women's labor market opportunities are also likely related to the decline in marriage, the increase in divorce, and the rise in cohabitation that have occurred since the 1960s. Corresponding to these changes is a noticeable, though modest, reallocation of household tasks and child care between married men and women. Even so, unless major changes take place in the availability and affordability of child care and elder care, and in the attitudes of men and women, women are likely to continue to shoulder the lion's share of home responsibilities for quite some time.

APPENDIX 3A

Specialization and Exchange: A Graphical Analysis

As discussed in Chapter 3, a complete analysis of the division of labor between the individuals who make up a couple takes into account both their production possibilities and their preferences for different goods. This appendix provides a fuller examination of the simple neoclassical model in the context of a graphical analysis and reaches the same conclusions as to the value of specialization and exchange as those based on the examples presented in Tables 3-1a and 3-1b.

For simplicity, we assume that individuals derive utility from only two types of goods—home goods, produced with inputs of home time, and market goods, purchased with market income. In Figure 3-1, H and M measure the dollar value of household output and market goods, respectively. Two persons, Kathy and Jim, each allocate their time between market work (M production) and housework (H production).[91]

---

[91] We also assume fixed proportions production functions for H and M for each individual. For example, an additional hour spent on the production of H by Kathy increases output by the same amount, regardless of how much H she already produced. This simplifying assumption results in the straight-line production possibility frontiers shown in Figure 3-1. For a discussion of this point, along with a consideration of other ways the standard theoretical model might be made more realistic, see Pollak, "Gary Becker's Contributions to Family and Household Economics."

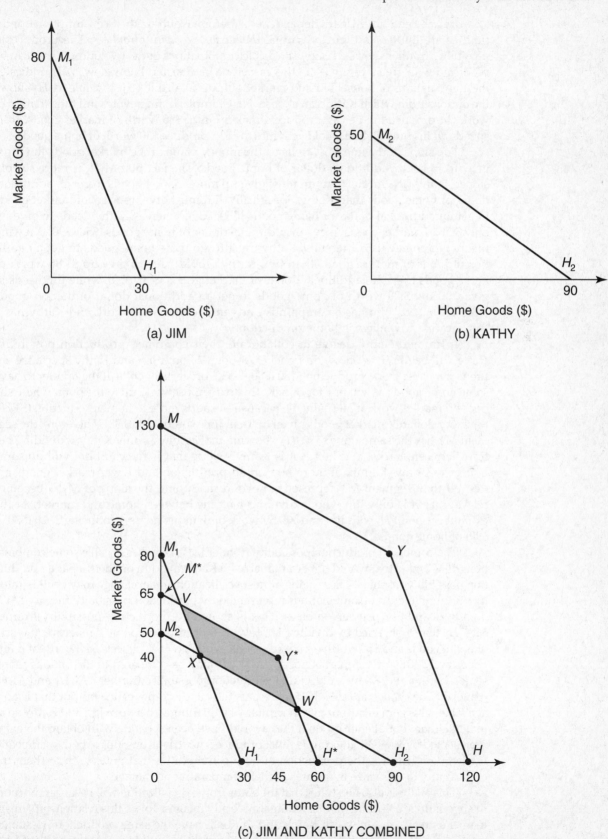

FIGURE 3-1 Separate and Combined Production Possibility Frontiers

If Kathy and Jim are each dependent on their own output, their consumption opportunities are limited to their individual *production possibility frontiers.* The production possibility frontier shows the largest feasible combinations of the two outputs that can be produced with given resources (in this case, time inputs) and know-how. M_1H_1 indicates the combinations of household and market outputs available to Jim, while M_2H_2 shows the options from which Kathy can choose. For example, if Jim devotes full time to market work (M production), he can produce a maximum of $80 worth of market goods. If he spends all his time on household activities, he can produce $30 worth of home goods.

The slope of the line M_1H_1 tells us the money value of the market goods Jim must give up to get an additional dollar of home goods. The fact that M_1H_1 is more steeply sloped than M_2H_2 means that Jim must give up more market goods to get an additional dollar of home goods than Kathy. Specifically, Jim must give up $2.67 of market goods to get an additional dollar of home goods ($80/$30), whereas Kathy needs to give up only $.56 of market goods to get an additional dollar of home goods ($50/$90). Viewing the matter somewhat differently, Kathy must forgo more home goods to get an additional dollar of market goods than Jim. Kathy would have to give up $1.80 worth of home goods to get an additional dollar of market goods ($90/$50), while Jim needs to give up only $.38 worth of home goods to get an additional dollar of market goods ($30/$80). Thus, Jim has a comparative advantage in market work and Kathy has a comparative advantage in home production.

If Jim and Kathy decide to collaborate, their combined production possibility curve will be MYH, as shown in panel c. At point M both Jim and Kathy specialize entirely in market work, producing $130 ($80 + $50) of market goods. If they prefer to have some home goods, it will pay for only Kathy to do housework, up to the point where she does no market work at all (point Y), because she adds more to home production ($1.80) for every dollar of market goods given up than Jim would add ($.38). Therefore, the segment MY has the same slope as M_2H_2, showing that as long as only Kathy is dividing her time between market and home, it is Kathy's slope that is relevant. Jim will do some housework only if a mix of more household production and fewer market goods are desired than segment MY represents. Beyond that point, the slope of M_1H_1 becomes relevant, as it is only Jim who is dividing his time between home and market. At the extreme, at point H, both Jim and Kathy work only in the home, producing $120 ($30 + $90) of home goods.

The combined production possibility frontier (MYH) makes feasible some combinations of M and H that would not be attainable by Kathy and Jim on their separate production possibility frontiers. These gains from specialization and exchange may be illustrated by putting the output combinations represented by production possibility frontier MYH on a per capita or per person basis. This is shown by production possibility frontier $M^*Y^*H^*$ that is obtained by dividing MYH by 2. (For instance, point Y reflects $90 worth of home goods and $80 worth of market goods, while point Y^* reflects $45 worth of home goods and $40 worth of market goods). $M^*Y^*H^*$ may be compared to the options represented by Jim and Kathy's individual production possibility frontiers, M_1H_1 and M_2H_2 (panel c). The shaded area $WXVY^*$ represents the increased per capita output that is now available. This gain in output may potentially be distributed between Jim and Kathy so as to make them both better off than they would have been separately. To obtain the gains represented by $WXVY^*$, the couple must produce a nontrivial amount of both market and home goods, for it is the production of both commodities that gives each of them the opportunity to specialize in the area of their comparative advantage.

This analysis also illustrates that the gains from specialization will be larger the more the two individuals differ in their comparative advantages. To see this relationship, imagine the extreme case in which Kathy and Jim both have the same production possibility frontier, say M_1H_1. The combined production possibility frontier would then be $2 \times M_1H_1$. On a per capita basis (dividing the combined production possibility frontier in half), we would simply be left with M_1H_1. Kathy and Jim would do no better combining forces than they would each do separately. Based on this simple analysis alone, it is not clear what the economic gains of collaborating are for such a couple. However, as we saw in Chapter 3, economic gains are likely even in this case, mainly because two people can use many goods and services more efficiently than a single person can. Here, however, we focus on a couple that can potentially increase its income through joint production.

To provide a link between the potential increase in output due to collaboration and the goal of maximizing satisfaction, we need to introduce an additional tool of economic analysis and pursue our inquiry one step further. So far we established the various combinations of the two types of outputs that Kathy and Jim could produce. Which of these they would choose depends on their tastes, that is to say, on their preferences for market goods compared to home goods. To considerably simplify the analysis, we will assume that they have identical tastes. If home goods are valued more highly than market goods, the couple will be willing to give up a considerable amount of market goods in order to get an additional dollar of home goods, and vice versa if market goods are valued more highly. This relationship can be illustrated using indifference curves, as seen in Figure 3-2.

Let us assume that Kathy and Jim have been told that they could have the combination of market and home goods represented by point A in panel a. They are then asked to find various other combinations of H and M from which they would derive exactly the same amount of satisfaction or utility. These other points can all be connected into one indifference curve, U_2, called that because the couple is indifferent about being at various points on the curve. The U_2 curve is *negatively sloped;* the reason for the negative slope is that if the amount of market or home goods is decreased, the amount of the other good must be increased for the couple to remain equally well off.

Notice too that indifference curve U_2 is convex to the origin. That is, it gets steeper as we move to the left and flatter as we move to the right. What this means is that at a point like C, where M goods are relatively plentiful and H goods are relatively scarce, it takes a fairly large amount of M ($15 worth) to induce the couple to give up a fairly small amount of H ($5 worth) and still remain equally well off. On the other hand, at a point like E, where M goods are relatively scarce and H goods are relatively plentiful, the couple is willing to give up a fairly large amount of H ($20 worth) to get even a small additional amount of

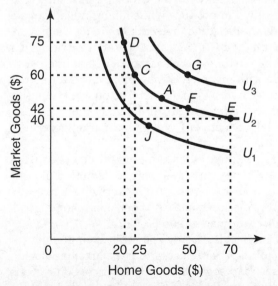

(a) RELATIVELY STRONG PREFERENCES
FOR MARKET GOODS

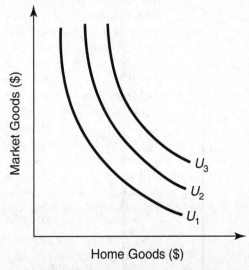

(b) RELATIVELY STRONG PREFERENCES
FOR HOME GOODS

FIGURE 3-2 Indifference Curves

scarce M ($2 worth). The convex shape depicted here is generally realistic to the extent that relatively scarce goods are valued more highly.

However, Kathy and Jim do not have just one indifference curve, but rather a whole family of higher and lower indifference curves. For it is possible to choose a point like G on curve U_3 that offers more of both M and H and is therefore clearly preferable to point A on curve U_2. Hence, all points on curve U_3 will, by extension, be preferable to (give more satisfaction than) all points on curve U_2. Similarly, it is possible to choose a point like J on curve U_1 that offers less of both M and H than at point A. Point J is clearly less desirable than point A and, by extension, all points on curve U_1 are less desirable (give less satisfaction) than all points on curve U_2. It should be clear that indifference curves can never intersect. All points on any one curve represent an equal amount of utility, while any point above (below) represents a larger (smaller) amount of utility. At the point where two curves intersect, they clearly represent the same amount of utility, yet at all other points they do not. This is a logical impossibility.

On the other hand, another couple's preferences might look like those depicted in panel b of Figure 3-2. These indifference curves are steeper and show that this couple places a relatively higher value on home goods, compared with market goods, than Kathy and Jim do. In general, it would take a larger amount of market goods to induce them to give up a dollar's worth of home goods while remaining equally well off.

To determine the division of labor (or time allocation) a couple will actually choose, we must consider both their production possibilities and their tastes or preferences. In Figure 3-3, we superimpose the couple's hypothetical indifference map on the production possibility frontier shown in Figure 3-1, panel c. It is then readily possible to determine the combination of home-produced and market-produced goods that a rational couple with those tastes (indifference curves) will choose. It will always be the point where the production possibility curve just touches the highest indifference curve it reaches. The reason is simple—the couple always prefers to be on a higher indifference curve (by definition, as we have seen), but because they are constrained to the possible combinations of output represented by the production possibility frontier, they cannot realistically reach an indifference curve that at all points lies above the frontier.

In Figure 3-3, we illustrate the impact of the couple's preferences on their time allocation. The combined production possibility curve for the couple, MYH, shows the various combinations of H and M the couple can produce while taking full advantage of their combined resources and the comparative advantage each has in producing one of the goods. Let us continue to assume that the wife has a comparative advantage in home production and that the husband has a comparative advantage in market work.

As may be seen in panel a, a couple with relatively strong preferences for market goods will maximize satisfaction at point A along segment MY. The husband will specialize entirely in market production and the wife will do all the housework and also supply some time to the market. They will consume M_a dollars of market goods and H_a dollars of home goods.

Panel b shows a couple with stronger preferences for home-produced goods. They will maximize utility at point B. The wife will devote herself entirely to household production, while the husband will do some housework as well as supplying time to the market. Such a couple will consume fewer market goods (M_b) and more home goods (H_b) than a couple with stronger preferences for market goods.

Finally, panel c shows a couple with intermediate tastes. They will maximize utility at point Y. Both wife and husband will each fully specialize in home and market production, respectively, and will consume M_c dollars of market goods and H_c dollars of home goods.

Couples may differ in their allocation of tasks within the family, not solely due to differences in tastes. The relative productivity of each member of the family in the production of market and home goods will also be an important factor. We already noted that if both husband and wife are equally productive in each endeavor, they will not realize any gains

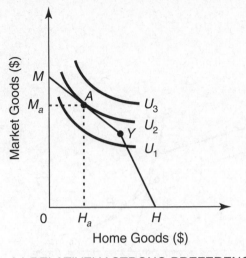

(a) RELATIVELY STRONG PREFERENCES
FOR MARKET GOODS

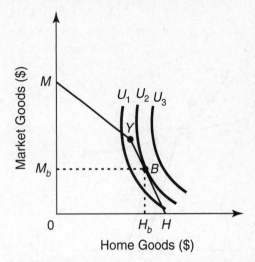

(b) RELATIVELY STRONG PREFERENCES
FOR HOME GOODS

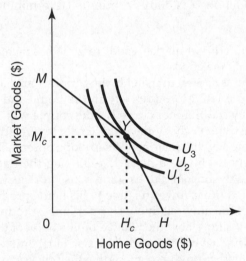

(c) INTERMEDIATE PREFERENCES

FIGURE 3-3   The Role of Tastes in Determining the Household Division of Labor

from specialization or division of labor within the family. However, even if we assume that the wife has a comparative advantage in household production and that the husband has a comparative advantage in market work, the relative productivities of each individual in home and market production are still relevant, which is illustrated in Figure 3-4.

Panel a shows two hypothetical production possibility frontiers. In MYH, the segment corresponding to the wife's frontier (MY) is relatively flat, indicating that she is considerably more productive in the home than in the market. For given tastes (represented by indifference curve U), the couple maximizes utility at point Y, where the wife specializes entirely in home production and the husband specializes completely in market work. However, if the couple's production possibility frontier were $MY'H'$, even with the same tastes (indifference curve), they would choose point A along segment $M'Y'$. Here the wife will continue to do all the housework but will do some market work as well. This is because MY' is steeper than MY, indicating a higher ratio of the wife's market productivity relative to her home productivity. The opportunity cost of

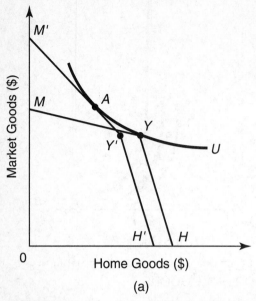

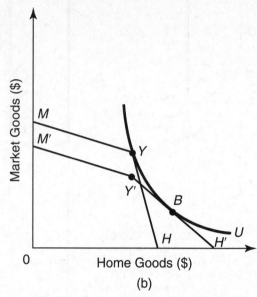

FIGURE 3-4 The Role of the Production Possibility Frontier in Determining the Household Division of Labor

home goods in terms of market goods forgone has increased and as a result the family consumes less home goods.

Similarly, as shown in panel b, the couple's time allocation may also depend on the husband's relative productivity in the home and the market. For given tastes (represented by indifference curve U), the couple will choose point Y when the husband's productivity in the home is extremely low relative to his market productivity. (This is indicated by the relatively steep slope of segment YH on frontier MYH.) They are more likely to choose a point like B along the flatter segment $Y'H'$ on frontier $M'Y'H'$, where the husband does some housework as well as market work, when his market productivity is lower relative to his home productivity. At B, the couple consumes more of the now relatively cheaper home-produced goods than at Y.

Figure 3-4 shows how the relative productivity of the husband and the wife in the home and the market influences the division of labor in the family and the combination of home- and market-produced goods that they choose to consume. Nonetheless, as long as the comparative advantages of husband and wife differ in this simple model, some degree of specialization will be efficient. As we have seen, the greater the difference between the two in their comparative advantage, the greater the gains to specialization and exchange.

Thus, the fuller analysis presented here supports the conclusions reached on the basis of the numerical example provided in Chapter 3. In this case too, however, the same qualifications hold. First, potential economic benefits to marriage include more than just specialization and exchange, and, second, the traditional division of labor is not without its disadvantages, particularly for women.

Questions for Review and Discussion

1. Explain why husbands and wives benefit from specialization and exchange. Under what conditions are these benefits likely to be large?
2. Jason and Jennifer are married. If Jason works in the labor market, he can earn a wage of $20 per hour, while Jennifer can earn a wage of $10 per hour.

a. Who has an absolute advantage in the labor market? How do you know?
b. Suppose we want to know who has a comparative advantage in the labor market. What specific information do we need to know? Discuss.

3. In view of the advantages of specialization and exchange pointed out by Becker, why are families increasingly moving away from the traditional division of labor?
4. To what extent is the presumption that women have a comparative advantage in housework justified?
5. Explain under what conditions it would be rational for a woman who could earn more than her husband in the labor market to specialize in housework.
6. For a long time, economists did not include housework in their analyses. In what respect was this omission justified or not?
7. Why have women been so eager to increase their participation in the labor market, and why have men been so reluctant to increase their participation in housework?
8. Clearly nonmarket production has some value. Discuss the merits of estimating its value.
9. It is frequently pointed out that each method of valuing nonmarket production is far from perfect. Explain what the main advantages and deficiencies of each method are.
10. What is a "bargaining approach" to decision making? Why is this approach more realistic than the standard neoclassical model?
11. Suggest some factors that would improve the bargaining power of married women.

Suggested Readings

Becker, Gary S. *A Treatise on the Family.* Cambridge, MA: Harvard University Press, 1981, enlarged edition, 1991.

Bianchi, Suzanne M., John P. Robinson, and Melissa A. Milkie. *Changing Rhythms of American Family Life.* New York: Russell Sage Foundation, 2006.

Bergmann, Barbara. *The Economic Emergence of Women*, 2nd edition. New York: Palgrave Macmillan, 2005.

Blau, Francine D. "Trends in the Well-Being of American Women, 1970–1995." *Journal of Economic Literature* 36, no. 1 (March 1998): 112–65.

Ferber, Marianne A., "A Feminist Critique of the Neoclassical Theory of the Family." In *Women, Family, and Work,* edited by Karine S. Moe. Oxford: Blackwell, 2003, Chapter 1.

Ferber, Marianne A., and Bonnie G. Birnbaum. "The New Home Economics: Retrospects and Prospects." *Journal of Consumer Research* 4, no. 1 (June 1977): 19–28.

Ferber, Marianne A., and Julie A. Nelson, eds. *Beyond Economic Man.* Chicago: University of Chicago Press, 1993.

Ferber, Marianne A., and Julie A. Nelson, eds. *Feminist Economics Today.* Chicago: University of Chicago Press, 2003.

Folbre, Nancy. *Valuing Children: Rethinking the Economics of the Family.* Cambridge, MA: Harvard University Press, 2008.

Folbre, Nancy, and Julie A. Nelson. "For Love or Money—Or Both?" *Journal of Economic Perspectives* 14, no. 4 (Fall 2000): 123–40.

Hartmann, Heidi I. "The Family as the Locus of Gender, Class and Political Struggle: The Example of Housework." *Signs: Journal of Women in Culture and Society* 6, no. 3 (Spring 1981): 366–94.

Jefferson, Therese, and John E. King. "Never Intended to Be a Theory of Everything: Domestic Labor in Neoclassical and Marxian Economics" *Feminist Economics* 7, no. 3 (November 2001): 71–101.

Juster, F. Thomas, Hiromi Ono, and Frank P. Stafford. "An Assessment of Alternative Measures of Time Use," *Sociological Methodology* 33 (2003): 19–54.

Katharine G. Abraham, and Christopher Mackie, *Beyond the Market: Designing Nonmarket Accounts for the United States.* Washington, DC: National Research Council, 2005.

Lundberg, Shelly, and Robert A. Pollak. "The American Family and Family Economics." *Journal of Economic Perspectives* 21, no. 2 (Spring 2007): 3–26.

Perlmann, Joel, and Mary C. Waters, eds. *The New Race Question: How the Census Counts Multiracial Individuals.* New York: Russell Sage Foundation, 2002.

Key Terms

commodities *35*
comparative advantage *35*
absolute advantage *36*
economies of scale *39*
public good *39*
externalities in consumption *40*
marriage-specific investments *40*
bargaining models *46*
American Time Use Survey *51*
gross domestic product *60*
opportunity cost approach *61*
market cost approach *61*
family *65*

CHAPTER 4

The Allocation of Time between the Household and the Labor Market

Chapter Highlights

- The Labor Force: Some Definitions
- Trends in Labor Force Participation
- Trends in Labor Force Attachment of Women
- Trends in Hours Worked
- Trends is Gender Differences in Unemployment
- The Labor Supply Decision
- Analyzing Trends in Women's Labor Force Participation: An Overview

- Analyzing Trends in Women's Labor Force Participation: A Look at Subperiods
- Analyzing Trends in Men's Labor Force Participation
- Black and White Participation Differentials: Serious Employment Problems for Black Men
- Appendix: The Income and Substitution Effects: A Closer Look

---

The rapid growth in women's labor force participation is one of the most significant economic and social developments in the post–World War II period, in the United States and elsewhere. One reason for our interest in women's participation trends is that they underlie the transformation in gender roles that has occurred in much of the world in recent years. However, other reasons also prompt an examination of women's labor force participation.

First, the economic well-being of women and their families is obviously significantly influenced by their participation in the labor force and their earnings levels, given participation. Such issues have gained in importance with the increase in the incidence of female-headed families and the growing dependence of married-couple families on the contributions of employed wives. Second, the family bargaining models reviewed in Chapter 3 suggest that, in married-couple families, women's participation in the labor force and their level of earnings while employed are expected to affect their bargaining power and thereby alter the distribution of resources within marriage. Third, shifts in participation are of importance for women's wages in that they influence the average levels of labor market experience of women and, as we shall see in Chapter 6, experience is an important determinant of wages.

In this chapter, we first review the definition of the labor force and summarize trends over time in female and male labor force participation. We shall see that, while female participation rates have been increasing, male rates have been declining, albeit not as dramatically. As a consequence of both types of changes, men's and women's labor force participation rates and their patterns of involvement in market work over the life cycle are becoming increasingly similar. We then turn to the development of some economic concepts for analyzing these trends and use them to provide a better understanding of the reasons for the remarkable influx of women into the labor market. Finally we use economic theory to analyze the reasons behind the decrease in male labor force participation and conclude with an examination of factors contributing to differences in labor force participation trends between blacks and whites.

THE LABOR FORCE: SOME DEFINITIONS

Each month, the U.S. Census Bureau conducts a survey to gather statistics on the labor force. These statistics are collected for the civilian noninstitutional population over age 16; thus they exclude individuals who are in the active-duty military as well as those who are incarcerated or in other institutions such as nursing homes. According to the official definition, the **labor force** includes all individuals 16 years of age and over who worked for pay or profit during the reference week or actively sought paid employment during the four weeks prior to the reference week. That is, the labor force is comprised of both the *employed* and the *unemployed*.

The **employed** group includes all those who worked one hour per week or more as paid employees or were self-employed in their own business or profession or on their own farm. This definition includes part-time workers who worked fewer than 35 hours per week, as well as those who worked full time, 35 hours or more. It also includes all those temporarily absent from paid employment because of bad weather, vacation, family leave, labor-management disputes, or personal reasons, whether or not they were paid. An exception to the emphasis on paid employment is that those who worked at least 15 hours as unpaid workers in an enterprise operated by a family member are also included.[1] The **unemployed** include those who do not have a job but who have made specific efforts to find a job within the past four weeks, as well as those not working but waiting to be called back to work or to report for a new job within 30 days. The relationships among these labor force concepts are illustrated in Figure 4-1.

The **labor force participation rate** of a particular group is equal to the number of its members who are in the labor force divided by the total number of the group in the population. Thus, for example, a labor force participation rate of 60 percent for women means that 60 percent of women 16 years of age and over are labor force participants.

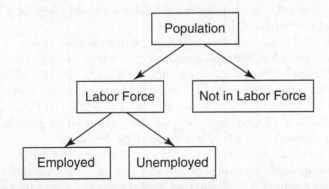

FIGURE 4-1   An Illustration of Labor Force Definitions

---

[1] The labor force excludes people engaged in illegal activities such as prostitution and drug trafficking. Furthermore, employment ranging from baby-sitting to yard work, which is paid for in cash and not reported for tax purposes (the so-called underground economy), is likely to be underreported in labor force statistics.

The **unemployment rate** of a particular group is equal to the number of individuals who are classified as unemployed divided by the size of the relevant labor force. An unemployment rate of 5 percent for women, for example, means that 5 percent of women who are in the labor force are unemployed.

A careful reading of the definition of the labor force makes it clear that being in the labor force is not synonymous with working. Individuals who work fewer than 15 hours a week as unpaid family workers and those who do only unpaid work in the household or as volunteer workers—no matter how many hours—are excluded. On the other hand, persons temporarily not working, or unemployed, are included. In large part, this results from the emphasis in the official definition of the labor force on being employed in or actively seeking *market* work. Because women have tended to have primary responsibility for nonmarket work, they constitute a high proportion in the categories that are left out. Thus, their share of the labor force considerably understates their share of work. This understatement was particularly true in earlier days when family enterprises were more common and when most married women were homemakers.[2] In fact, as discussed in the following inset, until surprisingly recently the official definitions were not even applied in the same way to men and women. In spite of these reservations, women's labor force participation rate is an important indicator of women's status in a market economy.

Although the unemployment rate provides an important indicator of the health of the economy, it is an incomplete tool for fully assessing either economic hardship for workers or the loss of output for the economy. First, measured unemployment rates fail to include individuals who would like a job, but did not look for work during the prior four weeks. Instead, they are among those classified as **not in the labor force.** For this reason, the Bureau of Labor Statistics also provides supplemental data on alternative measures of labor market difficulty and underutilization that are broader than the official unemployment rate and include some individuals who are otherwise classified as not in the labor force. **Marginally attached workers** are defined as those who are currently neither working nor looking for work but indicate that they want and are available for a job and have searched for work sometime in the last year (though not in the last four weeks). As this term suggests, marginally attached workers are considered to be the most likely to resume their search, and hence reenter the labor market, when the economy picks up. **Discouraged workers** are the subset of marginally attached workers who specifically stated that their reason for being out of the labor force is that they do not think labor market opportunities are available for them given their skills, or express concerns about labor market discrimination.

The unemployment rate also fails to provide information about underemployed workers. One type of **underemployment** occurs when workers have to take jobs for which they are clearly overqualified. Examples would be an MBA taking a job as a sales clerk or a skilled automobile mechanic working as a janitor. Another type of underemployment occurs when individuals would prefer to work full time but can only find part-time work. Individuals in this situation are classified as **part time for economic reasons** or sometimes called **involuntary part-time workers**.

Because the unemployment rate is so sensitive to the definition of who is counted among the unemployed, some economists also rely on broader measures of joblessness that include marginally attached workers, and in some cases, also involuntary part-time workers, in addition to those officially classified as unemployed.

---

[2] Historically, work of married women done at home, and even seasonal work done in factories frequently went unreported, especially when it was the husband who was interviewed; see, for instance, Milton Cantor and Bruce Laurie, eds., *Class, Sex, and the Woman Worker* (Westport, CT: Greenwood Press, 1977).

NO MORE GUESSING ABOUT WHO IS A HOMEMAKER

It has only been since January 1994 that the Current Population Survey, the major survey used by the Bureau of Labor Statistics to collect data on work activity in the labor market, asked men and women the same questions regarding their activities in the previous week. Prior to this time, if an adult woman opened the door, it was assumed that she might well be a homemaker. Accordingly, she was asked the question, "What were you doing most of last week—working, keeping house, or something else?" If an adult man opened the door, he was asked about "working, or something else." As a consequence of this type of stereotyping, women were more likely to be classified as out of the labor force (i.e., keeping house) rather than as unemployed (currently without a job, but searching). Now all individuals are asked the same questions, thus avoiding any potential bias from this source.

The Current Population Survey was also reworded to distinguish hours spent at home-based work for pay from hours spent doing unpaid work around the house. Specifically, the question asking "Did you do any work at all last week, not counting work around the house?" was changed to "Last week did you do any work for pay?"

Because the revised survey better captures the full range of women's paid work activities and their unemployment, these changes resulted in higher estimates of women's labor force activity than found with the previous survey. During a test period in 1993 when the old and new sets of questions were used, the estimate of women's employment-to-population rate (i.e., the number of women who were employed as a share of the female population) was 54.2 percent based on the old questions, and 54.9 percent using the new set. This might seem like a small difference, but it translates into thousands of women who were previously uncounted.

SOURCE: U.S. Department of Labor, Bureau of Labor Statistics, "Revisions in the Current Population Survey Effective January 1994," *Employment and Earnings* (February 1994).

TRENDS IN LABOR FORCE PARTICIPATION

The purpose of this section is to briefly review the trends in female and male labor force participation. The reasons for the observed changes are considered later, but here we may obtain an overview of just how substantial these changes have been. Labor force participation rates for selected years since 1890 are shown in Table 4-1.[3] The figures indicate a relatively slow rate of increase in the labor force participation rates of women in the pre-1940 period. After 1940, however, considerably larger increases occurred. In 1940, 28 percent of women were in the labor force; by 2007, the figure had risen to 59 percent of women 16 years of age and over, and three-quarters of women between the ages of 25 and 54 were labor force participants. During this time, women workers increased from 25 to 46 percent of the labor force.

Table 4-1 also suggests the sizable effect that the mobilization for World War II had on female labor force participation. As men left their civilian jobs to join the armed forces, women entered the labor force in unprecedented numbers. Between 1940 and 1945, the female participation rate increased from 28 to 36 percent. As suggested by the 1947 figures, some decline occurred in the immediate post–World War II period, but the upward trend in female participation quickly resumed. As may be seen in Figure 4-2,

---

[3] We begin with 1890 because, until that year, published census volumes contained few tabulations of the labor force participation and occupations of women. We omit 1910 because data on the labor force participation of women from the 1910 census are not comparable to other years. See Claudia Goldin, *Understanding the Gender Gap: An Economic History of American Women* (New York: Oxford University Press, 1990).

TABLE 4-1	Labor Force Participation Rates of Men and Women, 1890–2007	
Year	Percent of Men in the Labor Force	Percent of Women in the Labor Force
1890	84.3	18.2
1900	85.7	20.0
1920	84.6	22.7
1930	82.1	23.6
1940	82.5	27.9
1945	87.6	35.8
1947	86.8	31.5
1950	86.4	33.9
1960	83.3	37.7
1970	79.9	43.3
1980	77.4	51.5
1990	76.4	57.5
2000	74.8	59.9
2007	73.2	59.3

Notes: Based on the total population prior to 1950 and the civilian population thereafter. Rates are for individuals 14 years of age and over before 1947, and 16 years and over thereafter.

Sources: U.S. Department of Commerce, Bureau of the Census, *Historical Statistics of the United States Colonial Times to 1970*, Bicentennial Edition, Part 1, 1975, pp. 131–32; and *Employment and Earnings,* various issues.

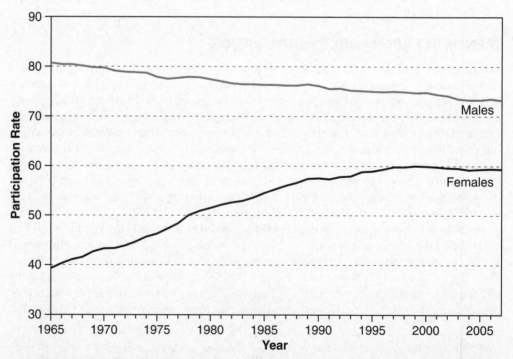

FIGURE 4-2   Trends in Female and Male Labor Force Participation Rates, 1965–2007
Source: U.S. Department of Labor, Bureau of Labor Statistics, *Employment and Earnings,* (various issues).

however, the steep rise in female participation rates slowed in the early 1990s, and female participation rates have been roughly constant since the mid-1990s, even declining very slightly.

In contrast to the long-term increase in labor force participation for women, male participation rates began to decline in the 1950s, from 86 percent in 1950 to 73 percent in 2007. As a consequence of these opposing trends, the *difference* between the male and female participation rates has decreased sharply from 55 percentage points in 1940 to 14 percentage points in 2007. This growing convergence in male and female participation rates is also illustrated in Figure 4-2.

We gain a fuller picture of labor force participation patterns by examining them separately for different subgroups. Table 4-2 shows trends in labor force participation since 1955 by race and Hispanic origin for years in which the data are available. The participation rate declined for both white and black men, but much more so for blacks. In 1955, participation rates for white and black men were roughly equal at 85 percent, but in recent years the rate for blacks is considerably lower, 67 percent compared to 73 percent for whites. In contrast, in recent years, Hispanic men are considerably more likely, and Asian men somewhat more likely, to be in the labor force than whites.

Participation rates have risen for all groups of women except Asians (for whom we have only a few years of data), but they have increased substantially more for whites and Hispanics than for blacks. Thus, while black women traditionally had far higher labor force participation rates than white women, the black-white gap in participation had closed by the mid-1980s. Black women's participation again drew ahead of that of white women in the late 1990s due to a substantial increase in their participation rate

TABLE 4-2 Labor Force Participation Rates of Men and Women by Race and Hispanic Origin, 1955–2007 (percent)

Year	Males				Females			
	Whites	Blacks	Hispanics	Asians	Whites	Blacks	Hispanics	Asians
1955	85.4	85.0	n.a.	n.a.	34.5	46.1	n.a.	n.a.
1965	80.8	79.6	n.a.	n.a.	38.1	48.6	n.a.	n.a.
1975	78.7	70.9	80.7	n.a.	45.9	48.8	43.1	n.a.
1985	77.0	70.8	80.3	n.a.	54.1	53.1	49.3	n.a.
1995[a]	75.7	69.0	79.1	73.6	59.0	59.5	52.6	58.6
2000	74.6	69.0	80.6	74.0	59.8	63.2	56.9	59.3
2005	72.9	67.3	80.1	74.8	59.5	61.6	55.3	58.2
2007	72.7	66.8	80.5	75.1	59.5	61.1	56.5	58.6

[a] Data for Asians are for 1996.

Notes: Civilian labor force; includes population aged 16 and over. Hispanics may be of any race. Prior to 1975, other nonwhites are included with blacks; and prior to 2005, Pacific Islanders are included with Asians. For 2000 and beyond, data on whites are for white, non-Hispanics. Prior to 2005, persons who reported more than one race (white, black, or Asian) were included in the group they identified as the main race. Subsequently, whites, blacks and Asians are defined as persons who selected this race group only; persons who selected more than one race group are not included.

n.a. = Not available.

Sources: U.S. Department of Labor, Bureau of Labor Statistics, *Working Women: A Databook*, 1977, pp. 44–45; U.S. Department of Labor, *Handbook of Labor Statistics* (August 1989), pp. 25–30; U.S. Department of Labor, *Employment and Earnings* (various issues); and unpublished data from the Bureau of Labor Statistics. Asian data for 1996 and 2000 are from U.S. Census Bureau, Current Population Survey, available at http://www.census.gov/population/www/socdemo/race/api.html.

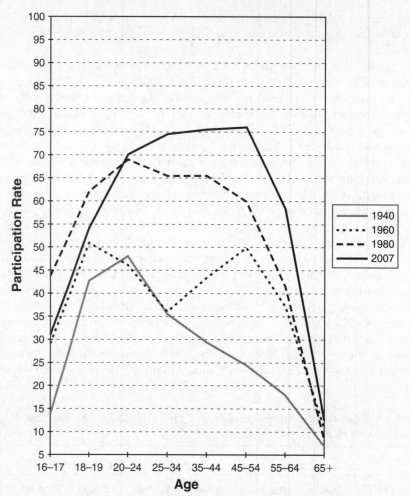

FIGURE 4-3   Civilian Labor Force Participation Rates of Women by Age

Source: U.S. Department of Labor, Bureau of Labor Statistics, *Employment and Earnings*, (various issues).

during that time, and remains slightly higher than that of whites today. In contrast, Hispanic women's participation rates are consistently lower than those of whites in all years. And, for years when data are available, Asian women's participation rate is about the same or slightly lower than that of white women.

The growth in female labor force participation that has occurred since World War II has been accompanied by pronounced changes in the patterns of women's employment over the life cycle. Before 1940, the typical female worker was young and single; most women tended to leave the labor force permanently upon marriage and childbearing. As Figure 4-3 shows, at that time, the peak age-specific participation rate occurred among women 20 to 24 years of age and declined for each successive age group after that.[4] Over the next 20 years, older married women with school-age or grown children entered or reentered the labor force in increasing numbers, while little change occurred

---

[4] Note that when labor force participation rates are changing, cross-sectional data on participation rates by age, as shown in Figure 4-3, may give a misleading impression of the actual experiences of individual women over the life cycle. For a fuller explanation of this issue, as well as an interesting analysis of cohort patterns of married women's participation, see Goldin, *Understanding the Gender Gap*, pp. 21–23.

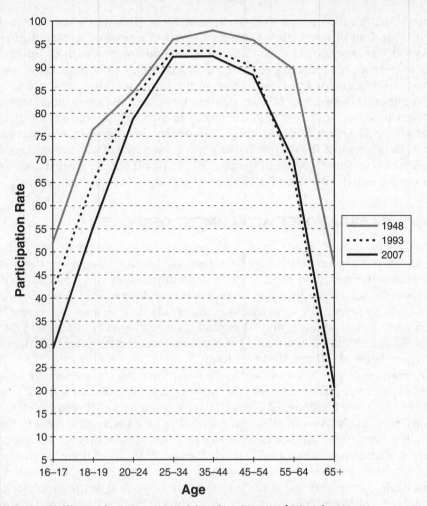

FIGURE 4-4   Civilian Labor Force Participation Rates of Men by Age

Source: U.S. Department of Labor, Bureau of Labor Statistics, *Employment and Earnings*, (various issues).

in the labor force participation rates of women between the ages of 20 and 34, who were more likely to have preschool-age children at home. The proportion of women workers who were married increased from 30 percent in 1940 to 54 percent in 1960. The World War II experience may have played a part in encouraging this shift in the behavior of married women, because during the war, for the first time, large numbers of older married women worked outside the home.

Between 1960 and 2007, participation rates increased for all age groups of women, but particularly for women ages 25 to 44. This increase in part reflects declines in the birthrate and increases in the divorce rate over this period. Most notable, however, is the large increase in the participation rates of married women with small children. Among those with children less than 6 years old, only 19 percent worked outside the home in 1960, compared to 61 percent in 2007. More than half (55 percent) of married mothers who had a child in the previous year were in the labor force. In contrast to the participation gains for women in the other age groups, participation rates of women less than 20 have scarcely risen since 1960 and have even declined a bit since 1980.

As a result of these changes, the pattern of age-specific participation rates among women has come to more closely resemble the male pattern shown in Figure 4-4, peaking in the so-called prime working ages of 25–54. This figure also shows that the long-term decline in male labor force participation rates that occurred during the post–World War II period was concentrated among younger men, those under 20, and among older men, aged 55 and over. Since the 1960s, smaller but notable decreases also occurred in the participation rates of men in the prime working ages, not only those 45 to 54 but even those 25 to 44. Participation rates for these age groups remain relatively high, however, with over 90 percent of 25- to 44-year-olds, and 88 percent of 45- to 54-year-olds in the labor force. An interesting recent development, also shown in the figure, is the reversal of the decline in the participation rate of older men (aged 55 and over). After decreasing throughout the post-World War II period, participation rates for this group bottomed out in the mid-1980s and then began to increase in the early 1990s.[5]

TRENDS IN LABOR FORCE ATTACHMENT OF WOMEN

The changes in women's labor force participation rates by age since 1940 suggest that rising female participation rates have been associated with an increase in the labor force attachment of women over the life cycle. This impression is reinforced by data on increases in the labor force attachment of women over the course of a year. So, for example, in 1970, 53 percent of women worked at some time during the year. Of these women with work experience, only 41 percent were employed full time and year round. By 2006, 62 percent of women worked at some time during the year, and 61 percent of them were employed full time and year round.[6]

Women's increased commitment to the labor force can also be seen by comparing women's labor force attachment near the time of a first birth in the early 1960s with the late 1990s. One notable difference between the two periods is that women are now substantially more likely to work while pregnant. Of women who gave birth to their first child in the early 1960s, only 44 percent worked during their pregnancy, compared to 67 percent of women who had a first birth in the late 1990s. In addition, women are now much more likely to return to work soon after a first birth. For instance, of those who worked during pregnancy in the early 1960s, only 17 percent returned to work within 3 months and just 21 percent within 6 months, while in the late 1990s, these figures were 60 percent and 75 percent, respectively.[7]

This growing labor force attachment of women contributed to the increase in their labor force participation rate. The labor force group is increased by entries into the labor force and decreased by exits from the labor force. When the number of entrants exceeds the number of those who leave the labor force, the size of the labor force is increased. Thus, both *increases* in flows of *entrants* and *decreases* in flows of *exits* potentially contribute to the growth of the female labor force. Both of these factors appear to have played a role in increasing the female participation rate.

As we shall see in greater detail in Chapter 6, work experience is an important determinant of labor market earnings. The lesser amount of work experience of women relative to men has traditionally been cited as an important reason for their lower

[5] U.S. Department of Labor, Bureau of Labor Statistics, "Spotlight on Statistics: Older Workers" (July 2008), available at www.bls.gov; and Alicia H. Munnell and Steven A. Sass, "The Labor Supply of Older American Men," in *Labor Supply in the New Century*, edited by Katharine Bradbury, Christopher L. Foote, and Robert K. Triest (Boston, MA: Federal Reserve Bank of Boston, 2008).

[6] "Work Experience of the Population in 2006," U.S. Department of Labor, Bureau of Labor Statistics, *News Release*, December 19, 2007, www.bls.gov/news.release/work.toc.htm, accessed June 27, 2008; and *Women in the Labor Force: A Databook*, U.S. Department of Labor, Bureau of Labor Statistics, February, 2004, www.bls.gov/cps/wlf-databook.htm, accessed June 27, 2008.

[7] Julia Overturf Johnson, Barbara Downs, and Martin O'Connell, "Maternity Leave and Employment Patterns: 1961–2000," U.S. Census Bureau, Washington, DC (October 2005). The early 1960s refer to 1961–1965 and the late 1990s refer to 1996–2000.

earnings. It is not immediately obvious, however, whether recent increases in women's labor force participation are associated with increases or decreases in the *average* amount of work experience of the female labor force. On the one hand, the growing number of new entrants, with little or no work experience, negatively affects the average labor market experience of women workers. On the other hand, the growing tendency for women to remain in the labor force for longer periods of time has a positive effect.

Unfortunately, the usual published statistics on labor force participation do not help to answer the question about the net effect of women's increased labor force participation on their average experience. This is because data on work experience are not routinely collected. However, estimates are made from time to time based on special surveys that explicitly ask respondents about their labor market experience, as well as less directly from information on labor force entry and exit rates. The evidence suggests that, before the late 1960s, rising female labor force participation rates were associated with constant or slowly increasing average levels of work experience among women workers, but since then, notable gains in women's average experience levels have occurred.[8] These trends are discussed in greater detail in Chapter 6.

TRENDS IN HOURS WORKED

The main focus of this chapter is on labor force participation. However, another important aspect of the labor supply decision is *hours worked*. In Chapter 3 we considered trends in the allocation of time of women and men between housework and market work. Here we focus on trends in hours among the employed. Hours worked can be measured as hours worked per day, per week, or annually. One particularly notable trend is that the full-time workweek declined from 60 hours at the turn of the nineteenth century to about 40 hours in the 1940s and, notably, remains at about that level today. Similarly, the average number of hours worked per week (including both full- and part-time workers) has shown considerable stability for both male and female workers; male workers have averaged about 42 hours per week since the 1940s, while women have averaged about 36 hours, since at least the 1970s.[9] The lower figure for women in part reflects their continued greater likelihood of working part time than men. For example, in 2006, 27 percent of employed women usually worked part time (fewer than 35 hours per week) compared to 12 percent of employed men.[10] In addition, although, as already noted, the proportion of employed women working full time and year round has increased over time, even among this group, women tend to work fewer hours than men.

Trends in annual work hours are more difficult to measure because they may be influenced by workers' difficulty obtaining a job (as reflected in spells unemployed or out of the labor force), decisions to work part time or part year, and how paid vacation time is counted. Not surprisingly then, there has been some controversy about these trends and how they should be measured, with some studies finding little

---

[8] Goldin, *Understanding the Gender Gap*, pp. 37–41; James P. Smith and Michael P. Ward, "Time Series Changes in the Female Labor Force," *Journal of Labor Economics* (January 1985, supp.); June O'Neill and Solomon Polachek, "Why the Gender Gap in Wages Narrowed in the 1980s," *Journal of Labor Economics* 11, no. 1, pt. 1 (January 1993): 205–28; and Francine D. Blau and Lawrence M. Kahn, "The U.S. Gender Pay Gap in the 1990s: Slowing Convergence," *Industrial and Labor Relations Review* 60, no. 1 (October 2006): 45–66.
[9] See Thomas J. Kniesner, "The Full-Time Work Week in the U.S.: 1900–1970," *Industrial and Labor Relations Review* 30, no. 1 (October 1976): 3–15; Mary T. Coleman and John Pencavel, "Changes in Work Hours of Male Employees, 1940–1988," *Industrial and Labor Relations Review* 46, no. 2 (January 1993): 262–83; Mary T. Coleman and John Pencavel, "Trends in Market Work Behavior of Women Since 1940," *Industrial and Labor Relations Review* 46, no. 4 (July 1993): 653–76; and Jerry A. Jacobs and Kathleen Gerson, *The Time Divide : Work, Family, and Gender Inequality* (Cambridge, MA: Harvard University Press, 2004).
[10] "Work Experience of the Population in 2006."

change in annual hours for women and men and others finding modest positive or negative trends.[11]

While in the aggregate relatively little change has occurred in weekly and annual work hours, an important development is that trends in work hours of both men and women have diverged by skill level, with a rising trend for more highly skilled workers and a declining trend for the less skilled.[12] For instance, the length of the workweek generally decreased for employees with less than a high school education, while it rose for those who completed four or more years of college, as well as for those in professional, managerial, and technical occupations. This increase in work hours for some individuals, combined with the fact that many Americans are single parents with responsibility for children or are members of a dual-earner family, leads to more families facing a growing "time squeeze," a topic discussed further in Chapter 11.

TRENDS IN GENDER DIFFERENCES IN UNEMPLOYMENT

Those participating in the labor force are not always able to find employment. Thus, although our main focus in this chapter is on labor force participation, we briefly review trends in gender differences in unemployment here. In fact, the gender difference in the unemployment rates of men and women has changed over time. Although women traditionally had higher unemployment rates than men, since the early 1980s, women's unemployment rates have tended to be about the same as men's, or, during recessions, even lower. The small gender gap in unemployment rates since 1980 is the net result of various factors working in opposing directions.

First, women have lower *labor force attachment* than men. On the one hand, the larger proportion of entrants and reentrants among women in the labor force tends to increase female relative to male unemployment because many will experience a period of unemployment as they search for jobs. On the other hand, the weaker labor force attachment of women means that women are considerably more likely than men to exit the labor force when they lose their jobs and hence to be counted as out of the labor force rather than unemployed. Particularly in recessions, this works to lower women's unemployment relative to men's.

Second, there are *gender differences in occupations and industries*. On the one hand, men are more heavily represented in blue-collar jobs and in durable manufacturing, sectors with above-average layoff and unemployment rates. Women are more likely to be employed in white-collar jobs, which experience lower layoff and unemployment rates. On the other hand, women are also disproportionately represented in service occupations, which have above-average unemployment rates. On balance, the occupational distribution appears to lower the female unemployment rate relative to the male rate. The fact that blue-collar jobs and durable-goods manufacturing industries are subject to greater cyclical variation in employment tends to particularly increase men's unemployment during recessions.

Prior to the 1980s, the net result of these opposing forces was that women's unemployment rates were higher than men's. An added factor during this earlier period was the growing number of young workers who were also seeking employment, as the large baby boom cohort entered the job market. Since adult women are more likely than adult men to be labor market entrants (as they return from periods of time out of the labor

---

[11] For reviews, see Deborah M. Figart and Lonnie Golden, "The Social Economics of Work Time: Introduction," *Review of Social Economy* 54, no. 4 (Winter 1998): 411–24; and Jerry A. Jacobs and Kathleen Gerson, *The Time Divide*.

[12] Coleman and Pencavel, "Changes in Work Hours of Male Employees, 1940–1988"; Coleman and Pencavel, "Trends in Market Work Behavior of Women Since 1940"; Jacobs and Gerson, *The Time* Divide; and Peter Kuhn and Fernando Lozano, "The Expanding Workweek? Understanding Trends in Long Work Hours among U.S. Men, 1979–2006," *Journal of Labor Economics* 26, no. 2 (April 2008): 311–43.

force), they were likely in greater direct competition with youth for entry-level positions and hence more negatively affected.

Factors that have lowered women's unemployment relative to men's since the 1980s and contributed to the convergence of men's and women's unemployment rates may include rising labor force attachment of women, decreasing demand for manufacturing workers and increasing demand for workers in services due to structural changes in the economy, and a declining number of young people competing with women for entry-level jobs as the "baby bust" cohort entered the job market.

The impact of these factors is illustrated in recent unemployment statistics. In 2007, the average female unemployment rate over the year was 4.5 percent, very close to the male rate of 4.7 percent. However, as the recession that began in December 2007 set in, the pattern of men having greater employment problems than women during downturns became evident in the unemployment statistics. By December 2008, the male unemployment rate was 8.1 percent, over two percentage points higher than the female rate of 6.0 percent.[13]

It is worth noting that in many other economically advanced countries, women do have higher unemployment rates than men. For example, in 2007, the average unemployment rate of women in the European Union was 7.8 percent compared to 6.3 percent for men.[14] The higher unemployment rates of women in these countries may be due to a different balance of the opposing forces that we outlined earlier. Further, in many of these countries, unions and the government play a larger role in setting wages than in the United States. While such wage policies tend to raise the wages of low-wage workers at the bottom of the wage distribution, and therefore especially benefit women (a disproportionately a low-wage group), the gain in wages may come at the price of higher unemployment rates for women.[15]

Finally, while differences in unemployment rates between men and women tend to be small in the United States, differences across a number of other demographic categories can be quite sizable. Particularly notable are the extremely high unemployment rates of African Americans. Among both men and women, unemployment rates are about twice as high for blacks as for whites. In 2007, for example, among white, non-Hispanics, the unemployment rate was 4.0 percent for men and 3.7 percent for women, while among blacks it was 9.1 percent for men and 7.5 percent for women. Possible explanations for the higher unemployment rates of blacks include lower average levels of education and skills, a lack of jobs located in or near communities where many of them live, and employment discrimination.[16] The higher incarceration rates of young black men may also contribute, since ex-offenders have difficulty finding employment.[17]

---

[13] The gender gap was smaller for the seasonally adjusted unemployment rate which was 7.9 percent for men and 6.4 percent for women. The unemployment data are from, U.S. Department of Labor, Bureau of Labor Statistics, "The Employment Situation: December 2008" (January 9, 2009).

[14] OECD.StatExtracts at http://stats.oecd.org/; data are for the "EU 15." In some cases the gender differences are quite large, including unemployment rates of 7.9 percent for women and for 4.9 percent for men in Italy; 10.9 percent for women and 6.4 percent for men in Spain; and 9.6 percent for women and 6.6 percent for men in Portugal.

[15] See, Giuseppe Bertola, Francine D. Blau, and Lawrence M. Kahn, "Labor Market Institutions and Demographic Employment Patterns," *Journal of Population Economics* 20, 4 (October 2007): 833–67.

[16] See Harry Holzer, "Black Employment Problems: New Evidence, Old Questions," *Journal of Policy Analysis and Management* 13, no. 4 (Fall 1994): 699–722; and Robert W. Fairlie and William A. Sundstrom, "The Emergence, Persistence, and Recent Widening of the Racial Unemployment Gap," *Industrial and Labor Relations Review* 52, no. 2 (January 1999): 252–70.
Unemployment rates tend to understate the employment difficulties of blacks because a higher fraction of blacks as compared to whites are not captured in this statistic because they have given up on job search and hence are "not in the labor force."

[17] See Harry J. Holzer, Paul Offner, and Elaine Sorensen, "Declining Employment Among Young Black Less-Educated Men: The Role of Incarceration and Child Support," *Journal of Policy Analysis and Management* 24, no. 2 (Spring 2005): 329–50.

For some of the same reasons, Hispanics also tend to have higher unemployment rates than whites, although the difference is generally smaller than between blacks and whites. In 2007, among Hispanics, the unemployment rate was 5.4 percent for men and 6.9 percent for women. Another group with considerably higher unemployment rates is teens. In 2007, when the overall unemployment rate was 4.6 percent, the rate for teens was 15.7 percent. Black teens had especially high rates, with 29.4 percent unemployed.[18]

THE LABOR SUPPLY DECISION

In Chapter 3, we examined the division of housework and market work between husband and wife. Here we focus upon the closely related question of how an individual, whether married or single, decides on the allocation of his or her time between the home and the labor market. We again use a neoclassical model and assume that the individual's goal is to maximize utility or satisfaction.[19] A brief preview of our conclusions may be helpful in understanding the more detailed analysis that follows. The economic model suggests that individuals decide whether or not to participate in the labor force by comparing the value of their time in the market given by their hourly wage rate (w) to the value they place on their time spent at home (w^*). If the value of market time is greater than that of home time ($w > w^*$), they choose to participate in the labor force. Alternatively, if the value of home time is greater than or equal to that of market time ($w^* \geq w$), they choose to remain out of the labor force. In this section, we trace out the reasoning behind this decision rule.

Individuals are viewed as deriving utility from the consumption of *commodities* (goods and services) that are produced using inputs of market goods and nonmarket time.[20] For example, the commodity, a family dinner, is produced using inputs of market goods (groceries, cooking equipment, etc.) and the individual's own time in preparing the meal. In order to keep this model reasonably simple, we make the following three additional assumptions.

First, we assume that all income earned in the labor market is spent on market goods. This assumption avoids the need to consider the determinants of savings and also means that we may use the terms *market income* and (the money value of) *market goods* interchangeably.

Second, we assume that all nonmarket time is spent in the production of commodities, whether the output is a loaf of bread, a clean house, a healthy child, or a game of tennis. This approach not only avoids the need for analyzing a three-way choice among market work, housework, and leisure but also makes the often difficult distinction between nonmarket work (including volunteer work) and leisure unnecessary.[21] We do not wish to suggest, however, that in reality no difference separates the two.

---

[18] Data are from U.S. Bureau of Labor Statistics, *Employment & Earnings* 55, no. 1 (January 2008) and unpublished data from the same source.

[19] As before, the underpinnings of the analysis are derived from the work of Gary S. Becker; see "A Theory of the Allocation of Time," *Economic Journal* 75, no. 299 (September 1965): 493–517; and Jacob Mincer, "Labor Force Participation of Married Women," in *Aspects of Labor Economics,* edited by H. Gregg Lewis, Universities National Bureau of Economic Research Conference Studies, no. 14 (Princeton, NJ: Princeton University Press, 1962), pp. 63–97. James Heckman and Reuben Gronau, among others, also made significant contributions to the development of statistical techniques for estimating the theoretical relationships.

[20] Students who have read the appendix to Chapter 3, where a graphical analysis of specialization and exchange was presented, will recognize the basic approach employed here as quite similar. However, in this analysis, we do not need to make the rigid distinction between home goods (produced exclusively with inputs of home time) and market goods (produced entirely with market-purchased goods) that was used to simplify the analysis in the appendix to Chapter 3. Indeed, not only can we recognize that market goods and nonmarket time are both inputs into the production of commodities, but also that more than one way may be used to produce the same commodity.

[21] Market work is relatively easy to distinguish as any activity that results in material, usually monetary, reward. However, it is quite problematic to determine whether preparing a gourmet meal, going to a meeting of young professionals, growing flowers, or taking a child to the zoo is work or leisure.

Indeed, one of the concerns about the impact of married women's increased labor force participation on their welfare is that it has not been accompanied by a comparable real-location of household chores. As a result, women are often saddled with the "double burden" of home and market work. Working a "double shift" may reduce the leisure time available to women, impede their ability to compete with men in the labor market, or both. Data on time spent in housework and child care were presented in Chapter 3.

Third, we focus here on the individual rather than on the family as a whole. This focus is quite realistic when the individual is the only adult in the family. However, as we saw in Chapter 3, where more than one adult is present, the division of labor among them, and thus the labor supply decision of each, is reasonably expected to be a family decision. We do not introduce all the complexities of family decision making here because it would cause the exposition to become unduly complex. We do, however, view the individual in a family context by taking into account the impact of the earnings of other family members on each person's labor supply decision; but the labor supply of other members of the household is taken as given and is assumed not to be influenced by the individual's own choice. This assumption is probably not too unreasonable when we consider women's labor supply decisions since, in most American families, husbands are still likely to remain in the labor market full time regardless of their wives' participation decision.[22]

Now that we have reviewed some of the assumptions of the model, we are ready to turn to an analysis of the labor supply decision itself. In the model, both market goods and nonmarket time are used in the production of the commodities from which the individual derives satisfaction. Thus, the goal of the individual is to select the utility-maximizing combination of market goods and nonmarket time. Because market goods are purchased with income earned through market work, and all time available is spent either on market work or nonmarket activities, this choice of the utility-maximizing combination of market goods and nonmarket time is the basis of the labor supply decision. In making this choice, the individual must take into account both the options that are open to him or her, given by the *budget constraint* shown in panel a of Figure 4-5, and his or her tastes or preferences expressed in the set of *indifference curves* shown in panel b of Figure 4-5. Let us trace out this decision for the hypothetical case of a married woman named Mary.

The Budget Constraint

The **budget constraint** in panel a shows the various combinations of nonmarket time and market goods from which Mary can choose, given her market wage rate and the nonlabor income available to her. The **wage** is the amount of money an individual earns for each hour he or she works; that is, the wage is an hourly rate of pay. **Nonlabor income** is any income an individual receives, apart from his or her own labor market earnings. The amount of nonlabor income is thus unrelated to the amount of time the individual devotes to the labor market. Nonlabor income may include the earnings of a spouse, as well as any income received from interest, dividends, or rental property. For simplicity, government transfer payments, such as welfare or unemployment insurance, may also be considered nonlabor income, although the amount of income received from such sources is in fact influenced by the amount of time a person supplies to the labor market. Hours of **nonmarket time** are measured from left to right along the horizontal axis.

[22] An indicator of this is that the responsiveness of husbands' labor supply decisions to their wives' wages tends to be quite low. Wives' labor supply decisions are much more responsive to their husbands' wages. See, for example, Francine D. Blau and Lawrence M. Kahn, "Changes in the Labor Supply Behavior of Married Women: 1980–2000," *Journal of Labor Economics* 25, no. 3 (July 2007): 393–438; for additional results on men, see their March 2005 NBER Working Paper No. 11230 by the same title.

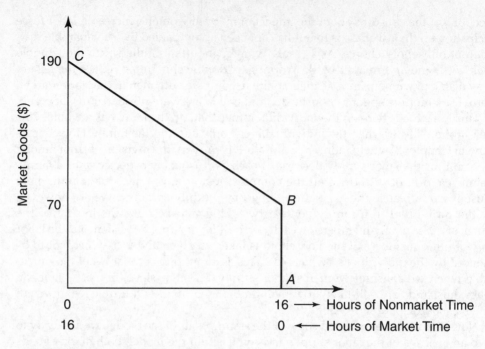

(a) THE BUDGET CONSTRAINT

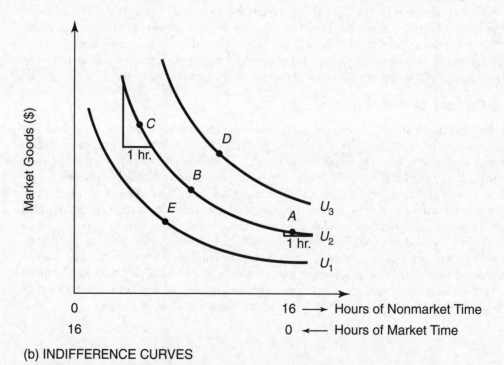

(b) INDIFFERENCE CURVES

FIGURE 4-5   The Budget Constraint and the Indifference Curves

We assume that Mary has a total of 16 hours available to her in a day to allocate between market and nonmarket activities (allowing 8 hours for nondiscretionary activities like sleeping). Since any of this time that Mary does not spend in nonmarket activities is spent in the market, hours of **market time** are measured from right to left along the horizontal axis.

Mary's nonlabor income is $70 a day. The vertical segment BA of the budget constraint shows that Mary has this income available to her even if she supplies no time to the labor market. She may increase her money income by participating in the labor force. For each additional hour she supplies to the market, she must give up an hour of nonmarket time. In return she receives $7.50, her hourly market wage (w). Thus, segment CB is negatively sloped. Its slope is equal to -7.50 or $-w$. If Mary devotes all her time to the market, her total earnings will be $120 ($7.5 \times 16$). Her total daily income, including her nonlabor income, will be $190 ($120 + $70).

Indifference Curves

Mary's preferences for market goods and nonmarket time are represented by her indifference map, shown in panel b. As discussed previously, we can incorporate the family context of decision making into the budget constraint by including the income of other family members as part of the individual's nonlabor income. This issue is more difficult when we consider the indifference curves. One possibility would be to view the indifference curves in Figure 4-5 as representing the family's preferences for various combinations of market goods and Mary's nonmarket time. We do not adopt this approach because, as we saw in Chapter 3, preferences among family members may differ, and the process of arriving at family decisions is complex. However, it is important to recognize that our discussion of indifference curves as representing the individual's preferences is only an approximation. In fact, we expect that the individual's decisions are made in the context of the family and that the preferences of other family members are taken into account in the decision-making process. Bearing this point in mind, we now take a closer look at the indifference curves.

Suppose Mary is told that she could have the combination of market goods and nonmarket time represented by point B. She is then asked to find various other combinations of market goods and nonmarket time from which she would get exactly the same amount of satisfaction or utility and identifies the combinations represented by points A and C. These and other points, which represent equal satisfaction, can all be connected into one **indifference curve**, so named because Mary is indifferent about being at various points on the curve. Thus, each indifference curve indicates the various combinations of market goods and nonmarket time that provide Mary with the same amount of utility or satisfaction.

However, Mary does not have just one indifference curve, but a whole set of higher and lower curves. A point like D on indifference curve U_3 is clearly preferable to B because it offers more of both market goods and nonmarket time. Thus, by extension, all points on U_3 are preferred to all points on U_2. Similarly, B is preferred to E and, thus, all the points on U_2 are preferred to all the points on U_1.[23] As we move out from the origin in a northeasterly direction, consumption possibilities, and thus potential satisfaction, increase.

Indifference curves are generally assumed to be convex to the origin. That is, they become flatter as we move from left to right and steeper as we move from right to left.

---

[23] It should be clear that indifference curves can never intersect. All points on any one curve represent an equal amount of utility, while any point above (below) represents a larger (smaller) amount of utility. At the point where two curves intersect, they represent the same utility. Yet at all other points they do not. This is a logical impossibility.

This shape occurs because it is believed that individuals generally value additional units of relatively scarcer commodities more highly than additional units of relatively more plentiful ones. At point *A*, where nonmarket time is relatively plentiful and market goods are relatively scarce, Mary would be willing to exchange an hour of nonmarket time for a relatively small amount of income (market goods) and still feel equally well off. However, at a point like *C*, where market goods are relatively plentiful and nonmarket time is relatively scarce, it would take a lot of income (market goods) to induce her to give up an additional hour of scarce nonmarket time.

It is interesting to consider more closely the way in which an individual like Mary may substitute market goods for nonmarket time (or vice versa) along an indifference curve while still remaining equally well off. It is important to recognize that we assume she does not derive satisfaction directly from market goods and nonmarket time. Rather, she values them only insofar as they can be used to produce commodities.[24] Thus, broadly speaking, two types of substitution are involved.

SUBSTITUTION IN CONSUMPTION   Some commodities are relatively *goods intensive* to produce. That is, they are produced using relatively large amounts of market goods and relatively little nonmarket time. Examples include buying expensive furniture and clothing or recreational activities such as dining at an elegant restaurant or flying to the Caribbean for a short vacation.

Other commodities are relatively *time intensive*. That is, they are produced using relatively greater amounts of nonmarket time and relatively fewer inputs of market goods. Examples of these commodities include recreational activities like hiking, bird watching, or taking a cycling trip. Also, as anyone who has spent time caring for children can attest, small children are a relatively time-intensive "commodity."

Substitution in consumption involves choosing among commodities so as to substitute goods-intensive commodities for time-intensive ones or time-intensive commodities for goods-intensive ones. When such substitutions are made along a given indifference curve, the implication is that the individual is indifferent between the two alternatives. So, for example, an individual may be indifferent between a goods-intensive vacation like staying for a short time at an expensive resort or a more time-intensive one of spending a longer period hiking and backpacking. Or, more broadly, an individual might be indifferent between having a large family of time-intensive children and spending more time in recreational activities that are more goods intensive.

SUBSTITUTION IN PRODUCTION   In many instances, the same commodity can be produced using a relatively time-intensive technique or a relatively goods-intensive technique. For example, a meal may be prepared from scratch at home, made using convenience foods, or purchased at a restaurant. A clean house may be produced by individuals doing the work themselves or by hiring cleaning help. A small child may be cared for entirely by a parent, by a babysitter for a few hours a day, or may spend all day at a child care center.

Substitution in production involves choosing among various ways of producing the same commodity so as to substitute goods-intensive production techniques for time-intensive ones or time-intensive production techniques for goods-intensive ones. Again, when such substitutions are made along a given indifference curve, the implication is that the individual is indifferent between the two alternatives. Examples here

---

[24] The indifference curves used in this chapter are a graphical representation of what has been termed the individual's *indirect utility function*; see Becker, "A Theory of the Allocation of Time." Students who read the appendix to Chapter 3 will recognize that we took a different approach in the analysis presented there and simply assumed that families derive utility *directly* from market and home goods.

include those already described: preparing a meal at home versus eating out, hiring cleaning help versus doing it oneself, taking a child to a child care center versus taking care of the child oneself.

SUBSTITUTION BETWEEN MARKET GOODS AND NONMARKET TIME   As an individual like Mary moves from point A to point B to point C along indifference curve U_2 in Figure 4-5, she is likely to exploit opportunities for substitution in both consumption and production. That is, she will substitute goods-intensive commodities for time-intensive commodities in consumption, and goods-intensive for time-intensive production techniques. As she continues to do so, she will exhaust many of the obvious possibilities. It will take larger increments of market goods to induce her to part with her scarcer nonmarket time, which explains why indifference curves are believed to get steeper as we move from right to left.

Comparing across individuals, the steepness of the indifference curve is influenced by how easy or difficult it is for them to substitute market goods for nonmarket time while remaining equally well off. This ease or difficulty, in turn, will depend on their opportunities for substituting one for the other in production or consumption or both. For example, those who enjoy hiking a great deal will not easily be induced to decrease the time they spend on it. They will have steeper indifference curves, reflecting that they have greater difficulty in substituting market goods for nonmarket time in consumption than those who care less for such time-intensive activities.

Similarly, we would expect those whose services are in greater demand in the home (say, because small children are present) to have steeper indifference curves, reflecting their greater difficulty in substituting market goods for nonmarket time in production. Tastes and preferences will be a factor here, too. People who feel strongly that children should be cared for full time by their own parent and that alternative care is an extremely poor substitute will have steeper indifference curves than those who believe that adequate alternative care can be provided.

This analysis assumes a degree of substitutability between market goods and nonmarket time.[25] However, some commodities cannot be purchased in the market. Various personal services and management tasks provided in the home may be of this nature. Similarly, some commodities available in the market cannot be produced at home. Examples range from sophisticated medical care and advanced education to means of transportation and communication, insurance, and many consumer durables. Nonetheless, it is highly likely that, when all commodities are aggregated together (as in the indifference curves shown in Figure 4-5), some substitution possibilities between market goods and nonmarket time exist. The ease or difficulty of substitution, then, is represented by the steepness of the indifference curves.

TASTES   Beyond considerations of this kind, economists generally do not analyze the determinants of individuals' preferences for income (market goods) versus nonmarket time. However, it is important to point out that individuals do not operate in a social vacuum. Their tastes and behaviors are undoubtedly influenced by social attitudes and norms.[26] For example, the willingness of a woman to substitute purchased services for her own time in child care is undoubtedly influenced by the social acceptability of doing so. Yet it is probably true that attitudes follow behavior to some extent, as well. Thus, it is likely, for example, that it is more acceptable for mothers of

---

[25] For and interesting discussion, see Nancy Folbre and Julie A. Nelson, "For Love or Money—Or Both?" *Journal of Economic Perspectives* 14, no. 4 (Fall 2000): 123–40.
[26] The importance of social norms is particularly emphasized by Clair Brown, "An Institutional Model of Wives' Work Decisions," *Industrial Relations* 24, no. 2 (Spring 1985): 182–204.

small children to work outside the home than it used to be in part because it is more common for them to do so.

A woman's relative preference for income (market goods) versus nonmarket time also reflects a variety of other factors not generally emphasized by economists. As we saw in Chapter 3, women may value earning their own income for the economic independence it brings and to enhance their relative power position in the family. In addition, an increasing number of women value career success in much the same way their male counterparts do, which also affects the shape of their indifference curves.

Although such considerations do not invalidate the use of this model in analyzing women's labor supply decisions, they do serve to make us aware that the term *tastes* (or preferences), as economists use it, covers a lot of ground. This awareness is particularly important as we attempt to explain women's rising labor force participation over time.

While, as noted, economists have generally not focused their attention on the determinants of tastes or of gender differences in these tastes, these topics have been the subject of some recent research. Perhaps not surprisingly, the evidence suggests that family background influences tastes. For example, in families where mothers have less traditional attitudes about gender roles, daughters and sons tend to share these views. Moreover, mothers' less traditional attitudes are not only positively associated with their daughter's labor force participation decision, but they appear to have an equally strong positive association with the labor force participation of their daughter-in-law (their son's wife). One explanation is that if a son is raised by a mother with less traditional attitudes, he may be more favorably disposed toward his wife working or perhaps more willing to share housework duties, thus facilitating his wife's employment.[27]

Research on immigrant women's labor force participation rates, which shows that these rates are influenced by patterns in their countries of origin, also points to the role of family background and cultural factors in influencing tastes.[28] Specifically, women migrating from countries with relatively high female labor force participation rates work greater hours than women coming from countries with lower relative female participation rates. Further, even though both groups assimilate toward native-born women's labor supply patterns as they spend more time in the United States, the gap in their labor supply tends to persist. Similarly, the labor supply behavior of U.S.-born daughters of immigrants (the second generation) has been found to be positively associated with both female participation rates in their parents' country of origin and the participation patterns of immigrants from those origin countries.[29] Nonetheless, considerable assimilation to native-born patterns occurs with successive generations in the United States.

---

[27] Lídia Farré and Francis Vella, "The Intergenerational Transmission of Gender Role Attitudes and Its Implications for Female Labor Force Participation," IZA Discussion Paper No. 2802 (May 2007); and Arland Thornton, Duane F. Alwin, and Donald Camburn, "Causes and Consequences of Sex-Role Attitudes and Attitude Change," *American Sociological Review* 48, no. 2 (April 1983): 211–27. Raquel Fernández, Alessandra Fogli, and Claudia Olivetti were the first to identify the link between a mother's behavior and the behavior of her son's wife; see their "Mothers and Sons: Preference Formation and Female Labor Force Dynamics" *Quarterly Journal of Economics* 119, no. 4 (November 2004): 1249–99.

[28] Francine D. Blau, Lawrence M. Kahn and Kerry L. Papps, "Gender, Source Country Characteristics and Labor Market Assimilation Among Immigrants: 1980–2000," NBER Working Paper 14387 (October 2008); and Heather Antecol "An Examination of Cross-Country Differences in the Gender Gap in Labor Force Participation Rates," *Labour Economics* 7, no. 4 (July 2000): 409–26.

[29] Racquel Fernández and Alessandra Fogli, "Culture: An Empirical Investigation of Beliefs, Work, and Fertility," *American Economic Journal: Macroeconomics* 1, No. 1 (January 2009): 146–177; Francine D. Blau, Lawrence M. Kahn, Albert Yung-Hsu Liu, and Kerry L. Papps, "The Transmission of Women's Fertility, Human Capital, and Work Orientation Across Immigrant Generations," NBER Working Paper 14388 (October 2008); see also, Antecol, An Examination of Cross-Country Differences in the Gender Gap," who examined the impact of ancestry.

The Labor Force Participation Decision

Let us suppose that Mary's indifference curves and her budget constraint are those shown in panel a of Figure 4-6. Mary will maximize utility or satisfaction at point Y where the budget constraint just touches the highest attainable indifference curve, U_2. At Y, the amount of income needed to induce her to give up an additional hour of non-market time, given by the slope of the indifference curve at Y, exactly equals the market wage she is offered for that hour, given by the slope of the budget constraint. That is, the budget constraint is *tangent* to the indifference curve at Y. Mary, therefore, supplies 8 hours per day to the market and spends 8 hours on nonmarket activities. Her daily earnings of $60 ($7.50 × 8) plus her daily nonlabor income of $70 give her (and her family) a total income of $130 per day.

It is interesting to consider in greater detail why Mary does not select point A, where she would supply no time to the labor market. At A, where indifference curve U_1 intersects the budget constraint, it is *flatter* than the negatively sloped portion of the budget constraint (which passes through point A and point 190 on the market goods axis). This means that, at point A, Mary values her nonmarket time *less* than the wage the market is willing to pay her for it. Thus, she will certainly choose to supply some time to the market.

Another woman, Joyce, faces the same budget constraint as Mary but has steeper indifference curves (shown in panel b of Figure 4-6). Perhaps she has more young children to care for than Mary. In Joyce's case, the budget constraint touches the highest attainable indifference curve at point A. At A, the indifference curve is steeper than the budget constraint. This means that Joyce sets a *higher* value on her nonmarket time than the wage rate she is offered in the market. She will maximize her utility by remaining out of the labor force, spending all 16 hours available to her on nonmarket activities. Her consumption of market goods will be limited to her nonlabor income of $70 per day.

The slope of the indifference curve at zero hours of market work (point A in panels a and b of Figure 4-6) is termed the **reservation wage** or the **value of home time** (w^*). It is equal to the value an individual places on his or her time at home. If the market wage is greater than the reservation wage (i.e., $w > w^*$), as in panel a, the individual will choose to participate in the labor market. If the reservation wage is greater than or equal to the market wage ($w^* \geq w$), as in panel b, the individual will choose not to participate. This decision rule can be summarized by the following simple equations:

$$w > w^* \Rightarrow \text{in the labor force}$$
$$w^* \geq w \Rightarrow \text{out of the labor force}$$

This economic analysis suggests that factors that increase the value of market time (w) tend to increase the probability that the individual will choose to participate in the labor force, all else equal. In other words, labor force participation is *positively related* to the wage or the value of market time. On the other hand, factors that increase the value of nonmarket time (w^*) tend to lower the probability of labor force participation, other things being equal. Therefore, labor force participation is *negatively related* to the reservation wage or the value of nonmarket time.

THE VALUE OF NONMARKET TIME (w^*)

As our previous discussion suggests, the value of nonmarket time is influenced by tastes and preferences and also by the demands placed on an individual's nonmarket time. Given adherence to the traditional division of labor in most families, the presence of small children, and other circumstances that increase the housework burden and caregiving responsibilities, particularly influence women's participation decisions.

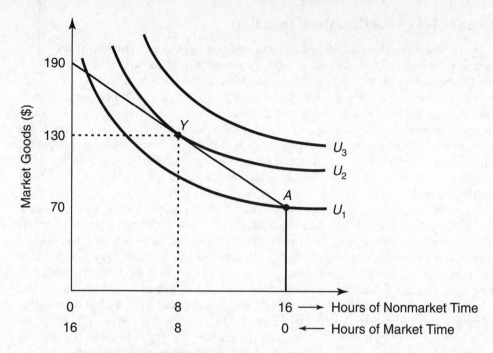

(a) $w > w^*$ PARTICIPATES IN THE LABOR MARKET

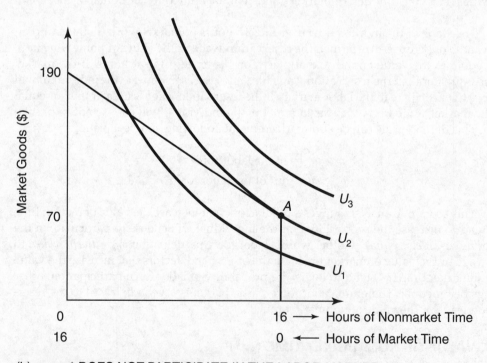

(b) $w < w^*$ DOES NOT PARTICIPATE IN THE LABOR MARKET

FIGURE 4-6 The Labor Force Participation Decision

Another factor that influences the value placed on nonmarket time is the availability of income from sources other than the individual's own work efforts. Figure 4-7 shows the impact of changes in nonlabor income on the labor force participation decision. Let us suppose that the figure represents the budget constraint and indifference curves for Susan, a married woman with two small children. Suppose that her husband is unemployed and that initially her budget constraint is *ABC*. This represents $30 of nonlabor income (from interest on some bonds the family owns) and her market wage of $7.50. She maximizes utility at point *D*, where she supplies five hours a day to the market and earns $37.50. This brings the family's total daily income to $67.50. Now suppose Susan's husband finds a job. When his earnings ($50) are added to the interest received from the bonds ($30), her nonlabor income becomes $80. Her new budget constraint is *AB'C'*. Note that segment *B'C'* is parallel to segment *BC*. This is because Susan's market wage rate, which is the slope of segment *BC*, remains unchanged at $7.50.

At the higher income level, Susan's consumption possibilities increase, and she is able to reach a higher indifference curve. She maximizes utility at *B'* where she has more of both market goods and nonmarket time, and supplies less time to the market; in fact, in this example, she withdraws from the labor force entirely. This example represents the impact of the **income effect**. Ordinarily, when individuals' incomes go up, they demand more of all commodities from which they derive utility. To the extent that nonmarket time is used to produce these commodities, an increase in income will increase the value of nonmarket time and result in less time spent in the labor market. The income effect will be relatively large when the demand for time-intensive commodities increases sharply with income. The individual then needs to transfer more time from market to nonmarket activities in order to produce them. This shift is likely to occur when market goods are not considered to be good substitutes for home-produced items. So Susan, whose wage rate has not changed while her income increased, may choose to consume more recreation or spend more time caring for her children.

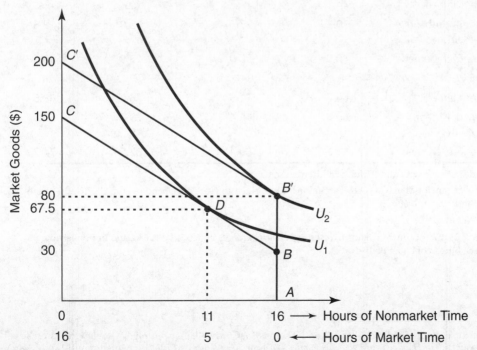

FIGURE 4-7   Impact of Nonlabor Income on Labor Force Particpation

Table 4-3 illustrates the impact of the value of nonmarket time (w^*) on women's labor force participation decisions, using data on female participation rates by marital status and presence and age of children. Marital status reflects in part the availability and level of alternative sources of income. Thus, we see that, within children's age categories, women who are married, with spouse present, are generally less likely to work outside the home than never-married women and other ever-married women. (The latter includes women who are separated from their husbands, divorced, or widowed.) Further evidence for the importance of the value of home time is provided by studies that find that, among married women, labor force participation is negatively related to husband's income, all else equal.[30] Recall that we expect an increase in the wife's nonlabor income to raise the value of her nonmarket time (w^*).

The impact of children on women's labor force participation may be discerned by comparing the participation rates of women with small children (children under 6) to the rates for women with school-age children (children 6–17), within each marital status category. We see that the presence of small children has a negative effect on women's participation, no doubt because they greatly increase the value of time spent at home. Of course, the causation may, to some extent, run in the opposite direction: Women who are more committed to the labor market or who have more attractive labor market opportunities may choose to have fewer children. It is difficult to distinguish between these two possible explanations for the negative association between women's labor

TABLE 4-3 Labor Force Participation Rates of Women by Marital Status, and Presence and Age of Children, 1960 and 2006

Marital Status	Total[a]	Women with Children		
		Under Age 18	6 to 17 only	Under 6
1960				
Never Married	44.1	n.a.	n.a.	n.a.
Married, Husband Present	30.5	27.6	39.0	18.6
Other Ever-Married	40.0	56.0	65.9	40.5
2006				
Never Married	64.7	71.5	76.2	68.6
Married, Husband Present	60.8	68.4	75.3	60.3
Other Ever-Married	49.1	80.4	82.5	74.3

[a]Inlcudes women with and without children present.

Notes: Data are for March of each year and include women 16 years of age and over in 2007, and 14 years of age and over in 1960.

n.a. = Not available.

Sources: U.S. Census Bureau, *Statistical Abstract of the United States: 1995*, Table 638; and unpublished data from the Bureau of Labor Statistics.

[30] See, for example, Richard Blundell and Thomas MaCurdy, "Labor Supply: A Review of Alternative Approaches," in *Handbook of Labor Economics*, Volume 3A edited by Orley Ashenfelter and David Card (Amsterdam: Elsevier, 1999), pp. 1559–1695.

supply and the presence of children, but the evidence generally suggests that children do have a negative effect on women's labor supply.[31]

It may at first seem surprising that participation rates in the "total" column (which include women with and without children under age 18 present) are generally lower than for the group of women with children present. One reason for this is that the married women and especially the other ever-married women with no children under 18 tend to be older, in some cases widows, whose children have left home. Older women tend to have lower participation rates because many have retired. At the other end of the age distribution, never-married women with no children present tend to be younger women, who may still be attending school and thus out of the labor force for that reason.

Table 4-3 also illustrates some interesting trends in the impact of marital status and the presence of children on labor force participation. Although the presence of small children is strongly negatively associated with women's labor force participation in each year, women with small children were considerably more likely to work outside the home in 2006 than in 1960. For example, in 2006, 60 percent of married women with children under 6 years old were in the labor force, compared to only 19 percent in 1960. Participation rates have also increased dramatically for women with older children: 75 percent of married women with children between the ages of 6 and 17 were labor force participants in 2006, compared to 39 percent in 1960.[32]

The differences in participation rates by marital status are also considerably smaller today than they were over 40 years ago. That is, married women's participation rates in each presence of children category are considerably closer to those of ever-married women in 2006 than they were in 1960. In addition, within the group of married women, wives' participation decisions are less sensitive to their husbands' income than they were in the past.[33] In other words labor force participation rates of today's wives are quite high, even for those whose husbands have relatively high earnings. In this way too, married women's behavior is now more similar to that of their nonmarried counterparts.

Figure 4-8 shows trends in participation rates of women with children under age 18 by marital status in more detail. Prior to the early 1990s, increases in the labor force participation rates of married mothers were especially large compared to those of never-married and other ever-married mothers. For example, in 1960, participation rates of married mothers were 28 percentage points lower than those of other ever-married mothers, but by 1992 married women's participation rates lagged by only five percentage points. Data on never-married mothers have only been available since 1975. At that time their participation rates were about the same as those of married mothers; however, by 1992 married mothers were *considerably more* (15 percentage points more) likely to be in the labor force than never-married mothers.

---

[31] The statistical problem in identifying the causal effect of children on labor supply is that, as in any problem of this type, it is necessary to find a variable that determines the number of children but does not directly influence labor supply. For an interesting approach using variation in the sex mix of the first two children as well as twin births as predictors of fertility, see Joshua D. Angrist and William N. Evans, "Children and Their Parents' Labor Supply: Evidence from Exogenous Variation in Family Size," *American Economic Review* 88, no. 3 (June 1998): 450–77; and Joyce P. Jacobsen, James Wishart Pearce III, and Joshua L. Rosenbloom, "The Effects of Childbearing on Married Women's Labor Supply and Earnings: Using Twin Births as a Natural Experiment," *Journal of Human Resources* 34, no. 3 (Summer 1999): 449–74.

[32] Statistical analyses controlling for other factors affecting the labor force participation of wives confirm that children exert a smaller negative influence on wives' participation than formerly; see, for example, Arleen Leibowitz and Jacob Klerman, "Explaining Changes in Married Mothers' Employment Over Time," *Demography* 32, no. 3 (August 1995): 365–78; and Heather Boushey. "'Opting Out'? The Effect of Children on Women's Employment in the United States," *Feminist Economics* 14, no. 1 (January 2008): 1–36.

[33] Blau and Kahn, "Changes in the Labor Supply Behavior of Married Women"; and Bradley T. Heim, "The Incredible Shrinking Elasticities: Married Female Labor Supply, 1978–2002," *Journal of Human Resources* 42, no. 4 (Fall 2007): 881–918.

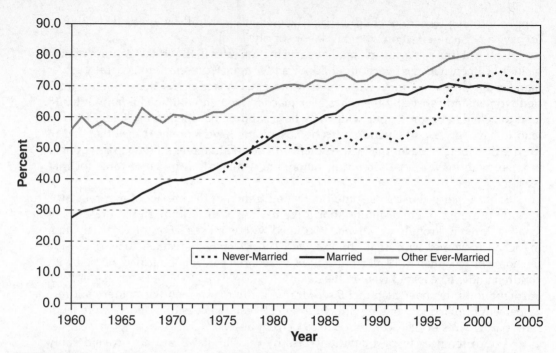

FIGURE 4-8 Labor Force Participation Rates of Women with Children Under 18, 1960–2007

Source: Statistical Abstract of the United States, 2004 (Table 597) and 2008 (Table 580); *BLS Bulletin 2340* (August 1989); Bernan Press, *Handbook of U.S. Labor Statistics*, 1st ed. (1997); and unpublished data from the BLS.

In contrast, after 1990, the growth in labor force participation of married mothers slowed and, after the mid-1990s, their participation rates began to level off and actually decline somewhat. On the other hand, beginning in the early 1990s, participation increased sharply among never-married and other ever-married mothers,[34] although the participation rates of these groups too began to level off and decline a bit after the early 2000s. As a consequence, both never-married and other ever-married mothers are now *more* likely to be in the labor force than married mothers. The factors behind these recent trends are explored further later in this chapter.

Even though most attention has been focused on the effect of the presence of children on women's labor supply, some research has examined the impact of children on male labor supply. Perhaps not surprisingly given traditional gender roles, fatherhood has been found to *increase* the labor supply of men. What may be surprising, however, is that men have been found to increase their labor supply more in response to the birth of sons than daughters.[35] Although, as discussed in Chapter 11, preference for male children is quite pronounced in a number of Asian countries including India,

---

[34] Rebecca M. Blank, "Distinguished Lecture on Economics in Government—Fighting Poverty: Lessons from Recent U.S. History," *Journal of Economic Perspectives* 14, no. 2 (Spring 2000): 3–19; and Bruce D. Meyer and Dan T. Rosenbaum, "Making Single Mothers Work: Recent Tax and Welfare Policy and Its Effects," *National Tax Journal* 53 (December 2000): 1027–62.

[35] Shelly Lundberg and Elaina Rose, "The Effects of Sons and Daughters on Men's Labor Supply and Wages," *Review of Economics and Statistics* 84, no 2 (May 2002): 251–68.

China, and Korea, this and other recent research suggests it is by no means entirely absent in the United States.[36]

The Value of Market Time (*w*)

In addition to the impact of the value of nonmarket time, the labor force participation decision is influenced by the labor market opportunities an individual faces, particularly the wage rate available in the labor market. To see this effect in greater detail, let us consider the case of Ellen, who initially faces the budget constraint, *ABC*, shown in Figure 4-9. Her potential market wage is $8.00 per hour, while her nonlabor income (say, equal to her husband's earnings) is $100 per day. Given her tastes (represented by her indifference map), she maximizes utility at point *B* where she devotes all her time to nonmarket activities. Note that at point *B* the indifference curve (U_1) is steeper than the budget line (*BC*)—Ellen's reservation wage (w^*) is higher than the wage rate offered to her by the market (*w*).

Now suppose that Ellen's market opportunities improve and her potential market wage increases to $12.00. Her new budget constraint is *ABC'*. Segment *BA* of her

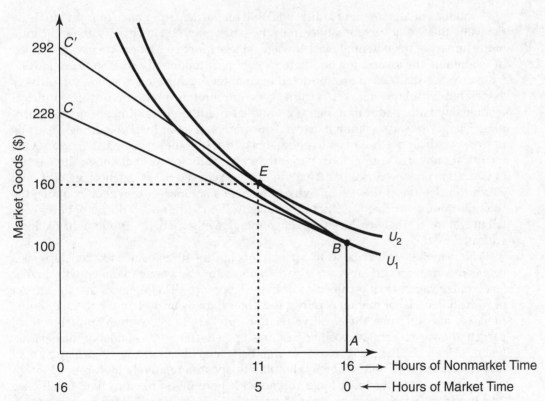

FIGURE 4-9 Impact of the (Potential) Market Wage on Labor Force Participation

---

[36] For example, the birth or expected birth of a son has been found to increase the probability that unmarried biological parents will marry, and the presence of sons to reduce the probability that married couples will divorce. Studies also find that in families with at least two children, the probability of having another child is higher in all-girl families than in all-boy families. See Gordon B. Dahl and Enrico Moretti, "The Demand for Sons: Evidence from Divorce, Fertility, and Shotgun Marriage," *Review of Economic Studies* 75, no. 4 (October 2008): 1085–120; and Shelly Lundberg and Elaina Rose, "Child Gender and the Transition to Marriage," *Demography* 40, no. 2 (May 2003): 333–49.

budget constraint remains unchanged because it is still the case that if she remains out of the labor market entirely, she (and her family) will receive $100 a day of nonlabor income. However, BC' is steeper than BC because she now receives $12.00 for each hour she supplies to the market rather than $8.00. Another way to see this is to realize that C' must lie above C because, if Ellen devotes all her time to market work, her total income at a wage of $12.00 per hour ($292) will be higher than it would have been at a wage of $8.00 per hour ($228).

At the higher wage, the budget constraint (BC') is now steeper than the indifference curve at point B—the market wage (w) is greater than the reservation wage (w^*), and Ellen maximizes her utility at point E on indifference curve U_2, where she supplies 5 hours to the market. Thus, Ellen now chooses to participate in the labor force.

This example illustrates the **substitution effect**. An increase in the wage rate, all else equal, raises the opportunity cost of time spent in nonmarket activities and, hence, the "price" of nonmarket time. Individuals are expected to respond by supplying more time to the market and substituting market goods for nonmarket time in consumption or production. Because the wage increase clearly enables Ellen to reach a higher indifference curve, we may conclude that she feels better off with the combination of commodities represented by point E, even though she has less nonmarket time available at E than at B.

Published data are not readily available on participation rates of individuals by the wage they could potentially earn in the labor market. However, some indication of the impact of the potential market wage on labor force participation may be gained by examining the association between educational attainment and labor force participation. As we shall see in greater detail in Chapter 6, education is strongly positively associated with labor market earnings. A common interpretation of this empirical relationship is that education increases market productivity and hence market earnings. The positive association between education and labor market earnings leads us to expect education to be positively associated with labor force participation. One qualification worth noting, however, is that, especially for women, the positive effect of education on labor force participation may be reduced to the extent that additional education also raises the productivity of women's nonmarket time. For example, the time that more-educated mothers spend with their children could potentially contribute more to their children's achievement levels than the time spent by less-educated mothers.[37]

Nonetheless, as may be seen in panel a of Figure 4-10, a positive relationship exists between education and labor force participation among women. Women with higher levels of education are more likely to be in the labor force. This suggests that the impact of education on labor market earnings is greater than its impact on the value of home time. We may interpret this positive relationship between education and labor force participation as reflecting a positive relationship between wages and labor force participation. However, the positive relationship between education and participation may also reflect self-selection: Women who plan to spend a relatively high proportion of their adult years in the labor force are more likely to invest in education. Finally, we may note that the jobs held by more educated individuals usually offer greater nonpecuniary (or nonmonetary) attractions—such as a more pleasant environment, more challenging work, more prestige, and so on—as well as higher wages. Consideration of such job features serves to emphasize that the value of market work should ideally take into account not only pecuniary benefits but also other aspects of the job.

---

[37] Interestingly, more educated parents (mothers and fathers) spend more time with their children than less-educated parents do, all else equal; see Jonathan Guryan, Erik Hurst, and Melissa Kearney, "Parental Education and Parental Time with Children," *Journal of Economic Perspectives* 22, no. 3 (Summer 2008): 23–46.

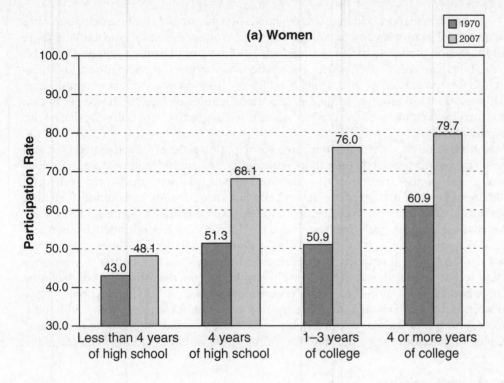

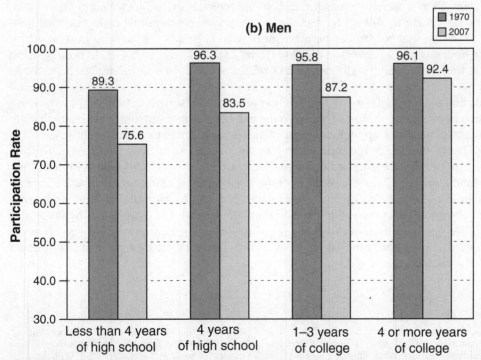

FIGURE 4-10   Labor Force Participation by Education, 1970 and 2007, Ages 25–64

Note: Educational categories are defined somewhat differently in 2007.

Source: U.S. Dept of Labor, *Handbook of Labor Statistics*, 1989 and author's tabulations from the 2007 microdata file of the March Current Population Survey.

Arguably, the most striking pattern shown in Figure 4-10 is that participation rates of high school graduates and of college-educated women increased substantially more over the period than they did for women who did not complete high school. These differential increases resulted in a stronger relationship between participation and education in 2007 than existed in 1970. Panel b of Figure 4-10 indicates a similar strengthening of this relationship among men. One important gender difference, however, is that labor force participation of men fell for all education groups, especially for those with less education.

At the same time that the labor force participation rates of less-educated men and women decreased relative to their more educated counterparts, their relative labor market wages also fell. A trend toward widening wage inequality in the United States and to a lesser extent in many other economically advanced nations resulted in widening wage differentials between more-skilled and less-skilled workers. Some evidence indicates that the declining relative labor force participation of less-educated women and men is due at least in part to their declining market wage opportunities.[38] The trend toward rising wage inequality is considered in more detail in Chapter 8, where we review recent developments in earnings. In addition to the negative effect of declining relative participation and wages on the economic status of less-educated women, single headship increased considerably more for this group than for their more highly educated counterparts. This development also adversely affected their economic status.[39] Chapter 10 discusses the considerable economic disadvantages faced by such families.

The Hours Decision

The impact of a change in the wage rate on the number of *hours* supplied to the market by those who are already labor force participants is a bit more complex than the impact of a wage change on *labor force participation*. This complexity is illustrated in Figure 4-11. As we saw in Figure 4-9, an increase in the wage rate corresponds to an outward rotation of the budget constraint, because more market goods can now be purchased for every hour worked, shown as a rotation from CD to CD' in Figure 4-11. In both panels a and b, the individual initially maximizes utility at point A on indifference curve U_1. At a higher wage, he or she is able to reach a higher indifference curve and selects point B on indifference curve U_2, resulting in either an increase (shown in panel a) or a decrease (shown in panel b) in hours supplied to the market.[40] These outcomes illustrate that, *for labor force participants*, an increase in the wage rate produces two distinct effects.

On the one hand, the increase in the wage is like an increase in income. For any given amount of time supplied to the market *greater than 0 hours*, income is higher along CD' than along CD. This gives rise to an *income effect* that, other things equal, increases the demand not only for most market goods, but also for nonmarket time, and hence lowers hours supplied to the market. On the other hand, the increase in the wage also raises the opportunity cost of nonmarket time, resulting in a *substitution effect* that, all else equal, causes a reduction in nonmarket time and an increase in the supply of hours to the market.

---

[38] Chinhui Juhn, "Decline of Male Labor Market Participation: The Role of Declining Market Opportunities," *Quarterly Journal of Economics* 107, no. 1 (February 1992): 79–121; and Juhn and Kevin M. Murphy, "Wage Inequality and Family Labor Supply," *Journal of Labor Economics* 15, no. 1, pt. 1 (January 1997): 72–97.

[39] Francine D. Blau, "Trends in the Well-Being of American Women: 1970–1995," *Journal of Economic Literature* 36, no. 1 (March 1998): 112–165; and Sara McLanahan, "Diverging Destinies: How Children Are Faring under the Second Demographic Transition," *Demography* 41, no. 4 (Nov. 2004): 607–27.

[40] The diagrammatic representation of the effect of a wage change on work hours is shown in greater detail in the appendix to this chapter (Appendix 4A).

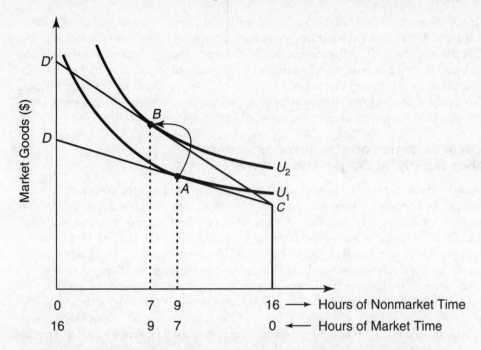

(a) THE SUBSTITUTION EFFECT DOMINATES THE INCOME EFFECT

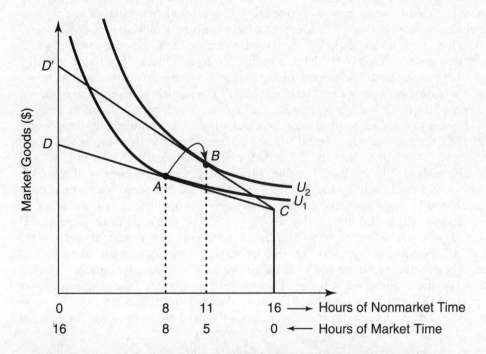

(b) THE INCOME EFFECT DOMINATES THE SUBSTITUTION EFFECT

FIGURE 4-11   Impact of the Market Wage on Labor Hours

Thus, when the wage rate rises, the substitution effect operates to increase labor hours supplied, but the income effect operates to reduce labor hours supplied. The net effect is theoretically indeterminate. If the substitution effect dominates the income effect, work hours increase (panel a). If the income effect dominates the substitution effect, work hours are reduced (panel b). Again, recall that *a wage increase unambiguously raises the probability of labor force participation* because, in this case, there is only a positive substitution effect; no offsetting income effect occurs.

Empirical Evidence on the Responsiveness of Labor Supply to Wages and Income

Our consideration of the labor supply decision suggests that both the wages that workers can earn in the labor market and the nonlabor income available to them should influence their labor supply decisions. This is what economic theory predicts, but what has actually been found when economists have looked at the data? How responsive is labor supply really to an individual's wages and nonlabor income? Does this responsiveness differ between women and men? Has this responsiveness changed over time?

The research to date especially focuses on married women because, given traditional gender roles, their labor supply behavior is most likely to be affected by the family context. As explained in greater detail in the following inset, economists measure the magnitude of this responsiveness with **elasticities**. The **wage elasticity** measures the responsiveness of an individual's labor supply to a change in his or her own wage. The **income elasticity** measures the responsiveness of an individual's labor supply to a change in his or her nonlabor income. For married couples, the largest source of nonlabor income is their spouses' wages (or income), and so much of the focus is on how a change in a husband's wage (or income) affects his wife's labor supply and how a change in a wife's wage (or income) affects her husband's labor supply.

As a baseline, let us begin by considering research findings for the 1970s and 1980s. An extensive survey of the labor supply literature, with most of the data in the studies cited coming from that period, found that men's wage elasticity was 0.08, while women's wage elasticity was much larger, at 0.78.[41] For nonlabor income, the evidence is a bit more bit mixed, but again suggests that women's labor supply is more responsive to changes in their husbands' wage than vice versa. For example, one study found that, in 1980, the elasticity of married women's labor supply to their husband's wage was about −0.4, while the elasticity of married men's labor supply to their wife's wage was considerably smaller in absolute value, with estimates ranging from −0.01 to 0.04.[42]

These empirical findings suggest that, at least circa 1980, women's labor supply was considerably more sensitive to their own wages and to their spouse's wage or income than was men's. This gender difference is likely related to the traditional division of labor in the family. As Jacob Mincer pointed out in important early work, women may be seen as substituting among market work, home production, and leisure, while men may be viewed as substituting only or primarily between market work and leisure.[43] Although it is possible to substitute market goods for nonmarket time in leisure activities, these possibilities are relatively limited. In contrast, because purchased goods and services are in many cases useful substitutes for nonmarket

---

[41] These were the medians across the studies surveyed; see, Blundell and MaCurdy, "Labor Supply: A Review of Alternative Approaches."

[42] See, Blau and Kahn, "Changes in the Labor Supply Behavior of Married Women" (and additional results in their NBER Working Paper No. 11230). For men, these elasticities were also not always statistically significant. See also Paul J. Devereux, "Changes in Relative Wages and Family Labor Supply," *Journal of Human Resources* 39, no. 3 (Summer 2004): 696–722. A review by Mark Killingsworth, however, finds larger elasticities (in absolute value) for men than women (although relatively small elasticities for both), see, *Labor Supply* (New York: Cambridge University Press, 1983).

[43] Mincer, "Labor Force Participation of Married Women."

time in producing the commodities the family wants, women have closer substitutes for time spent in market work than men do. Thus, changes in market wages are expected to have a larger substitution effect on women's labor supply, yielding a larger wage elasticity for them than for men.[44] One might also reason that, given traditional gender roles, women would generally be perceived as the secondary earner within the family and, thus, that their labor supply would be more responsive to changes in their husband's wage than vice versa. An interesting extension of this reasoning is that, to the extent that the traditional division of labor is breaking down and men and women are more equally sharing home and market responsibilities, we would expect women's labor supply elasticities to become more similar to men's over time.

A similar conclusion is reached by Claudia Goldin who provides an insightful analysis of changes in women's labor supply elasticities over the twentieth century.[45] She reports that, around 1900, when relatively few attractive labor market options were available to women and there was considerable stigma against wives working, married women's labor supply was largely determined by their husbands' labor market opportunities, rather than their own. That is, they might increase hours worked substantially if their husbands' wage fell, but not respond very much, if at all, when their own potential market wage rose. However, as women's education levels increased and white-collar employment opportunities became available to them, the stigma against married women working diminished. As a consequence, their responsiveness to their own labor market opportunities increased (e.g., a higher wage for themselves), while their responsiveness to changes in their husband's income decreased. Goldin further reasoned that, as divorce rates rose and women's jobs increasingly became careers as opposed to merely a means to earn income, not only should the effect of husbands' income continue to decline, but wives' labor supply would eventually become less responsive to changes in their own wages as well. That is, as women became more strongly attached to the labor force and more committed to their careers, they would be less likely to move in and out of the labor force or greatly change their hours worked in response to changes in their wages. Putting this somewhat differently, they would begin to behave more like men.

The expectation that women's labor supply behavior would become more similar to men's has indeed been realized, although significant gender differences remain. Francine Blau and Lawrence Kahn found that, between 1980 and 2000, women's wage elasticity fell from around 0.8 to about 0.4, while their responsiveness to their husbands' wage declined in absolute value from around −0.4 to about −0.2 (that is, each elasticity was cut roughly in half).[46] While substantial gender differences in labor supply

---

[44] Another reason for the gender difference in wage elasticities that is also related to the traditional division of labor is that many more women than men are out of the labor force. Thus, when the dependent variable is annual hours, women's wage elasticity reflects both (1) the responsiveness to a change in the wage of the participation decision as well as (2) the responsiveness to a change in the wage of the hours worked decision. For men, there is usually only the latter effect. Evidence suggests that the participation elasticity tends to be quite large, while the responsiveness of hours worked of labor force participants to a wage change tends to be fairly small, thus contributing to women's larger wage elasticity compared to men's. See, James J. Heckman, "What Has Been Learned About Labor Supply in the Past Twenty Years," *American Economic Review* 83, no. 2 (May 1993): 116–21. Nonetheless, even for the hours of work decision of labor force participants, married women's responsiveness to wages and nonlabor income tends to exceed men's. Readers should also note that the discussion in the text abstracts from issues of complementarity and substitutability of the home and work time of husband and wife. There is some evidence of complementarity for older couples, which we discuss later when we consider trends in male participation.

[45] Goldin, *Understanding the Gender Gap*, Ch. 5.

[46] Blau and Kahn "Changes in the Labor Supply Behavior of Married Women." They obtain a range of elasticities for each year based on various specifications of the labor supply equations. Thus, more precisely, they found that women's own wage elasticity fell by 50 to 56 percent, while their income (husband's wage) elasticity declined by 38 to 47 percent in absolute value. See also Heim, "The Incredible Shrinking Elasticities."

elasticities between men and women remain, Goldin sees the substantial changes that have occurred so far as manifestations of a "quiet revolution" in women's relationship to the labor market in which most women, like most men, view their employment as part of a long-term career, rather than as a series of disconnected jobs.[47]

LABOR SUPPLY ELASTICITIES

Economists use a concept called **elasticity** to describe how one variable responds to a change in another variable. Is this response very large or relatively small? In the case of labor supply analysis, economists focus on two specific elasticities: **wage elasticity** and **income elasticity**. The wage elasticity measures the responsiveness of an individual's labor supply to a change in his or her own wage. The income elasticity measures the responsiveness of an individual's labor supply to a change in his or her nonlabor income (for married couples, this is often their spouse's income or wage). Elasticities are useful because they provide information not only about the direction of a change, for example that an increase in the wage increases hours worked, but also about the magnitude or size of the change.

Specifically, the *wage elasticity of labor supply* is defined as the percentage change in hours worked by an individual induced by a 1 percent increase in an individual's own wage.

Wage Elasticity: % change in hours worked/% change in wages

The *income elasticity of labor supply* is defined as the percentage change in hours worked by an individual induced by a 1 percent increase in an individual's nonlabor income.

Income Elasticity: % change in hours worked/% change in nonlabor income

Let us suppose that a study finds that the wage elasticity of married women is 0.78. To understand what this means, we can rewrite this as 0.78/1. This figure tells us that a 1 percent increase in wages (the denominator) leads to a 0.78 percent increase in hours worked (the numerator). Let us say the same study finds that the wage elasticity of labor supply of married men is 0.08. This is clearly a considerably smaller response than for married women—for married men, a 1 percent increase in wages induces only a 0.08 percent increase in hours worked.

Our consideration of the labor supply decision leads us to expect the income elasticity of labor supply to be negative. That is, an *increase* in nonlabor income (e.g. spouse's income) is expected to *reduce* work hours. So, for example, an income elasticity of −0.4 for married women means that a 1 percent increase in nonlabor income leads to a 0.4 percent decrease in hours worked. An income elasticity of −0.01 for married men means that a 1 percent increase in nonlabor income leads to only a 0.01 percent decrease in hours worked.

When an elasticity exceeds 1(in absolute value*), we say that the relationship is relatively "elastic." When an elasticity is less than 1(in absolute value), we say that the relationship is relatively "inelastic." When an elasticity is just equal to 1(in absolute value), we say that the relationship is "unit elastic," with the magnitude of the response (a 1 percent change) exactly equal to the magnitude of the change in the variable that caused it (a 1 percent change). In the examples above, the wage and income elasticities are inelastic for both married men and married women, although women's elasticities are considerably larger than men's in absolute value.

*Absolute value refers to the value of a number, regardless of its sign. For example, the absolute value of both −2 and 2 is 2.

---

[47] Claudia Goldin, "The Quiet Revolution That Transformed Women's Employment, Education, and Family," *American Economic Review* 96, no. 2 (May 2006): 1–20.

Economic Conditions

Fluctuations in economic conditions also affect labor force participation. These effects are likely to be largest among so-called secondary workers. Economists view the response of labor force participation to changes in the level of economic activity as being the net result of two opposing effects.

The **added worker effect** predicts that during economic downturns, if the primary earner becomes unemployed, other family members may enter (or postpone their exit from) the labor force in order to maintain family income. The decline in their nonlabor income due to the unemployment of the primary earner lowers the value of other family members' nonmarket time (w^*). (This effect is shown as a movement from point B' to point D in Figure 4-7.) Such individuals may leave the labor force when economic conditions improve and the primary earner is again employed on a regular basis.

At the same time, the **discouraged worker effect** holds that during times of high unemployment, when individuals lose their jobs, they may become discouraged and drop out of the labor force after a fruitless period of job search. Others who are out of the labor force may postpone labor force entry until economic conditions improve. Discouragement is due to the decline in the expected reward to market work (w) because of the difficulty of locating an acceptable job. (This effect is shown as a movement from point E to point B in Figure 4-9.) As economic conditions improve, previously discouraged workers may renew their job search and enter the labor force.

Both these effects can operate at the same time for different households. The *net* effect of economic conditions on labor force participation depends on whether the discouraged or added worker effect predominates in the aggregate. This is an empirical question. The data suggest that the discouraged worker effect is dominant. Thus, the labor force tends to shrink or grow less rapidly in recessions and to expand or grow more rapidly during upturns in the economy.[48]

Some Applications of the Theory: Taxes, Child Care Costs, and Labor Supply

TAXES AND THE DECISION TO WORK   Not all money earned is actually at the disposal of the worker. Some of it has to be paid out in taxes. Because earnings are taxed and the value of home production is not, labor force participation among married women is discouraged. Two features of the U.S. income tax system further discourage married women's labor force participation: The tax system is progressive (additional increments of income are taxed at higher rates) and these tax rates are applied to family, not individual, income.[49] One consequence is that married women, often regarded as secondary earners within the family, face relatively high tax rates on the first dollar of their labor market earnings since it is "added on" to their husbands' earnings in calculating taxes. In general, we expect that the higher the tax rate (the lower the after-tax wage), the more likely a woman is to decide not to participate in the labor force.

---

[48] For some recent evidence, see Luca Benati, "Some Empirical Evidence on the 'Discouraged Worker' Effect," *Economics Letters* 70, no. 3 (2001): 387–95. There is evidence that the added worker effect also exists, though it is small; see Shelly Lundberg, "The Added Worker Effect," *Journal of Labor Economics* 3, no. 1 (January 1985): 11–37. One reason the added worker effect may be so small is that receipt of unemployment insurance helps to counteract the negative effect on family income that would otherwise occur when the primary breadwinner becomes unemployed; see Jonathan Gruber and Julie Berry Cullen, "Does Unemployment Insurance Crowd Out Spousal Labor Supply?" *Journal of Labor Economics* 18, no. 3 (July 2000): 546–72.

[49] Illustrative numerical examples of these concepts are discussed in Chapter 11 using tax information for 2008 provided in Table 11-4.

These points may be illustrated by Figure 4-9. Suppose Joan earns $12.00 per hour and faces budget constraint ABC'. If she has to pay out, say, one-third (33.3 percent) of her income in taxes, her after-tax wage (or hourly take-home pay) will be only $8.00. This situation is represented by budget constraint ABC. At this lower wage, Joan chooses to stay out of the labor market.[50]

Some empirical evidence on the potential impact of taxes on labor supply is provided by research on the effect of the **Earned Income Tax Credit (EITC)** on the labor force participation of single and married women in families with children. As explained in greater detail in Chapter 11, the EITC, which is part of the federal tax code, targets low-earning families with children and subsidizes their earnings through a refundable tax credit. Consider Dawn, a low-earner single mother. For individuals like Dawn, the amount of the EITC increases with additional hours worked. This is in effect a wage subsidy, raising their wage rate and hence their probability of participating in the labor force. Again looking at Figure 4-9, this increase in the wage rate corresponds to a change in the budget constraint from ABC to ABC' and hence encourages participation. The EITC has been found to strongly promote employment among low-earner single mothers. It has been estimated that nearly 60 percent of the very large increase in the employment of single mother from 1984 to 1996 was due to the expansion of the EITC alone.[51]

However, since the EITC is targeted on low-earning families, it is gradually phased out as total family earnings rise.[52] For instance, consider the situation of a low-income married couple with children. Depending on the level of husband's earnings, the EITC could either encourage or discourage the labor force participation of a wife in such a family. In the case in which the husband has very low earnings, his wife's participation is encouraged by the wage subsidy provided by the EITC for which the family is still eligible. (This is similar to the case of Dawn, the single mother discussed earlier.) However, at higher levels of husband's income, the decrease in the EITC with additional hours worked is like a decrease in the wage of a secondary worker contemplating labor force entry—as in the case of Joan. In such families, employment of wives will be discouraged. Evidence suggests that, on net, the EITC modestly discourages labor force participation by wives in low-earning families, decreasing their participation by about one percentage point.[53] Further consideration of the impact of the federal income tax and the EITC on the labor supply of wives is provided in Chapter 11.

GOVERNMENT SUBSIDIES OF CHILD CARE AND WOMEN'S LABOR FORCE PARTICIPATION

Young children are still a significant deterrent to the entry of their mothers into the labor market. Child care subsidies by the government could lower the cost of child care. What would be the expected effect on women's labor supply? We can use economic theory to see that a reduction in child care costs is expected to increase women's labor force participation.

---

[50] We simplified the representation of a progressive tax in Figure 4-8 in that we show only one tax rate—the one Joan faces given her level of family income—and assume that additional hours worked do not push her into a higher tax bracket. In fact, as long as individuals are below the maximum rate, it is possible that as they work more hours their higher total income will push them into a higher tax bracket. Thus, the after-tax budget constraint may be "kinked," its slope becoming flatter each time the individual enters a higher tax bracket.

[51] Bruce D. Meyer and Dan T. Rosenbaum, "Welfare, the Earned Income Tax Credit, and the Labor Supply of Single Mothers," *Quarterly Journal of Economics* 116, no. 3 (August 2001): 1063–1114. See also Nada Eissa and Jeffrey B. Liebman, "Labor Supply Response to the Earned Income Tax Credit," *Quarterly Journal of Economics* 111, no. 2 (May 1996): 606–37.

[52] For a fuller diagrammatic representation of the impact of the EITC on the individual's budget constraint, including the phase out range, see Ronald G. Ehrenberg and Robert S. Smith, *Modern Labor Economics: Theory and Evidence*, 10th edition (Boston: Pearson/Addison Wesley, 2009), Chapter 6.

[53] Nada Eissa and Hilary Williamson Hoynes, "Taxes and the Labor Market Participation of Married Couples: The Earned Income Tax Credit," *Journal of Public Economics* 88, issues 9–10 (August 2004): 1931–58.

Recall that so far we have assumed that individuals do not value market goods and nonmarket time in and of themselves, but rather because they can be used to produce the commodities people do value. This framework yields valuable insights into the possibilities of substitution in consumption and in production, which help determine the steepness of the indifference curves. However, to examine the impact of the cost of child care explicitly, it is more convenient to simply assume that the indifference curves represent the individual's preferences for market goods (income) versus nonmarket time.

Suppose Figure 4-9 represents the situation of Nancy, a woman with small children. To examine the impact of child care costs, we may view the hourly cost of child care that Nancy must pay if she works as a "tax" on her market earnings. If the budget constraint shows the wage Nancy receives after child care costs are subtracted out, it is clear that a decrease in child care costs is equivalent to an increase in her wage rate. For example, suppose Nancy can earn $14.00 an hour but must pay $6.00 an hour in child care costs. This results in a *net* wage of $8.00 per hour ($14.00 – $6.00 = $8.00), given by segment BC. At this wage, she chooses not to participate in the labor market. However, if her child care costs were to fall to $2.00 per hour, her net wage rises to $12.00 per hour ($14.00 – $2.00 = $12.00), given by segment BC', and she would participate.

In this example, the decrease in child care costs results in Nancy deciding to enter the labor force. In general, we would expect the availability of child care at a lower price to increase the labor force participation rate of women with small children. The empirical evidence supports this expectation. For example, one study that examined the effect of receiving a child care subsidy on the employment of single mothers found a substantial positive effect, ranging from 13 to 33 percentage points.[54] Consistent with this, another study found that provision of free public kindergarten (which is like a large public subsidy of child care costs for 5 year olds) had a substantial positive effect on the labor supply of mothers of 5 year olds, increasing labor supply by 6 to 15 percent for married mothers and 6 to 24 percent for unmarried mothers.[55]

A decline in child care costs is also likely to have long-run effects on women's labor supply and wages. Because women would experience shorter (and possibly fewer) labor force interruptions, they would accumulate longer and more continuous labor market experience. This is expected to enhance their career progression and increase their earnings, which would in turn further reinforce the tendency to spend more time in the labor market.[56] Therefore, in the long run, a reduction in child care costs is likely not only to raise women's labor force participation but also to enhance their occupational attainment and earnings. Thus, child care subsidies could contribute to a reduction in labor market inequality between men and women. Whether such subsidies are desirable on other grounds is considered in greater detail in Chapter 11.

---

[54] David Blau and Erdal Tekin, "The Determinants and Consequences of Child Care Subsidies for Single Mothers in the USA," *Journal of Population Economics* 20, no. 4 (October 2007): 719–41.

[55] Jonah Gelbach, "Public Schooling for Young Children and Maternal Labor Supply," *American Economic Review* 92, no. 1 (March 2002): 307–22. In a similar vein, it has been found that the adoption by the Canadian province of Quebec of a public policy offering generous child care subsidies in combination with free full-time kindergarten had a substantial positive effect on the labor supply of mothers with young children; see, Pierre Lefebvre and Philip Merrigan, "Child-Care Policy and the Labor Supply of Mothers with Young Children: A Natural Experiment from Canada," *Journal of Labor Economics* 26, no. 3 (July 2008): 519–48.

[56] For evidence that current work experience increases the probability of future participation due to its effect on wages, see Zvi Eckstein and Kenneth I. Wolpin, "Dynamic Labour Force Participation of Married Women and Endogenous Work Experience," *Review of Economic Studies* 56, no. 3 (July 1989): 375–90. Evidence that rising labor market returns to experience between the 1970s and the 1990s contributed to the observed increase in the labor force participation of married women is provided in Claudia Olivetti, "Changes in Women's Aggregate Hours of Work: The Role of Returns to Experience," *Review of Economic Dynamics* 9, no. 4 (October 2006): 557–87.

ANALYZING TRENDS IN WOMEN'S LABOR FORCE PARTICIPATION: AN OVERVIEW

In the remaining sections of this chapter we apply the theoretical model of labor supply to analyze some of the major trends in labor force participation described at the beginning of this chapter. In this section, we provide an overview of the factors responsible for the long-term increase in women's labor force participation over the twentieth and into the early twenty-first century. In the following sections, we take a closer look at a number of subperiods of particular interest. We first consider explanations for the dramatic rise in female labor force participation during World War II and the further increase that occurred during the post–World War II baby boom. We then analyze the period of the 1960s to the 1980s when especially sharp increases occurred in the labor force participation rates of married mothers of young children and then the 1990s through the 2000s when growth in the participation rates of married mothers slowed while that of single mothers increased substantially. Next, we consider explanations for the long-term decrease in men's labor force participation rates and conclude with an examination of some of the reasons for differences in labor force participation trends of blacks and whites.

Why did female labor force participation rise over the course of the twentieth and early twenty-first centuries? Drawing upon the analysis presented earlier in this chapter, the obvious answer is a rise in the wage rate (w), a decrease in the value of time spent in the home (w^*), or a combination of both. Considerable evidence shows various developments that would be expected to cause each of these effects, as well as complex interactions that reinforce the original results.[57]

Factors Influencing the Value of Market Time (w)

A variety of factors caused the real (inflation-adjusted) wages of women to increase over time. The result was an outward rotation of the budget constraint, as shown in Figure 4-9. Under these circumstances, more women are expected to find that the wage offered them by the market exceeds their reservation wage and hence choose to enter the labor force. This process does not require that women's wages increase relative to men's wages. During the 1950s and 1960s both men's and women's real wages were rising and the gender gap remained roughly constant. For much of the period since the early 1970s, however, men's real wages were stagnant or declining, while women's real wages increased. During this time the gender pay gap narrowed.

RISING QUALIFICATIONS: EDUCATION AND EXPERIENCE   As women obtained more education, the wage rate they were able to earn by working in the market went up and they were more likely to work outside the home. At the same time, once women were more inclined to work for pay, they sought more schooling, and also more market-oriented schooling in order to be able to obtain better-paying jobs.

The magnitude of this phenomenon can be gauged by the enormous increase in the proportion of the population that graduated from high school or obtained college degrees. Between 1940 and 2007, the proportion of women who completed at least four years of high school increased from 26 to 86 percent; and the proportion of men, from 23 to 85 percent. During this same period, the proportion of women who completed four

---

[57] See Goldin, *Understanding the Gender Gap*, for an interesting econometric analysis of these trends in labor force participation.

or more years of college increased from 3.8 to 28.0 percent, whereas for men the proportion rose from 5.5 to 29.5 percent.[58]

The statistics for higher education reflect the fact that traditionally more young men than young women completed college and pursued graduate study. However, this gender differential began to decline in the late 1960s. Since that time, women have greatly increased their share of college, graduate, and professional degrees, as well as their representation in traditionally male fields of study. Hence, although men's educational attainment has also increased, gender differences in higher education in the general population have narrowed substantially, and, in fact, since the 1980s, young women have been more likely to graduate college than young men. Data on these trends and explanations for them are presented in Chapter 6.

THE DEMAND FOR FEMALE LABOR   It is also the case that, first with industrialization and then with the movement to the postindustrial economy, the demand for workers in traditionally female clerical and service jobs increased and caused their wages to be higher than they otherwise would have been.[59] As discussed in Chapter 2, married women were barred from clerical employment by many large firms in the 1920s and 1930s, and they did not fully benefit from this expansion in demand until these marriage bars were abandoned in the 1950s.[60] In addition to the labor market offering women higher wages, the reward to labor market experience rose during the latter part of the twentieth century, further increasing women's incentives to work in the labor market.[61] It is also quite likely that antidiscrimination legislation has increased the demand for women in traditionally male jobs since its passage in the mid-1960s.

OVERALL PRODUCTIVITY INCREASES   Female as well as male workers benefited from increases in labor productivity due to growth over time in the capital stock and technological change, which exerted upward pressure on wages, all else equal.

Factors Influencing the Value of Nonmarket Time (w^*)

It would be a mistake, however, to ascribe the impetus for the persistent influx of women into the labor market entirely to higher wage rates and to overlook those changes that influenced the relative value of nonmarket time. Even though changes in w^* are not directly measurable, a review of the changes in the various factors influencing w^* suggests that their net effect was to decrease the value of nonmarket time. In any case it seems clear the value of nonmarket time did decline *relative to* market time, thus causing the proportion of women working for pay to increase.

---

[58] The statistics presented on educational attainment here, which are from the *Statistical Abstract of the United States* (2009), differ somewhat from those presented later in Chapter 6. This discrepancy is due to the age range, which is 25 years or over here, but 25–64 in Chapter 6.

[59] Valerie Oppenheimer, *The Female Labor Force in the United States: Demographic and Economic Factors Governing Its Growth and Changing Composition* (Westport, CT: Greenwood Press, 1976; originally published 1970); Goldin, *Understanding the Gender Gap*; Mary C. Brinton, "Gendered Offices: A Comparative-Historical Examination of Clerical Work in Japan and the U.S.," in *The Political Economy of Low Fertility: Japan in Comparative Perspective*, edited by Frances McCall Rosenbluth (Stanford, CA: Stanford University Press, 2007); and Francine D. Blau and Lawrence M. Kahn, "The US Gender Pay Gap in the 1990s."

[60] Goldin, *Understanding the Gender Gap*. Both Oppenheimer and Goldin attribute the increased willingness of employers to hire older married women in the 1950s to a decrease in the supply of young, single female workers, caused by the small size of the cohort born during the 1930s, coupled with the decline in the marriage age that occurred during the 1950s.

[61] Claudia Olivetti, "Changes in Women's Hours of Market Work."

AVAILABILITY OF MARKET SUBSTITUTES AND TECHNOLOGICAL CHANGE   Among the most obvious changes was the increase in the availability of **market substitutes** as goods and services previously produced in the home became increasingly available for purchase in the market. Not only did fruits and vegetables, in earlier days grown in the family garden, come to be available at the grocery, but in time they were canned, frozen, or packaged for immediate use. Similarly, first yarn, earlier spun at home, became commonly available; next it was cloth, and then ready-made clothing. Schools extended the hours, and years of care provided for older children. For young children, nursery schools and, later, day care centers became more prevalent, while hospitals increasingly cared for the sick, and various types of care for the infirm and aged became more common. These are only a few examples of commodities that in earlier days were produced with large inputs of home time but that today require mainly expenditures of money.

At the same time, **technological change** made housework easier and less time-consuming. Important innovations include indoor plumbing and electrification of houses, as well as the rapid diffusion of appliances, ranging from vacuum cleaners, washing machines, and refrigerators to dishwashers and microwave ovens.[62] Technological changes in other areas were beneficial as well. In the first half of the twentieth century, advances in medical technology reduced the time associated with childbearing, and the development and commercialization of infant formula provided an effective substitue for breast milk.[63] Later, in the 1960s, the development and dissemination of more effective contraceptive techniques, most importantly the birth control pill, gave women greater control not only over their fertility but also the timing of births, allowing them to reduce the educational and labor force disruptions caused by childbearing and childrearing.[64]

To be sure, some changes did have the opposite effect, such as the considerably higher cost and greater difficulty of finding domestic help. By and large, however, market goods offered more substitutability for nonmarket time, and technological change made doing housework and bearing and rearing children less time consuming. As a result, women would be expected to be more willing to give up time at home in order to be able to do more market work, a change illustrated in Figure 4-6 by the flatter indifference curves shown in panel a as compared to the steeper indifference curves shown in panel b.

Thus, we see that the greater availability of goods and services for purchase as well as labor-saving technological change resulted in a decrease in the value of women's nonmarket time (w^*) and caused their labor force participation to increase. At the same time, women's rising labor force participation tended to increase the demand for market goods and services that substitute for their time in the home or make housework tasks easier, further encouraging development and production of such products.

DEMOGRAPHIC TRENDS   Another important change that influenced relative preferences for home versus market time was the long-run decline in the birthrate, from 30.1 births per 1,000 population in 1910 to 14.3 per 1,000 by 2006. Because the rearing of young children, generally considered to be women's responsibility, is extremely time intensive, especially in the absence of adequate provision for their care outside the

---

[62] For evidence on the impact of the increased availability of consumer durables on female labor force participation, see Jeremy Greenwood, Ananth Seshadri, and Mehmet Yorukoglu, "Engines of Liberation," *Review of Economic Studies* 72, no. 1 (January 2005): 109–133.

[63] Stefania Albanesi and Claudia Olivetti, "Gender Roles and Technological Progress," NBER Working Paper 13179 (June 2007).

[64] Claudia Goldin and Lawrence F. Katz, "The Power of the Pill: Oral Contraceptives and Women's Career and Marriage Decisions," *Journal of Political Economy* 110, no. 4 (August 2002): 730–70; and Martha J. Bailey, "More Power to the Pill: The Impact of Contraceptive Freedom on Women's Lifecycle Labor Supply," *Quarterly Journal of Economics* 121, no. 1 (February 2006): 289–320.

home, their presence has traditionally been one of the strongest barriers to women's entry into the labor market. As already described, only since the 1960s have mothers of preschoolers worked outside the home to any significant extent, and even now their participation remains lower than that of mothers with school-age children.

Not only is the period during which young children are present in the home more protracted as their numbers rise, but the longer the woman is at home, the less favorable the terms she is likely to encounter in the labor market upon her return, and the more likely she is to remain out permanently. Women are, of course, aware of this cost and to some extent adjust family size to their work plans, as well as vice versa.

Just as women's labor force participation is influenced by, and in turn influences, their fertility, the same is true of marital stability. The divorce rate per 1,000 population per year went from 0.9 in 1910 to 3.6 in 2006. The divorce rate influences women's labor force participation in part due to its impact on the composition of the female population: Divorced women have considerably less nonlabor income than married women and are thus more likely to participate in the labor force. However, married women's behavior is affected by rising divorce rates as well. As married women become aware of the increasing probability of divorce, their participation increases as a means of safeguarding their standard of living in case of a marital breakup.[65] The other side of the coin is that a two-earner couple can more readily afford to get divorced. The woman can count on her own income, rather than being completely dependent on the often uncertain support of an ex-husband; the man need not spend resources to fully support, or to avoid support of, an ex-wife.

CHANGING ROLE OF HUSBAND'S INCOME   Not all changes have operated in the direction of lowering the value of nonmarket time. In particular, earnings of men increased more rapidly than the cost of living for most of the twentieth century. As their husbands' real income goes up, all else equal, married women's labor force participation is reduced due to the income effect (Figure 4-7). For women, however, the positive substitution effect of their own rising real wages tends to more than offset the negative income effect due to the increasing real incomes of their husbands.[66] Also, as we have seen, perhaps due to changing gender roles, the responsiveness of married women's participation to their husbands' income has declined over time. Moreover, since the 1970s, men's real wages have been stagnating overall, and those of the less educated and unskilled have declined in real terms. Given these trends, along with the decline in the responsiveness of wives' participation to husbands' income, this factor has had little effect on women's labor supply trends in recent years.[67]

TASTES   Over time, the development of many desirable market products, such as automobiles, air conditioning, television, personal computers, CD players, and iPods, that could not be produced in the home likely increased people's preferences for market-produced goods and reduced the relative value placed on nonmarket time.[68] Such changes in tastes may be related to broader trends such as the growing urbanization of

[65] William R. Johnson and Jonathan Skinner, "Labor Supply and Marital Separation," *American Economic Review* 76, no. 3 (June 1986): 455–69. The terms under which divorce is available can also affect the labor supply of married women; see, for example, H. Elizabeth Peters, "Marriage and Divorce: Informational Constraints and Private Contracting," *American Economic Review* 76, no. 3 (June 1986): 437–54; and Jeffrey S. Gray, "Divorce-Law Changes, Household Bargaining, and Married Women's Labor Supply," *American Economic Review* 88, no. 3 (June 1998): 628–42.

[66] This phenomenon was first pointed out by Mincer in "Labor Force Participation of Married Women."

[67] For analyses of the impact of these developments on labor supply trends, see, Juhn and Murphy, "Wage Inequality and Family Labor Supply"; and Blau and Kahn "Changes in the Labor Supply Behavior of Married Women."

[68] This factor is particularly emphasized by Brown, "An Institutional Model of Wives' Work Decisions."

the population. The movement from country to city reduced the opportunity for household production and increased the convenience of market purchases as well as access to market work. Even leisure activities changed from those that mainly required time—hiking, swimming in the waterhole, and chatting on the front porch—to others that required substantial expenditures, such as going to the theater, concerts, and sporting events; watching television; listening to CDs and iPods; and surfing the web.

It is also entirely possible that the trend toward rising female participation rates itself was responsible for further changes in tastes. It was probably far more difficult for women to enter the labor force in the past when it was the exception rather than today when it is the rule. In addition, shifting cultural norms, encouraged in part by the example of more women working in the market, led women to place a higher value on the independence and autonomy that their own earnings bring, and, increasingly, many women value career success in much the same way as their male counterparts. Finally, to the extent that people want to keep up with the Joneses in their consumption standards, it takes two paychecks to keep pace today.[69]

ANALYZING TRENDS IN WOMEN'S LABOR FORCE PARTICIPATION: A LOOK AT SUBPERIODS

The World War II Experience: Women's Surge in Labor Force Participation

As we saw in Table 4-1, a sharp rise in the female labor force participation rate occurred during World War II, particularly among married women. The rate declined in the immediate post–World War II period, but it remained above prewar levels and began its long-term rise shortly after that. In this section we explain these changes by considering factors influencing the value of market time (w) and nonmarket time (w^*). Overall, the World War II experience illustrates the importance of both economic and social factors in causing changes in female labor force participation.

As men were mobilized to serve in the armed forces and the need for civilian production workers to produce military goods rose at the same time, the demand for women to fill the available positions increased greatly. This surge in labor market opportunities, including relatively high-paying, traditionally male jobs, drove up the potential market wages of women. At the same time, married women were urged to work outside the home to contribute to the war effort, raising the nonpecuniary benefits of market work for women and lowering their subjective assessment of the value of nonmarket time. In addition, the birthrate, already relatively low in the Depression years of the 1930s, remained low during the war because many young men were away in the armed forces. In addition, many of the women whose husbands joined the military experienced a decrease in their nonlabor income, because working for "Uncle Sam" often did not pay as much as civilian employment. (On the other hand, those whose husbands had been unemployed might have experienced an increase in income.)

A further factor that worked to lower the value of home time for married women was that the government and some employers opened day care centers for children of employed mothers.[70] Even though not enough places were available to accommodate

---

[69] For evidence suggesting that women's labor force participation decisions are influenced by those of other women, see David Neumark and Andrew Postlewaite, "Relative Income Concerns and the Rise in Married Women's Employment," *Journal of Public Economics* 70, no. 1 (October 1998): 157–83.

[70] Given public concern, both about stimulating maternal employment in war industries and about possible neglect of children, during the 1941–1943 period the U.S. federal government provided matching funds to induce states to provide day care centers. An estimated 1.6 million children attended these programs. The best-known centers established by large private employers were those by Curtiss-Wright in Buffalo and by Kaiser in Portland. See Bernard Greenblatt, *The Changing Role of Family and State in Child Development* (San Francisco: Jossey Bass, 1977), pp. 58–60.

all the children whose mothers were employed, this action increased both the supply and the acceptability of alternative care of children, at least for the duration of the war. Thus, the combination of an increase in the value of market time and a reduction in the value of nonmarket time induced a large increase in the proportion of women working outside the home.

In the immediate postwar period, each of these factors was reversed, helping to bring about the observed decline in women's participation rates. As men returned from the war, many were able to reclaim their former jobs from the women who held them during the war. For example, many union contracts reserved their former jobs for men who had left them for military service. Even in the absence of union agreements, some employers voluntarily restored veterans' jobs because they felt it was the appropriate recompense for the veteran's wartime contribution. Moreover, whether or not a returning veteran claimed a specific job held by a woman during the war, the influx of returning males into the labor market lowered the demand for women workers. Also, the increase in earnings as husbands resumed civilian employment boosted wives' nonlabor income.

In addition, social values changed and the employment of married women outside the home was once again frowned upon, now that the wartime emergency was over. Indeed, after enduring the major dislocations of the Great Depression of the 1930s followed by a world war of unprecedented proportions, there may have been a keen desire to return to "normalcy," including traditional gender roles. This swing in attitudes also likely played a part in producing the upsurge in birthrates during the postwar period, discussed in the next section. Finally, when the wartime labor shortage was over, day care centers were perceived to be no longer needed and were closed. These changes combined to lower the benefits of market work relative to the value of home time and to reduce women's labor force participation rate in the immediate post–World War II period.

The operation of the long-term factors discussed in the preceding section meant that the postwar female labor force participation rate, while lower than the wartime peak, exceeded prewar levels. The long-term rise in participation rates that followed the war was primarily due to fundamental economic and social factors. Yet the wartime experience may have hastened this process by helping to break down the attitudinal barriers to married women's employment outside the home and giving many women a taste of the benefits of earning their own income. Historian William H. Chafe argues that the notion that woman's appropriate sphere was in the home was so deeply embedded that it took a cataclysmic event like World War II to break down this normative barrier.[71] Moreover, although data indicate that more than half of the the female wartime entrants left the labor force again by the end of the decade,[72] this means that a substantial number also remained. A recent study suggests that there was indeed a significant longer-term effect of the war: in states with greater mobilization of men during the war, women worked more both immediately after the war and in 1950.[73] And, in line with Chafe's

---

[71] William H. Chafe, *The American Woman: Her Changing Social, Economic, and Political Role, 1920–1970* (Oxford: Oxford University Press, 1972). Similarly, Dorothy Sue Cobble emphasizes the dramatic impact the war years had on the attitudes of women workers, particularly the emergence of a new consensus on equal pay and a breakdown of the formerly near-universal consensus in favor of protective legislation for women; see Dorothy Sue Cobble, "Recapturing Working-Class Feminism: Union Women in the Postwar Era," in *Not June Cleaver: Women and Gender in Postwar America, 1945–1960,* edited by Joanne Meyerowitz, (Philadelphia: Temple University Press, 1994), pp. 57–83.

[72] Claudia Goldin, "The Role of World War II in the Rise of Women's Work," *American Economic Review* 81, no. 4 (September 1991).

[73] Daron Acemoglu, David H. Autor, and David Lyle, "Women, War, and Wages: The Effect of Female Labor Supply on the Wage Structure at Midcentury," *Journal of Political Economy* 112, no. 3 (June 2004): 497–551.

argument, there may have also been *longer-term* effects of the war on social views of women's roles or on the subsequent behavior of young women who were employed during the war and later returned to the labor force after dropping out for a time.

The Post–World War II Baby Boom: Increased Participation of Married Mothers with Older Children

As noted previously, the long-run downward trend in birthrates was interrupted by the post–World War II baby boom. From 1946 to the mid-1950s, birthrates rose steadily and remained at relatively high levels until the early 1960s. Although some of this rise in birthrates was simply a result of the postponement of childbearing that occurred during the Depression and the war years, much of it did indeed reflect an increase in family size in comparison to earlier periods. At the height of the baby boom in the mid-1950s, women averaged three births, considerably more than the replacement-level fertility rates of their Depression-era mothers. This means that the decline in the birthrate, which did contribute to the rise in female labor force participation over the long run, does not help to explain the increase in participation that occurred during the baby boom era.

How did participation rates increase in the face of the negative effect of high birthrates? The first point to be made is that the rising female participation rates during this period were *not* due to the labor force entry of young women with small children, the group who would have been most affected by higher birthrates, but rather reflect the entry of older women (over age 35) with school-age or grown children. While it was still a sharp departure from the past for mothers to work outside the home, it was easier for women with older children to take on market work. Moreover, these older women were desirable workers from the employer's perspective, because they were from a generation that received considerably more education than their elders had: The rate of high school completion increased from 29 percent in 1930 to 49 percent in 1940.[74]

Second, during this period, economic factors were particularly favorable for rising female participation rates. Real wages were steadily increasing and economic conditions were relatively good.[75] Thus, both the continued rise in participation rates in this period and its concentration among older women can be explained in significant part by economic and demographic factors.

The 1960s to the 1980s: Increased Participation of Married Mothers with Younger Children

Female labor force participation rates rose sharply from the 1960s to the 1980s, and, as we saw in Figure 4-8, the increase was especially large for married mothers; this included those with small children. In this section, we again use the tools of economic analysis to understand the factors responsible for this increase.

We begin by considering demographic factors that are expected to affect the value of home time (w^*). The post–World War II baby boom was followed by a baby bust, when birthrates fell. By the late 1970s, total fertility rates had fallen below the replacement level and relatively low rates continued after that time. This decrease in fertility would be expected to lower w^* and thus increase the labor force participation of women. In addition, increasing numbers of women began to postpone marriage and

---

[74] Goldin, *Understanding the Gender Gap.*
[75] Goldin, *Understanding the Gender Gap,* finds that demand factors, in conjunction with the particularly large wage elasticity of supply that prevailed at that time for married women, largely account for the increase in participation that occurred during this period.

childbirth into their late twenties, thirties, or even early forties. This pattern of child-bearing appears to be associated with stronger attachment to the labor market and a reduction in time spent out of the labor force for childrearing. Another demographic trend that encouraged rising participation rates was a sharp increase in the divorce rate that occurred during this time. As discussed earlier, this increased female participation rates both because divorced women are more likely to be in the labor force than married women, and also because rising divorce rates increase the participation rates of married women, as they seek to protect their family income in the face of a rising probability of marital breakup. Although the divorce rate leveled off and even began to fall slightly in the 1980s, it remains at a high level.

These demographic shifts, particularly the decline in fertility, would most affect the labor force participation of younger women, and it was exactly this group, women under age 45, who posted the largest gains in participation rates over this period.[76] Nonetheless, even though these demographic factors undoubtedly are important,[77] a major factor contributing to rising female labor force participation rates during this period was the increase in the participation rates of married mothers, including those with small children.

Economic conditions are another possible factor contributing to the rising labor force attachment of married mothers during this period, but here the picture is mixed. During much of the 1960s, real wages were rising and unemployment was relatively low, favorable conditions for increases in female labor force participation rates. However, during the 1970s and the early 1980s, the situation was more complex. A stagnating economy resulted in frequent bouts of high unemployment and little increase in real wages.[78] Moreover, while the economy expanded during the mid- to late-1980s, overall real wages continued to stagnate. This raises the question of why married women's participation rates continued to rise despite these unfavorable economic conditions.

One obvious explanation is that, although real wages were not rising overall, they were increasing for women, particularly well-educated women. This increase may help to explain not only rising participation rates for women as a group but also why participation rates increased more slowly for less-educated women whose real wages lagged. It further points to rising educational attainment of women as an additional factor increasing the wages they could earn in the labor market and hence their labor force participation. In addition, as previously noted, the return to labor market experience increased, encouraging women to remain in the labor force more continuously.[79] It is also possible that stagnating male incomes increased the impetus of married women to enter the labor force. However, research suggests that, just as rising real incomes of husbands did not forestall the rise in participation of their wives during earlier, more pros-perous, times, the poor income performance of husbands does not explain much of the

---

[76] One reason for the decline in marriage rates for the baby boom cohort was the so-called marriage squeeze. During the early part of the baby boom, from 1946 to 1955, the birthrate for each successive year was higher than the previous year's. This meant that women born during this period faced a worse "marriage market," that is, a shortage of men 2 years older whom they would traditionally marry. Some evidence suggesting that this development contributed to the rise in female participation; see Shoshana Grossbard-Schechtman and Clive W. Granger, "Women's Jobs and Marriage, Baby-Boom versus Baby-Bust," *Population* 53 (September 1998): 731–52 (in French).

[77] Jacobsen, Pearce, and Rosenbloom, "The Effects of Childbearing," estimate that declining fertility explains between 6 and 13 percent of the increase in married women's labor supply between 1970 and 1980.

[78] The unstable economic conditions of the 1970s and early 1980s perhaps contributed to the growth in participation by giving married women an incentive to enter the labor market as soon as possible rather than wait-ing to supply labor in a more uncertain future; see Francine D. Blau and Adam J. Grossberg, "Wage and Employment Uncertainty and the Labor Force Participation Decisions of Married Women," *Economic Inquiry* 29, no. 4 (October 1991): 678–95.

[79] Olivetti, "Changes in Women's Aggregate Hours of Work."

increase in wives' participation during the 1970s and 1980s. In both cases, the dominant factor was women's own labor market prospects.[80]

Rising real wages for a large proportion of women in conjunction with the demographic factors discussed previously and the continued increase in women's educational attainment all contributed to the rise in participation rates over this period. However, a number of studies suggest that these factors cannot fully explain the increase in married women's participation during this time.[81] This increase also reflects, in part, changes in women's responses to these factors, perhaps due to changing social attitudes, as women's participation became less sensitive to the presence of small children and to their husband's income and more responsive to their own market opportunities (wages).

One may speculate that changes in the work expectations of younger women help to explain some portion of the participation increase not due to changes in measurable factors. It may be recalled that prior to World War II, most women left the labor force permanently upon marriage and childbearing. It is quite likely that the older married women who entered or reentered the labor force during World War II and the early postwar period had not anticipated working during this stage of the life cycle but were drawn into the labor market by prevailing economic and social conditions.

As the reentry pattern became firmly established, however, young women could increasingly anticipate spending a substantial portion of their mature years in the labor force. They likely also learned, by observing the experiences of older women, that time spent out of the labor force was costly in terms of career advancement and earnings. To maximize their labor market earnings and to secure the more attractive jobs that were increasingly becoming available to women, they would have to increase their investment in market-oriented human capital and keep work force interruptions to a minimum. The development and dissemination of the birth control pill mentioned earlier was undoubtedly important in facilitating this.[82] As young women entered the labor force with greater training and higher work expectations, they were more likely to remain employed after the birth of a child or to return shortly thereafter. Further, once it was socially acceptable for mothers of older children to work outside the home, it was not long before it was socially permissible for women with increasingly younger children to do so as well.

The 1990s and 2000s: Diverging Participation Trends for Married and Single Mothers

Another important trend discussed earlier and illustrated in Figure 4-8 is that trends in labor force participation rates of married and single mothers diverged considerably during the 1990s and 2000s. During the 1990s, growth in the participation rate of married mothers slowed, and participation rates of this group began to level off in the mid-1990s and decline somewhat in the early and mid-2000s. In stark contrast, participation rates of single mothers expanded rapidly during the 1990s, especially during the latter

---

[80] In fact, the married women with the largest increase in market hours were those with high-wage husbands. See, Juhn and Murphy, "Wage Inequality and Family Labor Supply"; and Ellen R. McGrattan and Richard Rogerson, "Changes in the Distribution of Family Hours Worked Since 1950," Working Paper, Federal Reserve Bank of Minneapolis and Arizona State University (April 2008).

[81] See David Shapiro and Lois Shaw, "Growth in the Labor Force Attachment of Married Women: Accounting for Changes in the 1970s," *Southern Economic Journal* 50, no. 2 (October 1983): 461–73; Juhn and Murphy, "Wage Inequality and Family Labor Supply"; Blau and Kahn, "Changes in the Labor Supply Behavior of Married Women; and Leibowitz and Klerman, "Explaining Changes."

[82] Claudia Goldin and Lawrence F. Katz, "The Power of the Pill"; and Bailey, "More Power to the Pill."

part of the decade, although their participation rates also began to level off and decline a bit after the early 2000s. How do we explain these contrasting trends?

We know much more about the reasons behind the trends for single mothers. Analyses suggest that the increasing participation of this group reflects the impact of some important changes in government policy combined with a buoyant economy.[83] By the time of its peak in March 2001, the record U.S. economic expansion that began in the 1990s had lasted 10 years. Single-female family heads are disproportionately low skilled, and an expanding economy disproportionately benefits less-skilled individuals. Two government policies reinforced the positive effects of the booming economy on the employment of this group. As explained in greater detail in Chapter 11, changes in welfare policies, including a new work requirement for welfare recipients, led to an increase in single mothers' labor force participation, and also contributed to a substantial decline in the welfare rolls. In addition, the EITC was expanded several times in the 1990s. These expansions raised the subsidy received by low-income single mothers, and thus, as explained earlier, increased their incentive to work outside the home.

The reasons for the slowing growth in the participation rates of married mothers with children during the 1990s and 2000s are not as well understood. Evidence indicates that the somewhat improved labor market opportunities for husbands in the 1990s relative to the 1980s play only a small role in explaining this slowing growth.[84] This finding is consistent with evidence discussed earlier that the dominant economic factor explaining the increase in married women's labor force participation in prior decades was their own labor market opportunities, not changes in their husbands' incomes. Recent emphasis in the popular press claiming that married mothers, especially highly educated ones, are increasingly "opting out" of the labor force also appears to be misplaced. (See the following inset on the "opt-out" revolution.) In fact, as we have seen, the negative effect of children on married women's participation has, if anything, decreased. Another factor to be considered is prevailing labor market conditions. Weakness in the labor market likely explains the slowdown and even declines in labor force participation rates for both single and married mothers following the 2001 recession.[85] Further declines may occur in the wake of the recession that began in December 2007. However, prior to 2001, the economy was in its longest peace time expansion (including a period when the national unemployment rate was less than 4 percent), so weakness in the labor market cannot explain the slowing growth and leveling off of married mothers' participation rates that started in the 1990s.

Although the slowing growth in married women's labor force participation prior to 2001 remains something of a puzzle, it is perhaps not surprising that growth in the participation rates of married mothers would eventually taper off as those women who could most readily participate in the labor force, and had the greatest incentives to do so, were already in the labor force. However, in this respect, it is useful to note that a number of European countries have higher participation rates of women than does the United States.[86]

---

[83] This section draws heavily on Blank, "Fighting Poverty"; and Rebecca Blank, "Evaluating Welfare Reform in the United States," *Journal of Economic Literature* 60, no. 4 (December 2002): 1105–66. See also Meyer and Rosenbaum, "Making Single Mothers Work"; and Eissa and Liebman, "Labor Supply Response to the Earned Income Tax Credit."

[84] Blau and Kahn, "Changes in the Labor Supply Behavior of Married Women." They found that the increase in husbands' real wages in the 1990s compared to the slight decrease that occurred in the 1980s explained only 16 to 21 percent of the slowdown in labor supply growth between the 1980s and the 1990s.

[85] Boushey. "'Opting Out'?'

[86] Ariane Hegewisch and Janet C. Gornick, *Statutory Routes to Workplace Flexibility in Cross-National Perspective* (Washington, DC: Institute for Women's Policy Research, 2008).

IS THERE AN "OPT-OUT REVOLUTION"?

Are record numbers of college-educated mothers with very young children choosing to leave their professional lives behind and opting out of the paid labor force? The possibility of such an "opt out revolution" was initially suggested in a 2003 *New York Times Magazine* article and there has been considerable discussion and debate since then.* In this inset we examine the extent of recent trends and attempt to put them in context.

This issue first received media attention in 2003 after the Census Bureau reported a notable decline in the labor force participation rate of all mothers with infants from 58.7 percent in 1998 to 54.6 percent in 2002. This decline was surprising in light of the fact that the rate had increased steadily from 31 percent in 1976 through 1998. Observers also noted a marked decline in labor force participation among college-educated mothers with infants.

More data are now available and so it is possible to put these trends in better perspective. First, despite the decrease in their labor force participation rate from 1998 to 2002, the labor force participation rate of mothers with infants has stood at greater than 50 percent since 1987, and was 56 percent as of 2006 (a slight increase over the 2002 figure). Further while trends in participation rates of college-educated mothers with infants have received substantial scrutiny by the media, data show that the decline in participation rates from 1998 to 2002 was not unique to college-educated mothers with infants: Participation rates also declined for new mothers with less than or just a high school education.

Claudia Goldin has further investigated the extent to which recent college graduates are "opting out" of the labor market using a unique data set that follows the career and family patterns of female graduates of selective colleges from around 1980 (when they graduated) until 15 years later. These data provide information about the length of time they spent out of the labor force, something that cannot be discerned from Census Bureau data. She found considerable evidence of strong labor force attachment for this group. For instance, on average, women with children spent just 2 of the 15 years elapsed out of the labor market, and half of women with children had not been out of the labor market (or an educational institution) for more than six months.** Census Bureau data confirm the strong labor force commitment of highly educated women. In 2006, 56 percent of mothers of infants who completed just high school were in the labor force, as compared to 61 percent of mothers who completed a bachelor's degree, and 74 percent who completed education beyond a bachelor's degree.

In short, the evidence presented here suggests that we are not seeing a surge in opting out of the labor force among college-educated women. The small declines that occurred for this group in the early 2000s seem to be part of a broader pattern affecting less-educated mothers as well, and even women without children. They are most likely due to weakness in the labor market.*** Whatever the reasons for labor force withdrawals, an important disadvantage of leaving the labor force for women (as well as for men who withdraw to raise children full time), particularly for those who are more highly educated, is the loss of work experience and firm-specific human capital. In other words, there may be perceived short-term benefits to staying home but the opportunity cost can be quite significant from a longer-term perspective. For this reason, it makes sense to promote policies that support women's ability to remain attached to the labor force and raise a family, if they so choose.

*See Lisa Belkin, "The Opt-Out Revolution," *New York Times Magazine*, October 26, 2003. For an interesting discussion of the "disconnect" between media portrayals of women opting out and research findings, see Arielle Kuperberg and Pamela Stone, "The Media Depiction of Women Who Opt Out," *Gender & Society* 22, no. 4 (August 2008): 497–519. Data on participation rates for mothers with infants reported in this inset are from U.S. Census Bureau, Fertility of American Women, "Women 15–44 Years Old Who Have Had a Child in the Last Year and Their Percentage in the Labor

Force by Selected Characteristics," supplemental Table 6 (October 2008), available at www .census.gov. See also, Sharon R. Cohany and Emy Sok, "Trends in Labor Force Participation of Married Mothers with Infants," *Monthly Labor Review* 130, no. 2 (February 2007): 9–16. For discussions of explanations behind the trends and implications for women, see Katharine Bradbury and Jane Katz, "Women's Rise: A Work in Progress," *Regional Review* 14 no. 3 (Q1 2005): 58–67; Anne Marie Chaker and Hilary Stout, "Stay-At-Home Moms Struggle to Revive Their Careers," *Wall Street Journal,* May 19, 2004; Sylvia Ann Hewlett and Carolyn Buck Luce, "Off-Ramps and On-Ramps: Keeping Talented Women on the Road to Success," *Harvard Business Review* 83, no. 3 (March 2005); and Barbara Kantrowitz and Pat Wingert, "The Parent Trap," *Newsweek,* January 29, 2004.
**Claudia, Goldin, "The Quiet Revolution that Transformed Women's Employment, Education, and Family," *American Economic Review* 96, no. 2 (May 2006): 1–20.
***Heather Boushey, "Opting Out?: The Effect of Children on Women's Employment in the United States," *Feminist Economics* 14, no. 1 (January 2008): 1–36.

ANALYZING TRENDS IN MEN'S LABOR FORCE PARTICIPATION

The changes in men's labor force participation patterns, while less dramatic than women's, are nonetheless quite significant. The decline in the participation rates of younger men (Figure 4-4) is mainly due to their tendency to remain in school longer. This trend in turn reflects the increasing skills demanded by our advanced economy. Young people's behavior is especially affected because expenditures on education are more profitable to the individual when they are made relatively early in the life cycle, resulting in a longer period over which to reap the returns to this investment in the form of higher earnings. Moreover, with rising real incomes, families are able to keep their children in school longer not only because they can better afford to pay the bills, but also because they can better afford to forgo the contribution their children might otherwise make to family income.

The long-term decrease in participation rates of older males (Figure 4-4) is often viewed as evidence of the dominance of the income effect over the substitution effect. As real wages rose over the course of the last century, men's demand for nonmarket time increased. This is suggested by the early decline (and subsequent stability) of the average full-time workweek discussed earlier. The increased propensity of men to retire at earlier ages is also seen as part of this pattern. In addition, the provision of Social Security and the growing coverage of private pension schemes, while in part a transfer of income from earlier to later years, also created an income effect that encouraged older males to retire.[87]

Interestingly, as also shown in Figure 4-4, the long-term decline in older men's labor force participation rates ceased in the mid-1980s and, since the late 1990s rates have modestly increased.[88] One reason for this development relates to the growth in the labor force participation of older women. While in general husbands and wives appear to substitute their time in household activities, there is evidence of complementarity of time use among older couples, with couples tending to make joint retirement decisions. Since husbands are on average 3 years older than their wives, they have responded to the higher likelihood of their wives being employed by remaining in the labor force longer themselves.[89] There have also been significant changes in the Social Security program that have increased the benefits that older individuals can receive while working and

---

[87] See Patricia M. Anderson, Alan L. Gustman, and Thomas L. Steinmeier, "Trends in Male Labor Force Participation and Retirement: Some Evidence on the Role of Pensions and Social Security in the 1970s and 1980s," *Journal of Labor Economics* 17, no. 4, pt. 1 (October 1999): 757–83.

[88] For an excellent analysis of recent and longer-term trends in the labor force participation of older men, see Alicia H, Munnell and Steven A. Sass, "The Labor Supply of Older American Men," in *Labor Supply in the New Century,* edited by Katharine Bradbury, Christopher L. Foote, and Robert K. Triest (Boston, MA: Federal Reserve Bank of Boston, 2008), pp. 83–138. Our discussion draws heavily on this article.

[89] Tammy Schirle, "Why Have the Labor Force Participation Rates of Older Men Increased since the Mid-1990s?" *Journal of Labor Economics* 26, no. (October 2008): 549–94. See also, Munnell and Sass, "The Labor Supply of Older American Men."

thus made employment more attractive.[90] In addition, changes in private pension schemes have made the exact amount of benefit payments individuals receive after retirement more uncertain.[91] Finally, with the growth of service employment and shifts in the nature of jobs in the manufacturing sector, jobs have become less physically demanding, making them more attractive to older individuals.

The same factors that have influenced the labor force participation of younger and older men have also affected the participation of women in these age groups. As shown in Figure 4-3, the long-term increase in the participation rates for women over 65 remains quite modest. In addition, the participation of younger women has declined somewhat since 1980 as greater numbers of them remain in school for longer periods.

Figure 4-4 also shows a decline in the participation rate of prime-age males (25 to 54), which is smaller than that for younger and older men, but is notable because this is the age group most likely to be actively engaged in the labor force. While participation rates of older and younger males declined by 20 percentage points or more, rates for prime age males fell by 4 to 8 percentage points. This development appears closely connected to the declining relative demand for less-skilled workers, which depressed their relative wages.[92] This trend is suggested by Figure 4-10b, which shows that participation rates decreased most markedly for less-educated males. Another contributing factor is the expansion of government programs that provide disability income to men below conventional retirement age.[93] In the absence of such programs, more men with disabilities would probably be forced to seek employment. Less-skilled men are disproportionately affected by the provision of disability income because the opportunity cost of leaving the labor force is lower for low-wage workers. Finally, part of the explanation for prime-age men's declining participation rate may be women's increased employment outside of the home. As the two-earner family becomes the norm, the additional income may induce some (albeit still relatively few) males to leave the labor force for periods of time, say, to care for small children or to retool for a midlife career change.[94]

BLACK AND WHITE PARTICIPATION DIFFERENTIALS: SERIOUS EMPLOYMENT PROBLEMS FOR BLACK MEN

As we saw in Table 4-2, since the 1950s, black male participation rates declined faster than those of white males, while black female participation rates increased at a slower pace than those of white females (though the period from 1995 to 2000 is a recent exception). The result is that now black male participation rates are considerably below those of white males, while black female participation rates, which used to greatly exceed those of white women, are now only a few percentage points higher.

---

[90] Chief among these is the liberalization of the social security "earnings test" (the earnings limit for receiving benefits) and its complete elimination for beneficiaries older than the full retirement age. For more explanation and a summary of additional changes in the program, see, Munnell and Sass, "The Labor Supply of Older American Men."

[91] Specifically, there has been a decline in the share of workers covered by defined benefit programs and a corresponding increase in the share covered by defined contribution programs. For a fuller explanation and assessment, see, Munnell and Sass, "The Labor Supply of Older American Men"; and BLS, Spotlight on Statistics, "Older Workers: Are There More Older people in the Workplace?" (July 2008), available at http://www.bls.gov/spotlight/2008/older_workers/.

[92] See Juhn, "Decline of Male Labor Market Participation." A smaller role for wage changes in explaining the trends is found by Paul Devereux, "Changes in Male Labor Supply and Wages," *Industrial and Labor Relations Review* 56, no. 3 (April 2003): 409–28.

[93] Donald Parsons, "The Decline in Male Labor Force Participation," *Journal of Political Economy* 88, no. 1 (February 1980): 117–34; and David H. Autor and Mark G. Duggan, "The Rise in the Disability Rolls and the Decline in Unemployment," *Quarterly Journal of Economics* 118, no.1 (February 2003): 157–205. These programs expanded first in the 1960s and 1970s and then again since the mid-1980s.

[94] Nonetheless, even recent analyses find little evidence of responsiveness of husbands' labor supply decisions to their wives' wages in the prime working ages; see, for example, Blau and Kahn, "Changes in the Labor Supply Behavior of Married Women."

Focusing first on the more serious employment problems of black men, one explanation for the differential trend in black and white participation rates is that since blacks obtain less education, on average, and are more likely to drop out of high school than whites, they are disproportionately negatively affected by the overall trends toward lower participation among less-educated individuals. However, even when comparing participation rates of less-skilled white and black men, these trends are less favorable for blacks. This observation suggests that while declining labor market opportunities for the less educated in general may explain a portion of the race trends in male participation, other factors also play a role.[95] One such factor may be the expansion of government disability programs. Because black men are less educated, on average, they would be particularly affected by the expansion of these programs—and, to the extent that, due to discrimination, their wages are lower than those of white men with similar education, the attractiveness of these programs to them is further increased. Higher rates of unemployment also likely reduce African-American's labor force participation. Even in the midst of a boom year like 1999, for example, when the white unemployment rate stood at 3.7 percent, the black rate was more than twice as high, at 8.0 percent.

Two other factors have also been identified in recent research as contributing to the decrease in the employment of less-educated, young black men (ages 16 to 34) relative to their white counterparts.[96] One is the dramatic increase in incarceration rates, which have been rising more rapidly for blacks than whites. Individuals who are incarcerated are not included in statistics on labor force participation and employment, implying that such statistics may understate the employment problems faced by blacks. However, ex-offenders are included in the statistics and are likely to have poorer employment prospects than nonoffenders due both to the negative effect of incarceration itself (e.g., loss of work experience) as well as employer reluctance to hire ex-offenders. Another factor that may contribute to relatively lower employment rates of less-educated young African-American men is the stronger enforcement of child support laws in recent years. Although this policy may be desirable on other grounds, mandated child support payments are equivalent to a "tax" on the income of noncustodial fathers. This "tax" is expected to reduce work incentives, especially for those with low incomes. Here again, young African-American males are likely to be disproportionately affected, because they are a low income group and female headship is much more pronounced in the black than in the white community.

The relative participation picture for black women is considerably more favorable than that for black men, with participation rates of black women slightly higher than those of white women. Nonetheless, participation growth has been considerably faster for white women than black women since the mid-1950s. Indeed, as we noted earlier in this chapter, white women had completely closed the race gap in participation by the mid-1980s. Since 1995, however, the labor force participation rates of African-American women have again drawn ahead of those of white women, largely as a result of an increase in participation among less-educated black women.[97] This increase was likely tied to the growth in participation rates of single mothers during this period that we discussed previously, because within each education category, black women are more likely to be single-family

[95]Juhn, "Decline of Male Labor Market Participation"; and Chinhui Juhn, "Black-White Employment Differential in a Tight Labor Market," in *Prosperity for All? The Economic Boom and African Americans,* edited by Robert Cherry and William M. Rodgers III (New York: Russell Sage Foundation, 2000), pp. 88–109; see also, Amitabh Chandra, "Labor-Market Dropouts and the Racial Wage Gap: 1940–1990," *American Economic Review* 90, no. 2 (May 2000): 333–38.

[96]Harry J. Holzer, Paul Offner, and Elaine Sorensen, "Declining Employment Among Young Black Less-Educated Men: The Role of Incarceration and Child Support," *Journal of Policy Analysis and Management* 24, no. 2 (Spring 2005): 329–50; see also, Steven Rafael, "The Socioeconomic Status of Black Males: The Increasing Importance of Incarceration," in Alan J. Auerbach, David Card, and John M. Quigley, eds., *Poverty, the Distribution of Income, and Public Policy* (Russell Sage Foundation: New York, 2006), pp. 319–58.

[97]See Francine D. Blau, Marianne A. Ferber, and Anne E. Winkler, *The Economics of Women, Men, and Work,* 4th edition (Upper Saddle River, NJ: Prentice Hall, 2002), Table 4-5, p. 127.

heads than are white women.[98] In addition, given their extremely high unemployment rates, blacks as a group are likely to have benefited disproportionately from the decline in unemployment that occurred over the late 1990s. Notably, however, as the economy cooled and the 2001 recession set in, the increase in black female labor force participation halted and a small reduction occurred in black women's participation rates.

Conclusion

We began by reviewing the trends in male and female participation rates. We found that while female labor force participation rates have increased over the course of the past century—from 20 percent in 1900 to 28 percent in 1940 and 59 percent in 2007—male participation rates declined from 87 percent in 1950 to 73 percent in 2007. We then turned to the economic theory of labor supply to gain insight into the determinants of labor force participation in order to better understand these trends, as well as differences in participation across various groups.

After decades of substantial increase, growth in female labor force participation slowed in the early 1990s and overall female participation rates have remained roughly constant, even declining very slightly since then. There have also been some recent small decreases in participation rates not only of married mothers, but of single mothers as well. What do these developments portend for the future? Taking into account the recent plateauing of the increase in female labor force participation, as well as shifts in the age composition of the population and other factors, the Bureau of Labor Statistics (BLS) projects that the participation rate of adult women will remain roughly constant at 59 percent in 2016. The male participation rate is expected to fall slightly to 72 percent.[99]

This projection of constancy in female participation rates seems reasonable to us given recent trends. Moreover, now that 75 percent of women in the prime working ages (25–54) are in the labor force, it is perhaps to be expected that the female labor force will grow more slowly or cease growing entirely. Nonetheless, we do not believe it to be entirely out of the question that the rise in female participation rates will resume at some point, albeit at a modest pace. As noted previously, participation rates in a number of European countries surpass those in the United States. And, as women continue to accumulate more market-oriented education and increasingly enter nontraditional fields with higher earnings, their incentives to enter and remain in the labor force should continue to grow.

Of course, some women have always chosen to leave market work for the traditional homemaking role, at least for a period of time, and we expect this to continue. Most recently, as we have seen, there has even been a small decline in the participation rates of mothers, both married and single, predominantly related to economic conditions. If this trend continues, or even intensifies, further declines in the female participation rate cannot be ruled. Moreover, younger and older women are subject to the same forces as their male counterparts toward remaining in school longer and retiring earlier, also working to reduce the aggregate female participation rate slightly. But, given the strong, fundamental shifts in the labor market and in the family that have produced the substantial rise in female participation rates since the turn of the twentieth century, we consider it extremely unlikely that women's overall participation rate will decline *substantially* in the foreseeable future.

The BLS projection of a further very small decline in the overall male labor force participation rate of men also seems reasonable given past trends. While the picture for men is not expected to change much in the aggregate, there are two areas

---

[98] Blau, "Trends in the Well-Being of American Women."

[99] Mitra Toossi, "Labor Force Projections to 2016: More Workers in their Golden Years," *Monthly Labor Review* 130, no. 11 (November 2007): 33–55.

of potential concern. First, there is concern about the decline in participation of less-educated prime age men, to the extent that this decline is caused by a decrease in labor market opportunities for them. Second, as we have seen, employment difficulties remain a particularly serious concern for African-American men.

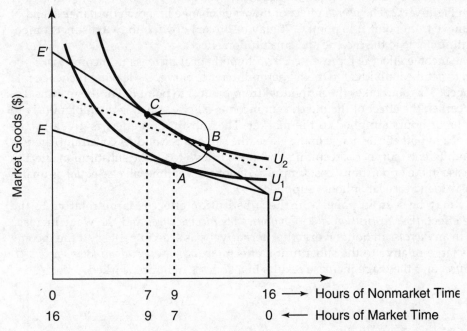

(a) THE SUBSTITUTION EFFECT DOMINATES THE INCOME EFFECT

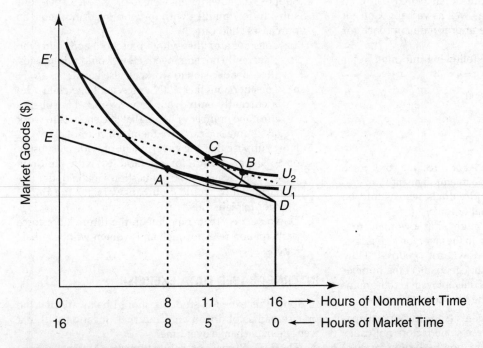

(b) THE INCOME EFFECT DOMINATES THE SUBSTITUTION EFFECT

FIGURE 4-12 Impact of the Market Wage on Labour Hours: A Closer Look

APPENDIX 4A

The Income and Substitution Effects: A Closer Look

As discussed in Chapter 4, for labor force participants, an increase in the wage rate causes an uncertain effect on hours supplied, all else equal. This is illustrated in greater detail in Figure 4-12. The *overall* effect of the wage change is shown (in panels a and b) by the move from point A to point C. It may be broken down into two distinct components, attributable to the income and substitution effects.

The income effect is represented by a hypothetical increase in income just large enough to get the individual to the higher indifference curve, U_2, leaving the wage rate unchanged. This shift takes the individual from point A to point B. For the reasons discussed earlier, the effect of the increase in income, all else equal, is unambiguously to reduce labor hours supplied to the market. The substitution effect is given by the impact of a hypothetical change in the wage (the slope of the budget constraint) along a given indifference curve, U_2, resulting in a move from B to C. The substitution effect of an increase in the opportunity cost (or price) of nonmarket time, all else equal, is unambiguously to increase labor hours supplied.

As may be seen in panel a, if the substitution effect is large relative to the income effect, *the substitution effect dominates the income effect* and the wage increase results in an *increase* in hours worked. Alternatively, as seen in panel b, if the income effect is large relative to the substitution effect, *the income effect dominates the substitution effect* and the wage increase results in a *decrease* in hours worked.

Questions for Review and Discussion

*Indicates that the question can be answered using an indifference curve framework as well as verbally. Consult with your instructor about the appropriate approach for your class.

1. Suppose that you have the following information for Country X:

Population:	100,000
Employed:	60,000
Unemployed:	3,000
Not in labor force:	37,000

   a. Calculate the size of the labor force, the labor force participation rate, and the unemployment rate.
   b. Provide examples of individuals who would be classified as "not in the labor force."
   c. What economic factors might shift a woman from "not in the labor force" to in the labor force? Discuss.
   d. Suppose an economic downturn occurred. How would you expect this change to affect the number employed, the number of unemployed, and the number classified as "not in the labor force"? Explain.

2. Explain the reasons why men's labor force participation decreased. Why do these same factors not cause women's labor force participation to decline as well?

3. Use economic reasoning (economic theory) to explain why the labor force participation rate for married women and never-married women might differ.*

4. Suppose the government were to provide a $2-per-hour subsidy for families with an employed mother who purchases child care.
   a. Consider a mother with a preschool-age child who is currently not employed. How would this subsidy affect her decision to work, all else equal?*
   b. Consider a mother with a preschool-age child who is currently employed. How would this subsidy affect the number of hours that she chooses to work (assuming she can vary them), all else equal?*

5. Now suppose that the government provides a subsidy of $300 per month for all families with children. Answer part a and part b of question 4 again under this scenario. How would your answers to question 4 change? Explain fully.*

6. Do you expect that sometime in the future labor force participation rates for men and women will be equal? Discuss.

INTERNET-BASED DATA EXERCISE

In doing this exercise, students should be aware that the precise names of documents and their location within a web site may change over time.

The U.S. Bureau of Labor Statistics is the primary source of U.S. government data on labor force statistics. These figures are reported monthly in the BLS Economic News Release titled "The Employment Situation."

Visit the home page of the U.S. Bureau of Labor Statistics at http://www.bls.gov/.

Find "The Employment Situation." For all questions, provide answers based on data for the most recent month (seasonally unadjusted):

(a) Using Table A-1, confirm that you understand how to calculate the labor force participation rate and the unemployment rate using the definitions provided at the start of Chapter 4. Show your work.

(b) Using Table A-1, what is the current unemployment rate? How does it compare to the rate for 1 year ago? What are the current rates for women 16+ and men 16+?

(c) Table A-4 provides current labor force statistics by educational attainment. What patterns do you see and what might explain them?

(d) Table A-12 provides statistics on labor force underutilization. What is the current range of estimates of unemployment (lowest to highest)? Are you surprised and if so, why?

Suggested Readings

Becker, Gary S. "A Theory of the Allocation of Time." *Economic Journal* 75, no. 299 (September 1965): 493–517.

Blank, Rebecca M. "Distinguished Lecture on Economics in Government—Fighting Poverty: Lessons from Recent U.S. History." *Journal of Economic Perspectives* 14, no. 2 (Spring 2000): 3–19.

Blau, Francine D., and Lawrence M. Kahn. "Changes in the Labor Supply Behavior of Married Women: 1980–2000." *Journal of Labor Economics* 25, no. 3 (July 2007): 393–438.

Goldin, Claudia. *Understanding the Gender Gap: An Economic History of American Women*. New York: Oxford University Press, 1990.

Goldin, Claudia. "The Quiet Revolution That Transformed Women's Employment, Education, and Family." *American Economic Review* 96, no. 2 (May 2006): 1–20.

Heckman, James J. "What Has Been Learned About Labor Supply in the Past Twenty Years." *American Economic Review* 83, no. 2 (May 1993): 116–21.

Jacobs, Jerry A., and Kathleen Gerson. *The Time Divide: Work, Family, and Gender Inequality*. Cambridge, MA: Harvard University Press, 2004.

Juhn, Chinhui. "Decline of Male Labor Market Participation: The Role of Declining Market Opportunities." *Quarterly Journal of Economics* 107, no. 1 (February 1992): 79–121.

Juhn, Chinhui, and Kevin M. Murphy. "Wage Inequality and Family Labor Supply." *Journal of Labor Economics* 15, no. 1, pt. 1 (January 1997): 72–97.

Mincer, Jacob. "Labor Force Participation of Married Women." In *Aspects of Labor Economics*, edited by H. Greg Lewis. Universities National Bureau of Economic Research Conference Studies, no. 14. Princeton, NJ: Princeton University Press, 1962, pp. 63–97.

Munnell, Alicia H, and Steven A. Sass, "The Labor Supply of Older American Men." In *Labor Supply in the New Century*, edited by Katharine Bradbury, Christopher L. Foote, and Robert K. Triest. Boston, MA: Federal Reserve Bank of Boston, 2008, pp. 83–138.

Key Terms

labor force 77
employed 77
unemployed 77
labor force participation rate 77
unemployment rate 78
not in the labor force 78
marginally attached workers 78
discouraged workers 78

underemployment 78
part time for economic reasons 78
involuntary part-time workers 78
budget constraint 89
wage 89
nonlabor income 89
nonmarket time 89
market time 91
indifference curve 91

substitution in consumption 92
substitution in production 92
reservation wage 95
value of home 95
income effect 97
substitution effect 102
elasticity 106, 108
wage elasticity 106, 108

income elasticity 106, 108
added worker effect 109
discouraged worker effect 109
Earned Income Tax Credit (EITC) 110
market substitutes 114
technological change 114

CHAPTER 5

Differences in Occupations and Earnings: Overview

Chapter Highlights

- Occupational Differences
- Trends in Occupational Segregation
- Female-Male Earnings Ratio

Chapter 4 reviewed the large increase in women's labor force participation that has occurred since World War II. This increase, in conjunction with a decline in male labor force participation rates, resulted in a steady narrowing of gender differentials in paid work. Further, as women have become more committed to market work, their labor force attachment has increased and they have been employed more continuously over the life cycle. We now turn to the question of how women fare in the labor market. In this chapter, we review the extent of gender differences in the two main indicators of labor market status—occupational attainment and earnings. As we shall see, despite important recent gains, substantial differences between men and women remain.

Our major focus here is simply in describing the extent of and trends in these gender differences in labor market outcomes. In the next three chapters we provide detailed explanations. In Chapter 6, we focus on supply-side explanations for the observed gender differences in outcomes, particularly the human capital model, which emphasizes the role of women's preferences and the choices that they may make to invest less in job-related education and training, as well as to spend a smaller share of their adult years in the labor force. These explanations can also include premarket discrimination, or societal discrimination, in which various types of social pressures influence women's choices adversely.

In Chapter 7, we consider demand-side explanations for the observed gender differences in outcomes. We focus on the results of gender discrimination in the labor market, which occurs when men and women with equal qualifications are treated differently. We also point out that labor market discrimination can indirectly lower women's earnings and occupational attainment by reducing their incentives and opportunities to acquire education and training.

Finally, in Chapter 8, we use what we learned in Chapters 6 and 7, as well as some additional insights, to explain the reasons for the narrowing of the gender earnings gap in recent years. This trend is considered in the context of other recent changes that significantly affected earnings outcomes in the labor market.

OCCUPATIONAL DIFFERENCES

We can get a general idea of the differences in occupations between men and women by comparing the distribution of male and female workers across the 10 broad occupations shown in Table 5-1 for 1983 and 2007. (These major occupational classifications are based on data for more than 400 detailed occupations.)[1] Traditionally, and to a considerable extent today, women are concentrated in office and administrative support and service occupations. **Office and administrative support occupations** include clerical jobs like secretary and administrative assistant, file clerk, data-entry keyer, and bookkeeper, as well as other support jobs such as computer operator, customer service representative, and postal service clerk. Examples of **service occupations** are child care workers, firefighters and police, waiters and waitresses, hairdressers and cosmetologists, cooks, maids and housekeeping cleaners, and grounds maintenance workers. In 2007, 22 percent of women workers were in office and administrative support occupations compared to only 6 percent of men; another 20 percent of women were in service jobs compared to 13 percent of men.

Women are also considerably more likely than men to be in **professional occupations**. Examples of jobs in this category are architects, engineers, lawyers, physicians, computer programmers, teachers, registered nurses, pharmacists, librarians, social workers, actors, and athletes, and coaches. About one quarter of women were in such jobs in 2007 compared to 17 percent of men.

Men, on the other hand, are considerably more likely than women to be in blue-collar occupations, which span skilled production, craft and repair work, as well as semiskilled and unskilled manual jobs. These include (1) **construction and extraction occupations** such as electricians, carpenters, plumbers, and mining machine operators;

TABLE 5-1   Distribution of Men and Women by Major Occupation, 1983 and 2007[a]

	1983		2007	
Occupation	Men (%)	Women (%)	Men (%)	Women (%)
Management, business, and financial operations occupations	14.7	8.6	15.8	13.6
Professional and related occupations	14.7	19.5	16.9	25.1
Service occupations	12.7	19.9	13.2	20.4
Sales and related occupations	10.5	12.2	10.8	12.2
Office and administrative support occupations	6.8	28.3	6.2	21.6
Farming, fishing, and forestry occupations	1.6	0.5	1.0	0.3
Construction and extraction occupations	11.0	0.4	11.9	0.4
Installation, maintenance, and repair occupations	6.5	0.4	6.4	0.3
Production occupations	10.6	7.4	8.4	4.2
Transportation and material-moving occupations	10.7	2.8	9.5	2.0
Total Employed	100.0	100.0	100.0	100.0

[a]Data refer to civilian workers 16 years of age and older.

Source: 2007 data from U.S. Department of Labor, Bureau of Labor Statistics, *Employment and Earnings* (January 2008), Table 10. Historical data retrieved from http://www.bls.gov/cps/constio198399.htm and associated links.

---

[1] A listing of most of the detailed categories included in each major occupation is provided in U.S. Department of Labor, *Employment and Earnings* (January 2008), Table 11.

(2) **installation, maintenance, and repair occupations** such as automotive service technicians and mechanics; computer, automated teller, and office machine repairers; and telecommunications line installers and repairers; (3) **production occupations** such as bakers, butchers, machinists, tool and die makers, and sewing machine operators; and (4) **transportation and material moving occupations** such as truck, taxi, and bus drivers; aircraft pilots; parking lot and service station attendants; and refuse and recyclable material collectors. In 2007, fully 36 percent of male workers were employed in such jobs, as compared to just 7 percent of women.

There are some gender differences in the remaining broad occupations listed in Table 5-1, as well, but they are quite a bit smaller.[2] In 2007, a somewhat higher percentage of men (16 percent) than of women (14 percent) were employed in **management, business, and financial occupations**. Examples of such jobs include chief executives, financial managers, human resources managers, education administrators, medical and health services managers, accountants and auditors, insurance underwriters, and wholesale and retail buyers. And, a very slightly higher share of men than women were in **sales occupations** in 2007. Examples of occupations in this varied category include cashiers; retail salespersons; securities, commodities, and financial services sales agents; travel agents; wholesale and manufacturing sales representatives; and telemarketers.

Some notable changes have occurred over time in the extent of gender differences in occupations. These changes can be seen by comparing the percentage of women in a given occupation in 2007 with the percentage in 1983. For instance, women are less concentrated in office and administrative support occupations than they were in 1983 when 28 percent of women held such jobs compared to 22 percent in 2007. On the other hand, women increased their representation in professional jobs by more than men did between 1983 and 2007. They are also much more likely to be in management, business, and financial operations occupations than they were in the past. Only 9 percent of women were in those jobs in 1983 compared to 14 percent in 2007; during that time, the percentage of male workers in management jobs was roughly constant. Women used to be even more underrepresented in management. In 1972, for example, just one in five managerial workers (21 percent) was female, rising to over two in five (43 percent) by 2007.[3]

The industries in which men and women work also differ considerably. As may be seen in Table 5-2, in 2007, men were more heavily concentrated in the areas of construction, manufacturing, and transportation and utilities—36 percent of men worked in those industries, as compared to 12 percent of women. In contrast, women were considerably more likely to be employed in education and health services—34 percent of women were in these industries, compared to 10 percent of men. To some extent, these differences in distribution by industry reflect gender differences in occupations. For example, as we have seen, men are more likely to hold blue-collar jobs than women, and a high proportion of such jobs are in construction, manufacturing, and transportation. Women are considerably more likely than men to be elementary and middle school teachers, and those jobs are in the education industry. However, substantial differences

---

[2] There are also gender differences in the occupation of farming, fishing and forestry, but these are not discussed in the text given the small size of this category; just 1 percent of employed men and 0.3 percent of employed women are in these jobs.

[3] The Census occupational classifications changed considerably in 2000 and these changes were adopted by the Current Population Survey (the data source for Table 5-1) in 2003. The 1983 data reported in Table 5-1 and in the text have been adjusted by the Bureau of Labor Statistics to permit meaningful comparisons. The figure for 1972 reported in the text, however, is based on occupational categories that are not strictly comparable with the 2007 categories.

TABLE 5-2 Distribution of Men and Women by Major Industry, 2007[a]

Industry	Men (%)	Women (%)
Agriculture, forestry, fishing, and hunting	2.0	0.7
Mining	0.8	0.1
Construction	13.7	1.7
Manufacturing	14.6	7.2
Wholesale and retail trade	14.7	13.9
Transportation and utilities	7.4	2.8
Information	2.6	2.2
Financial activities	6.0	8.6
Professional and business services	11.5	9.8
Education and health services	9.9	33.8
Leisure and hospitality	7.7	9.4
Other services	4.3	5.4
Public administration	4.8	4.5
Total employed	100.0	100.0

[a]Data refer to civilian workers 16 years of age and over.

Source: Department of Labor, Bureau of Labor Statistics, *Employment and Earnings* (January 2008), Table 17.

exist in the employment of men and women by firm or industry even *within* occupational categories,[4] further contributing to the observed industry differences by gender.

In order to examine occupational differences by race and ethnicity as well as by gender, Table 5-3 provides data separately for non-Hispanic whites, and for black, Asian, and Hispanic workers. African American and Hispanic men and women were less likely than non-Hispanic whites of the same sex to be employed in higher-paying managerial and professional positions. At the other end of the pay scale, they were overrepresented in service jobs, as well as in production and transportation and material moving occupations. The occupational distribution of Asian men and women compares much more favorably to that of whites than is the case for the other minority groups. Asians were about as likely as whites of the same sex to be employed in management, business, and financial operations occupations and more likely than whites to be employed as professionals. They were only slightly more likely than whites to be in service jobs, and Asian men were less likely than white men to be in blue-collar occupations.

Within each race or ethnic group, however, the broad outlines of occupational differences by gender show considerable similarities. Women were heavily overrepresented in office and administrative support, as well as service occupations, and, except among Asians, more likely than men to be in professional jobs. At the same time, women tended to be underrepresented in blue-collar occupations compared to men—though Asian women were slightly more likely to be in production occupations than Asian men. However, in contrast to the situation among whites and Asians, black and

---

[4] See, for example, Francine D. Blau, *Equal Pay in the Office* (Lexington, MA: Lexington Books, 1977); Erica L. Groshen, "The Structure of the Female/Male Wage Differential: Is It Who You Are, What You Do, or Where You Work?" *Journal of Human Resources* 26, no. 3 (Summer 1991): 457–72; and Kimberly Bayard, Judith Hellerstein, David Neumark, and Kenneth Troske, "New Evidence on Sex Segregation and Sex Difference in Wages from Matched Employee–Employer Data," *Journal of Labor Economics* 21, no. 4 (October 2003): 887–922. For historical evidence, see Claudia Goldin, *Understanding the Gender Gap: An Economic History of American Women* (New York: Oxford University Press, 1990).

TABLE 5-3 Distribution of Workers by Occupation, Race, Hispanic Origin, and Gender, 2007

Occupation	Non-Hispanic Whites		Blacks		Asians		Hispanics	
	Men (%)	Women (%)	Men (%)	Women (%)	Men (%)	Women (%)	Men (%)	Women (%)
Management, business, and financial operations occupations	18.7	14.8	9.2	11.0	15.8	15.7	7.2	8.6
Professional and related occupations	18.5	27.4	13.1	20.3	33.5	31.1	7.1	14.5
Service occupations	10.8	17.5	19.2	26.8	13.5	18.9	19.7	30.7
Sales and related occupations	11.8	12.3	8.8	11.7	11.5	11.4	7.2	12.4
Office and administrative support occupations	5.6	22.4	10.0	21.0	6.9	14.7	6.0	20.7
Farming, fishing, and forestry occupations	0.7	0.2	0.4	0.2	0.2	0.3	2.5	1.0
Construction and extraction occupations	10.5	0.4	8.1	0.3	3.1	0.1	22.8	0.6
Installation, maintenance, and repair occupations	6.9	0.3	5.5	0.3	4.1	0.5	5.7	0.2
Production occupations	7.9	3.2	9.6	5.4	6.7	6.3	10.4	8.0
Transportation and material-moving occupations	8.4	1.6	16.1	3.1	4.7	1.0	11.3	3.3
Total employed	100.0	100.0	100.0	100.0	100.0	100.0	100.0	100.0

Notes: Data refer to civilian workers 16 years of age and older. Hispanics may be of any race.

Source: U.S. Department of Labor, Bureau of Labor Statistics, *Employment and Earnings* (January 2008), Table 10, and unpublished data on non-Hispanic whites from the Bureau of Labor Statistics.

Hispanic women were more likely than black and Hispanic men to be managerial workers, and were also more likely than their male counterparts to be in sales jobs.[5]

Occupational Segregation

So far, we have discussed gender differences in occupational distributions for broadly defined occupational categories, but data on these major occupations do not reveal the full extent of occupational differences by gender. For example, while Table 5-1 indicates that about the same proportion of men and women are in sales and related occupations, women are more likely to be cashiers, retail salespersons, travel agents, and telemarketers, whereas men are more likely to be securities, commodities, and financial services sales agents, and wholesale and manufacturing sales representatives. Information

---

[5] Analyses of detailed occupational categories indicate that occupational differences by race (i.e., between blacks and whites) are considerably less pronounced than those by sex, and declined more rapidly between 1960 and 1990; see Victor Fuchs, *Women's Quest for Economic Equality* (Cambridge, MA: Harvard University Press, 1988); and Joyce P. Jacobsen, "Trends in Work Force Sex Segregation, 1960–90," *Social Science Quarterly* 75, no. 1 (March 1994): 204–11.

is, in fact, available on the large set of detailed occupations that underlie these broad categories. The precise number varies over time but, as already noted, is generally well in excess of 400. Women's representation in these more narrowly defined occupations varies considerably more. This is illustrated in Table 5-4, which shows percent female (i.e., the percentage of workers in the occupation who are women) for a selection of professional occupations, chosen because we tend to be familiar with the nature and function of the various professions and because both men and women are substantially represented in the category as a whole.

As evident from the table, many of the jobs in the professional category are either predominantly female or predominantly male. In 2007, women comprised more than 80 percent of workers in six of the professions shown in the table—dietitians and nutritionists, librarians, preschool and kindergarten teachers, elementary and middle school teachers, registered nurses and social workers. Men comprised more than 80 percent of the workers in all but one of the engineering occupations listed and among clergy, as well as more than 70 percent of architects, computer scientists and systems analysts, and dentists. Although considerable occupational differences by gender remain within the professional category, it is important to note that women have made considerable inroads into traditionally male professions since 1970. By 2007, women constituted more than 20 percent of workers in such formerly highly male occupations as architects, chemists, chemical engineers, computer scientists and systems analysts, dentists, lawyers, pharmacists, and physicians and surgeons.

One way to assess the magnitude of differences in the distribution of women and men across occupational categories is the **index of segregation**.[6] It gives the percentage of female (or male) workers who would have to change jobs in order for the occupational distribution of the two groups to be the same. The index would equal zero if the distribution of men and women across occupational categories were identical; it would equal 100 if all occupations were either completely male or completely female.

Researchers have calculated the index of segregation for various years using a detailed breakdown of all occupations (over 400 occupational categories). These studies show that, for much of the twentieth century, occupational segregation was well in excess of 60 percent. Significant declines in the index began in the 1970s, and we shall consider this important trend in greater detail later. Nonetheless, the extent of occupational segregation remains substantial: the segregation index for 2000 was estimated to be 52 percent, indicating that more than half of women (or men) would have had to change their jobs for the occupational distribution of the two groups to be the same.[7] Moreover, measures like the segregation index likely underestimate the full extent of employment segregation by sex. Job categories used by employers are far more detailed than the census occupational categories, and researchers find that particular firms often employ mostly men or mostly women, even in occupations where both sexes are substantially represented. Restaurants, for instance, commonly employ only waiters or waitresses, but not both. Or, women may be well represented as sales workers in clothing stores but not in stores selling electronics, computers, and televisions.[8]

---

[6] Otis Dudley Duncan and Beverly Duncan, "A Methodological Analysis of Segregation Indexes," *American Sociological Review* 20, no. 2 (1955): 210–17. The index of occupational segregation by sex is defined as:

$$\text{Segregation index} = 1/2\sum_i |M_i - F_i|$$

where M_i = the percentage of males in the labor force employed in occupation i, and F_i = the percentage of females in the labor force employed in occupation i.

[7] Jerry A. Jacobs, "Detours on the Road to Equality: Women, Work and Higher Education," *Contexts* 2, no. 1 (Winter 2003): 32–41.

[8] Blau, *Equal Pay*; Groshen, "The Structure of the Female/Male Wage Differential"; and Bayard et al., "New Evidence on Sex Segregation."

TABLE 5-4   Percent Female in Selected Professional and Related Occupations, 1970 and 2007

Occupations	1970	2007
Architects, except naval	4.0	24.7
Biological scientists	37.8	42.6
Chemists and materials scientist	11.7	40.8
Clergy	2.9	15.1
Computer scientists and systems analysts[a]	13.6	27.1
Dentists	3.5	28.2
Dietitians and nutritionists	92.0	87.6
Engineering occupations[b]		
Aerospace engineers[a]	1.8	10.5
Chemical engineers	1.3	21.2
Civil engineers	1.3	11.5
Electrical and electronics engineers	1.7	8.6
Industrial engineers, including health and safety	2.6	17.5
Mechanical engineers	1.0	7.3
Lawyers	4.9	32.6
Librarians	82.1	83.2
News analysts, reporters and correspondents, editors[c]	41.6	42.1
Pharmacists	12.1	53.3
Physicians and surgeons	9.7	30.0
Psychologists	38.8	64.4
Public relations specialists	26.6	63.3
Registered nurses	97.3	91.7
Social workers	63.3	82.0
Teaching occupations[b]		
Preschool and kindergarten teachers	97.9	97.3
Elementary and middle school teachers	83.9	80.9
Secondary school teachers	49.6	56.9
Postsecondary teachers	29.1	46.2

[a]There were especially large changes in the definition of this occupation in 2000 compared to 1970.

[b]Occupations listed here are illustrative and do not include all those in this category.

[c]In the 1970 occupational categories (based on 1980 codes), "Editors and reporters" is one category but in the 2000 occupational categories "Editors" and "Reporters" are separate categories; thus we combine the two categories here.

Notes: There were substantial changes in the Census occupational categories in 2000. Thus, the 2007 and 1970 occupational categories are not strictly comparable. 1970 data are from the 1970 Census and are for the experienced civilian labor force aged 16 and over, and use the 1980 occupational codes. 2007 data are annual averages from the *Current Population Surveys* and are for employed civilians aged 16 and over.

Sources: U.S. Census Bureau, *Detailed Occupation of the Experienced Civilian Labor Force by Sex for the United States and Regions: 1980 and 1970,* Supplementary Report PC80-S1-15 (March 1984); and U.S. Department of Labor, Bureau of Labor Statistics, *Employment and Earnings* (January 2008), Table 11.

Hierarchies Within Occupations

Not only do men and women tend to work in different occupations, they also tend to be employed at different levels of the hierarchy within occupations. A good example is the representation of women at various levels of the faculty hierarchy in colleges and universities. Despite considerable growth in the representation of women in academia over the past 30 years, women are still more highly represented at the lower echelons than at the top. In academic year 2007–2008, women constituted 60 percent of instructors and 48 percent of assistant professors (the lowest ranks), compared to 40 percent of associate and 26 percent of full professors at the upper ranks.

The academic case is not unique. Although women have markedly increased their share of managerial jobs, their representation in top positions is still extremely sparse. According to a report by *Catalyst* on Fortune 500 companies, only 15.4 percent of all corporate officers were women in 2007; and women held just 6.7 percent of top-earner spots comprised of the five highest-paid executives in each company. These figures did, however, represent a substantial increase from 8.7 percent of officers and 1.2 percent of top earners in 1995. Among corporate officers, women are also much less likely to hold positions that directly affect the company's bottom line ("line" positions), which tend to be key stepping-stones for rising up the corporate ladder. In 2007, women comprised 6 percent of those in such positions, a figure that was up only slightly from 5.3 percent 10 years earlier.[9]

The type of disparities described here prompt the claim that women face a "glass ceiling," or a set of subtle barriers impeding their efforts to move up the hierarchy. We return to this issue in Chapter 7, where we more closely examine the evidence on women's representation at the upper levels of industry, government, and academia, as well as possible explanations for the observed gender differences.

Evaluating the Extent of Occupational Segregation

However segregation is measured, and whatever the numerical value of the index arrived at, how can any figure in excess of zero and short of 100 be classified as modest or excessive? The answer depends, in part, on one's perception of how great the differences are in men's and women's talents, tastes, and motivation and how relevant they are to their occupational distribution and achievements.

On one side are those who argue that occupational segregation is natural and appropriate. In this view, efforts to change the existing situation will merely lead to economic inefficiency and personal frustration. Its proponents emphasize the similarities among individuals within each sex and the differences between the two groups. Those who emphasize the similarities between men and women and the variations among individuals within each sex group are on the other side. In this view, if men and women were not constrained by gender stereotyping and various barriers to individual choice but were free to follow their own inclinations, they would be far less concentrated in separate occupations. In this case, removing existing barriers would increase efficiency and decrease frustration because individuals could seek work more suited to their particular aptitudes.

However, even if the present level of occupational segregation is deemed excessive, it would be unreasonable to conclude that the optimal situation would necessarily be a precisely proportional distribution of men and women. Apart from whatever

---

[9] *2007 Catalyst Census of Women Corporate Officers and Top Earners in the Fortune 500* available at http://www .catalyst.org/; and *2002 Catalyst Census of Women Corporate Officers and Top Earners in the Fortune 500* (New York). Line officers are responsible for a company's profits and losses; staff officers are responsible for the auxiliary functioning of the business. Catalyst determines how to classify corporate officers based on the officer's title and functional area. See also, *1997 Catalyst Census of Women Corporate Officers and Top Earners* (New York).

innate differences may exist, past socialization and the prevalent allocation of household responsibilities would make such an outcome unlikely for some time to come.

In addition, the rate of change is limited by the time it takes for new people to be trained and hired. Large numbers of people cannot be expected to change jobs on short notice, as the computation of the segregation index perhaps implies. The most that could reasonably be expected is that the underrepresented group would be more highly represented among new hires, to the extent that they are qualified for the available positions, than among those presently employed in the occupation—at best, a slow process.

TRENDS IN OCCUPATIONAL SEGREGATION

The same issues confronted in measuring current occupational segregation arise in determining the extent to which it has changed over time. However, in addition to concerns over how detailed the categories are, and whether women are included in the upper ranks of occupational hierarchies, there is also the question of whether the same occupational categories are used for the various periods to be compared. The main difficulty is that the definition and number of occupational categories often undergo significant changes. Given the constant flux in the economy, this shift in definitions and included occupations is inevitable. For example, if the Census Bureau rigidly adhered to the occupational categories of an earlier era, jobs such as computer scientist and computer programmer would not be included. Thus, regardless of the best efforts of those who compile the data and the researchers who use them, data are not entirely comparable over the years and are less so as the years get further apart.

Despite these difficulties, results from numerous studies provide convincing evidence that the degree of segregation was largely unchanged during the decades prior to 1960. In fact, the index of segregation was actually reported to have increased by 1.1 percentage points between 1950 and 1960, as employment in predominantly female clerical and professional jobs increased relative to other occupations. Between 1960 and 1970, however, an inflow of men into female professions and of women into male sales and clerical jobs produced a modest drop in the segregation index, of 3.1 percentage points.[10]

Table 5-5 shows the larger declines in the index in the 1970s and 1980s. Estimates based on detailed census data indicate that the index fell from 67.7 in 1970 to 59.3 in 1980 and 53.0 in 1990.[11] Even though the level of segregation that remained was considerable, the cumulative reduction of nearly 15 percentage points over the two decades is substantial, especially when considered in light of the stability of the index in earlier decades. Some indication of trends over the 1990s may be obtained using *Current Population Survey* data based on a somewhat different set of detailed occupations and workers. The index of segregation computed from this source decreased from 56.4 in 1990 to 52.4 in 2000,[12] yielding a 4 percentage point decrease over the 1990s, compared

---

[10] For the pre-1960 period, see Edward Gross, "Plus Ça Change? The Sexual Structure of Occupations over Time," *Social Problems* 16, no. 1 (Fall 1968): 198–208; for 1950 to 1970, see Francine D. Blau and Wallace E. Hendricks, "Occupational Segregation by Sex: Trends and Prospects," *Journal of Human Resources* 14, no. 2 (Spring 1979): 197–210. The changes in the index presented for the 1950s and 1960s are not strictly comparable to those given for later years because of changes in the number and composition of occupational categories that are included.

[11] These figures are for a comparable set of occupations in each of the years. See Francine D. Blau, Patricia Simpson, and Deborah Anderson, "Continuing Progress? Trends in Occupational Segregation over the 1970s and 1980s," *Feminist Economics* 4, no. 3 (Fall 1998): 29–71. See also Andrea H. Beller, "Changes in the Sex Composition of U.S. Occupations, 1960–1981," *Journal of Human Resources* 20, no. 2 (Spring 1985) 235–50; Jacobsen, "Trends in Workforce Sex Segregation"; and David A. Macpherson and Barry T. Hirsch, "Wages and Gender Composition: Why Do Women's Jobs Pay Less?" *Journal of Labor Economics* 13, no. 3 (July 1995): 426–71.

[12] Jerry A. Jacobs, "The Sex Segregation of Occupations: Prospects for the 21st Century," in *Handbook of Gender in Organizations*, edited by Gary N. Powell (Newbury Park, CA: Sage Publications, 1999), pp. 125–41; and Jerry A. Jacobs, "Detours on the Road to Equality: Women, Work and Higher Education," *Contexts* 2, no. 1 (Winter 2003): 32–41.

TABLE 5-5   Trends in Occupational Segregation by Sex, 1970–2000

Year	Census	Current Population Survey
1970	67.7	
1980	59.3	
1990	53.0	56.4
2000		52.4

Sources: Francine D. Blau, Patricia Simpson, and Deborah Anderson, "Continuing Progress? Trends in Occupational Segregation over the 1970s and 1980s," *Feminist Economics* 4, no. 3 (Fall 1998): 29–71; and Jerry A. Jacobs, "Detours on the Road to Equality: Women, Work and Higher Education," *Contexts* 2, no. 1 (Winter 2003): 32–41.

to 8 and 6 percentage point decreases in the 1970s and 1980s, respectively. In sum, the figures indicate that there was a substantial decline in the amount of segregation by occupation between 1960 and 2000, with the pace of change accelerating markedly over the 1970s and 1980s and continuing at a slower pace in the 1990s.[13]

Changes in the extent of segregation may be due to changes in the sex composition of individual occupations as a result of the integration of previously male or female jobs, or to shifts in the occupational mix of the economy through greater employment growth in occupations that are already integrated relative to segregated male and female jobs. Research suggests that changes in the sex composition of occupations were the principal cause of the reduction in segregation over the 1970s and 1980s. Although such shifts in sex composition could have been due either to women entering formerly male jobs or men entering previously female jobs or a combination of both, the major factor was the movement of women into predominantly male jobs. As a result of this movement, these occupations became more integrated and the degree of segregation in the labor market, overall, was diminished. Women were especially successful in entering formerly male white-collar jobs, particularly professional and managerial occupations. Examples of the gains for women in the professional category were shown in Table 5-4 where we saw that women significantly increased their representation in a number of formerly highly segregated male professions. The impact of these changes in the sex composition of occupations was supplemented by some important shifts in the occupational mix of the economy, which also decreased segregation. Employment in integrated jobs increased compared to employment in predominately female and predominately male jobs. Examples of segregated jobs that declined in relative importance include a number of female administrative support jobs (e.g., secretary, typist, bookkeeper, and telephone operator) and male farm and blue-collar occupations.[14]

Despite recent gains, numerous predominantly single-sex occupations remain. Many of the predominantly male jobs are blue-collar occupations: examples of these include carpenters, electricians, plumbers, sheet metal workers, truck drivers and automotive service technicians and mechanics—all occupations in which women comprise 5 percent or less of workers. Predominantly female categories include, in addition to the traditionally female professions noted earlier, a number of jobs in the administrative

---

[13] Another interesting trend is that gender segregation by workplace—the extent to which women and men work in different firms—also declined between 1990 and 2000. See, Judith Hellerstein, David Neumark, and Melissa McInerney, "Changes in Workplace Segregation in the United States between 1990 and 2000: Evidence from Matched Employer–Employee Data," in *The Analysis of Firms and Employees: Quantitative and Qualitative Approaches*, Stefan Bender, Julia Lane, Kathryn L. Shaw, Fredrik Andersson, and Till Von Wachter, eds. (Chicago, IL: The University of Chicago Press, 2008).

[14] See Blau, Simpson, and Anderson, "Continuing Progress?"

support and service areas, such as secretaries and administrative assistants, receptionists and administrative clerks, bookkeeping, accounting and auditing clerks, child care workers, and dental assistants—all occupations where women comprise more than 90 percent of workers.

The areas where substantial occupational integration has occurred and those that have tended to remain segregated are linked to different trends in the reduction of occupational segregation across education groups. More substantial progress was made by highly educated women, who succeeded in moving into formerly male managerial and professional occupations. Gains were smaller for less-educated women, reflecting the slower progress in integrating blue-collar occupations. So, for example, as recently as 1971, the level of occupational segregation was fairly similar across educational groups. However, between 1971 and 1997, while the segregation index declined by 20 percentage points among college graduates and by 18 percentage points among those with some post-college education, it fell by 12 percentage points among high school dropouts and by only 5 percentage points among high school graduates.[15] The finding that gender differences in occupations narrowed less for less-educated groups is yet another piece of evidence of increasing differences in trends and outcomes by educational attainment. As discussed in Chapter 4, the labor force participation rates of less-educated women and men fell substantially relative to the more highly educated, and, as we shall see in Chapter 8, their wages declined relative to the more highly educated as well. In addition, single headship rates increased considerably more among less-educated women than among their more highly educated counterpart; as discussed in Chapter 10, such families face considerable economic difficulties.

In considering the overall long-term decrease in occupational segregation, it is also important to consider whether the observed trends reflect real improvements in opportunities for women. In some cases, firms responded to government pressures by placing women in token management positions that involve little responsibility and little contact with higher levels of management. In other instances, jobs became increasingly female when skill requirements declined because of technological changes. In such cases, integration may turn out to be a short-run phenomenon, as resegregation occurs and women increasingly come to dominate such jobs. One example of this phenomenon is the case of insurance adjusters and examiners. One study found that although women dramatically increased their share of this occupation after 1970, they were employed primarily as "inside adjusters" whose decision making was, to a considerable extent, computerized and involved little discretion. "Outside adjusters," a better-paid and more prestigious job, remained largely male. In yet other instances, women may gain access to a sector of an occupation that was always low paying. For example, the same study found that even though the representation of women among bus drivers increased substantially after 1970, men continued to comprise the majority of full-time workers in metropolitan transportation systems, whereas women were concentrated among part-time school bus drivers.[16]

At the same time, it is important to point out that women are expected to benefit from the increase in the demand for female labor that results when they are able to enter additional occupations from which they were previously excluded, even when the new jobs are qualitatively similar to those formerly available to them. Moreover, it is highly

---

[15] Jacobs, "The Sex Segregation of Occupations: Prospects for the 21st Century." These same patterns have been identified in other industrialized countries, as discussed in Chapter 12.

[16] These examples are from Barbara F. Reskin and Patricia A. Roos, *Job Queues, Gender Queues: Explaining Women's Inroads into Male Occupations* (Philadelphia: Temple University Press, 1990). See also Paula England, Paul Allison, Su Li, Noah Mark, Jennifer Thompson, Michelle Budig, and Han Sun, "Why Are Some Academic Fields Tipping Toward Female? The Sex Composition of U.S. Fields of Doctoral Degree Receipt, 1971–2002," *Sociology of Education* 80, no. 1 (January 2007): 23–42.

likely that much of the observed decline in occupational segregation does indeed represent enhanced labor market opportunities for women.

FEMALE-MALE EARNINGS RATIO

For many years, the single best-known statistic relevant to the economic status of women in this country was probably that women who worked full-time, year-round, earned about 59 cents to every dollar earned by men full-time, year-round workers.[17] One reason for the public awareness of this figure was that the **gender earnings ratio** persisted at that level for two decades, with only modest fluctuations and no significant trend. (The gender earnings ratio is equal to female earnings divided by male earnings.) This is shown in Table 5-6 and Figure 5-1, which indicate that the female-to-male earnings ratios (or gender earnings ratios) based on annual data hovered close to the 59 percent figure throughout the 1960s and 1970s.[18] And, the ratio had actually been somewhat higher in the 1950s than it was in these decades. However, a marked change occurred in the early 1980s, when the gender earnings ratio began to rise. Between 1981 and 2007 it increased substantially, from 59 percent to 78 percent.[19]

Table 5-6 and Figure 5-1 also show the gender earnings ratio calculated using data on the usual weekly earnings of full-time workers. For a variety of reasons, the earnings ratio computed on the basis of weekly earnings is generally higher than the annual figure.[20] Of more interest, however, is that the data for weekly earnings also show an upward trend, in this case dating from the late 1970s. Between 1978 and 2007, the earnings ratio, defined in these terms, increased from 61 to 80 percent.

Looking more closely at the trends in Figure 5-1, we see a substantial and steady narrowing of the gender earnings gap over the 1980s. However, during the 1990s, the pace of convergence in both the annual and weekly earnings series slowed and both series behaved more erratically. The pace of change grew a bit more robust in 2000s, though it still lagged behind the 1980s pace.[21] The long-run significance of the 2000s experience is unclear. It may signal a resumption of a somewhat stronger, long-run trend toward convergence in male–female earnings or may prove to be of only short duration. Nonetheless, the renewed growth in the gender earnings ratio at the start of the new century is an encouraging development.

Evidence on changes in the gender earnings ratio over the life cycle is shown in Table 5-7 for the 1970 to 2007 period. Data are presented on mean earnings ratios of

---

[17] *Full-time* is defined as 35 hours or more per week; *year-round* is defined as 50 weeks or more per year. The focus on full-time, year-round workers is an effort to adjust published government data on annual earnings for gender differences in hours and weeks worked. However, because even women who are employed full time tend to work fewer hours per week than male full-time workers, a finer adjustment for hours would raise the earnings ratio; see June O'Neill, "Women & Wages," *American Enterprise* 1, no. 6 (November/December 1990): 25–33.

[18] Median rather than mean earnings are shown because more government data are presented that way. The definition of the median is that half the cases fall above it and half below. In this case, half the individuals have higher earnings and half have lower. The mean, or arithmetic mean, is calculated by adding up the total earnings of all the individuals concerned and dividing by their number. Because a relatively small number of persons report extremely high earnings, the mean tends to be higher than the median.

[19] Focusing on all workers, rather than simply those employed full-time and year-round, Francine D. Blau and Andrea H. Beller found evidence of some earnings gains for women during the 1970s, after adjustment for hours and weeks worked; see "Trends in Earnings Differentials by Gender, 1971–1981," *Industrial and Labor Relations Review* 41, no. 4 (July 1988): 513–29.

[20] For example, annual earnings include overtime pay and bonuses, and men tend to receive greater amounts of this type of pay; see Nancy Rytina, "Comparing Annual and Weekly Earnings from the Current Population Survey," *Monthly Labor Review* 106 (April 1983): 32–38.

[21] Between 1980 and 1990, the average annual increase in the ratio was 1.14 percentage points for annual earnings and 0.74 percentage points for weekly earnings, while, between 1990 and 2000, it was only 0.16 percentage points for annual earnings and 0.42 percentage points for weekly earnings. As noted in the text, relative earnings growth in the 2000s was more robust: between 2000 and 2007, the average annual increase in the ratio was 0.65 percentage points for annual earnings and 0.59 percentage points for weekly earnings.

TABLE 5-6	Female-to-Male Earnings Ratios of Full-Time Workers, Selected Years, 1955–2008	
Year	Annual Earnings of Full-Time Year-Round Workers[a]	Usual Weekly Earnings of Full-time Workers[b]
1955	63.9	
1960	60.8	
1965	60.0	
1970	59.4	62.3
1975	58.8	62.0
1980	60.2	64.4
1985	64.6	68.2
1990	71.6	71.8
1995	71.4	75.5
2000	73.3	76.0
2005	77.0	81.0
2007	77.8	80.2
2008		79.9

[a]Workers aged 16 and over. Prior to 1979, workers aged 14 and over.

[b]Workers aged 16 and over.

Sources for Table 5-6 and Figure 5-1: U.S. Department of Labor, Women's Bureau, Bulletin 298, *Time of Change: 1984 Handbook on Women Workers*; Earl F. Mellor, "Investigating the Differences in Weekly Earnings of Women and Men," *Monthly Labor Review* 107, no. 6 (June 1984); U.S. Department of Labor, Bureau of Labor Statistics, *Handbook of Labor Statistics*, Bulletin 2340 (August 1989); U.S. Census Bureau, Current Population Reports, P60, *Income, Poverty, and Health Insurance Coverage in the United States* (and related titles), various issues; *Employment and Earnings*, various issues.

full-time, year-round workers for four age groups: 25–34, 35–44, 45–54, and 55–64. The age range 25–64 was selected because individuals in this age group have generally completed their formal schooling but have not yet retired from paid employment. The table indicates that, for example, in 1970 the ratio was 64.9 percent for 25- to 34-year-olds. Reading across the row, we see that this ratio increased over time and that, by 2007, 25- to 34-year-old women were earning 86.1 percent of what men in that age group earned.

Looking across the other rows in Table 5-7, we see that the gender earnings ratio for each age group increased substantially starting in the 1980s; little further change occurred over the 1990s, but gains resumed again in the 2000s. This is a similar pattern to what we observed for the overall gender earnings ratio. The separate data by age in Table 5-7 indicates that the earnings ratio began to rise as early as the 1970s for younger women (especially the youngest group aged 25 to 34), but that, even for this group, the 1980s gains were considerably larger. Younger women also experienced the largest cumulative increases: between 1970 and 2007, the earnings ratio rose by 21 percentage points for 25- to 34-year-olds, compared to 16 percentage points for 35- to 44-year-olds, and 13 percentage points for 45- to 54-year-olds.

The increase in the earnings ratio that occurred for each age group suggests that one mechanism by which women have narrowed the aggregate gender earnings gap is the entry of new cohorts of women who have higher relative earnings than their predecessors. (For example, those who were aged 25–34 in 1980 had higher relative earnings than 25–34 year olds did in 1970.) These higher relative earnings may reflect better

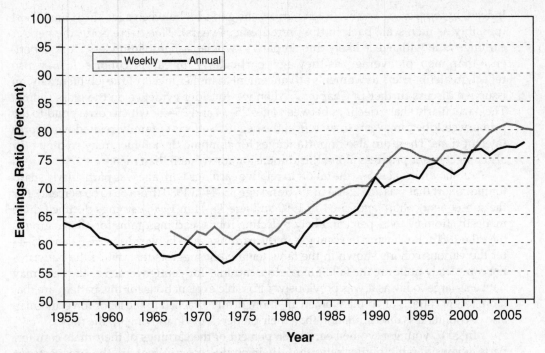

FIGURE 5-1   Female-to-Male Earnings Ratios of Full-Time Workers 1955–2008

TABLE 5-7   Female-to-Male Ratios of Mean Earnings for Full-Time, Year-Round Workers by Age, 1970–2007

Age	1970	1980	1990	2000	2007
25–34	64.9	68.5	76.9	74.4	86.1
35–44	53.9	55.3	64.4	66.0	70.0
45–54	56.3	52.0	58.2	60.4	69.2
55–64	60.3	54.9	57.1	53.6	64.2

Sources: 1970: June O'Neill, "Women & Wages," *American Enterprise* 1 (November/December 1990), p. 29; 1980 and 1990: U.S. Census Bureau, Consumer Income Series P-60, *Money Income of Households, Families, and Persons in the United States,* 1981 and 1991; 2000 and 2007: PINC03 Tables of the Current Population Survey Annual Social and Economic Supplement, 2001 and 2008, from http://pubdb3.census.gov/macro/032001/perinc/new03_000.htm and http://pubdb3.census.gov/macro/032008/perinc/new03_000.htm.

educational preparation, greater commitment to market work, and perhaps less discrimination against them as well.

The data in Table 5-7 may also be used to see what happens to the gender ratio of a particular cohort of women as they age. To do this, we may follow the progress of individual "birth" cohorts by looking diagonally down the rows of the table. So, for example, we may compare the earnings ratio for 25- to 34-year olds in 1970 to the earnings ratio for 35- to 44-year olds ten years later in 1980. We have shaded the entries in the table that trace out the experience of this cohort until they were 55–64 years old in 2000. This is the only cohort whose work life we may fully observe in the table, although we can see portions of the work life of a number of other cohorts.

For all cohorts for which we are able to make the comparison, we see a noticeable falloff in the earnings ratio as the cohort ages from 25–34 to 35–44, although the extent of that decline varies. Declines in relative earnings with age tend to be less pronounced at older ages (say comparing 35- to 44-year-olds to 45- to 54-year-olds a decade later).

Indeed, in some cases, women even narrow the gap a bit between ages 45–54 and 55–64 (possibly as men scale back in the preretirement years). This decrease in the gender earnings ratio with age is likely due, in part, to women accumulating less work experience than men, on average, as they age, particularly for earlier cohorts. It may also reflect greater barriers to women's advancement at higher levels of the job hierarchy, an issue we discuss further in Chapter 7 when we consider evidence on the glass ceiling. The particularly sharp declines between ages 25–34 and 35–44, which correspond to the primary childbearing years, may reflect the negative effects of family-related work force interruptions. These are also important ages for climbing the job hierarchy so they may also reflect lesser progress along this dimension for women than men.[22]

As shown in Table 5-7, the falloff in relative earnings with age was particularly sharp for the cohort that was age 25–34 in 1970 and age 35–44 in 1980 (from 65 to 55 percent). For the subsequent cohort, age 25–34 in 1980 and age 35–44 in 1990, earnings declined quite modestly, from 69 to 64 percent, likely reflecting robust earnings gains for all age groups over the 1980s. Reviewing the changes in the earnings ratio between age 25–34 and 35–44 for the various cohorts shown in the table tentatively suggests that, while the pattern is not completely uniform, the falloff in relative earnings for young women as they age may not be as large today as it was previously.[23] Possible explanations for this pattern are that more recent cohorts of young women are more firmly attached to the labor force and may also encounter less discrimination than their predecessors in moving up the ranks.

In 2007, younger women earned 86 percent of the earnings of their male counterparts, a considerably higher ratio than their predecessors. What are the prospects for their relative earnings as they age? Our consideration of the data in Table 5-7 suggests that their earnings ratio is likely to decline as they age, but they may well retain much, though likely not all, of this relatively high ratio.[24]

Table 5-8 provides information on the earnings of workers by level of education. Although education has a strong positive effect on the earnings of both men and women, men continue to earn substantially more than women within each educational category. In 1974 and indeed through much of the 1970s, the gap was so large that it was often noted that women college graduates earned less than male high school dropouts. While differences remain, as was the case for the overall earnings gap and the earnings differentials by age, the gender gap within educational categories has also narrowed considerably over time. And, as we shall see in Chapter 6, the earnings of female college graduates have pulled considerably ahead of their less-educated male counterparts.

Table 5-9 reviews the trends in the median earnings of women relative to men separately by race and Hispanic origin. Within each group, women earned less than men in 2007, but the gender earnings ratio was considerably higher among African Americans (86 percent) and Hispanics (88 percent) than among non-Hispanic whites (73 percent); Asians comprised an intermediate case (with the ratio standing at 80 percent).

---

[22] Gender earnings ratios for four-year age groups (rather than 10-year age groups, as in Table 5-7) indicate that women's earnings lose the most ground relative to men's through the mid-to-late thirties and that there is little relative change thereafter. See U.S. Congress, Joint Economic Committee, Democrats, "An Overview of the Gender Earnings Gap" (April 2006).

[23] Increases in women's rate of age-related wage growth relative to men have been found to account for about one-third of the narrowing of the gender wage gap between 1960 and 2000; see Catherine Weinberger and Peter Kuhn, "Changing Levels or Changing Slopes? The Narrowing of the U.S. Gender Earnings Gap, 1959–1999," Working Paper, University of California, Santa Barbara (February 2008).

[24] One caveat in interpreting data like those presented in Table 5-7 is that comparisons of this type may be influenced by which men and women choose to seek paid employment in each year, as well as by their relative success in locating jobs. Due to this problem of "selection bias," we cannot be completely certain that data on those who are employed accurately measure shifts in labor market opportunities for all women. Nobel laureate James J. Heckman greatly increased economists' awareness of problems of this type; see, for example, James J. Heckman, "Sample Selection Bias as a Specification Error," *Econometrica* 47, no. 1 (January 1979): 153–61.

TABLE 5-8 Ratio of Female-to-Male Mean Earnings by Education for Workers 18 Years Old and Over, 1974 and 2007

Education	1974	2007
High school		
1–3 years	55.1	68.5
4 years	57.5	72.9
College		
1–3 years	57.0	76.6
4 or more years	54.6	65.4

Notes: Definitions of educational categories are not exactly comparable for the two years. In 2007, mean earnings for 1–3 years of college is computed as a weighted average of the means for "some college, no degree" and "associate degree."

Sources: 1974 : U.S. Census Bureau Historical Income Tables-People Series, Table P-35, from www.census.gov/hhes/income/histinc/p35.html; 2007: CPS Annual Demographic Survey, March Supplement, PINC04 Series, from http://pubdb3.census.gov/macro/032008/perinc/toc.htm.

TABLE 5-9 Female-to-Male Ratios of Median Earnings by Race and Hispanic Origin for Full-Time, Year-Round Workers, 1955–2007

Year	Whites	Blacks	Asians	Hispanics
1955	65.3	55.1	n.a.	n.a.
1960	60.6	62.2	n.a.	n.a.
1965	57.9	62.5	n.a.	n.a.
1970	58.7	69.8	n.a.	n.a.
1975	57.6	74.6	n.a.	68.3
1980	58.9	78.8	n.a.	71.4
1985	63.0	81.9	n.a.	76.6
1990	67.6	85.4	79.7	81.9
1995	68.8	84.6	78.8	84.3
2000	72.3	83.3	75.1	86.9
2005	73.5	90.0	76.4	90.5
2007	73.0	86.0	79.7	88.1

Notes: Prior to 1970, data are for income rather than earnings. Data for 1980 onwards refer to workers 15 years of age and older; and for 1955–1975 to workers 14 years of age and older. Hispanic individuals may be of any race. Prior to 1970, blacks include blacks and other nonwhites; prior to 2005, Asians include Asians and Pacific Islanders. Beginning in 1990, data on whites are for white, non-Hispanics. After 2000, individuals were able to report more than one race. In this table, *whites* are defined as persons who selected this race group only, *blacks* are defined as persons who selected black alone or in combination with other races, *Asians* are defined as persons who selected Asian alone or in combination with other races.

n.a. = Not available

Sources: 1955–1965: U.S. Census Bureau, Current Population Reports, Consumer Income Series P-60, various issues; 1970 and beyond: U.S. Census Bureau, Historical Income Tables-People, Table P-40 "Women's Earnings as a Percentage of Men's Earnings by Race and Hispanic Origin" from, http://www.census.gov/hhes/www/income/histinc/incpertoc.html.

Not surprisingly, the trends in earnings ratios by gender among whites roughly mirror the overall trends because whites still comprise a substantial majority of the population. For whites, the gender ratio declined from 1955 to 1965, changed little from 1965 until 1980, and then increased at a rapid pace through 1990. Thereafter, progress was slower and more erratic. In contrast, the gender earnings ratio among African Americans increased considerably starting in the mid-1950s, rising by fully 31 percentage points by 2007. A sizable increase in the gender earnings ratio (20 percentage points) is also apparent among Hispanics since the mid-1970s when data first became available for this group. The data on Asians not only show a relatively high gender gap compared to the other minority groups but also no particular trend since data became available in 1990.[25]

Table 5-10 provides earnings comparisons for male and female minority group members relative to their white counterparts. Since most Hispanics are white, the inclusion of this growing low-earning group among whites would artificially inflate the relative progress of minority groups. Thus, in Table 5-10, data on whites are for white, non-Hispanics after 1990, when that breakdown became available, but for all whites in prior years.

TABLE 5-10   Minority-to-White Ratios of Median Earnings by Gender for Full-Time, Year-Round Workers, 1955–2007

Year	Black-to-White Ratios		Asian-to-White Ratios		Hispanic-to-White Ratios	
	Males	Females	Males	Females	Males	Females
1955	60.9	51.4	n.a.	n.a.	n.a.	n.a.
1960	66.1	67.8	n.a.	n.a.	n.a.	n.a.
1965	62.8	67.9	n.a.	n.a.	n.a.	n.a.
1970	69.0	82.2	n.a.	n.a.	n.a.	n.a.
1975	74.4	96.3	n.a.	n.a.	72.1	85.6
1980	70.7	94.6	n.a.	n.a.	70.8	85.8
1985	69.7	90.6	n.a.	n.a.	68.0	82.7
1990	70.1	88.6	88.8	104.8	63.5	77.0
1995	71.0	87.3	91.8	105.1	59.2	72.6
2000	73.0	84.1	98.3	102.1	57.6	69.2
2005	71.0	87.0	101.4	105.5	57.6	71.0
2007	71.7	84.6	100.4	109.6	60.0	72.4

Notes: Prior to 1970, data are for income rather than earnings. Data for 1980 onwards refer to workers 15 years of age and older; and for 1955–1975 to workers 14 years of age and older. Hispanic individuals may be of any race. Prior to 1970, blacks include blacks and other nonwhites; prior to 2005, Asians include Asians and Pacific Islanders. Beginning in 1990, data on whites are for white, non-Hispanics. After 2000, individuals were able to report more than one race. In this table, *whites* are defined as persons who selected this race group only, *blacks* are defined as persons who selected black alone or in combination with other races, *Asians* are defined as persons who selected Asian alone or in combination with other races.

n.a. = Not available

Sources: 1955–1965: U.S. Census Bureau, Current Population Reports, Consumer Income Series P-60, various issues; 1970 and beyond: U.S. Census Bureau, Historical Income Tables-People, Table P-38" Full-Time, Year-Round Workers by Median Earnings and Sex" from, http://www.census.gov/hhes/www/income/histinc/incpertoc.html.

---

[25] Trends for this group should be regarded with some caution, however, because underlying sample sizes are small and, prior to 2005, the data on Asians in the table (based on available government data) also included Pacific Islanders.

In terms of the racial and ethnic differences shown in the table, we see that blacks and Hispanics of both sexes earned less than whites in 2007, but the differential was considerably smaller among women than among men.[26] In 2007, black males earned 72 percent of white males' earnings, and the figure for Hispanic males was 60 percent. These figures were considerably lower than the earnings ratios of 85 percent for black women and 72 percent for Hispanic women, both compared to white women. In contrast, the median earnings of Asian men has been about the same as that of white men since 2000, and Asian women's earnings have been higher than their white counterparts' since data became available for this group in 1990. This may reflect the higher educational attainment of Asians than whites, which will be discussed in Chapter 6.

The earnings ratio for black relative to white women increased substantially from the mid-1950s, when it stood at only 51 percent, to the mid-1970s, when it was 96 percent. Black men also gained relative to white men, although not nearly as rapidly, from 61 percent of white men's earnings in 1955 to 74 percent in 1975. There has been no further convergence in earnings for black women or men since then.

Some caution is warranted in interpreting the trends for black males in Table 5-10 because the data are based on measured earnings of employed individuals. As discussed in Chapter 4, the participation and employment rates of black males relative to white males have decreased substantially since the 1950s, and it is likely that those who dropped out of the labor force are the individuals with the least favorable labor market opportunities. If the least successful blacks are leaving the labor force at a faster rate than comparable whites, observed black–white earnings ratios may rise (or show less of a decline than is actually the case), simply because of a change in the composition of employed blacks, rather than due to a true improvement in their labor market opportunities. Existing research suggests that this factor is important, but the general outlines of the trends shown in Table 5-10 remain.[27]

A similar issue potentially affects trends in the black–white earnings ratio among women, because, although black women traditionally had higher labor force participation rates than white women, the participation gap has narrowed considerably since the 1950s. However, the participation decision of women is considerably more complex than men's, and researchers find it more difficult to estimate the likely effects of shifting participation patterns on the black–white earnings ratio for women.[28] Earnings trends by race will be considered further in Chapter 8.

Earnings ratios for Hispanics relative to whites are considerably lower than black–white ratios for both men and women. Moreover, they have been declining since the mid-1970s, when this data first became available. One reason for this decrease may

[26] For a review of trends in the black-white gap in labor market outcomes and their sources, see Derek Neal, "Black–White Labour Market Inequality in the United States," in Steven Durlauf and Lawrence Blume, eds., *The New Palgrave Dictionary of Economics*, 2nd edition (London: Palgrave Macmillan, 2008), *The New Palgrave Dictionary of Economics Online*, Palgrave Macmillan, accessed on 19 January 2009 <http://www.dictionary ofeconomics.com/article?id=pde2008_B000306> doi:10.1057/9780230226203.0139.

[27] This is another example of selection bias; and again, James Heckman was the first to call it to the attention of economists in his work with Richard Butler, "The Impact of the Economy and State on the Economic Status of Black Americans: A Critical Review," in *Equal Rights and Industrial Relations*, edited by Farrell E. Bloch (Madison, WI: Industrial Relations Research Association, 1977), pp. 235–81. Other work includes, for example, Chinhui Juhn, "Labor Market Dropouts and Trends in the Wages of Black and White Men," *Industrial and Labor Relations Review* 56, no. 4 (July 2003): 643–63; and Amitabh Chandra, "Labor-Market Dropouts and the Racial Wage Gap: 1940–90," *American Economic Review* 90, no. 2 (May 2000): 333–38.

[28] For an insightful consideration of the selection issues, see, Derek Neal, "The Measured Black–White Wage Gap Among Women is Too Small," *Journal of Political Economy* 112 (February 2004, Supplement): S1-S28. For a study of trends, see Francine D. Blau and Andrea H. Beller, "Black–White Earnings over the 1970s and 1980s, Gender Differences in Trends," *Review of Economics and Statistics* 74, no. 2 (May 1992): 276–86. For an interesting historical analysis, see Martha J. Bailey and William J. Collins, "The Wage Gains of African-American Women in the 1940s," *Journal of Economic History* 66, no. 3 (September 2006): 737–777.

THE GENDER PAY GAP IN THE NEWS

We are bombarded in the press with a multitude of figures regarding how much women earn relative to men. Compounding this information overload are often inaccurate or misleading interpretations of the data presented. Here we provide a source and context for two figures that have received particular media attention.

The most common figure cited is based on the median earnings of year-round, full-time workers. It is readily available from the Census Bureau web site and, as shown in Table 5-6, was 78 percent in 2007. While this figure *does* pertain to men and women who all work full-time and year-round, it is important to bear in mind that they may well differ, on average, in their age, experience, educational attainment, seniority, occupation, industry, and other characteristics related to earnings. This is frequently misunderstood, and the lower earnings of women for this broad group are sometimes interpreted as an indicator of discrimination. As we shall see in more detail in Chapter 7, it is necessary to control for measured qualifications in assessing the extent of discrimination, and even then it may be difficult to reach definitive conclusions.

Another figure that has received substantial media attention, for instance by columnist George Will and in a book entitled *Women's Figures* by Diana Furchtgott-Roth and Christine Stolba, is the estimate of a 98 percent female–male earnings ratio for women and men ages 27 to 33 who have never had a child.* Should we take this statistic to mean that discrimination has been virtually eliminated, as these authors do? This conclusion does not appear to be warranted. First, it represents women's and men's earnings at the start of their careers. Hence, it does not reflect pay differences that may arise later as a result of gender differences in promotions and advancement. As we saw in Table 5-7, the gender earnings ratio tends to decrease with age. Second, the 98 percent statistic compares men and women who do not have children. As we shall see in Chapters 6 and 10, research indicates that mothers incur a wage penalty compared to other women, even when they have the same measured qualifications such as education and experience. No such wage penalty is found for fathers; indeed, researchers generally find a wage premium for them, meaning that they earn more than men with similar qualifications. Thus, family status has very different labor market implications for women and men, even with the same human capital. While it is not necessarily the case that these gender differences in the impact of family status on wages are due to discrimination, their magnitude and sources are worthy of serious consideration.

Identifying the sources of the gender pay gap, and particularly whether or not labor market discrimination plays a role, is a complex undertaking and involves more than an inspection of one or two statistics, including either or both of the two discussed above. First, it is important to be clear about what economists mean by labor market discrimination. **Labor market discrimination** exists when employers treat men and women differently, even when there are no productivity differences between them. One of the challenges of measuring the extent of labor market discrimination is that differential treatment of men and women, or the anticipation of it, may adversely influence a woman's decisions, including her decisions about the level and type of qualifications to acquire, as well as her subsequent labor market choices. Our review of the evidence in Chapter 7 suggests that discrimination against women in the labor market does exist and, while it may not be as severe as in the past, it continues to represent more than an occasional anomaly.

*George Will, "Lies, Damned Lies," *Newsweek*, March 29, 1999, p. 84; Diana Furchtgott-Roth and Christine Stolba, *Women's Figures: An Illustrated Guide to the Economic Progress of Women in America* (Washington DC: AEI Press: 1999); and June O'Neill, "The Shrinking Pay Gap," *Wall Street Journal*, October 7, 1994.

be that a large and growing proportion of Hispanics are recent immigrants to the United States. Hence their earnings are reduced because they tend to be relatively young, may not speak English well, and face other difficulties in adjusting to their new environment. Of course discrimination may also play a role in Hispanic–white earnings differences, just as it may for black–white differences.

Conclusion

In this chapter, we presented data on gender differentials in occupations and earnings for women overall, as well as for various subgroups. Although gender differences in occupations and earnings remain substantial, both have declined significantly. Reductions in occupational segregation by gender actually date back to the 1960s, though more rapid progress occurred in subsequent decades. The overall gender earnings gap for full-time workers started to narrow in the late 1970s or early 1980s. The trend toward earnings convergence was particularly dramatic during the 1980s, slowed in the 1990s, but picked up again in the 2000s. The next two chapters thoroughly investigate the possible explanations for the gender differences described here, while Chapter 8 focuses in part on explaining the reasons for the long-term convergence in the gender earnings gap.

Questions for Review and Discussion

1. Why have women been increasingly eager to move into men's occupations? Why do you think men generally show less enthusiasm about moving into women's occupations?

2. Consider the following hypothetical information about the occupational distribution in Country Y. Assume that 100 employed men and 100 employed women work in either Occupation A or Occupation B.

	Employed Women (%)	Employed Men (%)
Occupation A	70	20
Occupation B	30	80
Total	100	100

   a. Calculate the index of occupational segregation by sex using the formula given in footnote 6, Chapter 5.
   b. Explain exactly what the number you obtained in (a) means in light of the verbal definition of the segregation index.

3. Calculate the segregation index for 2007 for the 10 major occupational categories shown in Table 5-1. Why is the figure you obtain lower than the values that are obtained when a large set of detailed occupations are considered as in Table 5-5?

4. Explain why the female–male earnings ratio is likely to be higher for full-time, year-round workers than for all workers.

INTERNET-BASED DATA EXERCISE

Note: In doing this exercise, students should be aware that the precise names of documents and their location within a web site may change over time.

The U.S. Census Bureau is the primary source of government data on many topics included in this text including income, education, health insurance, and poverty.

Visit the home page of the U.S. Census Bureau at http://www.census.gov

Click on "Income". On the income page, look for the most recent document titled "Income, Poverty, and Health Insurance Coverage" (or a similar title). Find "Table 1" which provides income and earnings summary measures by selected characteristics.

(a) What are the most recent estimates of median earnings for full-time, year-round women and men workers? Using these data, compute the female–male earnings ratio.

(b) How does the current female–male earnings ratio compare to figures in Table 5-6?

Key Terms

occupational
   segregation *134*

index of segregation *135*
gender earnings ratio *141*

labor market
   discrimination *148*

CHAPTER 6

Differences in Occupations and Earnings: The Human Capital Model

Chapter Highlights

- What Is Human Capital?
- Gender Differences in Educational Attainment
- The Educational Investment Decision
- Gender Differences in Educational Investment Decisions
- Explaining Women's Rising Educational Attainment
- On-the-Job Training
- Gender Differences in Labor Market Experience

- The On-the-Job Training Investment Decision
- Gender Differences in Training Investment Decisions
- Occupations and Earnings
- Other Supply-Side Factors
- The Human Capital Explanation: An Assessment

In this chapter, we present supply-side explanations for the gender differences in occupations and earnings described in Chapter 5. We first summarize the arguments of scholars who emphasize this point of view, beginning with a consideration of the determinants of the decision to invest in formal education and on-the-job training and an analysis of the sources of gender differences in these decisions within the human capital framework. Next we apply these concepts to understanding gender differences in occupations and earnings. We then consider other supply-side factors that may produce gender differences in economic outcomes. We conclude by presenting a brief evaluation of the contributions of the human capital approach to understanding the sources of the gender pay gap. We return to this question in Chapter 7 in the context of our consideration of labor market discrimination. The possibility of labor market discrimination provides an alternative explanation for gender differences in occupations and earnings. The human capital and discrimination explanations are not mutually exclusive and it is our view that both provide valuable insights into the sources of male–female differences in occupations and earnings.

Supply-side explanations focus on the observation that men and women may come to the labor market with different tastes and with different qualifications, such as education, formal training, or experience. Gender differences in tastes might mean, for example, that one group or the other shows greater tolerance for an unpleasant, unhealthy, or dangerous work environment, for longer work hours or inflexible work schedules, for physical strain, or for repetitive tasks, and is more willing to accept any or all of these working conditions in return for higher wages. An example of a gender difference in qualifications would be a woman with a college degree in English and a man with a college degree in engineering. Or, as another example, a woman might move in and out of the labor force as her family situation changes, whereas a man's attachment might be more continuous.

To the extent that such differences in men's and women's tastes and qualifications exist, they could cause women to earn less and to be concentrated in different occupations. Little is known about tastes and their effects on occupational choices and rewards; however, a great deal of research has looked at job-related qualifications. Hence, we too shall concentrate on qualifications here.

Before considering the effects of gender differences in qualifications on earnings and occupations, one issue that arises is whether such differences in qualifications should be viewed as the result of the voluntary choices men and women make or as the outcome of what is termed *prelabor market* or **societal discrimination**. Societal discrimination denotes the multitude of social influences that cause women to make decisions that adversely influence their status in the labor market. Because we are all products of our environments to a greater or lesser extent, it is often difficult to draw the line between voluntary choice and this type of discrimination.

This distinction may in part reflect disciplinary boundaries. Economics tends to view individual decisions as determined by economic incentives and individual preferences (or tastes). It generally does not analyze the formation of preferences, and choices are generally viewed as being at least to some extent voluntary. In contrast, sociologists and social psychologists are more apt to examine the role of socialization and social-structural factors in producing what economists classify as individual preferences.[1] Thus, within the context of sociology or social psychology, individual choices are more likely to be seen as stemming from social conditioning or constraints rather than as voluntary.

The tendency to emphasize the role of choice versus societal discrimination may also reflect an implicit value judgment. Those who are reasonably content with the status quo of gender differences in economic outcomes tend to speak mainly of voluntary choices, whereas those who decry gender inequality in pay and occupations are inclined to focus on societal discrimination.

We tend toward the view that at least some of the gender differences in qualifications that currently exist stem from undesirable societal discrimination, although we acknowledge that, particularly in the past and to a lesser extent today, many individuals regarded this type of gender differentiation as perfectly appropriate. The important point is that even if societal discrimination is a problem, it is essentially different from **labor market discrimination** (discussed in Chapter 7), and a different set of policies is required to deal with it.

A second issue that deserves attention is that distinguishing between supply- and demand-side factors is not as easy as it appears at first. Labor market discrimination can affect women's economic status *indirectly* by reducing their incentives to invest in themselves and to acquire particular job qualifications. Thus, gender differences in productivity-related characteristics may reflect not only the voluntary choices of men and women and the impact of societal discrimination but also the indirect effects of labor market discrimination. This point will also be developed further in Chapter 7.

---

[1] Sociologists might question the appropriateness of the term *discrimination* in the context of gender socialization. We use it here only to the extent that the socialization process adversely affects the labor market success of young women.

WHAT IS HUMAN CAPITAL?

Within the economics literature, the human capital model provides the major supply-side explanation for gender differentials in economic outcomes. Most of us are familiar with the notion of investments in physical capital. For example, businesspeople expend resources today to build new plants or to purchase new machinery. This augments their firms' productive capabilities and increases output in the future. They make such decisions based upon a comparison of the expected costs and benefits of these investments. Important early work by Nobel laureates Theodore Schultz and Gary Becker, and by Jacob Mincer, pointed out that individuals and their families make analogous decisions regarding **human capital** investments.[2] In this case, resources are invested in an individual today in order to increase his or her productivity and earnings in the future. Examples of human capital investments include investments in formal education, on-the-job training, job search, and geographic migration.

Although the analogy between physical and human capital is compelling, some differences between the two are important. Chiefly, an individual's human capital investment decisions will be influenced to a greater extent by nonpecuniary (nonmonetary) considerations than is typically the case for physical capital investment decisions. Some people enjoy going to school; others do not. Some find indoor, white-collar work attractive; others would prefer to do manual work in the fresh air. Another important difference is that, in the absence of government intervention, it is generally more difficult to borrow to finance human capital investments than to finance physical ones. These differences between physical and human capital illustrate the general point that although labor markets are similar to other markets, they are not identical to them—in large part because labor services cannot be separated from the individuals who provide them. This distinction does not invalidate the use of economic analysis in the study of labor markets, but it does require us to be aware of the significant differences between labor markets and other markets.

We first focus upon the pecuniary aspects of the human capital investment decision and then consider how nonpecuniary factors might influence the analysis. We emphasize two major kinds of human capital investments: formal schooling and on-the-job training. According to the pioneering work of Jacob Mincer and Solomon Polachek, and others that followed, gender differences in these areas—in both the amount and the type of investments made—can produce substantial differences in the pay and occupations of men and women in the labor market.[3]

GENDER DIFFERENCES IN EDUCATIONAL ATTAINMENT

Gender differences in educational attainment in the United States are not large. They are, for example, considerably smaller than educational differences between minorities and whites in the United States and smaller than gender differences in educational attainment in many parts of the developing world. However, there are some notable differences and some significant changes over time. These are shown in Table 6-1, which provides figures on the educational attainment of the population aged 25 to 64 in 1970 and 2007.

---

[2] See, for example, Theodore W. Schultz, "Investment in Human Capital," *American Economic Review* 51, no. 1 (March 1960): 1–17; Gary S. Becker, *Human Capital: A Theoretical and Empirical Analysis, with Special Reference to Education*, 3rd ed. (Chicago: University of Chicago Press, 1993); and Jacob Mincer, "On-the-Job Training: Costs, Returns and Some Implications," *Journal of Political Economy* 70, no. 5, pt. 2 (October 1962): 50–79.

[3] Jacob Mincer and Solomon W. Polachek, "Family Investments in Human Capital: Earnings of Women," *Journal of Political Economy* 82, no. 2, pt. 2 (March/April 1974): 76–108; and Solomon W. Polachek, "Occupational Self-Selection: A Human Capital Approach to Sex Differences in Occupational Structure," *Review of Economics and Statistics* 63, no. 1 (February 1981): 60–69.

TABLE 6-1   **Educational Attainment of the Population by Gender: 1970 and 2007 (Ages 25–64)**

	1970		2007	
	Males (%)	Females (%)	Males (%)	Females (%)
Less than 4 years of high school	39.3	38.2	11.7	9.6
4 years of high school only	33.5	42.3	33.1	30.7
Some college	11.9	10.5	24.8	28.4
4 or more years of college	15.3	9.0	30.5	31.3
Total	100.0	100.0	100.0	100.0

Notes: There have been some changes in the coding of education in the Current Population Survey (CPS) data so that the 1970 and 2007 data are not strictly comparable. In making the two series as compatible as possible, we follow the suggestions of David A. Jaeger, "Reconciling the Old and New Census Bureau Education Questions: Recommendations for Researchers," *Journal of Business and Economic Statistics* 15, no. 3 (July 1997): 300–09. In particular, as recommended by Jaeger, both individuals with a high school degree and those with 12 years of high school but no degree are coded as having 4 years of high school only.

Source: Tabulated from the 1970 and 2007 microdata files of the March CPS.

First, we turn to patterns of educational attainment for women and men at the lower end of the educational distribution—high school dropouts and those who have completed only high school. The table indicates rising educational attainment for both men and women in terms of a falling share of the population that has not graduated from high school. In both 1970 and 2007, a somewhat higher proportion of men than women were high school dropouts—but these gender differences are small. However, it is important to bear in mind that data like those in Table 6-1 understate the gender difference in the share of high school dropouts because they do not include incarcerated individuals, who tend to be less educated and are overwhelmingly male. This understatement is larger in 2007 than in earlier years due to rising incarceration rates.[4] Further, the category "4 years of high school only" increasingly includes individuals who earned GED certificates, many of whom earned this certificate while in prison. (Indivduals who have been incarcerated are included in the table once they are released.) Evidence suggests that the GED certificate is worth less than a high school diploma in the labor market,[5] and so grouping certificate earners with high school graduates (increasingly) overstates men's educational qualifications at the lower end of the educational distribution. A further troubling recent trend, which is not adequately reflected in Table 6-1 due to the broad age range and the data problems mentioned earlier, is the stagnation in overall high school graduation rates of young people since 1970 (when high school graduation is comparably measured in each year). In fact, the high school graduation rate actually declined for males, halting what had been a steady upward trend in secondary education in the United States.[6]

---

[4] The Current Population Survey, the source of these data, surveys the civilian, noninstitutional population, thus excluding incarcerated persons.

[5] James J. Heckman and Paul A. LaFontaine, "The American High School Graduation Rate: Trends and Levels," NBER Working Paper No. 13670 (December 2007); and James J. Heckman and Paul LaFontaine, "Bias Corrected Estimates of GED Returns," *Journal of Labor Economics* 24, no. 3 (July 2006): 661–700.

[6] See Heckman and LaFontaine, "The American High School Graduation Rate," for this recent trend. The earlier strong growth in high-school graduation and its economic importance is documented in Claudia Goldin and Lawrence F. Katz, *The Race Between Education and Technology* (Cambridge, MA: Harvard University Press, 2008).

Table 6-1 also points to a large increase in college education for both men and women. Particularly notable is that male–female differences in college attendance have undergone dramatic changes among younger cohorts, changes that are becoming increasingly evident in the statistics for the full population shown in the table. Traditionally, men were considerably more likely than women to get a college education or higher degree.[7] For example, in the 1960s and early 1970s, women received only 40 percent of bachelor's degrees.[8] Thus, it is not surprising that the data for the full population in Table 6-1 show that, in 1970, men were 1.7 times more likely than women to have completed a college education or more. However, female college attendance had been increasing at a faster pace than male college attendance for quite some time, and the pace of change picked up in the late 1960s. By 1980, women caught up to men, and, in subsequent years, they surpassed them. Young women are now substantially *more* likely to graduate college than young men. And, by 2007, as shown in Table 6-1, for the full population (aged 25 to 64), the proportion of women who had completed a college education or more was slightly higher than the proportion of men.

Table 6-2 next provides a more detailed breakdown of educational attainment for the population aged 25 to 64 by race and Hispanic origin. For each of the groups shown, with the exception of Asians, women were less likely to be high school dropouts than men. Gender differences in the share of high school dropouts were generally small, but they were more substantial for Hispanics. We again note that gender differences at this end of the educational distribution are likely understated in the data. There were also differences across groups in college completion. Among non-Hispanic whites, men and women were nearly equally likely to complete college, whereas among Asians, men showed a clear edge in college completion. In contrast, among blacks and, particularly, among Hispanics, women were more likely to be college graduates.

Noticeable differences are also evident in educational attainment across minority groups. Blacks and Hispanics had lower educational attainment than non-Hispanic whites: They were less likely to have completed high school and less likely to have graduated from college. The differences between blacks and non-Hispanic whites were considerably smaller than the differences between Hispanics and non-Hispanic whites, reflecting a substantial increase in the relative educational attainment of the black population since the 1960s. The large influx of immigrants with low levels of education explains some of the sizable Hispanic–white difference in educational attainment; however, the numbers also reflect considerably higher high school dropout rates even for native-born Hispanic students.[9] Data on high school graduation rates again suggest some troubling trends, with little convergence for blacks and Hispanics relative to non-Hispanic whites since 1970, when high school graduation is measured comparably.[10] In contrast to other minorities, Asians had *higher* educational attainment than non-Hispanic whites, with an especially high proportion graduating college among both men and women.

Table 6-3 shows the trends in higher education in greater detail and highlights the rising educational attainment of women. During the 1960s and early 1970s, women received just two out of five bachelor's degrees. Table 6-3 indicates that this is about the

---

[7] While we call this the traditional pattern, early in the twentieth century, the ratio of male to female undergraduates in the United States was closer to parity than it would be in mid-century. See Claudia Goldin, Lawrence F. Katz, and Ilyana Kuziemko, "The Homecoming of American College Women: The Reversal of the College Gender Gap," *Journal of Economic Perspectives* 20, no. 4 (Fall 2006): 133–56. However, men always received a majority of bachelor's degrees.

[8] Figures on degrees awarded are presented in Table 6.3.

[9] Heckman and LaFontaine, "The American High School Graduation Rate"; and George J. Borjas, "Assimilation and Changes in Cohort Quality Revisited: What Happened to Immigrant Earnings in the 1980s?" *Journal of Labor Economics* 13, no. 2 (April 1995): 201–45.

[10] Heckman and LaFontaine, "The American High School Graduation Rate."

TABLE 6-2   Educational Attainment of the Population by Gender, Race, and Hispanic Origin, 2007 (Ages 25–64)

	Non-Hispanic Whites		Blacks		Hispanics		Asians	
	Males (%)	Females (%)	Males (%)	Females (%)	Males (%)	Females (%)	Males (%)	Females (%)
Less than 4 years of high school	6.5	5.2	11.8	11.0	37.2	31.9	7.0	8.9
4 years of high school only	32.6	29.9	41.7	37.1	32.5	31.7	21.8	20.8
Some college	26.3	29.8	27.2	31.4	18.4	21.8	15.2	17.1
4 or more years of college	34.6	35.1	19.4	20.6	11.8	14.5	56.1	53.2
Total	100.0	100.0	100.0	100.0	100.0	100.0	100.0	100.0

Notes: Whites are defined as white only; blacks are defined as black only as well as black in combination with another race; Asians are defined as Asian only as well as Asian in combination with another non-black race. Hispanics may be of any race. As in Table 6.1, the category of 4 years of high school only includes those with a high school degree as well as those with 12 years of high school but no degree.

Source: Tabulated from the 2007 microdata file of the March Current Population Survey (CPS).

TABLE 6-3   Degrees Awarded to Women by Level, 1929–30 to 2005–2006 (Selected Years)

Years	Associate (%)	Bachelor's (%)	Master's (%)	Ph.D. (%)	First professional (%)
1929–1930	n.a.	39.9[a]	40.4	15.4	n.a.
1960–1961	n.a.	38.5	31.7	10.5	2.7
1970–1971	42.9	43.4	40.1	14.3	6.3
1980–1981	54.7	49.8	50.3	31.1	26.6
1990–1991	58.8	53.9	53.6	37.0	39.1
2000–2001	60.0	57.3	58.5	44.9	46.2
2005–2006	62.1	57.5	60.0	48.9	49.8

[a]Includes first professional degrees.
n.a., not available.

Source: U.S. Department of Education, National Center for Education Statistics, *Digest of Education Statistics, 2007*, Table 258, "Degrees Conferred by Degree-Granting Institutions, by Level of Degree and Sex of Student: Selected years, 1869–70 through 2016–17," from http://nces.ed.gov/programs/digest/.

same as their share in 1930. By 1980, women were receiving about half of bachelor's degrees. And, by 2007, fully 58 percent of bachelor's degrees were awarded to women, as were 60 percent of master's degrees. Similarly, although women received 43 percent of associate degrees in the early 1970s, they received a majority of such degrees by the 1980s and 62 percent by 2007. Women were awarded nearly half of doctorate (Ph.D.) and first professional degrees in 2007, up from 11 percent of Ph.D.s and just 3 percent of first professional degrees in 1961. First professional degrees are those awarded in postcollege professional training programs, including medicine, law, dentistry, pharmacy, veterinary medicine, and theology.[11]

The figures on educational attainment, however, reveal only part of the story of gender differences in formal schooling. Beginning in high school, male and female students tended to differ in the types of courses taken and fields of specialization. This difference was especially true in the past and remains the case to some extent even today, especially at the college level.

At the secondary level, in the past, girls did achieve higher class rank than boys and did better than boys in reading, but they took fewer courses in mathematics and natural sciences and lagged substantially behind boys in math achievement test scores.[12] In recent years, girls not only continue to have higher grade point averages, but they have widened their lead in reading, and, most notably, narrowed the test score gap with boys in math. A recent government report found that "overall, females' high school academic programs in mathematics and science are at least as challenging as those taken by males."[13] Gender differences in high school math coursework are potentially important. Although differences in the number of courses taken in math and science have been found to have little effect on gender differences in pay for high school graduates, taking more high school math increases the wages of female college graduates, as well as their likelihood of entering technical and nontraditional fields.[14]

Differences between men and women in fields of specialization at the college level are more substantial and persistent, as illustrated in Table 6-4. Here too, however, the gender difference has narrowed considerably since the mid-1960s. The trend toward gender integration, primarily the result of women entering traditionally male fields, was most rapid through the mid-1980s and has slowed since then.[15] Similarly, the considerable increase in the percentage of women receiving first professional degrees, which we saw in Table 6-3, reflects large gains in their representation among students in traditionally male fields such as medicine, law, and business (a specific breakdown is shown in Table 6-5). Nonetheless, women remain extremely underrepresented in some college fields relative to their proportion of bachelor's degrees (58 percent in 2006). They comprised only one in five graduates in computer and information sciences and engineering and were also underrepresented in other areas, including economics (31 percent of majors), physical sciences and science technologies (42 percent of majors), and mathematics (45 percent of majors). At the same time they comprised the vast majority—about 80 percent or more—of graduates in education, health and home economics, and were about 70 percent or more of graduates in English and English literature, foreign languages, psychology and sociology.

In summary, traditionally, girls were somewhat more likely than boys to complete high school, but higher proportions of men than women completed four or more years of

---

[11] Master's degrees in business are also generally thought of as first professional degrees; however, the Department of Education, which provides the data for Table 6-3, includes them with master's degrees. In Table 6-5, we include master's degrees in business with first professional degrees.

[12] Goldin, Katz, and Kuziemko, "The Homecoming of American College Women."

[13] Catherine E. Freeman, "Trends in Educational Equity of Girls and Women," National Center for Educational Statistics (NCES) Working Paper No. 2005-016 (November 2004), p. 7. See also Goldin, Katz, and Kuziemko, "The Homecoming of American College Women"; and Christine Corbett, Catherine Hill, and Andresse St. Rose, *Where the Girls Are: The Facts About Gender Equity in Education* (Washington, DC: AAUW Educational Foundation, May 2008). For an analysis of gender differences in mathematics, see Sheila Tobias, *Overcoming Math Anxiety* (New York: W.W. Norton, 1993), chap. 3.

[14] See Charles Brown and Mary Corcoran, "Sex-Based Differences in School Content and the Male/Female Wage Gap," *Journal of Labor Economics* 15, no. 3, pt. 1 (July 1997): 431–65; and Phillip B. Levine and David J. Zimmerman, "The Benefit of Additional High-School Math and Science Classes of Young Men and Women," *Journal of Business and Economic Statistics* 13, no. 2 (April 1995): 137–49.

[15] Paula England and Su Li, "Desegregation Stalled: The Changing Gender Composition of College Majors, 1971–2002," *Gender and Society* 20, no. 5 (October 2006): 657–77; and Jerry A. Jacobs, "Gender and Academic Specialties: Trends Among Recipients of College Degrees in the 1980s," *Sociology of Education* 68, no. 2 (April 1995): 81–98.

TABLE 6-4   Bachelor's Degrees Awarded to Women by Field, 1965–1966, and 2005–2006 (Selected Fields)

Discipline	1965–1966 (%)	2005–2006 (%)
Agriculture and natural resources	2.7	47.7
Architecture and related services	4.0	43.1
Biological sciences/life sciences	28.2	61.5
Business management, administrative sciences, and marketing	8.5	49.8
Computer and information sciences	13.0[a]	20.6
Education	75.3	79.1
Engineering	0.4	19.4
English and English literature	66.2	68.6
Foreign languages	70.7	69.9
Health	76.9	86.0
Home economics	97.5	95.1
Mathematics	33.3	45.1
Physical sciences and science technologies	13.6	41.8
Psychology	41.0	77.5
Social sciences	35.0	52.2
Economics	9.8	31.1
History	34.6	41.4
Sociology	59.6	70.1

[a]Data are for 1969, the earliest year available.

Source: U.S. Department of Health, Education and Welfare, Office of Education, *Earned Degrees Conferred: 1965-66*; U.S. Department of Education, National Center for Education Statistics, *Digest of Education Statistics, 2007*, Tables 265 and 275, from http://nces.ed.gov/programs/digest/d07/tables/dt07_265.asp and http://nces.ed.gov/programs/digest/d07/tables/dt07_275.asp.

TABLE 6-5   First Professional Degrees Awarded to Women by Field, 1966, 1981 and 2006 (Selected Fields)

Field	1966 (%)	1981 (%)	2006 (%)
Business[a]	3.2[b]	23.8	42.9
Dentistry	1.1	14.4	44.5
Medicine	6.7	24.7	48.9
Pharmacy	16.4	42.6	67.4
Veterinary medicine	8.0[c]	35.2	77.4
Law	3.8	32.4	48.0
Theology	4.1	14.0	33.6

[a]Master's degree in business.
[b]Data are for 1964–1965.
[c]Data are for 1967–1968.

Source: U.S. Department of Health, Education and Welfare, Office of Education, *Earned Degrees Conferred: 1965–66*; U.S. Department of Education, National Center for Educational Statistics, *Digest of Education Statistics*, 1983 and 2007, from http://nces.ed.gov/programs/digest/.

college. Further, girls took fewer math and science courses than boys in high school, and college men and women differed greatly in their fields of study. Much has changed. Girls do retain an edge in high school completion, but the other gender differences we have enumerated have been narrowed, eliminated, or even reversed in recent years. The high school academic programs of girls and boys in math and science now tend to be equally challenging; young women are actually more likely to get a college degree than young men; and while gender differences in fields of study at the college level persist, they are much smaller than they were in the past. Despite these positive developments, the education gap between women and men continues to affect labor market outcomes. For more recent cohorts, the gender differences in fields of study that remain are of concern because they negatively affect women's earnings and occupational attainment. Moreover, these women are just one segment of the female labor force. The remainder of women workers are from earlier cohorts who completed their education at a time when the gender difference in college attendance was considerably larger (and favored men) and when there were much greater gender differences in fields of study.

We now turn to the explanation provided by the human capital model for the historic tendency of men and women to acquire different amounts of education and to specialize in different fields. We then consider some of the other factors that may account for these differences. We follow this with an examination of the reasons why women caught up to and then actually surpassed men in college attendance in more recent cohorts.

THE EDUCATIONAL INVESTMENT DECISION

We begin by considering an individual's decision whether to invest in formal education, as illustrated in Figure 6-1. Here we consider Daniel's choice between going to college and ending his formal education with high school. Initially, we focus solely upon the pecuniary costs and benefits of investing in education, although later we consider nonpecuniary costs and benefits as well. The investment decision entails a comparison between the expected **experience-earnings profiles** (the annual earnings at each level of labor market experience) associated with each type of schooling.

In this case, Daniel expects his profile to be DF if he enters the labor market after completing high school. Alternatively, if he goes on to college, he will incur out-of-pocket expenses on tuition and books of OA dollars per year (negative "earnings") for the four-year period. (He does not anticipate taking a job while he goes to school.) Upon graduation, he expects to earn OE' dollars. The investment in a college education is believed to increase his productivity, and hence, his earnings above what he could have earned if he entered the labor force directly after high school (OD). His experience-earnings profile, if he goes to college, is $ABCEG$.

As indicated in Figure 6-1, the earnings of both high school and college graduates are expected to increase with labor market experience over much of the individual's work life. Human capital theory attributes this increase to the productivity-enhancing effects of on-the-job training, which we discuss later in this chapter. Note that Figure 6-1 shows the college graduate's profile as rising more steeply than the high school graduate's. As we shall see later, this has indeed been found to be the case empirically and suggests that college graduates acquire more training informally on the job as well as formally in school.

Now let us consider how Daniel can use the information in Figure 6-1 to make his investment decision. To do so he considers both the incremental costs and the incremental benefits associated with graduating from college. He must take into account two types of costs of schooling. **Direct costs** are expenditures on items such as tuition, fees, and books. Less obvious, but no less important than direct costs, are the earnings forgone during the time an individual is in school. These **indirect costs** correspond to the opportunity costs of time spent in schooling. We assumed that Daniel does not work for pay while attending college, but even if he did, his forgone earnings are still likely to be

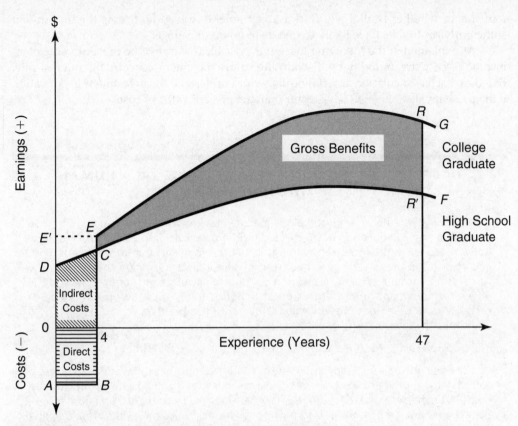

FIGURE 6-1 The Educational Investment Decision

substantial—college students are seldom employed for as many hours or for as high a wage as workers not enrolled in school. The full costs of a college education are equal to the sum of the direct and indirect costs, or area *ABCD*.

The gross benefits of a college education are equal to the excess of the expected earnings of a college graduate over those of a high school graduate over the individual's work life. Other things being equal, the size of these benefits depends on the length of the expected work life. If Daniel expects to work for 43 years after college until retirement at age 65, his gross benefits are equal to the shaded area *CERR′*.

For Daniel to decide in favor of a college education (on an economic basis), the *gross benefits* of this investment must exceed the costs; that is, the *net benefits* must be positive. Further, gross benefits must exceed costs by an amount sufficient to give him an adequate return on his investment. Individuals may differ on the rate of return required to induce them to undertake this investment, but all are likely to require a positive rate of return.

For one thing, instead of investing resources in his human capital, Daniel could have put his money into a savings account or invested it in other assets. Those alternatives provide a positive rate of return, and thus, his human capital investment must also do so in order to be competitive. More fundamentally, Daniel, like most people, prefers income (and the opportunity to spend it) now to income (and the opportunity to spend it) later. To induce him to delay his gratification and receive his income later rather than sooner, the labor market has to offer him (and others like him) an inducement in the form of a positive rate of return. In Daniel's case, the investment does appear profitable, although we cannot tell simply by looking at the diagram because even though the benefit area appears to exceed the cost area, we do not know what the resulting rate of return is or whether Daniel will find it acceptable. If indeed he deems the investment sufficiently profitable, he is likely to decide to go on to college.

As explained in the following inset, it is possible to express the **present value** of an income or cost stream today by discounting future income or costs by the interest rate. Based on such a calculation, an individual would undertake the investment in education if the present value of benefits is greater than the present value of costs.

CALCULATING THE NET PRESENT VALUE OF A HUMAN CAPITAL INVESTMENT

To determine whether to undertake a human capital investment, such as acquiring an additional year of education or specialized training, we calculate the benefits (*B*), typically measured as the increased earnings in the coming years due to the investment, and costs (*C*) *in present value* terms. Present value (*PV*) is a method that tells us the value of an earnings stream received in the future calculated in today's dollars. The difference between the present value of benefits, *PV(B)*, and the present value of costs, *PV(C)*, is called **net present value** (NPV). If NPV is positive, an individual would undertake the investment.

Decision rule: If $PV(B) - PV(C) > 0$, then undertake the investment.

The key principle to keep in mind is that $1 in your pocket today is worth more to you than the promise of $1 tomorrow. The reason is that if you have $1 today, you can put it in the bank (or in stocks, bonds, or other financial instruments) and earn a positive return on it. So any promise to pay money in the future must also offer a similar return. And, again, more fundamentally, this is because people value money and the opportunity to spend it now more highly than waiting to receive money in the future. (This is why the interest rate is sometimes called the *reward to waiting*.)

Present value is the reverse of the concept of future value, which may be more familiar. Let us first recall how to calculate future value, where we have $1 today and want to know its value next year:

$$\text{Future value} = (FV_t) = PV_t(1 + r)^t$$

where *r* is the market interest rate (or the rate of return on the investment), *FV* is the future value, *PV* is the present value, and *t* is the time period being considered (1 = next year, 2 = two years from now, etc.).

If we assume we have $1 today (our *PV* = $1), *r* = .05, and *t* = 1 (next year), then *FV* = $1.05. Or, if we want to know the value of $1 in two years, the formula tells us the answer is $1.10.

Now consider the case in which we can earn $1 next year and want to know its value *today*. To determine this, all we need to do is rewrite the earlier equation as:

$$\text{Present value } (PV_t) = \frac{FV_t}{(1 + r)^t}$$

If we assume we will receive $1 next year (*FV* is $1), *r* = .05, and *t* = 1 (next year), then the present value of $1 received next year is $.95 today. If we want to know the value of $1 received two years from now, then we would use the same formula as above, where *t* = 2 (or $.91). Note that when used to express a future value in present value terms, the interest rate (*r*) is referred to as the **discount rate**.

Let us look at an example to better understand how to calculate the net present value of an educational investment. Suppose Denise, age 50, is considering whether to obtain one year of specialized training. To decide whether she should make this investment, she needs to know about the costs (both indirect and direct), the benefits (the increase in her future earnings due to this investment), how long she expects to work after the training (and hence reaps the benefits), and the discount rate. Her net present value calculation is:

$$NPV = -C + \frac{B_1}{1 + r} + \frac{B_2}{(1 + r)^2} + \frac{B_3}{(1 + r)^3} + \cdots + \frac{B_T}{(1 + r)^T}$$

where C = today's costs, B = benefits, r = discount rate, and T = end of work life.

Suppose Denise's direct costs for tuition, books, and supplies are $8,000, and her indirect costs, measured as the salary foregone during the one year of training, are $20,000. Thus her total costs (C), all assumed to be incurred during the current year, are $28,000. (Because the costs are all incurred in the current year, they are not discounted.) Once Denise receives the training, she will earn an additional $6,000 per year thereafter. Thus all the Bs in this equation are $6,000. Let us further suppose that Denise plans to work for 10 years after the training and then retire and that the discount rate is 5 percent.

Therefore Denise performs the following present value calculation:

$$NPV = -\$28{,}000 + \frac{\$6{,}000}{(1 + .05)^1} + \frac{\$6{,}000}{(1 + .05)^2} + \frac{\$6{,}000}{(1 + .05)^3} + \frac{\$6{,}000}{(1 + .05)^4}$$
$$+ \frac{\$6{,}000}{(1 + .05)^5} + \frac{\$6{,}000}{(1 + .05)^6} + \frac{\$6{,}000}{(1 + .05)^7} + \frac{\$6{,}000}{(1 + .05)^8}$$
$$+ \frac{\$6{,}000}{(1 + .05)^9} + \frac{\$6{,}000}{(1 + .05)^{10}} = \$18{,}330.41$$

Since Denise's *NPV* exceeds zero, it makes economic sense for Denise to invest in the training.

Alternatively, one can solve for the discount rate that exactly equates the present value of costs to the present value of benefits (most easily calculated using a spreadsheet program like Excel). If this rate, called the **internal rate of return**, represents an adequate rate of return for the individual (for Denise, the internal rate of return would have to equal or exceed 5 percent), then the individual will choose to make the educational investment.

A large literature in economics documents a positive private return to investments in education, and, interestingly, the evidence suggests a higher return for women than for men.[16] We consider this gender difference later in this chapter. Estimates of the average private rate of return to education also vary over time. As we shall see in Chapter 8, the return to education, particularly a college education, has risen over the past 30 years.

The relationship between education and earnings is illustrated in Figures 6-2a and b, which show age-earnings profiles of high school and college graduates for 1974 and 2007. In each year, the earnings of college graduates lie above those of high school graduates of the same sex. Moreover, the earnings profiles of college graduates of both

---

[16] Christopher Dougherty, "Why Are the Returns to Schooling Higher for Women than for Men?" *Journal of Human Resources* 40, no. 4 (Fall 2005): 969–88. There are a number of issues in estimating the returns to schooling; for insightful discussions, see David Card, "The Causal Effect of Education on Earnings," in *Handbook of Labor Economics*, Volume 3, edited by Orley Ashenfelter and David Card (Amsterdam: Elsevier, 1999), pp 1801–63; and James J. Heckman, Lance J. Lochner, and Petra E. Todd, "Earnings Functions and Rates of Return," *Journal of Human Capital* 2, no. 1 (Spring 2008): 1–31.

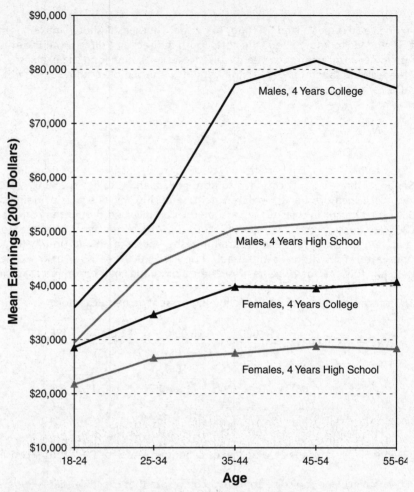

FIGURE 6-2A Age-Earnings Profiles of Year Round. Full-Time Workers by Gender and Education, 1974 (2007 Dollars)

sexes are steeper than those of their high school counterparts. Nonetheless, within each education group, women earn less than men and their earnings profiles tend to be flatter than men's. We consider these gender differences in greater detail later in this chapter.

Despite the general similarity of the profiles in each of the two years, there have been some changes that illustrate important labor market developments over the past 30 years. Earnings are shown in 2007 dollars in both years (i.e., they are adjusted for inflation), so levels of earnings and differences across groups are comparable in the two years. One striking difference between the mid-1970s and 2007 is that, for each sex, the earnings of college graduates rose relative to high school graduates, which means that the rate of return to education increased. This increase is part of a trend toward rising returns to skills like education and experience over this period.[17] As a consequence, college graduates experienced more favorable trends in real earnings than those with less education, with young, less-educated men particularly losing ground in real terms. These trends are considered in more detail in Chapter 8.

---

[17] Rising returns to education and other increases in the returns to skill over this period have been widely reported in the literature. See, for example, Lawrence F. Katz and David H. Autor, "Changes in the Wage Structure and Earnings Inequality," in *Handbook of Labor Economics*, pp. 1463–555. To be fully confident that the return to college has risen, we should also look at trends in out-of-pocket costs, but any changes there are likely to be dwarfed by the large shifts in earnings profiles.

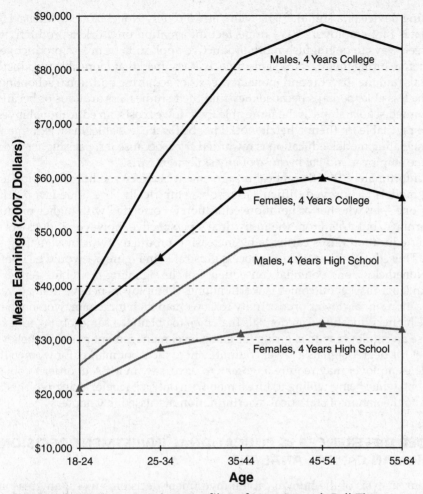

FIGURE 6-2B Age-Earnings Profiles of Year Round. Full-Time Workers by Gender and Education, 2007 (2007 Dollars)

Notes: The earnings profile of male high school graduates based on the 2007 data was somewhat out of line with previous years, so for both male and female high school graduates mean earnings have been calculated as the average of mean earnings in 2007 and mean earnings in 2006 (in 2007 dollars).

Source: U.S. Census Bureau Historical Income Tables—People, Tables P-32 and P-35 "Educational Attainment–Full-Time, Year-Round Workers 18 Years Old and Over by Mean Earnings, Age, and Sex," from http://www.census.gov/hhes/www/income/histinc/incpertoc.html.

EDUCATION AND PRODUCTIVITY

Human capital theory postulates that earnings rise with additional education because of the productivity-enhancing effects of education. Intuitively, it seems reasonable that education imparts a variety of skills and knowledge that could be useful on the job, ranging from specific skills, such as computer programming and accounting, to general skills, such as reasoning ability, writing skills, and proficiency in solving mathematical problems. Educational institutions may also teach certain behaviors that are valued on the job, such as punctuality, following instructions, and habits of predictability and dependability.

An alternative interpretation of the observed positive relationship between education and earnings that has been suggested is that education functions solely as a

screening device or a **signal**.[18] This view, advanced by Nobel laureate Michael Spence, postulates that employers have imperfect information on worker productivity and, thus, seek ways to distinguish more productive applicants from less productive applicants before hiring them. At the same time, it is assumed that more able (productive) individuals find the (psychic and monetary) costs of acquiring additional schooling lower than the less able, perhaps because they find their studies less arduous or because they are awarded scholarships. If the more able incur lower costs, an educational investment may be profitable for them when it would not be for the less able. In an extreme version of the signaling model, education is rewarded *solely* because it *signals* higher productivity to the employer and *not* because of any skills it imparts.

Unfortunately, this theoretical disagreement between the human capital and signaling models has proved difficult to resolve empirically. The issue is a particularly thorny one—*not* whether or not more education is correlated with higher productivity and earnings, but *why*. From the individual's perspective, however, it does not matter whether education raises earnings by increasing productivity or by signaling greater ability. Thus, the decision-making process illustrated in Figure 6-1 would be unaffected.

Nonetheless, one potential consequence of the signaling model for gender differences in labor market outcomes is worth noting. If employers believe that a given level of education signals lower productivity for a woman than for a man, women may have to have higher educational credentials than men to obtain the same job. So, for example, suppose an employer who is hiring for entry-level management positions believes that a bachelor's degree signals a lower commitment to the labor market for women than for men. The employer may require a woman to have, say, an MBA in order to obtain employment, while being willing to hire a man with only a bachelor's degree. This is quite similar to the notion of **statistical discrimination** discussed in Chapter 7.

GENDER DIFFERENCES IN EDUCATIONAL INVESTMENT DECISIONS: THE HUMAN CAPITAL ANALYSIS

Does our analysis of the human capital investment decision suggest any reasons why men and women might decide to acquire different amounts or types of formal education? According to the analysis we have presented, the major factors to consider are the expected costs and benefits of the investment. Thus, we will want to consider why men and women might differ in terms of costs or benefits. The definitions of costs and benefits may be extended to include nonpecuniary, as well as pecuniary, costs and benefits, and we do so later.

Expected Work Life

The major factor emphasized by human capital theorists as producing gender differences in human capital investments is that, given traditional gender roles in the family, many women anticipate shorter, more disrupted work lives than men. Such women reach the point sooner when additional investment is no longer worthwhile. Further, it will not pay for them to make the types of human capital investments that require sustained, high-level commitment to the labor force to make them profitable and that depreciate rapidly during periods of work interruptions.

The impact of these factors is illustrated in Figure 6-3, which reproduces the earnings profiles shown in Figure 6-1. Note that the horizontal axis now refers to potential experience or the total time elapsed since completing high school. We present it this way in order to represent periods of time out of the labor force on this diagram.

---

[18] See, Michael Spence, *Market Signalling* (Cambridge, MA: Harvard University Press, 1974).

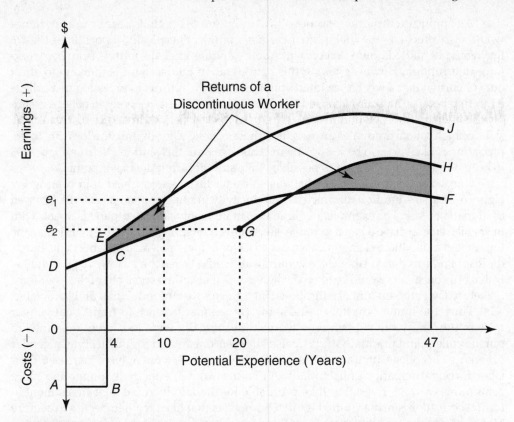

FIGURE 6-3 The Impact of Expected Work Life on the Educational Investment Decision

A career-oriented woman who anticipates working the same number of years as Daniel will find it equally profitable to invest in a college education, assuming she faces similar costs and has the opportunity to reap the same returns. However, a woman who expects to spend fewer years in the labor market will find her benefits correspondingly reduced.

Suppose Adele plans to be in the labor force for a time—6 years—after college and then to drop out for 10 years, say, for childrearing. If she, like Daniel, expects to retire at age 65, her expected work life is 33 years in comparison with his 43 years. Her shorter work life reduces the benefits of her human capital investment because she does not earn income during the time she spends out of the labor force. Further, it is generally believed that skills depreciate during time spent out of the labor force because they are not used. It is thus expected that, upon her return to the labor force after an interruption of 10 years, Adele's earnings of e_2 will be less in real terms than she was making when she left (e_1) and that she will be faced with profile *GH* rather than profile *EJ*. We show profile *GH* as approaching *EJ* over time, as Adele retools or becomes less rusty.[19] Nonetheless, her time out of the labor force costs her a reduction in earnings over the remainder of her working life. In this example, the benefits of the investment in a college education, the sum of the two shaded areas, may not be large enough to make it worthwhile.

---

[19] For evidence that earnings tend to "rebound" after workforce interruptions, see Jacob Mincer and Haim Ofek, "Interrupted Work Careers: Depreciation and Restoration of Human Capital," *Journal of Human Resources* 17, no. 1 (Winter 1982): 3–24; and Joyce P. Jacobsen and Laurence M. Levin, "Effects of Intermittent Labor Force Attachment on Women's Earnings," *Monthly Labor Review* 118, no. 9 (September 1995): 14–19.

A complication that we do not show in Figure 6-3 is that a break in experience would also affect *DF*, the high school earnings profile. Specifically, a portion of the *DF* line would be shifted down to represent Adele's options after she returns from her workforce interruption. However, taking this consideration into account is unlikely to affect our conclusion that a workforce interruption reduces the returns to investing in a college education because a major factor reducing the returns to the investment in college is simply the interruption itself and the loss of returns for that period. In addition, because the skills of high school graduates are less than those of college graduates, the loss due to depreciation is likely to also be less for them. Thus, we omit this shift in *DF* from Figure 6-3 to keep our diagram as simple as possible while still capturing the major points.

One factor that might somewhat offset the conclusions we arrived at in considering Figure 6-3 is that education may increase productivity in some nonmarket activities as well as in market work. For example, the time that more highly educated parents spend with their children may have a larger positive effect on their offspring's cognitive ability than the time of less well-educated parents. Were we to factor in these potential benefits in the home, the loss of returns due to labor force withdrawals would be reduced. However, it is unlikely that our conclusion would be altered: Higher anticipated time spent out of the labor force is likely to lower the amount of educational investments that the individual finds profitable.

Thus, the human capital model shows how an adherence to traditional gender roles in the family can explain why women traditionally were less likely than men to pursue college and graduate study. It also suggests one reason for the decline in gender differences in college attendance. As we saw in Chapter 4, women have increased their labor force participation substantially. As young women anticipate longer and more continuous working lives, it will be profitable for them to increase their investment in formal education. Furthermore, Figure 6-3 suggests that once women decide to acquire higher education, for whatever reason, their attachment to the labor force is reinforced because the opportunity cost of time spent out of the labor force is increased.

Although our application of the human capital model suggests a plausible explanation for the historical tendency of men to be more likely to pursue college and graduate study, it does not explain why in the past women were considerably *more* likely than men to complete high school. For example, in 1900, only two-thirds as many young men as young women graduated from high school. A likely explanation for this difference is that the opportunity cost of remaining in high school was lower for the young women than their male counterparts, because their potential labor market earnings were less. As job opportunities for young men who did not finished high school declined, so too did the gender differential in high school completion.

The human capital model also suggests a possible explanation for gender differences in fields of specialization, focusing on expectations of workforce disruptions. In some fields, such as science and engineering, technological change progresses rapidly. A woman returning from a labor force interruption will have to contend not only with her depreciation of skills over the interim but also with the advancement of the field during her absence. On the other hand, in fields such as teaching history or English, the pace of change is slower. A woman returning from a workforce interruption is likely to find that her earnings fall less steeply. Women anticipating traditional gender roles are, therefore, expected to avoid fields where the rate of technological change is rapid and to concentrate in fields where the cost of workforce interruptions is lower.[20] Thus,

---

[20] Solomon W. Polachek, "Sex Differences in College Major," *Industrial and Labor Relations Review* 31, no. 4 (July 1978): 498–508; Arthur F. Blakemore and Stuart A. Low, "Sex Differences in Occupational Selection: The Case of College Majors," *Review of Economics and Statistics* 66, no. 1 (February 1984): 157–63; and Daniel E. Hecker, "Earnings of College Graduates, 1993," *Monthly Labor Review* 118, no. 12 (December 1995): 3–17. Another issue is that some fields more easily accommodate part-time work, thus facilitating reentry.

women's increasing labor force attachment may partially explain their increased representation in traditionally male fields of study.

Another factor that has been pointed to as contributing to gender differences in college majors is gender differences in mathematical ability, as indicated, for example, by women's lower scores on standardized tests such as the math SAT.[21] Although the gender gap in math scores remains substantial, it has declined as the high school coursework of young men and women has grown more similar. In 1977 when the gender difference in SAT math scores was at its highest level in recent years, girls' scores lagged 46 points below boys' scores, on average. By the mid-1990s, the difference was 35 points and remained at about that level through 2008 (when it was 33 points). The SAT verbal scores of boys also exceed those of girls, though these differences (4 points as of 2008) are much smaller and have also declined.[22]

Whatever their source, gender differences in college major are strongly related to the wages of college graduates and help account for the male–female wage differential among this group. Moreover, the growing similarity in college majors between men and women has contributed to the narrowing of the gender wage gap for college graduates over time.[23]

GENDER DIFFERENCES IN EDUCATIONAL INVESTMENT DECISIONS: OTHER FACTORS

Although expected working life is a factor that has been particularly emphasized by human capital theorists, a variety of other factors may also contribute to gender differences in educational attainment and field of specialization. We consider these factors in this section. We begin by reviewing the overt discrimination by educational institutions that women faced in the past. We then turn to a variety of more subtle barriers that may adversely affect women's educational outcomes even today. To see how social influences may impact women's decision making, it is helpful to consider the nonpecuniary as well as the pecuniary costs and benefits of human capital investments. Societal influences may raise the costs of, or lower the returns to, specific types of education for women relative to men. Given these higher costs or lower returns, the investment in education may not prove profitable for many women. This situation is particularly apt to arise in traditionally male-dominated fields.

It is also important to bear in mind that social pressures may help cause the gender differences in labor force participation patterns, which are identified as being the primary cause of gender differences in educational investment decisions in the human capital model. In addition, women's lower labor force participation may to some extent be due to the discrimination they face in the labor market, which reduces their opportunities and lowers their earnings. Such feedback effects of labor market discrimination are considered in greater detail in Chapter 7.

---

[21] Morton Paglin and Anthony M. Rufolo, "Heterogeneous Human Capital, Occupational Choice, and Male–Female Earnings Differences," *Journal of Labor Economics* 8, no. 1, pt. 1 (January 1990): 123–44.

[22] See "College Board Reports Continuing Upward Trend in Average Scores on SAT 1," Press Release, College Board, August 22, 1996, and the College Board Web site at www.collegeboard.org. There was virtually no difference in the mean ACT scores of young men (21.2) and women (21.0) in 2008. The ACT score represents a combined assessment of English, math, reading, and science reasoning; see www.act.org. In a similar vein, Goldin, Katz, and Kuziemko in "The Homecoming of American College Women" present evidence that girls narrowed the gender gap in high school math achievement tests between 1972 and 1992.

[23] See Judith A. McDonald and Robert J. Thornton, "Do New Male and Female College Graduates Receive Unequal Pay?" *Journal of Human Resources* 42, no. 1 (Winter 2007): 32–48; Brown and Corcoran, "Sex-Based Differences"; and Eric Eide, "College Major Choice and Changes in the Gender Wage Gap," *Contemporary Economic Policy* 12, no. 2 (April 1994): 55–64.

Historical Background: Overt Discrimination by Educational Institutions

While now largely eliminated, overt discrimination against women in admission to college and professional school was pervasive in the not-too-distant past. Such discrimination placed serious limits on the educational options of older women and thus its impact continues to be reflected in the *current* occupational distribution of these women. Moreover, such discrimination not only limited the educational opportunities of the women directly affected by these barriers, but also contributed to a dearth of female role models for subsequent generations.

While options for higher education for American men date back to the colonial period,[24] American women were excluded from higher education until 1837 when Oberlin College, founded a few years previously, opened its doors to women and Mount Holyoke, a female seminary, was established.[25] Women did not gain entrance to medical school until 1847, and it was not until 1915 that the American Medical Association accepted women members. As late as 1869, the U.S. Supreme Court upheld the refusal of the Illinois State Bar to admit a woman. One of the justices declared that "the natural and proper timidity and delicacy which belongs to the female sex evidently unfit it for many of the occupations of civil life."[26] Nonetheless, a year later, in 1870, the first woman did succeed in graduating from an American law school.

Even after these "firsts," women were not universally admitted to all institutions of higher education in all fields for a long time. The prestigious Harvard Medical School did not admit women until 1945, while Harvard Law School excluded women until 1950. Similarly, many highly respected undergraduate institutions, such as Princeton and Yale, remained male-only until the late 1960s or early 1970s. Others, such as Harvard, granted women access to classes and some facilities but officially restricted them to a separate college.

Moreover, the opening of doors to women did not necessarily mean that the doors opened as widely for women as for men. Often women continued to be discriminated against in admissions and financial aid policies long after they gained formal admittance. In some cases, women were held to higher standards than men; in others, overt or informal quotas limited the number of places available to them.[27] Often course requirements for male and female high school students were different and, at all levels, gender-based counseling was prevalent.

While, fortunately, overt barriers to women in higher education have largely been eliminated, other factors such as the way girls and boys are socialized, stereotyped views of "masculine" and "feminine" traits, biased evaluations of male and female performance, and various subtle barriers to female success may still slow the advancement of women relative to men. These factors, discussed in the next sections, may well have

---

[24] The oldest institution of higher education, Harvard University, was founded in 1636 and, the second oldest, the College of William and Mary, was founded in 1693; see http://www.hno.harvard.edu/guide/intro/index.html and http://www.wm.edu/about/wmataglance/index.php.

[25] Three graduates of Oberlin in 1841 were the first women in the United States to receive AB degrees. The chemist and educator Mary Lyon, who founded Mount Holyoke Female Seminary, famously said, "Go where no one else will go, do what no one else will do." See http://cms.oberlin.edu/inauguration/history.dot and http://www.mtholyoke.edu/cic/about/history.shtml. The remaining information in this section on admissions of women is from Michelle Patterson and Laurie Engleberg, "Women in Male-Dominated Professions," in *Women Working: Theories and Facts in Perspective*, edited by Ann H. Stromberg and Shirley Harkess (Mountain View, CA: Mayfield, 1978), pp. 266–92.

[26] Cited in Patterson and Engleberg, "Women in Male-Dominated Professions," p. 277.

[27] See, for example, Ann Sutherland Harris, "The Second Sex in Academe," *AAUP Bulletin* 56, no. 3 (Fall 1970): 283–95; and Mary Frank Fox, "Women and Higher Education: Gender Differences in the Status of Students and Scholars," in *Women: A Feminist Perspective*, 3rd ed., edited by Jo Freeman (Palo Alto, CA: Mayfield, 1984), pp. 217–35.

contributed to women's lower participation in higher education in the past, as well as past and continuing gender differences in fields of study.[28]

Socialization

Socialization is the name given to the process by which the influence of family, friends, teachers, and the media shapes an individual's attitudes and behavior.[29] The socialization process influences the self-esteem of men and women, as well as their perceptions of gender-appropriate competencies and behavior. It may, for example, affect boys' and girls' perceptions of their mathematical abilities or the appropriateness of their interest in this subject. The socialization process also helps shape the role boys and girls expect work to occupy in their lives. We have already seen how gender differences in the expected importance of market work in their lives may influence men's and women's educational investment decisions, in the past deterring women from investing in college. Negative attitudes of family, teachers, or friends toward women's college attendance may have also reduced their college attendance by comprising a nonpecuniary cost that lowered their subjective evaluation of the net value of this investment.[30] The consequences of gender differences in occupational orientation, also influenced by the socialization process, are likely to be important as well. To a greater extent in the past, and even today, boys and girls are taught from an early age to aspire to and train for gender-appropriate lines of work. Here too, disapproval by or lack of support from family, teachers, or friends may be a factor discouraging girls and women from venturing into nontraditional areas. It is likely that gender differences in socialization have diminished with the growing social acceptance of women's employment outside the home and their participation in what were formerly viewed as male occupations, but it is unlikely that such gender differences have disappeared entirely.

CHILDREN'S TOYS: THE SELLING OF STEREOTYPES

Children's toys expose both boys and girls to gender stereotypes from an early age,* whether as a result of their parents' selection of toys for them; what they see when they go to toy stores, look through catalogs, or watch television; or the kinds of toys that they see at the homes of friends and relatives.

    For girls, toy stores, of course, offer ubiquitous dolls: babies they can take care of, children they can dress up, glamorous young women they can try to emulate, and, of

---

[28] A discussion of barriers to women's advancement in the sciences and policies that might improve their representation is presented in Jo Handelsman, Nancy Cantor, Molly Carnes, Denice Denton, Eve Fine, Barbara Grosz, Virginia Hinshaw, Cora Marrett, Sue Rosser, Donna Shalala, and Jennifer Sheridan, "Policy Forum: More Women in Science," *Science* 309 (August 19, 2005): 1190–91, available at www.sciencemag.org.

[29] See, for example, Francine D. Blau, Mary C. Brinton, and David B. Grusky, "The Declining Significance of Gender?" in *The Declining Significance of Gender?* edited by Francine D. Blau, Mary C. Brinton, and David B. Grusky (New York: Russell Sage Foundation, 2006), pp. 3–34; Cynthia Fuchs Epstein, *Deceptive Distinctions: Sex, Gender, and the Social Order* (New Haven, CT: Yale University Press, 1988); and Margaret M. Marini and Mary C. Brinton, "Sex Stereotyping in Occupational Socialization," in *Sex Segregation in the Work Place: Trends, Explanations, and Remedies,* edited by Barbara Reskin (Washington, DC: National Academy Press, 1984), pp. 192–232.

[30] Evidence on one aspect of the family environment, impact of sibling sex composition on women's educational attainment, is mixed. Kristin Butcher and Anne Case found that women with at least one sister have lower educational attainment than women raised only with brothers. They suggest that this finding is consistent with a "reference group" model in which the presence of a sister affects either parents' educational goals for their daughters or the skills that the young woman develops; see "The Effect of Sibling Sex Composition on Women's Education and Earnings," *Quarterly Journal of Economics* 109, no. 3 (August 1994): 531–65. In contrast, Robert M. Hauser and Hsiang-Hui Daphne Kuo found no evidence of a relationship between sibling sex composition and women's educational attainment when they examined three data sets not used in the Butcher and Case study; see "Does the Gender Composition of Sibship Affect Women's Educational Attainment?" *Journal of Human Resources* 33, no. 3 (Summer 1998): 644–57.

course, Barbie, the most popular doll ever. Even though Barbie is now available with wardrobes and accessories for various careers, she still has a body few girls will ever have; to be exact, only 1 young woman out of 100,000 will have such a shape. Ken's proportions, though also rare in the general population, are more realistic; 1 in 50 young men will have his shape.**

When it comes to dress up for occasions such as Halloween, toy store aisles and catalogs are still replete with ballerina and princess costumes, but now costumes are also available for girls wanting to be superheroes. This might suggest progress toward gender equity except that superhero costumes for girls tend to be highly form-fitting feminine outfits, a stark contrast to the macho black ninja costumes marketed for boys. Other toys intended for girls include kitchen accessories and makeup.***

The message that comes through loud and clear is that girls want to be pretty and that they are interested in having boyfriends, even at an early age. They also want to prepare themselves for a life in which being a good mother and competent household manager is primary. Video games, cartoons, and movies assign girls the same role. As just one example, "Powerpuff Girls" on the Cartoon Network has Bubbles, Blossom, and Buttercup who are "cute little preschoolers with big eyes and a tendency to play house."**** The few toys that show a connection to careers come in a poor second. Finally, of course, *the* girl toy colors—pink and light purple—are, of course, strictly off-limits to boys.

Enter a "boy aisle" in the toy store or click on a web site that lists toys boys might like and you will be barraged by light sabers, swords, and the TV and movie action figures that go with them. Traditional superheroes Batman, Superman, and Spiderman are joined by "Star Wars" characters, Iron Man, and others. Watch a cartoon or movie directed at boys and you will see plenty of violence as good battles evil. These characters are far from the nurturing role models given to girls. Moreover, it remains far less socially acceptable for boys to cross the gender barrier in stores and choose a Barbie than it is for a girl to choose a Batman figure.

It is unlikely that sex-stereotyping of toys will abate anytime soon. There are those who argue that merchants are merely responding to children's preferences, that placing toys for girls and boys in distinct areas is more convenient for shoppers, and that playing with these toys does no real harm to either boys or girls. Also, some gender-neutral toys and games such as Monopoly and Rollerblades are quite popular with children of both sexes. Nonetheless, separate toy aisles for girls and boys help perpetuate traditional gender roles by limiting children's visions of who they can be and what they should do at an early age.

*This inset draws on Crispin Sartwell, "The Gender Gap Remains—for Boys," *Baltimore Sun*, May 28, 2000; Megan Rosenfeld, "Games Girls Play: A Toy Chest Full of Stereotypes," *Washington Post*, December 22, 1995, p. A1; C. Estelle Campenni, "Gender Stereotyping of Children's Toys: A Comparison of Parents and Nonparents," *Sex Roles: A Journal of Research* 40, no. 1 (January 1999): 121–39; and Judith E. Owen Blakemore and Renee E. Centers, "Characteristics of Boys' and Girls' Toys," *Sex Roles* 53, no. 9/10 (November 2005): 619–33.
**Kevin I. Norton, Timothy S. Olds, Scott Olive, and Stephen Dank, "Ken and Barbie at Life Size," *Sex Roles: A Journal of Research* 34, nos 3–4 (February 1996): 287–94.
***Gary Strauss, "Princesses Rule the Hearts of Little Girls," *USA Today*, March 2, 2004, p. 1D.
****Sartwell, "The Gender Gap Remains."

Women's and Men's Traits and Abilities: Stereotyped Views and Evidence

Another way in which social influences may affect women's labor market outcomes is that women may be socialized to emphasize appropriate "feminine" traits, such as being subordinate, nurturing, and emotional. Traditionally male fields may be stereotyped as requiring "masculine" traits such as dominance, competitiveness, and rationality. Having internalized the idea of what is properly female, women may then avoid male fields because they perceive a nonpecuniary cost to acting in an "unfeminine" manner or because they feel unequipped to do so. In the latter case, they might expect to be less successful in the field, thus lowering their anticipated returns. Similarly, if women are raised to believe that they lack competence in "masculine" subjects like math and science, this belief would raise their perceived costs and lower their perceived returns to entry into fields emphasizing this knowledge. Men may see traditionally female fields as inappropriate for similar reasons.

The negative effects of stereotypical views are of concern even if men and women do differ on average in the direction these views suggest. One reason for concern is that it is not possible to know the extent to which social influences have caused or at least contributed to the observed gender differences. Therefore, one should not assume that all observed average differences between men and women on various traits are entirely due to biological factors.

For example, considerable attention has focused on gender differences in math test scores, in terms of both mean differences and differences at the highest levels of performance. And, in the United States, men do have an advantage on both dimensions,[31] although, as we have seen, the gender gap in math test scores has declined as girls have taken more math courses.

International comparisons may be instructive in shedding light on the nature and source of the gender difference in math scores in the United States, particularly the role of social influences. While girls' average math scores are below boys' in many countries, the gender difference in scores varies considerably across countries. In some countries, such as Sweden and Norway, there is no gender gap in math scores, and, in Iceland, girls' mean scores are higher than boys'. Similarly, there is considerable variation in the proportion of girls compared to boys scoring at the highest levels (above 95 or 99 percent) of each country's test score distribution. For example, in Iceland, more girls scored at the highest levels than boys. Indeed, a recent analysis of data from a variety of countries found that girls' math scores—whether measured at the means or based on performance at the highest levels—were positively related to indicators of country-level gender equity (as measured by various indicators of gender equity such as the World Economic Forum's Gender Gap Index).[32] This finding suggests that culture likely plays an important role in determining the gender math gap and may well affect gender differences in math scores in the United States.

The importance of cultural factors is also suggested by the considerable international variation found in a recent study that examined girls' participation in the most difficult math competitions for young people. The data in this study suggest that different cultures place different emphasis on the value of mathematics and that these differences affect girls' participation. For example, the United States has participated in the International Mathematical Olympiad since 1974, and, between 1974 and 2008, the various six-person teams fielded by the United States have included a total of 3 girls, compared to 9 for Bulgaria, 10 for East Germany/Germany, and 13 for the Soviet Union/Russia. As a further indicator of the importance of culture, the study found that half of recent U.S. team members were immigrants or the children of immigrants from countries where, according to the authors of the study, mathematics is more highly valued than it is in the United States.[33]

Analyses of other observed gender differences also suggest a possible role for social influences. For instance, researchers find that men's and women's propensity to negotiate differs, with women feeling much more apprehensive about negotiating and being much less likely to do so. So women may be less likely than men to negotiate over salaries, raises, or promotions, thus reducing their pay relative to men's. However,

---

[31] Luigi Guiso, Ferdinando Monte, Paola Sapienza, and Luigi Zingales, "Education Forum: Culture, Gender, and Math," *Science* 320 (May 30, 2008): 1164–65, available at www.sciencemag.org.

[32] The examples cited in the text and this finding are from Guiso, Monte, Sapienza, and Zingales, "Education Forum: Culture, Gender, and Math." They also found that girls had higher reading scores than boys in all countries and that the more gender equal the culture, the *higher* girls' reading scores were relative to boys'.

[33] Titu Andreescu, Joseph A. Gallian, Jonathan M. Kane, and Janet E. Mertz, "Cross-Cultural Analysis of Students with Exceptional Talent in Mathematical Problem Solving," *Notices of the American Mathematical Society* 55, no. 10 (November 2008): 1248–60; and Sara Rimer, "Math Skills Suffer in U.S., Study Finds," *New York Times*, October 10, 2008, available at www.nytimes.org.

a comprehensive examination of the gender gap in negotiating attributes the gender difference to social factors that hold women back. According to the authors, women are socialized to feel that they are being pushy or overbearing if they pursue their own goals in the face of conflict with others—say employers or coworkers. Women have learned that asserting their own needs can trigger a negative response from others. This negative response in turn may be tied to their departing from traditional gender roles.[34]

There is also some evidence from experiments conducted in Western cultures that women shy away from competition compared to men, suggesting that men are more competitively inclined than women.[35] This difference too could be a disability for women in the labor market, potentially lowering their relative pay and leading them to avoid certain occupations or business settings. However, related research comparing experimental results in two different cultures suggests that a key factor behind men's and women's behavior is the social organization of the society. Consistent with the results for Western cultures, in a traditional patriarchal society (the Maasai of Tanzania), men opted to compete at roughly twice the rate of women. However, in a matrilineal/matrilocal society where inheritance and residence is determined by the female lineage (the Khasi of India), women chose the competitive environment more often than men and even chose to compete a bit more often than Maasai men did.[36] This evidence further points to the role that social organization and culture play in women's and men's behavior.

Regardless of the source of observed gender differences—nature or nurture, there is generally considerable variation among men and women around the average. Stereotypical views may thus adversely impact behavior and outcomes for both women and men who do not conform to the stereotypes. So, for example, highly qualified individuals may not have the opportunity to enter a particular profession because they belong to a group that is, on average, less well qualified for it. In addition, as suggested in the following inset, the stereotypes themselves may adversely affect the performance of women, further compounding their negative effects.

WOMEN, MATH, AND STEREOTYPE THREAT

Research by psychologists Diane M. Quinn, Steven J. Spencer, and Claude M. Steele suggests that cultural stereotypes, such as the belief that girls and women have better verbal skills while boys and men are better at mathematics and science, may negatively affect girls' performance on math exams. Quinn explains how such "stereotype threat" situations can adversely affect girls' test performance and summarizes some of their findings:

> In the case of gender and math, imagine a boy and girl sitting down to take the SAT for the first time. They have equivalent math experience. Taking the SAT is a tense, sometimes frustrating experience for both of them. However, as the girl is taking the test she has an extra worry to contend with that the boy does not: A stereotype that she, as a girl, has

---

[34] In *Women Don't Ask: Negotiation and the Gender Divide* (Princeton: Princeton University Press, 2003), Linda Babcock and Sara Laschever document these gender differences in negotiating, present evidence that they are costly to women, and provide guidance on developing and exercising negotiating skills. See also Linda Babcock and Sara Laschever, *Ask for It: How Women Can Use the Power of Negotiation to Get What They Really Want* (New York: Bantam Books, 2008).

[35] See, for example, Muriel Niederle and Lise Vesterlund, "Do Women Shy Away from Competition?" *Quarterly Journal of Economics* 122, no. 3 (August 2007): 1067–101. For a review of experimental evidence on gender differences in preferences, see Rachel Croson and Uri Gneezy, "Gender Differences in Preferences," *Journal of Economic Literature* (forthcoming).

[36] Uri Gneezy, Kenneth L. Leonard, and John A. List, "Gender Differences in Competition: Evidence from a Matrilineal and a Patriarchal Society," NBER Working Paper No. 13727 (January 2008).

inferior math skills. As she experiences frustration and difficulty with the problems, she has the burden of knowing that her difficulty could be judged as proof of the veracity of the stereotype. The boy has none of these doubts or thoughts to interrupt his performance. It is important to note that in this situation neither the girl nor the boy have to believe that the stereotype is true. . . . Just the knowledge of the stereotype itself is enough to affect performance in the situation. How do we know this occurs?

My colleagues and I have tested the stereotype threat hypothesis in a series of studies. . . . In all of our experiments we bring university men and women matched for equivalent math backgrounds and interest into the laboratory. In the first of these studies we simply gave participants an easy or difficult math test. We found that women only performed worse than men on the difficult math test. To demonstrate that it was the threat of the stereotype that caused this underperformance, we gave a second group of men and women the same difficult math test. In order to make stereotypes about math explicit, half of the participants were told that the test had shown gender differences in the past. In order to eliminate a stereotype based inter-pretation of the situation, the other half of the participants were told that the test had been shown to be gender fair—that men and women performed equally on this test. In line with our predictions, when the stereotype was not applicable to the situation, when men and women were simply told that they were taking a gender fair test, men and women performed equally on the test. When told that the exact same test had shown gender differences in the past, women scored lower on the test than men. Just a simple change in the situation—a different line in the instructions—changed an outcome that many believed intractable. . . . We have also conducted studies where we have a condition in which we do not mention gender at all—we simply de-scribe the math test as a standardized test. In this situation, women also score lower on the test than men, suggesting that standardized mathematical test-ing situations are implicitly stereotype threat situations. . . .

When we look at what women and men are actually doing when working on the difficult test, we found that women and men primarily used the same strategies to solve the problems, however, women in stereotype threat situations were less likely to think of any way to solve a problem. That is, women were more likely to "blank out" or "choke" on a problem when they were in a stereotype threat condition. Thus research results so far point to the following scenario: When women with a strong interest and identification with math are in a situation in which their math skills could be negatively judged, their performance is undermined by the cognitive activation of gender stereotypes combined with some feelings of stress or anxiety. Women are not alone in being affected by negative stereotypes. Research on stereotype threat has demonstrated its effect on African–Americans and Latinos in intellectual situations, on the elderly in memory testing situations and even on White men in sports situations.*

Quinn also offers some suggestions to reduce stereotype threat and level the playing field for all students. For instance, stereotype threat is likely to be reduced when women (or minorities) are reassured that everyone struggles with difficult concepts and are as-sured that the exam is fair. Even small measures, such as these, may make a real difference.

*Reprinted from Diane M. Quinn, "Women, Math, and Stereotype Threat," *Newsletter of the American Economic Association Committee on the Status of Women in the Economics Profession* (Winter 2004), pp. 10–11, available at www.cswep.org. Reprinted by permission of the author. See also Diane M. Quinn and Steven Spencer, "The Interference of Stereotype Threat on Women's Generation of Mathematical Problem-Solving Strategies," *Journal of Social Issues* 57, no. 1 (Spring 2001): 55–71; and Steven J. Spencer, Claude M. Steele, and Diane M. Quinn, "Stereotype Threat and Women's Math Performance," *Journal of Experimental Social Psychology* 35, no. 1 (1999): 4–28.

Biased Evaluations

Even women's possession of "male" traits or competencies and their willingness to display them may not guarantee them equal success. Studies have found that, among both female and male college students, identical papers were given higher ratings on dimensions such as value, persuasiveness, profundity, writing style, and competence when respondents believed the author to be male rather than female. Similar findings are obtained in studies asking both women and men to evaluate the qualifications of applicants for employment, with men preferred over women in "male" and gender-neutral jobs.[37] The expectation of inferior performance may eventually cause that inferior performance. Even if it does not, it would lower the expected return to investments in educational credentials.

Subtle Barriers

Although *overt* barriers to women in higher education have been eliminated, *subtle* barriers to their success in the study of traditionally male fields remain a problem. In Chapter 7, we consider how these **subtle barriers** also block women's progress in the workplace.

Simply the fact that a field is predominantly male can discourage young women from attempting to enter it. In this way, past discrimination may continue to have an impact on young women today. Lacking contact with or firsthand knowledge of successful women, young women may assume (quite possibly erroneously) that they too would be unable to succeed. Even if they believe that times have changed and that their prospects for success are greater than indicated by the present low representation of women, the scarcity of women may still pose problems for them, limiting their eventual success and lowering their returns to entering predominantly male fields.

For example, without older women to serve as **role models**, female entrants lack adequate information about acceptable (or successful) modes of behavior and dress. They also lack access to the knowledge acquired by older women about successful strategies for combining work roles and family responsibilities. Thus, they are forced to be pioneers, and blazing a new trail is undoubtedly more difficult than following along a well-established path.

Women students may also be excluded from informal relationships that enhance the chances of career success. Older individuals who are well established in the field (mentors) often take promising young students (protégés) under their wing—informally socializing them into the norms of the field, giving them access to the latest research in the area, and tying them into their network of professional contacts. The **mentor–protégé relationship** is generally the result of the older individual identifying with the younger person. Male mentors may simply not identify with young women. The potential mentor may also fear that a close relationship with a young woman would be misunderstood by his colleagues or his wife. Thus, women students are likely to be at a disadvantage in predominantly male fields. Their problems will be further aggravated if male students neglect to include them in their **informal network**. Such informal contacts among students include study groups and discussions over lunches, sports, coffee breaks, or a Friday afternoon beer, where important information about coursework, the field, and career opportunities is often exchanged.

Thus, women often lack the support and encouragement, as well as the access to information and job opportunities provided by informal contacts between teachers and students and among students, as well as female role models to emulate. The absence of these opportunities raises the nonpecuniary costs to them in comparison

---

[37] Heather K. Davison and Michael J. Burke, "Sex Discrimination in Simulated Employment Contexts: A Meta-Analytic Investigation," *Journal of Vocational Behavior* 56, no. 2 (April 2000): 225–48, as cited in Alice H. Eagly and Linda L. Carli, *Through the Labyrinth* (Cambridge, MA: Harvard Business School Press, 2007). See also the summary of this line of research including the early study cited in the text in Eagly and Carli, chap. 5, pp. 76–80, and Virginia Valian, *Why So Slow? The Advancement of Women* (Cambridge, MA: MIT Press, 1998), chap. 7, pp. 125–44.

with otherwise similar male students, lowering their incentives to enter traditionally male fields. It may also result in their being less successful than comparable men when they complete their studies. To the extent that they foresee this, their entry into predominantly male fields is further discouraged.

Although it is widely believed that a lack of female role models and mentors is a significant problem for women students, it is difficult to obtain quantitative evidence. One approach uses self-reports and perceptions of young women, often, although not always, finding evidence that female role models and mentors are important.[38] Other studies use a different approach, examining the impact of the presence of women faculty on indicators of performance or choices of female students. One study finds that the percentage of female faculty at their undergraduate college or university is positively related to the probability that female students attain an advanced degree, and another finds that, for economics PhD students, additional female faculty may have beneficial effects for female students on completion rates and time to completion of the PhD.[39] Other results are less positive. For example, it has been reported that the race, gender, and ethnicity match between high school students, and their teachers did not affect how much students learned, but did sometimes positively affect the teacher's subjective evaluation of the students, suggesting, for example, that same-sex teachers might better serve as mentors.[40] Finally, for a sample of three schools, no evidence was found that an increase in the proportion of female college or university faculty in a department was associated with an increase in the proportion of undergraduate majors that were women.[41]

POLICY ISSUE: GOVERNMENT'S EFFORTS TO COMBAT DISCRIMINATION IN EDUCATIONAL INSTITUTIONS

To remedy discrimination in educational institutions, in 1972, Congress passed **Title IX** of the Educational Amendments to the Civil Rights Act of 1964. It prohibits discrimination on the basis of sex in any educational program or activity receiving federal financial assistance and covers admissions, financial aid, and access to programs and activities, as well as employment of teachers and other personnel.

The main provisions relevant at the high school level are that all courses and programs, except sex instruction, chorus, and contact sports, must be available to both males and females. At the university level, the most important provisions are for nondiscrimination in admissions and in faculty hiring and for equal availability of scholarships and fellowships, assistantships, research opportunities, and housing. Private, single-sex undergraduate schools are exempt from the nondiscrimination in admission requirements; however, once any women (or men) are admitted, no discrimination in admissions is permitted. Even though enforcement has not always been rigorous, it is likely that this legislation contributed to the substantial changes in the extent and type of participation of women in the educational system that we have reviewed.

---

[38] See, for example, Helen M. Berg and Marianne A. Ferber, "Men and Women Graduate Students: Who Succeeds and Why?" *Journal of Higher Education* 54, no. 6 (November–December 1983): 629–48; and Nancy E. Betz and Louise F. Fitzgerald, *The Career Psychology of Women* (Orlando, FL: Academic Press, 1987) and the references therein.

[39] Donna S. Rothstein, "Do Female Faculty Influence Female Students' Educational and Labor Market Attainments?" *Industrial and Labor Relations Review* 48, no. 3 (April 1995): 515–30; and David Neumark and Rosella Gardecki, "Women Helping Women? Role-Model and Mentoring Effects on Female Ph.D. Students in Economics," *Journal of Human Resources* 33, no. 1 (Winter 1998): 220–46.

[40] Ronald G. Ehrenberg, Daniel D. Goldhaber, and Dominic J. Brewer, "Do Teachers' Race, Gender, and Ethnicity Matter? Evidence from NELS," *Industrial and Labor Relations Review* 48, no. 3 (April 1995): 547–61.

[41] Brandice Canes and Harvey Rosen, "Following in Her Footsteps? Women's Choices of College Majors and Faculty Gender Composition," *Industrial and Labor Relations Review* 48, no. 3 (April 1995): 486–504.

Title IX has had a particularly dramatic impact on high school and collegiate athletics. Since its passage, support and facilities for women athletes have greatly increased, as has women's participation in athletic programs at both the high school and the college level.[42] Some research suggests that athletics has a positive effect on girls who participate. For example, looking across states, it has been found that in states where girls had a greater opportunity to play high school sports, female college attendance, labor force participation, and participation in previously male-dominated, typically high-skilled, occupations were also higher.[43] The implementation of Title IX in this area has not, however, been without controversy. The chief concern is that efforts to comply with the legislation, particularly at the collegiate level, have come at the expense of men's sports. However, research suggests that "institutions were more likely to add female teams or participants than to cut male teams or participants in order to move closer to compliance."[44] Indeed, both men's and women's participation in collegiate sports have increased since the early 1980s.[45]

Another controversial issue that has arisen is the desirability and legality of single-sex education. Some claim that, due to classroom issues, such as the tendency for males to dominate class discussion, women may benefit from single-sex schooling. Similar arguments favor predominantly black institutions. At the same time, two elite, state-financed, all-male military schools claimed that the benefits of their educational experience depended on an all-male environment.

From a legal perspective, different issues are raised depending on whether the educational institution involved is publicly funded. Single-sex, privately funded institutions are exempt from Title IX's admission requirements. However, constitutional issues come into play in single-sex, publicly funded schools. In 1996, the U.S. Supreme Court found that the exclusion of qualified women from the Virginia Military Institute (V.M.I.), a state-run, all-male military school, was not permissible. Writing for the majority, Justice Ruth Bader Ginsburg explained that the state must demonstrate an "exceedingly persuasive justification" for any official action that treats men and women differently. "The justification must be genuine, not hypothesized or invented *post hoc* in response to litigation.... And it must not rely on overbroad generalizations about the different talents, capacities, or preferences of males and females." This decision resulted in the admission of women into V.M.I. and a similar institution, the Citadel in South Carolina, which was not explicitly involved in the case.[46]

Private schools were not affected by the Supreme Court decision. However, all-male private colleges are nonetheless now quite rare, with only three in operation in 2005. All-female private colleges were much more prevalent, with 56 in 2005, though this figure was down considerably from 233 in 1960.[47]

Considerable controversy continues to surround the issue of single-sex public schools at the elementary and high school level. Despite concerns by some critics that

---

[42] Betsy Stevenson, "Title IX and the Evolution of High School Sports," *Contemporary Economic Policy* 25, no. 4 (October 2007): 486–505; and Welch Suggs, *A Place on the Team: The Triumph and Tradegy of Title IX* (Princeton, NJ: Princeton University Press, 2005).

[43] Betsy Stevenson, "Beyond the Classroom: Using Title IX to Measure the Return to High School Sports," *Review of Economics and Statistics* (forthcoming).

[44] Deborah J. Anderson and John J. Cheslock, "Institutional Strategies to Achieve Gender Equity in Intercollegiate Athletics: Does Title IX Harm Male Athletes?" *The American Economic Review* 94, no. 2 (May 2004): 307–11.

[45] John J. Cheslock, "Who's Playing College Sports? Money, Race and Gender," Women's Sports Foundation Research Report (September 2008), available at www.WomensSportsFoundation.org.

[46] Linda Greenhouse, "Military College Can't Bar Women, High Court Rules," *New York Times*, June 27, 1996, pp. A1, B8.

[47] Leslie Miller-Bernal and Susan L. Poulson, "The State of Women's Colleges Today," in *Challenged by Coeducation: Women's Colleges Since the 1960s*, edited by Leslie Miller-Bernal and Susan L. Poulson (Nashville, TN: Vanderbilt University Press, 2007), pp. 375–88.

single-sex schools are in violation of Title IX, the Bush administration supported giving public school districts freedom to create same-sex classes and schools as long as "substantially equal" opportunities are provided for the excluded sex. The number of single-sex public schools is growing; it is estimated that in 1995 there were only two single-sex public schools and that by 2007–2008 there were 49, with 65 percent having opened in the previous three years. In addition, an increasing number of coeducational public schools offer some single-sex classrooms.[48]

EXPLAINING WOMEN'S RISING EDUCATIONAL ATTAINMENT

Whatever the past barriers to women's access to higher education or the remaining gender differences in fields of study and in the acquisition of first professional and PhD degrees, the increase in women's representation in college and postgraduate study that we documented earlier is truly remarkable. How do we explain this change that began in earnest in the 1970s? One particularly puzzling feature of recent trends is that not only did women become half of those receiving bachelor's degrees in the early 1980s, but their representation continued to increase thereafter, reaching 58 percent by 2006. So, women are now *more* likely to go to college than men. While these developments are still not fully understood, we can point to a number of factors that have contributed to women's increased college attendance and, in some cases, have encouraged women's college attendance to exceed men's.

As we noted previously, the **increase in women's expected work life** is undoubtedly a central factor explaining the increase in women's college attendance. Looking at Figure 6-3, we see that as women anticipated spending longer periods in the labor market, the return on women's investment in higher education increased and with it their motivation to secure higher levels of education and more market-oriented education as well. And, indeed, the data suggest that women graduating from college in recent decades spend considerably less time out of the labor force than earlier cohorts. We saw, for example, in Chapter 4 that the labor force participation rates of female college graduates are quite high, 80 percent in 2007, up from 61 percent in 1970. In contrast, participation rates remain quite a bit lower for female high school graduates and have increased far less since 1970. In 2007, 61 percent of this group participated in the labor force up from 51 percent in 1970. Evidence of college-educated women's strong labor force attachment is also provided by a recent study of the work force experience of 1981 graduates of 34 highly selective colleges and universities. In the 15 or so years following their completion of college or more advanced schooling, fully 58 percent of the women surveyed were never out of the job market for more than six months in total. Overall, the group had spent a total of just 1.6 years out of the labor force, on average, or 11 percent of their potential working years.[49]

Labor market opportunities for women in traditionally male jobs expanded due to the passage of antidiscrimination legislation, which we discuss in Chapter 7, as well as shifting social attitudes toward women's work roles and their capabilities. Moreover, this increase in opportunities principally benefited college-educated

---

[48] See Elizabeth Weil, "Teaching Boys and Girls Separately," *New York Times*, March 2, 2008, available at www.nytimes.com, and Diana Jean Schemo, "Administration Proposes Same-Sex-School Option," *New York Times*, March 4, 2004, p. A16. See also the National Association for Single Sex Public Education (NASSPE) Web site at www.singlesexschools.org.

[49] Claudia Goldin, "Working It Out," *New York Times*, March 15, 2006, available at www.nytimes.org. For an extremely interesting study focusing on three cohorts of Harvard/Radcliffe graduates, see Claudia Goldin and Lawrence F. Katz, "Transitions: Career and Family Life Cycles of the Educational Elite," *American Economic Review* 98, no. 2 (May 2008): 363–69.

women. As we saw in Chapter 5, occupational segregation by sex particularly declined in managerial and professional jobs, high-earning occupations likely to provide opportunities for college women. In contrast, occupational segregation has declined very little in blue-collar occupations, thereby providing fewer new opportunities for high school–educated women.

There has also been an **increase in the returns to education** for women as well as men since 1980 due in part to technological change that has benefited more highly educated workers relative to their less skilled counterparts.[50] (We discuss this development in Chapter 8.) As a consequence, the gap between the college and high school profiles shown in Figure 6-1 has increased, raising the return to college education for both men and women. Moreover, not only have returns to education increased, but **the *returns* to education are higher for women than for men**, and this appears to have been the case for a considerable period of time. Although women earn less than men at each level of education, the wage gap between men and women with similar characteristics, like experience, is smaller for the more highly educated than for the less highly educated.[51] The reasons for this smaller gender gap at higher levels of education are not known, but it means that the gap between the high school and college profiles shown in Figure 6-1 is *larger* for women than for men.[52] This means that, in this respect at least, women have a greater incentive to invest in a college education than men. This may help explain why women are now more likely to go to college than men, especially now that their expected work life has become more similar to men's.

Two additional factors may have contributed to the ability of women to respond to these increasing economic incentives to go on to higher education and also reinforced those incentives. First, a study by Claudia Goldin and Lawrence F. Katz points to the development of oral contraception, otherwise known as **the pill**, and especially its growing availability to young, unmarried women beginning in the late 1960s and early 1970s.[53] The availability of the pill was associated with and facilitated a delay in marriage and childbearing, which in turn enabled women to pursue professional training after college. The authors argue that the pill led to important *direct* and *indirect* effects on women's career investments. The direct effect of the pill was that it increased the reliability of contraception and the ease of using it, thereby enabling women to postpone marrying and starting a family and more confidently embark on a lengthy professional education. The indirect effect of the pill was that, because it encouraged the delay of marriage for *all* young people (not just those acquiring professional training), a woman who postponed marriage to pursue professional studies would find a larger pool of eligible bachelors to choose from. Had this not occurred, a woman who put off marriage for professional studies would have faced a much smaller pool of potential mates and, given this smaller selection, would have had to settle for a lesser match if she wanted to marry. This would have raised the cost to women of professional study. Second, passage and enforcement of **Title IX**, which specifically banned

---

[50] For an excellent long-term analysis, see Goldin and Katz, *The Race Between Education and Technology.*

[51] Dougherty, "Why Are the Returns to Schooling Higher for Women than for Men?" See also Brian A. Jacob, "Where the Boys Aren't: Non-Cognitive Skills, Returns to School and the Gender Gap in Higher Education," *Economics of Education Review* 21, no. 6, pt. B. (2002): 589–98. Another study points to gender differences in the trends in anticipated earnings dispersion as a possible factor; see Kerwin Kofi Charles and Ming-Ching Luoh, "Gender Differences in Completed Schooling," *Review of Economics and Statistics* 85, no. 3 (August 2003): 559–77.

[52] This finding is based on studies estimated using controls and may not be apparent in descriptive data such as the figures presented in Figure 6-2a or b.

[53] Claudia Goldin and Lawrence F. Katz "The Power of the Pill: Oral Contraceptives and Women's Career and Marriage Decisions," *Journal of Political Economy* 110, no. 4 (August 2002): 730–70. See also Martha J. Bailey, "More Power to the Pill: The Impact of Contraceptive Freedom on Women's Lifecycle Labor Supply,' *Quarterly Journal of Economics* 121, no. 1 (February 2006): 289–320.

discrimination in educational institutions, likely led to changes in the admission practices of educational institutions thereby facilitating and encouraging women's increased participation in higher education.

For both women and men, a college education not only boosts their own income but also results in **family-related income gains**. One source of this family-related income gain is that college-educated individuals tend to marry others with the same level of education. As a result, not only do they reap the gains of their own higher education but they also reap the benefit of having a higher-earning spouse. Another factor, one that is of particular importance for women, is that college-educated women have lower divorce rates and a lower incidence of out-of-wedlock births. This means that they are less likely than their less-educated counterparts to become lower income, single family heads. One study finds that such family-related income gains increased more for women than for men, suggesting that this may be at least part of the reason for the dramatic increase in women's college completion rates.[54]

Finally, **girls may have lower nonpecuniary costs** of investing in college than boys. That is, investing in education may entail less disutility for girls than boys. These lower costs may explain why, with the elimination of social and labor market barriers, women's college attendance has not only increased, but come to surpass men's rates. Claudia Goldin, Lawrence F. Katz, and Ilyana Kuziemko present considerable evidence on this point. For one thing, as discussed earlier, girls have traditionally excelled relative to boys in overall secondary school academic performance and continue to do so today. They also appear more willing to put in effort; boys spend much less time doing homework than girls. In addition, boys have a much higher incidence of school disciplinary and behavior problems, ranging from more minor infractions to school suspensions and participation in criminal activity. Boys are also two to three times more likely to be diagnosed with attention deficit hyperactivity disorder (ADHD). The reasons for these gender differences have not been fully determined but one factor may be the later maturation of boys. Regardless of their sources, as the authors point out, "the slower social development and more serious behavioral problems of boys...allowed girls to leapfrog over them in the race to college."[55]

ON-THE-JOB TRAINING

One of the major insights of human capital theory is the observation that individuals can increase their productivity not only through their investments in formal education but also by learning important work skills while they are on the job.[56] Sometimes workers participate in formal training programs sponsored by their employers. More often, they benefit from informal instruction by their supervisors or coworkers and grow more proficient at their jobs through repetition and trial and error. Human capital theory suggests that the weaker attachment to the labor force of women who follow traditional gender roles means that they will acquire less of this valuable on-the-job training. As will be discussed in Chapter 7, women may also be denied equal access to this type of training due to employer discrimination.

---

[54] Thomas A DiPrete and Claudia Buchmann, "Gender-Specific Trends in the Value of Education and the Emerging Gender Gap in College Completion," *Demography* 43, no. 1 (February 2006): 1–24. These are gains in family income adjusted for family size.

[55] Goldin, Katz, and Kuziemko, "The Homecoming of American College Women," p. 154. See also Jacob, "Where the Boys Aren't." For statistics on how much time boy and girl teens spend in homework, among other activities, see Shirley L. Porterfield and Anne E. Winkler, "Teen Time Use and Parental Education: Evidence from the CPS, MTF, and ATUS," *Monthly Labor Review* 130, no. 5 (May 2007): 37–56.

[56] See, for example, Becker, *Human Capital*; Mincer, "On-the-Job Training"; and Walter Oi, "Labor as a Quasi-Fixed Factor," *Journal of Political Economy* 70, no. 6 (December 1962): 538–55.

GENDER DIFFERENCES IN LABOR MARKET EXPERIENCE

Before developing these ideas further, let us look at the actual extent of gender differences in work experience. Unfortunately, this information is not collected by government agencies on a regular basis but must be pieced together from various special surveys. The available data indicate that, on average, women in the labor market have less work experience than men, but that gender differences have narrowed considerably since 1980.

Data for an earlier period, 1960-1980, indicates that during this time the average level of experience for all women workers fell slightly.[57] Women's labor force attachment did increase and employed women increased their average labor market experience *within* each age group. However, the *average* level of experience for all women workers fell slightly because of the large increases in labor force participation of *younger* women (as discussed in Chapter 4). Even with women in each age group working more years than previously, because younger women have less experience than older women, this change in age mix resulted in a small decline in average experience for women as a whole.[58] Yet, it is precisely this pattern of growing labor force attachment of women during the childbearing years that would eventually cause women's average experience to increase. By the 1980s, overall female experience levels unambiguously began to rise relative to males'. Indeed, the gender gap in full-time experience decreased by more than 2 years (from 6.6 to 4.3 years) between 1979 and 1989 and declined nearly another year (to 3.5 years) by 1998.[59]

Another dimension of labor market experience is tenure, time spent with a specific employer. The gender difference in this variable has declined as well. So, for example, in 1966, men's median tenure was 2.4 years more than women's; by 2008, the gender gap had fallen to only .3 years. And the share of long-term workers, those with tenure of 10 or more years, was only slightly higher for men (33 percent) than for women (30 percent).[60]

To summarize, the view that women have, on average, less work experience than men is borne out by the evidence. However, the differences between men and women in the extent of involvement in paid employment have narrowed considerably since 1980. We examine next how, according to the human capital model, gender differences in labor force attachment and experience could lower women's pay and cause differences in occupational choices between men and women.

---

[57] James P. Smith and Michael P. Ward, "Women's Wages and Work in the Twentieth Century," RAND, R-3119-NICHD, 1984. These estimates are based on data on women's labor force participation and labor force turnover (entries and exits) rather than on direct information on actual work experience. However, direct data on experience, where available, suggest these estimates are reasonable. For complementary estimates that also include an earlier period, see Claudia Goldin, *Understanding the Gender Gap: An Economic History of American Women* (New York: Oxford University Press, 1990), chap. 2.

[58] Goldin, *Understanding the Gender Gap*, p. 41.

[59] Data are for full-time workers and are from Francine D. Blau and Lawrence M. Kahn, "The U.S. Gender Pay Gap in the 1990s: Slowing Convergence," *Industrial and Labor Relations Review* 60, no. 1 (October 2006): 45–66. A number of other studies also report rising experience levels for women; see, for example, Francine D. Blau and Lawrence M. Kahn, "Swimming Upstream: Trends in the Gender Wage Differential in the 1980s," *Journal of Labor Economics* 15, no. 1, pt. 1 (January 1997): 1–42; June O'Neill and Solomon W. Polachek, "Why the Gender Gap in Wages Narrowed in the 1980s," *Journal of Labor Economics* 11, no. 1, pt. 1 (January 1993): 205–28; and Alison J. Wellington, "Changes in the Male/Female Wage Gap, 1976–85," *Journal of Human Resources* 28, no. 2 (Spring 1993): 383–411. Another way to look at the experience gap is to cumulate it over the work life. For example, in a sample of men and women aged 51–61 in 1992, mean labor market experience at age 50 was 9.6 years less for women than for men; see Phillip B. Levine, Olivia S. Mitchell, and John W. Phillips, "Worklife Determinants of Retirement Income Differentials Between Men and Women," in *Innovations in Financing Retirement*, edited by Z. Bodie, B. Hammond, and O. S. Mitchell (Philadelphia: University of Pennsylvania Press, 2002), pp. 50–76. Of course, the lifetime gap is expected to be smaller for more recent cohorts of women who are more consistently attached to the labor force.

[60] U.S. Department of Labor, Bureau of Labor Statistics, "Job Tenure of Workers, January 1966," *Special Labor Force Report* No. 77 (1967); and U.S. Department of Labor, Bureau of Labor Statistics, "Employee Tenure in 2008," *Economic News Release* (September 26, 2008), available at http://www.bls.gov/news.release/tenure.toc.htm. Note median tenure data are for workers 16 and over; the share of long tenure is for workers 25 and over.

THE ON-THE-JOB TRAINING INVESTMENT DECISION

We begin with a general analysis of the training investment decision. On-the-job training may be divided into two types:

- General training
- Firm-specific training

General training increases the individual's productivity to the same extent in all (or a large number of) firms. For example, an individual may learn to use computer software or operate office equipment that is widely used by many firms. On the other hand, **firm-specific training**, as its name implies, increases the individual's productivity only at the firm that provides the training. For example, one may learn how to get things done within a particular bureaucracy or deal with the idiosyncrasies of a particular computer application or piece of equipment. Most training probably combines elements of both general and firm-specific training. However, for simplicity, we assume that training may be classified as being entirely general or entirely firm specific.

General Training

General training is, by definition, completely transferable from the firm providing the training to other firms. Employers will presumably not be willing to foot any part of the bill for such training because, in a competitive labor market, employers have has no way of making sure they will be able to collect any of the returns. This is because, after workers obtain training, employers must pay them what they are worth elsewhere, or they will simply leave the firm. Thus, if general training is to occur, employees must be willing to bear all the costs, since they will reap all the returns. As in the case of formal education, an individual decides whether to invest in general training by comparing the costs and benefits.

Let us consider Lisa's investment decision, illustrated in Figure 6-4. She will contrast the experience-earnings profile she can expect if she takes a job with no training

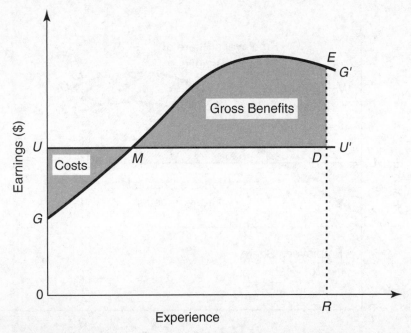

FIGURE 6-4 The On-the-Job Training Investment Decision:
General Training

(*UU'*) to the profile she can expect if she receives general training (*GG'*). On-the-job training, although often informal, still entails costs just as does formal schooling. Some of these costs may be direct. For example, in the cases with formal programs, expenses are incurred for instructors or for materials used in the training. Another portion of the costs is indirect, as the worker and his or her coworkers or supervisor transfer their attention from daily production to training activities. Such expenses arise even when, as is frequently the case, no formal program is in place. The resulting decline in output represents the opportunity cost to the firm of the training activity.

How does Lisa go about "paying" such costs if she decides to invest in general training? She does so by accepting a wage below what she could obtain elsewhere. This lower wage corresponds to her productivity (net of training costs) to the firm during the training period. The costs of the investment in general training are given by the area *UGM*. As Lisa becomes more skilled, her earnings catch up to and eventually surpass what she could earn without training. Assuming a total of *OR* years of labor market experience over her work life, her gross benefits will be equal to the area *MED*. As in the case of formal schooling, she is likely to undertake the investment if gross benefits exceed costs by a sufficient amount to yield the desired rate of return (as appears to be the case in Figure 6-4).

Firm-Specific Training

Figure 6-5 illustrates Don's decision of whether to invest in firm-specific training. His productivity on the job is shown by the profile *GG'*. It is also what his earnings profile would be in the case of general training. However, because firm-specific training is not transferable, Don will not be willing to bear all the costs of the training; his ability to reap the returns depends on continued employment at the firm that initially provided the training. If he were to lose his job, his investment would be wiped out. (The earnings profile available to him at another firm is *UU'*.) If Don paid for all his training, he would experience a strong incentive to remain with his employer, but his employer would have no particular reason to accord him any special protection from layoffs.

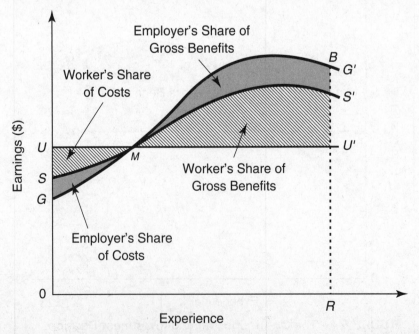

FIGURE 6-5 The On-the-Job Training Investment Decision: Firm-Specific Training

Similarly, the employer is unwilling to shoulder all the costs of firm-specific training because if Don were to quit, the firm would lose its investment. If the employer were to pay all the costs and receive all the returns, Don's profile would be UU'. He would have no special incentive to remain with the firm because he would be earning no more than he could get elsewhere. A temporary shift in demand that resulted in higher wages in another industry or even just more favorable working conditions at another firm might be sufficient to lure him away.

The solution is for the worker and the employer to share the costs of, and returns to, firm-specific training. In this case, the specifically trained worker's profile is SS'. The worker (Don) has an incentive to remain with the firm after completing training because he earns more there than he can get elsewhere (given by profile UU'). The firm also has an incentive to retain a worker who has completed specific training, even in the face of, say, a dip in the demand for its product. This incentive results because the specifically trained worker (Don in this case) is actually being paid less than his productivity—after point M, SS' lies below GG'.

This analysis of firm-specific training has two important implications. First, a relatively permanent attachment is likely to develop between the firm and the specifically trained worker. Such workers are less likely either to quit or to be laid off their jobs than untrained or generally trained workers. Second, because employers pay part of the costs of firm-specific training, they will be concerned about the expected employment stability of workers hired into jobs where such training is important. (This point is developed further later.)

As Figures 6-4 and 6-5 suggest, earnings will increase with experience for workers who have invested in training. Considerable empirical evidence does indeed show a positive relationship between labor market experience and earnings for workers of both sexes. Although the return to experience was lower for women than for men in the 1960s and 1970s, the return to experience for women subsequently increased relative to men's and currently little gender difference is found.[61]

EXPERIENCE AND PRODUCTIVITY

Human capital theory suggests that the reason earnings tend to increase with experience in the labor market is that on-the-job training augments worker productivity. However, critics of the human capital explanation argue that it is not clear that the productivity-enhancing effects of on-the-job training actually *cause* these higher earnings.[62]

For example, the rise in earnings with experience may simply reflect the widespread use of seniority arrangements, which appear to govern wage setting to some extent in the nonunion as well as in the union sector. Of course, this reasoning does not explain why firms would adhere to this practice, if more senior workers were not also generally more productive.

Another alternative to the human capital explanation is that upward-sloping earnings profiles, which reward experience with the firm (tenure), raise workers' productivity because employees are motivated to work hard so as to remain with the firm

---

[61] For evidence of higher returns to experience for men in earlier years, see, for example, Mincer and Polachek, "Family Investments in Human Capital." For studies pointing to a reduction or elimination of this gender difference over the 1980s and 1990s, see, for example, O'Neill and Polachek, "Why the Gender Gap in Wages Narrowed in the 1980s"; Blau and Kahn, "Swimming Upstream"; and Francine D. Blau and Lawrence M. Kahn, "The U.S. Gender Pay Gap in the 1990s," NBER Working Paper No. 10853 (October 2004).

[62] See, for example, James L. Medoff and Katherine G. Abraham, "Are Those Paid More Really More Productive? The Case of Experience," *Journal of Human Resources* 16, no. 2 (Spring 1981): 186–216.

until retirement and, thus, reap the higher earnings that come with longer tenure.[63] This relationship is in the interest of both workers and firms because the resulting increased productivity makes possible both higher earnings and higher profits. Note that, in this model, even though workers are induced to put forth extra effort and be more productive, higher productivity is *not* due to training and productivity does *not* rise with experience. Such alternative explanations focus on the return to tenure (experience with a particular employer), however, and do not necessarily challenge the human capital explanation for the return associated with *general* labor market experience.

It is difficult to obtain data to shed light on this controversy, because information on actual productivity of workers is seldom available. Empirical evidence is mixed, with some studies supporting the human capital explanation and others appearing to refute it.[64]

From the perspective of the individual, the factors influencing the investment decision are not affected by the reasons for the upward-sloping experience-earnings profile. It is the magnitude of costs *versus* benefits that is the individual's principal concern. When the upward-sloping experience-earnings profile reflects an incentive structure offered to the worker by a particular firm, the situation is similar to firm-specific training in that the higher earnings will only be available to the worker if he or she remains at that firm.

GENDER DIFFERENCES IN TRAINING INVESTMENT DECISIONS

Expected Work Life

Does our analysis of the training investment decision suggest that women will be less likely to invest in on-the-job training than men? Or, to put the question somewhat differently, would women be less willing to spend time in relatively low-paid, entry-level positions in order to reap a return in terms of higher earnings later? Again, human capital theory suggests that adherence to traditional gender roles would lower women's incentives to invest.

The impact of women's shorter work lives is illustrated in Figure 6-6. Let us assume TT' represents the earnings profile of a worker with general training who works continuously in the labor market. Here we see that, just as in the case of formal education, the gross return to on-the-job training depends upon the number of years over which the return is earned. Jane, who plans to be in the labor market for a shorter period of time than Lisa, will find the investment in on-the-job training less profitable. For example, suppose she expects to work R' years, and then return after an interruption of $R''-R'$ years. Her benefits are reduced by the time spent out of the labor force when her earnings are zero. Further, it is expected that, due to depreciation of skills, the workforce interruption will lower her earnings profile when she returns from the profile of a continuous worker (TT') to the postinterruption profile (II'), resulting in a further loss of benefits. Although we have again shown the post-interruption profile II' as approaching the profile of a continuous worker TT', a lifetime loss in earnings still occurs.

---

[63] Edward P. Lazear, "Why Is There Mandatory Retirement?" *Journal of Political Economy* 87 (December 1979): 1261–84. Another suggestion is that the observed return to tenure is just a statistical artifact: "Good matches" between workers and firms tend to last longer. So, at any point in time, workers with longer tenure will be higher paid, not because their earnings have risen with seniority but rather because workers with good, high-paying jobs are likely to keep them. See Katherine G. Abraham and Henry Farber, "Job Duration, Seniority, and Earnings," *American Economic Review* 77, no. 3 (June 1987): 278–97.

[64] Studies that do not support the training explanation include Medoff and Abraham, "Are Those Paid More Really More Productive?"; and Abraham and Farber, "Job Duration, Seniority, and Earnings." Those providing support for the training hypothesis include Robert Topel, "Specific Capital, Mobility and Wages: Wages Rise with Job Seniority," *Journal of Political Economy* 99, no. 1 (February 1991): 145–76, and James Brown, "Why Do Wages Increase with Tenure?" *American Economic Review* 79, no. 5 (December 1989): 971–91.

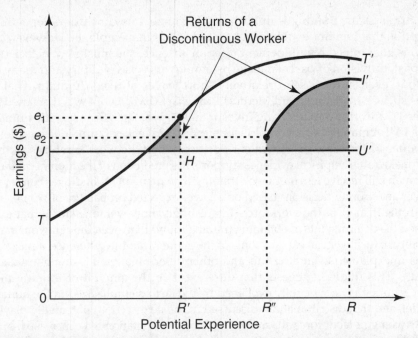

FIGURE 6-6   The Impact of Expected Work Life on the Training Investment Decision

Jane's gross return to her investment in general training is equal to the sum of the two shaded areas, considerably less than Lisa's return shown in Figure 6-4. Given these reductions in benefits, women following traditional gender roles are likely to find it less profitable to make large investments in general training than will career-oriented men or women. Moreover, as we noted in our discussion of field of educational specialization, if occupations differ in the amount of depreciation associated with them, women who anticipate discontinuous work lives are likely to be attracted to fields in which such depreciation is relatively small.[65]

Figure 6-6 may also be used to illustrate the consequences of the shorter and more discontinuous labor force participation of women following a traditional path for their incentives to invest in *firm-specific* training. Assume now that *TT'* is the earnings profile of a worker who obtained firm-specific training. The impact of work interruptions is potentially even more serious in this case, depending crucially on whether a woman is able to return to her initial employer.

Suppose Jennifer left the labor force for a substantial period of time and is unable to get her old job back. The firm-specific skills she acquired are useless in other firms. Her earnings upon her return to the labor force will be only *U* dollars (the earnings of an individual without training), and her new earnings profile will be *UU'* (the profile of an individual without training). The returns to Jennifer's previous investment in firm-specific training were completely wiped out by her withdrawal from the labor force! That is, the second shaded area shown in Figure 6-6 is eliminated, although she will still receive some returns for the brief period before she leaves the labor force. (She could start investing in training again, but the point remains that she will receive no returns from her earlier firm-specific training when she reenters the labor force.)

Thus, human capital theory suggests that women who anticipate workforce interruptions, particularly of long or uncertain duration, will particularly avoid jobs

---

[65] See, especially, Polachek, "Occupational Self-Selection."

where firm-specific training is important. Of course, this conclusion depends on our assumption that Jennifer could not return to her original employer. However, unless a woman is guaranteed reemployment after an absence, she must always face this risk. In the past, provision of parental leave by employers was voluntary and many did not provide it, even in the case of relatively short leaves of fixed duration. That is why policies such as the Family and Medical Leave Act (FMLA) of 1993, discussed later in Chapter 11, are critical to fostering investments in women's firm-specific human capital. The FMLA mandates that employers provide 12 weeks of unpaid leave, along with a guarantee of the same or equivalent position when the worker returns to the firm.

Considerable empirical evidence supports the prediction of the human capital model that women will receive less on-the-job training than men.[66] This finding is consistent with employer and worker decisions based on a lower expected probability of women remaining with the firm or in the workforce. Interestingly, however, one study that explicitly examined the determinants of obtaining training found that, even though women's higher probability of turnover can explain some of the gender training difference, a major portion remains unexplained even after this and other determinants of training are taken into account.[67] This finding suggests that differences in the amount of training men and women acquire may not be fully explained by the factors emphasized in the human capital model, and that discrimination (discussed in the next section) potentially plays a role.

As women's labor force attachment and career orientation have increased, so has the profitability of on-the-job training investments for them, both general and firm specific. This suggests that some of the reduction in occupational segregation by sex that we reviewed in Chapter 5 may be due to women's greater willingness to enter jobs that require considerable amounts of training, as well as the greater willingness of employers to hire them into such jobs. Moreover, as more women are employed in jobs with training opportunities, the opportunity cost of workforce interruptions is increased and their labor force attachment is further reinforced. The most important factor in the case of firm-specific training is attachment to a particular firm. Such an attachment most likely requires that women keep any workforce interruptions within the limits of their employers' leave policy and also raises the question of what such policies should be. We consider this issue in Chapter 11.

Discrimination

The explanation for gender differences in on-the-job training investment decisions suggested by human capital theory stresses differences between men and women in anticipated labor force participation over the life cycle. It is, however, important to point out that, just as in the case of men's and women's formal education decisions, societal discrimination may also be a factor increasing the (pecuniary and nonpecuniary) costs or decreasing the (pecuniary and nonpecuniary) returns to entry into traditionally male fields. Further, labor market discrimination, which is discussed in greater detail in Chapter 7, may also play a part in reducing women's representation in jobs where training is important. That is, overt or subtle discrimination on the part of employers, coworkers, or customers may prove an obstacle to women gaining access to jobs in such areas or reduce the pay of those who are able to obtain employment.

---

[66] See, for example, Joseph G. Altonji and James R. Spletzer, "Worker Characteristics, Job Characteristics, and the Receipt of On-the-Job Training," *Industrial and Labor Relations Review* 45, no. 1 (October 1991): 58–79; Lisa M. Lynch, "Private Sector Training and the Earnings of Young Workers," *American Economic Review* 82, no. 1 (March 1992): 299–312; John Barron and Dan A. Black, "Gender Differences in Training, Capital and Wages," *Journal of Human Resources* 28, no. 2 (Spring 1993): 342–64; and Reed Neil Olsen and Edwin A. Sexton, "Gender Differences in the Returns to and the Acquisition of On-the-Job Training," *Industrial Relations* 35, no. 1 (January 1996): 59–77.

[67] Anne Beeson Royalty, "The Effects of Job Turnover on the Training of Men and Women," *Industrial and Labor Relations Review* 49, no. 3 (April 1996): 506–21.

Firm-specific training provides a particular rationale for employer discrimination that may be important. As illustrated in Figure 6-5, the employer is expected to share some of the costs of firm-specific training. The returns to the firm's (as well as to the worker's) investment depend on how long the individual remains with the firm. Thus, if employers believe that women are less likely to stay at the firm than men, on average, they may prefer men for jobs that require considerable specific training. Employers' differential treatment of men and women on the basis of their perceptions of average gender differences in productivity or job stability has been termed **statistical discrimination**. Such behavior on the part of employers can restrict opportunities for career-oriented as well as noncareer-oriented women, if employers cannot easily distinguish between them.

Finally, labor market discrimination may indirectly lower women's incentives to invest in themselves by decreasing the rewards for doing so. The possibility of such *feedback effects* is considered in greater detail in the next chapter.

OCCUPATIONS AND EARNINGS

The analysis of gender differences in occupations and earnings based on the human capital model is quite straightforward. It is assumed that, given the traditional division of labor in the family, most women do indeed anticipate shorter and less continuous work careers than men. Thus, women are expected to select occupations requiring less investment in education and on-the-job training than those chosen by men. They will particularly avoid jobs in which firm-specific training is important, and employers will be reluctant to hire them for such jobs. Further, they will seek jobs where depreciation of earnings for time spent out of the labor force is minimal.

Hypothetical earnings profiles for predominantly male and predominantly female jobs are shown in Figure 6-7. For simplicity, we assume all workers have the same amount of formal schooling. Earnings profiles in predominantly male jobs are expected to slope steeply upward as does profile MM', because men are expected to undertake substantial investments in on-the-job training. Women, on the other hand, are expected to choose the flatter profile FF', representing smaller amounts of investment in on-the-job training. The existence of the crossover point, H, is crucial to this argument. Before H, profile FF' lies above profile MM'. It is argued that women choose higher earnings now in preference to higher earnings in the future because they do not expect to be in the labor market long enough for the larger human capital investment to pay off. Thus, we see that the human capital analysis of on-the-job training decisions, in conjunction with our previous discussion of formal education, can provide an explanation for the occupational segregation by gender detailed in Chapter 5.

The human capital analysis can also provide an explanation for gender differences in earnings. As we have seen, the human capital model suggests that women are less likely to make large investments in formal schooling. To the extent that women in the labor force were less likely than men to obtain a college or graduate education, their earnings would be reduced relative to men's. Because, even in the past, gender differences in educational attainment were fairly small, differences between men and women in fields of specialization would be of potentially more importance in explaining gender differences in earnings, to the extent that men are likely to enter more lucrative areas.

For given levels of formal education, our consideration of on-the-job training investments also gives us reasons to expect women to earn less, on average, as illustrated in Figure 6-7: Mean female earnings are $\overline{E}_f$ dollars and are less than male mean earnings of $\overline{E}_m$ dollars. Why do women earn less? First, on average they have less labor market experience than men—$\overline{X}_f$ is less than $\overline{X}_m$. Because earnings tend to increase with experience, women's lesser experience decreases their earnings relative to men's. Second, for reasons given

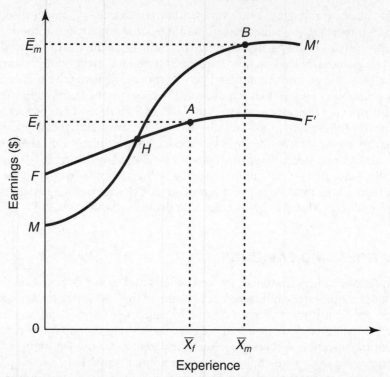

FIGURE 6-7 On-the-Job Training and Sex Differences in Occupations and Earnings

earlier, males have steeper profiles; they experience larger increases in earnings for additional years of experience. After crossover point H, this difference in returns produces a widening gap between male and female earnings with increasing labor market experience.

OTHER SUPPLY-SIDE FACTORS

Traditional gender roles, which result in women being viewed as the secondary earner in the family, may work to produce differences in economic outcomes in a variety of ways beyond their impact on human capital investments. For example, one study found that wives in dual-earner couples who have the "secondary" career in their family tend to earn lower wages than those who have the "primary" career, even controlling for any differences in levels of education or actual work experience, and the presence of children.[68] We briefly consider a number of ways in which adherence to traditional gender roles in the family could reduce women's wages relative to men's. This issue receives considerably more attention in Chapters 10 and 11.

First, the longer hours that women tend to spend on housework may reduce the effort that they put into their market jobs and thus decrease their hourly wage compared to men with similar qualifications.[69] Indeed, additional hours spent in

---

[68] Anne E. Winkler and David C. Rose, "Career Hierarchy in Dual-Earner Families," in *Research in Labor Economics*, edited by Solomon W. Polachek (Greenwich, CT: JAI Press, 2000), pp. 147–72.

[69] See Gary S. Becker, "The Allocation of Effort, Specific Human Capital, and the Differences Between Men and Women in Earnings and Occupations," *Journal of Labor Economics* 3, no. 1, pt. 2 (January 1985): 33–58.

housework by workers are associated with lower wages, all else equal.[70] Also consistent with women placing a greater priority on family responsibilities to the detriment of their labor market outcomes is the empirical evidence that women are more likely to quit their jobs for family-related reasons, which negatively affects their subsequent earnings.[71] Interestingly, some evidence shows that this gender difference in the pattern of quits is concentrated among workers with a high school education or less, while little gender difference is found for those who have attended college.[72] This finding suggests that workforce attachment of the latter group may be more nearly equal to their male counterparts.

Further evidence suggesting that women's nonmarket responsibilities may negatively affect their labor market outcomes is the finding that the presence of children negatively affects the wages of women.[73] To some extent this finding reflects the labor force disruptions mothers often experience. However, even after adjusting for differences in experience, mothers earn less. One explanation for this finding is that, in the past, the birth or adoption of a child often resulted in women severing their tie to the firm. They would thus lose the returns to any firm-specific training acquired and forgo what might have been an exceptionally good job match. Some evidence indicates that the availability of maternity leave significantly mitigates this negative effect, most likely because it enables women to take a short amount of time out but still maintain their attachment to the firm.[74]

In contrast to the finding that children negatively affect the wages of women, married men tend to earn a wage premium compared to single men, whether or not children are present.[75] While the positive association between marriage and wages for men might reflect a selection of men with higher earnings potential into marriage, or even discrimination in favor of married men by employers, the evidence suggests higher productivity is an important factor. This may in turn reflect the greater motivation or commitment of married men to their jobs, given some adherence to traditional gender roles in the family.

Second, to the extent that families place priority on the husband's, rather than on the wife's, career in determining the location of the family, her earnings are likely to be decreased. She may be a "tied mover," relocating when it is not advantageous for her to leave a job where she has accumulated considerable seniority and firm-specific training. Alternatively, she may be a "tied stayer," unable to relocate despite good opportunities elsewhere.[76] Anticipation of a lesser ability to determine the geographic location of the family may also lead women to select occupations in which jobs are likely to be readily obtained in any labor market, thus constraining their occupational choices.

---

[70] For evidence that housework reduces wages, see Joni Hersch and Leslie S. Stratton, "Housework, Fixed Effects and Wages of Married Workers," *Journal of Human Resources* 32, no. 2 (Spring 1997): 285–307. In other work, Leslie S. Stratton suggests that time spent in housework may reduce wages, not because of less effort, but because of time constraints created by the demands of household responsibilities; see "Why Does More Housework Lower Women's Wages? Testing Hypotheses Involving Job Effort and Hours Flexibility," *Social Science Quarterly* 82, no. 1 (March 2001): 67–76.

[71] Kristen Keith and Abagail McWilliams, "The Wage Effects of Cumulative Job Mobility," *Industrial and Labor Relations Review* 49, no. 1 (October 1995): 121–37.

[72] Anne Beeson Royalty, "Job-to-Job and Job-to-Nonemployment Turnover by Gender and Education Level," *Journal of Labor Economics* 16, no. 2 (April 1998): 392–443.

[73] See, for example, Victor R. Fuchs, *Women's Quest for Economic Equality* (Cambridge, MA: Harvard University Press, 1988), and Jane Waldfogel, "Understanding the 'Family Gap' in Pay for Women with Children," Journal of Economic Perspectives 12, no. 1 (Winter 1998): 157–70.

[74] See Waldfogel, "Understanding the 'Family Gap' in Pay for Women with Children." Considerably smaller effects of maternity leave are reported in Masanori Hashimoto, Rick Percy, Teresa Schoellner, and Bruce A. Weinberg, "The Long and Short of It: Maternity Leave Coverage and Women's Labor Market Outcomes," IZA Discussion Paper No. 1207 (July 2004).

[75] David C. Ribar, "What Do Social Scientists Know About the Benefits of Marriage? A Review of Quantitative Methodologies," IZA Discussion Paper No. 998 (January 2004).

[76] See, for example, Jacob Mincer, "Family Migration Decisions," *Journal of Political Economy* 86, no. 5 (October 1978): 749–73, and Thomas J. Cooke, Paul Boyle, and Kenneth Couch, "A Longitudinal Analysis of Family Migration and the Gender Gap in Earnings in the United States and Great Britain," *Demography* (forthcoming).

Third, if women tend to give greater priority than men to family concerns, they may restrict the amount of daily commuting they are willing to do,[77] their hours and work schedules, or their availability for work-related travel. Such constraints could adversely influence women's employment and occupational choices and reduce their earnings relative to men's. Finally, if women anticipate a shorter work life than men, they may invest less time in searching out the best possible job and, as a consequence, receive lower earnings.[78]

As with the human capital investment decisions we discussed earlier, it is important to bear in mind that women's decisions concerning the priority they place on their own versus their husbands' careers, the adaptations they make in response to family responsibilities, and so on may reflect social pressures as well as voluntary choices. Further, to the extent that women face discrimination in the labor market that decreases their wages relative to their husbands', traditional gender roles in the family are reinforced. This is the case because the opportunity cost of wives sacrificing their career objectives to family demands is reduced relative to their husbands'.

THE HUMAN CAPITAL EXPLANATION: AN ASSESSMENT

The human capital model provides a clear, consistent theoretical explanation for gender differences in earnings and occupations in terms of the voluntary choices women and men make. In assessing the contribution of the model, however, it is important to consider the extent to which the data support it. Specifically, we want to know the answers to two questions: Do the factors emphasized by human capital theorists help explain gender differences in labor market outcomes? If so, do they provide the *full* explanation? A voluminous literature in economics investigates these questions. Actual estimates vary depending on the sources of the data used and the types of qualifications examined. Nonetheless, most studies find that human capital factors, particularly women's lesser labor market experience, are important in explaining the gender pay gap. In addition to gender differences in overall experience, other important dimensions of work history include length of time employed on a particular job (tenure), work interruptions, and the timing of past work experience.[79] However, most studies also find that a substantial portion of the pay gap cannot be explained by gender differences in qualifications. The portion of the pay gap that is not explained by gender differences in qualifications is generally presumed to be due to labor market discrimination, although important measurement problems need to be taken into account before reaching such a conclusion. We discuss this evidence at greater length in Chapter 7.

Conclusion

In this chapter, we examined supply-side explanations for gender differences in occupations and earnings, chiefly focusing upon the human capital model and its explanation for gender differences in investment in formal education and on-the-job training. Although the evidence suggests that such factors are important, they are only part of

---

[77] Janice Madden suggested that the lesser willingness of women to commute increases the monopsony power of firms over their wages, thus decreasing their wages relative to men's; see "A Spatial Theory of Sex Discrimination," *Journal of Regional Science* 17, no. 3 (December 1977): 369–80. The monopsony model is discussed further in Chapter 7.

[78] Some evidence consistent with this possibility is found in Steven H. Sandell, "Is the Unemployment Rate of Women Too Low? A Direct Test of the Economic Theory of Job Search," *Review of Economics and Statistics* 62, no. 4 (November 1980): 634–38.

[79] See, for example, Mincer and Polachek, "Family Investments in Human Capital"; Blau and Kahn, "The U.S. Gender Pay Gap in the 1990s"; O'Neill and Polachek, "Why the Gender Gap"; Wellington, "Changes in the Male/Female Wage Gap"; and Audrey Light and Manuelita Ureta, "Early-Career Work Experience and Gender Wage Differentials," *Journal of Labor Economics* 13, no. 1 (January 1995): 121–54.

the story. Discrimination against women in the labor market is also an important factor, to which we turn in the next chapter. In Chapter 11, we broadly consider the conflicts that female and increasingly male workers face in coping with the dual demands of family and paid work, as well as the policies that government or private employers pursue, or might consider pursuing, to increase women's human capital and labor force attachment.

Questions for Review and Discussion

* Indicates that the question can be answered using a diagram illustrating the individual's human capital investment decision as well as verbally. Consult with your instructor about the appropriate approach for your class.

1. What are the main economic factors that underlie the decision to invest in a college education?
2. Carefully explain how the following hypothetical situations would affect the cost–benefit decision of whether it is worthwhile to invest in college.

   a. It is increasingly the case that full-time undergraduate students need five years to complete all of the requirements for a bachelor's degree.*
   b. The real earnings of college-trained workers increase while those of high school–trained workers decrease.*

3. As a future worker, explain the costs and benefits to you of obtaining highly specialized training from a particular firm.
4. What are the main reasons why women frequently invested less in their human capital than men? What changed this tendency? What government or employer policies would be likely to accelerate this change?
5. To what extent and how did economic factors influence the following:

   a. Your decision to attend college.
   b. Your choice of major.
   c. Your plans to go on or not to go on to graduate work.

   Would you expect any of these considerations to differ between men and women, and if so why?

6. It is claimed that employers are reluctant to hire women for some jobs because of their higher expected quit rates. Assuming women are more likely to quit, use human capital theory to explain what kind of jobs an employer would be especially reluctant to hire women for. Explain the reasons for the employer's reluctance.* How valid do you think such employer assumptions about women are today?

7. This problem revisits Denise's net present value calculation regarding the decision to invest in specialized training which was discussed in the inset entitled "Calculating the Net Present Value of a Human Capital Investment."(Consult with your instructor to find out if you are responsible for this material.) The calculation performed in the inset (referred to subsequently as the "initial calculation") was based on a set of assumptions. Recalculate the net present value of Denise's training investment for the following situations: [*Hint*: You can use a spreadsheet program like Excel to calculate net present value.]

   a. The discount rate is .10 instead of .05. (All other parts of the initial calculation remain the same). What does this tell you about the effect of an increase in the discount rate on the training decision, all else equal?
   b. Salary foregone during training is $30,000 instead of $20,000. (All other parts of the initial calculation remain the same.) What does this tell you about the effect of an increase in training costs on the training decision, all else equal?
   c. Additional earnings from training are expected to be $5,000 per year instead of $6,000. (All other parts of the initial calculation remain the same.) What does this tell you about the effect of a reduction in annual benefits on the training decision, all else equal?
   d. Expected work life after training falls from ten to five years. (All other parts of the initial calculation remain the same.) What does this tell you about the effect of a shorter work life on the training decision, all else equal?

Suggested Readings

Becker, Gary S. *Human Capital: A Theoretical and Empirical Analysis, with Special Reference to Education*, 3rd ed. Chicago: University of Chicago Press, 1993.

Blau, Francine D., and Lawrence M. Kahn. "Gender Differences in Pay." *Journal of Economic Perspectives* 14, no. 4 (Fall 2000): 75–99.

Corbett, Christine, Catherine Hill, and Andresse St. Rose. *Where the Girls Are: The Facts About Gender Equity in Education*. Washington, DC: AAUW Educational Foundation, May 2008.

Freeman, Catherine E. "Trends in Educational Equity of Girls and Women." National Center for Educational

Statistics (NCES) Working Paper No. 2005-016, November 2004.

Goldin, Claudia, Lawrence F. Katz, and Ilyana Kuziemko. "The Homecoming of American College Women: The Reversal of the College Gender Gap." *Journal of Economic Perspectives* 20, no. 4 (Fall 2006): 133–56.

King, Jacqueline E. *Gender Equity in Higher Education: 2006*. Washington, DC: American Council on Education, Center for Policy Analysis, 2006.

Mincer, Jacob, and Solomon W. Polachek. "Family Investments in Human Capital: Earnings of Women." *Journal of Political Economy* 82, no. 2, pt. 2 (March/April 1974): S76–S108.

Neumark, David. *Sex Differences in Labor Markets*. London: Routledge, 2004.

Stevenson, Betsy. "Title IX and the Evolution of High School Sports." *Contemporary Economic Policy* 25, no. 4 (October 2007): 486–505.

Tobias, Sheila. *Overcoming Math Anxiety: Revised and Expanded*. New York: W.W. Norton, 1995.

Waldfogel, Jane. "Understanding the 'Family Gap' in Pay for Women with Children." *Journal of Economic Perspectives* 12, no. 1 (Winter 1998): 157–70.

Key Terms

societal discrimination *151*
labor market discrimination *151*
human capital *152*
experience-earnings profiles *158*
direct costs *158*

indirect costs *158*
present value *160*
net present value *160*
discount rate *160*
internal rate of return *161*
screening device *164*
signal *164*

statistical discrimination *164*
socialization *169*
subtle barriers *174*
role models *174*
mentor–protégé relationship *174*

informal network *174*
Title IX *175*
general training *181*
firm-specific training *181*
statistical discrimination *187*

CHAPTER 7

Differences in Occupations and Earnings: The Role of Labor Market Discrimination

Chapter Highlights

- Labor Market Discrimination: A Definition
- Empirical Evidence of Labor Market Discrimination
- Models of Labor Market Discrimination
- Policy Issue: The Government and Equal Employment Opportunity
- Appendix: Regression Analysis and Empirical Estimates of Labor Market Discrimination

---

In the preceding chapter, we examined the role of supply-side factors in producing the gender differences in earnings and occupational attainment that we observe in the labor market and that were described in Chapter 5. We now focus upon the demand side, specifically the role of labor market discrimination. As we explained at the end of Chapter 6, the available evidence suggests that both supply- and demand-side influences are responsible for gender differences in economic outcomes.

In this chapter, we begin by providing a definition of labor market discrimination. Next, we examine the empirical evidence on the extent of gender discrimination in the labor market with respect to earnings and occupations. We then turn to a detailed consideration of the various explanations economists have offered for the existence and persistence of such discrimination. Although our focus is on gender discrimination, much of the analysis is equally applicable to discrimination based on other factors, such as race, ethnicity, age, or disability. In fact, most of the models of discrimination we discuss were initially developed to explain racial discrimination.

Our primary concern here is to determine to what extent discrimination exists and its possible effects on women's status in the labor market. This is partly an issue of equity or fairness. However, there is also an issue of misallocation of resources when workers are not hired, promoted, or rewarded on the basis of their qualifications. Thus, efficiency, as well as considerations of equity, provides an important rationale for government intervention to combat labor market discrimination. We conclude by reviewing the government's antidiscrimination policies and examining their possible effects.

LABOR MARKET DISCRIMINATION: A DEFINITION

Labor market discrimination exists when *two equally qualified individuals are treated differently solely on the basis of their gender* (race, age, disability, etc.).[1] As we saw in Chapter 1, in the absence of

---

[1] This definition is derived from the work of Gary S. Becker, *The Economics of Discrimination*, 2nd ed. (Chicago: University of Chicago Press, 1971).

discrimination, profit-maximizing employers in a competitive labor market pay workers in accordance with their productivity. For similar reasons, they also find it in their economic self-interest to make other personnel decisions, such as hiring, placement, or promotion, on the same objective basis. An individual's gender (or race, age, disability, etc.) would be an irrelevant consideration.

If labor market discrimination nonetheless exists, it is expected to adversely affect the economic status of women *directly* by producing differences in economic outcomes between men and women that are *not* accounted for by differences in their productivity-related characteristics or qualifications. That is, men and women who, in the absence of discrimination, would be equally productive and would receive the same pay (or be in the same occupation) do not receive equal rewards. As we shall see, in some economic models of discrimination, this inequality occurs because women are paid less than their marginal product due to discrimination. In other views of this process, labor market discrimination *directly* lowers women's productivity as well as their pay, as for instance, when a woman is denied access to an employer-sponsored training program or when customers are reluctant to patronize a female salesperson.

If such gender differences in *treatment* of equally qualified men and women are widespread and persistent, the behavior of women themselves may be adversely affected. As we saw in the preceding chapter, productivity differences among workers reflect, in part, the decisions they make whether to continue their schooling, participate in a training program, remain continuously in the labor market, and so on. Faced with discrimination in the labor market that lowers the returns to such human capital investments, women have less incentive to undertake them. To the extent that such *indirect* or **feedback effects** of labor market discrimination exist, they are also expected to adversely affect the economic outcomes of women compared to men.

Much of the theoretical and empirical work on labor market discrimination has focused on its more readily measured *direct* effects on pay or occupational differences between equally well-qualified (potentially equally productive) men and women. We follow that emphasis in this chapter. However, it is important to recognize that the *full* impact of discrimination also includes any feedback effects on women's behavior that result in their being less well qualified than men.[2] Thus, we also discuss such feedback effects.

EMPIRICAL EVIDENCE OF LABOR MARKET DISCRIMINATION

Having defined labor market discrimination, we now consider the empirical evidence as to the existence and extent of such discrimination. We restrict ourselves entirely to the direct effects of such discrimination and, thus, take as given any gender differences in qualifications. Our purpose is to address more fully the types of questions raised at the end of Chapter 6. Are gender differences in labor market outcomes *fully* explained by gender differences in qualifications or (potential) productivity? If not, how large is the unexplained portion of the gender differential? It is this differential that is commonly used as an estimate of the impact of labor market discrimination. Unfortunately, as we shall see, though the questions are relatively straightforward, the answers are not so easily obtained. We turn first to a consideration of gender differences in earnings and then to an examination of gender differences in occupations.

Earnings Differences

Economists and other social scientists have studied the sources of the earnings gap between men and women workers extensively. Estimates vary depending on the data

---

[2] Note that the argument is *not* that *all* differences in qualifications between men and women are due to the indirect effects of discrimination, but, rather, that *some* of these differences may be a response to such discrimination.

used and the types of qualifications examined. However, virtually all studies find that a substantial portion of the pay gap cannot be explained by gender differences in qualifications.[3]

EVIDENCE ON DISCRIMINATION FROM STATISTICAL ANALYSES   One standard method of decomposing gender differences in earnings is to use statistical methods. Here we discuss the general method and present findings from a representative study conducted by Francine Blau and Lawrence Kahn.[4] Essentially, the method decomposes the **gender wage gap** into two parts: the part of the gender difference that is due to differences in human capital or other qualifications (the **explained gap**) and the part that *cannot* be explained by these factors (the **unexplained gap**). The Blau-Kahn analysis is based on data from the Panel Study of Income Dynamics (PSID), which contains information on actual labor market experience for a large, nationally representative sample. The data used are for full-time workers aged from 18 to 65 in 1999. (Information on wages relates to the preceding calendar year, 1998.) The restriction to full-time workers is designed to focus on male and female workers who are as similar as possible.[5] Table 7-1 provides results of from this study and shows the contribution of each variable to explaining the gender wage differential of 20 percent. This procedure is explained in detail in Appendix 7A. The variables considered include indicators of human capital, that is, education and experience, as well as measures of occupation, industry, and union status. Race is also included as a control variable, but its effect is small because the proportion of each race group in the full-time sample is about the same for men and women.

As would be expected based on our discussion in Chapter 6, women's lesser amount of labor market experience is a significant determinant of the gender wage differential, explaining 11 percent of the gender gap in wages. This proportion reflects a 3.5-year difference in full-time experience between men and women, which, though smaller than in previous years, is still a substantial factor contributing to the wage gap.[6]

Interestingly, women in this sample had *more* education than men, which (as indicated by the negative sign in the table) works to *lower* the gender wage gap by 7 percent. In other words, gender differences in educational attainment do not help to explain the

---

[3] For summaries of this literature, see, for example, Francine D. Blau and Lawrence M. Kahn, "Women's Work and Wages," in *The New Palgrave Dictionary of Economics*, 2nd ed., edited by Steven N. Durlauf and Lawrence E. Blume (London: Palgrave Macmillan, 2008), pp. 762–72, available at The New Palgrave Dictionary of Economics Online (http://www.dictionaryofeconomics.com/dictionary); Joni Hersch, "Sex Discrimination in the Labor Market," *Foundations and Trends in Microeconomics* 2, no. 4 (2006): 281–361; Francine D. Blau and Lawrence M. Kahn, "Gender Differences in Pay," *Journal of Economic Perspectives* 14, no. 4 (Fall 2000): 75–99; Joseph G. Altonji and Rebecca M. Blank, "Race and Gender in the Labor Market," in *Handbook of Labor Economics*, edited by Orley C. Ashenfelter and David Card (Amsterdam: North-Holland, 1999), pp. 3C: 3143–259; and T. D. Stanley and Stephen B. Jarrell, "Gender Wage Discrimination Bias? A Meta-Regression Analysis," *Journal of Human Resources* 33, no. 4 (Fall 1998): 947–73.

[4] Francine D. Blau and Lawrence M. Kahn, "The U.S. Gender Pay Gap in the 1990s: Slowing Convergence," *Industrial and Labor Relations Review* 60, no. 1 (October 2006): 45–66.

[5] In addition to gender differences in qualifications and the extent of discrimination, the gender earnings differential may also be affected by the self-selection of women and men into the labor force and into full-time employment. In other words, those choosing to participate—or to work full time—may differ from those who choose to remain outside the labor force or to work part time in terms of both their measured and unmeasured characteristics. One possibility is that labor force participants are a positively selected group of those who received higher wage offers. Similarly, full-time workers may be more highly qualified and more committed to market work. Blau and Kahn find that, at a point in time, the gender pay gap is smaller if only full-time workers are considered than if part-timers and nonparticipants are included; in their paper, they examine the impact of changes in female and male selection into the labor force on trends in the gender pay gap. For further consideration of the selection issue, see Casey B. Mulligan and Yona Rubinstein, "Selection, Investment, and Women's Relative Wages," *Quarterly Journal of Economics* 123, no. 3 (August 2008): 1061–110. Research on the earnings differential between white and black women has found that, if self-selection is not accounted for, the race gap is underestimated; see Derek Neal, "The Measured Black-White Wage Gap Among Women Is Too Small," *Journal of Political Economy* 112, no. 1, pt. 2 (February 2004): S1–S28.

[6] Although women do have a bit more part-time experience than men, part-time experience is found to have a very low payoff in terms of current wages.

TABLE 7-1	Contribution of Measured Characteristics to the Gender Wage Differential, 1998	
Characteristics	**Percent Explained**
Educational attainment	–6.7
Labor force experience	10.5
Race	2.4
Occupational category	27.4
Industry category	21.9
Union status	3.5
Unexplained	41.1
Total	100.0
[Wage differential (%)	20.3]

Source: Calculated from data presented in Francine D. Blau and Lawrence M. Kahn, "The US Gender Pay Gap in the 1990s: Slowing Convergence," *Industrial and Labor Relations Review* 60, no. 1 (October 2006): 45–66; and NBER Working Paper No. 10853 of the same title (October 2004).

gender wage gap, but rather work slightly in the opposite direction. In the late 1990s, when the data for Table 7-1 were collected, women had an educational advantage among workers who were employed full time, though not yet among the full population (including those who are out of the labor force).[7]

Finally, as we would expect based on the data presented in Chapter 5, gender differences in occupation and industry remain substantial and help to explain a considerable portion of the gender wage gap. Recall that men are more likely to be in blue-collar jobs and a number of traditionally-male occupations in the professional category, and to work in mining, construction, durable manufacturing, or transportation and utilities; they are also more likely to be in unionized employment. Women are more likely to be in clerical and service jobs, as well as a number of traditionally-female professions, and to work in education and health services and financial activities. Taken together, occupation and industry differences explain 53 percent of the gender wage gap—27 percent for occupation, 22 percent for industry, and an additional 4 percent for union status.[8]

Although these findings suggest that gender differences in work-related characteristics are important, they also indicate that qualifications are only part of the story. The portion of the wage differential that is *not* explained by productivity-related characteristics serves as an estimate of labor market discrimination. In this case, 41 percent of the gender gap cannot be explained even when gender differences in education, experience, industries, occupations, and union status are taken into account. The portion of the pay gap that remains unexplained is potentially due to discrimination, though as we shall see shortly, the matter is not quite so simple.

We can consider the results of this study somewhat differently by focusing on the gender wage ratio. The actual ("unadjusted") gender wage ratio is 80 percent; that is, women's wages are, on average, 80 percent of men's wages. If women had the same human capital characteristics (i.e., education and experience), industry and occupational distribution, and union coverage as men, the "adjusted" ratio would rise to 91 percent of men's wages. Thus, although measured characteristics are important, women still earn less than similar men even when all measured characteristics are taken into account.

---

[7] As we saw in Chapter 4, labor force participation is positively correlated with education, more so for women than men. Thus, women in the labor force tend to be more highly educated relative to men than is the total female population.
[8] The study controls for 19 occupations and 25 industries.

BIASES IN THE ESTIMATE OF DISCRIMINATION   How conclusive are such estimates as indicators of labor market discrimination? Certainly not entirely so; a number of problems associated with these types of analyses may result in either upward or downward biases in the estimate of discrimination. One difficulty is that we lack information on all the qualifications of individuals that are associated with their (potential) productivity. Some of the factors that affect earnings, such as motivation or work effort, cannot easily be quantified. Others (e.g., college major) are frequently unavailable in a particular data set. Hence, in general, it is not possible to include all relevant job qualifications in a study of gender differences in wages.

For instance, although the study reported in Table 7-1 accounts for differences between men and women in many important work-related factors, it lacks data on others that are also potentially relevant. If men are more highly qualified with respect to the factors that are omitted from the analysis, the extent of labor market discrimination is likely to be *overestimated*. Some portion of the "unexplained" gender differential in Table 7-1 may, in fact, be due to men being more highly motivated or to gender differences in college major. However, it is also possible that women are more highly qualified in some respects not taken into account. They may possess greater interpersonal skills, for example. In that case, discrimination would be *underestimated*. In general, more attention has been focused on the possibility that discrimination may be overestimated due to omitted factors.[9]

An additional factor that could cause discrimination to be underestimated is that some of the lower qualifications of women may themselves be a direct result of labor market discrimination. For example, qualified women may be excluded from particular jobs due to discrimination in hiring or promotion. The results reported in Table 7-1 include controls for variables such as occupation and industry, which could themselves be affected by such discrimination. To the extent that studies of discrimination control for qualifications that themselves reflect the direct effects of discrimination, the impact of discrimination on the pay gap will be *underestimated*.[10] The results presented in Table 7-1 suggest that the unexplained gap would be considerably larger had we not controlled for occupation and industry. Indeed, according to estimates based on the Blau-Kahn study, the adjusted wage ratio would fall from 91 to 81 percent if these variables were excluded and only education, experience and race were controlled for.

Analyses of the type presented in Table 7-1 also neglect the feedback effects of labor market discrimination on the behavior and choices of women. For example, women traditionally received lower returns to labor market experience than men. The lesser amount of work experience that they accumulated may be due in part to their response to these lower returns. As another example, women were perhaps less likely to pursue college study in traditionally male fields because of their perception that they would encounter job discrimination in these areas.

---

[9] This problem is a bit less serious than it appears at first glance because the included factors likely capture some of the effects of those that cannot be controlled for because of lack of information. For example, it is likely that more highly educated individuals are also more intelligent and more able, on average, than the less educated. For an interesting explication of the statistical issues raised by imperfect measures of productivity, see Arthur Goldberger, "Reverse Regression and Salary Discrimination," *Journal of Human Resources* 19, no. 3 (Summer 1984): 293–318.

[10] For a consideration of such issues, see Alan Blinder, "Wage Discrimination: Reduced Form and Structural Estimates," *Journal of Human Resources* 8, no. 4 (Fall 1973): 436–55, and Ronald Oaxaca, "Male-Female Wage Differences in Urban Labor Markets," *International Economic Review* 14, no. 3 (October 1973): 693–709. For evidence on the issue of discrimination against women in access to on-the-job training, see Greg J. Duncan and Saul Hoffman, "On-the-Job Training and Earnings Differences by Race and Sex," *Review of Economics and Statistics* 61, no. 4 (November 1979): 594–603; John M. Barron, Dan A. Black, and Mark A. Lowenstein, "Gender Differences in Training, Capital and Wages," *Journal of Human Resources* 28, no. 2 (1993): 342–64; and Anne Beeson Royalty, "The Effects of Job Turnover on the Training of Men and Women," *Industrial and Labor Relations Review* 49, no. 3 (April 1996): 506–21.

SOME EVIDENCE ON POSSIBLE SOURCES OF THE UNEXPLAINED GENDER WAGE GAP While the existence of an unexplained pay gap in traditional statistical analyses is consistent with discrimination against women in the labor market, as we have seen, this does not mean that the full unexplained gap may be attributed to discrimination. In this section, we consider some of the factors apart from discrimination that may contribute to an unexplained pay gap between men and women in conventional analyses.

Some of the unexplained gap may be due to the impact of childbearing. Research suggests a negative effect of children on women's wages that is not simply due to the workforce interuptions associated with childbearing. This may reflect the fact that, particularly in the past, women often severed their ties to their employer and withdrew from the labor force entirely after the birth of a child. They thus gave up the returns to any firm-specific training they had acquired, as well as any rewards for having made an especially good job match.[11] Of course, as we discuss in a later section of this chapter, the division of labor in the family may itself be influenced by the market opportunities available to women and men in the labor market. The negative impact of children on women's labor market outcomes and possible policy responses are discussed further in Chapters 10 and 11.

Another possible source of the unexplained wage gap is gender differences in noncognitive skills such as work habits, behavioral traits, or preferences.[12] We noted some of these differences in Chapter 6. For example, evidence suggests that women tend to shy away from competition while men are drawn to it.[13] Similarly, there is evidence that women's propensity to negotiate is much less than men's.[14] These gender differences could plausibly negatively affect the performance and wages of women in certain settings. Further, the lesser value that women place on money and work than men has been found to lower their wages relative to men's.[15] While the impact of gender differences in noncognitive skills may contribute to the unexplained gender wage gap in studies that lack information on these factors, some caution must be used in broadly attributing the unexplained gap to the effects of noncognitive skills. For one thing, not all gender differences in noncognitive skills favor men. Interpersonal skills are an important noncognitive skill, and women tend to have better interpersonal skills than men. Indeed, one study has found that women's advantage in this area has helped to increase their wages relative to men's.[16] There may also be significant feedback effects from differential treatment in the labor market to noncognitive traits. So, for example, women's lesser focus on wages or reluctance to negotiate may be a result of anticipated discrimination.

---

[11] Complex issues are involved in measuring this effect because, as discussed in Chapter 10, it may be that children reduce women's productivity and hence their earnings, but it may also be the case that less productive women choose to have more children. For a review of the empirical findings, see Hersch, "Sex Discrimination in the Labor Market."

[12] Noncognitive skills are getting an increasing amount of attention by economists, see Bas ter Weel, "The Noncognitive Determinants of Labor Market and Behavioral Outcomes: Introduction to the Symposium," *Journal of Human Resources* 43, no. 4 (Fall 2008): 729–37; also see other articles in this special issue of the journal.

[13] Muriel Niederle and Lise Vesterlund, "Do Women Shy Away from Competition?" *Quarterly Journal of Economics* 122, no. 3 (August 2007): 1067–101. Some evidence also suggests that competition has a more positive effect on men's performance than on women's; see Uri Gneezy, Muriel Niederle, and Aldo Rustichini, "Performance in Competitive Environments: Gender Differences," *Quarterly Journal of Economics* 118, no. 3 (August 2003): 1049–74.

[14] Linda Babcock and Sara Laschever, *Women Don't Ask: Negotiation and the Gender Divide* (Princeton: Princeton University Press, 2003).

[15] Nicole M. Fortin, "The Gender Wage Gap Among Young Adults in the United States; The Importance of Money Versus People," *Journal of Human Resources* 43, no. 4 (Fall 2008): 884–918. The measure of the value placed on money and work that was used in this study was based on respondents' answers to questions about the importance in selecting a career of *Making of lot of money* and *The chance to be a leader* and about the importance in life of *Being successful at work* and *Having lots of money* (p. 888).

[16] Lex Borghans, Baster Weel, and Bruce Weinberg, "People People: Social Capital and the Labor-Market Outcomes of Underrepresented Groups," NBER Working Paper No. 11985 (January 2006).

THE EFFECT OF SEXUAL ORIENTATION ON EARNINGS

Statistical techniques similar to those used to analyze the gender wage gap have also been employed to study discrimination on the basis of sexual orientation. This research has found that gays earn less than heterosexual men, both married and unmarried, while lesbians earn more than married and unmarried heterosexual women (although less than either heterosexual or gay men).* One reason for this is probably that gays and lesbians are less likely to pursue a traditional division of labor with their partners than heterosexual men and women.** In most states in the United States, they are not permitted to marry, and their inability to form a legally sanctioned union makes specialization more risky for them. Therefore, gay men are not expected to reap the same benefits from specialization as married men and have lower incentives to specialize in market activities. Similarly, lesbian women may be more career-oriented than heterosexual women who are married or expect to marry, and they may even benefit to the extent that employers view unmarried women as more career minded.

At the same time, the finding that gay men earn less than heterosexual men with similar qualifications is certainly also consistent with discrimination. Even the earnings premium lesbians receive compared to heterosexual women with the same measured qualifications, such as education and work experience, might conceal some discrimination against them based on their sexual orientation. For if lesbians have traits that lead to higher productivity that are unmeasured in standard analyses, such as greater career orientation, then their observed wages, though higher than those of heterosexual women, may not fully reflect their higher average productivity. In addition, discrimination may lower the potential wages of both gays and lesbians by leading them to trade off high-wage jobs for positions that are more open to homosexuals.

A very interesting analysis of the experience of transgender individuals presents further evidence on gender discrimination in the labor market and also sheds light on the economic consequences of such transitions. The study, based on a special survey, examined the labor market outcomes of transgender individuals, that is, people who changed their gender, generally with hormone therapy and surgery. The study found that the average earnings of individuals who changed their gender from female to male increased slightly, while the average earnings of individuals who changed their gender from male to female fell by nearly one-third. The authors note that their findings are consistent with subjective reports that "for many male-to-female workers, becoming a woman often brings a loss of authority, harassment, and termination, but that for many female-to-male workers, becoming a man often brings an increase in respect and authority."***

---

*Dan A. Black, Hoda R. Makar, Seth G. Sanders, and Lowell Taylor, "The Effects of Sexual Orientation on Earnings," *Industrial and Labor Relations Review* 56, no. 3 (April 2003): 449–69; John M. Blandford, "The Nexus of Sexual Orientation and Gender in the Determination of Earnings," *Industrial and Labor Relations Review* 56, no. 4 (July 2003): 622-42; and M. V. Lee Badgett, "Testimony on HR 2015, The Employment Non-Discrimination Act of 2007," U.S. House of Representatives, Committee on Education and Labor, Subcommittee on Health, Employment, Labor, and Pensions, September 5, 2007, available at http://www.law.ucla.edu/williamsinstitute/publications/HR2015%20testimony.pdf.

**See, for example, Dan A. Black, Seth G. Sanders, and Lowell J. Taylor, "The Economics of Lesbian and Gay Families," *Journal of Economic Perspectives* 21, no. 2 (Spring 2007): 53–70.

***Kristen Schilt and Matthew Wiswall, "Before and After: Gender Transitions, Human Capital, and Workplace Experiences," *The B.E. Journal of Economic Analysis & Policy* 8, no. 1 (2008): Article 39, available at http://www.bepress.com/bejeap/vol8/iss1/art39/. The quotation is from the abstract.

ADDITIONAL EVIDENCE ON DISCRIMINATION Given the problems with traditional statistical studies, some particularly persuasive evidence of discrimination comes from other types of studies that take a different approach to identifying discrimination. In the first of these approaches, the studies apply the same statistical techniques as those already discussed, but focus on especially homogeneous groups. The advantage of this approach is that it minimizes the effect of gender differences in unmeasured characteristics.

One such study focused on two cohorts of graduates of the University of Michigan Law School 15 years after graduation; the first surveyed between 1987 and 1993 and the second between 1994 and 2000.[17] The results for the two cohorts were quite similar. The gap in pay between women and men was found to be relatively small at the outset of their careers, but 15 years later, women graduates earned only about 60 percent as much as men. Some of this difference reflected choices that workers themselves made, including the propensity of women lawyers to work shorter hours. However, even after accounting for differences in current hours worked, as well as an extensive list of worker qualifications and other factors, including grades while in law school, and detailed work history data, such as years practiced law, months of part-time work, and type and size of employer, men still earned 11 percent more.

Three other studies focused on the earnings gap of college graduates, also a relatively homogenous group. The first of these studies examined gender wage differences in 1985 among recent college graduates (who had graduated one to two years earlier).[18] After controlling for narrowly defined college major, college grade point average, and specific educational institution attended, this study still found an unexplained pay gap of 10 to 15 percent between men and women. Results reported for a 1993 survey of all college graduates were broadly similar for black and white women, but were mixed for Hispanic and Asian women (all relative to white, non-Hispanic men).[19] The final study used data collected from a 2006 survey to examine the gender earnings gap for three cohorts of Harvard graduates. This analysis included controls for educational performance (incuding GPA, SAT scores, and college major), time out of work, and current occupation and still found a very substantial unexplained gap of approximately 30 percent.[20]

While one must be cautious in interpreting the unexplained gaps identified in these studies as entirely due to discrimination for the reasons we discussed previously, these findings are consistent with discrimination against highly educated women.

An experimental approach is another method used to investigate labor market discrimination. In one such study, male and female pseudo-job seekers were given similar résumés and sent to apply for jobs waiting on tables at the same set of 65 Philadelphia restaurants.[21] The results provided statistically significant evidence of discrimination

---

[17] Mary C. Noonan, Mary E. Corcoran, and Paul Courant, "Pay Differences Among the Highly Trained: Cohort Differences in the Sex Gap in Lawyers' Earnings," *Social Forces* 84, no. 2 (December 2005): 853–72.

[18] Catherine J. Weinberger, "Race and Gender Wage Gaps in the Market for Recent College Graduates," *Industrial Relations* 37, no. 1 (January 1998): 67–84; see also Judy Goldberg Dey and Catherine Hill, *Behind the Gender Gap* (Washington, DC: American Association of University Women Educational Foundation, 2007).

[19] Dan A. Black, Amelia M Haviland, Seth G. Sanders, and Lowell J. Taylor, "Gender Wage Disparities Among the Highly Educated," *Journal of Human Resources* 43, no. 3 (Summer 2008): 630–59. In contrast, Judith A. McDonald and Robert J. Thornton found that college major explains up to 95 percent of the gap in starting salary offers of college graduates over the 1974 to 2001 period; see "Do New Male and Female College Graduates Receive Unequal Pay?" *Journal of Human Resources* 42, no. 1 (Winter 2007): 32–48. However, as Hersch ("Sex Discrimination in the Labor Market") points out, the sample they used in their study may not be representative since the data come from the salary offers made to students who were recruited through campus college placement centers.

[20] Claudia Goldin and Lawrence F. Katz, "Transitions: Career and Family Life Cycles of the Educational Elite," *American Economic Review* 98, no. 2 (May 2008): 363–69.

[21] David Neumark, with the assistance of Roy J. Blank and Kyle D. Van Nort, *Quarterly Journal of Economics* 111, no. 3 (August, 1996): 915–42.

against women in high-priced restaurants where earnings of workers are generally higher. In these restaurants, a female applicant's probability of getting an interview was 40 percentage points lower than a male's and her probability of getting an offer was 50 percentage points lower. A second study examined the impact of the adoption of "blind" auditions for musicians by symphony orchestras in which a screen is used to conceal the identity of the candidate.[22] The screen substantially increased the probability that a woman would advance out of preliminary rounds and be the winner in the final round. The switch to blind auditions was found to explain one quarter of the increase in the percentage female in the top five symphony orchestras in the United States, from less than 5 percent of all musicians in 1970 to 25 percent in 1996.

A third approach that has been employed is to identify an occupation or industry where productivity can be directly measured, such as the amount of output produced per worker. One such study focused on the manufacturing sector. This study attempted to estimate the productivity of women relative to men and then compare the magnitude of the productivity gap to the magnitude of the gender wage gap. It was found that women's estimated marginal product was somewhat lower than men's. However, women's wages fell short of men's by considerably more than what could be explained by their lower marginal productivity. This finding is consistent with discrimination against women in the labor market.[23]

Finally, evidence that labor market discrimination exists is provided by the many employment discrimination cases in which employers were found guilty of discrimination in pay or reached out-of-court settlements with the plaintiffs. A number of employment practices that explicitly discriminated against women used to be quite prevalent, including marriage bars restricting the employment of married women[24] and the intentional segregation of women into separate job categories with lower pay scales.[25] Although such overt practices no longer exist, recent court cases provide evidence that employment practices that produce discriminatory outcomes for women still exist.

As an illustration, we may consider a number of recent cases that involve the financial services industry. In 2008, for example, there was a $33 million settlement of a sex discrimination lawsuit against Smith Barney charging discrimination against female financial consultants. The complaint charged that Smith Barney routinely assigned smaller and less valuable accounts to female brokers (including those who outperformed their male counterparts) and thereby lowered their pay, provided women with less sales and administrative support than it provided to men, and maintained "a corporate culture hostile to female professionals."[26] Similarly, in a sex discrimination lawsuit against Morgan Stanley, which was settled in 2004 for $54 million, the plaintiffs claimed that the firm underpaid and did not promote women. Allegations of sexist

---

[22] Claudia Goldin and Cecilia Rouse, "Orchestrating Impartiality: The Impact of 'Blind' Auditions on Female Musicians," *American Economic Review* 90, no. 4 (September 2000): 715–41. See also Blair Tindall, "Call Me Madame Maestro," *New York Times*, January 14, 2005, available at www.nytimes.com.

[23] See Judith K. Hellerstein, David Neumark, and Kenneth R. Troske, "Wages, Productivity, and Worker Characteristics: Evidence from Plant-Level Production Functions and Wage Equations," *Journal of Labor Economics* 17, no. 3 (July 1999): 409–46. See also Jonathan S. Leonard, "Antidiscrimination or Reverse Discrimination: The Impact of Title VII, Affirmative Action, and Changing Demographics on Productivity," *Journal of Human Resources* 19, no. 2 (Spring 1984): 145–84.

[24] Claudia Goldin, *Understanding the Gender Gap: An Economic History of American Women* (New York: Oxford University Press, 1990).

[25] See, for example, *Bowe v. Colgate-Palmolive Co.*, 416 F.2d 711 (7th Cir., 1969), and *IUE v. Westinghouse Electric Co.*, 631 F.2d 1094 (3rd Cir., 1980).

[26] "Women Employees Sue Smith Barney for Sex Discrimination," March 31, 2005, available at http://www.genderlawsuitagainstsmithbarney.com/press_release_01.htm; and "Court Grants Final Approval to $33 Million Gender Class Action Settlement with Smith Barney," August 13, 2008, available at http://www.genderlawsuitagainstsmithbarney.com/press-release-03.htm.

practices included claims that Morgan Stanley withheld raises and desirable assignments from women who took maternity leave, and that it condoned a hostile workplace where men made sexist comments and organized trips to topless bars and strip clubs.[27] Another example of a major case in this industry was the $31 million settlement of sex bias charges against American Express Financial Advisors in 2002, where it was also claimed that female employees were underpaid and given fewer job opportunities. According to the plaintiffs, the company steered the most profitable accounts to male financial advisers and, corporate-wide, men were given preferential treatment in training, mentoring, and promotion. It was claimed that these gender differences were "the product of a stereotype—pervasive both inside Amex and throughout the industry—that women do not have what it takes to succeed in the financial planning business and that only young males have the temperament and the ability to achieve aggressive sales."[28]

Where do these findings, taken as a whole, leave us? They suggest that pinpointing the exact portion of the pay gap that is due to labor market discrimination is difficult. Nonetheless, the findings of traditional statistical studies provide strong evidence of pay differences between men and women that are *not* accounted for by gender differences in measured qualifications, even when the list of qualifications is quite extensive. The inference from these results that discrimination exists is backed up by the results of studies that take a different approach, as well as by evidence from court cases. We conclude that discrimination does indeed exist. Although precisely estimating its magnitude is difficult, the evidence suggests that the *direct* effects of labor market discrimination may explain 40 percent or more of the pay differential between men and women.

Occupational Differences

As we saw in Chapter 5, not only do women earn less than men, they also tend to be concentrated in different occupations. In this section, we address two questions:

- What are the consequences for women of occupational segregation? In particular, what is its relationship to the pay gap between men and women?
- What are the causes of gender differences in occupational distributions? Specifically, what role does labor market discrimination play? Does the evidence indicate a "glass ceiling" that limits the upward mobility of women?

From a policy perspective, an understanding of the consequences of segregation is crucial for assessing its importance, and an analysis of its causes helps us to determine the most effective tools for attacking it.

CONSEQUENCES OF OCCUPATIONAL SEGREGATION   In Chapter 5, we saw that women are concentrated in clerical and service jobs, whereas men are more likely than women to work in higher-paying, skilled blue-collar occupations. Similarly, although the representation of women in the professional category actually exceeds men's, men are more likely to work in lucrative professions such as law, medicine, and engineering, whereas women are more often employed in lower-paying ones such as elementary and secondary school teaching and nursing. Such observations suggest that women are concentrated in relatively low-paying occupations and that this gender difference in occupations helps to explain the male–female pay gap.

---

[27] "Sex Suit Costs Morgan Stanley $54M," July 12, 2004, available at www.cbsnews.com. See also Patrick McGeehan, "Discrimination on Wall St.? Run the Numbers and Weep," *New York Times*, July 14, 2004, sec. C, pp. 1, 7.
[28] Bureau of National Affairs, "American Express Financial Advisors Reach $31 Million Agreement on Sex Bias Charges," *Employment Discrimination Report* 18, no. 9 (February 27, 2002), p. 251.

On the other hand, factors other than gender composition may help to account for pay differences between male and female jobs. For example, male jobs may tend to require more education and training than female jobs or call for the exercise of skills, such as supervisory responsibility, that are more valuable to the employer. Also, some require more physical strength, inconvenient hours, and so on.

Such characteristics are important, but occupational differences appear to be a significant factor in explaining the earnings gap, even when productivity-related characteristics of workers are held constant. The findings reported in Table 7-1, for example, suggest that differences in the employment of men and women across the 19 occupational categories included in the study account for 27 percent of the pay difference between men and women. A substantial body of research that takes into account a large number of detailed occupational categories—over 400—finds a negative relationship between percent female in an occupation and the wage of the occupation, even after controlling for the measured qualifications of workers. In other words, predominantly female jobs pay less than predominantly male jobs for both men and women. Moreover, even *within* female-dominated occupations, which tend to pay less on average, women tend to earn less than their male counterparts.[29]

While the census regularly collects data on 400 occupations, employers use considerably finer breakdowns of occupations and job titles. It is likely that, were such extremely detailed categories available for the economy as a whole, an even higher proportion of the pay gap would be attributed to occupational segregation. Moreover, within the same occupational category, women tend to be employed in low-wage firms and industries. In the study reported in Table 7-1, for example, gender differences in industry and union status together account for an additional 25 percent of the gender gap. More generally, a substantial body of research finds evidence of negative effects on women's wages of segregation by industry and firm, within occupational categories.[30]

Moreover, when evaluating the negative consequences of occupational segregation for women, it is important to bear in mind that the focus upon earnings does not take into account any adverse nonpecuniary consequences of such segregation. For one, it is likely that occupational segregation reinforces cultural notions of exaggerated differences between men and women in capabilities, preferences, and social and economic roles. Such beliefs may adversely affect the opportunities and outcomes even of women in predominantly male jobs.

CAUSES OF OCCUPATIONAL SEGREGATION   As with earnings differences, the causes of occupational segregation may be classified into supply-side versus demand-side factors. Only the latter—differences in treatment—represent *direct* labor market discrimination. Of course, here again, the anticipation of, or experience with, labor market discrimination may indirectly influence women's choices via feedback effects.

As we explained in Chapter 6, human capital theory suggests that, because women generally anticipate shorter and less continuous work lives than men, it will

---

[29] For a recent study, see Stephanie Boraas and William M. Rodgers III, "How Does Gender Play a Role in the Earnings Gap? An Update," *Monthly Labor Review* 126, no. 3 (March 2003): 9–15. See also David A. Macpherson and Barry T. Hirsch, "Wages and Gender Composition, Why Do Women's Jobs Pay Less?" *Journal of Labor Economics* 13, no. 3 (July 1995): 426–71, and Elaine Sorensen, "The Crowding Hypothesis and Comparable Worth Issue," *Journal of Human Resources* 25, no. 1 (Winter 1990): 55–89.

[30] See, for example, Francine D. Blau, *Equal Pay in the Office* (Lexington, MA: Lexington Books, 1977); Erica L. Groshen, "The Structure of the Female/Male Wage Differential: Is It Who You Are, What You Do, or Where You Work?" *Journal of Human Resources* 26, no. 3 (Summer 1991): 457–72; and Kimberly Bayard, Judith Hellerstein, David Neumark, and Kenneth Troske, "New Evidence on Sex Segregation and Sex Difference in Wages from Matched Employee-Employer Data," *Journal of Labor Economics* 21, no. 4 (October 2003): 887–923.

be in their economic self-interest to choose predominantly female occupations, which presumably require smaller human capital investments and have lower wage penalties for time spent out of the labor market. We also discussed the supply-side factors that could influence women's occupational choices, including the socialization process and constraints placed by traditional gender roles on women's ability to work long hours, travel extensively as part of their jobs, and relocate to new labor markets, and considered various subtle barriers that may impede women's access to training in traditionally male fields. On the demand side, employers may contribute to occupational segregation by discriminating against equally qualified women in hiring, job placement, access to training programs, and promotion for traditionally male jobs.

Considerable evidence supports the belief that gender differences in preferences play some role in gender differences in occupations.[31] The claim that discrimination is also important is more controversial, but here too quite a bit of evidence suggests that discrimination plays a role as well. Of course, it is not an easy matter to distinguish between preferences and discrimination empirically because both likely contribute to observed differences.

Some persuasive evidence of the importance of discrimination comes from descriptions of institutional barriers that historically excluded women from particular pursuits or impeded their upward progression.[32] Also, many studies, although not all, find that women are less likely to be promoted, all else equal.[33] Another finding is that a major portion of the gender difference in on-the-job training remains unexplained, even after gender differences in the probability of worker turnover and other variables are taken into account.[34] This finding suggests that women may encounter discrimination in access to on-the-job training. This is important because on-the-job training may be valuable in providing an entrée to higher-paying jobs.

Although such findings regarding promotion and training are consistent with discrimination, it is important to note that they suffer from the same types of problems raised earlier in our analysis of the determinants of the gender wage gap. They may overstate discrimination if other important nondiscriminatory factors are omitted from the analysis, such as tastes for particular types of work, availability for travel, and so forth, which could help to account for the observed gender differences. On the other hand, discrimination would be understated to the extent some of the variables that are controlled for, such as initial job category in a promotion study, reflect the impact of labor market discrimination.

Given these types of concerns, it is not possible to use these findings to ascribe a specific portion of gender differences in occupations to the choices individual men and

[31] Morley Gunderson, "Male-Female Wage Differentials and Policy Responses," *Journal of Economic Literature* 27, no. 1 (March 1989): 46–72.

[32] See Barbara F. Reskin and Heidi I. Hartmann, eds., *Women's Work, Men's Work: Sex Segregation on the Job* (Washington, DC: National Academy Press, 1986), and Patricia A. Roos and Barbara F. Reskin, "Institutional Factors Contributing to Occupational Sex Segregation," in *Sex Segregation in the Workplace: Trends, Explanations, Remedies,* edited by Barbara Reskin (Washington, DC: National Academy Press, 1984),pp. 235–60.

[33] For examples of studies that find evidence of lower promotion rates, see Francine D. Blau and Jed DeVaro, "New Evidence on Gender Differences in Promotion Rates: An Empirical Analysis of a Sample of New Hires," *Industrial Relations* 46, no. 3 (July 2007): 511–50; Deborah A. Cobb-Clark, "Getting Ahead: The Determinants of and Payoffs to Internal Promotion for Young U.S. Men and Women," in *Worker Wellbeing in a Changing Labor Market,* edited by Solomon W. Polachek, *Research in Labor Economics,* vol. 20 (Amsterdam: Elsevier Science, JAI, 2001), pp. 339–72; and Kristin McCue, "Promotions and Wage Growth," *Journal of Labor Economics* 14, no. 2 (1996): 175–209. For an example of a study that does not find evidence of discrimination, see Joni Hersch and W. Kip Viscusi, "Gender Differences in Promotions and Wages," *Industrial Relations* 35, no. 4 (October 1996): 461–72.

[34] Royalty, "The Effects of Job Turnover"; see also Barron, Black, and Lowenstein, "Gender Differences", and Duncan and Hoffman, "On-the-Job Training."

women make versus labor market discrimination (i.e., to supply-side vs. demand-side factors).[35] However, as in the case of our review of evidence on the pay gap, the evidence suggests that both are important. And, as in the case of pay differences, evidence of discrimination may be found not only in statistical analyses, but also in the experimental data discussed earlier for wait staff and musicians and in discrimination cases in which employers were found guilty of gender discrimination or settled the cases out of court.

IS THERE A GLASS CEILING?　　The **glass ceiling** is the name given to the set of subtle barriers believed by many to inhibit women and minorities from reaching the upper echelons of corporate America, government, and academia. To the extent such barriers exist, they constitute a form of labor market discrimination. Is there a glass ceiling impeding women's occupational advancement?[36] Substantial disparities in the representation of women at the upper levels of most hierarchies are easy to document. As our preceding discussion suggests, however, the reasons for them are harder to pin down. Here we consider the extent of the gender differences in representation at the top, focusing first on management jobs and high-level government positions, and then on academia, and summarize what is known about the reasons for women's underrepresentation.

The extremely low representation of women in the senior ranks of management was already noted in Chapter 5. According to data from *Catalyst*, in 2007, only 15.4 percent of all corporate officers in Fortune 500 companies were women, and women held just 6.7 percent of the top-earner spots, defined as the five highest-paid executives in the company. These figures did, however, represent a substantial increase from 8.7 percent of officers and 1.2 percent of top earners in 1995. Another issue noted earlier in Chapter 5 is that, among corporate officers, women are particularly underrepresented in "line" positions (those that affect the firm's "bottom line"), which are more likely to lead to the highest level of leadership positions in the corporation. Among the Fortune 500, women comprised 6 percent of those in line positions in 2007, up only slightly from 5.3 percent 10 years earlier.[37] This may be one of the reasons that women's representation at the very highest ranks, among chief executive officers (CEOs), was especially sparse. Just four of the CEOs in the Standard & Poor's (S&P) 1500 were women in 1992. While this figure had increased to 34 by 2004, it still represents a very low share (2.3 percent) of the total.[38] Women were also sparsely represented on corporate boards of directors in Fortune 500 firms, holding 14.8 percent of board seats in 2007, up from 8.3 percent in 1993.[39] The underrepresentation of women at the highest levels is similar in

---

[35] For additional evidence on the sources of gender differences in occupations, see Barbara F. Reskin and Denise D. Bielby, "A Sociological Perspective on Gender and Career Outcomes," *Journal of Economic Perspectives* 19, no. 1 (Winter 2005): 71–86; Barbara F. Reskin and Patricia A. Roos, *Job Queues, Gender Queues: Explaining Women's Inroads into Male Occupations* (Philadelphia: Temple University Press, 1990); Virginia Valian, *Why So Slow? The Advancement of Women* (Cambridge, MA: MIT Press, 1998); Paula England, "Socioeconomic Explanations of Job Segregation," in *Comparable Worth and Wage Discrimination: Technical Possibilities and Political Realities*, edited by Helen Remick (Philadelphia: Temple University Press, 1984), pp. 28–46; and Reskin and Hartmann, *Women's Work, Men's Work.*

[36] For insightful examinations of this issue and related questions, see Valian, *Why So Slow?* and Alice H. Eagly and Linda L. Carli, *Through the Labyrinth: The Truth About How Women Become Leaders* (Cambridge, MA: Harvard Business School Press, 2007).

[37] *2007 Catalyst Census of Women Corporate Officers and Top Earners in the Fortune 500*, available at http://www .catalyst.org/; and *2002 Catalyst Census of Women Corporate Officers and Top Earners in the Fortune 500* (New York). Line officers are responsible for a company's profits and losses; staff officers are responsible for the auxiliary functioning of the business. *Catalyst* determines how to classify corporate officers based on the officer's title and functional area; see *1997 Catalyst Census of Women Corporate Officers and Top Earners* (New York).

[38] Justin Wolfers, "Diagnosing Discrimination: Stock Returns and CEO Gender," *Journal of the European Economic Association* 4, nos. 2–3 (May 2006): 531–41.

[39] See *Catalyst*, "2007 Catalyst Census of Women Board Directors," and previous issues.

government. For example, in 2008, women comprised 16 percent of U.S. Senators, 17 percent of members of the U.S. House of Representatives, 16 percent of governors, and 24 percent of state legislators.[40]

We focus our attention on the underrepresentation of women in top-level management positions[41] due to the complexities of identifying the source of gender disparities in elective offices. Even in the case of corporate America, however, it is difficult to determine whether the scarcity of women at the top is simply due to the fact that women are relative newcomers and it takes time to move up through the ranks or whether it represents particular barriers to women's advancement. The "pipeline" argument is certainly credible. Women received only 5 percent of master's degrees in business in 1970, a figure little changed from 1960. While their representation in these programs grew sharply thereafter, reaching 24 percent in 1981 and 43 percent in 2006, a lag is to be expected in woman's representation in top-level positions. Thus, it is difficult to ascertain whether progress to date has been adequate, particularly given the absence of information on available candidates for such jobs as well as on norms regarding the typical speed of movement up the corporate ladder. Nonetheless, given that the growth of women in top-level managerial jobs has been so much slower than the expansion in female receipt of MBA degrees, which dates back to the 1970s, it seems reasonable to conclude that the pipeline effect can only partly explain the low representation of women at the top.[42]

Work–family conflicts provide another plausible nondiscriminatory explanation for the scarcity of women in top corporate jobs. Consistent with this, a survey of top executives at 10 major U.S. firms with global operations found that, while 90 percent of male executives had children, only 65 percent of female executives did. And, although the majority of both the male and the female executives were married or in a couple relationship, this was true of a considerably higher proportion of men (94 percent) than of women (79 percent). Another indication of the greater work–family conflict female executives face is that, among those who were married or in a couple relationship, nearly 75 percent of the women had a spouse/partner who was employed full time; in contrast, 75 percent of the men had a spouse/partner who was *not* employed outside the home.[43] A 2008 study of graduates from a top MBA program also suggests that work–family issues are important. The study finds that women were more likely to have taken time out since graduation and, moreover, that there were huge wage penalties for taking *any* time out. As one of the authors of the study notes, this is "consistent with the view that a

---

[40] "A Paradox in Public Attitudes, Men or Women: Who's the Better Leader," *A Social & Demographic Trends Report*, Pew Research Center, August 25, 2008, available at http://pewresearch.org; this report contains some very interesting recent attitudinal data on perceptions about men and women as political leaders. For additional data on women's representation in elective office, see http://www.cawp.rutgers.edu/fast_facts/index.php. As we shall see in Chapter 12, for the most part, the situation is not very different in other countries. For example, only 17.7 percent of all the legislators in parliaments around the world were women. On the other hand, there are a few countries where women are doing far better, including Rwanda with 49 percent, followed by Sweden with 47 percent, Finland with 42 percent, Argentina with 40 percent, and Costa Rica with 37 percent. See "Women in Politics: 2008—Room for Improvement Despite Significant Gains," Inter-Parliamentary Union, Press Release No. 297, New York, February 29, 2008.

[41] For an excellent consideration of this issue, see Marianne Bertrand, "CEOs," unpublished working paper, University of Chicago Graduate School of Business (2008). We draw heavily on this paper in our discussion of this issue.

[42] This is Bertrand's assessment; see "CEOs." The 1970 figure cited in the text is from Bertrand, and the rest of the statistics are from Table 6-5 of Chapter 6.

[43] The Families and Work Institute, *Catalyst*, and the Boston College Center for Work and Family, "Leaders in a Global Economy: A Study of Executive Women and Men," January 2003, available at http://familiesandwork.org/site/research/summary/globalsumm.pdf. As the study points out, although there has been considerable speculation in the press about "trophy husbands" of high-level female executives based on anecdotal evidence, in this data only 17 percent of the women had husbands who were not employed, just slightly more than the average of 11 percent for all employed married women.

continuous commitment to the workforce is pretty much a sine qua non condition to make it to the very top in corporate America."[44]

The possibility that pipeline effects and work–family conflicts account for some of the extremely low representation of women at the very top of corporate American does not rule out a role for discrimination or other subtle barrriers in limiting women's opportunities. Notably, the study of top corporate executives discussed earlier found that while women are less likely to have children than men at all levels of the corporate hierarchy, likely reflecting the challenges of balancing work and family, women at the very top echelons were actually more likely to have children than women at the lower echelons.[45] This finding suggests that the presence of children and the associated demands are not the full explanation for women's underrepresentation higher up the ladder. The possibility of discrimination is also suggested by a study of S&P 1500 firms that found that women were more highly represented in top-level jobs when the CEO or the chairman of the board was a woman (women-led firms), than in men-led firms, and further that female top-level executives in women-led firms earned 10 to 20 percent more than comparable executive women in male-led firms.[46]

What are the economic consequences of women's lower representation at the top? A 2001 study of gender differences in pay among the five highest-paid executives in S&P 1500 firms suggests that they are substantial.[47] It was found that the 2.5 percent of executives in their sample who were women earned 45 percent less than their male counterparts. Female executives were younger and thus had less seniority, a factor contributing to the gender pay difference. However, three-quarters of the gender pay gap was due to the fact that women managed smaller companies and were less likely to be the CEO, chair, or president of their company.

Even though there is not sufficient evidence to fully resolve the sources of the disparities of the type we have outlined here, it is important to recognize that, to the extent discrimination plays a role, it need not manifest itself through overt and conscious behavior. The barriers women face are often subtle and difficult to document, let alone to remove. For example, recruiting practices may involve the use of personal contacts from an "old boys' network" that leaves women "out of the loop." Women may also remain outsiders to a "male" workplace culture. A prime example is that, because sports have traditionally been a male domain, successful women are often those who learn to play golf and talk sports.[48] As a final example, women may be disadvantaged by a perception that men make better bosses. A survey of female executives from Fortune 1000 companies by *Catalyst* found that 40 percent believed that men have difficulty being

---

[44] Marianne Bertrand, Claudia Goldin, and Lawrence F. Katz, "Dynamics of the Gender Gap for Young Professionals in the Financial and Corporate Sectors," unpublished working paper, University of Chicago Graduate School of Business (2008), cited in Bertrand, "CEOs"; the quotation is from Bertrand.

[45] Families and Work Institute, *Catalyst*, and Boston College Center for Work and Family, "Leaders in a Global Economy."

[46] Linda A. Bell, "Women-Led Firms and the Gender Gap in Top Executive Pay," Institute for the Study of Labor Working (IZA) Working Paper No. 1689 (July 2005). Although, as Bertrand points out, this may reflect an industry effect (woman may be more highly represented in particular industries at all levels of the hierarchy), this seems a less likely explanation for the higher pay of female executives in women-led firms. There is also some evidence that greater representation of women in high-level management narrows the overall gender wage gap among workers; see Philip N Cohen and Matt L. Huffman, "Working for the Woman? Female Managers and the Gender Wage Gap," *American Sociological Review* 72, no. 5 (October 2007): 681–704.

[47] Data are for the 1992-1997 period; see, Marianne Bertrand and Kevin F. Hallock, "The Gender Gap in Top Corporate Jobs," *Industrial and Labor Relations Review* 55, no. 1 (October 2001): 3–21. Blau and Kahn, "The U.S. Gender Pay Gap in the 1990s," present some evidence consistent with a greater negative effect of glass ceiling barriers on women's relative wages in the 1990s than in the 1980s and speculate that women's 1980s gains placed more of them into the higher-level positions where glass ceiling barriers hindered their further upward progression.

[48] Tory Johnson, "Sports in the Office: How to Make Sure You Have Your Bases Covered," October 15, 2008, available at http://diversityblog.experience.com.

managed by women.[49] Or, as reported in another study, although "women, more than men, manifest leadership styles associated with effective performance as leaders, ... more people prefer male than female bosses."[50]

There may also be stereotyped views about women's qualifications and preferences that result in well-qualified women receiving fewer opportunities. For example, many people believe that women are not aggressive enough, are unwilling to relocate for higher positions, and, when they have families, are less committed to their jobs than their male counterparts. A number of additional preconceptions may especially limit women's access to top-level jobs in the increasingly important arena of international business. Among these are that international clients are not as comfortable doing business with women as with men.[51]

The status of women in academia, discussed briefly in Chapter 5, is a subject that has attracted a great deal of attention among researchers. This attention may in part be due to the role faculty members can play as potential mentors and role models for students. Another reason is that there is a clear hierarchy for faculty, along with relatively well-defined criteria for progressing within this hierarchy. These factors make the status of women in academia a particularly instructive case.

Table 7-2 shows data on the distribution of men and women in academia by rank in the mid-1970s and the late 2000s. In its broad outlines, the situation is quite clear. In each year, women were concentrated at the lower end of the occupational hierarchy as lecturers, instructors, and assistant professors, whereas they were less highly represented at the upper ranks as associate professors and full professors. Instructor and lecturer positions are less desirable in terms of pay, promotion prospects, and job continuity, whereas associate professor and full professor positions tend to pay more and provide job security in the form of tenure. Assistant professor positions fall somewhere in the middle; this is typically the rank where academics must prove themselves for promotion to associate professor. Other data indicate women are considerably underrepresented at the most highly ranked research universities and much more heavily represented at

TABLE 7-2   Percent Female of Faculty in Institutions of Higher Education by Academic Rank, 1976–77 and 2007–08

Academic Rank	1976–1977	2007–2008
Professors	8.4	25.9
Associate professors	16.7	40.4
Assistant professors	29.7	48.4
Instructors	49.0	60.0
Lecturers	41.9	54.8
All ranks	22.4	40.3

Source: 1976–1977: from *Academe*, August 1981; 2007–2008: calculated from "The Annual Report on the Economic Status of the Profession: 2007–08," *Academe*, March–April 2008, Table 12, available at http://www.aaup.org.

---

[49] See *Catalyst*, "Women in U.S. Corporate Leadership," New York, 2003, p. 6. Alice H. Eagly and Steven J. Karau argue that a perceived incongruity between the female gender role and leadership roles results in women being viewed less favorably than men as potential leaders and being evaluated less favorably than men for behavior that fits with a leadership role; see "Role Congruity Theory of Prejudice Toward Female Leaders," *Psychological Review* 109, no. 3 (July 2002): 573–98. See also *Catalyst*, "The Double-Bind Dilemma for Women in Leadership: Damned if You Do, Doomed if You Don't," New York, 2007.
[50] Alice H. Eagly, "Female Leadership Advantage and Disadvantage: Resolving the Contradictions," *Psychology of Women Quarterly* 31, no. 1 (February 9, 2007, published online): 1–12.
[51] *Catalyst*, "Passport to Opportunity: U.S. Women in Global Business," news release, October 18, 2000.

less research-oriented, as well as smaller, liberal arts institutions and two-year colleges.[52] Women also tend to be concentrated in less lucrative fields, often in the humanities, while men tend to dominate in the higher-paying scientific and technical fields.

As in the case of women in management, disparities in the representation of women and men by level of the academic hierarchy may reflect the pipeline effect: it will take time for recent cohorts of women in academia to move up the ladder. Consistent with this argument, the data in Table 7-2 do suggest some female gains over time. So, although women are underrepresented at the higher ranks in both years, their representation has increased markedly over time with their progression up through the ranks. Nevertheless, most studies find that the underrepresentation of women at the higher levels cannot be entirely explained by lags as women work their way through the pipeline. Rather, the pipeline tends to be "leaky"; at each step of the hierarchy, the representation of women decreases—from completion of graduate school to entry-level assistant professorships and from assistant professorships to tenured associate and then to full professor positions.[53]

Detailed studies further suggest that discrimination plays a role in academia. For example, a study of faculty promotion in the economics profession found that, even after accounting for quality of Ph.D. training, publishing productivity, major field of specialization, current placement in a distinguished department, age, and post-Ph.D. experience, female economists were still significantly less likely to be promoted from assistant to associate and from associate to full professor.[54] Other types of disparities in treatment may also adversely affect the success of women in academia. A pathbreaking 1999 report on faculty at the Massachusetts Institute of Technology (MIT) found evidence of differential treatment of senior women in the sciences that included differences not simply in salary but also in space, committee and teaching assignments, and resources, "with women receiving less despite professional accomplishments equal to those of their male colleagues."[55] A follow-up report issued in 2006 indicated that progress has been made, but it would nonetheless take some time for disparities, especially in hiring, to disappear.[56] In 2006 as well, the National Academy of Sciences examined the underrepresentation of women among science and engineering faculty at a broader set of research universities and pointed to ongoing biases concluding that "It is not lack of talent, but unintentional biases and outmoded institutional structures that are hindering the access and advancement of women."[57]

---

[52] For example, in 2007–2008, women constituted 51 percent of faculty at two-year colleges but were only 36 percent at research universities that grant doctorates ("The Annual Report on the Economic Status of the Profession: 2007-08," *Academe* (March–April 2008), Table 12, available at http://www.aaup.org). See also Marianne A. Ferber and Jane W. Loeb, "Introduction," in *Academic Couples, Problems and Promise*, edited by Marianne A. Ferber and Jane W. Loeb (Champaign: University of Illinois Press, 1997).

[53] See the Reports of the American Economic Association Committee on the Status of Women in the Economics Profession (CSWEP), available at http://www.cswep.org/annual_reports.htm; and *Beyond Bias and Barriers: Fulfilling the Potential of Women in Academic Science and Engineering*, Committee on Maximizing the Potential of Women in Academic Science and Engineering, National Academy of Sciences, National Academy of Engineering, and Institute of Medicine (Washington, DC: National Academy of Sciences, 2006), Executive Summary available at http://www.nap.edu/catalog/11741.html.

[54] John M. McDowell, Larry D. Singell Jr., and James P. Ziliak, "Cracks in the Glass Ceiling: Gender and Promotion in the Economics Profession," *American Economic Review* 89, no. 2 (May 1999): 392–96. See also Shulamit Kahn and Donna K. Ginther, "Women in Economics: Moving Up or Falling Off the Academic Career Ladder," *Journal of Economic Perspectives* 18, no. 3 (Summer 2004): 193–214; Massachusetts Institute of Technology, "A Study on the Status of Women Faculty in Science at MIT," *MIT Faculty Newsletter* 11, no. 4 (March 1999); Donna K. Ginther and Kathy J. Hayes, "Gender Differences in Salary and Promotion in the Humanities," *American Economic Review* 89, no. 2 (May 1999): 397–402; and Sharon G. Levin and Paula E. Stephan, "Gender Differences in the Rewards to Publishing in Academe: Science in the 1970s," *Sex Roles* 38, nos. 11–12 (June 1998): 1049–64.

[55] Massachusetts Institute of Technology, "A Study on the Status of Women Faculty," p. 4.

[56] Nancy Hopkins, "Diversification of a University Faculty: Observations on Hiring Women Faculty in the Schools of Science and Engineering at MIT," *MIT Faculty Newsletter* XVIII, no. 4 (March/April 2006): 1, 15–23.

[57] *Beyond Bias and Barriers*, the quotation is from the Executive Summary.

In light of the gender disparities of the type we have outlined here, employers have experimented with a number of approaches to promoting diversity in management and other higher-level positions. A recent study, which focused on private sector firms, found that the most effective strategy was for the organization to take specific measures, such as setting forth an affirmative action plan or establishing a committee or manager in charge of creating and maintaining a diverse workplace. Efforts to reduce the social isolation of women and minorities through mentoring and networking also showed some modest effects. Least effective were efforts to moderate managerial bias through diversity training and evaluating managers on their diversity performance.[58]

MODELS OF LABOR MARKET DISCRIMINATION

The empirical evidence suggests that there are indeed pay and occupational differences between men and women that are not accounted for by (potential) productivity differences. We now turn to an examination of how labor market discrimination can produce such gender differences in economic outcomes and why this inequality has persisted over time. Economists have developed a variety of models that may be used to analyze these issues. Empirical research in this area has not, however, established which of these approaches most accurately describes the labor market. Indeed, for the most part, these explanations are *not* mutually exclusive and each may shed some light on how labor market discrimination affects women's economic outcomes. Specifically, we focus on the following theoretical explanations:

- Tastes for Discrimination (employee, employer, and customer)
- Statistical Discrimination
- Overcrowding Model
- Institutional Models (including dual labor markets)

Unless otherwise indicated, the analyses presented here assume that male and female workers are equally well qualified and, in the absence of discrimination, would be equally productive and receive the same pay. Of course, we know that this assumption is not an accurate description of reality—gender differences in qualifications exist and explain some of the pay gap. However, this assumption is appropriate in that models of discrimination are efforts to explain the portion of the pay gap that is *not* due to differences in qualifications; that is, they are intended to explain pay differences between men and women who are (potentially) equally productive.

Tastes for Discrimination

The foundation for the neoclassical analysis of labor market discrimination was laid by Nobel laureate Gary Becker.[59] Becker conceptualized discrimination as a personal prejudice, or what he termed a *taste* against associating with a particular group. In his model, employers, coworkers, and customers may all potentially display such **tastes for discrimination**. In contrast to the case of racial discrimination that Becker initially analyzed, it may at first seem odd to hypothesize that men would not like to associate with women when, in fact, men and women generally live together in families. The

---

[58] Alexandra Kalev, Frank Dobbin, and Erin Kelly, "Best Practices or Best Guesses? Assessing the Efficacy of Corporate Affirmative Action and Diversity Policies," *American Sociological Review* 71, no. 4 (August 2006): 589–617.

[59] Becker, *The Economics of Discrimination*. In our presentation of the tastes for discrimination model, we also incorporate some of the insights of another Nobel prize winner, Kenneth Arrow; see "The Theory of Discrimination," in *Discrimination in Labor Markets*, edited by Orley Ashenfelter and Albert Rees (Princeton, NJ: Princeton University Press, 1973), pp. 3–33.

issue here may be more one of socially appropriate roles than of the desire to maintain social distance, as Becker postulated was the case with race.[60]

Employers who show no reservations about hiring women as secretaries may be reluctant to employ them as plumbers. Men who are willing to work with women in complementary or subordinate positions may dislike interacting with them as equals or superiors. Customers who are delighted to purchase pantyhose from female clerks may avoid women who sell cars or are attorneys. If such discriminatory tastes reflect a dislike for interacting with women in these positions, rather than beliefs that women are less qualified than men for traditionally male pursuits, they are appropriately analyzed as a taste for discrimination.[61] The possibility that women are less qualified or less productive is considered later under the theory of statistical discrimination.

In order for such discriminatory tastes to result in negative consequences for women's earnings and employment, tastes must actually influence people's behavior. According to Becker, individuals with tastes for discrimination against women act as if there were nonpecuniary costs of associating with women—say, in what is viewed as a socially inappropriate role.[62] The strength of the individual's discriminatory taste is measured by his or her **discrimination coefficient** (i.e., the size of these costs in money terms). We now examine the consequences of discrimination based on employer, employee, and customer preferences.

EMPLOYER DISCRIMINATION   In the case of **employer discrimination**, an employer who has a taste for discrimination against women will act as if there were a nonpecuniary cost of employing women equal in dollar terms to d_r (the discrimination coefficient). To this employer, the costs of employing a man will be his wage, w_m, but the *full* costs of employing a woman will be her wage *plus* the discrimination coefficient ($w_f + d_r$). A discriminating employer will hire a woman only if the full cost of employing her ($w_f + d_r$) is no greater than the cost of employing a man (w_m) and will be indifferent between hiring a man or a woman if the full cost of a woman exactly equals the cost for a man. This implies that the discriminating employer will hire a woman only at a lower wage than a man ($w_f = w_m - d_r$). Further, if we assume that men and women are equally productive, that is, their marginal products (MPs) are the same, and that men are paid in accordance with their productivity, then women will be hired only if they are paid less than their productivity.[63]

Becker's analysis showed that the consequences of this situation for female workers depend on the prevalence and size of discriminatory tastes among employers, as well as on the number of women seeking employment. Nondiscriminatory employers are willing to hire men and women at the same wage rate (i.e., their discrimination coefficient equals 0). When the number of such nondiscriminatory employers is relatively large or relatively few women are seeking employment, women workers may all be absorbed by the nondiscriminatory firms. In this case, no discriminatory pay differential occurs based on gender, even though some employers have tastes for discrimination against women.

---

[60] The notion of socially appropriate roles may also be a factor in racial discrimination, as when blacks experience little difficulty in gaining access to menial or lower-level jobs but encounter discrimination in obtaining higher-level positions.

[61] However, as we shall see, such discriminatory preferences on the part of workers or customers for men will cause women to be less productive from the point of view of the employer.

[62] Throughout, we assume that employers, coworkers, or customers have tastes for discrimination against women. It is also possible that they have positive preferences for employing, working with, or buying from men. This may be termed *nepotism*. See Matthew Goldberg, "Discrimination, Nepotism, and Long-Run Wage Differentials," *Quarterly Journal of Economics* 97, no. 2 (May 1982): 307–19, for an interesting analysis of the consequences of nepotism for the persistence of discrimination in the long run. See also David Neumark, "Employers' Discriminatory Behavior and the Estimation of Wage Discrimination," *Journal of Human Resources* 23, no. 3 (Summer 1988): 279–95.

[63] That is, if $w_m = MP$, where MP is equal to the marginal productivity of men (or women), then women will be paid $w_m - d_r$, which is less than their productivity.

However, if discriminatory tastes are widespread, or the number women seeking employment is relatively large, some women will have to find jobs at discriminatory firms. These women obtain such employment only if w_f is less than w_m. If we assume that the labor market is competitive, all employers will pay the (same) going rate established in the market for workers of a particular sex. No employer would be willing to pay more than the going rate, because additional workers are always available at that wage. No worker will accept less than the going rate, because jobs at other firms are always available to him or her at that wage. In equilibrium, then, the market wage differential between men and women must be large enough so that all the women who are looking for employment are able to obtain it—including those who must find work at discriminatory firms. Thus, the more prevalent and the stronger employers' discriminatory tastes against women and the larger the number of women seeking employment, the larger will be the marketwide wage gap ($w_m - w_f$) between men and women.

This model of employer tastes for discrimination is consistent with some of the inequalities between men and women that we observe in the labor market. Under this model, a wage differential may exist between equally qualified male and female workers because discriminatory employers will hire women workers only at a wage discount.[64] Further, because less discriminatory employers will hire more women workers than more discriminatory employers, male and female workers may be segregated by firm—as also appears to be the case. Finally, if, as seems likely, employer tastes for discrimination vary across occupations, occupational segregation by sex can also occur.

However, one problem that economists have identified with this model is that discrimination is not costless to the employer who forgoes the opportunity to hire more of the lower-priced female labor and less of the higher-priced male labor. Therefore, less discriminatory firms should have lower costs of production. Such a competitive advantage would enable them to expand and drive the more discriminatory firms out of business in the long run. As the less discriminatory firms expand, the demand for female labor would be increased and the male–female pay gap would be reduced. If there were enough *entirely* nondiscriminatory firms to absorb all the women workers, the gender pay gap would be eliminated. Hence, the question is how discrimination, which represents a departure from profit-maximizing behavior, can withstand the impact of competitive pressures.

One answer is that discrimination may result from a lack of such competitive pressures in the economy. For this reason, Becker hypothesized that, on average, discrimination would be less severe in competitive than in monopolistic industries, and some research supports this prediction. For example, with the deregulation of the banking industry beginning in the mid-1970s, the gender pay gap in banking declined and the representation of women in managerial positions increased.[65] These findings suggest that

---

[64] Some researchers have proposed testing the employer discrimination model by comparing the gender pay gap between self-employed workers and employees. The claim is that if *employer* discrimination is responsible for the pay differential, female self-employed workers should fare relatively better than female employees, all else equal. See Victor R. Fuchs, "Differences in Hourly Earnings Between Men and Women," *Monthly Labor Review* 94, no. 5 (May 1971): 9–15, and Robert L. Moore, "Employer Discrimination: Evidence from Self-Employed Workers," *Review of Economics and Statistics* 65, no. 3 (August 1983): 496–501. Although such studies do not support the employer discrimination model, they do not provide an ideal test because self-employment and wage and salary employment differ in a number of important dimensions. Among these dimensions, self-employment requires access to capital, and there may be discrimination against women by lenders. Discrimination by customers is another possibility.

[65] Sandra E. Black and Philip E. Strahan, "The Division of Spoils: Rent-Sharing and Discrimination in a Regulated Labor Market," *American Economic Review* 91, no. 4 (September 2001): 814–31. See also Sandra E. Black and Elizabeth Brainerd, "Importing Equality? The Effects of Globalization on Gender Discrimination," *Industrial and Labor Relations Review* 57, no. 4 (July 2004): 540–59, and Orley Ashenfelter and Timothy Hannan, "Sex Discrimination and Product Market Competition: The Case of the Banking Industry," *Quarterly Journal of Economics* 101, no. 1 (February 1986): 149–73. Another possible reason for the persistence of employer discrimination in the long run is that it is based on a positive preference by employers for male workers (or "nepotism") rather than a disutility for employing female workers; see Goldberg, "Discrimination, Nepotism, and Long-Run Wage Differentials."

employers in banking were able to discriminate in part due to the monopolistic nature of the industry, but that their ability to do so was reduced when competition was increased (by deregulation).

Also consistent with Becker's reasoning is another recent study that finds that, among plants with high levels of product market power (and hence an ability to exercise their tastes for discrimination in the Becker model), those employing relatively more women were more profitable.[66] This correlation suggests that, among these firms, there is some discrimination against women and that less discriminatory firms benefit from the lower costs of production resulting from hiring more women.

Finally, unions may also, to some extent, be considered a barrier to competition in that wages may be set above the competitive level in the union sector. Unions are also more likely to arise in less competitive industries, and it is indeed the case that women are less highly represented in unionized employment, although such gender differences have decreased substantially. Thus, historically women have not benefited from the wage advantage of unionism to the same extent as men.[67] For this reason, as we shall see in greater detail in Chapter 9, declining gender differences in union representation have boosted the wages of women relative to men.

It has also been suggested that *monopsony* power by employers in the labor market plays a role in producing and perpetuating the gender pay differential. One way in which a firm gains monopsony power is when it is a large buyer of labor relative to the size of a particular market.

To see how monopsony power can adversely affect women, consider the not uncommon case of a one-university town. In the past, when the husband's job prospects usually determined the location of the family, the faculty wife with a Ph.D. had little choice but to take whatever the university offered her—most considered themselves fortunate if they were able to obtain employment at all. Even the growing numbers of egalitarian Ph.D. couples cannot entirely avoid this problem. Although an increasing number of two-career couples, in academia and elsewhere, work in different locations and see each other, say, on weekends, most seek jobs in the same location. In order to change jobs, such couples must find *two* acceptable alternatives in a single location. This will obviously be harder to do than to find *one* desirable alternative. Thus, the Ph.D. couple will have fewer options than those with only one Ph.D. in the family. (Similar problems can arise for two-career couples in other fields.) This situation gives the employer a degree of monopsony power and is likely to lower the pay of both members of the couple relative to Ph.D.s who can relocate more easily. Among such Ph.D. couples, both the husband's *and* the wife's salary may be adversely affected.[68]

The monopsony model has also been offered as a general explanation for the gender pay gap. Some argue that employers hold greater monopsony power over women than men due to factors such as occupational segregation that may limit women's options. Further, as we saw in Chapter 6, women who adopt more traditional gender roles will tend to seek jobs that are closer to home.[69]

Consideration of job search suggests that another way in which firms may gain monopsony power is if workers lack perfect information about employment

---

[66] Judith K. Hellerstein, David Neumark, and Kenneth Troske, "Market Forces and Sex Discrimination," *Journal of Human Resources* 37, no. 2 (Spring 2002): 353–80.

[67] For an analysis of the impact of unions on gender pay differences, see William E. Even and David A. MacPherson, "The Decline of Private-Sector Unionism and the Gender Wage Gap," *Journal of Human Resources* 28, no. 2 (Spring 1993): 279–96.

[68] For early evidence consistent with monopsony in one academic institution, see Marianne A. Ferber and Jane W. Loeb, "Professors, Performance and Rewards," *Industrial Relations* 13, no. 1 (February 1974): 67–77.

[69] Janice F. Madden, *The Economics of Sex Discrimination* (Lexington, MA: Lexington Books, 1973). See also Alan Manning, "The Equal Pay Act As an Experiment to Test Theories of the Labour Market," *Economica* 63, no. 250 (May 1996): 191–212.

opportunities.[70] In a competitive labor market with perfect information, even a slightly higher wage at another firm will induce workers to move to that better opportunity. However, when information is imperfect, workers must search among employers for a good job match, thus incurring "search costs." These costs include the opportunity cost of the time spent looking for a job, as well as out-of-pocket costs for printing up a resume, transportation expenses to employment interviews, and so on. Because search is costly, workers will be less mobile across firms than they would be if information was perfectly and costlessly available, and it will take larger wage premiums at other firms to bid them away. Thus, the presence of search costs gives employers a degree of monopsony power over workers. If we further assume that some employers discriminate against women and are not willing to hire them, we see that women will face higher search costs than men. As a consequence, employers can exploit this greater monopsony power over women and offer them lower wages than men. Thus, when information is imperfect and search costs exist, it is more credible that employer discrimination can persist in the long run.[71]

Evolving views of the nature of prejudice may also shed light on the persistence of discrimination in the long run. As we noted in our discussion of a possible glass ceiling curtailing women's upward progress, discrimination against women need not be overt or even conscious. Social cognition theory developed by social psychologists suggests that unconscious biases can cause people to ". . . think, feel, and behave in ways that oppose their explicitly expressed views, and even, explicitly known self-interests."[72] For example, they may automatically categorize others and treat them in a manner consistent with the stereotypes they hold about the social category to which the individuals belong. They may also tend to remember evidence that is consistent with their preexisting stereotypes and ignore, discount, or forget evidence that undermines them.[73] So, for example, a manger might sincerely profess a belief in gender equity, but still tend to undervalue the qualifications of female job applicants, based on unconscious biases. Or, such an individual might tend to remember when female employees leave for family-related reasons but dismiss as exceptional examples of female employees that remained committed workers after having a child. Such **implicit discrimination** may be less likely to be eliminated by competitive forces, or, at a minimum, the impact of competitive forces may operate more uncertainly and slowly.

Finally, models of statistical discrimination, developed after Becker's work, suggest another possible reason for the persistence of discrimination in the labor market: employers are motivated to discriminate against women not simply by personal prejudice, but

---

[70] We draw heavily here on Dan A. Black, "Discrimination in an Equilibrium Search Model," *Journal of Labor Economics* 13, no. 2 (April 1995): 309–34.

[71] Some evidence consistent with the monopsony model as an explanation for gender wage differentials in the grocery industry is provided in Michael R Ransom and Ronald L. Oaxaca, "New Market Power Models and Sex Differences in Pay," Industrial Relations Section, Princeton University, Working Paper No. 540 (January 2009). However, an earlier review of results from three studies of the quit behavior of men and women found no evidence that men's labor supply is more sensitive to wages than women's at the firm level (as required by the monopsony model); see , Francine D. Blau and Lawrence M. Kahn, "Institutions and Laws in the Labor Market," in *Handbook of Labor Economics*, edited by Orley Ashenfelter and David Card (The Netherlands: Elsevier Science, B.V., 1999), pp. 3A: 1399–461.

[72] Marianne Bertrand, Dolly Chugh, and Sendhil Mullainathan, "Implicit Discrimination," *American Economic Review* 95, no. 2 (May 2005): 94–98; quotation is from p. 94. These authors suggest the term *implicit discrimination*.

[73] See Barbara F. Reskin, "The Proximate Causes of Employment Discrimination," *Contemporary Sociology* 29, no. 2 (March 2000): 319–28; Susan T. Fiske, "Stereotyping, Prejudice, and Discrimination," in *Handbook of Social Psychology*, edited by D. T. Gilbert, S. T. Fiske, and G. Lindzey (New York: McGraw-Hill: 1998), pp. 357–411; and Francine D. Blau, Mary C. Brinton, and David B. Grusky, "The Declining Significance of Gender?" in *The Declining Significance of Gender?* edited by Francine D. Blau, Mary C. Brinton, and David B. Grusky (New York: Russell Sage Foundation, 2006), pp. 3–34.

rather by actual or perceived differences between male and female workers in productivity or behavior. We consider such models of statistical discrimination later in this chapter. Before turning to such models, however, we consider two further possible sources of discrimination in the Becker model. A major insight of Becker's was the realization that, even if employers themselves have no tastes for discrimination against women, profit-maximizing behavior by employers may result in gender discrimination in the labor market if employees or customers have such tastes. No conflict arises here with profit maximization by employers. Hence, there is no economic reason why this type of discrimination cannot continue.[74] We now consider the possibility of employee and customer discrimination.

EMPLOYEE DISCRIMINATION   In the case of **employee discrimination**, a male employee who has a taste for discrimination against women will act as if there were nonpecuniary costs of working with women equal to his discrimination coefficient, d_e. This is the premium he must be paid to induce him to work with women. Thus, if a discriminating male worker would receive w_m if he did not work with a woman, he would only be willing to work with a woman at a higher wage ($w_m + d_e$). This higher wage is analogous to the compensating wage differential that economists expect workers to be offered for unpleasant or unsafe working conditions.

What will be the profit-maximizing employer's response to this situation? One solution would be for the employer to hire a sex-segregated workforce and thereby eliminate the necessity of paying a premium to male workers for associating with female workers. If all employers responded in this way (but had no taste for discrimination themselves), male and female workers would be paid the same wage rate, although they would work in segregated settings.

However, complete segregation may not be profitable when substantial costs of adjustment arise from the previous situation.[75] For example, the hiring of new workers entails recruitment and screening costs for the firm. Further, for jobs in which firm-specific training is important, the firm must incur the costs of these investments as well. Where such costs are involved in changing from the current situation, history matters. Given rising female participation rates over time, women, as relatively new entrants, will find men already in place in many sectors. Further, as we saw in Chapter 2, women were heavily concentrated in a few female-dominated activities even when they constituted a small proportion of the labor force. Regardless of the various factors initially causing this segregation, adjustment costs in conjunction with employee tastes for discrimination could help to perpetuate it.

Given employee tastes for discrimination and adjustment costs, marketwide wage differences between male and female workers may result. Again, the size of the wage differential depends on the distribution and intensity of, in this case, *employees'* discriminatory tastes, as well as the relative number of women seeking employment. If employees with no taste for discrimination against women represent a large proportion or relatively few women are seeking jobs, then it may be possible for all the women to work with nondiscriminatory men; and no pay differential would occur.

However, if discriminatory tastes are widespread or relatively large numbers of women are seeking jobs, some of the women will have to work with discriminating male workers. Those males will require higher compensation to induce them to work with women. The result will be a wage differential between male and female workers,

---

[74] Lawrence M. Kahn presents a model that shows that customer discrimination can produce persistent discriminatory wage differentials in "Customer Discrimination and Affirmative Action," *Economic Inquiry* 29, no. 3 (July 1991): 555–71.

[75] Arrow, "The Theory of Discrimination."

on average, because some males will receive this higher pay. Moreover, it is also possible that women will be paid less to compensate. In addition, more variation will occur in male workers' wage rates than would otherwise be the case. Discriminating male workers who do not work with women do not need to be paid a wage premium, nor do nondiscriminating males, regardless of whether or not they are employed with women.

In an empirical test of this prediction, one study compared the wages of men and women (within the same narrowly defined white-collar occupations) in sex-integrated and sex-segregated firms.[76] The study found that, contrary to what was expected on the basis of the employee discrimination model, men earned *more* in sex-segregated than in integrated firms, and women earned *more* when they worked with men than when they worked only with other women. These findings are more consistent with a situation in which high-wage (e.g., monopolistic or unionized) employers are better able to indulge their preferences for hiring men than one in which the pay differentials are due to employee discrimination. There may, however, be other cases in which employee discrimination has played an important role.

If such employee tastes for discrimination do in fact exist, and if they vary by occupation, employee discrimination may be a factor causing occupational segregation as well as pay differentials. For example, one reason why women may not be hired for supervisory and managerial positions may be that even male employees who do not mind working with women do not like being supervised by them. As we have seen, there is some evidence of this. This could create a barrier to the employment of women in such jobs.[77]

Barbara Bergmann and William Darity have suggested that employee discrimination may also adversely affect the morale and productivity of discriminating male workers who are forced to work with women, a possibility not initially considered by Becker.[78] This possibility would make employers reluctant to hire women, especially when their male employees require considerable firm-specific training and are hard to replace. Further, if employers do hire women under such circumstances, they may pay them less to compensate for the reduction in the productivity of the discriminating male employees. In a sense, a woman's marginal productivity is lower than a man's because adding her to the workforce causes a decline in the productivity of previously employed male workers. Adding an additional male worker causes no such decline in output.

Two recently proposed models of discrimination suggest additional motivations for male employees to discriminate against female coworkers and provide rationales as to why men may resist female inroads into traditionally male occupations beyond simply a "taste" for discrimination. In both cases, men believe they will be negatively affected if women enter their traditionally male occupation. In George A. Akerlof and Rachel E. Kranton's **identity model**, occupations are associated with societal notions of "male" and "female." In this model, men oppose the entry of women into traditionally male jobs out of concern that they will lose their male identity or sense of self.[79] In

---

[76] Blau, *Equal Pay in the Office*.

[77] However, one study found that both male and female employees earned *less* when they had a female supervisor, which is not consistent with employee discrimination against female supervisors and suggests rather that the presence of a female supervisor is associated with less favorable characteristics of the job. See Donna S. Rothstein, "Supervisor Gender and the Early Labor Market Outcomes of Young Workers," in *Gender and Family Issues in the Workplace*, edited by Francine D. Blau and Ronald G. Ehrenberg (New York: Russell Sage, 1997): 210–55.

[78] Barbara R. Bergmann and William A. Darity Jr., "Social Relations in the Workplace and Employer Discrimination," in *Proceedings of the Thirty-Third Annual Meetings of the Industrial Relations Research Association* (Madison: University of Wisconsin, 1981), pp. 155–62.

[79] George A. Akerlof and Rachel E. Kranton, "Economics and Identity," *Quarterly Journal of Economics* 115, no. 3 (August 2000): 715–53.

Claudia Goldin's **pollution theory of discrimination**, the entry of women into traditionally male jobs is seen by male incumbents as reducing the prestige of the occupation, based on general social perceptions that women are, on average, less productive.[80]

A final way in which employee discrimination could depress women workers' pay, also not initially considered by Becker, is that it could directly reduce the productivity of women in comparison with men. This is most likely to be a problem in traditionally male fields where the majority of workers are male. For example, on-the-job training frequently occurs informally as supervisors or coworkers demonstrate how things are done and give advice and assistance. When male employees have tastes for discrimination against women, they may be reluctant to teach them these important skills. Consequently, women may learn less and be less productive.

CUSTOMER DISCRIMINATION   In the case of **customer discrimination**, customers or clients who have tastes for discrimination against women will act as if there were a nonpecuniary cost associated with purchasing a good or a service from a woman equal to their discrimination coefficient, d_c. That is, they will behave as if the full price of the good or service is $p + d_c$ if sold or provided by a women, but only p if sold or provided by a man. Then, at the going market price, women will sell less. Alternatively, in order to sell as much as a comparable male, a woman would have to charge a lower price $(p - d_c)$. Again, discrimination, this time on the part of possible customers or clients, can result in potentially equally productive women being less productive (in terms of revenue brought in) than comparable males. They are, thus, less desirable employees and receive lower pay. If, as we speculated earlier, such customer discrimination exists in some areas but not in others, occupational segregation may also result.

SUBTLE BARRIERS   As we noted previously, discrimination against women is not always or even usually conscious and overt. In Chapter 6, we outlined subtle barriers that may limit women's acquisition of formal schooling. Such **subtle barriers** may also operate in the labor market, as suggested in our discussion of the glass ceiling. For instance, as in educational institutions, women in the workplace may participate less in the beneficial *mentor–protégé* relationships that often develop between senior and junior workers and may be excluded from the *informal networks* that tend to arise among peers at the workplace. As a result, they will be denied access to important job-related information, skills, and contacts, as well as the informal support systems that male workers generally enjoy. In these cases, although women are *potentially* equally productive, discrimination reduces both their productivity and their pay.

Discrimination may also result from the perception that a woman would not "fit in" with the group as well as a man would and evaluations of a female employee's competence may be tainted by gender stereotypes of appropriate female behavior. Discrimination by employers, employees, and customers may also be reinforced by habitual behavior that has the effect of disadvantaging women, even though its link to discriminatory outcomes may not be apparent at first. A good example of this is the role that all-male clubs traditionally played for business executives, high-level professionals, and civic leaders.[81] While some mistakenly perceive such clubs as "social" in their orientation, there is increased recognition that much business is transacted and many professional contacts are made in these settings. For this reason, many clubs, under legal pressure or voluntarily, have opened their doors to women. In addition, although

---

[80] Claudia Goldin, "A Pollution Theory of Discrimination: Male and Female Differences in Occupations and Earnings," National Bureau of Economic Research Working Paper No. 8985 (June 2002).

[81] For further discussion of this issue, see Robin L. Bartlett and Timothy I. Miller, "Executive Earnings by Gender: A Case Study," *Social Science Quarterly* 69, no. 4 (December 1988): 892–909.

no federal law prohibits gender discrimination by private clubs, a number of major cities and several states, including New York, Florida, Michigan, and Minnesota, have taken action and banned the exclusion of women by business-oriented private clubs.[82] However, this issue is by no means entirely one of the past. In 2002, a firestorm of negative media attention surrounded the male-only membership restriction of the exclusive Augusta National Golf Club, which hosts the Masters Tournament. As of 2008, this club still did not allow women members.[83]

Statistical Discrimination

As noted earlier, models of **statistical discrimination** developed by Edmund Phelps and others[84] attribute a different motivation to employers for discrimination, one that is potentially more consistent with profit maximization and, thus, with the persistence of discrimination in the long run. In this view, employers are constantly faced with the need for decision making under conditions of incomplete information and uncertainty. Even if they carefully study the qualifications of applicants, they never know for certain how individuals will perform on the job or how long they will stay with the firm after being hired. Mistakes can be costly, especially when substantial hiring and training costs are involved. Promotion decisions entail similar risks, although in this case employers have additional firsthand information on past job performance with the firm.

PERCEPTIONS OF AVERAGE GENDER DIFFERENCES CAN RESULT IN A PAY GAP   In light of these uncertainties, it is not surprising that employers often use any readily accessible information that may be correlated with productivity or job stability in making difficult personnel decisions. If they believe that, *on average*, women are less productive or less stable employees, *statistical discrimination* against *individual* women may result. That is, employers may judge the individual woman on the basis of their beliefs about group averages. The result may be discrimination against women in pay or in hiring and promotion.

For example, suppose an employer is screening applicants for an entry-level managerial position and that the two major qualifications considered are level of education and grades. Assume further that the employer believes that at the same level of qualifications (e.g., an MBA with an A– average), women as a group will be less likely to remain with the firm than men. Then, for a given level of qualifications, the employer would hire a woman only at a lower wage or, perhaps, simply hire a man rather than a woman for the job. More careful screening of applicants might enable the employer to distinguish more from less career-oriented women (e.g., a consideration of the candidate's employment record while a student or of her extracurricular activities while in school), but it may not be cost-effective for the employer to invest the additional resources necessary for this screening.

Judged on the basis of statements employers themselves make, such beliefs regarding differences in average ability or behavior by sex are quite common. For example, employers are often concerned that women do not take their careers as seriously as

---

[82] Tom McNichol, "Is There a 'Glass Ceiling'?" *USA Weekend*, November 16, 1997, p. 8; and Cailin Brown, "Private Clubs Less Restrictive," *Times Union*, May 14, 1995, p. B1.

[83] Alex Kuczynski, "It's Still a Man's, Man's, Man's World," *New York Times*, July 21, 2002, sec. 9, pp. 1–2; and Jennifer Steinhauer, "Phoenix Journal: Nice Spot to Eat After Golf, but Women Are Barred," *New York Times*, June 28, 2008, available at www.nytimes.org. The latter article describes the controversy over the Phoenix Country Club's policy of forbidding women in the men's grill room, regarded as "a center of power dining in Phoenix"; women are, however, permitted to become members.

[84] See, for example, Edmund S. Phelps, "The Statistical Theory of Racism and Sexism," *American Economic Review* 62, no. 4 (September 1972): 659–61, and Dennis J. Aigner and Glen G. Cain, "Statistical Theories of Discrimination in Labor Markets," *Industrial and Labor Relations Review* 30, no. 2 (January 1977): 175–87.

men and fear that they will quit their jobs when they have children. Other perceptions of average differences in behavior or performance of men and women were noted in our consideration of issues related to the glass ceiling.

If such employer beliefs are simply incorrect or exaggerated or reflect time lags in adjusting to a new reality, actions based on them are clearly unfair and constitute labor market discrimination as we define it. That is, they generate wage and occupation differences between men and women that are not accounted for by (potential) productivity differences. If such views are not simply rationalizations for personal prejudice, it might be expected that, over time, they will yield to new information. However, this process may be more sluggish than one would like, and, in the meantime, employers make less than optimal choices. Moreover, as noted previously, some discrimination may be unconscious and, thus, that much less susceptible to change by new information.

The situation is different, and a bit more complicated, if the employer views *are* indeed correct *on average.* Employers make the best choices possible with imperfect knowledge, and, in a sense, at the marketwide level, labor market discrimination does not exist in this case: Any resulting wage and employment differences between men and women, on average, would be accounted for by *average* productivity differences.

Yet the consequences for *individual* women are far from satisfactory. A particular woman who would be as productive and as stable an employee as her male counterpart is denied employment or paid a lower wage. It seems fairly clear from a *normative* perspective that basing employment decisions on a characteristic such as sex—a characteristic that the individual cannot change–is unfair. Indeed, the practice of judging an *individual* on the basis of *group* characteristics rather than upon his or her own merits seems the very essence of stereotyping and discrimination. Such behavior is certainly not legal under the antidiscrimination laws and regulations that we discuss later in this chapter. Yet it most likely still plays a role in employer thinking. Moreover, statistical discrimination, which is based on employers' *correct* assessment of average gender differences, is not likely to be eroded by the forces of competition.

STATISTICAL DISCRIMINATION AND FEEDBACK EFFECTS   As Nobel laureate Kenneth Arrow pointed out, the consequences of statistical discrimination are particularly pernicious when accompanied by *feedback effects.*[85] For example, if employers' views of female job instability lead them to give women less firm-specific training and to assign them to jobs where the costs of turnover are minimized, women experience little incentive to stay with the employer and may respond by exhibiting exactly the unstable behavior that employers expect. Employers' perceptions are confirmed, and they see no reason to change their discriminatory behavior. Yet if employers believe women to be stable workers and hire them into positions that reward such stability, they might well be stable workers!

Hence, where statistical discrimination is accompanied by feedback effects, employer behavior that is based on *initially* incorrect assessments of average gender differences may persist in the long run and be fairly impervious to competitive pressures.

EMPIRICAL EVIDENCE ON GENDER DIFFERENCES IN QUITTING   Some indication that such feedback effects are important is provided by studies of male and female quitting. This possibility is especially important because employer views that women are more likely to quit their jobs than men tend to be fairly widespread. A number of studies find that although women are on average more likely to quit their jobs than men, most of this difference is explained by the types of jobs women are in and other individual

---

[85] Arrow, "The Theory of Discrimination."

characteristics.[86] These findings suggest that, when a woman worker is confronted with the same incentives to remain on the job in terms of wages, advancement opportunities, and so on, a woman is no more likely to quit than a comparable male worker. Moreover, while some research suggests that employers might have had greater difficulty predicting the quit behavior of women than the quit behavior of men for earlier cohorts, this was not found to be the case for women born after 1950. Indeed, for college-educated workers, little difference was found between men and women even in overall turnover rates.[87]

Even though these studies of gender differences in turnover offer little justification for employers to practice statistical discrimination against women based on presumed differences in quit rates, this does not necessarily mean that gender differences in quit behavior are not related to the pay gap. While the overall quit rates of women and men with similar characteristics are similar, women and men tend to quit their jobs for *different* reasons. Women are more likely than men to quit their jobs for family-related reasons or to exit the labor force entirely and they are less likely than men to quit in order to move to another job. Such behavioral differences between men and women and the resulting greater workforce interruptions of women will contribute to the gender pay gap. Interestingly, however, even in this aspect of quitting—the reasons for quits, college women's behavior now appears more similar to their male counterparts.[88]

The Overcrowding Model

The **overcrowding model**, developed by Barbara Bergmann, is of interest because it gives a more central role to occupational segregation in causing a wage differential between men and women than the discrimination models we have considered so far.[89] Bergmann's overcrowding model demonstrates that, regardless of the reason for segregation (e.g., socialization, personal preferences, or labor market discrimination), the *consequence* may be a male–female pay differential. This differential will occur if demand (job opportunities) in the female sector is small relative to the supply of women available for such work. The overcrowding model is consistent with the evidence presented earlier that, all else equal, earnings tend to be lower in predominantly female than in predominantly male jobs. The fact that men in predominantly female occupations also receive low wages is not necessarily inconsistent with the overcrowding hypothesis. Although men as a group are obviously not excluded from the male sector, some of them may, nonetheless, enter female occupations because they have a strong preference or particular skills for this type of work. Or they may be simply unlucky or poorly informed about alternative opportunities. They will accept the lower wages paid in female jobs. However, this lower pay is primarily caused by the many women who "crowd" into these jobs due to their preferences for the work or a lack of alternative opportunities.

---

[86] See, for example, Francine D. Blau and Lawrence M. Kahn, "Race and Sex Differences in Quits by Young Workers," *Industrial and Labor Relations Review* 34, no. 4 (July 1981): 563–77; W. Kip Viscusi, "Sex Differences in Worker Quitting," *Review of Economics and Statistics* 62, no. 3 (August 1980): 388–98; Nachum Sicherman, "Gender Differences in Departures from a Large Firm," *Industrial and Labor Relations Review* 49, no. 3 (April 1996): 484–505; and Anne Beeson Royalty, "Job-to-Job and Job-to-Nonemployment Turnover by Gender and Education Level," *Journal of Labor Economics* 16, no. 2 (April 1998): 392–443.

[87] Audrey Light and Manuelita Ureta, "Panel Estimates of Male and Female Job Turnover Behavior: Can Female Nonquitters Be Identified?" *Journal of Labor Economics* 10, no. 2 (April 1992): 156–81; and Royalty, "Job-to-Job and Job-to-Nonemployment Turnover."

[88] Sicherman, "Gender Differences in Departures from a Large Firm"; Royalty, "Job-to-Job and Job-to-Nonemployment Turnover"; and Kristin Keith and Abagail McWilliams, "The Wage Effects of Cumulative Job Mobility," *Industrial and Labor Relations Review* 49, no. 1 (October 1995): 121–37.

[89] Barbara R. Bergmann, "Occupational Segregation, Wages and Profits When Employers Discriminate by Race or Sex," *Eastern Economic Journal* 1, nos. 1–2 (April–July 1974): 103–10.

This model is illustrated in Figure 7-1. F jobs and M jobs are considered. As in the previous models of discrimination, it is assumed that male and female workers are (potentially) equally productive. The hypothetical situation of no discrimination is represented by demand curves D_f and D_m and supply curves S_{f0} and S_{m0}. The nondiscriminatory equilibrium points in the two markets (E_{f0} and E_{m0}) are determined so that the wage rate (W_0) is the same for both types of jobs.

To see why, in the absence of discrimination, the wage rate will be the same for both types of jobs, recall that we assumed all workers are equally well qualified for F and M jobs and that employers are indifferent between hiring male and female workers. Suppose that, by chance, the equilibrium wage in F jobs is higher than the equilibrium wage in M jobs. Then workers attracted by the higher wage rates would transfer from M jobs to F jobs. This process would continue until wages in F jobs were bid down to the level of wages in M jobs. Similarly, if by chance wages in M jobs were set above those in F jobs, workers would move from F jobs to M jobs until the differential was eliminated. Thus, in the absence of discrimination, worker mobility ensures that the wages paid for both types of work are the same, at least after allowing time to make adjustments. This outcome, of course, assumes that no *nonpecuniary* differences exist in the relative attractiveness of the two jobs that would result in a compensating wage differential.

In the hypothetical example given in Figure 7-1, demand conditions are such that, in the nondiscriminatory equilibrium, L_{f0} workers (25 percent of the labor force) are employed in F jobs and L_{m0} workers (75 percent of the labor force) work in M jobs. F and M jobs have no sex labels associated with them, and both women and men are randomly divided between the two sectors.

How does the situation differ when there is discrimination against women in "male" occupations or when, for a variety of reasons, women choose to concentrate in typically female jobs? The consequences of such segregation may be ascertained by comparing this situation to the hypothetical situation of no segregation. In our example, the restriction of M jobs to men results in an inward shift of the supply curve to M jobs

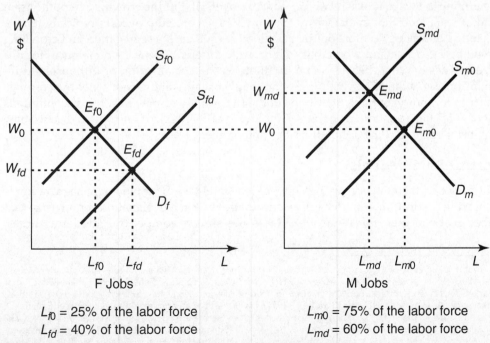

L_{f0} = 25% of the labor force
L_{fd} = 40% of the labor force

L_{m0} = 75% of the labor force
L_{md} = 60% of the labor force

FIGURE 7-1   An Illustration of the Overcrowding Model

from S_{m0} to S_{md}, causing wages to be bid up to W_{md}. At this higher wage, only L_{md} workers (60 percent of the labor force) are employed in M jobs. The exclusion of women from M jobs means that all the women must (or choose to) "crowd" into the F jobs. The expanded supply of labor in F jobs, represented by an outward shift of the supply curve from S_{f0} to S_{fd}, depresses wages there to W_{fd}. Now L_{fd} workers (40 percent of the labor force) are employed in F occupations.

The overcrowding model shows how gender segregation in employment may cause a wage differential between otherwise equally productive male and female workers. This differential will occur if the supply of women seeking employment is large relative to the demand for labor in the F jobs. This may well be what takes place in the labor market. Nevertheless, the analysis also shows that gender segregation in employment need not always result in a wage differential between men and women. If it so happens that the wage rate that equates supply and demand in the F sector is the same as the wage that equates supply and demand in the M sector, no wage differential will result (i.e., if the F sector is not overcrowded). However, this will happen only by chance. Labor market discrimination (or some other barrier) eliminates the free mobility of labor between the two sectors that would otherwise ensure wage equality between M and F jobs.

Returning to the more likely situation illustrated in Figure 7-1, in which segregation does lower women's pay, we may examine its impact on the *productivity* of women relative to men. Employers of women in F jobs accommodate a larger number of workers (L_{fd} rather than L_{f0}) by substituting labor for capital. The relatively low wages of the women, W_{fd}, make it profitable to use such labor-intensive production methods. On the other hand, the higher wage in the male sector, W_{md}, encourages employers to substitute capital for labor to economize on relatively high-priced labor. In the overcrowding model, women earn less than men, but both are paid in accordance with their productivity. Discrimination causes differences in both wages and productivity between *potentially* equally productive male and female labor—women are less productive than men because, due to segregation and crowding, they have less capital to work with.

The claim that the supply of labor to a particular occupation (or industry) helps to determine the wage rate is relatively noncontroversial. But the crowding hypothesis, in and of itself, does not explain why so many women are employed in typically female sectors. Controversy centers on the question of whether this segregation and crowding result because men and women have inherently different talents or preferences for different types of work; because, due to differences in socialization or in household responsibilities, women are willing to trade higher wages and steeper lifetime earnings profiles for more favorable working conditions and lower penalties for discontinuous labor force participation; or because employers, coworkers, or customers discriminate against women in some occupations but not in others.

Institutional Models

The idea that the male-female pay gap is closely related to employment segregation is echoed in **institutional models of discrimination**.[90] Such explanations emphasize that labor markets may not be as flexible as the simple competitive model assumes.

---

[90] For important early work on this concept, see Peter B. Doeringer and Michael J. Piore, *Internal Labor Markets and Manpower Analysis* (Lexington, MA: D.C. Heath and Co., 1971), and Michael J. Piore, "The Dual Labor Market: Theory and Implications," in *Problems in Political Economy: An Urban Perspective*, edited by David M. Gordon (Lexington, MA: D.C. Heath and Co., 1971), pp. 90–94. For an application to gender, see Francine D. Blau and Carol L. Jusenius, "Economists' Approaches to Sex Segregation in the Labor Market: An Appraisal," *Signs: Journal of Women in Culture and Society* 1, no. 3, pt. 2 (Spring 1976): 181–99. For a thoughtful consideration of concepts and evidence, see George Baker and Bengt Holmstrom, "Internal Labor Markets: Too Many Theories, Too Few Facts," *American Economic Review* 85, no. 2 (May 1995): 255–59.

Rigidities are introduced both by the institutional arrangements found in many firms and by various barriers to competition introduced by the monopoly power of firms in the product market or of firms or unions in the labor market.

THE INTERNAL LABOR MARKET   Institutionalists point out that the job structure of many large firms looks like the illustration in Figure 7-2a. Firms hire workers from the outside labor market for entry jobs. The remaining jobs are internally allocated by the firm as workers progress along well-defined promotion ladders by acquiring job-related skills, many of which are firm specific in nature. When firm-specific skills are emphasized and a high proportion of jobs are filled from internal sources, the firm has an **internal labor market**. That is, it determines wages for each job category and the allocation of workers among categories and is insulated to some extent (although not entirely) from the impact of market forces.

To administer their personnel systems, larger firms often take the occupational category as the decision unit, establishing pay rates for each category (with some allowance for seniority and merit considerations), and linking jobs together into promotion ladders. Thus, group treatment of individuals is the norm, and it will be to the employer's advantage to make sure that workers within each job category are as similar as possible. If it is believed that men and women (as well as, say, whites and nonwhites) differ in their productivity-related characteristics (like quit and absenteeism rates), statistical discrimination is likely to result in their being channeled into different jobs.

PRIMARY AND SECONDARY JOBS   The **dual labor market model** developed by Peter Doeringer and Michael Piore takes this analysis a step further and emphasizes the distinction between primary and secondary jobs.[91] Primary jobs emphasize high levels of firm-specific skills and, thus, pay high wages, offer good promotion opportunities, and encourage long-term attachment between workers and firms. In secondary jobs, firm-specific skills are not as important. Such jobs pay less, offer relatively fewer promotion opportunities, and have fairly high rates of labor turnover. This situation is depicted in

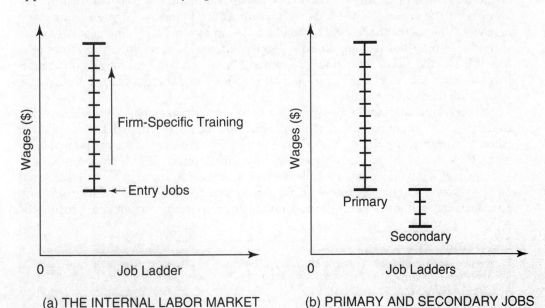

(a) THE INTERNAL LABOR MARKET   (b) PRIMARY AND SECONDARY JOBS

FIGURE 7-2   An Illustration of the Institutional Model

---

[91] Doeringer and Piore, *Internal Labor Markets*; and Piore, "The Dual Labor Market."

Figure 7-2b. Applying the dual labor market model to gender discrimination leads us to expect that men would be more likely to be in primary jobs and women in secondary jobs.

The distinction between primary and secondary jobs may occur within the same firm—say, between the managerial and clerical categories. In addition, it is believed that primary jobs are more likely to be located in monopolistic industries that are generally higher paying and have traditionally offered more stable employment[92] and that secondary jobs are more likely to be found in lower-paying, competitive industries with more labor turnover. This is an additional reason for expecting women to be more concentrated in the competitive sector.

Segmentation of male and female workers into primary and secondary jobs is likely to produce both pay and productivity differences between them due to unequal access to on-the-job training. Institutionalists also point out that feedback effects are likely to magnify any initial productivity differences, as women respond to the lower incentives for employment stability in the secondary sector.

Institutional analyses also reinforce the point made earlier that labor market discrimination against women is not necessarily the outcome of conscious, overt acts by employers. Once men and women are channeled into different types of entry jobs, the normal, everyday operation of the firm—"business as usual"—will virtually ensure gender differences in productivity, promotion opportunities, and pay. This process is termed **institutional discrimination**.[93] Even gender differences in initial occupational assignment may be in part due to adherence to traditional practices that tend to work against women; for example, referrals from current male employees or an informal network of male colleagues at other firms, sexist recruitment materials picturing women in traditionally female jobs and men in traditionally male jobs, and lack of encouragement of female applicants to broaden their sights from traditional areas.

Feedback Effects

As noted several times already, labor market discrimination or unequal treatment of women in the labor market may adversely affect women's own decisions and behavior.[94] These **feedback effects** are illustrated in Figure 7-3. Human capital theory and other supply-side explanations for gender differences in economic outcomes tend to emphasize the role of the gender division of labor in the family in causing differences between men and women in labor market outcomes and are indicated by the arrow pointing to the right in the figure.

This relationship undoubtedly exists; however, such explanations tend to neglect the impact of labor market discrimination in reinforcing the traditional division of labor (shown by the arrow pointing to the left). Even a relatively small amount of initial labor market discrimination can result in greatly magnified effects if it discourages women from making human capital investments, weakens their attachment to the labor force, and provides economic incentives for the family to place priority on the husband's career. Although labor market discrimination is not responsible for initially causing the

---

[92] The original formulation emphasized that these would be union jobs as well, but as we shall see in Chapter 9, there has been a steep decline in the extent of unionization in the United States.

[93] See Roos and Reskin, "Institutional Factors," for a description of business practices that tend to adversely affect women.

[94] A number of authors emphasize the importance of feedback effects in analyzing discrimination in pay and employment. See, for example, Arrow, "The Theory of Discrimination"; Shelly J. Lundberg and Richard Startz, "Private Discrimination and Social Intervention in Competitive Labor Markets," *American Economic Review* 73, no. 3 (June 1983): 340–47; and Yoram Weiss and Reuben Gronau, "Expected Interruptions in Labour Force Participation and Sex-Related Differences in Earnings Growth," *Review of Economic Studies* 48, no. 4 (October 1981): 607–19.

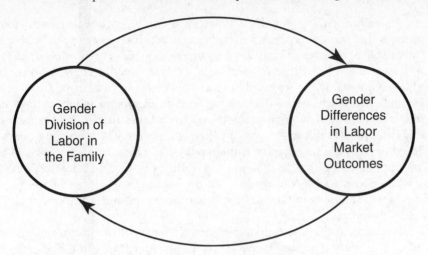

FIGURE 7-3   An Illustration of Feedback Effects

traditional division of labor in the family, which clearly predates modern labor markets, it may well help to perpetuate it by inhibiting more rapid movement toward egalitarian sharing of household responsibilities today.

The net result is what might be viewed as a vicious circle. Discrimination against women in the labor market reinforces traditional gender roles in the family, while adherence to traditional roles by women provides a rationale for labor market discrimination. However, this also means that effective policies to end labor market discrimination can be expected to have far-reaching effects, particularly when combined with simultaneous changes in social attitudes toward women's roles. A decrease in labor market discrimination will have feedback effects as the equalization of market incentives between men and women induces further changes in women's supply-side behavior. These changes in turn are likely to further encourage employers to reduce statistical discrimination against women. In addition, as more women enter previously male-dominated fields, the larger number of female role models for younger women is likely to induce still further increases in the availability of women for such jobs. Thus, demand-side policies can be expected to play an important role in sustaining a process of cumulative change in women's economic status.

POLICY ISSUE: THE GOVERNMENT AND EQUAL EMPLOYMENT OPPORTUNITY

Government policies to combat labor market discrimination against women can potentially be justified on at least two grounds. One is equity or fairness—"a matter of simple justice."[95] Thus, government intervention may be rationalized to assure equal treatment for all participants in the labor market, regardless of gender (or race, ethnic origin, etc.).

In addition to being unfair, unequal treatment on the basis of gender may result in an inefficient allocation of resources. This inefficiency provides a second rationale for government intervention. Consider the case where equally productive men and women are hired for different jobs and women's jobs are lower paid (as in the overcrowding model). Under these circumstances, prices do not serve as accurate indicators of social

---

[95] This phrase provided the title of the Report of the President's Task Force on Women's Rights and Responsibilities (Washington, DC: U.S. Government Printing Office, April 1970).

costs. In comparison with the nondiscriminatory situation, society produces "too little" of the outputs that use "overpriced" male labor, given that equally productive female labor is available at a lower price to expand production. Society produces "too much" of the outputs that use "underpriced" female labor, given that the contribution of equally productive labor is valued more highly in the male sector (as measured by its price).

The inefficiency caused by discrimination is even greater when we take into account feedback effects. If women are deterred from investing in their human capital because of discrimination, society loses a valuable resource. Thus, opening doors previously closed (or only slightly ajar) to women potentially benefits society as well as individual women by bringing their talents and abilities to bear in new areas. As Nobel laureate Paul A. Samuelson commented, "To the degree that women are getting an opportunity they didn't have in the past, the economy is tapping an important and previously wasted resource."[96]

Weighed against these potential gains are the costs of the increased government intervention in society that may be necessary to produce this result. These costs loom large indeed to those who are skeptical of the evidence of labor market discrimination against women presented earlier. Some may also fear what they regard as the possible excesses of antidiscrimination policies in the form of reverse discrimination or preferential treatment for women and minorities, although, as we shall see, research to date provides no evidence that the increased employment of women and minorities encouraged by legislation entailed such efficiency costs.[97] We examine the record of government intervention in this area next.[98]

Equal Employment Opportunity Laws and Regulations

There is a long history of government involvement in shaping conditions encountered by women in the labor market. During the period following the Civil War, in response to concern and agitation by workers and their sympathizers, a number of states passed protective labor laws limiting hours and regulating other terms of employment for all workers. At first, the Supreme Court struck down these laws as unconstitutional on the basis that they interfered with the freedom of workers to enter contracts. Subsequently, in its 1908 decision in *Muller v. Oregon*,[99] the Court upheld such laws when they were confined to women alone, arguing that individual rights may be abridged because the state has a legitimate interest in the possible social effects of women's work. Louis Brandeis, later to become a Supreme Court Justice known for his support of individual human rights, wrote the following about the case:

> The two sexes differ in structure of body, in the functions performed by each, in the amount of physical strength, in the capacity for long-continued labor,

---

[96] *Business Week*, January 28, 1985, p. 80. For evidence on the efficiency costs of gender discrimination, see Tiago V. de V. Cavalcanti and José A. Tavares, "Gender Discrimination Lowers Output Per Capita (A Lot)," VOX, October 16, 2007, available at http://voxeu.org.

[97] Leonard, "Antidiscrimination or Reverse Discrimination"; and Harry Holzer and David Neumark, "Are Affirmative Action Hires Less Qualified? Evidence from Employer-Employee Data on New Hires," *Journal of Labor Economics* 17, no. 3 (July 1999). For a helpful review of the evidence on this question and other issues related to affirmative action, see Harry J. Holzer and David Neumark, "Affirmative Action: What Do We Know?" *Journal of Policy Analysis and Management* 25, no. 2 (Spring 2006): 463–90.

[98] For excellent summaries of the legal situation, see Mack A. Player, *Federal Law of Employment Discrimination*, 5th ed. (St. Paul, MI: Thomson/West, 2004), and Susan Deller Ross, Isabelle Katz Pinzler, Deborah A. Ellis, and Kary L. Moss, *The Rights of Women: The Basic ACLU Guide to a Woman's Rights*, 3rd ed. (Carbondale: Southern Illinois University Press, 1993). For a useful description of the legal setting, including a discussion of how lawyers and economists view discrimination and the role of economists in employment litigation, see Joni Hersch, "Employment Discrimination, Economists and the Law," in *Women, Family and Work: Writings on the Economics of Gender*, edited by Karine S. Moe (Oxford: Blackwell Publishers, 2003), pp. 217–333.

[99] *Muller v. Oregon*, 208 U.S. 412 (1908).

particularly when done standing, the influence of vigorous health upon the future well-being of the race, the self-reliance which enables one to assert full rights, and in the capacity to maintain the struggle for subsistence. The difference justifies a difference in legislation, and upholds that which is designed to compensate for some of the burdens which rest upon her.

In time, however, the concern shifted from protection to equal opportunity. Indeed, protective laws eventually came to be viewed as undesirable impediments to the advancement of women. Supreme Court Justice Brennan expressed this view well in a 1973 case: "Traditionally, discrimination was rationalized by an attitude of romantic paternalism which in practical effect put women not on a pedestal but in a cage."[100]

As early as 1961, President Kennedy issued an executive order calling for a presidential commission on the status of women. Two years later, the **Equal Pay Act** of 1963 was passed, which requires employers to pay the same wages to men and women who do substantially equal work, involving equal skill, effort, and responsibility, and performed under similar conditions in the same establishment. This law, for instance, made it illegal for a firm to have separate pay scales for women and men doing the same job. It applied only to wage discrimination for the same job in the same firm and did not address discrimination in hiring, promotion, training programs, and so on.

More comprehensive legislation was enacted in 1964 when **Title VII of the Civil Rights Act** was passed. This legislation was originally written to prohibit discrimination in employment on the basis of race, religion, and national origin but was changed at the last minute to include the word *sex*.[101] Title VII prohibits sex discrimination in virtually all aspects of employment, including hiring and firing, training, promotions, wages, fringe benefits, or other terms and conditions of employment. As amended, it covers all businesses employing 15 or more workers, including federal, state, and local governments and educational institutions. It also prohibits discrimination by employment agencies and labor organizations. The **Equal Employment Opportunity Commission (EEOC)** is the federal agency charged with enforcing the Equal Pay Act and Title VII.

Executive Order 11246 issued in 1965, and amended in 1967 to include sex, bars discrimination in employment by all employers with federal contracts and subcontracts. It also requires affirmative action for classes of workers disadvantaged by past discrimination. Contractors are required to analyze their employment patterns to determine where women and minorities are underrepresented. Whenever such deficiencies are found, they are to set up "goals and timetables" for the hiring of women and minorities and to make good faith efforts to reach their goals in the specified period. The Executive Order is enforced by the Office of Federal Contract Compliance. Violators face possible loss of their government contracts, although this sanction is seldom invoked.

In the years since their passage and implementation, the federal antidiscrimination laws and regulations have been interpreted and clarified by the courts, with the final arbiter being the U.S. Supreme Court. This process is especially important in understanding the provisions of Title VII of the Civil Rights Act, the broadest law and the centerpiece of the federal government's antidiscrimination enforcement effort. In some cases, the Court's interpretations of the law changed as the membership on the Court shifted, which is likely to continue to be the case in the future. Bearing this likelihood in mind, in order to better understand what activities are currently prohibited under Title VII, we turn to a brief summary of some of the more important Court decisions.

---

[100] *Frontiero v. Richardson*, 411 U.S. 677 (1973).
[101] Because it was Howard Smith, a conservative congressman from Virginia, who proposed this amendment, it is widely believed that his purpose in doing so was to increase opposition to the bill and reduce the chances of its passage.

Title VII permits exceptions to its ban on gender discrimination when sex is found to be a **bona fide occupational qualification** (BFOQ). When the law was passed in the mid-1960s, it was not entirely clear what this exemption would mean as a practical matter particularly as only gender could be a basis for a BFOQ in the legislation, not race, religion, or national origin. At that time, social views widely accepted the notion that a considerable number of jobs were particularly suitable for women and a goodly number of others especially appropriate for men. Indeed, newspapers routinely divided portions of their help wanted sections into "help wanted male" and "help wanted female." The former might include openings for jobs such as manager or construction worker, while the latter might include "girl Friday" (i.e., administrative assistant) or receptionist. Thus, the interpretation of the BFOQ exemption by the courts was extremely important. If interpreted broadly, to match the social views of the day, considerable gender discrimination would have been permissible under Title VII in that sex might have been viewed as a valid qualification for a host of traditionally male and traditionally female jobs.

However, both the EEOC and the courts have taken the position that the BFOQ exception should be interpreted narrowly. That is, men and women are entitled to consideration on the basis of their individual capabilities, rather than on the basis of characteristics generally attributed to the group. The Court, for example, has rejected the BFOQ exemption for predominately male jobs in which heavy lifting is required as well as for the predominately female position of flight attendant where it was argued by the employer that airline passengers preferred women in the job. Also, the Court has ruled that it is discriminatory to bar all women of childbearing age from jobs where they would work with substances that might be hazardous to a developing fetus.[102] In the only major case to date in which gender was found to be a BFOQ, the 1977 *Dothard v. Rawlinson* case, the Supreme Court allowed the hiring of only males for the position of prison guard in Alabama's maximum security male prisons. The Court reasoned that due to the nature of the prison population, as well as the atmosphere of the prison, women would be particularly subject to sexual assault, which would interfere with their job performance. Regardless of whether or not one agrees with this reasoning, this case has not resulted in substantially greater acceptance by the courts of the BFOQ exception for other jobs, given its unusual circumstances.[103]

The Court has also found that sex cannot be used in combination with some other factor as a legal basis for discrimination under Title VII. The Court has held, for example, that an employer cannot refuse to hire women with preschool-age children while men with preschool-age children are hired.[104] Furthermore, it is illegal to pay women lower monthly pension benefits than men.[105] In the past, this practice was justified on the basis that, on average, women live longer, and, thus, it would be more costly to provide them with the same monthly benefit. The courts ruled that each woman is entitled to be treated as an individual, rather than as a group member.

---

[102] Major cases in which the court has rejected a BFOQ exemption include *Weeks v. Southern Bell Telephone and Telegraph*, 408 F.2d 228 (5th Cir. 1969); *Rosenfeld v. Southern Pacific Company*, 444 F.2d 1219 (9th Cir. 1971); *Diaz v. Pan American World Airways, Inc.*, 442 F.2d 385 (5th Cir. 1971); and *United Auto Workers v. Johnson Controls, Inc.*, U.S. Sup. Ct., No. 89-1215 (1991). The Johnson controls case, which focused on workplace hazards, raised a particularly controversial issue. The Court found the exclusion of women of childbearing age from such employments to be discriminatory because "fertile men, but not fertile women, are given a choice as to whether they wish to risk their reproductive health for a particular job." It clarified that the BFOQ exemption of Title VII "must relate to ability to perform the duties of the job" rather than to any danger or risk to the woman herself. The Court also concluded that the risk of employer liability was slight given that "Title VII bans sex-specific fetal-protection policies, the employer fully informs the woman of the risk, and the employer has not acted negligently...." See Bureau of National Affairs, *Daily Labor Report*, no. 55 (March 21, 1991), pp. A1–A3 and D1–D11.

[103] *Dothard v. Rawlinson*, 433 U.S. 321 (1977); see Ross et al., *The Rights of Women*, for a consideration of this and other cases relating to the BFOQ exemption.

[104] *Philips v. Martin Marietta Corp.*, 400 U.S. 542 (1971).

[105] *City of Los Angeles, Dept. of Water v. Manhart*, 435 U.S. 702 (1978).

Disparate treatment of women and minorities, that is, differential treatment of these groups with the intention to discriminate, is a clear violation of Title VII. A more complex issue addressed by the courts in interpreting Title VII concerns unintentional discrimination. This type of discrimination arises when apparently neutral practices or policies of a firm, say with regard to hiring or promotion, result in a **disparate impact**, or have disproportionately adverse effects, on women or minorities. An example of disparate impact might be a minimum height and weight requirement for the position of police officer that screens out a higher proportion of women than men. Based on a 1971 Supreme Court decision in *Griggs*, apparently neutral practices resulting in a disparate impact on women and minorities may be illegal even if the discrimination is not intentional. Once the plaintiffs show that the practice creates a disparate impact, the burden of proof shifts to the employer to show that the practice is a matter of "business necessity" or that the requirement is job related; otherwise, the practice is discriminatory.[106]

In 1991, the Civil Rights Act was reauthorized, and several provisions were added. The new law permits women to obtain compensatory and punitive damages for *intentional* discrimination, in addition to back pay, although the amounts are limited. Prior to this law, only racial minorities had such rights. In addition, the new law allows discrimination cases to be argued before juries as well as judges. As we shall see shortly, these changes made it much more likely that private law firms would be willing to take on sex discrimination cases, particularly class action cases.

An issue at the center of considerable attention in recent years is sexual harassment.[107] **Sexual harassment** potentially encompasses a broad range of objectionable behaviors ranging from the making of sexual demands where a refusal results in an adverse action (e.g., dismissal, the loss of a promotion, reduced benefits), generally called *quid pro quo* harassment, to various actions that are sufficiently offensive to result in a hostile work environment. Deciding whether sexual harassment was indeed covered under Title VII and demarcating the conditions under which the behavior was egregious enough to be illegal has proved challenging for the courts. A major step forward was the Supreme Court's 1986 decision in *Meritor*, which held that sexual harassment is illegal under Title VII if it is unwelcome and "sufficiently severe or pervasive to alter the conditions of the victim's employment and create an abusive working environment."[108] Some controversy followed the Court's ruling over what constituted evidence of a hostile environment, with some lower courts requiring evidence of severe psychological injury or diminished job performance.

In its 1993 *Harris*[109] case, the Supreme Court clarified this issue, overturning a lower court ruling that an employee who was subjected to the company president's

---

[106] *Griggs v. Duke Power Co.*, 401 U.S. 424 (1971). A later 1989 Supreme Court decision (*Wards Cove Packing Co. v. Atonio*, 490 U.S. 642 (1989)) held that even after a disparate impact was demonstrated, the burden of proof remained with the plaintiffs to show that the employer had no business necessity justification for the practice. This decision was widely criticized by civil rights advocates and the original interpretation of the law that places the burden of proof on the *employer* was reestablished by Congress with the passage of the 1991 Civil Rights Act.

[107] This issue attracted particular attention during the 1991 confirmation hearings of Supreme Court Justice Clarence Thomas, when charges of sexual harassment were made against the nominee by Anita Hill, a law professor who had formerly worked as his assistant. Although Justice Thomas was confirmed, the airing of this issue in a national forum greatly heightened public awareness of the problem. Kaushik Basu provides an overview of the extent of and trends in sexual harassment and discusses the rationale for government intervention in this area in "The Economics and Law of Sexual Harassment in the Workplace," *Journal of Economic Perspectives* 17, no. 3 (Summer 2003):141–57. See also Heather Antecol and Deborah A. Cobb-Clark, "The Changing Nature of Employment-Related Sexual Harassment: Evidence from the U.S. Federal Government (1978–1994)," *Industrial and Labor Relations Review* 57, no. 3 (April 2004): 443–61.

[108] *Meritor Savings Bank v. Vinson*, 477 U.S. 57 (1986); the quotation was cited in "Ending Sexual Harassment: Business Is Getting the Message," *Business Week*, March 18, 1991, p. 99.

[109] *Harris v. Forklift Systems Inc.*, U.S., No. 92–1168, November 9, 1993. The summary of the case and quotation from the opinion are from Linda Greenhouse, "Court, 9–0, Makes Sex Harassment Easier to Prove," *New York Times*, November 10, 1993, pp. A1–A14; see also "Psychological Injury Not Needed to Prove Sex Harassment, Unanimous Supreme Court Rules," Bureau of National Affairs, *Daily Labor Report*, no. 216, November 10, 1993, pp. AA1–AA2.

repeated offensive and demeaning comments of a sexual nature was not entitled to redress under the law because she had not suffered sufficient psychological damage. The standard put forth by the Court in its decision is essentially that a hostile environment is one that a *reasonable person* would perceive to be "hostile or abusive." Writing for the majority, Justice Sandra Day O'Connor said that the protection of federal law "comes into play before the harassing conduct leads to a nervous breakdown." The Court has since ruled that Title VII prohibits sexual harassment between members of the same sex under the same legal standards as those used to evaluate claims of sexual harassment by a member of the opposite sex.[110]

Because sexual harassment generally results from interactions between employees, the question arises as to when employers are held liable for the actions of their employees. This issue is important because employers are regarded as having the "deep pockets"; that is, they can potentially pay financial compensation to individuals who are the victims of harassment. The stakes involved may be considerable. In 1998, in the largest sexual harassment settlement negotiated up to that point, Mitsubishi Motor Corporation agreed to pay $34 million to end a government lawsuit charging that hundreds of female employees at its automobile assembly plant in Normal, Illinois, had been sexually harassed.[111] Prior to two 1998 Supreme Court decisions,[112] it was believed, based on a lower court ruling, that employers could only be held liable for sexual harassment if they knew or should have known that the harassment had taken place. In its 1998 decisions, however, the Supreme Court extended the employer's liability well beyond this situation, making it clear that employers bear the fundamental responsibility for preventing and eliminating sexual harassment from the workplace. The Court ruled that when sexual harassment results in "a tangible employment action, such as discharge, demotion or undesirable assignment" (as in the quid pro quo type of case described earlier), the employer's liability is absolute. In cases of no tangible action (including hostile environment cases), an employer could still be liable but can defend itself by establishing that it took "reasonable care to prevent and correct promptly any sexually harassing behavior" and that the employee "unreasonably failed to take advantage of any preventive or corrective opportunities" provided. It is widely believed that a strong, well-publicized employer policy against harassment coupled with an effective grievance (complaint) procedure are the best tools currently available to employers to combat sexual harassment at the workplace and to safeguard themselves from liability. Such a policy cannot simply be "on the books." The employer must make sure that the policy is effectively communicated to employees, complaints are promptly investigated, and corrective action, where merited, is promptly taken.

A final substantive issue is employment discrimination based on sexual orientation. Title VII has not been interpreted to prohibit employment discrimination against individuals due to their sexual orientation. However, 17 states do prohibit such discrimination in private employment, and a sizable number of cities and counties do as well.[113] Efforts to address this type of discrimination have been made at the federal level as well. In 2007, the U.S. House of Representatives passed a bill to prohibit

---

[110] This ruling came in the 1998 case of *Oncale v. Sundowner Offshore Services, Inc.*; see Charles J. Muhl, "The Law at Work: Sexual Harassment," *Monthly Labor Review* 121, no. 7 (July 1998): 61–62.

[111] Barnaby J. Feder, "$34 Million Settles Suit for Women at Auto Plant," *New York Times*, June 12, 1998, available at www.nytimes.com.

[112] The two cases, both decided in 1998, are *Faragher v. City of Boca Raton* and *Burlington Industries, Inc. v. Ellerth*. The quotations are from Linda Greenhouse, "The Supreme Court: The Workplace; Court Spells Out Rules for Finding Sex Harassment," *New York Times*, June 27, 1998, available at www. nytimes. com. See also Muhl, "The Law at Work", and Steven Greenhouse, "Companies Set to Get Tougher on Harassment," *New York Times*, June 28, 1998, available at www.nytimes.com.

[113] See "Sexual Orientation Discrimination in the Workplace," available at www. nolo. com. See also "Laws Prohibiting Job Discrimination Based on Sexual Orientation and/or Gender Identity," June 9, 2003, available at www.aclu.org. Updated information on a state-by-state basis may also be found at www.lambdalegal.org.

employment discrimination on the basis of sexual orientation or gender identity;[114] as of 2008, no action had been taken in the Senate.

Judicial decisions on procedural as well as substantive matters can also have important consequences for the implementation of Title VII and thus its potential effects. A controversial 2007 decision by the Supreme Court in *Ledbetter v. Goodyear Tire & Rubber Co.*[115] was viewed by many as a setback in combating gender discrimination. Lilly Ledbetter, the plaintiff in the court case, worked as a supervisor at Goodyear Tire & Rubber for 19 years. When she began her job in 1979, she was paid the same as her male colleagues, but due to smaller raises, a disparity arose; by 1998 (when she brought suit), she was paid significantly (40 percent) less than her male counterparts. The Court held that employees alleging discrimination in pay under Title VII may not bring suit unless they have filed a formal complaint with the EEOC within 180 days after the original discriminatory pay-setting decision. Surprisingly to many observers, this timeline was found to apply, "even if the effects of the initial discriminatory act were not immediately apparent to the worker and even if they continue to the present day." It was widely believed that adherence to this standard would bar many of the pay discrimination cases that had been brought under Title VII and were still pending. The decision rejected the view of the EEOC that each (lower) paycheck received reflected the initial discrimination and in effect reset the 180-day clock.

In a strongly worded dissent, Supreme Court Justice Ruth Bader Ginsburg argued that many employees lack information on the salaries of their coworkers and thus would not know within the 180 day limit that they had been underpaid. Moreover, if the initial disparity is small, an employee, particularly a woman or minority "trying to succeed in a nontraditional environment," might disregard it so as not to "make waves," but small differences could cumulate to large ones over many pay periods (as they did in the Ledbetter case). In 2009, legislation was passed by Congress that restored the EEOC interpretation, that is, it defined the 180 days as starting each time discriminatory compensation is received, rather than when the employer discriminates for the first time.[116]

Effectiveness of the Government's Antidiscrimination Effort

Much remains to be learned about the functioning of these laws and regulations. Questions have been raised both about their effectiveness in improving opportunities for protected groups[117] and about the possibility that they might result in reverse discrimination against groups not covered.

It is highly likely that the impact of the Equal Pay Act is fairly minimal. The major reason is that, even today, men and women rarely do exactly the same kind of work in the same firm, and, moreover, as discussed above, the law does not address discrimination more broadly in hiring, promotion, training programs, and so on. However, as occupational segregation has declined and more women and men are working side by side, the protection offered by this law has likely grown more important and may be expected to continue to grow more important in future if there are further reductions in segregation.

---

[114] For information on this proposed legislation, see "H.R. 2015: Employment Non-Discrimination Act of 2007," available at www.govtrack.us.

[115] *Ledbetter v. Goodyear Tire & Rubber Co.*, U.S., No. 05-1074 (May 29, 2007). For more on this case, see "Ledbetter v. Goodyear Tire & Rubber Co. United States Supreme Court," available at www. bna. com, and Linda Greenhouse, "Justices Limit Discrimination Suits Over Pay," *New York Times*, May 29, 2007, available at www.nytimes.com. We draw heavily on Greenhouse, "Justices Limit Discrimination Suits Over Pay," and the quotations in the text are from that article.

[116] For more on the Lilly Ledbetter Fair Pay Act of 2009, see http://www.govtrack.us.

[117] A recent Government Accounting Office Report called for better monitoring of the performance of federal agencies in enforcing the antidiscrimination laws, see "Women's Earnings: Federal Agencies Should Better Monitor Their Performance in Enforcing Anti-Discrimination Laws," GA0-08-799 (August 2008), available at http://www.gao.gov/new.items/d08799.pdf.

Considerably less agreement exists on the effects of Title VII and the Executive Order. Although some empirical work looks at the effectiveness of the government's efforts, the results are not entirely conclusive, in large part because it is difficult to isolate the effect of legislation, regulations, and major Court decisions, from other changes that occurred.

A review of the trends in the male–female pay gap was presented in Chapter 5. It gave no indication of a notable improvement in women's economic status in the immediate post-1964 period that might be attributable to the effects of the government's antidiscrimination effort; the gender pay ratio remained basically flat through the late 1970s or early 1980s, after which it began to increase. In contrast, African Americans experienced considerable increases in their earnings relative to whites in the immediate post-1964 period that many ascribe, at least in part, to the impact of the antidiscrimination laws.

On the other hand, some detailed studies do find positive effects of the government's policies on women's earnings and occupations.[118] Studies focusing specifically on the impact of affirmative action also suggest modest employment gains for women attributable to this program. Such programs also appear to boost the relative wages of women, both because establishments using affirmative action are higher paying, controlling for the characteristics of workers employed in them, and because sex differences in wages are smaller in such establishments.[119] It might also be argued that the improvement in women's wages that began around 1980 could be due at least in part to the opportunities created by the government's antidiscrimination laws and regulations, which perhaps took some time to have an effect. This influence could potentially include both the direct effect of improving the treatment of women in the labor market and, in response to that, the indirect effect of increasing the incentives for women to train for non-traditional jobs.

The government's enforcement of antidiscrimination laws and regulations and the number of cases filed have varied considerably over time. In the 1980s, during the Reagan era, the government scaled back its antidiscrimination enforcement efforts. During that time, enforcement of affirmative action in the contract sector declined,[120] and the number of class action cases brought by the EEOC under Title VII (alleging a pattern and practice of discrimination against women or minorities on the part of an employer) also fell.[121] The resolution of class action suits on behalf of the plaintiffs potentially results in a much larger labor market impact than the resolution of individual complaints. However, the passage of the 1991 federal antidiscrimination law mentioned earlier ushered in a new era. This is because the 1991 law makes it more lucrative for

---

[118] For studies finding that antidiscrimination legislation improved women's earnings (relative to men's), see Ronald Oaxaca, "The Persistence of Male-Female Earnings Differentials," in *The Distribution of Economic Well-Being*, edited by Thomas F. Juster (Cambridge, MA: Ballinger Publishing Company, 1977), pp. 303–44, and Andrea H. Beller, "The Impact of Equal Employment Opportunity Laws on the Male/Female Earnings Differential," in *Women in the Labor Market*, edited by Cynthia B. Lloyd, Emily Andrews, and Curtis L. Gilroy (New York: Columbia University Press, 1979), pp. 304–30. Other research suggests that the antidiscrimination legislation and regulations resulted in positive employment effects for women and minorities; see, for instance, William J. Carrington, Kristin McCue, and Brooks Pierce, "Using Establishment Size to Measure the Impact of Title VII and Affirmative Action," *Journal of Human Resources* 35, no. 3 (Summer 2000): 503–23; or increased women's probability of being employed in a male occupation; see Andrea H. Beller, "Occupational Segregation by Sex: Determinants and Changes," *Journal of Human Resources* 17, no. 3 (Summer 1982): 317–92.
[119] Harry Holzer and David Neumark, "Assessing Affirmative Action," *Journal of Economic Literature* 38, no. 3 (September 2000): 483–568; see also Holzer and Neumark, "Affirmative Action: What Do We Know?" Holzer and Neumark, "What Does Affirmative Action Do?" and Jonathan S. Leonard, "Women and Affirmative Action," *Journal of Economic Perspectives* 3, no. 1 (Winter 1989): 61–75.
[120] Leonard, "Women and Affirmative Action."
[121] Erin Kelly and Frank Dobbin argue that employers' EEO/AA programs survived the Reagan era cutbacks because in the previous decade EEO/AA programs and practices had developed a constituency within the firm in the form of EEO/AA specialists. Increasingly, however, the rationale for these efforts was shifted from legal compliance to "diversity management." See "How Affirmative Action Became Diversity Management: Employer Response to Anti-Discrimination Law, 1961-1996," *American Behavioral Scientist* 41, no. 7 (April 1998): 960–84.

private law firms to represent employees alleging discrimination. Under the original antidiscrimination legislation, monetary redress was generally limited to back pay. Now, in cases of intentional discrimination, it is possible to sue for distress, humiliation, and punitive damages. In addition, the new law allows discrimination cases to be argued before juries, who tend to be more favorable to plaintiffs, also increasing the incentives for private firms to take them on.[122] After the passage of the law, the number of class action and other employment discrimination suits increased substantially and then remained fairly steady at this higher level between the late 1990s and 2003.[123]

Affirmative Action

Just as there is disagreement on the effectiveness of the government's antidiscrimination effort, so is there controversy about the form it should take. Debate particularly centers on the desirability of affirmative action to remedy the underrepresentation of women and minorities. **Affirmative action** may be defined as "...pro-active steps...to erase differences between women and men, minorities and nonminorities, etc." in the labor market and contrasts with laws and regulations that simply require employers not to discriminate against these groups.[124] Thus, affirmative action refers to a broad array of possible activities ranging from efforts to more vigorously recruit women and minorities for job openings to some sort of preferences for women and minorities.

Affirmative action plans are legally mandated in only two situations. First, as we have seen, the Executive Order requires affirmative action by government contractors who are found to underutilize women or minorities. Such employers are required to set goals based on estimates of the availability of protected groups for similar types of positions and to set reasonable timetables for meeting those goals. Thus, contrary to popular belief, the government contract compliance program under the Executive Order does not impose hiring quotas on employers. Second, affirmative action may be imposed by the courts in cases where employers are found guilty of discrimination or settlements are reached in discrimination suits. Although quotas may sometimes be ordered in such instances, quotas remain extremely rare in the labor market. In addition to these legal requirements, some employers have voluntarily adopted affirmative action programs. They may be motivated by a sincere desire to expand their utilization of women and minorities, the hope of heading off potential lawsuits by women and minorities, the potential public relations benefits of such efforts, or some combination of all of these factors.

There is considerable disagreement about affirmative action. First, some argue that there is no conclusive evidence that serious discrimination against women and minorities (still) exists and that, even if there were, removing it would be sufficient and

---

[122] Brooke A. Masters and Amy Joyce, "Costco Is the Latest Class-Action Target: Lawyers' Interest Increases in Potentially Lucrative Discrimination Suits," *Washington Post*, August 18, 2004, available at www. washington-post. com; see also Allen Myerson, "As U.S. Bias Cases Drop, Employees Take Up Fight," *New York Times*, January 12, 1997, available at www.nytimes.com. A 1999 Supreme Court ruling may, however, have made it less likely that employees who bring successful discrimination suits against their employers will be able to collect punitive damages. In *Kolstad v. American Dental Association*, the Court ruled that when a company makes "good faith efforts" to comply with the civil rights law, it cannot be required to pay punitive damages for the discriminatory actions of managers who violate company policy; see Linda Greenhouse, "Ruling Raises Hurdle in Bias-Award Cases," *New York Times*, June 23, 1999, available at www.nytimes.com.

[123] Detailed trends for the period 1992 to 2003 are provided in Donald L. Zink and Arthur Guttman, "Statistical Trends in Private Sector Employment Discrimination Suits," in *Employment Discrimination Litigation: Behavioral, Quantitative, and Legal Perspectives*, edited by Frank Landy (Hoboken, NJ: Wiley, 2005), pp. 101-31.

[124] Holzer and Neumark, "Assessing Affirmative Action," p. 484. The Holzer and Neumark article, as well as Holzer and David Neumark, "Affirmative Action: What Do We Know?" and Barbara R. Bergmann, *In Defense of Affirmative Action* (New York: Basic Books, 1996) provide extremely useful treatments of the issues surrounding affirmative action and assessments of the empirical evidence.

affirmative action is not needed. Second, others accept the need for some form of affirmative action but oppose the use of goals and timetables for fear that they will be too rigidly enforced and become de facto quotas. A difference of opinion, even among strong proponents of affirmative action, focuses on whether it should take the form of sincere efforts to find and encourage fully qualified candidates from the protected groups or go so far as to hire them preferentially. Some believe that preferential treatment may at times be needed to overcome the effects of past discrimination, while others do not believe such steps are warranted.

Although affirmative action programs that include preferences for women or minorities in employment are controversial in the public debate, such programs have generally been found by the courts to be legitimate approaches to remedying past discrimination in the labor market. The legal status of court-mandated affirmative action plans that include employment preferences is not in question. Similarly, those required by the Executive Order have generally not been challenged.[125]

The Supreme Court has also found that voluntary programs incorporating employment preferences are legal under certain circumstances. Specifically, employers can give employment preferences to women and minorities as a temporary measure to remedy manifest imbalances in traditionally segregated job categories.[126] A later Court ruling upholding affirmative action based on race in admission to the University of Michigan Law School was interpreted by some experts as possibly providing (through extension) an additional rationale for affirmative action in the employment arena, namely, achieving diversity. Specifically, the court's majority opinion, written by Justice Sandra Day O'Connor, cited the views put forward by a number of major companies in "friend of the court" briefs in finding that the educational benefits of diversity are "not theoretical but real, as major American businesses have made clear that the skills needed in today's increasingly global marketplace can only be developed through exposure to widely diverse people, cultures, ideas, and viewpoints."[127]

At the same time, the Court has stressed the need for affirmative action plans to be flexible, gradual, and limited in their adverse effect on men and whites; it has also tended to disapprove of strict numerical quotas except where necessary to remedy demonstrated cases of severe past discrimination. Furthermore, although the Court has ruled that employers may give preference to women and minorities in hiring and promotion under certain circumstances, it has rejected the use of such preferences to protect women and minorities from layoffs.[128] This distinction may be due to a concern over the rights of third parties, that is, members of nonprotected groups who may be adversely affected by an affirmative action program. Being denied a potential benefit such as being hired for a particular job, gaining admittance to a training program, or securing a promotion may be viewed as a less serious cost than being laid off from a job, especially after accumulating considerable seniority.

---

[125] The Supreme Court's ruling in the 1995 *Adarand* case placed significant limits on federal government programs that favor racial minorities (and presumably women). However, that case dealt with preferences for minority-owned firms in awarding contracts rather than with employment.

[126] *Steelworkers v. Weber*, 443 U.S. 193 (1979); and *Johnson v. Santa Clara County Transportation Agency*, 480 U.S. 616 (1987).

[127] Cited in Lisa E. Chang, "*Grutter v. Bollinger*, et al.: Affirmative Action Lessons for the Private Employer," *Employee Relations Law Journal* 30, no. 1 (Summer 2004): 3–15. This article includes a useful appraisal of the impact of the *Grutter* decision on employers. See also Steven Greenhouse and Jonathan D. Glater, "Companies See Court Ruling as Support for Diversity," *New York Times*, June 24, 2003, available at www. nytimes. com. Note that the Court struck down an affirmative action program used for *undergraduate* admissions at Michigan for giving too much weight to race, in contrast to the law school that considered race as one factor among many. This ruling was interpreted in the employment arena as reinforcing the Court's negative stance on quotas.

[128] Stuart Taylor, "Court's Change of Course," *New York Times*, March 27, 1987, p. 1; and Steven A. Holmes, "Quotas: Despised by Many, but Just What Are They?" *New York Times*, June 2, 1991, p. 20.

It is important to recognize, however, that most affirmative action programs do not require that employers favor one group. Rather, far more often, employers respond by improving their human resource management systems, such as by implementing wider and more systematic search procedures and developing more objective criteria and procedures for hiring and promotion.[129] Not only are such changes likely to make human resource management systems more effective, but they should also help to create more objective evidence when considering women and minority candidates for promotions or other employment opportunities.

In recent studies comparing workers in firms using affirmative action and firms that did not, little evidence indicated that women or minorities hired under affirmative action performed worse. Where affirmative action was used in *recruitment only* (rather than in hiring), the results indicated that women and minorities, if anything, performed better than white males. When affirmative action was used in the hiring process, it was found that new female hires possessed similar qualifications and job performance. Some evidence of lesser qualifications was found "on paper" for minorities, but once hired, most minority groups performed at a level equivalent to their white male peers.[130] These findings are consistent with empirical research, which strongly suggests that rigid employment quotas and reverse discrimination are not the norm in the labor market. One study found that the employment goals of government contractors covered under the Executive Order were not filled with the rigidity one would expect if they were really quotas. That is, firms tended to fall short of their employment goals for women and minorities. Nonetheless, the setting of goals had a positive effect on the employment of these groups in that establishments that promised to employ more women and minorities in the future tended to do so in subsequent years.[131]

As in the case of affirmative action, it has been found, with respect to the broader issue of antidiscrimination policy as a whole, that the increased employment of women has been achieved without substantial reverse discrimination. Specifically, no evidence at the industry level indicates that the productivity of women fell relative to men as their employment increased—as would be expected if there were substantial reverse discrimination. Direct tests at the company level of the effect of affirmative action pressure, Title VII litigation, and changing proportions of women and minorities on profits also fail to show any adverse effect.[132]

Given that there is little evidence that affirmative action has produced ill effects, one may wonder why affirmative action programs have excited so much public opposition. One reason may be that it is unclear who the "victims" of affirmative action efforts are, and, hence, it is easy to form exaggerated views of their numbers. So, for example, when a woman or minority gets a position, observers may leap to the conclusion that the individual is an "affirmative action hire," which may or may not be true in the first place. Then, since it is generally not known who would have otherwise been hired, all those who did not get the job may feel that it was "because" of affirmative action. Of course, in reality, no more than one of the rejected applicants would have been hired. A second possible reason for public concern about affirmative action is that, as we shall see in greater detail in Chapter 8, recent decades have been in some respects difficult and uncertain times for the less skilled, in particular. Affirmative action becomes a ready scapegoat for those who feel adversely affected by what are in truth broader economic trends that are unrelated to the government's antidiscrimination effort.

---

[129] Holzer and Neumark, "What Does Affirmative Action Do?"

[130] Holzer and Neumark, "Are Affirmative Action Hires Less Qualified?" and Holzer and Neumark, "What Does Affirmative Action Do?"

[131] Jonathan S. Leonard, "What Promises Are Worth: The Impact of Affirmative Action Goals," *Journal of Human Resources* 20, no. 1 (Winter 1985): 3–20.

[132] Leonard, "Antidiscrimination or Reverse Discrimination"; see also Holzer and Neumark, "Are Affirmative Action Hires Less Qualified?"

Exaggerated public perceptions of the negative effects of affirmative action and other government antidiscrimination programs constitute a serious concern, because they may adversely affect attitudes toward women and minorities in the workplace. A related problem is that women and minorities may, as noted earlier, be branded as affirmative action hires and stigmatized as less competent. Such perceptions could sap their confidence and make it difficult for them to function effectively in their jobs. On the other hand, if the alternative to affirmative action is greater discrimination against women and minorities, the absence of good advancement opportunities could, through feedback effects, discourage these groups from investing in job skills.

Comparable Worth

In the latter half of the 1970s, impatience with the slow progress in closing the male–female earnings gap, as well as some reluctance to accept the movement of women out of traditionally female occupations as a necessary component of the solution, led to considerable interest in a possible alternative approach to increasing women's wages. The idea that emerged, in simple terms, amounts to extending the notion of equal pay for equal work to the broader concept of equal pay for work of **comparable worth** within the firm.[133] Proponents argue that this is a reasonable interpretation of Title VII and a feasible way of achieving a more rapid reduction in the male–female pay gap. Opponents point to the difficulties involved in determining exactly what comparable worth means in practical terms. They are also concerned about interfering with the working of the market and the possibility of bringing about a substantial imbalance in the supply of and demand for female workers.

Comparing the value to the firm of workers employed in different jobs is a difficult task that involves the establishment of equivalences for various fields of education, different types of skill, and varying work environments. Nonetheless, a procedure that provides a mechanism to do this is available in the form of job evaluation. Job evaluation is widely used to determine pay scales, not only by governments, but also by many larger firms. This wide usage certainly shows that the approach is feasible. However, it should be noted that such a procedure is generally used in conjunction with information about market wage rates, rather than as a completely separate alternative to the market. Moreover, existing job evaluation schemes have themselves been criticized for undervaluing the skills and abilities that are emphasized in female jobs. Finally, when unions are involved in determining and implementing comparable worth or pay equity adjustments, alterations in pay rates across jobs may in part be determined through the negotiation process rather than solely through job evaluation.

Turning to the issue of setting wages at a level other than that determined by the market, the strongest opposition to such a policy comes primarily from those who believe that the existing labor market substantially resembles the neoclassical competitive model. In such a market, only the person's qualifications and tastes limit access to jobs, and all workers are rewarded according to their productivity. In this view, raising women's wages is not only unnecessary but would lead to excess supply, hence, unemployment and a misallocation of resources.

---

[133] For an early article articulating the legal basis for this approach, see Ruth G. Blumrosen, "Wage Discrimination, Job Segregation, and Title VII of the Civil Rights Act of 1964," *University of Michigan Journal of Law Reform* 12, no. 3 (Spring 1979): 399–502. For examinations of the economic and social issues involved, see, for example, Barbara R. Bergmann, *The Economic Emergence of Women*, 2nd ed. (New York: Palgrave, St. Martin's Press, 2002); Paula England, "The Case for Comparable Worth," *Quarterly Review of Economics and Finance* 39, no. 3 (Special Issue Fall 1999): 743–55; and Mark R. Killingsworth, "Comparable Worth and Pay Equity: Recent Developments in the United States," *Canadian Public Policy* 28, no. s1 (May 2002): S171–S186.

On the other hand, many of those in favor of the comparable worth approach begin with a view of a segmented labor market, where workers' access to highly paid positions is often limited by discriminating employers, restrictive labor organizations, entrenched internal labor markets, and differences in the prelabor market socialization of men and women. Under such circumstances, the crowding of women into traditional occupations is believed to represent a misallocation of resources, which is permitted to continue by societal and labor market discrimination against women. Mandating higher wages would bring the earnings of those who remain in women's jobs closer to the level of comparably qualified men.

However, raising women's wages without changing the underlying conditions that produced them could still result in job loss. This is illustrated in Figure 7-1. Suppose we begin with the discriminatory situation. The relevant supply curves are S_{fd} and S_{md}, and wages are W_{fd} and W_{md}, in the female and male sectors, respectively. Suppose further that a comparable worth system sets wages in female jobs at W_0, the rate that would prevail in the absence of discrimination. At that wage, only L_{f0}, rather than L_{fd}, workers would be demanded by employers. The remainder, $L_{fd} - L_{f0}$, would be displaced from their jobs.

If such shifts were major and abrupt, which of course need not be the case, the transition period might be quite protracted. To the extent that not only new entrants but experienced workers were involved, it would be disruptive and painful. Female unemployment rates might well be increased. The costs associated with this policy depend crucially on how many workers are displaced, how quickly, and what happens to them.

It is also worth noting that the alternative approach of raising women's pay through the principles of equal pay for equal work and equal employment opportunity also offers the potential for increasing the wages even of women who remain in female jobs. This scenario may also be illustrated in Figure 7-1. Suppose that we again begin with the discriminatory situation. If the barriers to entry into male jobs are reduced, women will transfer from F jobs to M jobs. The supply curve in F jobs will shift inward toward S_{f0}, while the supply curve in M jobs shifts outward toward S_{m0}. Wages in the female sector are increased by the reduction of overcrowding there. A completely successful antidiscrimination policy would result in a wage of W_0 being established for both types of jobs. Proponents of comparable worth contend, however, that existing policies have not achieved adequate success as yet and that a new strategy is called for.

Thus far, we have emphasized the economic issues relevant to the subject of comparable worth—issues that are paramount in concluding whether, and for whom, such a policy would be beneficial. However, the courts have made decisions concerning the issue on purely legal grounds. Currently, the status of comparable worth as a legal doctrine under Title VII is unclear because the matter has not been definitively addressed by the Supreme Court.[134] Nor is there much evidence of the adoption of comparable worth in the private sector, although some state and local governments have implemented some version of comparable worth.[135] In addition, some unions, particularly those in the public sector, have pressed for pay equity as a collective bargaining demand.

---

[134] In *County of Washington v. Gunther*, 452 U.S. 161 (1981), the Supreme Court removed a major legal stumbling block to the comparable worth doctrine by ruling that it is not required that a man and woman do "equal work" in order to establish pay discrimination under Title VII. However, many other issues remain unresolved, and the Court stopped short of endorsing the comparable worth approach. See Ross et al., *The Rights of Women*, pp. 26–29.

[135] See Susan E. Gardner and Christopher Daniel, "Implementing Comparable Worth/Pay Equity: Experiences of Cutting-Edge States," *Public Personnel Management* 27, no. 4 (Winter 1998), and Killingsworth, "Comparable Worth and Pay Equity."

Empirical evidence on the potential impact of comparable worth in the United States is based on analyses of its implementation for state and municipal government employees, since the private sector has little experience with comparable worth. Such studies tend to find positive effects on women's relative wages. When employment effects are also examined, adverse effects on the growth of women's relative employment are usually found, although such effects are generally small.[136] Some additional light can be shed on these issues by examining what happened in Australia when wages in female occupations were abruptly raised by introducing a comparable worth policy. The experience of that country is described in Chapter 12, but overall it tends to be relatively positive in that a considerable narrowing of the gender pay gap was achieved with relatively modest negative employment effects.

However, it may be difficult to extrapolate the results of studies that focus on government employees to the impact of the adoption of a nationwide comparable worth policy that includes the private sector. Even studies of comparable worth as implemented in Australia may be less than fully instructive because the labor market in that country tends to be highly centralized with a large role for government tribunals and unions in setting wage rates. This contrasts strongly with the highly decentralized U.S. labor market, which relies much more heavily on the market and generally gives firms considerable autonomy in setting wages. In this respect, the consequences of a pay equity initiative that was implemented in one Canadian province, Ontario, beginning in the early 1990s, may be of particular interest because the Canadian labor market is more similar to the United States in being relatively decentralized. The results of a study of the Ontario experience suggest some caution in implementing comparable worth in such circumstances. Substantial lapses in compliance and implementation of the law were found. These lapses tended to center on small firms that lacked the resources to undertake the necessary job evaluation programs and often did not have a sufficient sample of male and female jobs to make meaningful comparisons. Because such small firms employed the majority of both male and female workers in Ontario, little evidence was found of a positive impact of the pay equity policy on women's relative pay overall. Even among large firms, where compliance was fairly complete, estimated positive effects on women's pay in female jobs were modest and typically statistically insignificant.[137] It is also possible that the ineffectiveness of pay equity legislation in this case reflects additional factors specific to the situation in Ontario, such as the particular law implemented there or a change in the governing party that occurred a few years after the passage of the law.

JOB EVALUATION

The implementation of comparable worth requires an evaluation of the contribution of the many different jobs within an enterprise.* At present, formal **job evaluation** procedures are already used by the federal government, a number of state governments, and many large private firms as an aid in determining pay rates. Employers rely on such evaluations because, as explained in our discussion of internal labor markets,

---

[136] See, for example, Mark R. Killingsworth, *The Economics of Comparable Worth* (Kalamazoo, MI: W.E. Upjohn Institute for Employment Research, 1990); Peter F. Orazem and J. Peter Mattila, "The Implementation Process of Comparable Worth: Winners and Losers," *Journal of Political Economy* 98, no. 1 (February 1990): 134–52; and June O'Neill, Michael Brien, and James Cunningham, "Effects of Comparable Worth Policy: Evidence from Washington State," *American Economic Review* 79, no. 2 (May 1989): 305–09.

[137] Michael Baker and Nicole M. Fortin, "Comparable Worth Work in a Decentralized Labor Market: The Case of Ontario," *Canadian Journal of Economics* 37, no. 4 (November 2004): 850–78.

many positions, particularly in large firms, are filled entirely from within the firm itself through promotion and upgrading of the existing workforce. Job evaluation may be useful in setting pay rates in such jobs, especially since some of them are unique to a particular enterprise. This means that the "going rate" in the local labor market is often not known for such internally filled jobs. Thus, employers may find it necessary to use some other mechanism to determine wages for such jobs, since they cannot simply accept those determined by the market. However, it is important to bear in mind that, when wages are set in this way, it does not mean that market forces are ignored. In setting wages, most firms and governmental units that use job evaluation try to take into account whatever information is available to them on prevailing wages for different types of labor. At the same time, the existence of job evaluation and other procedures for setting wages tends to make wages less responsive to short-term shifts in market conditions than they would otherwise be.

The actual methods used differ in detail but share the same basic rationale and approach. The first step is always a description of all the jobs within the given organization. The next step is to rate each job according to all the various features that are believed to determine pay differences across jobs. Last, these ratings are combined to create a score for each job, which may then be used to help determine wages.

Among the factors used to construct job scores are characteristics such as level of education, skills, and responsibility needed for the job, as well as the environment in which the work is performed. Commonly, multiple regression is used to link these to the existing pay structure. At other times, weights are assigned according to the judgment of the experts constructing the scale. In theory, various jobs can be assigned values objectively, presumably not influenced by irrelevant factors such as the gender and race of the incumbents, and quite different jobs may be assigned equal values, if warranted.

It would be a mistake, however, to take the objectivity of such procedures for granted. Both prevailing wage structures and the judgments of individuals may be tainted by existing inequalities in the economy and in society. An additional problem with the job evaluation approach is that it is most readily implemented in large firms.

---

*Job evaluation is discussed in Donald J. Treiman and Heidi I. Hartmann, eds., *Women, Work and Wages: Equal Pay for Jobs of Equal Value* (Washington, DC: National Academy Press, 1981), pp. 71–74. Institutional models, discussed earlier, emphasize the importance of job evaluation and other administrative procedures for determining wages. See Peter B. Doeringer and Michael J. Piore, *Internal Labor Markets and Manpower Analysis* (Lexington, MA: D.C. Heath and Co., 1971).

Conclusion

Economists define labor market discrimination as a situation where two equally qualified individuals are treated differently on the basis of gender (or race, age, etc.). Such discrimination against a particular group is likely to be detrimental, both directly and indirectly through feedback effects on their accumulation of human capital. Empirical studies have used available evidence on differences in the characteristics of male and female workers to explain the pay gap and the differences in occupational distributions between the two groups. Productivity-related factors have not been able to account for all of the gender differences in economic outcomes, suggesting that discrimination does play a part, accounting for perhaps 40 percent of the male–female earnings differential.

As much attention as has been focused on the issue of whether discrimination exists, there has been almost equal interest in the question of who discriminates, why, and how. We have reviewed theories that focus on the following possible sources of discrimination:

- Employers, coworkers, or customers have tastes for discrimination against women.
- Employers judge individual women in terms of the average characteristics of the group (statistical discrimination).
- Women's wages are depressed because they are crowded into a few sectors.
- Women are concentrated in dead-end jobs with few opportunities for on-the-job training and promotion.

Last, we examined the government's equal employment opportunity policies and considered the pros and cons of comparable worth.

Each of the models of discrimination that we have considered contributes to our understanding of a complex reality, where the factors keeping women in segregated and poorly paid jobs, rather than being mutually exclusive, are likely to reinforce each other. By the same token, however, we pointed out that any improvements in women's labor market outcomes are likely to have positive feedback effects. By rewarding women more highly for their human capital, women are encouraged to accumulate more human capital on which they can gather rewards.

APPENDIX 7A

Regression Analysis and Empirical Estimates of Labor Market Discrimination

In Table 7-1, we presented empirical estimates of labor market discrimination. In this appendix,[138] we explain in more detail how economists arrive at such estimates. The goal is to be able to "decompose" the gender wage gap into a portion due to measured productivity-related characteristics and a portion that cannot be explained by differences in characteristics and is, therefore, potentially due to labor market discrimination.

The starting point of such analyses is the estimation of a wage regression, which expresses wages as a function of factors such as experience and education. For simplicity, let us begin with the case in which there is only one explanatory variable, experience. Figure 7-4 shows a hypothetical scatter of points, "observations," for individual women with each point representing one woman's wage rate and experience.

To better understand how wages are determined, we would like to use this information to estimate the effect of an additional year of work experience on wages. As can be seen, if we were to fit a straight line to the points in Figure 7-4, it would be an upward sloping line, suggesting that wages increase with additional years of labor market experience.

Before considering the technique that we would use to estimate the line shown in the figure, let us begin with the following equation that models the general relationship between wages and experience:

$$\text{WAGE}_i = a_0 + a_1 X_i + e_i$$

---

[138] In formulating this section, we benefited from reviewing Ronald G. Ehrenberg and Robert S. Smith, *Modern Labor Economics*, 6th ed. (Reading MA: Addison Wesley, 1996), Appendix 1A, pp. 17–24; and Mark Killingsworth, "Where Does the Pay Gap Come From?" Class Handout for Economics 375, Women in the Economy, Rutgers University. For a more detailed treatment of regression analysis, see a statistics or econometrics text.

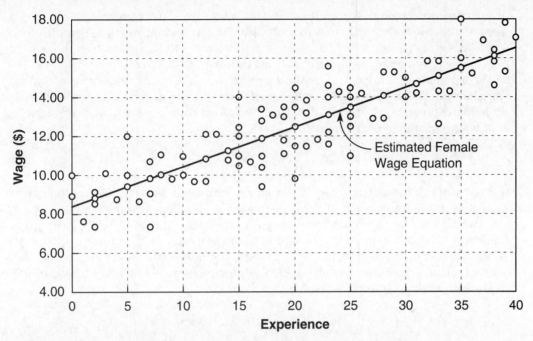

FIGURE 7-4   Scatter Plot and Regression Line for Women's Wages

In this equation, WAGE represents the wage rate of individual i and is called the **dependent variable**. The independent or **explanatory variable** is X, which represents the individual's level of experience. The regression coefficients, a_0 and a_1, specify the relationship between the dependent and explanatory variable: a_0 is the intercept of the line on the y-axis and a_1 is the slope of the line. The intercept gives the wage rate corresponding to zero years of work experience, that is, for a new entrant into the labor market. The slope of the line tells us how much wages increase for each additional year of experience. The last term, e, is a random error term. It is included because we do not expect each observation to lie along the straight line; random factors unrelated to experience are also likely to influence wages. (We shall see below that systematic factors such as education, which also affect wages, can be incorporated in multiple regression analysis.)

How do we find the straight line that best fits the points in the figure? This amounts to estimating a_0 and a_1. The statistical technique generally used is called **least squares regression analysis**. It is estimated by finding the line that minimizes the sum of the squared deviations (vertical differences) of each point from the line.

If we estimate a least squares regression using the points in Figure 7-4, we obtain the following estimated line:

$$\text{WAGE}_i = 8.5 + 0.2X_i$$

The estimate of $a_0 = 8.5$ and the estimate of $a_1 = 0.2$ mean that a new entrant into the labor market is expected to earn \$8.50 per hour, and an individual's wages are expected to increase by \$0.20 with each additional year of experience.

At least two potential problems arise with this estimate. First, the hypothetical and the actual earnings profiles we showed in Chapter 6 were not straight lines but rather curved lines, which suggests that even though earnings rise with experience, the rate of increase tends to fall over time. Such a relationship can readily be estimated using regression analysis and in fact most studies by economists allow for this.[139] We, however, will stick to a straight line as in Figure 7-4 to simplify our exposition.

Second, economic theory tells us that a number of other explanatory variables besides experience are important determinants of wages. These additional explanatory variables can be incorporated by using **multiple regression analysis**. We illustrate multiple regression analysis by adding education as an additional explanatory variable. Our wage equation now becomes:

$$\text{WAGE}_i = a_0' + a_1'X_i \times a_2'ED_i + e_i'$$

ED is a variable measuring years of schooling completed. Each regression coefficient now tells us the impact of a unit change in each explanatory variable on the dependent variable, *holding the other explanatory variable constant*. So, for example, a_1' gives the effect of an additional year of experience on wages, holding education constant. Thus, the regression coefficients a_0' and a_1' are not necessarily equal to a_0 and a_1, because their interpretation has changed. The new relationship estimated by multiple regression analysis is found to be:

$$\text{WAGE}_i = 2 + 0.3X_i + 0.5Ed_i$$

That is, we find that, holding education constant, each additional year of experience raises wages by $0.30; and, holding experience constant, each additional year of education raises wages by $0.50.

Note that including education changed our estimate of the effect of experience. This change occurs because education is *correlated* with experience: Given the trend toward rising educational attainment, younger women have higher levels of education, on average, but less experience than older women. The estimated experience coefficient in the simple regression (the one that includes only experience) is *smaller* than in the multiple regression because the positive effect of experience on earnings is offset somewhat by the tendency of older people (with higher levels of experience) to be less well educated. Thus, education is an important *omitted variable* and not taking it into account results in a *biased* estimate of the effect of experience; specifically, the estimated effect of experience is *biased downward* when education is omitted from the regression.

The results obtained with multiple regression analysis for the relationship between wages and experience can still be summarized in a simple diagram if we evaluate them at a specific level or specific levels of education, as shown in Figure 7-5 for $ED = 12$ (high school graduates) and $ED = 16$ (college graduates).

Now that the basics of regression analysis are clear, we can consider how it is used to obtain statistical estimates of the extent of labor market discrimination. We do this first in terms of a diagram and then present a general formula.

Figure 7-6 shows hypothetical male and female wage regression lines for college graduates. By focusing on one education group, we can proceed in terms of simple regression with one explanatory variable, experience. As may be seen in the figure, women's average wages, $\bar{w}_f$, are lower than men's, $\bar{w}_m$. At the same time, women have less experience on average, $\bar{x}_f$, than men do, $\bar{x}_m$. How much of the difference in average wages between men and women, $\bar{w}_m - \bar{w}_f$, is due to the gender difference

---

[139] To do this, we include experience squared (X^2), in addition to X, as an explanatory variable in the regression.

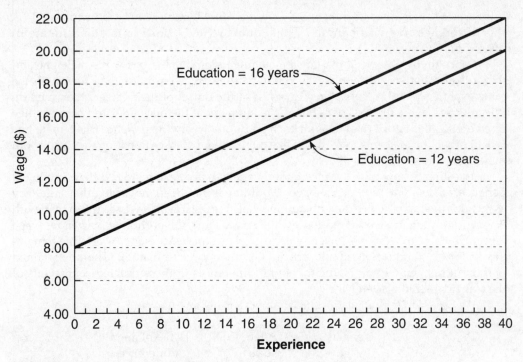

FIGURE 7-5 The Estimated Relationship between Wages and Experience for Women Evaluated at 12 and 16 Years of Education

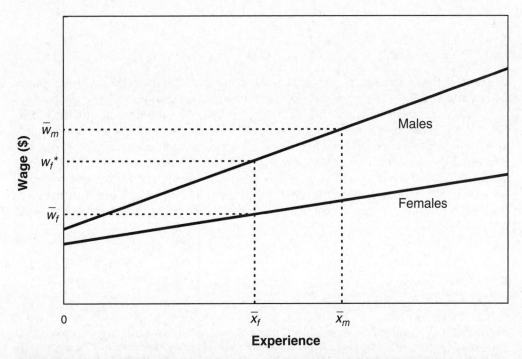

FIGURE 7-6 Hypothetical Regression Lines for Male and Female College Graduates

in average levels of experience, $\bar{x}_m - \bar{x}_f$, and how much cannot be explained by this difference in qualifications? This "unexplained" portion is our estimate of discrimination.

We begin by observing that the female regression line lies below the male line and that it is also flatter. This comparison shows that women earn less than men with the same experience both because they earn less at the outset of their careers than men do (the intercept of the female line is below the intercept of the male line) and because they receive a smaller return than men for each additional year of experience (the female line is flatter than the male line). We would like our estimate of discrimination to capture both these differences.

To estimate how much of the gender wage gap is due to gender differences in experience, we ask what women's wages would be if they were rewarded the same way as men for their experience. Reading off the male regression line, we see that a man with $\bar{x}_f$ years of experience would receive a wage of w_f^*. Thus, the portion of the gender wage gap attributable to women's lower average level of experience is $\bar{w}_m - w_f^*$. The remainder, $w_f^* - \bar{w}_f$, is unexplained and potentially due to discrimination. The unexplained portion of the gender gap is due to gender differences in the estimated coefficients of the wage regression (a_0 and a_1).

We can express this relationship mathematically as follows:

$$\begin{matrix} \text{Gender} & & \text{Difference} & & \text{Unexplained} \\ \text{wage} & = & \text{due to} & + & \text{difference} \\ \text{difference} & & \text{qualifications} & & \end{matrix}$$

$$= \bar{w}_m - \bar{w}_f = (\bar{w}_m - w_f^*) + (w_f^* - \bar{w}_f)$$

where

$$\bar{w}_m = a_{0m} + a_{1m} \times \bar{x}_m$$
$$\bar{w}_f = a_{0f} + a_{1f} \times \bar{x}_f$$
$$\bar{w}_f^* = a_{0m} + a_{1m} \times \bar{x}_f$$

In the preceding equations, a_{0m} and a_{1m} are the intercept and slope of the male regression, and a_{0f} and a_{1f} are the intercept and slope of the female regression.

The portion of the wage difference that is due to differences in qualifications, $(\bar{w}_m - w_f^*)$, in this case experience, is obtained by evaluating both men's and women's average levels of experience using the male regression coefficients. The unexplained portion of the gender difference is estimated by the difference between what women's wages are when their average experience is evaluated using the male regression versus when they are evaluated using the female regression. This approach can readily be applied in the multiple regression context and underlies estimates such as those presented in Table 7-1.[140]

---

[140] Our ability to perform this decomposition is aided by the property of least squares regression that the regression line passes through the means of the dependent and explanatory variables. Thus, the point $(\bar{w}_f, \bar{x}_f)$ will lie on the female regression line and the point $(\bar{w}_m, \bar{x}_m)$ will lie on the male regression line. This analysis is some times known as a *Oaxaca Decomposition*, after the economist who was one of the first to use it; he provides a detailed description in Ronald Oaxaca, "Male–Female Wage Differentials in Urban Labor Markets," *International Economic Review* 14 (October 1973): 693–709.

Questions for Review and Discussion

1. How do economists generally measure the extent of labor market discrimination against women statistically? What important qualifications need to be noted about such estimates? Do such studies indicate that discrimination against women in the labor market continues to exist? Is there any evidence that there is now reverse discrimination as a general pattern in the labor market?

2. What factors explain why some researchers conclude that labor market discrimination against women is small while others come to a different conclusion? [*Hint*: You may also want to consult the inset on the gender pay gap in Chapter 5.]

3. Suppose you are given data about a firm, indicating that the average wage of male employees is $15.00/hour and the average wage of female employees is $10.50/hour. Define *labor market discrimination* against women. Do the preceding data prove that the firm discriminates against women? What kind of additional information would you need to determine whether such discrimination exists?

4. Prohibition of discrimination, affirmative action, and comparable worth are all possible means of reducing the wage gap. Which, if any, are likely to be effective? Why or why not? Do you see them as substitutes or as complements and why?

5. To the extent that it is true that women earn less because they spend less time in the labor market and that they spend less time in the labor market because they are paid less, how can this vicious circle be broken?

6. Given the discussions in Chapters 6 and 7, why do you think the earnings ratio for black females to black males is so much higher than for all women relative to all men, as shown by data presented in Chapter 5?

7. "Excluding women from occupations that require physical strength is justified because men tend to be stronger than women." Evaluate the validity of this argument.

Suggested Readings

Akerlof, George A., and Rachel E. Kranton. "Economics and Identity." *Quarterly Journal of Economics* 115, no. 3 (August 2000): 715–53.

Altonji, Joseph G., and Rebecca M. Blank. "Race and Gender in the Labor Market." In *Handbook of Labor Economics*, edited by Orley C. Ashenfelter and David Card, pp. 3143–259. Amsterdam: North-Holland, 1999.

Basu, Kaushik. "The Economics and Law of Sexual Harassment in the Workplace." *Journal of Economic Perspectives* 17, no. 3 (Summer 2003): 141–57.

Becker, Gary S. *The Economics of Discrimination*, 2nd ed. Chicago: University of Chicago Press, 1971.

Bergmann, Barbara R. *In Defense of Affirmative Action*. New York: Basic Books, 1996.

Blau, Francine D., Mary C. Brinton, and David B. Grusky, eds. *The Declining Significance of Gender?* New York: Russell Sage Foundation, 2006.

Blau, Francine D., and Lawrence M. Kahn. "Gender Differences in Pay." *Journal of Economic Perspectives* 14, no. 4 (Fall 2000): 75–99.

Blau, Francine D., and Lawrence M. Kahn. "Women's Work and Wages." In *The New Palgrave Dictionary of Economics*, 2nd ed., edited by Steven N. Durlauf and Lawrence E. Blume. London: Palgrave Macmillan, 2008, pp. 762–72.

Darity, William A., Jr., and Patrick L. Mason. "Evidence on Discrimination in Employment: Codes of Color, Codes of Gender." *Journal of Economic Perspectives* 12, no. 2 (Spring 1998): 63–90.

Eagly, Alice H., and Linda L. Carli. *Through the Labyrinth: The Truth About How Women Become Leaders*. Cambridge, MA: Harvard Business School Press, 2007.

Fiske, Susan T. "Stereotyping, Prejudice, and Discrimination." In *Handbook of Social Psychology*, edited by D. T. Gilbert, S. T. Fiske, and G. Lindzey. New York: McGraw-Hill, 1998, pp. 357–411.

Goldin, Claudia. "A Pollution Theory of Discrimination: Male and Female Differences in Occupations and Earnings." National Bureau of Economic Research Working Paper No. 8985 (June 2002).

Hersch, Joni. "Employment Discrimination, Economists and the Law." In *Women, Family and Work: Writings on the Economics of Gender*, edited by Karine S. Moe. Oxford: Blackwell Publishers, 2003, pp. 217–333.

Hersch, Joni. "Sex Discrimination in the Labor Market." *Foundations and Trends in Microeconomics* 2, no. 4 (2006): 281–361.

Holzer, Harry J., and David Neumark. "Affirmative Action: What Do We Know?" *Journal of Policy Analysis and Management* 25, no. 2 (Spring 2006): 463–90.

Reskin, Barbara F., and Denise D. Bielby. "A Sociological Perspective on Gender and Career Outcomes." *Journal of Economic Perspectives* 19, no. 1 (Winter 2005): 71–86.

Valian, Virginia. *Why So Slow? The Advancement of Women*. Cambridge, MA: MIT Press, 1998.

Key Terms

labor market discrimination *193*

feedback effects *194, 224*

gender wage gap *195*

explained gap *195*

unexplained gap *195*

glass ceiling *205*

tastes for discrimination *210*

discrimination coefficient *211*

employer discrimination *211*

implicit discrimination *214*

employee discrimination *215*

identity model *216*

pollution theory of discrimination *217*

customer discrimination *217*

subtle barriers *217*

statistical discrimination *218*

overcrowding model *220*

institutional models of discrimination *222*

internal labor market *223*

dual labor market model *223*

institutional discrimination *224*

Equal Pay Act *227*

Title VII of the Civil Rights Act *227*

Equal Employment Opportunity Commission (EEOC) *227*

Executive Order *227*

bona fide occupational qualification *228*

disparate treatment *229*

disparate impact *229*

sexual harassment *229*

affirmative action *233*

comparable worth *236*

job evaluation *238*

dependent variable *241*

explanatory variable *241*

least squares regression analysis *241*

multiple regression analysis *242*

CHAPTER **8**

Recent Developments in Earnings

Chapter Highlights

- Trends in Female and Male Wages
- The Declining Gender Pay Gap
- The Rising Payoff to Education

I n previous chapters we documented a substantial wage gap between men and women and considered various explanations for the gender difference, focusing on the human capital model in Chapter 6 and models of labor market discrimination in Chapter 7. We also chronicled a significant decrease in the gender wage gap that began around 1980. This is only one of a number of dramatic shifts in earnings patterns that have taken place in recent years. Other changes include a flattening of the growth in real wages that American workers long took for granted, and a widening gap in the wages of high- and low-skilled workers associated with a rising payoff to education. In this chapter we focus on these developments, with particular emphasis on understanding the decrease in the gender wage gap that has occurred in recent decades. In doing so, we apply insights from models of human capital and labor market discrimination considered in Chapters 6 and 7, and we also consider a new factor, changes in the overall U.S. wage structure.

TRENDS IN FEMALE AND MALE WAGES

In examining trends in wage levels, researchers generally focus on **real wages**. These wages have been adjusted for changes in the cost of living or price inflation. A good starting point is to look at what is happening to trends in real wages for the average or typical worker, as well as trends for workers at the top and bottom of the earnings distribution. Distinguishing between trends at the top and the bottom is of interest because one of the most notable labor market trends in recent years is the pronounced increase in **wage inequality** that has occurred among both male and female workers since 1980. By an increase in wage inequality, we mean a widening dispersion in the distribution of earnings within each group (men and women), so that the wage gap between those at the bottom and those at the top has widened considerably. In the case of male workers, constant or falling real wages for males overall has meant that rising wage inequality has been associated with declines in the real wages of less-educated men who are at the lower end of the wage distribution.[1]

The declining relative labor market position of the less skilled is partly a consequence of an *increase* in the **returns to skills** or the rewards that the labor market gives for various worker skills or qualifications. For instance, consider an individual with a 4-year college education. If the payoff to this level of education is higher today than in earlier years, this constitutes an increase in the returns to this skill. There is not full consensus on the reasons for the increase in the returns to education and to skills more generally (education is just one example), but research points to factors on both the demand- and supply-side as playing a role.[2]

On the demand side, there has been an increase in the relative demand for skills, driven primarily by technological change. For example, the development of personal computers and related information technologies has increased the demand for college-educated workers, while increased computer use has largely been a substitute for less-skilled workers, reducing the demand for less-skilled workers.[3] Some research also suggests that growing international trade has had a similar effect, reducing the demand for less-skilled U.S. workers, although its role appears to be smaller than technological change. Supply-side shifts are also important, principally the sharp slowdown in the growth in the supply of college-educated workers since 1980, which "in the face of strong secular growth in the relative demand for more educated workers has been a driving force in the rise in the college wage premium."[4] Some also point to rising immigration as contributing to the widening wage gap between high- and low-skilled-workers by increasing the supply of the less-skilled, although there is less agreement about the importance of this factor.[5] In addition, institutional factors including the decline in unionism, which we discuss in Chapter 9, and the decreasing real value of the minimum wage also likely contributed.

The trends in real earnings for men and women since 1960 are shown in Figure 8-1 and summarized in Table 8-1. Both show trends in the median annual earnings of year-round, full-time workers after adjustment for inflation. Male real earnings rose

---

[1] For summaries of these trends, see, for example, Frank Levy, *The New Dollars and Dreams: American Incomes and Economic Change* (New York: Russell Sage Foundation, 1998); Francine D. Blau, "Trends in the Well-Being of American Women: 1970–95," *Journal of Economic Literature* 36, no. 1 (March 1998): 112–65; and David H. Autor, Lawrence F. Katz, and Melissa S. Kearney, "Trends in U.S. Wage Inequality in the 1990s: Revising the Revisionists," *Review of Economics and Statistics* 90, no. 2 (May 2008): 300–23.

[2] This discussion draws on Lawrence F. Katz and David H. Autor, "Changes in the Wage Structure and Earnings Inequality," in *Handbook of Labor Economics*, edited by Orley C. Ashenfelter and David Card (Amsterdam: Elsevier, 1999), pp. 3A:1463–555; Claudia Goldin and Lawrence M. Katz, *The Race Between Education and Technology* (Cambridge, MA: The Belknap Press of Harvard University Press, 2008); and John DiNardo, Nicole M. Fortin, and Thomas Lemieux, "Labor Market Institutions and the Distribution of Wages, 1973–1992: A Semiparametric Approach," *Econometrica* 64, no. 5 (September 1996): 1001–44.

[3] In explaining the trends since the 1990s, David H. Autor, Lawrence F. Katz, and Melissa S. Kearney have postulated a more complex situation, with computers complementary to nonroutine cognitive (high-education) tasks, substitutable for routine (middle-education) tasks, and having little impact on nonroutine manual (low-education) tasks. This is consistent with the observed empirical pattern in which wage inequality in the top half of the distribution has been rising since 1980 but inequality in the bottom half of the distribution has not increased since the late 1980s. See, "The Polarization of the U.S. Labor Market," *American Economic Review* 96, no.2 (May 2006): 189–194. See also, Autor, Katz, and Kearney, "Trends in U.S. Wage Inequality: Revising the Revisionists.* For an alternative perspective, see David Card and John E. DiNardo, "Skill-Biased Technological Change and Rising Wage Inequality: Some Problems and Puzzles," *Journal of Labor Economics* 20, no. 4 (October 2002): 733–83.

[4] Claudia Goldin and Lawrence M. Katz, "The Race Between Education and Technology: the Evolution of U.S. Educational Wage Differentials, 1890 TO 2005," NBER Working Paper No. 12984 (March 2007); the quotation is from p. 10.

[5] See, for example, George J. Borjas, Richard B. Freeman, and Lawrence F. Katz, "How Much Do Immigration and Trade Affect Labor Market Outcomes?" *Brookings Papers on Economic Activity* (1997: 1): 1–90; and David Card "Is the New Immigration Really So Bad?" *Economic Journal* 115, no. 507 (November 2005): F300–23.

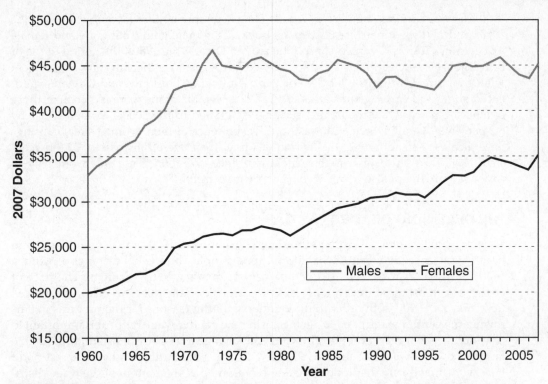

FIGURE 8-1 Median Earnings of Year-Round, Full-Time Workers by Sex, 1960–2007 (2007 Dollars)

Source: U.S., Census Bureau, Historical Income Tables—People, Table P-38 "Full-Time, Year-Round All Workers by Median Earnings and Sex: 1960 to 2007" from http://www.census.gov/hhes/www/income/histinc/p38AR.html.

TABLE 8-1 Change in Real Median Earnings of Men and Women, Year-Round, Full-Time Workers, Selected Periods, 1960–2007

Period	Men (%)	Women (%)
1960–1970	29.9	27.1
1970–1980	4.4	5.8
1980–1990	−4.5	13.6
1990–2000	5.4	8.5
2000–2007	0.6	6.2
1973–2007	−3.3	32.8
1960–2007	37.2	75.9

Notes: Persons 15 years old and over beginning in 1980, and persons 14 years old and over for previous years. Adjusted for inflation using the Consumer Price Index for All Urban Areas (CPI-U-RS).

Source: U.S. Census Bureau, Historical Income Tables—People, Table P-38 "Full-Time, Year-Round All Workers by Median Earnings and Sex: 1960 to 2007" from http://www.census.gov/hhes/www/income/histinc/p38AR.html.

substantially during the 1960s and moderately during the 1970s, reaching a peak in 1973. Progress in male real earnings has been fitful since then. Male real earnings declined over the 1980s, and, while they did increase moderately over the 1990s, they stagnated in the 2000s. Indeed, as may be seen in Table 8-1, from their 1973 peak to 2007, male real earnings failed to increase, and in fact declined slightly (by 3.3 percent).

The real earnings trends for women have been much more favorable. During the 1960s and 1970s, women's real earnings tracked the male gains, but male and female real earnings trends diverged sharply thereafter. During the 1980s, the period of major convergence in the gender wage gap, women's real earnings increased by 13.6 percent while men's real earnings fell by 4.5 percent. And, while both men and women experienced some real earnings increases in the 1990s, female gains were larger than those of males. Finally, while men's real earnings stagnated in the 2000s, women's rose by 6.2 percent. Overall, in stark contrast to the experience of men, women's real earnings have increased steadily over this period, leading to an overall increase of 32.8 percent since 1973. Thus, the decline in the gender gap since 1973 reflects not only women's real earnings growth but also men's weak real earnings trends.[6]

THE DECLINING GENDER PAY GAP

As we saw in Chapter 5, starting in the late 1970s or early 1980s, the **gender wage ratio** began to increase. Between 1978 and 2007, for example, the weekly earnings of women full-time workers rose from 61 to 80 percent of men's weekly earnings. The pace of change was most rapid over the 1980s, slowed considerably over the 1990s, and picked up again in the 2000s. In order to fully understand the reasons for the progress in narrowing the **gender wage gap** (i.e., in increasing the gender wage ratio), it is important to consider the labor market context in which this change took place, most importantly the fact that overall wage inequality increased. This consideration raises the question of how women, who are disproportionately represented at the bottom of the wage distribution, succeeded in narrowing the gender wage gap in the face of overall labor market trends that were unfavorable for low-wage workers in general.

We begin our analysis of the trends in the gender wage gap with a consideration of the determinants of the gender wage gap based on economic theory. We then apply these concepts to understanding the trends in the gender wage gap and review the results of research analyzing women's gains in recent decades. We also briefly consider what is known about the reasons for the trends in the race wage gap during this same period.

Determinants of Trends in the Gender Wage Gap

In analyzing the reasons for the decline in the gender wage gap, it makes sense to start with the two major explanations for the gender wage gap developed by economists, which we reviewed in previous chapters:

- **Differences in human capital investments** or other gender differences in qualifications (considered in Chapter 6)
- **Labor market discrimination** or differences in the treatment of equally qualified men and women (considered in Chapter 7)

As we have seen, these two explanations are not necessarily mutually exclusive—both may play a role in explaining the gender wage gap. In addition, feedback effects may occur if discrimination in the labor market lowers women's incentives to invest in their qualifications and women's lower qualifications reinforce statistical discrimination against them. The empirical research reviewed in previous chapters provides

---

[6] Estimated trends in real earnings vary to some extent depending on the earnings measure and price deflator used, the data set employed, and the starting and ending years selected. Although the trends reported here, based on government data, are broadly consistent with the findings in the literature, we note that considerable controversy has focused on the measurement of price changes. See, for example, Michael J. Boskin, "The CPI Commission: Findings and Recommendations," *American Economic Review* 87, no. 2 (May 1997): 78–83; and Katharine Abraham, John S. Greenlees, and Brent R. Moulton, "Working to Improve the Consumer Price Index," *Journal of Economic Perspectives* 12, no. 1 (Winter 1998): 27–36.

considerable support for each set of factors—differences in qualifications and discrimination—in explaining the gender wage gap.

Following this reasoning, we would expect the pay gap to decline if (1) women increased their qualifications relative to men's, or (2) labor market discrimination against women decreased. The evidence provides some reason to believe that both these developments have occurred. As we saw in Chapter 6, women have narrowed the gap in work experience with men and increased their share of college and professional degrees, as well as their representation in traditionally male fields of study. At the same time, women's increasing commitment to market work may have induced employers to reduce the extent of statistical discrimination against them. That is, employers may judge individual women less negatively than in the past for being members of a group they view as less committed to the labor market, on average.

Research on trends in the gender wage gap suggests that explaining these trends requires that we also consider a third factor, one not mentioned in earlier chapters— overall trends in wage structure:[7]

- **Wage structure** refers to the returns that the labor market offers for various skills and for employment in various industries or occupations.

If, for example, the difference in wages between high- and low-wage occupations (or for high-skilled and less-skilled workers) is relatively small, this is referred to as a "relatively compressed" wage structure. Countries with strong unions that raise the wages of less-skilled workers tend to have a relatively compressed wage structure, while, in the United States, wages are determined in a more decentralized manner, re-sulting in a more dispersed wage structure. Wage structure can also change over time as rewards to skills and premiums for employment in high-wage occupations and industries increase or decrease.

Both the human capital and discrimination explanations of the pay gap suggest a potentially important role for trends in wage structure in determining how women fare relative to men over time. For example, despite important recent gains, women still have less experience than men, on average. If the labor market return to experience (i.e., the increase in wages associated with each additional year of experience) rises over time, women will be increasingly disadvantaged by their lesser amount of experience. In addition, both the human capital and discrimination models suggest reasons why women are likely to be employed in different occupations and perhaps in different industries than men. This implies that an increase in the rewards for employment in "male" occupations or industries will also place women at an increasing disadvantage. In fact, the patterns of rising overall wage inequality in the labor market, particularly in the 1980s, resulted from precisely such increases in the market rewards to skill and to employment in high-wage male sectors. This means that women as a group were essen-tially "swimming upstream" in a labor market growing increasingly unfavorable for workers with below-average skills—in this case, below-average experience—and for workers employed in disproportionately female occupations and industries.

Explaining the Decline in the Gender Wage Gap

How can we explain the decrease in the gender wage gap in recent decades in the face of rising wage inequality overall and rising labor market returns to skill that worked against women as a group? A study by Francine Blau and Lawrence Kahn of full-time

---

[7] See, for example, Francine D. Blau and Lawrence M. Kahn, "Rising Wage Inequality and the U.S. Gender Gap," *American Economic Review Papers and Proceedings* 84, no. 2 (May 1994): 23–28; and Francine D. Blau, and Lawrence M. Kahn. "The U.S. Gender Pay Gap in the 1990s: Slowing Convergence," *Industrial and Labor Relations Review* 60, no. 1 (October 2006): 45–66.

workers sheds light on this question.[8] Their research and most of the other research results that we reference focus primarily on the 1980s and 1990s. Unfortunately, less is known about the 2000s at this point.

Blau and Kahn examined the effect of changes in women's and men's measured characteristics—experience, education, occupation, industry, and union status—and changes in wage structure on trends in the gender wage gap. The part of the change in the gender gap that cannot be explained by these factors is referred to as unexplained. As discussed in Chapter 7, the **unexplained gap** is often attributed, at least in part, to labor market discrimination, though it is acknowledged that it may reflect other factors, such as unmeasured skills, as well.

It appears that women were able to narrow the gender wage gap in part, by improving their qualifications relative to men. Thus, although women continued to have less labor market experience than men, on average, they *narrowed the gender difference in experience*. The gender gap in full-time experience fell from 6.6 years in 1979 to 3.5 years in 1998.[9] In the case of education, women not only closed the gap with men, but eventually *surpassed men in educational attainment* in this sample of full-time workers. In 1979, the incidence of a college or advanced degree was 4 percentage points higher among employed men than women; by 1998, women workers were 2 percentage points more likely to have a college or advanced degree than men workers. *Shifts in women's occupations* played an important role too, as the employment of women as professionals and managers rose, while their concentration in clerical and service jobs fell. Women's wages also increased relative to men's because of the *decrease in unionization* that occurred during this time. The decline in unions had a larger negative effect on male than female workers because men, who were traditionally considerably more likely than women to be unionized, experienced a larger decrease in unionization than women. Another factor that worked to decrease the gender wage gap substantially, especially during the 1980s, was a *decrease in the unexplained portion of the gender differential*, that is, a decline in the pay difference between men and women with the same measured characteristics (i.e., experience, education, occupation, industry, and union status).

Taken together, changes in qualifications and in the unexplained gap worked to decrease the gender wage gap substantially. Working in the opposite direction, however, especially during the 1980s, were changes in wage structure (or returns to characteristics) that favored men over women during this period. Of particular importance were a rise in the return to experience (since women have less of it) and increases in returns to employment in occupations and industries where men are more highly represented. The effect of these adverse shifts in labor market returns by themselves would have reduced the gender wage ratio substantially. Thus, in order for the gender wage gap to

---

[8] Blau and Kahn, "The U.S. Gender Pay Gap in the 1990s." Unless otherwise indicated, results cited in the text are from this study with some additional data drawn from Francine D. Blau and Lawrence M. Kahn, "The U.S. Gender Pay Gap in the 1990s: Slowing Convergence," NBER Working Paper No. 10853 (October 2004). Other research on the convergence of the gender gap includes, for example, Casey B. Mulligan and Yona Rubinstein, "Selection, Investment, and Women's Relative Wages," *Quarterly Journal of Economics* 123, no. 3 (August 2008): 1061–1110; Marigee Bacolod and Bernardo S. Blum, "Two Sides of the Same Coin: U.S. 'Residual Inequality' and the Gender Gap," *Journal of Human Resources* (forthcoming); Catherine Weinberger and Peter Kuhn, "The Narrowing of the U.S. Gender Earnings Gap, 1959-1999," Working Paper, University of California, Santa Barbara (February 2008); Finis Welch "Growth in Women's Relative Wages and in Inequality Among Men: One Phenomenon or Two?" *American Economic Review* 90, no. 2 (May 2000): 444–49; Nicole M. Fortin and Thomas Lemieux, "Are Women's Wage Gains Men's Losses? A Distributional Test," *American Economic Review* 90, no. 2 (May 2000): 456–60; and June O'Neill and Solomon W. Polachek, "Why the Gender Gap in Wages Narrowed in the 1980s," *Journal of Labor Economics* 11, no. 1, pt. 1 (January 1993): 205–28.

[9] Other studies that also find that the decline in the gender gap in experience contributed to the narrowing of the gender wage gap include, for example, O'Neill and Polachek, "Why the Gender Gap in Wages Narrowed in the 1980s," and Weinberger and Kuhn, "The Narrowing of the U.S. Gender Earnings Gap, 1959–1999."

decline, the factors favorably affecting women's wages needed to be large enough to more than offset the impact of unfavorable shifts in returns. This was indeed the case, so the gender wage gap declined.

What can we say about the reasons for the decrease in the unexplained gender wage gap that occurred during this period? Such a shift may reflect a decline in labor market discrimination against women, but could also be due to an upgrading of women's *unmeasured* labor market skills, a shift in labor market demand favoring women over men, or changes in the composition of the labor force due to the pattern of labor force entries or exits. Indeed all of these factors may have played a role, and all appear credible during this period.

First, since women improved the relative level of their *measured* skills, like full-time job experience and education, as well as their employment in higher-skilled managerial and professional jobs, it is plausible that they also enhanced their *unmeasured* skills compared to men. By unmeasured skills we mean skills that are not measured (or observed) in standard data sets used in statistical analyses like this one. But, in some cases, information on "unmeasured" skills may be available from other sources. For example, as we saw in Chapter 6, gender differences in college major— found to be strongly related to the gender wage gap among college graduates—have decreased, and the gender difference in SAT math scores has declined as well. Further, we as we saw in Chapter 7, the lower value that women have traditionally placed on money and work than men is a factor that has been linked to women's lower pay. It has been found that men's and women's attitudes toward money and work have become more similar in recent years and that this helps to explain the decrease in the gender wage gap.[10]

Second, it is possible that discrimination against women declined. For one thing, it is likely that the rationale for statistical discrimination against women has eroded, at least to some extent, as women have become more firmly attached to the labor force. Further, in the presence of feedback effects, employers' revised views can generate additional increases in women's wages by raising their returns to investments in job qualifications and skills—both measured and unmeasured. Another possible reason for a decline in discrimination against women is that changes in attitudes may have made such discriminatory tastes or prejudices increasingly less socially acceptable.

Third, the underlying labor market demand shifts that widened overall wage inequality appear to have favored women relative to men in certain ways, and thus also likely contributed to a decrease in the unexplained gender gap identified in the analysis above and other similar types of studies. Overall, manufacturing employment declined, particularly in the 1980s. In addition, some evidence indicates that technological change produced within-industry demand shifts that favored white-collar relative to blue-collar workers in general. Given that men have tended to hold a disproportionate share of manufacturing and blue-collar jobs, these shifts would be expected to benefit women relative to men.[11] Increased computer use, a key aspect of technological change, also seems to favor women compared to men. For one, women are more likely than men to use computers at work and computers also restructure work in ways that deemphasize

---

[10] Nicole M. Fortin, "The Gender Wage Gap Among Young Adults in the United States The Importance of Money versus People" *Journal of Human Resources* 43, no. 4 (Fall 2008):884–918.

[11] Eli Berman, John Bound, and Zvi Griliches, "Changes in the Demand of Skilled Labor Within U.S. Manufacturing Industries: Evidence from the Annual Survey of Manufacturing", *Quarterly Journal of Economics* 109, no. 2 (May 1994): 367–97; Blau and Kahn, "The U.S. Gender Pay Gap in the 1990s;" and Francine D. Blau and Lawrence M. Kahn, "Swimming Upstream: Trends in the Gender Wage Differential in the 1980s," *Journal of Labor Economics* 15, no. 1, pt.1 (January 1997): 1–42. Such demand shifts probably helped to offset the effects of the large increase in female labor supply that also occurred during this time.

physical strength.[12] In addition, with the spread of computers, some evidence suggests that interpersonal interactions have become more important; this is because teamwork is more important in occupations with greater computer use. Since women's interpersonal skills tend to exceed men's, on average, this factor is believed to have increased women's wages relative to men's.[13] Alongside these developments, there has also been an increase in the labor market return to cognitive skills and a corresponding decrease in the return to motor skills. This has also boosted women's wages relative to men's because women tend to be more highly represented in occupations where cognitive skills are important while men are more likely to be in jobs that emphasize motor skills.[14]

A final factor contributing to the considerable narrowing of the "unexplained" gender wage gap was favorable shifts in the composition of the female labor force. The female labor force expanded, particularly during the 1980s, and some evidence suggests that the women who entered the labor force tended to be those with relatively high (unmeasured) skills. These skills improved the quality of the female labor force and thus contributed to the narrowing of the gender wage gap.[15]

The experience of blacks in the 1980s and 1990s stands in sharp contrast to that of women. As we saw in Chapter 5, while the black-white earnings gap declined after the passage of civil rights legislation in the mid-1960s, it changed little after the mid- to late 1970s. Some research suggests that changes in wage structure may provide at least a partial explanation for the stalling of progress of African Americans. On average, blacks have lower educational attainment than whites (although the race gap in education has declined) and, as a consequence, blacks are more adversely affected than whites by declining relative wages for less-educated workers. Some evidence also indicates that the decline in blue-collar jobs in manufacturing particularly negatively affected black males. For black women, although their exit from extremely low-paying, private household employment was an important factor in narrowing the race gap in earlier years, this factor was no longer relevant by the 1980s, when their representation in these jobs approached levels for whites. Despite these interesting insights, the full explanation for the unfortunate lack of progress in narrowing the race gap in earnings since the 1970s remains elusive.[16]

The data presented in Chapter 5 also indicate that the wages of Hispanic women and men fell relative to those of whites of the same sex. Education gaps between Hispanics and whites are considerably larger than those between blacks and whites, so

---

[12] Alan B. Krueger, "How Computers Have Changed the Wage Structure: Evidence from Microdata, 1984–1989," *Quarterly Journal of Economics* 108, no. 1 (February 1993): 33–60; and Bruce Weinberg, "Computer Use and the Demand for Female Workers," *Industrial and Labor Relations Review* 53, no. 2 (January 2000): 290–308. The growing importance of "brains" relative to "brawn" as a factor narrowing the gender pay gap is particularly emphasized by Welch in "Growth in Women's Relative Wages and in Inequality Among Men."

[13] Lex Borghans, Baster Weel, and Bruce Weinberg, "People People: Social Capital and the Labor-Market Outcomes of Underrepresented Groups," NBER Working Paper No. 11985 (January 2006).

[14] Bacolod and Blum, "Two Sides of the Same Coin."

[15] Mulligan and Rubinstein, "Selection, Investment, and Women's Relative Wages" place particular emphasis on the role of selection in narrowing the gender wage gap. Blau and Kahn, "The U.S. Gender Pay Gap in the 1990s" suggest a more modest role for this factor; moreover, they find that female labor force entrants were less skilled during the 1990s than the 1980s, perhaps as a result of the entry of many relatively low-skilled, female single-family heads.

[16] For a useful overview of black-white differences, see, Derek Neal, "Black-White Labour Market Inequality in the United States," in The *New Palgrave Dictionary of Economics*, 2nd edition, edited by Steven Durlauf and Lawrence Blume (London: Palgrave Macmillan, 2008). For studies of black-white trends, see, for example, Chinhui Juhn, Kevin M. Murphy, and Brooks Pierce, "Accounting for the Slowdown in Black-White Wage Convergence," in *Workers and Their Wages*, edited by Marvin Kosters (Washington, DC: AEI Press, 1991), pp. 107–43 (this study is especially important for clarifying the role of changes in wage structure); and Francine D. Blau and Andrea H. Beller, "Black-White Earnings over the 1970s and 1980s, Gender Differences in Trends," *Review of Economics and Statistics* 74, no. 2 (May 1992): 276–86 (one of the few to examine women as well as men).

it is likely that Hispanics were especially negatively affected by the declining relative wages of less-educated workers. In addition, as noted in Chapter 5, a large and growing proportion of Hispanics are recent immigrants to the United States, hence the earnings of Hispanics as a whole are reduced because new immigrants tend to be relatively young, may not speak English well, and are likely to face other difficulties in adjusting to their new environment. This negative effect is exacerbated by the fact that the economic status of immigrants has deteriorated relative to the native born in recent decades.[17]

THE RISING PAYOFF TO EDUCATION

The more favorable trends in real earnings for women and the rising gender wage ratio since 1980 point to significant gender differences in earnings trends. However, when we compare how the less educated have fared relative to the more highly educated, the experiences of men and women are more similar. Among both women and men, the less educated are increasingly falling behind others, as earnings disparities by education grow. Among men, these disparities are associated with substantial declines in real wages for the less educated, while among women, real wages either declined slightly or at least grew considerably more slowly for the less educated.

These trends are seen in Tables 8-2 and 8-3. Table 8-2 gives the mean earnings of year-round, full-time workers in each educational category relative to those of high school graduates for 1974 (before the sharp rise in the returns to education) and 2007. It is clear that the earnings of those who did not complete high school fell relative to high school graduates, while the relative earnings of college graduates increased considerably. For instance, in 2007, women and men with a college degree or more earned about twice as much as high school graduates, compared to about 50 percent more in 1974.[18] Those with some college also increased their earnings relative to high school graduates, but to a lesser extent than college graduates did.

Interestingly, the ratios of each educational category's earnings relative to high school graduates are fairly similar for men and women in both years in Table 8-2, suggesting that the extent of earnings differentials by education is about the same for both. However, as we saw in Chapter 6, more detailed research indicates that women in fact get a higher return to education than men.[19]

Table 8-3 shows the consequences of widening inequality in earnings by education for trends in real earnings of education groups over the period from 1974 to 2007. For both men and women, more highly educated workers did considerably better in terms of real earnings changes. Among men, only college graduates experienced an increase in real earnings; for other education groups real earnings decreased. The largest decline was for high school dropouts whose real earnings fell by 21 percent over the period. The real earnings of men with some college decreased slightly, by 4 percent. In contrast, male college graduates experienced an *increase* in their real earnings of

---

[17] For analyses of Hispanic and immigrant earnings, see Maury B. Gittleman and David R. Howell, "Changes in the Structure and Quality of Jobs in the United States: Effects by Race and Gender, 1973–1990," *Industrial and Labor Relations Review* 48, no. 3 (April 1995): 420–40; Gregory DeFreitas, *Inequality at Work: Hispanics in the U.S. Labor Force* (Oxford: Oxford University Press, 1991); and George J. Borjas, "Assimilation and Changes in Cohort Quality Revisited: What Happened to Immigrant Earnings in the 1980s?" *Journal of Labor Economics* 13, no. 2 (April 1995): 201–45.

[18] Of course, the costs of going to college rose as well, but even taking this cost increase into account, the figures suggest an increase in the return to a college education.

[19] See, Christopher Dougherty, "Why Are the Returns to Schooling Higher for Women than for Men?" Journal of Human Resources 40, no. 4 (Fall 2005): 969–88. By detailed analyses, we mean statistical analyses of the rate of return to education that control for other factors that may be correlated with wages, such as age or experience, race and ethnicity.

TABLE 8-2 Mean Earnings of Education Groups Relative to High School Graduates, 1974 and 2007 (%)

Education	1974		2007	
	Men	Women	Men	Women
High School				
1–3 years	88.9	85.3	77.0	72.3
4 years	100.0	100.0	100.0	100.0
College				
1–3 years	113.6	112.6	119.2	125.2
4 or more years	155.0	147.2	210.8	189.2

Notes: Data refer to year-round, full-time workers 18 years of age and older. Definitions of educational categories are not exactly comparable for the 2 years. In 2007, mean earnings for 1–3 years of college is computed as a weighted average of the means for "some college, no degree" and "associate degree."

Source: U.S. Census Bureau Historical Income Tables—People, Tables P-32 and P-35 "Educational Attainment—Full-Time, Year-Round Workers 18 Years Old and Over by Mean Earnings, Age, and Sex," from http://www.census.gov/hhes/www/income/histinc/incpertoc.html.

TABLE 8-3 Change in Real Mean Earnings of Men and Women by Education for Year-Round, Full-time Workers, 1974–2007

Education	Men (%)	Women (%)
High School		
1–3 years	−20.8	−1.7
4 years	−8.6	16.0
College		
1–3 years	−4.1	29.1
4 or more years	24.4	49.1

Notes: Data refer to year-round, full-time workers 18 years of age and older. Definitions of educational categories are not exactly comparable for the 2 years. In 2007, mean earnings for 1–3 years of college is computed as a weighted average of the means for "some college, no degree" and "associate degree." Adjusted for inflation using the Consumer Price Index for All Urban Areas (CPI-U-RS).

Sources: U.S. Census Bureau Historical Income Tables—People, Tables P-32 and P-35 "Educational Attainment—Full-Time, Year-Round Workers 18 Years Old and Over by Mean Earnings, Age, and Sex," from http://www.census.gov/hhes/www/income/histinc/incpertoc.html.

24 percent. Women fared better than their male counterparts within each educational category in terms of real wage growth. However, for them too the more highly educated did a great deal better. Real earnings declined by 2 percent for female dropouts but rose by 49 percent for female college graduates. Note that real wage changes for men and women overall are determined not just by the wage trends for each education group but also by changes in the relative size of each education group. In this respect, rising educational attainment helped to boost the real earnings of both men and women, although overall male real earnings have nonetheless continued to stagnate since the early 1970s.

These trends indicate a rising payoff to a college education for both men and women. They also mean that, among both men and women, the earnings of the less educated fell compared to others. The deteriorating earnings situation of less-educated women and men tell only part of the story of the declining economic status of the less educated in the United States. To be included in these tabulations, an individual must not only be employed, but work year-round and full-time. As we saw in Chapter 4, less educated women and men are increasingly less likely to be in the labor force than the more highly educated over the past 30 years. Among women, this reflects considerably smaller increases in participation rates for those with less than 4 years of high school in comparison to substantial increases for those with higher levels of education. Among men, decreases in participation rates occurred among all education groups, but the declines were especially precipitous among those who did not complete high school. A final piece of the story is the rising incidence of families headed by single mothers that we shall examine in Chapter 10. This increase, particularly pronounced among the less educated, places them and their families at even greater economic disadvantage.[20]

Conclusion

In this chapter we began by considering overall trends in wage inequality and real wage growth for men and women. Wage inequality has risen dramatically since 1980, a development that is associated with an increase in the returns to skills including education. Despite overall increases in inequality, the gender wage gap has narrowed considerably over the same period and women's real wages have continued to rise while those of men have stagnated overall and have declined considerably for the low skilled. Women were able to narrow the gender wage gap in the face of rising wage inequality and increasing returns to skill by substantially upgrading their qualifications, especially their experience and education, as well as their occupations. They also benefited from a decrease in the unexplained gender wage gap (particularly in the 1980s), which may represent a decline in discrimination, an improvement in women's qualifications that we are not able to measure using conventional data sources, or demand shifts that favored women more than men. The evidence also suggests that as the labor force expanded, particularly in the 1980s, the women who entered the labor force tended to be those with relatively high (unmeasured) skills. This resulted in a favorable shift in the composition of the female labor force that also boosted women's wages.

Questions for Review and Discussion

1. What has happened to wage inequality since 1980? What factors account for the change?
2. Economists point to three major factors behind trends in the gender wage gap. Discuss each and explain the role each played in the narrowing of the gender wage gap since 1980.

3. Based on the research findings discussed in this chapter, can you conclude that discrimination against women in the labor market has definitely declined? Why or why not? Explain fully.

Suggested Readings

Blank, Rebecca M., Sheldon H. Danziger, and Robert F. Schoeni, eds., *Working and Poor: How Economic and Policy Changes are Affecting Low-Wage Workers*. New York: Russell Sage Foundation, 2006.

Blau, Francine D., and Lawrence M. Kahn. "The U.S. Gender Pay Gap in the 1990s: Slowing Convergence." *Industrial and Labor Relations Review* 60, no. 1 (October 2006): 45–66.

---

[20] This development is particularly emphasized in Blau, "Trends in the Well-Being of American Women."

Blau, Francine D., and Lawrence M. Kahn. "Gender Differences in Pay." *Journal of Economic Perspectives* 14, no. 4 (Fall 2000): 75–99.

Blau, Francine D., Mary C. Brinton, and David B. Grusky, editors, *The Declining Significance of Gender?* New York: Russell Sage Foundation, 2006.

Goldin, Caudia, and Lawrence F. Katz. *The Race between Education and Technology.* Cambridge, MA: The Belknap Press of Harvard University Press, 2008.

Katz, Lawrence F., and David H. Autor. "Changes in the Wage Structure and Earnings Inequality." In *Handbook of Labor Economics,* edited by Orley C. Ashenfelter and David Card. Amsterdam: Elsevier, 1999, pp. 3A:1463–555.

Levy, Frank. *The New Dollars and Dreams: American Incomes and Economic Change.* New York: Russell Sage Foundation, 1998.

Neal, Derek. "Black–White Labour Market Inequality in the United States." In The *New Palgrave Dictionary of Economics*, 2nd edition, edited by Steven Durlauf and Lawrence Blume. London: Palgrave Macmillan, 2008.

Salverda, Wiemer, Brian Nolan, and Timothy M. Smeeding, editors. *The Oxford Handbook of Economic Inequality.* Oxford, UK: Oxford University Press, 2009.

Key Terms

real wages *247*
wage inequality *247*
returns to skills *248*
gender wage ratio *250*

gender wage gap *250*
human capital investments *250*
labor market discrimination *250*

wage structure *251*
unexplained gap *252*

CHAPTER **9**

Recent Employment Trends

Chapter Highlights

- The Rise of the Nonstandard Workforce
- The Growth in Women's Self-Employment
- The Changing Face of Labor Unions

A central theme of the study of women's status in the labor market, the family, and the broader society is one of change. We are also living in a time of considerable change in labor market arrangements and outcomes. In Chapter 8 we examined the notable recent changes in earnings, principally the secular increase in women's earnings relative to men's that began in 1980 as well as the considerable decline in the real and relative wages earned by less-skilled workers that started around the same time. In this chapter we take a closer look at three highly significant recent employment trends and examine their impact on women and men. First we consider the growth in nonstandard employment arrangements that have resulted in a substantial share of the workforce being employed in arrangements that differ from regular, full-time jobs. Second, we examine the sources and significance of the growth in self-employment for women. Finally we consider the continued decline in the share of the workforce that is unionized and its consequences for women and men.

THE RISE OF THE NONSTANDARD WORKFORCE

The **nonstandard workforce** consists of individuals who do not have "regular" full-time jobs. While data on the trends in nonstandard employment are limited, the existing information suggests that there has been a long-term increase in the proportion of people in such jobs. For example, employment in the temporary help industry, a sector that is associated with nonstandard employment and for which consistent data are available, grew at an average annual rate of 11 percent per year from 1982 to 2002, as compared to a 1.9 percent annual growth rate for nonfarm employment overall during the same period.[1]

---

[1] Figures on employment in the temporary help industry are calculated from the U.S. Census Bureau, *Census of Service Industries* for 1982 and 2002 and figures on nonfarm employment are from U.S. Bureau of Labor Statistics, www.bls.gov. Another indicator that permanence of employment is decreasing is that the fraction of men holding long-term jobs (jobs lasting 10 to 20 years) has been declining, though there has been a slight increase for women; see, Henry S. Farber, "Is the Company Man an Anachronism? Trends in Long Term Employment in the U.S., 1973–2006" in *The Price of Independence: The Economics of Early Adulthood*, edited by Sheldon H. Danziger and Cecilia Elena Rouse (New York: Russell Sage Foundation, 2007), pp. 56–83.

Detailed data on a broader set of nonstandard work arrangements (with "temp" jobs as just one such arrangement) first became available in the mid-1990s. These data indicate only a slight recent expansion in the share of nonstandard workers as a percentage of the labor force; between 1995 and 2005, the share increased from 10 to 11 percent. When part-time workers are also included, the share of workers in nonstandard employment was roughly constant at 26 percent of the workforce over the same period.[2] Nonetheless, these figures mean that a sizable share of the workforce is in such jobs. This section defines the nonstandard workforce, examines recent data on its dimensions, and then looks at the consequences of the rise in nonstandard employment for workers and their families.

Definition and Characteristics of the Nonstandard Workforce

Nonstandard workers include individuals identified by the Bureau of Labor Statistics (BLS) as having "alternative" or nontraditional employment arrangements; that is, "individuals whose employment is arranged through an employment intermediary such as a temporary help firm, or individuals whose place, time, and quantity of work are potentially unpredictable."[3] Four major categories of workers in alternative arrangements are identified by the BLS: *temporary help agency workers (temps), on-call workers, contract workers,* and *independent contractors.*[4] Our definition of the non-standard workforce also includes *part-time workers.*

Temporary help agency workers are employed by agencies and sent out to other businesses as they are needed. **On-call workers** or limited duration hires are only employed as needed, generally for short periods of time; they include, for instance, substitute teachers and construction workers supplied by a union hiring hall. **Contract workers** are employed by firms that contract out employees or services to other companies; they supply such services as cleaning, security, landscaping, or computer programming.[5] **Independent contractors** or freelance workers are individuals who provide a product or service for their own customers. Management consultants, freelance writers, and textbook editors are all examples of occupations in which some individuals work on a freelance basis. These workers are most often self-employed. However, self-employed business operators, such as shop owners or restaurateurs, are not included among independent contractors.[6]

---

[2] See the data presented below and in Francine D. Blau, Marianne A. Ferber and Anne E. Winkler, *The Economics of Women, Men, and Work,* 3rd ed. (Upper Saddle River, NJ: Prentice Hall, 1998), Table 8-9, p. 256. For further discussion of trends, see Marianne A. Ferber and Jane Waldfogel, "The 'Contingent' Labor Force," in *The Elgar Companion to Feminist Economics,* edited by Janice Peterson and Margaret Lewis (Cheltenham, UK: Edward Elgar, 1999); and the contributions in Francoise Carre, Marianne A. Ferber, Lonnie Golden, and Steve Herzenberg, eds., *Nonstandard Work Arrangements and the Changing Labor Market: Dimensions, Causes, and Institutional Responses,* Industrial Relations Research Association Research Volume (2000).

[3] Anne E. Polivka, "Contingent and Alternative Work Arrangements, Defined," *Monthly Labor Review* 119, no. 10 (October 1996): 3–9. Regarding the distinction between an independent contractor and employee, see Charles J. Muhl, "What Is an Employee? The Answer Depends on Federal Law," *Monthly Labor Review* 125, no. 1 (January 2002): 3–11.

[4] Many of these workers, particularly those employed as temps and on-call workers, would be classified as holding "contingent" jobs, that is, jobs in which an individual "does not have an explicit or implicit contract for long-term employment; see, Polivka, "Contingent and Alternative Work Arrangements, Defined," p. 4. A recent government report estimated that 61 percent of temps, 25 percent of on-call workers, and 20 percent of contract workers were contingent. In contrast, less than 4 percent of independent contractors and just under 3 percent of workers in traditional employment arrangements were classified as contingent. See U.S. Bureau of Labor Statistics, "Contingent and Alternative Employment Arrangements: February 2005," *News,* USDL 05-1433, July 25, 2005, Table 12.

[5] To be included under alternative employment arrangements, contract workers had to report that they usually had only one customer and worked at the customer's worksite. These characteristics distinguish contract workers from those employed by companies that carry out work assignments, such as advertising agencies, equipment manufacturers, lawyers, or economic "think tanks." See Polivka, "Contingent and Alternative Work Arrangements, Defined," p. 8.

[6] See section titled "Concepts and Definitions" in U.S. Bureau of Labor Statistics, "Contingent and Alternative Employment Arrangements: February 2005."

The status of **part-time workers**, those who work fewer than 35 hours per week, is less clear because many are employed by a single employer and may be employed for an extended period of time. From this perspective, part-time workers should not be included in the definition of nonstandard employment. Nonetheless we include them in our estimates of the nonstandard workforce because they share a number of the problems of others in this category, such as often having limited training and promotion opportunities and receiving few if any fringe benefits.

Table 9-1 provides a breakdown of the employment arrangements included in our definition of nonstandard work.[7] In all, as noted earlier, nearly 11 percent of workers were employed as temps, on-call workers, independent contractors, and contract workers in 2005.[8] Including part-timers in otherwise traditional employment arrangements brings the total to almost 26 percent. Part-time workers are a longtime feature of the labor market. In the 1950s, they consisted of 12 percent of employed workers. That number had increased to 17 percent by 2007. Some individuals who work part time do so involuntarily, because they cannot find full-time jobs, while others voluntarily choose this schedule. Not surprisingly, the proportion of involuntary part-time workers rises considerably in recessions and falls in more prosperous times. Regardless of the business cycle, however, the proportion of voluntary part-time workers always remains quite large, especially among women.

As shown in Table 9-1, women are overrepresented among nonstandard workers; it is estimated that 57 percent of such workers were women, as compared to 46 percent of all employed workers. However, the representation of women varies considerably by employment arrangement. Women comprise the vast majority of part-time workers and

TABLE 9-1 Nonstandard Workers in the Labor Force, 2005

	Percent Female	Percent of All Employed
I. Alternative Employment Arrangements		
On-call workers	49.4	1.8
Temporary help agency workers	52.8	0.9
Independent contractors	35.3	7.4
Workers provided by contract firm	31.0	0.6
Subtotal	38.8	10.7
II. Part-Time Workers (not included above)	67.0[a]	15.1
III. Total Nonstandard Workers (sum of I and II)	57.0[a]	25.8

[a]Percentage female for "Part-Time Workers (not included above)" is based on all part-time workers.

Sources: U.S. Department of Labor, Bureau of Labor Statistics, "Contingent and Alternative Employment Arrangements, February 2005," Report 01-153 (May 2005); and U.S. Department of Labor, Bureau of Labor Statistics, *Employment and Earnings* (January 2006).

---

[7] In academia, a large and growing number of faculty are employed in nontenure track jobs, typically as instructors or lecturers. These individuals are not included by the Bureau of Labor Statistics in their figures but are in fact nonstandard workers. For instance, from academic year 1993–94 to 2005–06, the percentage of full-time faculty with a tenure-track position fell from nearly 56 to just under 50 percent. Moreover, in 2005–06 only 41 percent of full-time women employed in academe held tenured or tenure-track positions, as compared to 55 percent of men. See National Center for Education Statistics, *Digest for Education Statistics*, 2006, Table 254, available at www.nces.ed.gov.

[8] Additional workers who might be considered to have alternative employment arrangements are direct-hire temporaries who were hired into a temporary job directly by their employer rather than through a temporary agency. The Bureau of Labor Statistics does not provide information on this category.

are overrepresented among temps and on-call workers. They are, however, underrepresented among independent contractors and contract workers. In terms of labor market outcomes, contract workers and independent contractors tend to earn more, while other nonstandard workers, including part-timers, tend to earn less than those in traditional employment with similar qualifications and job characteristics.[9] Similarly, although workers in alternative arrangements are less likely than those in traditional employment to be covered by employer-provided health insurance and pensions, among those in alternative arrangements, contract workers are more likely to receive these benefits while on-call and temporary workers are less likely to be covered. Part-time workers also tend to receive fewer employer-provided benefits.[10] Because women are overrepresented among part timers, on-call workers, and temps, as a group, they are likely to have lower average earnings and fewer benefits.

Explanations for the Rise of Nonstandard Workers

In understanding the long-term rise in nonstandard workers, it is helpful to begin by examining the reasons why employers seek to hire workers for nonstandard jobs and why workers are interested in such employment. On the demand side, research points to a variety of reasons why firms make use of nonstandard workers. Small- and medium-sized firms, in particular, may find it cost-effective to use contracted services in specialized areas such as computer programming, rather than investing in their own in-house staff. This is especially the case if such skills are needed only occasionally. Also, if production is characterized by peak and off-peak periods or demand for the product is variable, firms, regardless of size, may find it cost-effective to hire temporary help workers during peak periods. By employing temporary workers, the firm avoids carrying surplus workers in slow times and the costs of repeatedly hiring and firing workers as business conditions change. In addition, the use of nonstandard workers provides a way to screen future employees—employees who prove to be successful may then be offered regular positions. Businesses may also replace regular jobs with nonstandard positions in an attempt to cut labor costs by paying lower wages or by not providing benefits to the nonstandard workers. Similarly, some high-wage companies contract out for services rather than using their regular workforce in order to pay lower wages or reduced benefits without creating inequities within the ranks of their own workers.[11]

From the supply-side perspective, nonstandard work may be attractive to workers for a variety of reasons. The flexibility of such jobs may be valued by students, homemakers who must also balance family responsibilities, and older people in transition to

---

[9] Arne L. Kalleberg et al., *Nonstandard Work, Substandard Jobs: Flexible Work Arrangements in the U.S.* (Washington, DC: Economic Policy Institute and Women's Research and Education Institute, 1997; figures subsequently updated by Ken Hudson, "No Shortage of Jobs," Briefing Paper #89 (Washington, DC: Economic Policy Institute, 1999).

[10] For instance, nearly 50 percent of contract workers but only 26 percent of on-call workers and 8 percent of temporary help workers had employer-provided health insurance. The issue of employer provision was not relevant to independent contractors (who are essentially self-employed), but 69 percent of this group did have health insurance coverage. As a point of comparison, 56 percent of workers with traditional employment arrangements had employer-provided coverage. See U.S. Department of Labor, Bureau of Labor Statistics, "Contingent and Alternative Employment Arrangements: February 2005," Table 9. For further evidence, including figures on part-timers see, Susan N. Housman, "The Benefit Implications of Recent Trends in Flexible Staffing Arrangements," in *Benefits for the Workplace of the Future*, edited by Olivia S. Mitchell, David S. Blitzstein, Michael Gordon, and Judith F. Mazos (Philadelphia: University of Pennsylvania Press, 2003), pp. 89–109.

[11] Katherine G. Abraham and Susan K. Taylor, "Firms' Use of Outside Contractors: Theory and Evidence," *Journal of Labor Economics* 14, no. 3 (July 1996): 394–424; Dale Belman and Lonnie Golden, "Contingent and Nonstandard Work Arrangements in the United States: Dispersion and Contrasts by Industry, Occupation and Job Type," in Carre et al., eds., *Nonstandard Work Arrangements*, pp. 167–212; and Susan N. Houseman, "Why Employers Use Flexible Staffing Arrangements: Evidence from an Establishment Survey," *Industrial and Labor Relations Review* 55, no. 1 (October 2001): 149–70.

retirement. Young people may also find nonstandard jobs a convenient way to explore career options. Individuals may be interested in working as independent contractors, in particular, for much the same reasons that other forms of self-employment are attractive, including greater autonomy and more flexible hours. Some nonstandard workers, most notably independent contractors and contract workers, may also earn higher wages than comparable workers in traditional employment, in part to compensate for the uncertainty and lower benefits. Finally, it is important to point out that some workers may take nonstandard jobs because they are unable to locate regular employment. The extent to which this is true tends to vary by type of alternative employment arrangement. More than four-fifths of independent contractors stated in a 2005 survey that they preferred their current work arrangement, while just one-third of temporary help workers did so.[12]

While there is not full agreement on the reasons for the rise in nonstandard employment, it is likely that both demand and supply factors of the sort we have reviewed played a role.[13] On the demand side, one likely explanation is the rise in the cost of benefits, health insurance especially, which has increased the incentive for firms to hire nonstandard workers to avoid these expenses.[14] In addition, a growing number of states now limit the right of employers to terminate employment "at will," which makes hiring regular workers riskier since it is harder to let them go.[15] Finally, the number of small firms is growing, and, as we noted previously, these firms are most likely to find it advantageous to purchase specialized skills from outside sources. On the supply side, it is notable that groups that are more heavily represented in some types of nonstandard employment, like women and older workers, have increased as a share of the labor force.

Consequences of Nonstandard Work for Workers and Their Families

Nonstandard work is likely to have a variety of consequences for workers and their families. Most obviously, such workers will tend to have less job security because the average duration of their jobs is relatively short as compared with regular full-time employment.[16] In addition, nonstandard workers generally lack the protection provided by labor unions, in part because they are especially difficult to organize and also because unions for a long time opposed part-time employment. Further, as noted earlier, nonstandard workers, regardless of type, usually receive substantially fewer employer-provided benefits. As a consequence they are more vulnerable in the event of a serious health problem, as well as during the retirement years, when they will have a lesser amount of pension income, if any. Part-time workers may be more attached to their

---

[12] See U.S. Department of Labor, Bureau of Labor Statistics, "Contingent and Alternative Employment Arrangements: February 2005," Table 11.

[13] One explanation that has been suggested, but has not been supported by the evidence, is that job growth was greater in industries where nonstandard work arrangements are more common. In fact, Marcello Estavao and Saul Lach found that for temporary help jobs, virtually all of the growth in such employment between 1977 and 1997 occurred due to an increase in the employment of temporary help workers *within* each industry, rather than to an expansion of industries that utilize temps more intensively. See "The Evolution of the Demand for Temporary Help Supply Employment in the United States," in Carre et al., eds., *Nonstandard Work Arrangements*, pp. 123–44.

[14] Susan Houseman and Machiko Osawa, "The Growth of Nonstandard Employment in Japan and the United States," in *Nonstandard Work in Developed Economies*, edited by Susan Houseman and Machiko Osawa (Kalamazoo, MI: W.E. Upjohn Institute, 2003), pp. 175–214.

[15] David H. Autor, "Outsourcing at Will: The Contribution of Unjust Dismissal Doctrine to the Growth of Employment Outsourcing," *Journal of Labor Economics* 21, no. 1 (January 2003): 1–42.

[16] Susan N. Houseman and Anne E. Polivka, "The Implications of Flexible Staffing Arrangements for Job Security," in *On the Job: Is Long-Term Employment a Thing of the Past?* edited by David Neumark (New York: Russell Sage Foundation, 2000), pp. 427–62.

employers than others in nonstandard jobs, but even they have shorter tenure on average than those who work full time, are more likely to be assigned to routine jobs, and often receive less training as well as fewer promotions.

Because some workers desire these employment arrangements and others may be unsuccessful in obtaining regular jobs, it would be counterproductive to impose restrictions on nonstandard jobs. However, as such arrangements continue to expand, policy makers should consider how important benefits such as health insurance and pensions might be provided to the growing numbers of workers who do not receive them from their employers.

THE GROWTH IN WOMEN'S SELF-EMPLOYMENT

In recent years, there has been some growth in **self-employment** for women. As shown in Table 9-2, women's self-employment rate (the percentage of women workers who are self-employed) increased from 5.1 to 6.9 percent between 1979 and 2006. Most of this increase occurred during the 1980s. Women's self-employment rate peaked in 1995 at 7.1 percent and actually declined slightly in the late 1990s. The rate rebounded to 6.9 percent in 2006, but it is unclear whether this portends further increases in the future. Men's self-employment rate is considerably higher than women's, at 12.5 percent in 2006, but because it has increased only slightly since the late 1970s, the "self-employment" gender gap has narrowed somewhat.[17]

Patterns similar to those identified in Table 9-2—higher rates of self-employment for men along with larger increases in self-employment rates for women—also hold for an extensive set of race and ethnic groups. However, self-employment rates for women and men vary considerably by race and ethnicity. For instance, the rate for Korean women was nine times higher than that for African American women. More generally, rates of self-employment among African Americans, both men and women, remain among the lowest of any group. Part of the reason for the race difference is that African Americans have fewer assets and less access to credit. Further, business ownership tends to "run in the family" and, since African American women and men are less likely to have a self-employed parent, they are also less likely to be self-employed themselves, all else equal.[18]

---

[17] *Self-employment* is defined here to include both those individuals who identify themselves as mainly working in their own unincorporated businesses, often sole proprietorships with no employees, and those running their own, typically larger, incorporated businesses. The figures reported here on self-employment rates by gender were calculated from Current Population Survey data by Robert W. Fairlie; see econ.ucsc.edu/~fairlie; for figures on self-employment rates by race, see Robert W. Fairlie and Alicia M. Robb, *Race and Entrepreneurial Success: Black-, Asian- and White-Owned Businesses in the United States* (Cambridge, MA: MIT Press, 2008). The definition of self-employment used by the U.S. Bureau of Labor Statistics (BLS) differs: It includes only individuals in an unincorporated business as self-employed and counts those running an incorporated business as wage and salary workers. A disadvantage of this latter measure is that the trend reflects changes in the rate of incorporation. The BLS definition indicates a decline in both men's and women's self-employment rates from the mid 1990s through 2006; see U.S. Bureau of Labor Statistics, *Women in the Labor Force: A Databook*, Report 1002 (Sept. 2007), Table 36. See also, Steven Hipple, "Self-Employment in the United States: An Update," Monthly Labor Review 127, no. 7 (July 2004): 13–23; Theresa J. Devine, "Characteristics of Self-Employed Women in the United States," *Monthly Labor Review* 117, no. 3 (March 1994): 20–34; and Marilyn E. Manser and Garnett Picot, "The Role of Self-Employment in U.S. and Canadian Job Growth," *Monthly Labor Review* 122, no. 4 (April 1999):10–25.

[18] Robert W. Fairlie and Bruce D. Meyer, "Ethnic and Racial Self-Employment Differences and Possible Explanations," *Journal of Human Resources* 31, no. 4 (Fall 1996): 757–93; Robert W. Fairlie and Alicia M. Robb, "Families, Human Capital, and Small Business: Evidence from the Characteristics of Business Owners Survey," *Industrial and Labor Relations Review* 60, no. 2 (January 2007): 225–45; and David G. Blanchflower, "Entrepreneurship in the United States," IZA Discussion Paper No. 3130 (October 2007). Magnus Lofstrom and Timothy Bates observe that not all self-employment requires large amounts of financial and human capital, and therefore argue that these factors cannot explain lack of entry by African Americans into what they term "low barrier" fields. See "African American's Pursuit of Self-Employment," IZA Discussion Paper No. 3156 (November 2007).

TABLE 9-2 Self-Employment Rates of Women and Men in the Nonagricultural Sector, Selected Years, 1979–2006

Year	Self-Employment Rate (%)		
	Total	Women	Men
1979	9.3	5.1	12.1
1985	10.2	6.4	13.0
1990	10.3	6.9	13.1
1995	10.1	7.1	12.7
2000	9.4	6.5	11.9
2006	9.9	6.9	12.5

Notes: Includes individuals 16 years of age and older who work 15+ hours per week.

Figures were calculated by Robert W. Fairlie of University of California, Santa Cruz, using data from the Current Population Survey. The self-employed include workers in both unincorporated and incorporated businesses. Due to a change in the underlying survey design, the series is not perfectly comparable before and after 1994.

Source: Unpublished data from Robert W. Fairlie and Robert W. Fairlie's home page, http://econ.ucsc.edu/~fairlie/.

A number of factors likely contribute to the growth in women's self-employment. A reasonable starting place may be to inquire what motivates people to enter self-employment in the first place. The ability to set one's own hours, at least to some extent, is likely to be attractive, especially to women seeking to combine family and work responsibilities. In addition, the presence of a spouse already covered by health insurance would also make the choice of self-employment more attractive.[19] Further, an increase in the labor market return to self-employment, all else equal, should increase entry into self-employment. Notably, one study found that the increase in women's self-employment earnings explains most of the substantial rise in women's self-employment rate during the 1980s,[20] suggesting that women's move into self-employment represents a desirable expansion in their opportunities.

Nonetheless, some women (like some men) may end up in self-employment as a last resort, when they encounter difficulty finding wage and salary employment perhaps after being displaced from their jobs.[21] In addition, some of the growth in self-employment likely reflects the increase in independent contractors, discussed in the previous section, who comprise one component of the nonstandard workforce.[22] Also, some women may choose self-employment to escape from a "glass ceiling" that limits

---

[19] Karen V. Lombard finds evidence for each of these explanations for married women's self-employment decision; see "Female Self-Employment and the Demand for Flexible, Nonstandard Work Schedules," *Economic Inquiry* 39, no. 2 (April 2001): 214–37. For evidence on the attractiveness to women of the greater flexibility offered by self-employment, see Greg Hundley, "Male/Female Earnings Differences in Self-Employment: The Effects of Marriage, Children, and the Household Division of Labor," *Industrial and Labor Relations Review* 54, no. 1 (October 2000): 95–114; and Allison J. Wellington, "Self-Employment: The New Solution for Balancing Family and Career," *Labour Economics* 13, no 3 (June 2006): 357–86. Regarding the role of health insurance coverage, see Allison J. Wellington, "Health Insurance Coverage and Entrepreneurship," *Contemporary Economic Policy* 19, no. 4 (October 2001): 465–78.

[20] Lombard, "Female Self-Employment." Consistent with this, Devine, "Characteristics of Self-Employed Women in the United States," reports that earnings of female self-employed workers rose relative to those of wage and salary workers between 1975 and 1990.

[21] Richard E. Mueller, "The Transition from Paid to Self-Employment in Canada: The Importance of Push Factors," *Applied Economics* 34, no. 6 (March 2002): 791–801.

[22] The Bureau of Labor Statistics estimates that one-half of all self-employed workers are independent contractors. They also find that 87 percent of independent contractors are self-employed. See "Concepts and Definitions" in Bureau of Labor Statistics, "Contingent and Alternative Employment Arrangements: February 2005."

their advancement in the wage and salary sector.[23] Finally, some poor women may see self-employment as a possible route out of poverty. In fact, a modest amount of financial and technical assistance is available to low-income women for starting their own businesses from Microenterprise Assistance Programs, funded by the federal government, nonprofit, and private organizations.[24] However, the success of such programs in raising incomes of poor women is mixed, as discussed further in an international context in Chapter 12.

Research generally finds that female self-employed workers earn less than their wage and salary counterparts with the same qualifications.[25] However, a recent study suggests that this aggregate finding may mask differential effects by occupation, depending on women's varied reasons for entry into self-employment.[26] Women in professional occupations appear to earn a premium from self-employment, even after accounting for marital status and children. This is consistent with the notion that self-employment reflects an expansion in career opportunities for them. In contrast, self-employed women in nonprofessional occupations, including those providing child care services, experience an earnings penalty. For many in this latter group, self-employment may serve as a means to increase workplace flexibility.

For men the evidence is more mixed, with some studies finding that self-employment boosts earnings but one detailed analysis reporting a negative effect.[27] All told, the available evidence suggests that many women, and possibly men as well, may forgo some income in exchange for expectations of greater freedom in determining their own hours and working conditions. Hence the lower earnings of the self-employed may be considered a compensating differential. In fact, this differential is likely to be even larger when total compensation, including benefits, is considered because self-employed workers are less likely than their wage and salary worker counterparts to have health care coverage in their own right, and are also likely to have lower retirement benefits.[28]

THE CHANGING FACE OF LABOR UNIONS

Over the past 30 years, **union membership** has undergone major changes; far fewer workers are union members than in the past and women comprise a growing proportion of union membership. This section discusses these trends, their impact, and prospects for the future.

---

[23] See, for example, Dorothy P. Moore and E. Holly Buttner, *Women Entrepreneurs Moving Beyond the Glass Ceiling* (Thousand Oaks, CA: Sage Publications, 1997). On the other hand, Theresa J. Devine provides evidence suggesting that a glass ceiling for women wage and salary workers does not explain the rise in female self-employment in "Changes in Wage-and-Salary Returns to Skill and the Recent Rise in Female Self-Employment," *American Economic Review* 84, no. 2 (May 1994): 108–13.

[24] Margaret Sherrard Sherrarden, Cynthia K. Sanders, and Michael Sherraden, *Kitchen Capitalism: Microenterprise in Low-Income Households* (Albany: State University of New York Press, 2004).

[25] See, for instance, Ferber and Waldfogel, "The Long-Term Consequences of Nontraditional Employment"; and Michele J. Budig, "Gender, Self-Employment, and Earnings: The Interlocking Structures of Family and Professional Status," *Gender and Society* 20, no. 6 (Dec. 2006): 725–53. Donald R. Williams further finds that women's self-employment negatively affects wage growth when they move back into the wage and salary sector but does not find the same negative effects for self-employed men. See "Consequences of Self-Employment for Women and Men in the United States," *Labour Economics* 7, no. 5 (September 2000): 665–87.

[26] Budig, "Gender, Self-Employment, and Earnings."

[27] Ferber and Waldfogel, "The Long-Term Consequences of Nontraditional Employment," among others, find that self-employed men earn more than their wage and salary counterparts. In contrast, using a detailed set of controls as well as accounting for selection into self-employment, Barton H. Hamilton finds evidence of lower earnings for self-employed men; see "Does Entrepreneurship Pay? An Empirical Analysis of the Returns to Self-Employment," *Journal of Political Economy* 108, no. 3 (June 2000): 604–31.

[28] Devine, "Characteristics of Self-Employed Women"; Ferber and Waldfogel, "The Long-Term Consequences of Nontraditional Employment"; and Wellington, "Health Insurance Coverage and Entrepreneurship."

Trends in Labor Union Membership

Overall union membership in the United States reached a high of more than one-quarter of the labor force in the mid-1950s (a figure far lower than in most other economically advanced countries). It declined steadily after that, especially since the 1970s. As may be seen in Table 9-3, by 2007 only 12 percent of workers were members of labor unions; this includes 13 percent of men and 11 percent of women. The decline in the overall unionization rate reflects the steep decrease that has occurred in private sector unionization. In contrast, unionization rates in the public sector actually *rose* during the 1970s and remained fairly steady subsequently. While debate continues about the precise causes of the decline in private sector unionization, most agree that the shift in industrial structure due to global competition is a contributing factor.[29] One consequence of the divergent trends in public and private sector unionization is that today nearly one-half of all union workers are employed in the public sector, as compared to just 17 percent in 1973.[30]

TABLE 9-3   Trends in Union Membership for Selected Years, 1956–2007

	Women's Share of		Union Members as a Percent of Employed Workers		
Year	All Employed Workers	Membership in Labor Organizations	Men	Women	Total
Unions only					
1956	32.0	18.5	32.2	15.7	27.0
1966	35.6	19.3	30.7	13.1	24.4
Unions and Associations					
1970	37.7	23.9	32.9	16.9	26.8
1980	42.4	30.1	25.1	14.7	20.7
1990	47.2	36.9	19.3	12.6	16.1
2000	48.0	42.3	16.5	13.1	14.9
2007					
All	48.0	44.1	13.0	11.1	12.1
Whites	47.1	42.9	12.8	10.8	11.8
Blacks	54.2	49.3	15.8	13.0	14.3
Asian	47.4	50.5	10.2	11.6	10.9
Hispanics	40.6	39.6	9.9	9.6	9.8

Notes: Persons whose ethnicity is Hispanic may be of any race.

Sources: U.S. Department of Labor, Bureau of Labor Statistics, "Earnings and Other Characteristics of Organized Workers," Bulletin 2105 (May 1980), Table 2, p. 2; Linda H. LeGrande, "Women in Labor Organizations: Their Ranks Are Increasing," *Monthly Labor Review* 101, no. 8 (August 1978), Table 1, p. 9; *Employment and Training Report of the President* (1981), Table A-16, pp. 144–46; *Employment and Earnings* 38, no. 1 (January 1991), p. 228; *Employment and Earnings* 48, no. 1 (January 2001), and U.S. Department of Labor, Bureau of Labor Statistics, "Union Members in 2007," USDL 04-53 (January 2008).

---

[29] Other explanations include firms' increased opposition to unions, differential growth in traditionally union and non-union sectors, and changes in legal and institutional factors that may have affected union organizing activity. See Henry Farber and Bruce Western, "Round Up the Usual Suspects: The Decline of Unions in the Private Sector, 1973-98," *Journal of Labor Research* 2, no. 2 (Summer 2001): 63–88.

[30] Figures are from Barry Hirsch and David Macpherson, "Union Membership and Coverage Database from the CPS," available at www.unionstats.com. For useful discussions, see Ruth Milkman, "Two Worlds of Unionism" in *The Sex of Class: Women Transforming American Labor* edited by Dorothy Sue Cobble (Ithaca: Cornell University Press, 2007); and Henry S. Farber, "Union Membership in the United States: The Divergence Between the Public and Private Sectors," in *Collective Bargaining in Education: Negotiating Change in Today's Schools*, edited by Joan Hannaway and Andrew Rotherham (Cambridge, Mass.: Harvard Education Press, 2006), pp. 27–52.

Traditionally, men were much more likely to be union members than women and the gender gap in unionization was extremely large, nearly 17 percentage points in 1956. Since then, men's unionization rate has fallen precipitously, from just over 32 to 13 percent, while women's rate has declined far less, only from nearly 16 percent to 11 percent. Trends in men's and women's unionization rates differ in large part because men and women tend to be employed in different occupations and industries. The sharp drop in men's rate reflects the shift in industrial structure away from more heavily unionized sectors such as manufacturing, which were largely the bastions of men. Women's unionization rates fell far less because a much greater fraction of female union workers are employed in the public sector, typically in the fields of health, education, and public administration, where, as we have seen, unions held their own. The result of these different trends is that the gender gap in unionization is now fairly small, and as the gender difference in unionization rates has narrowed, women's share of union membership has come to approach their share of the labor force as a whole. In 2007 they comprised 44 percent of union members, up from less than 20 percent in the mid-1950s.

Benefits of Union Membership for Workers and the Impact of Deunionization

Unions confer a range of benefits on their members, with the most cited benefit being a **union wage advantage**, though its size tends to vary by occupation and industry. Overall, the union wage advantage remained fairly constant at about 17–18 percent, from the early 1970s to the early 2000s, though it was briefly greater than 20 percent during the mid 1980s.[31] In the 1970s, women received a slightly higher union wage premium than men, adjusting for other factors, though by 2000 the situation had reversed and men received a slightly larger gain to unionization.[32] In evaluating the economic gains of unionization to workers, it should also be noted that the gains typically increase with labor force attachment, because unions tend to provide higher earnings and more generous benefits to workers with more seniority.[33] Indeed, the narrowing of the gender gap in unionization in recent years is likely a consequence of the fact that women's greater labor force attachment has increased the gain to them of becoming a union member.

Women's and men's participation rates in unions and changes in these rates are watched closely, in part because they directly affect the size of the gender wage gap. Men's traditionally higher unionization rate boosted their wages relative to women's

---

[31] Figures are from David G. Blanchflower and Alex Bryson, "What Effect Do Unions Have on Wages Now and Would Freeman and Medoff Be Surprised?" in *What Do Unions Do? A Twenty-Year Perspective*, edited by James T. Bennett and Bruce E. Kaufman (New Brunswick, NJ: Transaction Publishers, 2007), pp. 79–113. The earlier study referred to is Richard B. Freeman and James L. Medoff, *What Do Unions Do?* (New York: Basic Books, 1984). One difficulty in precisely identifying the union wage premium is that union status is not exogenously determined, but rather, firms and workers that become unionized are likely to exhibit characteristics that increase this likelihood. For instance, if high-wage firms are more likely to be organized, a higher union wage might be observed, but it would not be because of the union's presence. In a recent attempt to disentangle these factors, John DiNardo and David S. Lee compared wages in newly organized firms where unions barely won the union representation election (e.g., by one vote) to firms in which the union barely lost, essentially seeking to compare firms that had virtually the same likelihood of being organized. Contrary to the vast empirical literature, they find no difference in wages paid. See Dinardo and Lee, "Economic Impacts of Unionization on Private Sector Employers: 1984–2001," *Quarterly Journal of Economics* 119, no. 4 (November 2004): 1383–1441. This atypical result may, however, not be representative of outcomes in firms in which the union has stronger support; see David S. Lee and Alexandre Mas, "Long-Run Impacts of Unions on Firms: New Evidence from Financial Markets, 1961–1999," Princeton University Working Paper (July 2008).

[32] Blanchflower and Bryson, "What Effect Do Unions Have on Wages Now?" in Bennett and Kaufman, eds., *What Do Unions Do?*

[33] Milkman, "Two Worlds of Unionism"; and William E. Even and David A. Macpherson, "The Decline of Private Sector Unionism and the Gender Wage Gap," *Journal of Human Resources* 28, no. 2 (1993): 279–96.

thus increasing the gender wage gap. As men's and women's unionization rates have become more similar, the gender wage gap has been correspondingly reduced.[34]

The extent to which workers are unionized also has profound effects on wage inequality, more generally. Because unions provide relatively high-paying job opportunities for many less-skilled workers, their presence tends to reduce overall wage inequality, while deunionization has the opposite effect. Thus, the dramatic decline in men's unionization in recent years has contributed to rising male wage inequality in the United States. For women, this factor had little effect, in part because their initial rates of unionism were much lower and, subsequently, fell much less.[35] Further, unions tend to increase the fringe benefits of their members relative to their nonunion counterparts. Hence, another serious consequence of deunionization has been a reduction in health insurance coverage.[36]

Finally, advocates of unions argue that unions provide important nonpecuniary benefits to their members, chiefly by giving them a greater opportunity to shape their work environment by communicating their preferences to employers through the collective bargaining process and by providing grievance procedures.[37] In addition, unions offer the potential to help reduce the tension between work and family by negotiating for such benefits as family leave, on-site day care, and flexible schedules. These benefits are not only particularly important for women workers but also increasingly for men, as they share more household responsibilities.

Even though unions offer these advantages to workers, to the extent that the demand for labor is responsive to cost, unionization is also associated with lower employment. Hence, the gains of those who get greater rewards are at least in part at the expense of those who are not hired, or are displaced, as a result of unionization.

Reasons for the Historic Underrepresentation of Women in Unions

In light of the advantages workers gain from union membership, how do we explain the historic underrepresentation of women in unions? Interestingly, the evidence does not show that women exhibit a lesser "taste" or preference for unionism. In fact, considerable evidence indicates that among workers who are not currently unionized, women tend to be more supportive of collective action to achieve their goals than men and are more likely to vote for union representation.[38] However, women have tended to be concentrated in industries and occupations where rates of unionization were lower. As already noted, traditionally, unionization was highest among blue-collar workers in manufacturing, while women were concentrated in clerical and service occupations and in service industries, with lower unionization rates. Moreover, within the manufacturing

---

[34] Even and Macpherson, "The Decline of Private Sector Unionism"; Francine D. Blau and Lawrence M. Kahn, "The US Gender Pay Gap in the 1990s: Slowing Convergence," *Industrial and Labor Relations Review* 60, no. 1 (October 2006): 45–66; and Francine D. Blau, "Trends in the Well-Being of American Women: 1970–95," *Journal of Economic Literature* 36, no. 1 (March 1998): 112–65. In the latter paper, Blau reports that the decline in unionism lowered the real wages of men by 2.8 percent and of women by 1.6 percent, thereby narrowing the gender gap.

[35] David Card, Thomas Lemieux, and W. Craig Riddell, "Unions and Wage Inequality," in Bennett and Kaufman, eds., *What Do Unions Do?*, pp. 114–59; and Richard B. Freeman, "How Much Has De-Unionization Contributed to the Rise in Male Earnings Inequality?" in *Uneven Tides: Rising Inequality in America*, edited by Sheldon Danziger and Peter Gottschalk (New York: Russell Sage Foundation, 1993), pp. 133–64.

[36] Thomas C. Buchmeuller, John E. Dinardo, and Robert G. Valletta, "Union Effects on Health Insurance Provision and Coverage in the United States," *Industrial and Labor Relations Review* 55, no. 4 (July 2002): 610–27.

[37] Richard B. Freeman termed this process the *voice effect* of unions; see "Individual Mobility and Union Voice in the Labor Market," *American Economic Review* 66, no. 2 (May 1976): 361–68. For a recent discussion, see John T. Addison and Clive R. Belfield, "Union Voice," in Bennett and Kaufman, eds., *What Do Unions Do?*, pp. 238–74.

[38] Kate Bronfenbrenner, "Organizing Women: The Nature and Process of Union Organizing Efforts Among U.S. Women Since the Mid-1990s," *Work and Occupations* 32, no. 4 (Nov. 2005): 441–63.

sector, women are concentrated in the more competitive industries, while unionization occurs more frequently in monopolistic industries. Indeed, one study found that the major factor behind the decline in the gender gap in unionization between 1973 and 1988 was the decline of unionism in traditionally male sectors.[39] As discussed earlier, women's increasing labor force attachment, which has increased the gains to unionization for women, is an additional factor that has likely contributed to the narrowing of the gap in recent years.

Historically, the policies of unions themselves also contributed to women's underrepresentation among their ranks. Male craft unions did not begin to admit women until the late 1800s[40] and failed to be hospitable to women (or blacks) long after they no longer formally excluded them. Also, unions have been criticized for their less than vigorous efforts to organize women workers and lack of support for women's own efforts to unionize. Moreover, the tendency of unions to emphasize issues of greater concern to male workers, while neglecting women's concerns, likely decreased the appeal of unions for women.[41] For example, fringe benefits such as health insurance might be of less value to women workers because many of them are members of two-earner families and are frequently already covered under their husbands' plans. On the other hand, benefits such as parental leave and day care are generally of greater interest to women than to men.

The Glass Ceiling in Union Leadership

Although women now comprise 44 percent of all union members, they appear to face a glass ceiling here, as in corporate America, when it comes to leadership positions, especially top posts at the national level. For instance, in 2008 only 18 percent of AFL-CIO executive council members were women.[42] The Coalition of Labor Union Women (CLUW), an advocacy group, was formed in 1974 with the express goal of moving women into such positions. To date, women have made impressive gains in unions with large female memberships although they still rarely attain top positions in predominately male unions.[43] Women are also underrepresented among union organizers (those seeking to unionize currently unorganized workers). This is particularly striking in light of the fact that the majority of recently organized workers are women.[44]

The reasons for the lack of women in key leadership roles are not entirely clear, but most likely reflect the same types of barriers encountered by women in other organizations, from corporations and foundations to elective positions in government. First, because women still generally retain the primary responsibility for housework and children, many employed women must juggle family and job responsibilities, leaving little time for union activities. Such participation can require as much as 20 to 40 hours of work per week and, at the local level, is often unpaid. Further, election to top leadership positions often takes years of working with rank-and-file members. Many men begin

---

[39] Even and Macpherson, "The Decline of Private Sector Unionism."
[40] Barbara M. Wertheimer and Anne H. Nelson, "'Union Is Power': Sketches from Women's Labor History," in *Women: A Feminist Perspective,* 4th ed., edited by Jo Freeman (Palo Alto, CA: Mayfield, 1989), pp. 312–28. See also Alice Kessler-Harris, *Gendering Labor History* (Urbana, IL: University of Illinois Press, 2007); and Margaret S. Coleman, "Undercounted and Underpaid Heroines: The Path to Equal Opportunity Employment During the Twentieth Century," *Working USA* 3, no. 5 (January–February 2000): 37–65.
[41] For further discussion, see Anne Forrest, "Connecting Women with Unions: What Are the Issues?" *Industrial Relations* (Canadian) 56, no. 4 (Autumn 2001): 647–77.
[42] "About AFL-CIO," at www.aflcio.org, accessed January 2008.
[43] Milkman, "Two Worlds of Unionism."
[44] Bronfenbrenner, "Organizing Women."

these activities in their twenties, the same years where many women start childbearing. This makes it difficult for women to devote their time to union activities on an equal basis. Finally, evidence suggests that women tend to underestimate their abilities and are thus less likely to put themselves forward for leadership positions.[45]

As is true in other organizations, the existing underrepresentation of women in union leadership positions itself also hinders women's advancement because it reduces the opportunities for women to find role models and receive informal mentoring, and also makes them more likely to be perceived as "outsiders." In addition, women frequently lack the crucial education and experience required for leadership positions, such as negotiating skills and institutional knowledge about union offices. Finally, as is true for women who are trying to progress through hierarchies in corporate America and elsewhere, women must often contend with the perception that they are not "tough" enough to negotiate contracts or participate in bargaining, and in the case of unions, they may even face retaliation by bosses for union activism.[46]

Prospects for Women in Unions

In spite of all these problems, important recent efforts at the national level in the AFL-CIO and among international unions have been opening up leadership positions to women. Under the auspices of its president, John Sweeney, the AFL-CIO created the position of executive vice president to be filled by a woman trade union activist. In addition, the executive council was expanded to allow for greater female representation, and one position was designated for a representative from the CLUW, signaling the importance of this group. In 2005, the AFL-CIO passed a resolution to increase the racial and gender diversity of those serving as delegates at future constitutional conventions, and also to increase the representation of women and other underrepresented groups in leadership roles within the organization. Further, the resolution called for affiliated unions and councils to follow suit and increase diversity in the upper ranks of their organizations.[47] While such policies are intended to help members of underrepresented groups, they carry the risk that these individuals will be viewed as mere tokens, especially if they are appointed to such posts rather than elected. Nonetheless, these positions do provide them with an up-close view of the decision-making process and give them an opportunity to demonstrate they can do the job. Karen Nussbaum, the founder of the union "9 to 5" and a longtime labor activist, observes that another positive sign is that a woman serves as head of Change to Win (CTW), the new union federation created in 2005.[48]

Conclusion

In this chapter we examined a number of developments in the labor market, notably the growth of nonstandard work, women's rising self-employment, and the decline and changing role of labor unions, and considered the impact of each on women and men in the labor force. There have been some favorable developments such as women's rising self-employment, but other changes, such as the growth of nonstandard work, raise concerns for both women and men workers. Some developments have actually hurt men more, principally deunionization, because they had the highest rates of unionization and their rates declined most dramatically.

---

[45] *I Knew I Could Do This Work: Seven Strategies That Promote Women's Activism and Leadership in Unions* (Washington, DC: Institute for Women's Policy Research, 2007).

[46] *I Knew I Could Do This Work*; and contributions in Cobble, ed., *The Sex of Class*.

[47] Karen Nussbaum, "Working Women's Insurgent Consciousness," in Dorothy Sue Cobble, ed., *The Sex of Class*.

[48] Karen Nussbaum, "Working Women's Insurgent Consciousness."

Questions for Review and Discussion

1. It is said that various factors either "push" or "pull" individuals into self-employment. Provide an example or two of each.
2. What are the pros and cons of nonstandard employment for workers?

3. What obstacles are there to women rising to leadership positions in unions? How are these obstacles similar to or different from those facing women in business, academia, and government?

Suggested Readings

Bennett, James T., and Bruce E. Kaufman, eds. *What Do Unions Do? The Evidence Twenty Years Later.* New Brunswick, NY: Transaction Publishers, 2007.

Carré, Francoise, Marianne A. Ferber, Lonnie Golden, and Steve Herzenberg, eds. *Nonstandard Work Arrangements and the Changing Labor Market: Dimensions, Causes, and Institutional Responses.* Industrial Relations Research Association Research Volume, 2000.

Cobble, Dorothy Sue, ed. *The Sex of Class: Women Transforming American Labor.* Ithaca, NY: ILR Press, 2007.

Freeman, Richard B., and James L. Medoff. *What Do Unions Do?* New York: Basic Books, 1984.

Houseman, Susan, and Machiko Osawa, eds. *Nonstandard Work in Developed Economies.* Kalamazoo, MI: W.E. Upjohn Institute, 2003.

Kruse, Douglas, and Joseph Blasi. "The New Employee-Employer Relationship." In *A Working Nation: Workers, Work, and Government in the New Economy,* edited by David T. Ellwood, Rebecca M. Blank, Joseph Blasi, Douglas Kruse, William A. Niskanen, and Karen Lynn-Dyson, Chapter 2, pp. 42–91. New York: Russell Sage Foundation, 2000.

Key Terms

nonstandard workforce *259*

temporary help agency workers *260*

on-call workers *260*

contract workers *260*

independent contractors *260*

part-time workers *261*

self-employment *264*

union membership *266*

union wage advantage *268*

CHAPTER **10**

Changing Work Roles and the Family

Chapter Highlights

- Economic Explanations for Family Formation
- Marriage
- Divorce
- Cohabitation: Opposite-Sex and Gay and Lesbian Couples

- Fertility
- Changing Family Structure and Economic Well-Being

In earlier chapters, we discussed the family as an economic institution and the allocation of time of husband and wife between the household and the labor market. We then looked in detail at gender differences in labor market outcomes and their determinants. In this chapter, we return our attention to the family, but we now focus on describing and explaining the trends in family structure and also consider the consequences of the changes in family structure for the well-being of family members. One important difference between our approach here and in Chapter 4 is that there we accepted marital status and fertility as given, exogenous to our models, and focused on the effects of these factors on women's labor force participation. In this chapter, we turn the tables and examine the impact of economic factors, including women's labor force participation, on demographic outcomes.

The first sections of this chapter deal with the effect of economic factors on the incidence of marriage, divorce, and cohabitation by opposite-sex and gay and lesbian couples, and on fertility. Next, we look at the relationship between changing family structure and economic well-being, focusing on both dual-earner families and single-parent families. One of the most important issues raised by changes in family structure and increases in the labor market activity of women is the consequences of these developments for the well-being of children. Thus, we review the literature on the effect of maternal employment on children's development and then examine the effect of family structure on measures of children's future success.

ECONOMIC EXPLANATIONS FOR FAMILY FORMATION

What is the expected effect of economic factors, including women's increased labor force participation, on family formation? From the viewpoint of neoclassical economics, the determining factor in decisions concerning family issues such as marriage, divorce, and fertility is whether the benefits exceed

273

the costs.[1] Thus, the question arises as to the effect of women's increasing labor force participation and other economic factors on the costs and benefits associated with these decisions—do more or fewer couples choose to marry, divorce, or bear children? As we shall see, the answer to this question is not obvious from a theoretical point of view. That is, forces operate both to reduce and to increase the benefits and costs of these decisions leaving the outcome uncertain.

Marriage

Marriage offers a number of potential economic advantages. A useful starting point for our consideration of them follows from our discussion of specialization and exchange in Chapter 3. By facilitating specialization and exchange, marriage potentially increases the couple's productivity and economic well-being. In general, the larger the *difference* in comparative advantage in producing home and market goods between the two partners, the larger the potential gain to marriage, for each partner may then specialize mainly or entirely in his or her area of higher relative productivity. Further, as discussed in Chapter 3, even if a husband and wife do not differ in their comparative advantage, marriage confers a range of other potential benefits. For one, marriage provides economies of scale because the cost of housing and food is much lower on a per person basis if shared. Marriage also increases the enjoyment of public goods, such as a well-tended garden, because both spouses can take pleasure in the view together. Further, marriage allows spouses to share financial risk if one of them loses a job or wants to make a career switch. These benefits can also be reaped, at least to some extent, by unmarried couples, rommmates, or those living in extended families. A particular advantage of marriage, however, is that it offers greater legal protections than these alternatives if the relationsip were to end. As a result, it fosters investments in "marriage-specific" capital including children and each others' areas of recreational and cultural interest, which in turn enhance the gains from the partnership.

In years past, when the dominant married-couple paradigm was a homemaker wife and a breadwinner husband, the gains from specialization and exchange were large, as each partner had a considerable comparative advantage in his or her domain. With the rise in dual-earner couples, the gains to specialization and exchange have diminished. As discussed in Chapter 4 and subsequent chapters, women have acquired more job-oriented education and training, which has lead to higher potential market wages and rising rates of labor force participation. They have also encountered less discrimination in the labor market than in the past, further raising their market wage and spurring investments in their human capital. The availability of reliable contraceptive technology, particularly the birth control pill, which became available to married women in the early 1960s, has also permitted women to focus on their careers, without the risk of pregnancy.[2] As a result of these developments, women's market productivity has increased relative to the value of time spent in the home, reducing the gains from specialization and exchange and the attractiveness of marriage. Enhanced market opportunities for women also serve to reduce marriage by making the alternative of remaining single more economically feasible and attractive from a financial standpoint.

---

[1] Seminal work by neoclassical economists on the economics of the family was first done by Gary S. Becker and is summarized by him in *A Treatise on the Family* (Cambridge, MA: Harvard University Press, 1991). A good deal of work on this subject has also been done by Shoshana Grossbard-Shechtman, *On the Economics of Marriage* (Boulder, CO: Westview Press, 1993). For a recent discussion and evidence, see Shelly Lundberg and Robert A. Pollak, "The American Family and Family Economics," *Journal of Economic Perspectives* 21, no. 2 (Spring 2007): 3–26.

[2] Claudia Goldin and Lawrence F. Katz, "Career and Marriage in the Age of the Pill," *American Economic Review* 90, no. 2 (May 2000): 461–65.

Changes in men's market productivity also affect the gains from specialization and exchange, and hence marriage. Higher male earnings increase the gains to specialization and hence raise the likelihood of marriage.[3] As discussed in Chapter 8, economic outcomes for less-educated men, in particular, have deteriorated considerably since 1980. This fall in male market productivity, which has reduced the gains to specialization and exchange from marriage, is particularly relevant in explaining recent declines in marriage among the less educated.

Gains from specialization have also fallen as a result of changes in how household goods are produced. The near ubiquity of household appliances such as the microwave oven, along with the emergence of high-quality market substitutes for home cooked meals, have reduced the relative value of time spent on household production and hence the gains from specialization and exchange. A further factor reducing the gains from specialization is the liberalization of state divorce laws that started in the 1970s, including the introduction of no-fault and unilateral divorce. These changes, which increased the bargaining power of the partner most interested in exiting the marriage, reduce incentives for marriage-specific investments, including specializing in nonmarket production.[4]

Thus, a number of factors have substantially reduced the gains to marriage from specialization in production and this development is expected to have a negative effect on the incidence of marriage. However, even as the gains to specialization have declined, not only do other advantages to marriage remain, including economies of scale, the enjoyment of public goods and benefits from marriage-specific investments, but it may be argued that the gains from shared consumption have increased.[5] This is expected to be the case to the extent that two-earner couples have more similar tastes and experiences than traditional couples. With two incomes, spouses are also able to spend more money on leisure activities that they can engage in together further enhancing joint consumption. A further benefit reaped by two earners, which has likely become increasingly important given the uncertainties of our ever-changing global economy, is that the spouses are able to share risk and so are not entirely dependent on one income.

Thus we see that, on the one hand, women's increased labor force participation has reduced the gains to specialization and, from that perspective, it should reduce marriage. On the other hand, it has left a number of other potential benefits of marriage unaffected and has likely increased the gains to shared consumption. All told, without empirical evidence it is not possible to say whether the net impact of women's rising labor force participation has served to decrease or increase marriage rates.

Several other factors also affect the decision to marry. One of these is the availability of marriage partners. Demographic trends, for one, may lead to an insufficient supply of women or men and, in turn, reduce marriage rates.[6] As an example, consider the baby boom, the period when birth rates rose considerably, which lasted from the end of

---

[3] Further, as will be discussed shortly, the opportunities for specialization that marriage affords appear to increase men's market productivity and hence their earnings. Thus, for men, marriage and earnings likely have reinforcing effects. See Avner Ahituv and Robert I. Lerman, "How Do Marital Status, Work Effort, and Wage Rates Interact?" *Demography* 44, no. 3 (August 2007): 623–47.

[4] Betsy Stevenson, "The Impact of Divorce Laws on Marriage-Specific Capital," *Journal of Labor Economics* 25, no. 1 (January 2007): 75–94.

[5] Betsey Stevenson and Justin Wolfers, "Marriage and Divorce: Changes and their Driving Forces," *Journal of Economic Perspectives* 21, no. 2 (Spring 2007): 27–52; Lundberg and Pollak, "The American Family and Family Economics." Early discussions of the benefits of shared consumption include Francine D. Blau and Marianne A. Ferber, *The Economics of Women, Men, and Work*, 1st edition (Upper Saddle River, NJ: Prentice Hall, 1981), Chapters 3 and 5; and David Lam, "Marriage Markets and Assortative Mating with Household Public Goods," *Journal of Human Resources* 23, no. 4 (Fall 1988): 462–87.

[6] Grossbard-Shechtman, *On the Economics of Marriage*, Chapters 4 and 5; and Joshua Angrist, "How Do Sex Ratios Affect Marriage and Labor Markets? Evidence from America's Second Generation," *Quarterly Journal of Economics* 117, no. 3 (August 2002): 997–1038.

World War II to the early 1960s. Women born during the early part of the baby boom encountered a particular imbalance in the marriage market because the men that these women sought to marry, typically several years older than themselves, were from a smaller birth cohort. For these women, the number of available partners was lower, creating what has been called a "marriage squeeze."[7] William Julius Wilson has further observed that women's propensity to marry depends not only on the availability of men in the marriage market, but also on the availability of men with decent earnings prospects, who he has termed *marriageable men*.[8] Wilson's point is closely related to our earlier discussion of decreasing gains to specialization for the less educated due to declining labor market earnings of less-educated men. High incarceration rates of males have also been identified as a contributing factor to an insufficient supply of men and hence lower marriage rates.[9] These factors are particularly relevant in understanding marriage patterns among African Americans given that African American men tend to have lower average educational attainment as well as higher incarceration rates as compared to their white counterparts.

Government transfer programs and tax policies also have the potential to affect whether and when to marry. For instance, prior to the passage of the federal welfare reform legislation of 1996, there was considerable concern that the existing welfare program, Aid to Families with Dependent Children (AFDC), which largely provided benefits to single parents and their children, discouraged marriage. This was one of a number of reasons that changes in this program were advocated, leading to reform of the welfare system in 1996. However, a considerable amount of research strongly suggests that the AFDC program could not have lead to the large shift in family structure away from marriage toward single-parent families that began in the 1970s, even among the low-income women who would be expected to be particularly sensitive to this program.[10] The potential impact of tax policies on marriage is discussed at length in Chapter 11.

Finally, changes in social norms, principally the dramatic liberalization in attitudes toward divorce, cohabitation, and sex outside of marriage beginning in the 1960s and 1970s, have undoubtedly affected the decision to marry, its timing, and whether childbearing occurs within marriage or outside of it.[11] In particular, by reducing the benefits to marriage (or the costs of remaining unmarried), these trends have likely contributed to a delay of marriage and a reduction in marriage rates.

Table 10-1 show the net impact of these various factors on trends in marriage rates from 1960 to 2006. From 1960 to 1970, marriage rates rose from 8.5 to 10.6 marriages per 1,000 population; they remained at about that level until 1980 and have declined steadily since then, reaching 7.3 marriages per 1,000 population in 2006. Based on the research evidence, it appears that the rapid entry of women into the labor

---

[7] Paul Glick, "Fifty Years of Family Demography: A Record of Social Change," *Journal of Marriage and the Family* 50, no. 4 (November 1988): 861–73.

[8] This theory is presented in William J. Wilson and Kathryn Neckerman, "Poverty and Family Structure: The Widening Gap Between Evidence and Public Policy Issues," in *Fighting Poverty: What Works and What Doesn't*, edited by Sheldon Danziger and Daniel Weinberg (Cambridge, MA: Harvard University Press, 1986), pp. 232–59.

[9] Kerwin Kofi Charles and Ming Ching Luoh, "Male Incarceration, the Marriage Market and Female Outcomes," mimeo, University of Michigan (2006).

[10] Robert A. Moffitt, "The Temporary Assistance for Needy Families Program," in *Means-Tested Transfer Programs in the United States*, edited by Robert A. Moffitt (Chicago: University of Chicago Press, 2003), pp. 291–363; Carolyn M. Moehling, "The American Welfare System and Family Structure," *Journal of Human Resources* 42, no. 1 (Winter 2007): 117–55; and for a review, Robert A. Moffitt, "The Effect of Welfare on Marriage and Fertility" in *Welfare, the Family, and Reproductive Behavior: Research Perspectives*, edited by Robert A. Moffitt (Washington, DC: National Research Council, 1998), pp. 50–97.

[11] Arland Thornton and Linda Young-DeMarco, "Four Decades of Trends in Attitudes Toward Family Issues in the United States: The 1960s Through the 1990s," *Journal of Marriage and the Family* 63 (November 2001): 1009–37.

TABLE 10-1   Trends in Family Structure, 1960–2006

	1960	1970	1980	1990	2000	2006
Marriage rate per 1,000 population	8.5	10.6	10.6	9.8	8.3	7.3
Cohabitation rate (unmarried, opposite-sex couples per 100 married couples)	1.1	1.2	3.2	5.5	8.6	9.2
Divorce rate per 1,000 population	2.2	3.5	5.2	4.7	4.1	3.6
Dual-earner couples (as % of all married couples)	45.0	50.1	53.5	59.4	60.0	57.5

Notes: For dual-earners, 1960 figure is for 1968 and 1970 figure is for 1976.

Source: U.S. Census Bureau, detailed tables from www.census.gov: Table UC-1, "Unmarried-Couple Households by Presence of Children," Table HH-1, "Households by Type: 1940–Present," and Table F-13, "Work Experience of Husband and Wife—All Married-Couple Families by Median and Mean Income;" U.S. Census Bureau, *Statistical Abstract of the United States: 2007*, Table 76; U.S. Department of Health and Human Services, "Births, Marriages, Divorces, and Deaths: Provisional Data for 2006," *National Vital Statistics Reports* 55, no. 20, August 28, 2007; and Howard Hayghe, "Husbands and Wives as Earners: An Analysis of Family Data," *Monthly Labor Review* 104, no. 2 (February 1981): 46–59.

market important is responsible for at least part of the recent decline in marriage rates.[12] Returning to the earlier discussion, this finding suggests that the decline in the gains to specialization and exchange has been the dominant factor in determining marriage trends rather than any increase in the benefit of shared consumption that may have also occurred. Undoubtly, the liberalization of social attitudes has also played a role. However, some of the decline in the incidence of marriage reflects a postponement of marriage by young men and women rather than their forgoing it completely. Postponement can be seen in the rising median age of first marriage for both women and men, along with the dramatic increase in the fraction of young women and men who have never been married, as shown in Table 10-2. In 1970, for example, only 36 percent of women age 20 to 24 had never been married as compared with fully 75 percent in 2006.

   Women's rising economic opportunities, which encouraged young women to stay in school longer and, in many cases, to pursue careers, were the major factor behind this postponement. Claudia Goldin and Larry Katz also point to the pivotal role of the birth control pill, which became widely available to *single* women starting in the late 1960s and early 1970s, in fostering this delay. It allowed young women to postpone marriage and pursue college and professional training without incurring the cost of abstinence or facing a substantial risk of an unwanted pregnancy that could derail their studies. Further, as more and more women delayed marriage, the risk of waiting to marry and then losing out on finding a good marriage partner also fell.[13]

   As marriage rates have declined, cohabitation rates have increased. Table 10-1 shows that the ratio of unmarried to married couples increased from 1:100 in 1960 and

---

[12] Evidence that women's improved labor market opportunities lead to this decline is provided by T. Paul Schultz, "Marital Status and Fertility in the United States," *Journal of Human Resources* 29, no. 2 (Spring 1994): 637–69; and Francine D. Blau, Lawrence M. Kahn, and Jane Waldfogel, "Understanding Young Women's Marriage Decisions: The Role of Labor Market and Marriage Market Conditions," *Industrial and Labor Relations Review* 53, no. 4 (July 2000): 624–47. However, Valerie Kincade Oppenheimer and Vivian Lew question the emphasis placed on this factor; see "American Marriage Formation in the 1980s: How Important Was Women's Economic Independence?" in *Gender and Family Change in Industrialized Countries*, edited by Karen Oppenheim Mason and An-Magitt Jensen (Oxford: Clarendon Press, 1995).

[13] Goldin and Katz, "Career and Marriage in the Age of the Pill." See also Martha J. Bailey, "More Power to the Pill: The Impact of Contraceptive Freedom on Women's Life Cycle Labor Supply," *Quarterly Journal of Economics* 121, no. 1 (February 2006): 289–320.

TABLE 10-2 Timing of Marriage and Percentage Married, 1970–2006

	1970	1980	1990	2000	2006
Median Age at First Marriage					
Men	23.2	24.7	26.1	26.8	27.5
Women	20.8	22.0	23.9	25.1	25.5
% Never-Married Men					
Age 20–24	54.7	68.8	79.3	83.7	86.7
Age 40–44	6.3	7.1	10.5	15.7	18.5
% Never-Married Women					
Age 20–24	35.8	50.2	62.8	72.8	75.3
Age 40–44	4.9	4.8	8.0	11.8	13.1
% Married Adults, Ages 18+	71.7	65.5	61.9	59.5	58.1
Whites	72.6	67.2	64.0	62.0	60.6
Blacks	64.1	51.4	45.8	42.1	40.1
Asians	n.a.	n.a.	n.a.	n.a.	64.3
Hispanic origin	71.8	65.6	61.7	60.2	58.4

Notes: Person of Hispanic origin can be of any race.

n.a. Not available.

Source: U.S. Census Bureau, detailed tables from www.census.gov: Table MS-2, "Estimated Median Age at First Marriage, by Sex, 1890 to the Present" and Table A1, "Marital Status of People 15 Years and Over by Age, Sex, Personal Earnings, Race, and Hispanic Origin;" U.S. Census Bureau, *America's Families and Living Arrangements* (2000 and 2006); U.S. Census Bureau, "Marital Status and Living Arrangements: March 1994," *Current Population Report* P20–484 (Feb. 1996), Tables A-1, A-2, and A-3; and U.S. Census Bureau, U.S. *Statistical Abstract: 2008*, Table 55.

1970 to more than 9:100 in 2006 and many more individuals undoubtedly cohabited at some point, if only briefly. This increase suggests that cohabitation serves as an alternative to marriage, at least to some extent. Nevertheless, most individuals eventually marry; the proportion of people who never marry in their lifetime, in recent years about 5 percent, is not expected to increase to more than 10 percent in the foreseeable future.[14] One important difference from past patterns, however, is that more children are now being born to unmarried mothers.

Table 10-2 also provides figures on the fraction of adults currently married, which reflect trends in the rate and timing of first marriage, divorce, and remarriage.[15] As may be seen in the table, the fraction of currently married adults has declined most among blacks. This shift appears to reflect black women's rising economic opportunities combined with black men's often poor job prospects. In addition, especially in inner cities, high rates of homicide and incarceration have futher contributed to the decline by reducing the number of "marriageable" young black men.[16]

---

[14] Figure is from U.S. Census Bureau, "Number, Timing, and Duration of Marriages and Divorces: 1996," *Current Population Reports* P70–80 (February 2002).

[15] For detailed trends by race, see Adam Isen and Betsey Stevenson, "Women's Education and Family Behavior: Trends in Marriage, Divorce and Fertility," Wharton Working Paper (2008).

[16] T. Paul Schultz finds that black women's marriage rates are more greatly affected by their husband's economic prospects than by their own in "Eroding the Economic Foundations of Marriage and Fertility in the United States," *Structural Change and Economic Dynamics* 9, no. 4 (December 1998): 391–413. See also, Geoffrey L. Wallace, "An Assessment of Several Marriage Market Related Explanations for the Decline in Female Marriage Rates Between 1970 and 1980," LaFollette School of Public Affairs Working Paper No. 2006-030 (2006); and Charles and Luoh, "Male Incarceration, the Marriage Market and Female Outcomes."

A similar trend, not shown in the table, is the marked decline in first marriage and remarriage for less-educated women and men relative to their more highly educated counterparts.[17] While low earnings and employment difficulties pose a substantial obstacle to marriage among the less educated, researchers point to other barriers for this group as well.[18] Among these, disadvantaged women may be avoiding marriage because of concerns about future divorce. Such concerns are not unfounded given higher rates of divorce for this group. Another factor found to be important is women's concerns about whether they can fully rely on and trust male partners. These views are likely related, at least in part, to the fragile economic situation of many of these couples.

In conclusion, despite the decline in the overall marriage rate in the United States since 1980, marriage remains the norm in the United States and, as we shall see in Chapter 12, the U.S. marriage rate remains one of the highest among the economically advanced nations. Furthermore, most people who get divorced do eventually remarry, though the remarriage rate has also declined, no doubt for the same reasons that caused marriage rates to fall.[19] The continuing relatively high rates of marriage and remarriage rates in the United States suggest that marriage remains central to the lives of many Americans.

Divorce

A number of factors affect a couple's decision to **divorce**.[20] Again, the gains to specialization provide a useful starting place. For traditional married couples, the interdependence of husband and wife due to specialization and exchange is probably the single most important economic deterrent to divorce. Both partners have invested in a very specific set of skills in their sphere, whether the home or market. Over the years, the development of marriage-specific human capital further cements this interdependent relationship. With women's rising labor force participation, the gains from specialization and exchange are reduced and the propensity to divorce is likely to increase. On the other hand, as discussed in the case of marriage, the similar experiences of husbands and wives in dual-earner couples may enhance the quality of their married lives, thereby making their union more enduring.

Women's increased labor force participation not only reduces the gains within marriage, but it also increases the financial viability of exiting a marriage and supporting oneself. For partners in an unhappy marriage, a divorce may be an improvement for all concerned. In such instances, we may observe a positive relationship between women's paid work and and divorce, but it is not necessarily the case that paid employment *caused* the divorce, but rather that women's market earnings provide the means to exit an unhappy situation. For instance, one study found that the relationship between women's increased labor force participation and divorce depends on whether the spouses were happily married prior to the wife's entry into the labor market. The wife's labor force participation was found to have no effect on the likelihood of divorce for couples with a fulfilling marriage, but her participation was found to increase the likelihood of divorce in unhappy couples.[21]

---

[17] For detailed data by educational attainment, see Isen and Stevenson, "Women's Education and Family Behavior."

[18] Kathryn Edin and Joanna M. Reed, "Why Don't They Just Get Married? Barriers to Marriage Among the Disadvantaged," *The Future of Children* 15, no. 2 (2005): 117–37.

[19] See Department of Health and Human Services, Centers for Disease Control and Prevention, *Cohabitation, Marriage, Divorce, and Remarriage in the United States*, Series 23, no. 22 (July 2002). See also, Stevenson and Wolfers, "Marriage and Divorce"; and Andrew Cherlin, "American Marriage in the Early Twenty-First Century," *The Future of Children* 15, no. 2 (Fall 2005): 33–55.

[20] Gary S. Becker, Elisabeth M. Landes, and Robert T. Michael, "An Economic Analysis of Marital Instability," *Journal of Political Economy* 85, no. 6 (December 1977): 1141–87.

[21] Robert Schoen, Nan Marie Astone, Kendra Rothert, Nicola J. Standish, and Joung J. Kim, "Women's Employment, Marital Happiness, and Divorce," *Social Forces* 81, no. 2 (December 2002): 643–62.

Unanticipated events that occur in a marriage are another factor that may tip the decision toward divorce. One example is a sudden job loss for one or both partners.[22] Another example of an unexpected change is the shift in long-accepted norms regarding gender roles, such as the change that occured during the 1960s and 1970s. These changes, thrust upon husbands and wives who married under very different circumstances and assumptions, likely altered their preferences and needs, thereby increasing the propensity to divorce.

Considerable interest continues to surround the impact of the liberalization of state divorce laws in the 1970s on the divorce rate. These changes included the adoption of "no-fault" divorce, where the spouse who is seeking a divorce does not have to show that the other partner did something wrong in order to obtain it, and unilateral divorce, where divorce can proceed if just one spouse seeks to terminate the marriage rather than requiring both spouses to agree to termination. These changes not only made it easier to divorce, but effectively increased the bargaining power of the partner most interested in exiting the marriage. On the one hand, some have argued that these changes should not increase the divorce rate if spouses are able to make adequate adjustments within marriage, such as shifting resources toward the partner with the newly increased bargaining power. On the other hand, others have argued that divorce rates should rise either because bargaining within the marriage would be difficult or because the changes in the law reduced legal costs. While the research evidence is mixed, one recent study suggests that the liberalization of divorce laws directly increased the divorce rate, but only temporarily, for about 2 years after the changes in the law.[23] The changes in the rules governing divorce might also affect which couples marry in the first place. It has been argued that now that it is easier for either partner to dissolve a marriage, couples who choose to marry these days tend to be those who are better matched and thus have more to gain from marriage.[24] To the extent that this argument is valid, the propensity to divorce is expected to decline.

Given that many couples who divorce have children, changes in rules governing child support—income provided by noncustodial parents—may also affect spouses' decisions regarding divorce. In recent years enforcement of these provisions has become stricter, but the effect of this policy change on divorce is not clear a priori. On the one hand, if the expected payment increases, the spouse who expects to get the payments would presumably be more willing to terminate the marriage because these payments provide a financial cushion; at the same time the partner who must make such payments would be less likely to favor breaking up the marriage. Some research suggests that stricter child support enforcement discourages divorce while other research finds no net effect.[25]

---

[22] Interestingly, one recent study finds that the likelihood of divorce tends to increases after a layoff not so much due to the financial loss but rather due to the negative "signal" about the partner's employment prospects; see Kerwin Kofi Charles and Melvin Stephens, Jr., "Job Displacement, Disability, and Divorce," *Journal of Labor Economics* 22, no. 2 (April 2004): 489–522.

[23] Justin Wolfers, "Did Unilateral Divorce Raise Divorce Rates: Reconciliation and New Results," *American Economic Review* 96, no. 5 (December 2006): 1802–20. For earlier evidence that no-fault divorce did not increase the divorce rate, see H. Elizabeth Peters, "Marriage and Divorce: Informational Constraints and Private Contracting," *American Economic Review* 76, no. 3 (June 1986): 437–54; and Jeffrey S. Gray, "Divorce-Law Changes and Married Women's Labor Supply," *American Economic Review* 88, no. 3 (June 1998): 628–42. For earlier evidence on the other side, see Leora Friedberg, "Did Unilateral Divorce Raise Divorce Rates?" *American Economic Review* 88, no. 3 (June 1998): 608–27.

[24] Imran Rasul, "Marriage Markets and Divorce Laws, *Journal of Law, Economics, and Organization* 22, no. 1 (Spring 2006): 30–69.

[25] Lucia Nixon finds that the latter effect dominates, that is, more vigorous child support enforcement discourages divorce in "The Effect of Child Support Enforcement on Marital Dissolution," *Journal of Human Resources* 32, no. 1 (Winter 1997): 159–81; while Bradley T. Heim finds no effect in "Does Child Support Enforcement Reduce Divorce Rates? A Reexamination," *Journal of Human Resources* 38, no. 4 (Fall 2003): 773–91.

As would be expected, divorce is also influenced by religious beliefs and broad social attitudes. The role of broad social attitudes is illustrated by the results of a recent study, which finds that divorce in the United States occurs less frequently in families with sons. This finding suggests some preference for male children even in the United States, although this preference is not nearly as strong as in some other countries, notably those in East Asia.[26]

For some time, the factors that served to increase divorce appeared to dominate those that encouraged the continuation of marriage. As shown in Table 10-1, the divorce rate stood at 2.2 divorces per 1,000 population in 1960, rose to 3.5 in 1970, and then further increased to 5.2 in 1980. This suggests that, for this period, the reduction in the gains to specialization and the reduced economic dependence of wives associated with women's rising labor force participation outweighed any larger gains to joint consumption of dual-earner couples.[27] It may also be that divorce rates during this period were increased by the unexpected change in gender roles that wives' rising labor force participation entailed. After 1980, the divorce rate leveled off and then declined, decreasing from 5.2 divorces per 1,000 population to 3.6 in 2006.[28] One explanation for the leveling off and subsequent decline of the divorce rate is that, as we have seen, the marriage age has been rising. This delay of marriage may promote marital stability, as suggested by the fact that people who get married in their late twenties are less likely to break up than those who marry earlier.[29] Further, it is possible that couples increasingly marry with the expectation that the wife will work, so her entry into the labor force is not as disruptive. Another possibility is that rising cohabitation explains recent trends since breakups of these unions are not counted in the divorce statistics. However, a recent study found that this factor played only a minor role at most.[30] A final explanation might be changes in the "matching" of spouses, as individuals increasingly choose partners who share more similar interests, partly perhaps in response to changes in the divorce laws and also possibly related to the rising age at marriage.

While the overall divorce rate has declined since its peak in 1980, it has fallen considerably more for more highly-educated women than for their less-educated counterparts.[31] The factors causing this divergence are not yet fully determined, but at least part of the explanation likely lies with deteriorating labor market opportunities for less-skilled workers. Looking ahead, even though the overall divorce rate may continue to decline a bit, it is not likely to fall to the levels that prevailed when traditional marriages were the norm and attitudes toward divorce were extremely negative.

---

[26] The preference for sons in East Asia is discussed further in Chapter 12. For evidence on this point for the United States, see Shelly Lundberg, "Sons, Daughters, and Parental Behavior," *Oxford Review of Economic Policy* 21, no. 3 (Autumn 2005): 340–56; and Gordon Dahl and Enrico Moretti "The Demand for Sons," *Review of Economic Studies* 75, no. 4 (October 2008): 1085–1120.

[27] For papers that support the hypothesis that women's increased employment or rising wages caused a higher divorce rate, see Steven Ruggles, "The Rise of Divorce and Separation in the United States, 1890–1990," *Demography* 34, no. 4 (November 1997): 455–566; and Robert Michael, "Why Did the U.S. Divorce Rate Double Within a Decade?" *Research in Population Economics* 6 (1988): 367–99. For papers that come to a different conclusion, see Valerie Kincade Oppenheimer, "Comment on 'The Rise of Divorce and Separation in the United States, 1880–1990,'" *Demography* 34, no. 4 (November 1997): 467–72; and Saul D. Hoffman and Greg J. Duncan, "The Effect of Incomes, Wages, and AFDC Benefits on Marital Dissolution," *Journal of Human Resources* 30, no. 1 (Winter 1995): 19-41.

[28] For those married from the 1950s through 1970s, around one-half of marriage ended in divorce within 25 years. The figure for more recent cohorts is likely to be slightly lower, given recent declines in the divorce rate. See Stevenson and Wolfers, "Marriage and Divorce and the Driving Forces."

[29] Evelyn Lehrer, however, found that while waiting until the late 20s to marry has a stabilizing effect, waiting until the late 30s does not further increase marital stability. See "Age at Marriage and Marital Instability: The Becker-Landes-Michael Hypothesis Revisited," *Journal of Population Economics* 21, no. 2 (April 2008):463–84.

[30] Joshua R. Goldstein, "The Leveling of Divorce in the United States," *Demography* 36, no. 3 (August 1999): 409–14.

[31] See Steven P. Martin, "Trends in Marital Dissolution by Women's Education in the United States," *Demographic Research* 15, no. 20 (December 2006): 537–60; and Sara McLanahan, "Diverging Destinies: How Children Are Faring Under the Second Demographic Transition," *Demography* 41, no. 4 (November 2004): 607–27.

CUSTODY BATTLES: IT WOULD TAKE A SOLOMON*

As more and more women are increasingly committed to their work, and as fathers continue to become more involved with their children, legal battles that arise when both parents want custody of their children, or when the noncustodial parent does not want to permit the children to move out of their community, have become increasingly common. Such cases raise serious and complicated issues.

Traditionally, in custody cases, the mother was routinely awarded custody, barring overwhelming evidence that she was unfit, and, in general, this outcome remains most common. However, increasingly more fathers are aggressively seeking custody. One well-justified concern, prompted by this change, centers on the usual presumption that the mother should automatically be given preference, and that the father, especially when not married to the mother of the child, has few rights. Another equally justified concern is that courts appear to look askance at mothers who have a career, or aspire to one, but fail to show the same reservations about "career fathers." Further, inevitable difficulties arise when contestants and their respective supporters make charges and countercharges that are difficult to verify with any degree of certainty. A brief summary of two high-profile cases and recent court rulings concerning permission for the custodial parent to move illustrate the problems involved.

The first case attained celebrity status in part because Sharon Prost, the mother of two boys, worked as counsel to Republican Senator Orrin G. Hatch of Utah. Kenneth Greene, the father, was assistant executive director of the American Federation of Television and Radio Artists. They were married in 1984 and separated 8 years later. The judge awarded custody of the children to Mr. Greene in a sharply worded opinion that cited his friends and relatives who described his former wife as a driven workaholic, while claiming that he was a playful and affectionate parent. Partisans of Prost, including Senator Hatch, on the other hand, claimed that this picture was distorted and ignored the maximum efforts she made to be a responsible parent, while her husband chose not to take care of the children full time even while he was unemployed. They objected to the fact that the judge gave the father credit for any time he participated in activities at the children's kindergarten, and for coming home first in the evening, but ignored the teacher's description of Ms. Prost as "surrogate room mom" as well as the fact that she regularly got up at 5:30 A.M. to play with the children before she left for work at 8:00. In sum, they charged that the judgment involved sex bias. The judge, a mother herself, who had worked part time while her children were young, explained that a woman was entitled to put her career ahead of other demands in her life but, having made that decision, she must live with the consequences. Whether or not one agrees with the judge's decision, it must be expected to make some professional women fearful that courts may use a double standard, because they are likely to compare them to other mothers, who often are employed only part time, or not at all, while fathers will be compared to other men with children, who almost invariably are employed full time. Such comparisons would tend to make career mothers look bad as compared to similarly positioned fathers.

The second case involved different circumstances but also raised issues with implications for the role of women as mothers, albeit somewhat more indirectly. The mother had given birth to a daughter in 1991, when both she and the defendant were 16 years old and unmarried. She first agreed to give the baby up for adoption, but three weeks later changed her mind and decided to raise the child herself. Both mother and father lived with their respective families, continued to go to high school, and eventually graduated. The father had no contact with the infant during the first year of her life, but after that visited her regularly. In the fall of 1993 the plaintiff and her child moved to Ann Arbor, where she attended the University of Michigan on a scholarship.

They lived in university family housing and the child attended university-approved day care. Expenses were covered by the maternal grandmother, while the child received occasional gifts from the father and his family. At no time were any charges made that the child was less than adequately cared for, or that the relationship between mother and child was anything less than warm and satisfactory. The child had a strong emotional attachment to both parents.

There were no problems until the mother filed an action for child support. Only then did the father claim that he should obtain custody of his daughter because it would be better for her to be looked after by his mother (the child's paternal grandmother) rather than in a day care center. The court sided with the father, but the child was not removed from the mother's custody because she appealed the case. The decision was later reversed in a higher court. This reversal clearly stated that arrangements for the child's care while a parent works or goes to school are not an appropriate consideration.

The implications of this case go well beyond the custody issue. The initial decision, explicitly made on the grounds that it is preferable for a child to be cared for by a blood relative (her paternal grandmother) rather than by "strangers," ignored the substantial amount of contact parents and children have, and the parental care children receive, even when children spend eight hours a day, five days a week, at a day care center. Furthermore, this decision, which overruled the recommendations of two impartial child welfare groups, obviously implies that day care is always second best to having children taken care of by their own parents or, in this instance, even grandparents. It also suggests that a woman who really cares about her children would stay home and give up, or at least interrupt, her schooling or her career. Moreover, it means that if she does not stay home full time it might one day be held against her if anyone chooses to question her fitness as a mother. Wide acceptance of this view, even though it is contrary to evidence discussed later in this section and in Chapter 11 on the potential benefits of out-of-home care, especially for children over age 2, could prove to be an obstacle in the path of women's further progress toward greater equality in the labor market.

Another question that arises in custody cases that can be as difficult to resolve is whether and under what circumstances the custodial parent should be permitted to move out of state. On the one hand, the noncustodial parent will find it more difficult to maintain regular contact with children if they live further away; on the other hand, not being able to move may impose serious constraints on the custodial parent who needs to find a job, is transferred by his or her employer, is offered better opportunities elsewhere, or wants to marry someone who lives in another state. And, the best interests of the children must also be considered. In the past, a woman in this situation was permitted to move only under "exceptional" circumstances. In recent years courts have become somewhat more permissive, though rulings vary considerably from case to case.

* This inset draws on Susan Chira, "Custody Fight in Capital: A Working Mother Loses," *New York Times*, September 20, 1994, sec. A, p. 1; Anna Quindlen, "Sometimes You Just Can't Win for Losing. Particularly If You're a Single Mother in America," *New York Times*, July 10, 1994, sec. 1, p. 19; Raymond Hernandez, "Court Ruling Gives Divorced Parents Right to Leave the State," *New York Times*, March 27, 1996, sec. A, p. 1; Leslie Eaton, "Divorced Parents Move, and Custody Gets Trickier," *New York Times*, August 8, 2004, p. 1; *Jennifer Ireland, Plaintiff-Appellant, Cross Appellate v. Steve Smith a/k/a Steven J. Smith, Defendant-Appellee, Cross-Appellant*, Nos. 177431, 182369, Court of Appeals of Michigan, 214 Mich. App. 235; 1995 Mich. App. LEXIS 478, May 3, 1995, Submitted; November 7, 1995, Decided; and Sanford L. Braver, Ira M. Ellman, and William V. Fabricius, "Relocation of Children After Divorce and Children's Best Interests: New Evidence and Legal Considerations," *Journal of Family Psychology* 17, no. 2 (2003): 206–19.

Cohabitation: Opposite-Sex, Unmarried Couples

As previously mentioned, **opposite-sex cohabitation** represents an increasingly common living arrangement.[32] In some instances, cohabitors may be individuals who never marry, in other instances, women and men may cohabit prior to their first marriage or after they have been divorced or widowed. Studies on cohabitation were once rare, but now a good deal of research focuses on the economic and social explanations for the rise in cohabitation and its role vis-à-vis marriage.

We have already discussed the economic factors influencing the decision to form partnerships by marrying, and many of those same factors influence the decision to cohabit. Like marriage, cohabitation involves two individuals living together in a single household. Here again, the situation presents possibilities for specialization and economies of scale as well as the other gains derived from couples living together that were discussed earlier. Why then do some couples choose to cohabit while others marry? One factor may of course be the level of commitment of the partners, but beyond that a number of economic and social factors are likely to play a role.

The current financial and economic resources of the two partners, especially the male's, appear to be an important consideration. Many couples believe that they should be financially secure before taking the "next step" to marriage. This may further mean that some couples do not move to this "next step" if the male's economic situation does not improve. Related to this, a traditional wedding, desired by many couples, is costly and at least some may delay marriage until they have adequate funds to afford the type of wedding they envision.[33]

Marriage also provides a set of legal protections that are not available to opposite-sex cohabitors. For instance, it establishes property rights for each individual regarding assets brought into or acquired after setting up a joint household.[34] As another example, even if cohabitors have been together for a long time, neither partner in such a relationship is legally entitled to a spousal benefit under Social Security. Such legal considerations may play a role in the decision to cohabit vs. marry. For example, one would expect individuals who want to live together to be more likely to cohabit rather than marry if little or no legal protection of property is at issue. In addition, the desire for or presence of children may increase the importance of these property rights. Finally, the propensity to cohabit is influenced by prevailing social attitudes toward sex and childbearing outside of marriage which, except among the very religious, have grown more liberal.[35] Indeed, as cohabitation becomes more common, attitudes likely grow more tolerant, further encouraging couples to choose this arrangement.

Differences between the circumstances of married couples and cohabitors shed light on how long the partnership may be expected to last. Cohabitation is expected to be of shorter duration than marriage. One reason for this expectation is that an individual in a cohabiting relationship who specializes in homemaking and forgoes the opportunity to maintain and increase labor market skills does not receive the same legal protections as a married person would. Consequently, cohabitors are less likely to become as economically interdependent. In addition, the fact that cohabitation creates few, if any, legal commitments makes it more likely that any personal problems or economic setbacks that arise will lead to breakups. Consistent with these expectations, the median length of time

---

[32] Although the term *mixed-sex* or *different-sex* is used by some researchers to distinguish men–women couples from gay and lesbian couples, we use the term *opposite-sex* couple here because it is used by the U.S. Census Bureau and the general public.

[33] Pamela Smock, Wendy Manning, and Meredith Porter, " 'Everything's There Except Money': How Money Shapes Decisions to Marry Among Cohabitors," *Journal of Marriage and Family* 67, no. 3 (August 2005): 680–96.

[34] For a discussion of the legal standing of opposite-sex and same-sex cohabitors, see Cynthia Grant Bowman, "Legal Treatment of Cohabitation in the United States," *Law & Policy* 26, no. 1 (January 2004): 119–51.

[35] Thornton and Young-DeMarco, "Four Decades of Trends in Attitudes Toward Family Issues in the United States."

couples spend cohabiting is short—as brief as a year or so, with cohabitation ending either in marriage or a breakup. Indeed, more than 50 percent of cohabiting couples eventually get married, suggesting that cohabiting is often not so much an alternative to marriage as a prelude to it.[36] It might be expected that such premarital cohabitation would stabilize marriage by providing the partners with more information about each other. There is, however, little evidence that premarital cohabitation provides this stabilizing effect.[37]

Rates of cohabitation have increased substantially among all cohorts, but, consistent with cohabitation frequently being a prelude to marriage, they have increased especially among younger Americans. Indeed, as of 2002, an estimated 50 percent of the population aged 15 to 44 had cohabited at some time in their lives.[38] One consequence is that increasing numbers of children are living in these arrangements. In some cases, children are born to cohabiting parents, while in other cases, one or both partners may have children from a previous relationship.[39] For instance, in 2007, just under 40 percent of cohabiting couples included at least one child under age 18, a figure that is only slightly lower than the percent of married-couple families with children under age 18 present.[40] Moreover, it is projected that 40 percent of *all* children will spend at least some of their childhood in a cohabiting family.[41]

Rapidly rising rates of cohabitation raise some concerns. For one, cohabitors are considerably more likely to break up than married couples, putting children at greater risk of the often negative consequences of family disruption.[42] In addition, cohabiting couples, on average, have considerably lower incomes than married couples and a much larger fraction live in poverty.[43] As discussed in Chapter 11, these economic difficulties would not be fully remedied by simply having these couples marry; even if they were to do so, they would still have lower earnings, on average, than married couples mainly because they tend to have less education and work experience. Moreover, marriage, per se, would not likely reduce the breakup rate of couples who previously cohabited because cohabiting couples appear to be more susceptible to breakup in the first place.

It is interesting to note that cohabitation rates are quite a bit higher in a number of other economically advanced countries, particularly Sweden, where as many as 35 percent of individuals age 20 to 40 are cohabiting at a given point in time compared to just under 10 percent in the United States.[44] Some researchers have argued that there are several stages of cohabitation: In the first stage, cohabitation is rare; in the second stage, cohabitation serves as a prelude to marriage, but does not involve childbearing; in the third stage, cohabitation is even more socially acceptable and includes childbearing; and in the fourth stage, cohabitation and marriage become "indistinguishable" in terms

---

[36] Larry Bumpass and H.-H. Lu, "Trends in Cohabitation and Implications for Children's Family Context in the United States," *Population Studies* 54, no. 1 (March 2000): 29–41.

[37] Lee A. Lillard, Michael J. Brien, and Linda J. Waite suggest that one reason cohabitors may be less successful at marriage is that they tend to be less committed. Still even after accounting for this type of "selectivity," they do not find that cohabitation reduces marital dissolution in "Pre-Marital Cohabitation and Subsequent Marital Dissolution: Is It Self-Selection?" *Demography* 32, no. 3 (August 1995): 437–58.

[38] U.S. Department of Health and Human Services, "Fertility, Family Planning, and Reproductive Health of U.S. Women: Data from the 2002 National Survey of Family Growth," *Vital and Health Statistics* Series 23, no. 25 (2005), Table 48.

[39] See Michael J. Brien, Lee A. Lillard, and Linda J. Waite, "Interrelated Family-Building Behaviors: Cohabitation, Marriage and Nonmarital Conception," *Demography* 36, no. 4 (November 1999): 535–51.

[40] U.S. Census Bureau, "Families and Living Arrangements: 2007," Detailed Tables FG3 and UC3, available at www.census.gov. Accessed September 2008.

[41] Bumpass and Lu, "Trends in Cohabitation."

[42] Wendy D. Manning, Pamela J. Smock, and Debarun Majumdar, "The Relative Stability of Cohabiting and Marital Unions for Children," *Population and Research Review* 23, no. 2 (April 2004): 135–59.

[43] Wendy D. Manning and Susan L. Brown, "Children's Economic Well-Being in Married and Cohabiting Parent Families," *Journal of Marriage and Family* 68, no. 2 (May 2006): 345–62.

[44] The figure for Sweden is from OECD, *Society at a Glance 2007*, table SF8.1. The cohabitation figure for the United States is for ages 15–44 and is from U.S. Department of Health and Human Services, "Fertility, Family Planning and Reproductive Health of U.S. Women: Data from the 2002 National Survey of Family Growth," *Vital and Health Statistics*, series 23, no. 25, Table 47 (December 2005).

of duration and childbearing. The United States is believed to fall somewhere between the second and third stages, while Sweden and other Nordic countries are in the fourth stage.[45] While the United States is not expected to "reverse course," it is likely to remain in its current stage of cohabitation for some time to come given the continued central role of marriage in the lives of many Americans.

Cohabitation: Gay and Lesbian Couples

Like traditional married couples and unmarried opposite-sex couples, **gay and lesbian couples** also reap economic benefits, including the ability to share economic resources and to realize economies of scale. However, even though same-sex partners may also differ in terms of their comparative advantage in housework and market work, neither partner is likely to specialize in home production to the same extent as the average married woman.[46]

First, as in the case of unmarried opposite-sex couples, same-sex couples have far fewer legal protections than married couples, thereby making investment in homemaking skills particularly costly in the event that the couple breaks up. Opposite-sex couples in the United States have the option of marrying if they choose, whereas same-sex couples generally do not. As of 2008, the exceptions were Massachusetts and Connecticut where same-sex marriage is permitted. In 2008 the California Supreme Court permitted same-sex marriage but this ruling was revoked in a ballot initiative later that year.

Second, to the extent that young women know they are not likely to enter an opposite-sex relationship, they will have little incentive to specialize in homemaking skills. On the contrary, those expecting to have partnerships with other women are more likely, all else equal, to accumulate human capital useful for the labor market as compared with those expecting to be members of a more traditional household. For the same reason, they are also likely to choose more career-oriented, male-dominated occupations.

Turning to gay men, while they are also likely to acquire skills useful for the labor market, they are unlikely to be as specialized in market-oriented activities as their heterosexual male counterparts since they are not expecting to fulfill the traditional breadwinner role. Thus, both lesbian women and gay men are likely to be less specialized in traditional gender roles than their heterosexual counterparts.

Several surveys provide information about the number of gay men and lesbians in the United States, but there are difficulties in obtaining reliable estimates. One problem is that gay men and lesbians may be reluctant to identify themselves given prevailing attitudes. Another is that the definitions used vary considerably. According to one recent study, about 2.8 percent of men are gay and 1.4 percent of women are lesbians, based on self-reported information. The same study also finds that about 50 percent of gay men and 63 percent of lesbians live with a same-sex partner, and around 10 percent of gay couples and 22 percent of lesbian couples have children.[47] These figures suggest that children's living arrangements are far more diverse than many people realize.

It is expected that in the future the fraction of same-sex couples, including those with children, will increase to the extent that societal attitudes toward them become more tolerant and other states follow the lead of Massachusetts and Connecticut and permit gay marriage. Short of marriage, civil unions, which are available in a number of other states, do establish some legal rights for gay and lesbian couples, such as rights regarding adoption, pensions, and inheritance. However, civil unions are not generally

---

[45] Kathleen Kiernan, "Unmarried Cohabitation and Parenthood: Here to Stay? European Perspectives," in *The Future of the Family*, edited by Daniel P. Moynihan, Timothy M. Smeeding, and Lee Rainwater (New York: Russell Sage Foundation, 2004): 66–95.

[46] Dan A. Black, Seth G. Sanders, and Lowell J. Taylor, "The Economics of Lesbian and Gay Families," *Journal of Economic Perspectives* 21, no. 2 (Spring 2007): 53–70.

[47] All figures reported in this paragraph are from Black et al. "The Economics of Gay and Lesbian Families."

viewed as having the same social standing as marriage. Further, to the extent that alternative reproductive technologies become less expensive and more acceptable, the fraction of children raised in nontraditional households is likely to further increase.

Fertility

Neoclassical economic theory sheds considerable light on the determinants of **fertility**: people's decisions about whether to have children and how many to have. According to the economic approach, parents' **demand for children** depends not only on the benefits (or utility) they expect to derive from having children but also on the costs of raising them, including the "opportunity cost of time," and the family income available.[48]

With respect to the demand for children, one obvious economic consideration is the cost of clothing, housing, and education. For 2006, the U.S. Department of Agriculture estimated that the expenditures required for an average married couple to raise a child through age 17 amounted to $197,700.[49] This is a substantial sum and does not take into account the time parents devote to childrearing, which is a large part of their contribution to raising children. Even when a great deal of child care is purchased, parents, most often mothers, still spend a good deal of time finding suitable caregivers, taking care of emergencies, and helping with school work, as well as providing recreation and other enrichment. The time and energy parents devote to these purposes could otherwise be used to obtain more education or training for themselves, to advance their own careers, to earn more income by working longer hours, or to enjoy more leisure. Giving up some or all of these constitutes an important part of the the opportunity cost of rearing children.[50]

Higher income is expected to increase the couple's demand for all "commodities" from which they derive utility or satisfaction, including children. Moreover, higher income enables a family to more easily meet the money costs of raising more children. Thus, one might expect to see a positive relationship between income and fertility. In fact, however, fertility tends to decline with income. One reason is that higher income is believed to increase parents' demand for child *quality* (investment per child) rather than for child quantity (the number of children).[51] Child quality may be enhanced by expenditures on piano lessons, a spot at soccer camp, or advanced classes in science, as well as by providing tuition for college and perhaps graduate school later on. Because education and skills are particularly valued in today's labor market, these kinds of expenditures provide children with considerable advantages. Another dimension of child quality, children's health, also requires expenditures, either through paying insurance premiums or out-of-pocket costs. Parents with strong preferences for child quality are likely to have fewer children because higher expenditures on child quality increase the costs of child quantity. For instance, parents who are committed to providing a

[48] Richard A. Easterlin offers a different explanation for changes in fertility and female labor force participation. In his model, the driving force behind changes in these outcomes is that young people aspire to achieve at least the same income their parents had when they were growing up. If members of a particular birth cohort are worse off than their parents were, female labor force participation will rise to compensate and fertility will decline. If, on the other hand, their income is higher than what their parents' achieved, the effect on fertility will be positive. See Richard A. Easterlin, "On the Relation of Economic Factors to Recent and Projected Fertility Changes," *Demography* 3 (August 1966): 131–53. For a review of Easterlin's work and influence, see Diane J. Macunovich, "Fertility and the Easterlin Hypothesis: An Assessment of the Literature," *Journal of Population Economics* 11, no. (1998): 53–111. For a discussion of other ways to broaden the economic model of fertility, see Robert Pollak and Susan Cotts Watkins, "Cultural and Economic Approaches to Fertility: Proper Marriage or Mesalliance?" *Population and Development Review* 19, no. 3 (September 1993): 467–96.

[49] Mark Lino, *Expenditures on Children by Families, 2006* (U.S. Department of Agriculture, Center for Nutrition Policy and Promotion. Miscellaneous Publication no. 1528-2006, 2007), Table ES-1, available at www.cnpp .usda.gov. Accessed on February 28, 2008.

[50] See Nancy Folbre, *Valuing Children: Rethinking the Economics of the Family* (Cambridge, MA: Harvard University Press, 2008).

[51] Becker, *A Treatise on the Family*; Gary Becker and Nigel Tomes, "Child Endowments and the Quantity and Quality of Children," *Journal of Political Economy* 84, no. 4, part 2 (August 1976): S143–62.

college education for each of their children will find an additional child more costly than those committed to getting just their children through high school.

Changing economic opportunities of women and men are also expected to affect the fertility decision. As women's wages rise, the opportunity cost of the time they spend with children increases, leading to a negative substitution effect on their demand for children. In other words, as children become more expensive, the individual is likely to substitute away from children toward the consumption of other goods or services that provide utility. Even though a higher wage is expected to also have a positive income effect encouraging fertility (but see our discussion of child quality above), the substitution effect of the wage increase is likely to dominate for women because they continue to be the primary caregivers. Similarly, because women's wages are a key determinant of their labor force participation, we would expect to observe a negative relationship between fertility and women's labor market activity. Over the long term, the relationship between women's wages (or labor force participation) and fertility depends on the relative strength of competing factors. On the one hand, as women become better educated and more career-oriented, the opportunity cost of childrearing is increased, thereby reducing the demand for children.[52] On the other hand, the availability of affordable high-quality child care, as well as the increasing acceptance of using it, probably reduce the opportunity cost of childrearing to some extent. Certainly, access to child care makes it easier for women to combine employment with having a family.

For men, the income effect of a wage increase is likely to dominate the substitution effect because they generally do not give up as much of their time to provide child care. Therefore, as men's wages increase we would expect to see a rise in fertility, all else equal. However, as already discussed, families are also likely to use some of the added income to increase spending per child.

In addition to women's and men's wages and family income, the introduction of new and more effective methods of contraception, such as the birth control pill, has enhanced the ability to limit fertility. Contraceptive methods, along with reproductive technologies that facilitate births to women at older ages, also permit more control over the timing of births. Access to abortion, made legal in 1973, also has the potential to affect fertility rates and timing. Interestingly, a recent study found that legalized abortion reduced total fertility over women's childbearing years, rather than just delaying childbearing.[53] Government tax policies and transfer programs may also affect fertility. For instance, in the federal individual income tax, the personal exemption increases with the number of children, as do several tax credits including the Child Tax Credit and Earned Income Tax Credit. These tax features subsidize childbearing and thus provide positive incentives for fertility.[54]

Table 10-3 and Figure 10-1 show the considerable fluctuation in the **fertility rate** since the 1940s. The period that lasted from the end of World War II until the early 1960s is known as the **baby boom**. As shown in the figure, fertility rates for this cohort were considerably higher than for those in the prior and subsequent cohorts; rates reached a peak of 3.7 children per woman (3,690 children per 1,000 women) between 1955 and 1959, far above the replacement rate of 2.1 children per woman. By 1976, however, during the "baby bust," the rate

---

[52] For instance, McKinley L. Blackburn, David E. Bloom, and David Neumark found that late childbearers tend to invest more heavily in their human capital than early childbearers in "Fertility Timing, Wages and Human Capital," *Journal of Population Economics* 6, no. 1 (1993): 1–30. Late childbearing would also be expected to reduce the number of children per woman, all else equal. See also Steven P. Martin, "Women's Education and Family Timing: Outcomes and Trends Associated with Age of Marriage at First Birth" in *Social Inequality*, edited by Kathryn Neckerman (New York: Russell Sage Foundation, 2004), pp. 79–118.

[53] See, for instance, Goldin and Katz, "Career and Marriage in the Age of the Pill"; and Elizabeth Oltmans Ananat, Jonathan Gruber, and Phillip B. Levine, "Abortion Legalization and Life Cycle Fertility," *Journal of Human Resources* 42, no. 2 (Spring 2007): 375–97.

[54] In the case of the Earned Income Tax Credit, the credit does not increase further for three or more children. Regarding incentive effects of tax policies, see Stacey Dickert-Conlin and Reaghan Baughman, "The Earned Income Tax Credit and Fertility," *Journal of Population Economics* 22, no. 3 (2009): 537–63; regarding the effects of welfare programs, see Robert A. Moffitt, "The Temporary Assistance for Needy Families Program"; and Moffitt, "The Effect of Welfare on Marriage and Fertility."

TABLE 10-3 Total Fertility Rates, 1940–2005

Years	Total Fertility Rate[a]
1940–1944	2,523
1945–1949	2,985
1950–1954	3,337
1955–1959	3,690
1960–1964	3,449
1965–1969	2,622
1970–1974	2,094
1975–1979	1,774
1980–1984	1,819
1985–1989	1,899
1990–1994	2,042
1995–1999	2,022
2000–2004	2,038
2005	2,054

[a]The number of births that a cohort of 1,000 women would have if they experienced the age-specific birthrates occurring in the current year throughout their childbearing years. Dividing by 1,000 provides a measure of births per woman.

Source: U.S. Census Bureau, *Statistical Abstract of the United States*, 1984, 1999; U.S. Department of Health and Human Services, "Births: Final Data for 2005," *National Vital Statistics Reports* 56, no. 6 (December 5, 2007), available at www.cdc.gov/nchs.

declined to as low as 1.7, well below the replacement rate. The cohort that was born after the baby boom and includes the baby bust period is referred to in the media as **Generation X**. After a number of years of relatively low fertility, the fertility rate began to rise modestly in the mid 1980s; it reached approximately replacement rate by 1990 and remained around that level through the mid 2000s. In addition to the fertility rate, the total number of births is also related to the number of women in their childbearing years. One prime example is the very large recent cohort known as the *echo* of the baby boom or **Generation Y** by the media, who are the offspring of the baby boom cohort. While the start and end dates of Generation Y are not as well defined as for the baby boom, it generally includes those born in the early- to mid-1980s through the early- to mid-1990s. Generation Y is so large, not because the baby boom cohort had high birthrates, on the contrary birthrates were relatively low for this group, but rather because so many women were of childbearing age at the same time.

These fluctuations in the fertility rate occurred, in substantial part, as a result of variations in the strength of the factors discussed earlier. The baby boom took place during a time of prosperity and rising real wages of men and women. Because relatively few married women of childbearing age were employed in those days, the main effect of rising real wages was an increase in fertility due to the income effect of husbands' rising wages. For this period, a recent study also points to the role of falling prices of labor-saving appliances, such as the vacuum cleaner, washing machine and clothes dryer, in spurring the adoption of these conveniences, thereby reducing the burden of larger families.[55] Nonetheless, the magnitude of the baby boom probably cannot be fully explained without taking into account the postponement of births during the Great Depression of the 1930s and World War II, as well as a variety of social and cultural factors.

The subsequent sharp drop in fertility beginning in the early 1960s coincided with both rapid increases in the labor force participation rate of young women and advances

---

[55] "Jeremy Greenwood, Ananth Seshadri, and Guillaume Vandenbroucke, "The Baby Boom and Baby Bust," *American Economic Review* 95, no. 1 (March 2005): 183–207.

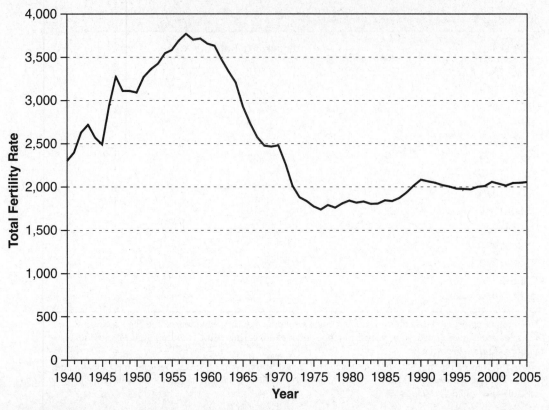

FIGURE 10-1   Total Fertility Rates, 1940–2005

Sources: U.S. Department of Health and Human Services, "Births: Final Data for 2005," *National Vital Statistics Report* 56, no. 6 (December 5, 2007); "Births: Final Data for 2002," *National Vital Statistics Report* 52, no. 10 (December 17, 2003); and *Vital Statistics of the United States* (1964 and 1969).

in contraceptive techniques. As labor market opportunitities opened up for women and as women became increasingly career oriented, their opportunity cost of dropping out of the labor force to bear and raise children was increased. The modest rise in fertility from the mid-1980s to the early 1990s may reflect a "catching up" phenomenon, as women who did not have children earlier chose to have them at a later time.[56] It may also, in part, reflect the decision of some couples to start their families earlier in light of publicity about the difficulties that some older women face in becoming pregnant. Since then, the level has fluctuated only modestly at about 2.1 children per woman.

Future trends in fertility are difficult to predict, but it is unlikely that the overall fertility rate will rise significantly from its present level, especially in light of the continued increase in women's educational attainment discussed in Chapter 6 and their continued commitment to market work discussed in Chapter 4. One might even speculate that the U.S. fertility rate could fall somewhat given that it is now higher than the rates in most other economically advanced countries, in some cases considerably so, as discussed in Chapter 12.[57] On the other hand, it is possible that the negative effect of rising

---

[56] Julie DaVanzo and M. Omar Rahman, "American Families: Trends and Correlates," *Population Index* 59, no. 3 (Fall 1993): 350–86. Blackburn, Bloom, and Neumark, "Fertility Timing, Wages and Human Capital," suggest that this postponement was associated with women's greater investment in their human capital.

[57] The substantial fertility decline that has occurred in some of these countries may, however, reflect greater challenges to combining work and family than in the United States; see James Feyrer, Bruce Sacerdote, and Ariel Dora Stern, "Will the Stork Return to Europe? Understanding Fertility Within Developed Nations," *Journal of Economic Perspectives* 2, no. 3 (Summer 2008): 3–22.

female education and continued high participation rates on fertility may be mitigated in the future by further increases in the involvement of fathers with their children and a greater availability of good child care, as well as any new tax provisions or subsidies reducing the financial burden of raising and educating children that may be enacted.

In the remainder of this section, we review recent trends in fertility for various subgroups. One notable trend has been the marked increased in the share of births to unmarried mothers starting in the 1970s. As shown in Table 10-4, the share of births to unmarried mothers rose sharply from 11 percent of all births in 1970 to 28 percent in 1990. The rate of increase has slowed since then. Still, by 2005, 37 percent of all births in the United States were to unmarried women. The share of all births that are to unmarried women depends on both the number of unmarried women (and hence the

TABLE 10-4   Selected Birth Rates, 1970–2005

	1970	1980	1990	2000	2005
Birth Rates (Births per 1,000 Women in Specified Group)[a]					
Overall birth rate, ages 15–44	87.9	68.4	70.9	65.9	66.7
Teen birth rate, ages 15–19	68.3	53.0	59.9	47.7	40.5
Older mother birth rate					
Ages 35–39	31.7	19.8	31.7	39.7	46.3
Ages 40–44	8.1	3.9	5.5	8.0	9.1
Unmarried Birth Rates (Births per 1,000 Unmarried Women in Specified Group)[b]					
Unmarried birth rate, ages 15–44	26.4	29.4	43.8	44.1	47.5
Whites	13.9	18.1	32.9	38.2	43.0
Blacks	95.5	81.1	90.5	70.5	67.8
Unmarried teen birth rate, ages 15–19	22.4	27.6	42.5	39.0	34.5
Whites	10.9	16.5	30.6	32.7	29.9
Blacks	96.9	87.9	106.0	75.0	60.6
Unmarried older mother birth rate					
Ages 35–39	13.6	9.7	17.3	19.7	24.5
Ages 40–44	3.5	2.6	3.6	5.0	6.2
Types of Births (%)					
Unmarried births as % of all births	10.7	18.4	28.0	33.2	36.9
Whites	5.7	11.2	20.4	27.1	31.7
Blacks	37.6	55.5	66.5	68.5	69.3
Unmarried teen births as % of all teen births	31.9	48.3	67.6	78.8	83.3
Unmarried teen births as % of all unmarried births	50.1	40.8	31.0	27.4	22.6

[a]For instance, birth rate for ages 15–44 refers to births to women ages 15–44 per 1,000 women in that age group.

[b]For instance, unmarried birth rate for ages 15–44 refers to births to unmarried women ages 15–44 per 1,000 unmarried women in that age group.

Notes: For data stratified by race, *race* refers to child's race for 1970; data refers to mother's race for other years.

Source: U.S. Department of Health and Human Services, "Births: Final Data for 2005," *National Vital Statistics Reports* 56, no. 6 (December 5, 2007); "Births: Final Data for 2000," *National Vital Statistics Reports* 50, no. 5 (February 12, 2002); and U.S. Department of Health and Human Services, *Nonmarital Childbearing in the United States, 1940–99*, 48, no. 16 (October 18, 2000), Table 4.

marriage rate) and the probability of married and unmarried women giving birth. The birthrate of unmarried women has indeed increased substantially, particularly between 1980 and 2005, when it rose from 29.4 to 47.5 births per 1,000 unmarried women. Nonetheless, the largest source of the increase in the share of births to unmarried women was actually the substantial increase in the *number* of unmarried women of childbearing age, rather than the rise in the birthrate of unmarried women.[58] Also quite notable is that while the birthrate of unmarried women has risen substantially among all women and whites since 1980, it has declined substantially among blacks since 1990. And, while the black rate remains quite a bit higher than the white rate, the race difference has declined considerably since 1980.

Births to unmarried women are related to many of the same factors that affect incentives to marry. Women's increased labor market opportunities have made it easier for them to financially support a family on their own, while at the same time men's ability to make a substantial economic contribution to their family has declined among the less educated.[59] In addition, premarital sex and unmarried childbearing have become much more widely accepted than in the past and unmarried mothers are now far less likely to get married before the baby's birth.[60] However, it should not be assumed that the father is absent in all cases. In fact, one study finds that as many as 40 percent of all nonmarital births in the United States in the early 1990s occurred to cohabiting couples, rather than to women living alone.[61] Government policies also have the potential to influence nonmarital fertility. For instance, stricter child support enforcement in recent years, which increased the costs of fatherhood, appears to have discouraged unmarried births.[62]

The figure that continues to receive perhaps the greatest attention is the rate of teen births in the United States, which is considerably higher than in other economically advanced countries.[63] Although the U.S. rate still remains quite high, it has declined substantially since the early 1990s, from a high of 62 births per 1,000 teens in 1991 to a historical U.S. low of 41 births per 1,000 in 2005.[64] And, as we have seen, the birthrate for unmarried women, including unmarried teens, has declined markedly for African Americans. Despite these encouraging trends, teen births remain a particular concern because a growing share of them are to unmarried mothers (fully 83 percent in 2006, up from only one-third in 1970). This shift is in large part due to the significant decline in the rate of teen marriage.

Teen pregnancy and births to unmarried teens are, in part, related to economic factors, including poor labor market prospects, which lower the opportunity cost of

[58] JoAnna Gray, Jean Stockard, and Joe Stone, "The Rising Share of Nonmarital Births: Fertility Choice or Marriage Behavior?" *Demography* 43, no. 2 (May 2006): 241–53.

[59] For evidence on the poor job prospects of low-skilled workers, see Chinhui Juhn, "Decline of Male Labor Market Participation: The Role of Declining Market Opportunities," *Quarterly Journal of Economics* 107, no. 1 (February 1992): 79–122. Robert J. Willis also suggests that unmarried fertility may be a result of an imbalance in the sex ratio in "The Economics of Fatherhood," *American Economic Review* 90, no. 2 (May 2000): 378–82.

[60] George A. Akerlof, Janet L. Yellen, and Michael L. Katz argue that the availability of the birth control pill and legal abortion reduced the cost of premarital sex as well as unmarried women's ability to "bargain" for marriage in the event of pregnancy. These changes, in turn, lead to a reduction in the number of marriages following pregnancy and a rise in nonmarital fertility; see "An Analysis of Out-of-Wedlock Childbearing in the United States," *Quarterly Journal of Economics* 111, no. 2 (May 1996): 277–317.

[61] Bumpass and Lu, "Trends in Cohabitation."

[62] Robert D. Plotnick, Irwin Garfinkel, Sara S. McLanahan, and Inhoe Ku, "The Impact of Child Support Enforcement Policy on Nonmarital Childbearing," *Journal of Policy Analysis and Management* 26, no. 1 (Winter 2007): 79–98; and Anna Aizer and Sara McLanahan, "The Impact of Child Support Enforcement on Fertility, Parental Investments, and Child Well-Being," *Journal of Human Resources* 41, no. 1 (Winter 2006): 28–45.

[63] Susheela Singh and Jacqueline E. Darroch, "Adolescent Pregnancy and Childbearing: Levels and Trends in Developed Countries," *Family Planning Perspectives* 32, no. 1 (Jan./Feb. 2000): 14–23.

[64] A preliminary figure for 2006 indicates the rate increased to 42 births per 1,000 teens, though whether this portends a renewed rise in the trend remains to be seen. See Frank F. Furstenberg, "Cause for Alarm? Understanding Recent Trends in Teenage Childbearing," *Pathways* (Stanford: Stanford Center for the Study of Social Inequality and Poverty, Summer 2008), pp. 3–6.

pregnancy for young women.[65] For very young women, access to and affordability of contraception and family planning services also likely play an important role in sexual activity, as well as pregnancy and births. One recent study specifically looked at this relationship by comparing teen outcomes in states that adopted a policy that raised the income eligibility for access to federally-funded family planning services, thereby expanding access to additional young women, with those who did not. The study found that adoption of this policy reduced teen births, largely as a result of greater use of contraception. In addition, contrary to the concerns of some, the study did not find that the expansion of family planning services increased the number of teens who were sexually active.[66]

Recent evidence also points to an increasing divergence in women's timing of childbearing by educational attainment. There has been a long-standing pattern of college-educated women delaying childbearing somewhat more than less-educated women, principally because they tend to be more career oriented, and the opportunity cost of having children early in their careers is likely to be quite substantial for them. In recent years, although the average age of first birth rose for all women, it increased substantially more for college-educated women.[67] The net result is that by 2006, among women ages 25 to 34, fully 52 percent of those with a bachelor's degree remained childless as compared to 26 percent of women who completed just high school.[68]

A final interesting trend revealed by Table 10-4 is a substantial rise in birthrates among women age 35 and older since 1980. Birthrates of older women are now higher than they were in 1970, substantially so for women aged 35 to 39. While Table 10-4 indicates birthrates for this age group were also fairly high in 1970, there are important differences. In earlier years, older mothers tended to be women with large families who started their childbearing in their twenties and continued to have children into their thirties and even into their early forties. In more recent years, women are much more likely to begin their childbearing at later ages. The pronounced rise in motherhood among older women since 1980, including older unmarried women, reflects this delay in childbearing.[69]

CHANGING FAMILY STRUCTURE AND ECONOMIC WELL-BEING

The U.S. labor force was once composed almost entirely of workers with few if any responsibilities for homemaking. The majority were married men with wives who were full-time homemakers, while most of the others were single. Today the labor force includes a growing proportion of workers from **dual-earner families**, in which both husbands and wives participate in the paid labor force, and from **single-parent families**, generally mothers and their children. As we shall see, family structure has substantial implications for the well-being of workers and their families. The policy issues raised by these changes will be discussed in Chapter 11.

---

[65] Barbara Wolfe, Kathryn Wilson, and Robert Haveman, "The Role of Economic Incentives in Teenage Nonmarital Childbearing Choices," *Journal of Public Economics* 81, no. 3 (September 2001): 473–511; and Shelly Lundberg and Robert D. Plotnick, "Adolescent Premarital Childbearing: Do Economic Incentives Matter?" *Journal of Labor Economics* 13, no. 2 (April 1995): 177–200.

[66] Melissa S. Kearney and Philip B. Levine, "Subsidized Contraception, Fertility and Sexual Behavior," *Review of Economics and Statistics* 91, no. 1 (February 2009): 137–51. See also, Wolfe, Wilson, and Haveman, "The Role of Economic Incentives in Teenage Nomarital Childbearing Choices."

[67] See, for instance, David T. Ellwood and Christopher Jencks, "The Spread of Single-Parent Families in the United States Since 1960," in *The Future of the Family*, edited by Daniel P. Moynihan, Timothy M. Smeeding, and Lee Rainwater (New York: Russell Sage: 2004), pp. 25–65; and Martin, "Delayed Marriage and Childbearing."

[68] "Fertility of American Women: June 2006," *Current Population Reports* P20–548 (August 2008), Detailed Table 3, available at www.census.gov. Accessed September 2008.

[69] See Lucie Schmidt, "Murphy Brown Revisited: Human Capital, Search, and Nonmarital Childbearing Among Educated Women," William College Working Paper (2007); and Emily Bazelon, "2 Kids + 0 Husbands = Family," *New York Times Magazine*, February 1, 2009, pp. 30–35.

Dual-Earner Families

As shown in Table 10-1, over the period 1960 to 2006 dual-earner families increased from 45 to 58 percent of all married couple families. Even more telling, Table 10-5, which provides more detailed statistics on dual-earner families for 2006, shows that as many as 68 percent of married couples *with children* were headed by dual earners. Morever, the labor force commitment of wives in such families is often quite substantial; in over half of dual-earner couples, including those with children, both spouses worked full time, full year. These developments are largely a result of labor market trends for women discussed in earlier chapters—women's rising labor force attachment, improved qualifications, and increasing labor market opportunities.

As further shown in Table 10-5, married women's earnings are an important source of family income today. The incomes of dual-earner married couples are, on average, 50 percent higher than those with just an employed husband. One consequence of recent labor market developments for women, in conjunction with declines in the real earnings of less-educated men, is that the earnings of employed wives rose relative to their husbands, on average,[70] and the percentage of wives with higher annual earnings than their husbands also increased, from only 16 percent in 1981 to 26 percent by 2006.[71] Both women's increased earnings and the increase in the fraction of wives who earn more than their husbands, would be expected to increase women's bargaining power within marriage.

An important question is how various dimensions of family—marriage, children, and employment of a spouse—affect women's and men's wages. Considerable

TABLE 10-5   Characteristics of Married and Dual-Earner Couples, by Presence of Children, 2006

	All Married Couples	With Children Under Age 18
Dual-Earner Couples (%)	57.5	67.5
% of dual-earner couples where both spouses employed full-time, full-year	54.9	51.6
% of dual-earner couples where wife has higher annual earnings than husband[a]	25.7	n.a.
Median Income ($2006)		
All married couples	69,404	74,049
Husband only employed	56,815	55,028
Dual earners	86,773	83,411
Both spouses employed full-time, full-year	95,018	91,706

[a]Dual-earner couple defined as married couple where both spouses have earnings.

n.a. Not available.

Source: U.S. Census Bureau, Table FINC-04, "Presence of Related Children Under 18 Years Old—Married Couple Families, by Total Money Income in 2006, Work Experience in 2006" and Table F-22, "Married-Couple Families with Wives' Earnings Greater than Husbands' Earnings: 1981 to 2006" from www.census.gov.

---

[70] Francine D. Blau, "Trends in the Well-Being of American Women, 1970–1995," *Journal of Economic Literature* 36, no. 1 (March 1998): 112–65.

[71] Anne E. Winkler, Timothy D. McBride, and Courtney Andrews find that in the majority of couples in which the wife earns more than her husband, this pattern persists for some period of time; see "Wives Who Outearn Their Husbands: A Transitory or Persistent Phenomenon for Couples?" *Demography* 42, no. 3 (August 2005): 523–35.

evidence suggests that men's earnings rise with marriage. This **male marriage premium** is most likely primarily due to the benefits husbands reap from specialization in the family: To the extent their wives have primary responsibility for the home and children, husbands can devote greater attention to their jobs. Further, with one career as the primary focus of the family, both spouses can concentrate on making that career as successful as possible. The positive association between men's wages and marriage may also reflect the personal characteristics of married men, such as a greater ability to get along with others, that make them both more likely to marry and to be successful at work. To the extent that this is the case, the observed positive relationship between marriage and male wages may not be causal. However, the majority of evidence suggests that marriage does cause men's wages to be higher.[72] The presence of children also appears to boost men's earnings, presumably because fatherhood increases the incentive to work harder to support the family.[73] Some evidence suggests that this effect is greater for fathers of male children, implying some preference for boys.[74]

The effect of family on women's earnings is quite different than in the case of men. For one, married women do not receive a premium as compared to unmarried women. Further, considerable evidence shows that mothers earn less than women without children, a finding commonly known as the **motherhood wage penalty**.[75] Much of the explanation for this penalty is that mothers tend to have lesser levels of labor market experience, either because of time out of the labor force or time spent in part-time work, which tends to be associated with lower wages and lower returns to experience. What continues to raise particular attention is that the motherhood penalty exists even for mothers with the same labor market experience and education as nonmothers. A variety of explanations have been offered, and it may well be that all play a role to some degree. For one, some mothers are not able to return to their previous employer after childbirth, but instead must change firms, especially if their employer does not provide adequate maternity leave. Women in this situation lose out on the benefits of firm-specific training and potential rewards from an especially good job match.[76] This explanation is likely to be less important in recent years as a result of the 1993 Family and Medical Leave Act. This Act provides 12 weeks of unpaid leave in the event of birth or adoption of a child, as well as in the case of illness of a family member, and employers are required to hold workers' jobs during this time. Nevertheless, as discussed further in Chapter 11, many workers are not covered by the legislation or a similar policy provided by their employer and so may have no alternative but to start over with a new firm after the birth of a child. Moreover, women may choose to stay out of the labor force for longer than the

---

[72] For a comprehensive review of studies on the marriage premium for men, see David C. Ribar, "What Do Social Scientists Know About the Benefits of Marriage? A Review of Quantitative Methodologies," IZA Discussion Paper No. 998 (January 2004).

[73] Shelly J. Lundberg and Elaina Rose, "Parenthood and the Earnings of Married Men and Women," *Labour Economics* 7, no. 6 (November 2000): 689–710.

[74] Shelly J. Lundberg and Elaina Rose, "The Effects of Sons and Daughters on Men's Labor Supply and Wages," *Review of Economics and Statistics* 84, no.2 (May 2002): 251–68.

[75] See Jane Waldfogel in "Understanding the 'Family Gap' in Pay for Women with Children," *Journal of Economic Perspectives* 12, no. 1 (Winter 1998): 137–56; Michelle J. Budig and Paula England, "The Wage Penalty for Motherhood," *American Sociological Review* 66 (April 2001): 204–25; and Wendy Sigle-Rushton and Jane Waldfogel, "Motherhood and Women's Earnings in Anglo-American, Continental European, and Nordic Countries," *Feminist Economics* 13, no. 2 (April 2007): 55–91.

[76] Jane Waldfogel points to this issue and the potential benefits of adequate family leave, in "Working Mothers Then and Now: A Cross Cohort Analysis of the Effects of Maternity Leave on Women's Pay," in *Gender and Family Issues in the Workplace*, edited by Francine D. Blau and Ronald Ehrenberg (New York, Russell Sage Foundation, 1997), pp. 92–126. The rest of the explanations offered here are nicely summarized in Sigle-Rushton and Waldfogel, "Motherhood and Women's Earnings in Anglo-American, Continental European, and Nordic Countries."

12 weeks leave time allowed by the law or any additional leave time offered by their employer.

The motherhood penalty may also arise from the fact that women, even those employed full time, continue to bear primary responsibility for the household and children. For instance, it has been suggested that mothers may trade off earnings for greater job flexibility in the form of more convenient hours or closer proximity to home, or perhaps may take a less-demanding position. In other cases, mothers may have no choice but to take a job with inflexible hours, but this may result in their having greater absenteeism, as, for example, when they take time off to care for a sick child or take their child to an appointment. Their job performance ratings and wages may consequently suffer.[77] Mothers' greater household and child care responsibilities may also simply leave them with less energy and time available for their jobs.[78] Even for mothers who are no less productive, employers may evaluate them negatively based on perceived, not actual performance.[79] Finally, as discussed earlier regarding the relationship between marriage and earnings, the relationship between parenthood and wages may not be causal. Rather, women (and men) who become parents may have different attributes than those who do not have children. For instance, it may be the case that women who are especially career oriented are more likely to remain childless.[80]

There is also evidence that having an employed spouse may cause both husbands' and wives' earnings to suffer, what might be termed an **employed spouse penalty**.[81] Wives' wages, especially, may suffer to the extent that typically the husband's career is given precedence, thereby limiting wives' job opportunities.[82] Some couples do try to accomodate both careers and make a joint location decision, but doing so may limit the career prospects advancement of both partners. One solution might be to live in a big city that would offer more job opportunities, and in fact, big cities are home to increasing numbers of highly educated couples. At present, it is not yet clear whether this growing fraction is a result of decisions by highly educated married couples to locate in

---

[77] Deborah J. Anderson, Melissa Binder, and Kate Krause, "The Motherhood Wage Penalty Revisited: Experience, Heterogeneity, Work Effort and Work-Schedule Flexibility," *Industrial and Labor Relations Review* 56, no. 2 (January 2003): 273–94; and Leslie S. Stratton, "Why Does More Housework Lower Women's Wages? Testing Hypotheses Involving Job Effort and Hours Flexibility," *Social Science Quarterly* 82, no. 1 (March 2001): 67–76.

[78] Gary Becker first theorized that household responsibilities may reduce available effort on the job in "Human Capital, Effort, and the Sexual Division of Labor," *Journal of Labor Economics* 3, no. 1, pt. 2 (January 1985): 33–58. For evidence, see Joni Hersch and Leslie Stratton "Housework, Fixed Effects, and Wages of Married Workers," *Journal of Human Resources* 32, no. 2 (Spring 1997): 285–307 and Stratton, "Why Does More Housework Lower Women's Wages?"

[79] Shelley J. Correll, Stephen Benard, and In Paik conduct a lab experiment in which they ask individuals to assess female job applicants who are equally qualified and differ only as to whether they are mothers or not (which can be inferred from information on the application such as PTA coordinator). They find that mothers are perceived less favorably than nonmothers. See "Getting a Job: Is There a Motherhood Penalty?" *American Journal of Sociology* 112 (2007): 1297–338.

[80] Lundberg and Rose, "Parenthood and the Earnings of Married Men and Women."

[81] For evidence that having an employed wife leads to a wage penalty see Hyunbae Chun and Injae Lee, "Why Do Married Men Earn More: Productivity or Marriage Selection?" *Economic Inquiry* 39, no. 2 (April 2001): 307–19; Julie L. Hotchkiss and Robert E. Moore, "Testing for and Decomposing the Working Spouse Effect: Accounting for Endogeneity of the Wife's Decision to Work," *Industrial and Labor Relations Review* 52, no. 3 (April 1999): 410–23; and Jeffrey S. Gray, "The Fall in Men's Return to Marriage: Declining Productivity Effects or Changing Selection?" *Journal of Human Resources* 32, no. 3 (Summer 1997): 481–504. On the other hand, Joyce P. Jacobsen and Wendy L. Rayack find no effect of wives' employment on husbands' wages in "Do Men Whose Wives Work Really Earn Less?" *American Economic Review* 86, no. 2 (May 1996): 268–73.

[82] For further discussion, see Anne E. Winkler and David C. Rose, "Career Hierarchy in Dual-Earner Families," *Research in Labor Economics*, edited by Solomon Polachek (Greenwich, Connecticut: JAI Press, 1999), pp. 147–72; Joyce Jacobsen and Laurence M. Levin, "Marriage and Migration: Comparing Gains and Losses from Migration for Couples and Singles," *Social Science Quarterly* 78, no. 3 (September 1997): 688–709; and Kristin Keith and Abagail McWilliams, "Job Mobility and Gender-Based Wage Growth Differentials," *Economic Inquiry* 35, no. 2 (April 1997): 320–33.

a big city or whether such cities are simply desirable locations for highly educated individuals, whether unmarried or married.[83]

Men, especially those with wives employed full time, may also bear a penalty to the extent that employers still look askance at men not in a "traditional" family or if employers believe these men do not need as much income. Also, husbands with employed wives may in fact bear greater home responsibilities that reduce the time and energy they spend on their jobs, thereby reducing some of the male gains to marriage discussed earlier.[84] It is even possible that the direction of causality runs in the other direction: The husband's lower earnings could in fact be the cause of the wife's employment. What is clear, however, is that, even if there is an employed spouse penalty, on balance, two paychecks increase total family income and frequently help raise families above the poverty line.

Finally, it is instructive to examine trends in earnings inequality among families, and causes for these changes. Evidence indicates that family earnings inequality has increased substantially since the 1980s. The primary factor producing this increase has been the rise in male earnings inequality we discussed in Chapter 8. An important question is whether married women's increasing labor force participation and the rise in dual-earner families has served to restrain this rise, or whether it has further contributed to it. On the one hand, the larger proportion of wives in the labor force works to reduce income inequality because there are now fewer couples in which the wife has no earnings. On the other hand, the correlation between the earnings of husbands and wives has increased. The positive relationship between the earnings of husbands and wives reflects the fact that men and women with higher earnings potential tend to be married to one another. While this association always existed, it has grown stronger.[85] To date, it appears that the rising employment and earnings of wives has caused family income inequality to rise less than might otherwise have been the case.[86]

Maternal Employment and Children's Outcomes

A particularly emotionally charged issue concerns the effect of maternal employment on children's development. Some decades ago, the increased labor force participation of married women with infants and small children prompted study of the effect of maternal employment on children's development. This question has become all the more important since the passage of the 1996 federal welfare legislation, which requires single (and married) parents to seek employment as a condition for receiving welfare benefits. In principle, the question should be asked about parental rather than just maternal employment but it is still commonly accepted that the father will be working for pay full

[83] Dora Costa and Matthew E. Kahn provide evidence that power couples choose to locate in big cities in "Power Couples: Changes in the Locational Choice of the College-Educated, 1940–1990," *Quarterly Journal of Economics* 115, no. 4 (November 2000): 1287–1315; while Janice Compton and Robert A. Pollak question this conclusion in "Why Are Power Couples Increasingly Concentrated in Large Metropolitan Areas?" *Journal of Labor Economics* 25, no. 3 (July 2007): 475–512.
[84] These reasons are cited in Hotchkiss and Moore, "Testing for and Decomposing the Working Spouse Effect."
[85] Christine R. Schwartz and Robert D. Mare, "Trends in Educational Assortative Marriage from 1940 to 2003," *Demography* 42, no. 4 (November 2005): 621–46.
[86] See, Maria Cancian and Deborah Reed, "The Impact of Wives' Earnings on Income Inequality: Issues and Estimates," *Demography* 36, no. 2 (May 1999): 173–84; John Pencavel, "Earnings Inequality and Market Work in Husband–Wife Families," in *Research in Labor Economics*, edited by Solomon W. Polachek and Olivier Bargain (Greenwich, Connecticut: JAI Press, 2007), pp. 1–37; and Richard Breen and Leire Salazar, "Educational Assortative Marriage and Earnings Inequality in the United States," paper presented at the Conference on "Work, Poverty, and Inequality in the 21st Century," Stanford University (July 2008).

time as is still generally the case. Even so, some limited attention is now being paid to the influence of fathers' employment as well.[87]

As would be expected, research clearly shows that children's development is determined by a great many factors in addition to mother's employment. These factors include the sex and other innate characteristics of each child; the number of children in the family; the family's level of resources; parents' characteristics, such as their level of educational attainment and their sensitivity and responsiveness to the children's needs; the role of their father, of other family members, and of close friends in their lives; the quality of their alternative care; and last but by no means least, the nature of the community where they live. In addition, many aspects of children's development merit consideration other than merely test scores, educational attainment, and whether a girl becomes pregnant in her teens, the criteria most frequently employed by economists to gauge child outcomes. Social and emotional development is obviously important as well, as are such long-term outcomes as the stability of their marriages and their success in raising their own children. Again the evidence shows that many different factors influence these various outcomes.[88]

It is also important to remember, as discussed in Chapter 3, that while employed mothers spend less time directly engaged with their children than those who are not employed, the difference tends to be fairly modest. Among the reasons, many mothers work only part time or take time from their own leisure activities to spend time with their children. In addition, increasing numbers of children attend preschool and hence are not at home, even if their mother is not employed. When considering the consequences of maternal employment for time spent with children, it is also important to bear in mind that fathers in two-parent families are spending more time with children, so mothers' employment does not translate into a one-to-one reduction in total parental time with children.[89]

The general consensus among researchers is that children between the ages of 2 and 4 tend to do better both intellectually and socially in center day care than children cared for entirely at home.[90] For infants, however, the evidence remains more mixed, with some recent studies, in particular, finding negative effects on their later cognitive development when their mother is employed.[91] An important qualification is that these studies are not able to fully account for the quality of nonmaternal care, which might attenuate any negative effects. Also, maternal employment provides additional economic resources to the families, which tend to benefit children and might help to offset any negative effects of such employment. In addition, researchers in this field and those interpreting their findings face the challenge that factors affecting children's outcomes are highly interrelated, making it extremely difficult to isolate the influence of a single factor.[92]

---

[87] See, for instance, Susan L. Averett, Lisa A. Gennetian, and H. Elizabeth Peters, "Paternal Child Care and Children's Development," *Journal of Population Economics* 18, no. 3 (September 2005): 391–414; Christopher J. Ruhm, "Parental Employment and Child Cognitive Development," *Journal of Human Resources* 39, no. 1 (Winter 2004): 155–92; and Joseph H. Pleck, "Why Could Father Involvement Benefit Children? Theoretical Perspectives," *Applied Development Science* 11, no. 4 (December 2007): 196–202.

[88] For a review of the issues, see Jack P. Shonkoff and Deborah A. Phillips, eds. *From Neurons to Neighborhoods: The Science of Early Child Development* (Washington, DC: National Research Council, 2000), especially Chapters 10 and 11.

[89] These arguments are drawn from Suzanne M. Bianchi, "Maternal Employment and Time with Children: Dramatic Change or Surprising Continuity?" *Demography* 37, no. 4 (November 2000): 401–14.

[90] Jane Waldfogel, *What Children Need* (Cambridge, MA: Harvard University Press, 2006).

[91] For an overview of the findings, see Waldfogel, *What Children Need*, Chapters 2 and 3. For specific studies, see Ruhm, "Parental Employment and Child Cognitive Development"; Charles L. Baum II, "Does Early Maternal Employment Harm Child Development? An Analysis of the Potential Benefits of Leave Taking," *Journal of Labor Economics* 21, no. 2 (April 2003): 409–48; and Jane Waldfogel, "Child Care, Women's Employment, and Child Outcomes," *Journal of Population Economics* 15, no. 3 (August 2002): 527–48.

[92] See, for instance, Tamar Lewin, "A Child Study Is a Peek. It's Not the Whole Picture," *New York Times*, July 21, 2002, p. 4; and Shonkoff and Phillips, eds. *From Neurons to Neighborhoods*, Chapter 11. Moreover, causation between mothers' employment and children's outcomes may go either way. For instance, mothers of children with developmental delays may be slower to return to employment.

As already mentioned, a critical dimension of this issue is to what extent the *quality* of nonmaternal child care affects children's development. Studies of specific child care programs provide evidence on this point. Quality is measured either in terms of institutional features of child care settings such as teacher training, group size, and child–teacher ratios, or in terms of children's experiences in child care, such as how much verbal interaction occurs between children and teachers or whether "developmentally appropriate" activities are provided. As might be expected, programs that tend to be of high quality in one dimension tend to also be of high quality in others. Although findings vary somewhat, evidence indicates that quality of care does matter. For instance, recent research found that the amount of verbal interaction between child care providers and children positively influences children's outcomes, though factors related to the child's own family environment are consistently stronger determinants of their development than attributes of day care. The conclusion that the quality of child care matters is also supported by the success of Head Start, a preschool program targeted at low-income children and funded by the federal government, as well as by positive results from other early intervention programs.[93] Even though children in low-income families are arguably in the greatest need of quality child care, regrettably, they are also the least able to get it because such care is expensive and hard to find, as discussed further in Chapter 11.

For adolescents, mothers' employment can have both positive and negative effects on their development. On the one hand, employed mothers provide positive role models, and they bring more income into the household. On the other hand, adolescents of employed mothers may have more home responsibilities, reducing time for homework, as well as less supervision, possibly leading to more risky behaviors.[94] Recent evidence regarding the net effect of mothers' employment on adolescent development is mixed, with some studies finding a negative effect and other research finding no effect overall.[95]

Single-Parent Families

Single-parent families are increasingly common in the United States, especially families maintained by mothers.[96] Table 10-6 indicates that, among families with one or more children under age 18 present, the percentage of mother-only families increased from slightly less than 12 percent to 26 percent between 1970 and 2006. In addition, just over 6 percent were father-only families, a figure that has quintupled since 1970. These figures include single parents who head their own household as well as those who live in someone else's household, whether with a parent or a nonrelative. One point to keep in mind in interpreting Census Bureau statistics on families, mentioned earlier in Chapter 3,

---

[93] For evidence that quality matters, see Shonkoff and Phillips, eds. *From Neurons to Neighborhoods*, Chapters 10 and 11; Chantelle J. Dowsett, Aletha C. Huston, Amy E. Imes, and Lisa Gennetian, "Structural and Process Features in Three Types of Child Care for Children from High and Low Income Families," *Early Childhood Research Quarterly* 2 (2008): 69–93; David Blau and Janet Currie, "Preschool, Day Care, and Afterschool Care: Who's Minding the Kids," in *Handbook of the Economics of Education*, Vol. 2, edited by Eric Hanushek and Finis Welch (North Holland: Elsevier, 2006), Chapter 20; and Jens Ludwig and Deborah A. Phillips, "The Benefits and Costs of Head Start," *Social Policy Report* XXI, no. 3 (2007): 3–14. Society for Research in Child Development.

[94] For extended discussions, see Robert Haveman and Barbara Wolfe, "The Determinants of Children's Attainments: A Review of Methods and Findings," *Journal of Economic Literature* 33, no. 4 (December 1995): 1829–78; and Waldfogel, *What Children Need*, Chapter 5.

[95] Studies finding evidence of negative effects of maternal employment on teens include P. Lindsay Chase-Lansdale et al., "Mothers' Transitions from Welfare to Work and the Well-Being of Preschoolers and Adolescents," *Science* 299, no. 5612 (March 7, 2003): 1548–62; and Charles L. Baum II, "The Long-Term Effects of Early and Recent Maternal Employment on a Child's Academic Achievement," *Journal of Family Issues* 25, no. 1 (January 2004): 29–60. In contrast, Alison Aughinbaugh and Maury Gittleman do not find negative effects in "Maternal Employment and Adolescent Risky Behavior," *Journal of Health Economics* 23, no. 4 (July 2004): 815–38.

[96] For an excellent discussion, see Ellwood and Jencks, "The Spread of Single-Parent Families in the United States Since 1960."

TABLE 10-6 Trends in Families with Own Children Under Age 18, 1970–2006

	As a % of All Families				
	1970	1980	1990	2000	2006
Mother-Only Families					
All races	11.5	19.4	24.2	25.8	26.4
White	8.9	15.1	18.8	20.7	21.4
Black	33.0	48.7	56.2	55.3	55.7
Hispanic origin	n.a.	24.0	29.3	28.4	28.3
Father-Only Families					
All races	1.3	2.1	3.9	5.5	6.4
White	1.2	2.0	3.8	5.4	6.2
Black	2.6	3.2	4.3	6.1	7.5
Hispanic origin	n.a.	1.9	4.0	5.7	6.1
Married-Couple Families					
All races	87.1	78.5	71.9	68.7	67.2
White	89.9	82.9	77.4	73.9	72.4
Black	64.3	48.1	39.4	38.6	36.7
Hispanic origin	n.a.	74.1	66.8	65.9	65.5

Notes: Families include those heading their own households and those living in the households of others (subfamilies). Cohabitors may be included among single-parent families. For 2006, *white* refers to those who reported race as white alone; *black* includes those who reported this race alone or in combination with one or more other race groups. For all years, persons of Hispanic origin may be of any race.

n.a. Not available.

Source: U.S. Census Bureau, Table FM-2, "All Parent/Child Situations by Type, Race, and Hispanic Origin of Householder or Reference Person: 1970 to Present" from www.census.gov.

is that cohabiting partners and their children are not counted as a family. This means that as cohabitation has risen, the count of mother-only and father-only families increasingly include families in which the parents of the child are cohabiting.[97]

Historically, mother-only families have been more common among African Americans, but as shown in Table 10-6 and Figure 10-2, the proportion of white mother-only families has increased considerably since 1970.[98] As of 2006, nearly 56 percent of black families with children were maintained by mothers as compared with just over 21 percent of white families and 28 percent of families of Hispanic origin. Single-parent families raise considerable concerns, particularly in relation to child well-being. First, such families, especially those maintained by women, experience a high incidence of poverty.[99] Second, as discussed in further detail in the next section, there is ongoing concern about the effect of growing up in a single-parent family on children's outcomes.

---

[97] See U.S. Census Bureau, "Living Arrangements of Children: 2004," *Current Population Reports* P70–114 (Washington, DC: U.S. Census Bureau, February 2008); and for more regarding trends in father-only families, see Steven Garasky and Daniel R. Meyer, "Reconsidering the Increase in Father-Only Families," *Demography* 33, no. 3 (August 1996): 385–93.

[98] Michael S. Rendall observes, however, that in contrast to black families, many white families still have two parents present, whether married or cohabiting, in "Entry or Exit? A Transition-Probability Approach to Explaining the High Prevalence of Single Motherhood Among Black Women," *Demography* 36, no. 3 (August 1999): 369–76.

[99] See Harry J. Holzer, Diane Whitmore Schanzenbach, Greg J. Duncan, and Jens Ludwig, "The Economic Costs of Poverty in the United States: Subsequent Effects of Children Growing Up Poor," *Journal of Children and Poverty* 14, no. 1 (March 2008): 41–61.

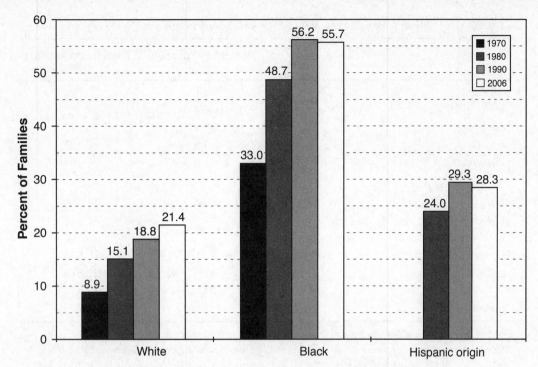

FIGURE 10-2   Mother-Only Families by Race and Ethnicity, 1970–2006 (%)

Table 10-7 shows the income and poverty status of families with children in 2006. Most strikingly, the median income of female-headed families was less than half that of married couples. As many as 36.5 percent were poor, compared to just 6.4 percent of married couples. These disparities explain why the "feminization" of poverty is at the center of a great deal of discussion.

Poverty rates are particularly high for African American and Hispanic female-headed families with children, with approximately 43 percent of both living in poverty in 2006, although these figures are well below the high of just over 60 percent in the early 1990s. Even among white, non-Hispanic female-headed families, the poverty rate for 2006 was 30 percent. Inevitably, the high rates of poverty among single-parent families are a major factor behind the high rates of poverty for children overall. In 2006, just over 17 percent of all children—10 percent of white, non-Hispanic, 27 percent of Hispanic, and 33 percent of black children—lived in poverty.[100]

When interpreting poverty statistics, it is important to understand the way the **official poverty rate** is currently determined. On the one hand, income used to determine poverty status does not include such items as food stamps, Medicaid, housing subsidies, and the Earned Income Tax Credit, so that it understates the total income of the low-income families that receive these benefits. On the other hand, although the poverty threshold is updated for changes in inflation, it remains a fixed multiple of the amount of money needed to provide food for the family. This measure, established in the 1960s, ignores the fact that expenditures on food have increased substantially less than costs for other items such as housing, health insurance, and education. In light of

---

[100] U.S. Census Bureau, Historical Poverty Tables, Table 3: "Poverty Status of People by Age, Race and Hispanic Origin: 1959–2006," available at www.census.gov. For discussion, see Hilary Hoynes, Marianne Page, and Ann Stevens, "Poverty in America: Trends and Explanations," *Journal of Economic Perspectives* 20, no. 1 (Winter 2006): 47–68.

TABLE 10-7   Income and Poverty Rates for Families with Children, 2006[a]

	Percent in Poverty 2006	Median Income ($) 2006
All Families	14.6	56,788
White, non-Hispanic	9.3	68,557
Black	28.1	35,138
Asian	9.5	80,131
Hispanic origin	23.4	37,163
Type of Family		
Married-couple families	6.4	74,049
Male householder, no wife present	17.9	37,388
Female householder, no husband present	36.5	24,394
White, non-Hispanic	30.2	27,540
Black	43.3	20,678
Asian	23.8	37,536
Hispanic origin	42.5	21,489

[a]Figures are for families heading their own households, with related children under age 18.

Notes: White, non-Hispanic refers to those who reported their race as white alone and reported Hispanic origin. *Black* (Asian) includes those who reported this race alone or in combination with one or more other race groups. Persons of Hispanic origin may be of any race.

Source: U.S. Census Bureau, Table POV04, "Families by Age of Householder, Number of Children, and Family Structure: 2006" and Table FINC-03 "Presence of Related Children Under 18 Years Old—All Families by Total Money Income in 2006, Type of Family, Experience in 2006, Race and Hispanic Origin of Reference Person" from www.census.gov.

these concerns, alternative measures of poverty are currently calculated as well. These alternatives, for instance, modify income by including the value of in-kind benefits such as food stamps and by deducting work-related expenses such as the cost of child care and out-of-pocket medical expenses. Some also include adjustments to the poverty threshold so that it better reflects regional differences in housing costs. Nevertheless, the official poverty rate continues to serve as a major indicator of economic well-being.[101]

It is not difficult to understand why single-parent families have incomes so much lower than families with two parents. First, they have a lower ratio of adults to children, and thus fewer potential earners. This also means that they have fewer caregivers per dependent, as well, making it far more difficult for the adult to do justice to both work and family, potentially lowering the adult's earnings. Second, the incidence of female-headed families is higher among the less educated, which further accounts for the lower income of such families.[102] Third, women tend to earn considerably less than men with comparable qualifications, and mothers tend to accumulate less labor force experience than other workers.

As noted earlier, single mothers may live independently or in extended households, with their parents (their children's grandparents), other relatives, or with an

---

[101] Since 1995, the U.S. Census Bureau has been tracking alternative measures alongside the official measure. For definitions and data, see reports included in the U.S. Census Bureau web page titled "Poverty Measurement Studies and Alternative Measures," available at http://www.census.gov/hhes/www/povmeas/povmeas.html. For further discussion, see Rebecca Blank, "How to Improve Poverty Measurement in the United States," *Journal of Policy Analysis and Management* 27, no. 2 (Spring 2008): 233–54.

[102] Francine D. Blau, "Trends in the Well-Being of American Women, 1970–1995"; and Sara McLanahan, "Diverging Destinies."

unmarried male partner.[103] Doubling up with parents does involve some loss of privacy, but also reduces costs, because of economies of scale. In addition, other household members often provide financial assistance and emotional support as well as in-house childcare. Notably, when a single mother cohabits with a male partner, U.S. Census Bureau figures do not take into account the partner's income in determining the family's income or poverty status because an unmarried partner is not counted as part of the family. The mother and her children may, nevertheless, benefit from some degree of income sharing with the partner.[104] Studies find that the poverty rate for children in cohabiting families would fall slightly if cohabitors' incomes were added, but that many of these families would remain poor because cohabitors often have low income themselves.[105]

Recent research has also focused attention on a previously overlooked group termed *fragile families*. In many cases, while a child's parents may not be living together (and thus not "cohabiting"), many fathers are around at the time of their child's birth, want to help raise them, and more often than not are romantically involved with the child's mother. What distinguishes these types of families is that quite often the parents have low levels of education, unstable employment histories, and low earnings; they are also quite susceptible to breakup.[106]

The economic circumstances of families maintained by women also vary considerably depending on the woman's age and marital status. Never-married mothers tend to have particularly low incomes, not only because they are less likely than divorced mothers to receive child support from absent fathers, but also because they are, on average, younger and have less education. Women who become parents as teenagers, most of whom are not married, tend to remain at a particular economic and social disadvantage throughout their lives. Many have little education and, if employed, they generally earn low wages. At first, researchers assumed that it was early childbearing itself that led to these negative outcomes. Subsequently, however, studies suggested that many of these women would not have done particularly well even if they delayed childbearing until their twenties, because many are, themselves, from economically and socially disadvantaged backgrounds. While the research evidence to date is mixed, it does appear that early childbearing, per se, has some detrimental effect on young women and their children.[107]

Divorced mothers tend to fare somewhat better than never-married mothers because they are more likely to receive child support payments. Nonetheless, many struggle financially. One recent study found that after the first year of divorce, children's family income was 40 percent lower, on average, than if their parents stayed together.

[103] See, for instance, Wendy Sigle-Rushton and Sara McLanahan, "The Living Arrangements of New Unmarried Mothers," *Demography* 39, no. 3 (August 2002): 415–33. For recent evidence on the rising number of children living with grandparents, see U.S. Census Bureau web page, America's Families and Living Arrangements, Historical Table CH-7, "Grandchildren Under Age 18 Living in the Home of Grandparents: 1970 to Present" at www.census.gov.

[104] Regarding pooling among cohabitors, see Anne E. Winkler, "Economic Decisionmaking Among Cohabitors: Findings Regarding Income Pooling," *Applied Economics* 29, no. 8 (August 1997): 1079–90. For a more general discussion, see Steven J. Haider and Kathleen McGarry, "Recent Trends in Resource Sharing Among the Poor," in *Working and Poor: How Economic and Policy Changes Are Affecting Low-Wage Workers*, edited by Rebecca M. Blank, Sheldon H. Danziger, and Robert F. Schoeni (New York: Russell Sage Foundation, 2006), pp. 205–32.

[105] See, for instance, Manning and Brown, "Children's Economic Well-Being in Married and Cohabiting Parent Families."

[106] Marcia Carlson and Sara McLanahan, "Early Father Involvement in Fragile Families" in *Conceptualizing and Measuring Father Involvement*, edited by Randal D. Day and Michael E. Lamb (Mahwah, NJ: Lawrence Erlbaum Associates, 2004), pp. 241–71.

[107] For a recent study see Jason M. Fletcher and Barbara L. Wolfe, "Education and Labor Market Consequences of Teenage Childbearing: Evidence Using the Timing of Pregnancy Outcomes and Community Fixed Effects," *Journal of Human Resources* 44, no. 2 (Spring 2009): 303-25. For a review of earlier research, see Saul D. Hoffman, "Teenage Childbearing Is Not so Bad After All...Or Is It? A Review of the New Literature," *Family Planning Perspectives* 30, no. 5 (September/October 1998): 236–43.

After 6 years, their economic situation was somewhat better, and their post-divorce family income was only 20 percent lower, on average, though the latter figure varies considerably depending on whether the mother remarries.[108]

An important reason for the low income of both never-married and divorced mothers is that if noncustodial parents provide any child support at all, they tend to contribute less than what would generally be considered their fair share. In 2005, only 57 percent of custodial parents were awarded child support; of those who were supposed to receive payments, fewer than half (47 percent) received the full amount they were awarded, 30 percent received partial payment, and the remaining 23 percent received no payment at all.[109] Nonetheless, child support payments provide a considerable supplement to income for parents who do receive them, and they reduce reliance on welfare.[110] Indeed, given the importance of this source of income, the government has stepped up efforts to increase such payments, as discussed further in Chapter 11.

A number of factors contribute to low rates of child support collection.[111] Some parents fail to pay child support they could well afford because they believe that the custodial parent does not spend the entire amount on their children. There is also the question of determining the appropriate share of overhead costs such as housing, maintenance, and so on. Others may withhold payments in retaliation for limited visitation rights or simply because of resentment against the other parent. In a few cases the other parent may be deceased. Far more frequently, however, absent parents are themselves poor and it would be genuinely difficult for them to pay more.[112] Unfortunately, it is most often mothers who are the least able to stand on their own, with little education, little or no labor market experience, and few other resources, who are also the least likely to receive any support from their children's father(s).

This review makes clear that single-parent families are at a particular economic disadvantage. In Chapter 11 we review government policies intended to raise incomes of these families, pointing to both the successes and limitations of these policies.

Family Structure and Children's Outcomes

As evident from the statistics, the share of single-parent families has increased considerably. Consequently, an increasing fraction of children are being raised in such families. For instance, in 2006, just 70 percent of children under age 18 lived in a married-couple family, and even fewer lived with both biological or adoptive parents (in the remainder a stepparent was present).[113] Children's living arrangements may affect their economic

---

[108] Marianne E. Page and Ann Huff Stevens, "The Economic Consequences of Absent Parents," *Journal of Human Resources* 39, no. 1 (Winter 2004): 80–107. See also, Suzanne M. Bianchi, Lekha Subaiya, and Joan R. Kahn, "The Gender Gap in the Economic Well-Being of Nonresident Fathers and Custodial Mothers," *Demography* 36, no. 2 (May 1999): 195–203.

[109] Figures are from U.S. Census Bureau, "Custodial Mothers and Fathers and Their Child Support: 2005," Table 1, available at www.census.gov.

[110] Regarding child support's effect on income, see Maria Cancian and Daniel R. Meyer, "Child Support and the Economy," in *Working and Poor: How Economic and Policy Changes Are Affecting Low-Wage Workers,* edited by Rebecca M. Blank, Sheldon H. Danziger, and Robert F. Schoeni, (New York: Russell Sage, 2006), pp. 338–65. For evidence it has reduced the welfare rolls, see Chien-Chung Huang, Irwin Garfinkel, and Jane Waldfogel, "Child Support Enforcement and Welfare Caseloads," *Journal of Human Resources* 39, no. 1 (Winter 2004): 108–34.

[111] For further discussion, see Andrea Beller and John W. Graham, "The Economics of Child Support," in *Marriage and the Economy: Theory and Evidence from Advanced Industrial Countries,* edited by Shoshana Grossbard-Schechtman (Cambridge: Cambridge University Press, 2003), pp. 153–76.

[112] Chien-Chung Huang, Ronald B. Mincy, and Irwin Garfinkel, "Child Support Obligations and Low-Income Fathers," *Journal of Marriage and Family* 67, no. 5 (November 2005): 1213–25.

[113] See U.S. Census Bureau, "Living Arrangements of Children: 2004," *Current Population Reports* P70–114 (February 2008).

and social well-being.[114] Studies, such as those cited here, examine effects of growing up in a singe-parent family on family income, as well as a number of outcomes for children, including their educational attainment, labor force participation, and likelihood of teen pregnancy.

A landmark 1994 study by Sara McLanahan and Gary Sandefur, which received considerable attention, found that children in married-couple families with both biological parents present do better in these respects than those from single-parent families.[115] This study also found that a number of outcomes are not as favorable for children in step-parent families as for those living with both biological parents. Among the specific findings regarding single-parent families, they report that children raised by single parents have a higher high school dropout rate and a higher rate of teen births than those raised by two biological parents, even after taking account of differences in parents' educational levels, race, and income. Stated another way, their findings suggest that, while differences in parents' education and incomes partly account for differences in children's outcomes, family structure also contributes to such differences. Among the reasons for this negative effect, they point to the fact that single-parent families tend to move more often, and so tend to form fewer connections to their local communities; community ties are often beneficial in helping to find a job or getting other help. Further, because children in single-parent families tend to receive less parental attention and supervision at home, this factor may also contribute to higher high school dropout rates and increased likelihood of teen pregnancy.

This study generated considerable interest and debate about whether, and to what extent, growing up in a single-parent family is the real cause of children performing poorly in school, among other negative outcomes. Some argue that other factors might lead to both children's poor school performance and parents' divorce, such as a parent's substance abuse problem or a high degree of family conflict. In these cases, the child might well perform poorly in school even if the parents did not separate. As a result, researchers continue to make efforts to disentangle causation from correlation.[116] Some of this research tends to confirm McLanahan and Sandefur's findings that living in arrangements other than an intact biological two-parent family, such as a single-parent or blended family, results in unfavorable effects on educational outcomes, but others find no such effect.[117] In interpreting the research findings, it is important to keep in mind that even if growing up in a single-parent family has negative effects, this only means that the risk of less desirable outcomes is increased, *not* that it is assured or nonexistent for children in families with both biological parents.

---

[114] For evidence on the impact of family instability, see Paula Formby and Andrew J. Cherlin, "Family Instsability and Child Well-Being," *American Sociological Review* 72, no. 2 (April 2007): 181–201.

[115] Sara McLanahan and Gary Sandefur, *Growing Up with a Single Parent: What Hurts, What Helps?* (Cambridge, MA: Harvard University Press, 1994). In this study, adopted children are included with biological children.

[116] For reviews of the methodological challenges, see Wendy Sigle-Rushton and Sara McLanahan, "Father Absence and Child Well-Being: A Critical Review," in *The Future of the Family*, edited by Daniel P. Moynihan, Timothy M. Smeeding, and Lee Rainwater (New York: Russell Sage Foundation, 2004), pp. 116–55; and Ribar, "What Do Social Scientists Know About the Benefits of Marriage?"

[117] For evidence that family structure influences educational attainment, after accounting for other factors, see Anne Case, I-Fen Lin, and Sara McLanahan, "Household Resource Allocation in Stepfamilies: Darwin Reflects on the Plight of Cinderella," *American Economic Review* 89, no. 2 (May 1999): 234–38; and Eirik Evenhouse and Siobhan Reilly, "A Sibling Study of Stepchild Well-Being," *Journal of Human Resources* 39, no. 1 (Winter 2004): 248–76. For evidence on the other side see Donna K. Ginther and Robert A. Pollak, "Family Structure and Children's Educational Outcomes: Blended Families, Stylized Facts, and Descriptive Regressions," *Demography* 41, no. 4 (November 2004): 671–96.

Conclusion

This chapter considered the effect of a woman's labor force participation and other factors on the formation, functioning, and possible breakup of families. It is clear that dual-earner families and female-headed families are becoming far more common, rapidly replacing the traditional married-couple family of the breadwinner husband and homemaker wife. Dual-earner families earn considerably more income, on average, than single-earner families. In addition, women's increased earnings most likely increase their bargaining power in the family. Nevertheless, some concern centers on whether maternal employment during a child's first year of life may negatively affect children's cognitive development. In evaluating this finding it is important to keep in mind that maternal employment is only one factor, of many, that affects children's well-being and achievement and, moreover, researchers cannot fully account for the quality of nonparental care, which may attenuate any negative effects. Out-of-home care for preschoolers, on the other hand, is generally found to be beneficial. We also looked at the difficulties faced by women who head families. In Chapter 11, we examine policies designed to raise incomes of these and other low-income families. Some evidence also indicates that children growing up in single-parent families do not, on average, fare as well as those raised in married-couple families with both biological parents present, though again this is an area of active research.

Questions for Review and Discussion

1. Describe the main changes in the typical family in the United States over the past 30–40 years and explain their causes.
2. Women's rising labor force participation might either increase or reduce marriage rates. Explain why the effect could go either way.
3. A negative relationship is observed between women's labor force participation and fertility. Is higher labor force participation the cause of the lower birthrate, or vice versa? Discuss.
4. Increasing numbers of children are being raised in families in which mothers are cohabiting, either with the child's father or with a boyfriend. Consider the pros and cons for children of these arrangements versus living with a single parent.
5. In what ways are marriage and cohabitation similar, and in what ways do they differ?
6. Explain why child support enforcement might encourage some married couples to stay together while it might encourage others to break up.
7. What are the advantages and disadvantages of the rising age of first marriage?
8. Women who become mothers when they are teenagers are less likely to obtain a college degree than those who delay their childbearing until at least their mid-twenties. Discuss why this outcome is generally the case and what the consequences for these women and their families are likely to be. (*Hint*: Refer back to the human capital model in Chapter 6.)
9. Explain why the distinction between causation and correlation is so important in understanding the relationship between family structure and children's well-being. Suggest another factor that may affect both children's outcomes and family structure.

INTERNET-BASED DATA EXERCISE

Note: In doing this exercise, students should be aware that the precise names of documents and their location within a web site may change over time.

The U.S. Census Bureau is the primary source of government data on many topics included in this text including income, education, health insurance, and poverty.

Visit the home page of the U.S. Census Bureau at http://www.census.gov.

1. Click on "Poverty" on the Census Bureau home page. On the poverty page, look for the most recent document titled "Income, Poverty, and Health Insurance Coverage" (or a similar title). (This is the same publication used in the data exercise for Chapter 5). Find Table 3, which provides information on people and families in poverty by selected characteristics.

   a. What is the current poverty rate for families? How does this figure compare with the rate in Table 10-7?
   b. Look at differences in poverty rates by age, race, nativity, and work experience. What might explain these differences given discussions in this chapter and earlier ones?

2. The U.S. Census Bureau home page also provides a link to an annual publication called the *Statistical Abstract of the United States*. This publication provides information

on a broad range of topics, from topics covered in this book such as birth, marriage, and divorce, to crime, natural resources, and science and technology.

a. Find the most recent statistics on the marriage rate per 1,000 population and divorce rate per 1,000 population. Compare these to the figures in Table 10-1. (Also, for these statistics and those in the following questions, be sure to write down the precise names of the table(s) where you found them).

b. This publication also provides information on marriage rates and divorce rates by state. For the state in which you are currently located, what are these rates and how do they compare with the national average?

c. The fertility rate reported in Table 10-3 is technically called the "total fertility rate." Using these data, update Table 10-3. How do figures for different race and ethnic groups compare to the replacement rate level of 2,100 (or 2.1 children per mother)? Discuss.

Suggested Readings

Black, Dan A., Seth G. Sanders, and Lowell J. Taylor. "The Economics of Lesbian and Gay Families." *Journal of Economic Perspectives* 21, no. 2 (Spring 2007): 53–70.

Blank, Rebecca. "How to Improve Poverty Measurement in the United States," *Journal of Policy Analysis and Management* 27, no. 2 (Spring 2008): 233–54.

Blau, Francine D. "Trends in the Well-Being of American Women, 1970–1995." *Journal of Economic Literature* 36, no. 1 (March 1998): 112–65.

Edin, Kathryn, and Laura Lein. *Making Ends Meet: How Single Mothers Survive Welfare and Low-Wage Work.* New York: Russell Sage Foundation, 1997.

Ellwood, David T., and Christopher Jencks. "The Spread of Single-Parent Families in the United States Since 1960." In *The Future of the Family,* edited by Daniel P. Moynihan, Timothy M. Smeeding, and Lee Rainwater. New York: Russell Sage Foundation, 2004.

England, Paula, and Kathryn Edin, eds. *Unmarried Couples with Children.* New York: Russell Sage Foundation, 2007.

Grossbard-Schechtman, Shoshana, ed. *Marriage and the Economy.* Cambridge: Cambridge University Press, 2003.

Hoynes, Hilary, Marianne Page, and Ann Stevens. "Poverty in America: Trends and Explanations." *Journal of Economic Perspectives* 20, no. 1 (winter 2006): 47–68.

Lundberg, Shelly. "Men and Islands: Dealing with the Family in Empirical Labor Economics." *Labour Economics* 12 (2005): 591–612.

Lundberg, Shelly, and Robert A. Pollak. "The American Family and Family Economics." *Journal of Economic Perspectives* 21, no. 2 (Spring 2007): 3–26.

McLanahan, Sara. "Diverging Destinies: How Children Are Faring Under the Second Demographic Transition." *Demography* 41, no. 4 (November 2004): 607–28.

McLanahan, Sara, and Gary Sandefur. *Growing Up with a Single Parent: What Hurts, What Helps?* Cambridge, MA: Harvard University Press, 1994.

Moffitt, Robert A., ed. *Welfare, the Family, and Reproductive Behavior: Research Perspectives.* Washington, DC: National Research Council, 1998.

Moynihan, Daniel P., Timothy M. Smeeding, and Lee Rainwater, eds. *The Future of the Family.* New York: Russell Sage Foundation, 2004.

Shonkoff, Jack P., and Deborah A. Phillips, eds. *From Neurons to Neighborhoods: The Science of Early Child Development.* Washington, DC: National Research Council, 2000.

Thornton, Arland, William Axinn, and Yu Xie. *Marriage and Cohabitation.* Chicago, IL: University of Chicago Press, 2007.

Waite, Linda, ed. *The Ties That Bind: Perspectives on Marriage and Cohabitation.* New York: Aldine de Gruyter, 2000.

Waldfogel, Jane. *What Children Need.* Cambridge, MA: Harvard University Press, 2006.

Key Terms

marriage *274*
divorce *279*
opposite-sex cohabitation *284*
gay and lesbian couples *286*

fertility *287*
demand for children *287*
fertility rate *288*
baby boom *288*
Generation X *290*
Generation Y *290*

dual-earner families *293*
single-parent families *293*
male marriage premium *295*

motherhood wage penalty *295*
employed spouse penalty *296*
official poverty rate *301*

CHAPTER 11

Policies Affecting Paid Work and the Family

Chapter Highlights

- Policies to Alleviate Poverty
- Taxes, Specialization, and Marriage
- The Competing Demands of Work and Family

- Rationales for Government and Employer Policies to Assist Workers
- Government and Employer Family-Friendly Policies

A host of programs and policies have emerged and evolved over time that influence the well-being of individuals and families. This chapter begins where Chapter 10 left off, by discussing government policies to alleviate poverty, especially those that affect mother-only families, because these families often face the greatest difficulties. Next, we review some major features of the U.S. federal income tax and Social Security systems and point to some of their potential effects on paid work and family formation decisions. The remainder of the chapter discusses the competing demands of paid work and family faced by more and more individuals as single-parent and dual-earner families swiftly replace the traditional family of a breadwinner husband and homemaker wife. We next discuss the potential role for government and employers in alleviating these conflicts and review family-friendly policies, including family and medical leave and child care, as well as alternative work schedules offered by firms.

POLICIES TO ALLEVIATE POVERTY

This section examines a number of policies designed to help raise the incomes of people living in poverty in the United States, with emphasis on those that assist mother-only families. We begin by describing Aid to Families with Dependent Children (AFDC), the federal program that, for more than 60 years, guaranteed cash assistance to poor children and their families, and then turn to the program that replaced it in 1996, Temporary Assistance for Needy Families (TANF).[1] We next examine the Earned Income Tax Credit (EITC), government employment programs, and policies designed to

---

[1] For overviews of the AFDC and TANF programs, see Robert A. Moffitt, "Welfare Reform: The U.S. Experience," Institute for Research on Poverty Discussion Paper 1334-08 (February 2008); Robert A. Moffitt, "The Temporary Assistance for Needy Families Program," in *Means-Tested Transfer Programs in the United States*, edited by Robert A. Moffitt (Chicago: University of Chicago Press, 2003), pp. 291–363; Rebecca M. Blank, "What We Know, What We Don't Know and What We Need to Know About Welfare Reform" in *Welfare Reform and Its Long-Term Consequences for America's Poor*, edited by James Ziliak (Cambridge, UK: Cambridge University Press, forthcoming); and Jeffrey Grogger, and Lynn A. Karoly, *Welfare Reform: Effects of a Decade of Change* (Cambridge, MA: Harvard University Press, 2005).

increase child support paid by noncustodial parents. In light of recent legislation, we also review marriage promotion initiatives intended to improve economic well-being.

Aid to Families with Dependent Children: The Former U.S. Welfare Program

AFDC, initiated in 1935 as part of the Social Security Act, was a federal entitlement program that provided all eligible families, principally those headed by single mothers, with cash assistance. As the program evolved, AFDC recipients also generally qualified for in-kind benefits, including food stamps and Medicaid. Many were eligible for housing subsidies as well.

AFDC came to be one of the most hotly debated government transfer programs, despite the fact that it made up only about 1 percent of the federal budget. One concern was that because AFDC mainly provided benefits to single mothers, it might create an incentive for couples not to get married or to break up, in order for the mother and her children to be eligible for welfare.[2] Public concern was heightened when it became clear that the program, originally intended to help families of poor widows, in fact mainly served divorced women and, over the years, increasing numbers of never-married mothers. This trend can be seen in Table 11-1, which provides data on AFDC for 1970

TABLE 11-1   Statistics on the AFDC/TANF Program, Selected Years

	AFDC Program		TANF Program	
	1970	**1993**	**2000**	**2005**
Benefits				
AFDC/TANF guarantee for three-person family[a]				
In current dollars	$194	$414	$446	$468
In 2005 dollars	$878	$549	$505	$468
AFDC/TANF tax rate (rate at which benefits are reduced)	67.0%	100.0%	varies	varies
Recipient Characteristics				
Average monthly number of recipients (in thousands)	7,415	14,143	6,324	5,124
Recipients as % of population	4.0%	5.4%	2.1%	1.7%
Adults with earnings (%)[b]	n.a.	7.4%	23.6%	19.5%
Adults who are never-married (%)[c]	27.9%	53.1%	65.3%	68.8%
Average family size	4.0	2.9	2.6	2.4

[a]Weighted average monthly benefit computed as the benefit for each state weighted by that state's share of total AFDC/TANF families.

[b]The 1970 and 1993 figures indicate percentage of AFDC families with earnings.

[c]For 1970 and 1993, figures indicate percentage of AFDC children with never-married parent.

n.a. Not available.

Source: U.S. Department of Health and Human Services, *Indicators of Welfare Dependence,* Annual Report to Congress (2007 edition), available at http://aspe.hhs.gov.

---

[2] Starting in 1961, states were also permitted to offer AFDC benefits to two-parent families with an unemployed spouse and, beginning in 1988, all states offered such benefits. However, single mothers remained the overwhelming majority of welfare recipients. See Anne E. Winkler, "Does AFDC-UP Encourage Two-Parent Families?" *Journal of Policy Analysis and Management* 14, no. 1 (Winter 1995): 1–24.

and 1993 (when caseloads were at their peak level), and for TANF for 2000 and 2005. Table 11-1 shows that from 1970 to 1993 the percentage of families on AFDC headed by never-married mothers increased from 28 to 53 percent. It was, therefore, argued that this program discouraged marriage and encouraged unmarried women to have children. Recent evidence suggests, however, that even though AFDC appears to have affected these decisions, it cannot explain the dramatic rise in female headship or in births to unmarried women since the 1970s.[3]

AFDC also created potential disincentives for paid work because it provided the maximum benefit, termed the *AFDC guarantee*, for recipients who were not employed. As we saw in Chapter 4, the availability of nonlabor income increases the reservation wage, thereby reducing the probability of labor force participation. Furthermore, in the later years of AFDC, if a recipient entered the labor force, the AFDC guarantee was reduced by a dollar for each dollar earned on the job. This is equivalent to a 100 percent tax rate on earnings.[4] Needless to say, for any individual, on welfare or not, this would provide a considerable disincentive to work. Evidence indicates that AFDC did reduce labor supply, but again the effects were found to be relatively small. Further, altering the tax rate was not found to have much impact on recipients' propensity to work.[5]

AFDC also discouraged paid work because, by keeping their hours low, recipients could remain on the AFDC program and thus retain access to Medicaid. Their Medicaid benefits would be lost if they were no longer AFDC recipients. However, changes that started in the late 1980s reduced this disincentive by allowing pregnant women, infants, and young children to receive Medicaid even if their income rose somewhat so they no longer qualified for AFDC.[6] Another concern was that AFDC promoted welfare dependency because benefits were not time limited. Evidence indicates, however, that most recipients did not rely on AFDC for long periods of time.[7]

Finally, AFDC and other transfer programs were also subject to much criticism because they produced only modest success in alleviating poverty. Part of the reason that AFDC and other programs were not more successful was that the amount of money available became increasingly inadequate. As Table 11-1 shows, the value of the AFDC guarantee (averaged across the states) fell by well over 50 percent between 1970 and 1993 in inflation-adjusted terms. Although the impact of this decline was cushioned somewhat by an increase in the real value of food stamps, as of 1993, the combined value of the two benefits for a family of three still provided only two-thirds of the amount needed to reach the poverty threshold. The decline in real wages for less-educated individuals, which we discussed in Chapter 8, further compounded the difficulty of raising low-income households out of poverty.

---

[3] For a comprehensive review of the literature, see Robert A. Moffitt, "The Effect of Welfare on Marriage and Fertility," in *Welfare, the Family, and Reproductive Behavior: Research Perspectives,* edited by Robert A. Moffitt (Washington, DC: National Research Council, 1998), pp. 50–59; and for an updated view of the evidence, Moffitt, "Temporary Assistance to Needy Families Program"; For evidence that AFDC may also have encouraged cohabitation, see Robert A. Moffitt, Robert Reville, and Anne E. Winkler, "Beyond Single Mothers: Cohabitation and Marriage in the U.S. Welfare System," *Demography* 35, no. 3 (August 1998): 359–78.

[4] Starting in 1981, the AFDC tax rate was set at 67 percent for four months and then rose to 100 percent thereafter.

[5] Robert A. Moffitt, "The Temporary Assistance for Needy Families Program."

[6] Anne E. Winkler, "The Incentive Effects of Medicaid on Women's Labor Supply," *Journal of Human Resources* 26, no. 2 (Spring 1991): 308–37; Robert A. Moffitt and Barbara Wolfe, "The Effect of the Medicaid Program on Welfare Participation and Labor Supply," *Review of Economics and Statistics* 74, no. 4 (November 1992): 615–26; and Aaron S. Yelowitz, "The Medicaid Notch, Labor Supply, and Welfare Participation: Evidence from Eligibility Expansions," *Quarterly Journal of Economics* 110, no. 4 (November 1995): 909–39.

[7] See, for instance, Moffitt, "The Temporary Assistance for Needy Families Program."

The Iron Triangle of Welfare

Redesigning welfare is particularly difficult because three often-sought policy goals are in conflict: alleviating poverty, providing incentives to work, and limiting costs by keeping down the number of recipients. This conflict is sometimes referred to as the "**iron triangle of welfare.**" It is impossible to simultaneously achieve more than two of the following three desirable features: a low **welfare tax rate** on additional earnings of welfare recipients to encourage work, an adequate **welfare guarantee** (the amount received by an individual with no earnings) that is high enough to provide a sufficient safety net, and a low **break-even level of income** to limit the number of program recipients and hence program costs. The break-even level of income is the maximum level of income individuals can earn in the labor market and still be eligible for welfare. Thus, the lower the break-even level of income, the fewer individuals will be eligible for the program.

Table 11-2 illustrates this dilemma. Consider a hypothetical welfare program in which benefits are computed as the welfare guarantee minus taxable earnings.[8] The first row of Table 11-2 shows the case where the annual welfare guarantee is set at $10,000 and the tax rate on welfare benefits is 100 percent; families are eligible for assistance provided their earnings are below the break-even level of $10,000.[9] We assume, for purposes of this example, that the $10,000 guarantee level is viewed as providing an adequate safety net. In this case, two program goals are achieved: The welfare guarantee is high enough to provide an adequate safety net and the break-even level of income is low enough so that eligibility for the program is limited to families with $10,000 of income or less. However, the incentive to work is low because benefits are reduced dollar for dollar with labor market earnings.

Next, suppose the government seeks to address the work incentive problem by reducing the tax rate to 50 percent (as shown in case 2 of the table). This encourages people to work because now benefits are reduced by only $.50 for each dollar of labor market earnings. In this case, again, two program goals are achieved: Work incentives are strengthened (by the lower tax rate) and the welfare guarantee for families without earnings remains adequate at $10,000. Now, however, the break-even level of income increases from $10,000 to $20,000, meaning that many more families—those with incomes between $10,000 and $20,000—are eligible for transfers. Thus, although work incentives for welfare recipients are increased, program costs rise as a result of the increase in the eligible population.

TABLE 11-2   Illustration of the Iron Triangle of Welfare

	Annual Welfare Guarantee	Welfare Tax Rate	Break-even Income
Case 1	$10,000	100%	$10,000
Case 2	$10,000	50%	$20,000
Case 3	$5,000	50%	$10,000

Definitions: Benefit formula: Benefits received = Guarantee − (tax rate × earnings).

Guarantee: Maximum welfare benefit (provided if earnings are zero).

Break-even income: Maximum earnings level that qualifies for benefits.

---

[8] A simple mathematical representation is as follows: benefits received = $G - t^*Y$, where G is the welfare guarantee as defined in the text, t is the welfare tax rate or the amount by which benefits are reduced for each additional dollar in income, and Y refers to income. Breakeven income (the income level at which benefits fall to zero) is equal to G/t.

[9] This tax rate applies only to the earnings of *welfare recipients;* it differs from federal income tax rates, which will be discussed shortly.

Finally, suppose the government keeps the tax rate at 50 percent (to encourage work) but seeks to reduce program costs by cutting the welfare guarantee in half from $10,000 to $5,000 (as shown in case 3 of the table). In this case, again, two program goals are achieved: The higher incentive to work remains and the break-even level of income is kept relatively low at $10,000. But families without earnings must subsist on $5,000 rather than $10,000. Thus, while the number of eligible individuals is kept low, as in the first case, this also means that many more families have inadequate income and so the goal of an adequate safety net is not achieved.

The conflicts represented by the iron triangle of welfare were present in AFDC. As we shall see, the TANF program differs from this earlier welfare program by using mandatory work requirements, with sanctions for those who do not comply, to create work incentives. This feature increases employment for welfare recipients, but, unlike a reduction in the tax rate, it also keeps down the number of recipients without requiring a reduction in the guarantee level. However, due to other aspects of the program, TANF, unlike AFDC, does not function as a true "safety net." As discussed further later, TANF provides states with considerably more latitude in setting eligibility rules than under AFDC. Further, recipients who fail to comply with TANF program rules may face termination of benefits for their family as a whole.[10]

Temporary Assistance to Needy Families: The Current U.S. Welfare Program

In 1996 AFDC was replaced with a new program called **TANF**, which altered the federal provision of welfare transfers in a number of important ways. For one, it changed the way welfare is funded. AFDC was a federal entitlement program, meaning that the federal government provided assistance to families deemed needy by federal rules. Under TANF, states are given fixed block grants and have greater discretion regarding program rules, eligibility, and how funds are used. This shift was based on the view that states would be better able to tailor aid to their population because of their greater knowledge of their residents' needs. As of 2008, 50 percent of single parents receiving welfare were required to be employed in some capacity for a minimum of 30 hours.[11] One argument for the work requirement is that most married women, including those with small children, are now employed so that it is not unreasonable to require single women maintaining families to also be employed. To put "teeth" into these rules, the legislation gave states greater authority to sanction recipients who do not follow program rules. TANF is also designed to reduce welfare dependency; it mandated a 5-year cumulative time limit on receiving federally funded welfare, albeit with exemptions possible for up to 20 percent of families. In addition, it restricted eligibility for teen parents, so that only those who stay in school and live with their parents can receive benefits, stepped up enforcement of child support by noncustodial parents, most often fathers, and limited eligibility for food stamps for some adults.[12]

Pressure to restructure welfare grew, beginning in the 1980s, as reflected in the emphasis on work in the 1988 Family Support Act, and President Clinton's promise during the 1992 campaign to "end welfare as we know it." To this end, early in his presidency, President Clinton encouraged states to experiment with welfare reform. In response, more than two-thirds of the states sought and received waivers from the federal government,

---

[10] See Moffitt, "The Temporary Assistance for Needy Families Program," p. 341. While sanctions have long been a part of welfare policy, sanctions under TANF are more frequent and have much greater financial ramifications. See Dan Bloom and Don Winstead, "Sanctions and Welfare Reform," *Welfare Reform and Beyond*, Policy Brief No. 12 (Brookings Institution: Washington, DC, January 2002).

[11] In the case of two-parent families, 90 percent of such families were required to have an employed adult, and minimum work hours were set higher than for single-parent families.

[12] U.S. House of Representatives, *2004 Green Book.*

which allowed them to try alternative approaches to welfare, including time limits for welfare receipt, requiring recipients to work after a certain period, limiting AFDC benefit increases for those who had additional children while receiving aid, providing sanctions or bonuses to encourage completion of high school, and cutting off benefits to teen mothers who did not live with their parents. The 1996 welfare legislation embodied many features of this earlier wave of reform. Nonetheless one fundamental difference is that the 1996 legislation ended the federal guarantee of assistance. Under TANF, states provide benefits to needy families only if they are willing and able to do so.

As might be expected, the states (and the District of Columbia) have taken advantage of the greater latitude given to them by the federal government under TANF and are now essentially running 51 different welfare experiments. For instance, in calculating welfare benefits, states now differ greatly as to the tax rate applied to a welfare recipient's earnings, with some states choosing very low tax rates in an effort to increase work incentives.[13] States have also made different choices regarding eligibility for two-parent families, and whether benefits are reduced if recipients have additional children. Because the state-level policies generally include both "carrots" and "sticks" in an effort to encourage or discourage certain behaviors, it is virtually impossible to classify individual states as more harsh or generous across the board. Also, program evaluation is difficult because it is hard to isolate the influence of individual policies.

It is, however, possible to draw some conclusions about the initial success of the 1996 welfare reform. Most dramatically, as shown in Table 11-1, it resulted in more than a 50 percent reduction in the national welfare caseload from 1993, when numbers were at or near their most recent peak, to 2005. This decrease was unprecedented in the history of the program, and far larger than policy makers anticipated. By 2005, just 1.7 percent of the U.S. population were receiving welfare benefits, as compared with 5.4 percent in 1993. This dramatic decline was a result of three major factors: (1) changes in welfare, which began with the waivers in the early 1990s, (2) the expansion of the EITC (to be discussed shortly), and (3) the booming U.S. economy of the late 1990s.[14] These factors contributed to a considerable reduction in the rate of families entering welfare, as well as an increase in the rate of families exiting the program.[15]

A critical issue is to what extent the changes in welfare are associated with increased employment, earnings, and income, and hence reductions in the poverty rate of the target population. TANF and the other changes do appear to have had some success at moving individuals from welfare to work. As shown in Figure 4-8, starting in the mid-1990s, the labor force participation rate of single mothers increased considerably more rapidly than for married mothers. Since 2001, the labor force participation rate for single mothers has declined slightly but continues to remain relatively high.[16] Recent welfare changes also appear to have led to increases in family earnings and reductions in poverty. However, some evidence indicates that the economic well-being of women on the lowest rungs of the economic ladder may have worsened.[17]

---

[13] Jordan D. Matsudaira and Rebecca M. Blank, "The Impact of Earnings Disregards on the Behavior of Low Income Families," NBER Working Paper No. 14038 (May 2008).

[14] Numerous studies have sought to untangle the role of each factor. For reviews, see, for instance, Moffitt, "The Temporary Assistance for Needy Families Program"; and Grogger and Karoly, *Welfare Reform*.

[15] Jeffrey Grogger, Steven J. Haider, and Jacob Klerman, "Why Did the Welfare Rolls Fall During the 1990s? The Importance of Entry," *American Economic Review* 93, no. 2 (May 2003): 288–92; and Moffitt, "Welfare Reform."

[16] Participation rates for married mothers also declined slightly, suggesting that the slight decline for single mothers reflects a broader weakness in the labor market.

[17] For overviews of findings, see Moffitt, "Welfare Reform"; Blank, "What We Know?"; and Grogger and Karoly, *Welfare Reform*. Economists have also examined the impact of welfare reform on a broader range of outcomes, including aspects of children's well-being, consumption patterns, and access to health insurance as discussed extensively in Blank, "What We Know." For a feminist critique of this research, see Karen Christopher, "Welfare as We [Don't] Know It: A Review and Feminist Critique of Welfare Reform Research in the United States," *Feminist Economics* 10, no. 2 (July 2004): 143–71.

One difficulty in drawing definitive conclusions from available data is that there are a number of serious methodological challenges in identifying the impact of TANF, in part because it was instituted during a period of economic expansion. Hence, although much of the evidence regarding the impact of welfare reform appears positive, numerous questions and concerns remain. For one, there is concern about the long-term wage prospects of women who leave welfare, given the types of jobs they tend to find. Also, states are required to find employment for a growing fraction of welfare recipients, many of whom will likely encounter greater employment difficulties than those initially placed into jobs.[18] A related issue is the availability of affordable, quality day care, as more women move into employment. This issue has not gone unnoticed at the federal level. When Congress reauthorized the TANF program in 2005, it somewhat increased federal funds for child care. Nevertheless, some suggest that these funds remain inadequate given current child care needs.[19] Another concern surrounds the fate of families that reach the federal 5-year cumulative time limit for TANF benefits. On this point, evidence to date suggests that while some families have confronted this "wall," their numbers are fewer than anticipated. Among the reasons, some states continued benefits through the use of state funds, while other states utilized the provision that allows them to exempt 20 percent of the caseload from the time limit. Moreover, some families left welfare of their own accord before reaching this point.[20]

There is also some question as to how states will respond and how individuals will fare in a prolonged economic downturn. This issue is particularly serious because in times of people's greatest economic need, states will be least able to provide economic assistance. The experience from the 2001 recession provides some evidence. Contrary to past recessions, the national welfare caseload did not rise. This difference may in part be due to the fact that the unemployment rate increased only modestly, along with the fact that families were perhaps deterred from entering TANF as a result of the work requirements and the time-limited nature of the benefits. Nonetheless, during this period a majority of states faced fiscal crises, in many cases leading to cuts in TANF benefits and related support programs targeted at needy families. The impact would have likely been greater, if not for the fact that states were able to draw upon TANF surpluses that accumulated during the boom years of the 1990s. The difficulties faced by states, even during this rather mild recession, point to the much graver difficulties that will likely arise during a more prolonged, serious recession such as the one that began in December 2007.[21]

BEYOND TRADITIONAL INCOME AND WORK SUPPORT POLICIES: MARRIAGE PROMOTION

Efforts to alleviate poverty among families and improve children's well-being have long relied on welfare programs including AFDC and, more recently, TANF. As discussed further shortly, these efforts were buttressed by expansions in the federal EITC, a tax credit that supplements the income of families with low earnings, as well as by policies to strengthen child support enforcement. More recently, considerable attention has

[18] Rebecca M. Blank, "Improving the Safety Net for Single Mothers Who Face Serious Barriers to Work," *Future of Children* 17, no. 2 (Fall 2007): 183–97.
[19] Mark Greenberg, "Next Steps for Federal Child Care Policy," *Future of Children* 17, no. 2 (Fall 2007): 73–96.
[20] Moffitt, "Welfare Reform."
[21] This discussion is drawn from Howard Chernick and Andrew Reschovsky, "State Fiscal Responses to Welfare Reform During Recessions: Lessons for the Future," *Public Budgeting and Finance* 23, no. 3 (2003): 3–21; and Sharon Parrott and Nina Wu, "States Are Cutting TANF and Child Care Programs: Supports for Low-Income Working Families and Welfare-to-Work Programs Are Particularly Hard Hit," (Washington, DC: Center on Budget and Policy Priorities, June 2003).

focused on another strategy—promoting and supporting healthy marriages. As discussed in an inset in Chapter 3, the 1996 welfare legislation explicitly mentioned **marriage promotion** as a goal and a substantial number of states began marriage initiatives. These have ranged from providing bonuses to married recipients in state welfare programs to funding local marriage education programs. In 2005, Congress reaffirmed its commitment to this effort, providing $150 million annually for such purposes.*

Proponents point to a range of benefits of marriage,** including the fact that married-couple families are, on average, on a considerably better financial footing than single-parent families, as shown earlier in Table 10-6. Married couples also have considerably higher incomes than cohabiters. In addition, Chapter 10 pointed to evidence that suggests that children tend to do better in married families with both biological parents present than when raised by a single parent.[22] When comparing the economic well-being of married and unmarried couples, it must, however, be kept in mind that they have very different characteristics, on average. For instance, parents in married-couple families tend to be older and more highly educated. Thus, it is not reasonable to assume that if all cohabiting couples were to marry that they would achieve the same economic well-being as married couples. One study does find that when marriage is "simulated" among cohabiting couples, the poverty rate of children in these families falls from over three to two times the rate for children in married-couple families. Nonetheless, this improvement would still leave a considerable fraction of children in poverty.***

While there is a considerable pro-marriage constituency, concerns have been raised about such an emphasis, even by some of those favoring marriage promotion.**** A major concern is that such a focus may divert government funds from traditional assistance programs for lower-income families. Also, if marriage were more actively promoted, what might be the implications for the success of these marriages? At worst, it might even lead to an increase in domestic violence. Further, as discussed in Chapter 10, some research finds negative effects associated with growing up with a stepparent, suggesting that all marriages may not be equally beneficial for children. Looking toward the future, in light of these concerns, marriage promotion programs will likely continue to play just a small role in the government's effort to support families.

*Information on the TANF reauthorization legislation is from U.S. Department of Health and Human Services, "The Next Phase of Welfare Reform: Implementing the Deficit Reduction Act of 2005," Fact Sheet (December 2006). For the George W. Bush administration's perspective, see Wade F. Horn, "Marriage, Family, and the Welfare of Children: A Call for Action," in *The Future of the Family*, edited by Daniel P. Moynihan, Timothy M. Smeeding, and Lee Rainwater (New York: Russell Sage Foundation, 2004), pp. 181–97. For further discussion of the argument that government should play a role in promoting marriage, see Nancy R. Burstein, "Economic Influences on Marriage and Divorce," *Journal of Policy Analysis and Management* 26, no. 2 (Spring 2007): 387–429.

**For a review, see Robert Lerman, "Marriage and the Economic Well-Being of Families with Children: A Review of the Literature" (Washington, DC: U.S. Department of Health and Human Services, July 2002); and David C. Ribar, "What Do Social Scientists Know About the Benefits of Marriage? A Review of Quantitative Methodologies," IZA Discussion Paper No. 998 (January 2004).

***Gregory Acs and Sandi Nelson, "Should We Get Married in the Morning?" Discussion Paper (Washington, DC: Urban Institute, 2004). See also Adam Thomas and Isabel Sawhill, "For Richer or Poorer: Marriage as an Antipoverty Strategy," *Journal of Policy Analysis and Management* 21, no. 4 (Fall 2002): 587–99.

****The remainder of the inset draws from discussions by Theodora Ooms, "Marriage and Government: Strange Bedfellows?" *Policy Brief*, no 1, Center for Law and Social Policy (August 2002); Daniel T. Lichter, "Marriage as Public Policy," Progressive Policy Institute (September 2001); and Daniel Lichter and Deborah Roempke Graefe, "Men and Marriage Promotion: Who Marries Unwed Mothers?" *Social Service Review* 81, no. 3 (September 2007): 397–421.

---

[22] In such studies, adopted children are included with biological children.

The Earned Income Tax Credit

The **Earned Income Tax Credit** (EITC), mentioned briefly earlier, is a refundable tax credit based on household earnings that both raises income and encourages individuals with low potential wages to seek employment. In contrast to many tax credits, which benefit only households with an income high enough to pay taxes, the refundable feature of the tax credit means that the government provides a refund if the amount of the credit exceeds taxes owed. Thus, unlike these other tax policies, the EITC transfers income to low-income households. Further, unlike the minimum wage, it targets only low-wage workers living in poor and near-poor households.[23]

The EITC was established in 1975 to offset the Social Security payroll tax for low-earner households with children and was expanded considerably in the early 1990s. It has become the largest cash transfer program for low-income families in the United States, dwarfing TANF. The amount of the credit varies according to the presence of children as well as the level of family earnings.[24] The size of the credit differs for three income ranges: in the low-income range, the amount of the credit increases with earnings; in the middle-income range, the maximum credit is provided; and in the high-income range, the value of the credit declines with earnings. As a case in point, consider a single-parent family with two children in 2008. For those with earnings between zero and $12,060 (the low-income range), earnings were subsidized at a rate of 40 percent; at $12,060 the family received the maximum credit available of $4,824 (.40 × $12,060). For those with earnings between $12,060 and $15,740 (the middle-income range), they received the maximum credit of $4,824. For earnings between $15,740 through $38,646 (the high-income range), the credit fell by 21 cents for every additional dollar earned, reaching zero at $38,646.

The impact of the EITC on raising families out of poverty is substantial.[25] For instance, as shown in Table 11-3, in 2008, the EITC increased the income of an employed single parent with two children who worked full time, full year at the minimum wage from $13,100 to $17,924, a figure just above the amount of the relevant poverty threshold. This family would also be eligible for food stamps, which increases net income, and may receive some federal child care assistance as well,

TABLE 11-3 Making Ends Meet for a Low-Earner Single-Parent Family with Two Children, 2008

Earnings (assume employed at minimum wage job full time, full year)[a]	$13,100
EITC (maximum credit)	$4,824
Earnings plus EITC	$17,924
Poverty threshold[b]	$17,165
Ratio of earnings plus EITC to poverty threshold	1.04

[a]Earnings are computed as $6.55 per hour multiplied by 40 hours per week multiplied by 50 weeks per year.
[b]This figure, calculated by the U.S. Census Bureau, is the preliminary estimate of the weighted average poverty threshold for a family of 3 for 2008; see www.census.gov.

[23] See, for instance, Bruce D. Meyer, "The U.S. Earned Income Tax Credit, Its Effects, and Possible Reforms," *Swedish Economic Policy Review* 14, no. 2 (Fall 2007): 55-80; and Richard V. Burkhauser and Joseph J. Sabia, "The Effectiveness of Minimum Wage Increases in Reducing Poverty: Past, Present, and Future," *Contemporary Economic Policy* 25, no. 2 (April 2007): 262–81.
[24] Since 1994, low-income households without children have also been eligible, though only for a small credit.
[25] For evidence, see Craig Gunderson and James P. Ziliak, "Poverty and Macroeconomic Performance Across Space, Race, and Family Structure," *Demography* 41, no. 1 (February 2004): 61–86.

though likely not enough to fully cover child care costs. Also, while this family would not owe federal income taxes (their income is too low), they would have to pay federal payroll taxes on earnings. One study found that these factors, taken together, nearly offset one another, leaving income at about the level reported in Table 11-3 (for "Earnings plus EITC").[26] Children under age 15 may also receive federally funded health care, either through Medicaid or through the Children's Health Insurance Program (CHIP) though their parents may or may not have health care coverage, depending on their employers.

In contrast to AFDC, which provided maximum payments to those not employed and imposed a high marginal tax rate on earnings for program participants, the EITC encourages individuals to seek employment by subsidizing earnings of recipients.[27] For individuals in the low-income range, the amount of the EITC increases with additional hours worked. At the same time, however, the EITC may cause some workers to reduce the number of hours worked. The provision of a fixed credit over the middle-income range, for instance, provides these workers with a pure increase in income. As discussed in Chapter 4, with higher nonlabor income, individuals tend to work fewer hours. The work disincentive is even greater for individuals in the highest income range eligible for the EITC. For them, the credit and thus the net wage are reduced as earnings increase. Individuals with earnings in this range are expected to substitute toward nonmarket time and away from paid work because of the decrease in the opportunity cost of nonmarket time. At the same time, total income is still higher than it would otherwise be without the EITC program, also providing an incentive for individuals to work less. Hence, in this range, both the substitution and income effects operate to reduce hours worked.

The effect of the EITC program thus varies depending on the family's earnings. Overwhelming evidence indicates that the EITC provides a strong incentive for single mothers to enter the paid labor force. In fact, one study finds that nearly 60 percent of the increase in single mother's employment from 1984 to 1996 was due to the expansion of the EITC.[28] On the other hand, as discussed in Chapter 4, the design of the EITC also causes some secondary earners in married-couple families, typically wives, to leave the labor force.[29] Wives' additional earnings would often place the family's income in the high-income range of the credit or even above it, thereby leading to receipt of a lower EITC or none at all. The EITC's secondary earner penalty was eased slightly by the Bush administration in 2003, though by no means eliminated.

The EITC not only results in a "second-earner" penalty for some married-couple families, but it also alters incentives for couples to marry or stay married because eligibility is largely based on family income. For instance, a single mother with children who is employed full time, full year at the minimum wage and her employed male partner may be better off cohabiting because then only her income is counted in the EITC calculation. If instead they were to marry, both incomes would be counted. Interestingly,

[26] David T. Ellwood, "The Plight of the Working Poor," Children's Roundtable Report #2 (Washington, DC: Brookings Institution, November 1999).

[27] Most discussions on incentive effects, such as the one here, assume that the EITC is received on a regular basis throughout the year. However, virtually all recipients receive it as a lump sum, which may affect their response; see Timothy Smeeding, Katherine Ross Philips, and Michael O'Connor, "The EITC: Expectation, Knowledge, Use and Economic and Social Mobility," *National Tax Journal* 53, no. 4, pt. 2 (December 2000): 1187–209.

[28] Bruce D. Meyer and Dan T. Rosenbaum, "Welfare, the Earned Income Tax Credit, and the Labor Supply of Single Mothers," *Quarterly Journal of Economics* 116, no. 3 (August 2001): 1063–114; and for a review of this and other studies, Meyer, "The U.S. Earned Income Tax Credit."

[29] Nada Eissa and Hilary Williamson Hoynes, "Taxes and the Labor Market Participation of Married Couples: The Earned Income Tax Credit," *Journal of Public Economics* 88, no. 9–10 (August 2004): 1931–58.

the EITC might also encourage marriage for others. For instance, if a nonemployed mother with children who is ineligible for the EITC marries a low-earner male, the family will gain eligibility.

Employment Strategies

The employment outlook for welfare recipients tends to be especially bleak because, as a rule, they have little education and few job skills. Many also face other barriers to employment, including discrimination and often physical or mental health problems.[30] In addition they may encounter problems getting to work due to a lack of transportation. The government could, of course, assist people in finding jobs, which tends to be quite inexpensive to do, but jobs alone are not likely to help many of them escape poverty. The alternative is to provide education and skills that raise the earnings of both welfare recipients and those who are poor but not on welfare. However, this approach involves considerable costs in the short run, as compared with merely maintaining welfare payments, and it takes some time for such expenditures to pay off. Unfortunately, resources for this purpose from state and local governments have been scarce, not only during times when obtaining additional funds would require raising taxes, but even in the late 1990s and 2000, when many state governments and the federal government experienced budget surpluses.

The federal government has been active to some extent in providing training and employment programs for at least some disadvantaged and unemployed workers since the 1960s. The current program, the **Workforce Investment Act** (WIA), provides funds for job training and job support services at the local level.[31] Beginning in the 1980s, states and subsequently the federal government initiated some education and training programs explicitly designed to move AFDC recipients from welfare to work. Analyses of a number of these welfare-to-work programs indicate that, in some cases, such programs increased earnings, but generally not enough to lift individuals out of poverty.[32] The 1996 welfare legislation that followed largely shifted the emphasis of the employment strategy for helping welfare recipients away from job training and education and toward a focus on employment. Many states now pursue a "work first" strategy, which emphasizes job search and tries to get welfare recipients into paid employment as quickly as possible. If this effort is unsuccessful, states may place welfare recipients in unpaid work or subsidized employment or offer them limited opportunities for education and training. The success of a "work first" approach depends most notably on a sustained healthy economy that creates sufficient jobs for lower-skilled workers. Also, this approach must be sufficiently flexible to assist individuals who lack adequate qualifications or face any of the other types of employment barriers mentioned earlier.[33] The EITC, which raises earnings in the low-paying jobs that such workers usually obtain, is another crucial ingredient needed for success.

Self-employment can be another employment strategy. However, even for those with a promising idea, access to credit often poses a substantial barrier, and they may

---

[30] Blank, "Improving the Safety Net for Single Mothers Who Face Serious Barriers to Work."

[31] See contributions in Harry J. Holzer and Demetra Smith Nightingale, eds., *Reshaping the American Workforce in a Changing Economy* (Washington, DC: Urban Institute Press, 2007); regarding future prospects of the WIA, see Harry J. Holzer, "Workforce Development and the Disadvantaged," *Perspectives on Low-Income Working Families*, Brief 7 (Washington, DC: The Urban Institute, September 2008).

[32] The most-often cited example of success is the Riverside California GAIN program. See, Moffitt, "The Temporary Assistance to Needy Families Program."

[33] See David E. Card and Rebecca M. Blank, eds., *Finding Jobs: Work and Welfare Reform* (New York: Russell Sage Foundation, 2000); and Holzer and Nightingale, eds., *Reshaping the American Workforce in a Changing Economy.*

also lack the financial and management skills needed to be successful. Following efforts in developing countries, such as the Grameen Bank in Bangladesh (discussed further in Chapter 12), microenterprise assistance programs, funded by the federal government, foundations, and private organizations, have been developed in the United States to meet these needs. These programs provide start-up funds, training, and mentoring to assist low-income individuals in becoming entrepreneurs. Notably, programs in the United States have failed to show the same success as those in developing countries. Among the explanations, developing countries tend to have a large "informal" sector that provides self-employment opportunities for those with relatively few skills. Also, self-employment in developing countries is subject to fewer regulations, so it does not tend to require as much business "know-how."[34]

Child Support Enforcement

Child support enforcement is another strategy for aiding single-parent families. Over the last 25 years, child support enforcement in the United States has changed considerably, shifting from a "complaint-driven, court-enforced system" subject to considerable discretion by judges to a system guided by state and federal laws and regulations.[35] The first major child support legislation, enacted in 1975, was aimed at enforcing payments by noncustodial parents. Additional legislation in 1984 and 1988 considerably strengthened this law by requiring states to adopt numerical guidelines in setting child support awards and allowing them to collect income withheld by employers (garnish wages) and retain income tax refunds from noncustodial parents who do not make the required payments. The 1996 welfare legislation went further and instituted rules that make the establishment of paternity faster and easier, added a national registry system that makes tracking down delinquent parents across state lines possible, and set forth tough new penalties for nonpayment, including revoking professional licenses and seizing assets. Subsequently, a law passed in 1998 made the sanctions even tougher, including penalties of up to 2 years in prison, for "deadbeat" parents.

Mothers who receive welfare are required to pursue child support as one of the conditions for receiving cash benefits. States may keep these funds to cover the costs of public assistance but they also have the option to allow at least some portion of the child support monies received to "pass through" to children. The *pass-through* provides at least a modest incentive for noncustodial parents to make child support payments because they could assume that their children would get some benefit from their payments. States vary considerably in the amount of the pass-through allowed, although many states increased the allowable amount following federal welfare changes in 2005, which increased their financial incentives to do so. Even prior to this change, Wisconsin was one of the most generous states in this regard, permitting welfare families to keep *all* of the child support monies received.[36]

Recent evidence indicates that the government policies outlined here (in the case of the child support pass-through, a policy that retains it) do lead to higher rates of child

[34] See, for instance, Mark Schreiner, "Microenterprise Development Programs in the United States and in the Developing World," *World Development* 31, no. 9 (September 2003): 1567–80.
[35] This characterization is from Elaine Sorensen and Ariel Halpern, "Child Support Reforms: Who Has Benefited?" *Focus* 21, no. 1 (Spring 2000): 38–41. For a concise review of the major changes in the relevant federal laws see "Child Support Enforcement Policy and Low-Income Families," *Focus* 21, no. 1 (Spring 2000): 3.
[36] See Maria Cancian and Daniel Meyer, "Child Support and the Economy," in *Working and Poor: How Economic and Policy Changes Are Affecting Low-Wage Workers*, edited by Rebecca M. Blank, Sheldon H. Danziger, and Robert F. Schoeni (New York: Russell Sage Foundation, 2006), pp. 338–65; and Laura Wheaton and Elaine Sorensen, "The Potential of Increasing Child Support Payments to TANF Families." *Perspectives on Low Income Working Families*, Brief 5 (Washington, DC: The Urban Institute, December 2007).

support receipt by families, especially by those on welfare. Not surprisingly, these effects are even stronger when combined with greater state expenditures on enforcement. Even so, the success of recent enforcement efforts is not apparent in aggregate statistics on child support received, which show that the proportion of single-mother families who received child support remained remarkably steady from the late 1970s to 2001, at just over 30 percent. One reason this figure changed so little is that, at the same time enforcement efforts were increased, the proportion of never-married mothers also rose; never-married mothers are much less likely to get child support awards, let alone actual payments, as compared with divorced women. Nevertheless, child support award rates for never-married mothers, while still quite low, continue to rise, no doubt as a result of the many new policies targeted at this group.[37]

While recent policies have had the intended effect of increasing child support awards, these positive gains have been accompanied by concerns that the current system is not sufficiently flexible to deal with the diverse economic circumstances of non-custodial parents, typically fathers. The current guidelines are designed for those with stable employment and adequate incomes, while many fathers face a different economic reality of little education, unstable employment, and consequently low earnings. These fathers, sometimes labeled *dead-broke dads*, may simply not be able to financially support their children and so, for them, existing policies may be counterproductive. For instance, such men may shift from legal employment to "under-the-table" work, with all its attendant disadvantages, or they may give up employment altogether. In addition, such policies may lead some fathers to avoid social contact with their children because they are unable to pay support.[38] To address these concerns, the federal government has funded a variety of initiatives to improve the labor market opportunities of young unmarried fathers.[39]

One alternative to the patchwork of child support policies in the United States would be to establish a **child support assurance system** similar to the one that exists in Sweden, where both parents and government are responsible for the support of children.[40] Under such a system, awards from nonresident parents could be set as a percentage of their income and withheld from their earnings, just as taxes are. If the parent cannot meet this obligation, the government would provide the minimum assured benefit. Such a program, however, faces little chance of being adopted in the United States in the near future given the reluctance of many to see the role of the federal government expanded.

TAXES, SPECIALIZATION, AND MARRIAGE

Up to this point we have largely ignored the role of the **federal income tax system**, but it is in fact quite important in this context. Income taxes help to finance the federal programs discussed here, along with many others. At the same time, when income is taxed, this means that individuals do not retain all their labor market earnings. Hence, the

---

[37] Figures and evidence are from Cancian and Meyer, "Child Support and the Economy."

[38] See contributions in Irwin Garfinkel, Sara McLanahan, Daniel Meyer, and Judith Seltzer, eds., *Fathers Under Fire: The Revolution in Child Support Enforcement* (New York: Russell Sage Foundation, 1998); and Harry J. Holzer, Paul Offner, and Elaine Sorensen, "Declining Employment Among Young Black Less-Educated Men: The Role of Incarceration and Child Support," *Journal of Policy Analysis and Management* 24, no. 2 (Spring 2005): 329–50.

[39] Karin Martinson and Demetra Nightingale, "Ten Key Findings from Responsible Fatherhood Initiatives," *Policy Brief* (Washington, DC: Urban Institute, February 2008).

[40] For a discussion of child support systems elsewhere, see Anne Corden and Daniel R. Meyer, "Child Support Policy Regimes in the United States, United Kingdom, and Other Countries: Similar Issues, Different Approaches," *Focus* 21, no. 1 (Spring 2000): 72–79.

structure of the federal income tax affects take-home pay and consequently decisions regarding whether and how much to work, as well as decisions about family formation. Similarly, payroll taxes and the Social Security payments they fund also affect these decisions.[41] Both the federal income tax system and the Social Security program evolved when the one-earner family was the norm and, in effect, subsidize married women who stay home. Thus, both programs have been criticized for favoring the traditional, one-earner family. In this section, we examine the ways in which these programs may discourage married women's employment. In addition, concerns have been raised about the equity of these programs. One of the primary rules proposed by economists for fair taxation is **horizontal equity**, which means that those in similar circumstances should be treated similarly.[42] Thus, we also specifically consider whether the current income tax and Social Security systems violate this rule in their treatment of one-earner and two-earner families.[43]

Income Taxation Policy

First and foremost, the present federal income tax system may be considered inequitable because the value of goods and services produced in the home is not taxed, whereas money income is subject to taxation. As a result, two couples with different levels of economic well-being may have the same taxable incomes. Suppose, for instance, that Ellen and Ed earn $25,000 each and produce $10,000 worth of goods and services in the household. Suppose too that Jim earns $50,000 and Jane, a full-time homemaker, produces $30,000 worth of goods and services in the home. Although Jim and Jane produce a total income of $80,000, including the value of home production, while Ellen and Ed only produce an income of $60,000, taxable income is $50,000 for both. Thus, because home production is not taxed, the tax system favors the traditional one-earner family such as Jim and Jane.

The federal income tax structure further provides a disincentive for married women to participate in the labor force because of two specific features. First, the *family is the unit of taxation*, which means that there are separate schedules depending on a taxpayer's family status. For the typical married couple, the spouses sum their incomes and taxes are determined using the "married filing jointly" schedule. There are also schedules for single individuals and single heads of household (such as heads of single-parent families).[44] Second, the United States has a **progressive income tax** structure, meaning that higher levels of income are taxed at a higher *rate* than lower levels. As shown in panel a of Table 11-4, this means that if a married couple earns $50,000, part of this amount is subject to a 10 percent tax rate and the remainder is subject to a 15 percent rate. In general, progressive tax rates are considered to be desirable because they result in wealthier families paying a proportionately larger share of their incomes in taxes.

The degree of progressivity in the tax system has varied considerably in recent years. The Tax Reform Act of 1986 enacted during the Reagan administration reduced

[41] Here we focus on two major federal programs only, but most states also have their own income tax, and an array of other taxes are imposed at the federal, state, and local levels.

[42] The view that "there is a generally accepted standard of equity or fairness with respect to public finance measures: equal treatment of those equally circumstanced" was first expressed by Carl S. Shoup, *Public Finance* (Chicago: Aldine Publishing Company, 1969), p. 23 and has been widely shared ever since.

[43] These topics have been discussed by economists for some time, from Nancy R. Gordon, "Institutional Responses: The Federal Income Tax System" and "Institutional Responses: The Social Security System," in *The Subtle Revolution*, edited by Ralph E. Smith (Washington, DC: Urban Institute, 1979), pp. 201–21, 223–55; to Edward J. McCaffery, *Taxing Women* (Chicago: University of Chicago Press, 1997).

[44] There is also a schedule that permits married couples to file separately. (This is distinct from the "single" schedule—using the single schedule is not an option for married couples.) However, the vast majority of couples file jointly because the taxes owed using this schedule are generally lower. The married filing jointly schedule is the one discussed in the text and shown in Table 11-4.

TABLE 11-4 Federal Individual Income Tax Rates and Calculation of Marriage Penalty/Bonus

(a) 2008 Federal Individual Income Tax Rate Schedules[a]

Single Schedule		Married Filing Jointly Schedule	
Taxable Income	Tax Rate	Taxable Income	Tax Rate
$0–$8,025	10%	$0–$16,050	10%
$8,025–$32,550	15%	$16,050–$65,100	15%
$32,550–$78,850	25%	$65,100–$131,450	25%
$78,850–$164,550	28%	$131,450–$200,300	28%
$164,550–$357,700	33%	$200,300–$357,700	33%
$357,700+	35%	$357,700+	35%

(b) Calculation of Marriage Penalty/Bonus Using 2008 Tax Rate Schedule[b]

Couple	Value of Home Production (not taxable)	Husband's Income (taxable)	Wife's Income (taxable)	Combined Income (taxable)	Tax Liability if: Married Couple	Both Single	Marriage Penalty or Bonus
Ellen and Ed	$10,000	$ 25,000	$25,000	$ 50,000	$ 6,698	$ 6,698	$ 0 penalty
Jane and Jim	$30,000	$ 50,000	$ 0	$ 50,000	$ 6,698	$ 8,844	$2,146 bonus
Gina and Greg	$10,000	$ 70,000	$70,000	$140,000	$27,944	$27,688	$ 257 penalty
Debra and Dave	$30,000	$140,000	$ 0	$140,000	$27,944	$33,178	$5,234 bonus

[a]There are two other schedules not shown here, the head of household schedule for single individuals with a dependent child and a married filing separately schedule for couples who are separated.

[b]This table makes several simplifying assumptions. It assumes that there are no children and that taxable income equals gross income. In actual practice, taxable income is calculated as gross income less personal exemptions and less the standard deduction.

the number of tax brackets from 15 brackets, with a top rate of 50 percent, to only 2 brackets, with stated rates of 15 and 28 percent. Under President Clinton, the top tax rate was 39.6 percent. In 2001, President Bush introduced a 10 percent bracket, and lowered all other rates, including the top rate, which stood at 35 percent in 2008, as shown in Table 11-4.

The current tax structure means that a married woman, still generally considered to be the secondary earner by most families, will often face a high marginal tax rate on her potential income, should she decide to enter the labor market. This is because the first dollar of her earnings is taxed at her husband's top marginal tax rate. This reduces her incentive to enter the labor market. In the case of Jane and Jim, for example, if Jane decides to work for pay, the first dollar she receives is taxed at a 15 percent rate, rather than at the lowest rate of 10 percent. This is because her income will be added on to Jim's and their tax liability will be determined using the married filing jointly tax schedule. This disincentive increases considerably with couples' income. For instance, consider a couple in which the husband, Dave, has $140,000 in earnings and his wife, Debra, is presently a full-time homemaker. If Debra were to enter the labor market, her first dollar of pay would be taxed at a 28 percent rate, not at the bottom tax rate of 10 percent. Further, as noted earlier, the EITC, which is part of the federal tax code, discourages participation by a secondary earner in low-earning families, because the value of the EITC eventually declines as family earnings rise.

The "marriage penalty" is another disincentive created by the current structure of the U.S. tax system. A **marriage penalty** refers to the additional taxes a couple owes if they are married as compared to the taxes they would pay if they remained single. Couples could also possibly receive a **marriage bonus**, which refers to tax savings due to marriage compared to remaining single. As explained later, under our current tax system, two-earner couples may incur a marriage penalty, while single-earner couples receive a marriage bonus. Because single-earner couples receive a marriage bonus, the tax system provides incentives for such couples to marry. On the other hand, the marriage penalty that arises for some dual-earner couples may discourage such couples from marrying.[45]

The marriage penalty occurs when the income brackets for married couples are less than twice as wide as the brackets for singles. The marriage penalty came about as the result of a policy change initiated in 1969 to reduce taxes paid by single taxpayers relative to married couples. This change inevitably increased the relative tax liability for some married couples as compared to single taxpayers. In 2001 President Bush introduced tax changes to partly deal with this situation. The Bush changes made the new 10 percent bracket for married couples twice as wide as for singles and instituted the same change for the existing 15 percent bracket. The value of the standard deduction for married couples was also increased so that it is now twice the value for singles. Importantly, although these changes eliminated the marriage penalty for some two-earner married couples, and reduced it for others, they also had the effect of considerably *increasing* the marriage bonus for traditional couples.

To get a better idea of how marriage bonuses and subsidies arise, let us look at panel b of Table 11-4, which illustrates the size of the bonus or penalty for different types of married couples using 2008 tax rates. For instance, consider again Jim and Jane and Ellen and Ed, but now suppose that they are unmarried. If Jim earns $50,000 and marries Jane, who has no earnings, their combined tax liability declines by $2,146, providing a marriage bonus of this amount. Conversely, if Ellen and Ed each earn $25,000

---

[45] Regarding the impact of taxes and subsidies on fertility, marriage, and divorce decisions, see James Alm, Stacey Dickert-Conlin, and Leslie A. Whittington, "Policy Watch: The Marriage Penalty," *Journal of Economic Perspectives* 13, no. 3 (Summer 1999): 193–204; and Adam Carasso and C. Eugene Steurle, "The Hefty Penalty on Marriage Facing Many Households with Children," *Future of Children* 15, no. 2 (Autumn 2005): 157–75.

and marry, they receive no bonus. Because their top tax bracket is 15 percent, they also do not face a marriage penalty as a result of the Bush tax changes described earlier.

Marriage penalties remain, however, for couples whose income is taxed in brackets higher than 15 percent. For instance, Gina and Greg, who each earn $70,000, face a marriage penalty of $257. In contrast, consider the situation of Debra and Dave, who have the same combined family income of $140,000, but Dave brings in all the earnings. They receive a *bonus* of $5,234. What explains the very different tax consequences for Debra and Dave versus Gina and Greg (or for that matter, Jane and Jim versus Ellen and Ed)? The simplest answer points to the two features of our tax structure reviewed earlier: progressive taxation combined with separate schedules for married couple and single taxpayers. Debra and Dave receive such a large bonus because, as a married couple, a larger portion of their income is taxed at a lower rate in the married-couple tax schedule than in the single schedule. These examples illustrate the general pattern we noted earlier: Single-earner couples generally receive a marriage bonus, while two-earner couples receive no marriage bonus and may bear a penalty. Indeed, as we have seen, marriage penalties persist for those in higher tax brackets; they also tend to be larger when the spouse's incomes are fairly equal.[46] Finally, as discussed earlier in this chapter, the marriage penalty is also quite large (as a percentage of income) for low-earning couples with children who qualify for the EITC.[47]

It is also instructive to compare the examples in Table 11-4 to a system that taxes each person as an individual, as is the case of countries like Canada, Sweden, and the United Kingdom, and as was the case in the United States prior to 1948. This alternative eliminates the secondary earner penalty because each individual's first dollar is taxed at the same rate they would pay if they were single. It also eliminates marriage bonuses (and penalties) because there is one tax schedule regardless of family structure. Such a change would clearly be to the advantage of two-earner couples such as Gina and Greg, who face a penalty under the current system. On the other hand, single-earner couples (Jane and Jim and Debra and Dave) would no longer receive large marriage bonuses. Which system is viewed as more equitable in its treatment of money income (in the sense of establishing horizontal equity) depends on whether the individual or the family is viewed as the appropriate tax unit.[48] The fact that single-earner families would be made worse off under individual taxation than under the current arrangement points to the considerable political challenges involved in changing from one regime to another. Another option that would also meet the goal of horizontal equity and surfaces periodically is a "flat tax," which imposes the same rate on all incomes and provides a personal exemption. Still, even with a large personal exemption such a tax would be much less progressive than the current system.

The Social Security System

The **Social Security system** also poses problems of equity between one-earner married couples, on the one hand, and two-earner married couples, unmarried couples, and single people, on the other hand.[49] The problem arises because payroll taxes paid by

---

[46] Couples cannot get around this "penalty" by filing separate returns. The tax rates for married filing separately are higher than those for single individuals.

[47] For a discussion of penalties and bonuses in the EITC, see Carasso and Steurle, "The Hefty Penalty on Marriage Facing Many Households with Children."

[48] For instance, some argue that the family should be the unit of taxation because it is a basic economic unit in society and because husbands and wives pool income. However, recent evidence weakens the latter argument. See McCaffery, *Taxing Women,* Chap. 1.

[49] Useful overviews of these issues are provided in Melissa M. Favreault and C. Eugene Steurle, "Social Security Spouse and Survivor Benefits for the Modern Family," The Retirement Project Discussion Paper 07-01 (Washington, DC: Urban Institute, March 2007); McCaffery, *Taxing Women;* and Marianne A. Ferber, "Women's Employment and the Social Security System," *Social Security Bulletin* 56, no. 3 (Fall 1993): 33–55.

workers are based on each individual's employment history, while the Social Security benefits they will later receive are family based.

As of 2008, individuals in jobs covered by Social Security (and Medicare) faced a 15.3 percent tax rate on earnings up to a specified maximum level, half to be paid by the employer, half by the worker. To receive benefits, individuals must work in jobs covered by Social Security for at least 40 calendar quarters. Benefits received reflect contributions paid, so low-wage workers and those with long periods out of the labor force receive correspondingly lower benefits. The Social Security system has special rules for married couples: Spouses of covered workers are entitled to receive Social Security benefits equal to 50 percent of the amount received by the covered worker, and survivor benefits of 100 percent if the covered worker dies, even if they have never paid payroll taxes.[50] Alternatively, the spouse may receive benefits based on his or her own earnings record if that amount is greater.

One consequence of these various rules is that married couples fare very differently under Social Security in terms of taxes paid in (contributions) and benefits received, depending on how much each spouse earns. To illustrate this point, we look at three more or less traditional situations: (1) the husband is the sole earner, (2) both spouses are employed but the wife works intermittently or at low wages, and (3) both spouses are employed and both have considerable earnings records.[51]

In the case of a married couple where the husband is the sole earner, only the husband pays payroll taxes, while the family (husband and wife) receives 150 percent of his individual Social Security benefit. In this situation, the difference between payroll taxes paid in and benefits received is the greatest, and hence this family structure is most favored by the Social Security system.

Next, consider a couple where the wife is employed, but she earns substantially lower wages or has a shorter worklife than her husband. In this case, the family is likely to maximize benefits by claiming the spouse benefit. In this case, although the wife pays payroll taxes into the system too, the family still receives 150 percent of the husband's Social Security benefit, precisely the same amount as they would have if she had not been employed and had paid no payroll taxes. Nevertheless, the husband and wife together receive more benefits than they would if they were each single.

Finally, consider the case of the wife who earns enough to receive larger benefits in her own right than she would receive as a spouse.[52] The benefits received by this family (calculated as the wife's individual benefit plus the husband's individual benefit) are somewhat larger than the amount received by the married couples in the prior two cases. However, the couple in this case does not benefit from being married. She and her husband receive exactly the same amount in benefits as if they were both single.

The results in the preceding descriptions violate the rule of horizontal equity, namely that equal contributions should secure equal returns. Each employed wife pays in as much as she would if she were single, but only the one who earns considerably less than her husband receives additional benefits as a spouse. Moreover, a wife who is not employed receives benefits as a spouse without making any tax payments. Clearly this system provides secondary earners, typically wives, with yet another disincentive to work for pay.

---

[50] Since 1977, spouses divorced after at least 10 years of marriage are entitled to the same benefit as current spouses. For more discussion on program changes over the years, see Patricia P. Martin and David A. Waver, "Social Security: A Program and Policy History," *Social Security Bulletin* 66, no. 1 (2005): 1–15.

[51] The rules are gender neutral and would apply equally if the wife were the sole wage earner.

[52] Phillip B. Levine, Olivia S. Mitchell, and John W. Phillips find that two-thirds of wives nearing retirement who have 40 calendar quarters of employment will receive benefits based on their own work history in "A Benefit of One's Own: Older Women's Retirement Entitlements Under Social Security," *Social Security Bulletin* 63, no. 3 (2000): 47–53.

One way to bring about equity among couples under the Social Security system would be through **earnings sharing**.[53] This approach assigns an equal share of total household earnings to each spouse and eliminates dependent benefits. Earnings sharing recognizes that the division of labor in the home represents a joint decision and that both spouses contribute to family welfare through their market and/or nonmarket work. Unlike the present system, earnings sharing would not penalize dual-earner couples. In addition, the Social Security system would move in the direction of greater horizontal equity, in that equal contributions to Social Security would yield equal benefits.[54] No couple would have an advantage as compared to any other type of couple or as compared to an unmarried individual. Such a change would, however, create problems for traditional couples who presumably made their labor supply decisions under the existing rules. This difficulty could, however, be overcome by giving couples who married before the new policy was adopted the option of remaining under the current system. A change to earnings sharing might also raise concerns about the adequacy of benefit levels for single-earner families. Although such issues remain to be addressed, continued growth of the two-earner family is likely to increase support for policies that eliminate the advantages single-earner families realize under the current structure of Social Security.

Under the current system, concern has also been raised about the adequacy of Social Security benefits for never-married, divorced, and widowed women because these groups have the highest poverty rates among the elderly. Their high poverty rates are in part due to the fact that women, on average, earn lower wages, work fewer hours per week, and are much more likely to have spent time out of the labor market to raise children or take care of other family members.[55] For this reason, they are also much less likely to have pensions from employers and are thus much more likely to have to rely on Social Security as their major source of income in their old age. Widows, for instance, receive just 50 to 75 percent of the combined benefit of a married couple, which results in a considerable drop in their standard of living because the cost of maintaining a one-person household is considerably more than half of the cost of maintaining a household of two.[56] Never-married women and divorced women who were married fewer than 10 years receive benefits based on their own earnings record only. Elderly women at greatest risk of poverty are those who spent a good deal of time on welfare in earlier years. Their shorter work lives and most often low earnings lead to extremely low Social Security benefits. Even though they are likely to be eligible for **Supplemental Security Income** (SSI), which provides cash benefits for the low-income elderly, the combined benefits of the two programs are generally insufficient to lift them out of poverty.[57] One way to address these problems would be to increase the value of the minimum Social Security benefit. Others advocate increasing the size of the spousal and survivor benefit or perhaps giving women "credit" for time spent out

---

[53] For details on this alternative, see Marianne Ferber, Vanessa Rouillon, and Patricia Simpson, "The Aging Population and Social Security: Women as the Problem and the Solution," *Challenge* 49, no. 3 (May/June 2006): 105–19; and Favreault and Steurle, "Social Security Spouse and Survivor Benefits."

[54] No Social Security taxes are paid on the value of what is produced in the household, but neither does the family accumulate benefits.

[55] See, for instance, Janet C. Gornick, Eva Sierminska and Timothy M. Smeeding, "The Income and Wealth Packages of Older Women in Cross-National Perspective," *Journal of Gerontology: Social Science* 64B, no. 3 (2009): 402-14; and Madonna Harrington Meyer, Douglas A. Wolf, and Christine L. Himes, "Linking Benefits to Marital Status: Race and Social Status in the United States," *Feminist Economics* 11, no. 2 (July 2005): 145–62.

[56] Another inequity of the current system is that widows from one-earner families receive a survivor benefit of 75 percent of the couple's previous benefit while widows who had earned about as much as their husbands only receive 50 percent of the couple's previous benefit.

[57] Sheila R. Zedlewski and Rumki Saha, "Social Security and Single Mothers," in *Social Security and the Family: Addressing Unmet Needs in an Underfunded System*, edited by Melissa M. Favreault, Frank J. Sammartino, and C. Eugene Steurle (Washington, DC: The Urban Institute, 2002), pp. 89–121.

of the labor force to raise children, but these changes would further increase the advantage of one-earner over two-earner families and increase incentives for women to stay out of the labor force.[58]

During the 2000s, the majority of reform proposals for Social Security focused on ensuring that the program will be financially able to meet the demands of the baby boom cohort, which is quickly nearing retirement. To address this concern, payroll taxes could be raised, the cap on the maximum amount of earnings subject to Social Security taxes could be increased or even removed, benefits could be cut, the eligibility age for receiving benefits could be further increased, or some combination of these reforms could be instituted.[59] In addition to such reforms, a number of proposals include a "two-tier" system, comprised of a Social Security program much like the present one, coupled with a second tier of private investments.[60] The merits of this specific reform remain the subject of a lively debate, particularly because it is such a radical departure from the existing system. Part of the discussion focuses on the implications of such a change for women.[61] One concern is that women who spend time out of the labor market to rear children, and especially those who were never employed, would be disadvantaged because they would have accumulated little in the investment program. Even employed women would likely accrue smaller amounts than men because of their lower earnings levels. However, if the two-tier system were combined with earnings sharing (discussed earlier), these concerns would be mitigated.

THE COMPETING DEMANDS OF WORK AND FAMILY

As noted in Chapter 10, today a growing share of the workforce has family responsibilities. There are greater numbers of two-earner families, including those with small children, more single-parent families, and more people with elderly parents. In the United States, the burden of balancing the competing demands of work and family is still largely borne by individuals. Nonetheless, government and employers offer some policies to assist workers as discussed in the latter part of this chapter.

Many individuals inevitably confront a trade-off between doing full justice to their job and fully meeting family responsibilities. Balancing these demands is generally most difficult for employed women with families. Before they start their work day and after it ends, they typically do most of the housework, as well as child and elder care, essentially working a "second shift."[62] As seen in Chapter 3, employed wives spend nearly twice as much time in housework as their husbands. Further, as discussed in Chapter 10, this appears to reduce their wages, perhaps by limiting the energy and time they are able to expend on market work. In addition, the need for elder care, mainly provided by women, is placing increasing demands on women's time. The

[58] For a comparison of the effects of these alternatives, see Gornick et al., "The Income and Wealth Packages of Older Women in Cross-National Perspective."
[59] Carole Green points out that a seemingly neutral policy such as raising the eligibility age for Social Security may have a disparate impact by race and ethnicity, given differences in health status, financial need, and occupation. See "Race, Ethnicity, and Social Security Retirement Age in the US," *Feminist Economics* 11, no. 2 (July 2005): 117–43.
[60] For details on one proposal, see John F. Cogan and Olivia S. Mitchell, "Perspectives from the President's Commission on Social Security Reform," *Journal of Economic Perspectives* 17, no. 2 (Spring 2003): 149–72. For a critique of this and other similar proposals, see Ferber et al., "The Aging Population and Social Security."
[61] U.S. General Accounting Office, "Social Security Reform: Implications for Women," Report T-HEHS-99–52 (Washington, DC: U.S. General Accounting Office, February 1999). Although many concerns have been raised, a simulation by Rudolph G. Penner and Elizabeth Cove suggests that women might actually benefit from such a change. See "Women and Individual Accounts," in *Social Security and the Family*, edited by Favreault, Sammartino, and Steurle, pp. 229–70.
[62] The pioneering book on this subject is Arlie Hochschild, *The Second Shift* (New York: Viking Press, 1989).

Census Bureau projects that, by 2050, the U.S. population age 65 and older will increase by 80 percent, a figure substantially greater than the expected increase in the population of working-age adults. In addition, as a result of improved health care and nutrition, the proportion of the "old old" population, typically defined as those age 85 and older, is increasing and they are even more likely to require care.[63] Demands are especially great on women responsible for both the care of their parents and their children at the same time, typically those who delayed childbearing until their thirties or forties.[64]

Some women respond to these competing demands by taking part-time rather than full-time jobs, in many cases effectively putting their careers on hold. Indeed, as Table 11-5 shows, in 2007 just under one-half of all married mothers with children under 18 years of age were employed full time, while this was true of only 39 percent of married mothers with a child under age 3. Those who do work full time are more securely attached to the labor force and earn higher incomes, but many undoubtedly face a time squeeze.

It is, however, low-income single mothers who are likely to face the most serious time squeeze. As of 2008, those on welfare are required to work for pay for no less than 30 hours per week, and their earnings, even supplemented by the EITC, are often inadequate to pay for essentials such as child care, let alone purchase help with housecleaning. In addition, their jobs often offer less flexibility, limiting their ability to tend to sick children or go to parent–teacher conferences.[65]

In the absence of adequate provisions for maternity leave, women in the labor force who bear children also face a number of unique challenges. For instance, as a general rule, pregnant women must be careful to avoid heavy lifting and excessive physical exertion. If employers do not accommodate the needs of pregnant women in such jobs by assigning them to alternative duties, these women may not be able to keep their jobs.[66] Also, breastfeeding, a practice strongly encouraged by the American Academy of

TABLE 11-5 Work Experience of Mothers, by Age of Youngest Child, 2007

	All Mothers	Married Mothers
With Child Under Age 18		
% employed	67.8	66.7
% employed full time[a]	51.3	48.8
With Child Under Age 3		
% employed	55.4	55.4
% employed full time[a]	39.2	38.9

[a]*Full time* refers to usually works 35 hours or more per week at all jobs.

Source: Bureau of Labor Statistics, *Employment Characteristics of Families in 2007*, USDL 08-0731 (May 9, 2008), Tables 5 and 6.

[63] U.S. Census Bureau, "Census Bureau Frames U.S. in Global Context; Identifies Aging, Fertility Trends," CB02-CN53 (February 2002). For evidence on the extent and impact of elder care responsibilities see, for example, Richard W. Johnson and Anthony T. Lo Sasso, "The Employment and Time Costs of Caring for Elderly Parents," *Inquiry* 43, no. 3 (Fall 2006): 195–210.
[64] See, for example, Charles R. Pierret, "The 'Sandwich Generation': Women Caring for Parents and Children," *Monthly Labor Review* 129, no. 9 (September 2006): 3–9.
[65] Randy Albeda, "Welfare-to-Work, Farewell to Families? U.S. Welfare Reform and Work/Family Debates," *Feminist Economics* 7, no. 1 (March 2001): 119–35.
[66] Sue Shellenbarger, "Pregnant Workers Clash with Employers over Job Inflexibility," *Wall Street Journal* (February 10, 1999): B1.

Pediatrics, especially during the first months of children's lives, is often impossible or at least difficult for employed mothers.[67]

Given women's primary role as caregivers, they would be the main beneficiaries of more family-friendly policies. Adoption of such policies would make it easier for them to remain attached to the labor force and to succeed on the job, while also continuing to take care of their families. Such policies would, in turn, increase the incentives for women and their employers to invest in women's human capital. In addition, men who already shoulder sizable housework and child care responsibilities would benefit as well, and others would find it easier to take on a larger share.[68] Thus, family-friendly policies would also be expected to promote a more equal division of labor in the household.

RATIONALES FOR GOVERNMENT AND EMPLOYER POLICIES TO ASSIST WORKERS

As we have seen, many workers face difficulties doing full justice to the demands of paid work and family. The question arises as to whether the government or employers have a role in easing such conflicts. In the following sections we examine the rationales that might justify a role for each.

Rationales for Government Policies

In all economically advanced countries, government plays some role in child care through such policies as mandated or government-provided parental leave, providing or financing of day care, and so on. However, there is considerable variation across countries and, in contrast to most other economically advanced countries, the government's role in the United States remains quite limited. Even unpaid family leave was not mandated until the passage of the Family and Medical Leave Act (FMLA) in 1993, while all other economically advanced nations provide *paid* leave, and most have been doing so for a long time. Also, the U.S. government does not provide day care, although it does subsidize child care for poor families and offers tax deductions to others. Consequently, families must make their own arrangements or take advantage of benefits offered by some firms such as on-site child care or help in finding child care. In comparison, France, Sweden, and Denmark, among others, provide free or heavily subsidized day care through the government sector.

The question of how the costs of raising children should be shared among parents, the government, and employers is controversial.[69] One economic argument for government to play a role is that there are **externalities** associated with bearing and raising

---

[67] Brian Roe, Leslie A. Whittington, Sara Beck Fein, and Mario F. Teisl, "Is There Competition Between Breast-Feeding and Maternal Employment?" *Demography* 36, no. 2 (May 1999): 157–71. These authors find that mothers who have longer leaves breastfeed their infants longer, but they also find that many mothers who return to the workplace do manage to do both, with key factors being provision of access to a private area and break time.

[68] For a discussion of men's difficulties in balancing work and family, see Joseph H. Pleck, "Balancing Work and Family," *Scientific American Presents* 10, no. 2 (Summer 1999): 38–43.

[69] For excellent discussions of these issues, see Arleen Leibowitz, "Child Care: Private Cost or Public Responsibility?" in *Individual and Social Responsibility: Child Care, Education, Medical Care, and Long-Term Care in America*, edited by Victor R. Fuchs (Chicago: University of Chicago Press, 1996), pp. 33–57; Nancy Folbre, "Children as Public Goods," *American Economic Review* 84, no. 2 (May 1994): 86–90; and James J. Heckman, "Skill Formation and the Economics of Investing in Disadvantaged Children," *Science* 312, no. 5782 (June 30, 2006): 1900–02.

children. For instance, while children's parents undoubtedly receive a direct benefit from their own children and thus bear a special responsibility for their care, the nation also benefits when children grow up to be healthier, better-educated, and better-trained adults. They are likely to be more productive and contribute more both as workers and as taxpayers, and are less likely to be a burden on the public. These benefits suggest that government should help finance the costs of raising children.

Issues of equity provide another rationale for government to play a role. Government support for young children through such policies as subsidies for day care, parental leave, and infant nutrition serve to ensure that all children have a more equal chance at life, regardless of the economic status of the family into which they are born. Currently, various levels of government in the United States subsidize primary, secondary, and, to some extent, higher education. Arguably, it makes little sense to help educate children from age 5 or 6 on, but not to help ensure that they will be ready to benefit from that education. Parental leave, when taken by fathers as well as mothers, and subsidized day care also enhance equity because they place female and male workers on a more equal footing.

Another argument for government to provide or mandate benefits such as family leave and health insurance relates to a phenomenon called **adverse selection**. Adverse selection may occur if only some but not all firms offer such policies. It arises because those workers who expect to benefit most from these policies are most likely to seek employment with firms that provide them; that is, workers will be adversely selected from the firm's perspective. To understand the problem adverse selection poses, consider the following example. Suppose no federal family leave policy exists and instead only one firm offers it, basing its estimate of costs on the percentage of the total workforce that might use it. It would then provide the benefit and offer its workers a somewhat lower wage that would cover its costs. Given the scarcity of this benefit, however, this firm would likely attract workers with a higher probability of using family leave than the workforce at large. Hence, it would face higher costs than anticipated, and might well try to reduce wages even more. This would further aggravate the adverse selection problem because those willing to work for these lower wages would increasingly consist of those who are most likely to take advantage of leave. In the end, the firm might well stop offering this benefit because it is too costly. More generally, adverse selection is likely to result in too few firms offering family leave relative to the optimal number, given workers' preferences. A government mandate requiring all firms to provide such a policy would, however, eliminate this problem and thus be desirable on these grounds.[70]

The preceding discussion provides both efficiency and equity reasons as to why the government should play a role in raising children. However, in fully assessing the issue, potential costs should be considered as well. For one, government financing of any program requires tax collection. Some research suggests that taxes cause individuals to work and save less than they would otherwise, thus reducing output.[71] For this reason, employer-mandated leave may be more efficient than leave paid for by the government, especially if the group that benefits from the mandate bears the cost of the leave in the form of lower wages. At least one study provides some evidence that wages

---

[70] This example is drawn from Christopher J. Ruhm and Jackqueline L. Teague, "Parental Leave Policies in Europe and North America," in *Gender and Family Issues in the Workplace,* edited by Francine D. Blau and Ronald G. Ehrenberg (New York: Russell Sage Foundation, 1997), pp. 133–56. For a discussion of the adverse selection problem in general, see Harvey Rosen, *Public Finance,* 4th ed. (Chicago: Irwin, 1995).

[71] For evidence of the negative effect of taxes on labor supply, see, for instance, Jerry A. Hausman, "The Effect of Taxes on Labor Supply," in *How Taxes Affect Economic Behavior,* edited by Henry Aaron and Joseph Pechman (Washington, DC: Brookings, 1981), pp. 27–84.

do adjust and, thus, the policy is efficient.[72] Mandates would also boost economic efficiency to the extent that they encourage women to stay in the labor force, thereby raising the firm-specific human capital of the labor force.[73] On the other hand, mandates for unpaid leave, financed through wage reductions of the affected groups, eliminate any subsidy for parents. Recall that there is a case for such subsidies because of the benefits that society as a whole derives from children who become the next generation of productive citizens and workers. In addition, lower wages would reduce the incentive for mothers to stay in the labor force and thus might diminish the positive effects of such policies in encouraging women's labor force attachment. Finally, such a policy is particularly burdensome for low-income workers whose wages would be reduced further.

This discussion shows that the issues regarding family leave and subsidized day care are complex. It is therefore not surprising that the extent of government's involvement differs considerably across countries, as do the manner in which policies are instituted and the generosity of these policies.

Rationales for Employer Policies

Employers may institute family-friendly policies in lieu of wage increases and other benefits or because they expect the gains of the policies to outweigh the costs. Possible benefits for employers include improved recruitment and retention of workers and greater productivity as a result of better morale and reductions in lateness and absenteeism. The improvement in worker retention is likely to be beneficial to the firm because it is often much less costly to provide workers with family-friendly benefits than to train new employees.[74] On the other hand, firms are also likely to incur additional costs because they may need to hire replacements and also deal with scheduling problems. In addition, the costs of such policies tend to rise to the extent that more workers take advantage of them. On balance, however, we would expect that employers' incentives to adopt policies of this type to increase as more women and also more men must cope with the difficulties of combining market work with home responsibilities.

It is also becoming increasingly clear that family-friendly policies lead to many positive results for employees. Such policies can dramatically increase workers' satisfaction with the firm, and they may also reduce work–family conflict by lowering stress.[75] Even so, they are, nonetheless, being introduced only at a rather slow pace in the United States. One reason is that their adoption requires a change in corporate "culture." Currently, family issues are seen as separate from the work sphere. For example, workers may be deemed unprofessional if they admit that they are delayed due to child

[72] Jonathan Gruber, "Incidence of Mandated Maternity Benefits," *American Economic Review* 84, no. 3 (June 1994): 622–41. Note, however, that to the extent that mandates are efficient, they do not increase equity because the group who benefits from the policy also bears its cost. For further discussion, see Susan N. Houseman, "The Effects of Employer Mandates," in *Generating Jobs: How to Increase Demand for Less-Skilled Workers*, edited by Richard B. Freeman and Peter Gottschalk (New York: Russell Sage Foundation, 1998), pp. 154–91.

[73] Christopher J. Ruhm, "The Economic Consequences of Parental Leave Mandates: Lessons from Europe," *Quarterly Journal of Economics* 113, no. 1 (February 1998): 285–318.

[74] See, for instance, Harry J. Holzer, "Work and Family Life: The Perspective of Employers," in *Work, Family, and Well-Being*, edited by Suzanne M. Bianchi, Lynne M. Casper, and Rosalind Berkowitz King (Mahwah, NJ: Lawrence Erlbaum, 2005), pp. 83–96; and Regan Baughman, Daniela DiNardi, and Douglas Holtz-Eakin, "Productivity and Wage Effects of 'Family-Friendly' Fringe Benefits," *International Journal of Manpower* 24, no. 3 (2003): 247–59. One study even found that the announcement of a firm's new work-family policy increased the value of its stock; see Michelle M. Arthur and Alison Cook, "Taking Stock of Work-Family Initiatives: How Announcements of 'Family Friendly' Human Resource Decisions Affect Shareholder Value," *Industrial and Labor Relations Review* 57, no. 4 (July 2004): 599–613.

[75] See, for instance, James A. Breaugh and N. Kathleen Frye, "Work-Family Conflict: The Importance of Family-Friendly Employment Practices and Family-Supportive Supervisors," *Journal of Business and Psychology* 22, no. 4 (June 2008): 345–53.

care problems rather than car problems. Second, in many firms, workers are evaluated on the basis of "face time" (i.e., the number of hours spent at the office or plant) rather than on output. There is also concern that with more flexible policies, including home-based work and flextime, it may be harder to monitor employees. Thus, work may have to be organized differently to accommodate increased flexibility.[76]

Large firms, and especially those with a high proportion of women, have often been at the forefront of implementing family-friendly policies. Perhaps the main reason is that they can reap the advantages of economies of scale in setting up programs because of the large number of workers who can potentially take advantage of them. Also, large firms are not as dependent on one or a few highly trained and specialized individuals as is more often the case for small businesses.

GOVERNMENT AND EMPLOYER FAMILY-FRIENDLY POLICIES

As discussed earlier, in the United States, government plays a much smaller role in social policy than in many other economically advanced countries. Nevertheless, the United States has initiated some **family-friendly policies** to help families juggle family and paid work, including mandated family leave and a variety of subsidies for child care.[77] Many, though by no means all, employers in the United States also make some effort to ease the conflict between work and family. They may offer paid or unpaid leave; assist workers with child care; and perhaps provide other family-friendly benefits, such as alternative work schedules, flexible benefit plans, and policies to assist couples. These various policies are discussed here.

Family Leave

Family leave allows workers to take time off from their job for such reasons as pregnancy, childbirth, infant care, and tending to ill family members. Without such a policy, workers may have to deal with these problems by giving up their jobs, with loss not only of earnings, but of accrued benefits and seniority as well. The availability of family leave, even a relatively short and unpaid one, with provisions for job security and some other entitlements, is often helpful in enabling workers, particularly women workers, to avoid these high costs. It also increases incentives for women to invest in firm-specific training and for employers to provide them with opportunities to do so.

The U.S. government mandates two specific policies regarding leave.[78] The **Pregnancy Discrimination Act** of 1978 (an amendment to Title VII of the Civil Rights Act of 1964) prohibits employers from discriminating against workers on the basis of pregnancy. An employer may not, for example, terminate or deny a job to a woman because she is pregnant. Employers who have a short-term disability program must provide paid disability leave for pregnancy and childbirth on the same basis as for other medical disabilities.[79]

The second is the **FMLA** of 1993, which allows eligible workers to take up to 12 weeks of unpaid leave for birth or adoption; acquiring a foster child; illness of a

---

[76] Holzer, "Work and Family Life"; and Charlene Marmer Solomon, "Work/Family's Failing Grade: Why Today's Initiatives Aren't Enough," *Personnel Journal* 73, no. 5 (May 1994): 72–87.

[77] Michelle Hoyman and Heidi Duer prefer the term *worker-friendly policies* because many of these policies benefit childless and single workers too; see "A Typology of Workplace Policies: Worker Friendly vs. Family Friendly?" *Review of Public Personnel Administration* 24, no. 2 (June 2004): 113–32.

[78] For details see Eileen Trzcinski and William T. Alpert, "Pregnancy and Parental Leave Benefits in the United States and Canada," *Journal of Human Resources* 29, no. 2 (Spring 1994): 535–54.

[79] Employers who do not have a short-term disability program, however, are not required to provide paid disability for pregnancy and childbirth.

child, spouse, or parent; or their own illness.[80] Workers may also take shorter leaves intermittently, pending the firm's approval. During the leave, the firm must continue health insurance coverage and, afterwards, the employee must be given the same or an equivalent position, with the same benefits, pay, and other conditions of employment. The FMLA applies to public and private sector workers who have been with the same employer for at least one year and worked at least 1,250 hours. However, the Act applies only to establishments with at least 50 workers. To the extent that some states mandate more generous benefits, they supersede the federal law.

Initially, the FMLA was hotly debated. Opponents of the measure were particularly concerned about the costs imposed on employers, who must continue to pay for health insurance for workers on leave and also bear the costs of training replacement workers. (Pay for replacement workers, however, is not an added cost because workers on leave do not draw a paycheck.) The net costs of implementing the policy are reduced, however, to the extent family leave reduces the costs of turnover; such costs can be quite substantial when hiring and training expenses are considered. Also, this policy may enhance workers' commitment to the firm and hence their productivity. A 1995 bipartisan Commission on Leave, as well as a study commissioned by the Department of Labor in 2000, found that providing short, unpaid leaves has not been unduly onerous for business in terms of profitability or growth.[81] Nonetheless, in a 2000 survey, firms reported an increase in the administrative burden of complying with the FMLA, citing difficulties ranging from determining what qualifies as a "serious health problem" to coordinating with rules for the Americans with Disabilities Act (ADA).[82]

The overall effect of family leave on women's labor force attachment and wages is ambiguous a priori. On the one hand, availability of leave is likely to increase labor force attachment by enabling workers to return to the same employer following an absence, and thus to maintain job continuity. This would be expected to result in a positive effect on wages by encouraging longer job tenure and associated investments in firm-specific training, the maintenance of a good "job match," and the opportunity to continue climbing the firm's career ladder. On the other hand, to the extent that leave encourages women to stay out of the labor market longer than they would without such a policy, leave or the extension of leave time might have a negative effect due to the depreciation of human capital. This is probably more of a concern in other countries where leaves may be as long as 12 months or more, but is less likely to be an issue in the United States where the mandated length of leave is quite short. As noted earlier, however, there is concern that even short leaves might reduce women's relative wages to finance the benefit, although this negative effect would be mitigated if men were to avail themselves of leave as well. Finally, it is possible that employers might respond to increased costs by cutting back on employment.

Empirical evidence thus far indicates that the effect of the FMLA has been modest; it has been found to have a small positive effect on employment and no effect on

---

[80] From the late 1980s until the time the legislation passed, approximately one-half of states adopted their own legislation. See Jacob Klerman and Arleen Leibowitz, "Labor Supply Effects of State Maternity Leave Legislation," in *Gender and Family Issues in the Workplace,* edited by Francine D. Blau and Ronald G. Ehrenberg (New York: Russell Sage Foundation, 1997), pp. 65–85. Information about the debate over federal family leave is provided in Andrew E. Scharlach and Blanche Grosswald, "The Family and Medical Leave Act of 1993," *Social Service Review* 71, no. 3 (September 1997): 335–59.

[81] Commission on Leave, *A Workable Balance: Report to Congress on Family and Medical Leave Policies* (Washington, DC: U.S. Department of Labor, 1996); and David Cantor et al., *Balancing the Needs of Families and Employers: The Family and Medical Leave Surveys: 2000 Update* (Rockville, MD: Westat, 2001), available at www.dol.gov.

[82] Cantor et al., *Balancing the Needs of Families and Employers.*

wages.[83] These findings probably reflect the situation in the United States, where leaves are generally unpaid and of short duration. Analyses of international differences in leave mandates have also found that leave of short duration has few, if any, negative effects, but where leave is paid and of medium or long duration, some evidence indicates negative effects on earnings.[84]

Turning next to the effect of leave on children, it has also been argued that children may be the beneficiaries of generous family leave policy. With such a policy, parents are able to spend more time with their children during infancy, when bonding is likely to be most important. Moreover, longer leave encourages breastfeeding, which has been found to have beneficial effects for children.[85] The effect of the FMLA on the length of leave taken is, however, not clear a priori. Since the FMLA offers the advantage of allowing parents to return to their previous job after taking leave, some workers may take more time out than without this policy. However, others who might have quit their jobs rather than return to work immediately postbirth might stay with their employer and return to work sooner. For a third group, the FMLA may have no effect on the amount of leave taken because they may not be able to afford to take time off without pay. Evidence suggests that, on balance, family leave increases the length of time away from work, but chiefly for college-educated parents, perhaps because they have greater financial means to support themselves temporarily without a paycheck coming in.[86]

Family leave, if taken by men as well as women, tends to promote greater gender equality by encouraging fathers to share in caring for infants and meeting family emergencies. Nevertheless, while both men and women are eligible to take advantage of the FMLA, female workers are still much more likely to seek time off under this policy than their male counterparts,[87] and so this policy has not been fully successful in this regard.

From the point of view of workers, a major problem with the FMLA is that it provides limited coverage. It does not cover workers in establishments with fewer than 50 employees, workers who fail to meet the 1,250 hours per year requirement, or workers employed for less than a year. Hence, it is estimated that the FMLA covers just under 50 percent of private-sector workers.[88] For the remainder, coverage depends on state- and firm-specific parental leave policies. One promising development is that for the period 1995 to 2000, one study found that an increasing number of firms not covered by the FMLA voluntarily offered such policies, perhaps to be able to better compete for workers.[89] Still, leaves are less likely to be available in smaller firms and for those working part time.

---

[83] See, for example, Charles L. Baum II, "The Effects of State Maternity Leave Legislation and the 1993 Family and Medical Leave Act on Employment and Wages," *Labour Economics* 10 no. 5 (October 2003): 573–96; and Jane Waldfogel, "The Impact of the Family and Medical Leave Act," *Journal of Policy Analysis and Management* 18, no. 2 (Spring 1999): 281–302. Also, see contributions in Francine D. Blau and Ronald G. Ehrenberg, eds., *Gender and Family Issues in the Workplace* (New York: Russell Sage Foundation, 1997).

[84] Ruhm and Teague, "Parental Leave Policies"; and Ruhm, "The Economic Consequences."

[85] Lawrence M. Berger, Jennifer Hill, and Jane Waldfogel find that children's health is better when mothers delay their return to work in "Maternity Leave, Early Maternal Employment and Child Outcomes in the US," *Economic Journal* 115, no. 501 (February 2005): F29–47.

[86] For instance, Charles L. Baum II finds that being able to take leave increases the likelihood that women will return to their original firm after the birth of a child and also increases the length of leave they take in "The Effects of Maternity Leave Legislation on Mothers' Labor Supply After Childbirth," *Southern Economic Journal* 69, no. 4 (April 2003): 772–99. Further, Wen-Jui Han, Christopher Ruhm, and Jane Waldfogel find that the FMLA increases leave-taking for both women and men in "Parental Leave Policies and Parents' Employment and Leave-Taking," *Journal of Policy Analysis and Management* 28, no. 1 (Winter 2009): 29–54.

[87] Han et al., "Parental Leave Policies and Parents' Employment and Leave-Taking."

[88] Jane Waldfogel, "Family and Medical Leave: Evidence from the 2000 Surveys," *Monthly Labor Review* 124, no. 9 (September 2001): 17–23.

[89] Cantor et al., *Balancing the Needs of Families and Employers*.

As already noted, another problem with the FMLA is that provides for only unpaid leave, which limits the ability of many covered workers, particularly those with low incomes, to take advantage of its provisions. Few firms offer paid leaves, though, in the case of pregnancy and childbirth, some workers have access through their employers' short-term disability plan. Others must use vacation time or sick leave. Even though paid leave is not mandated at the federal level, several states, including California, provide paid leave for pregnancy under the state's short-term disability program.[90] Moreover, in 2004, California became the first state to expand the availability of this leave to include those who must care for an ill family member, including a spouse, parent, or domestic partner. The leave is financed by an additional payroll deduction. The program replaces 55 percent of earnings, up to a specified maximum, and leave can be taken for up to 6 weeks per year.[91] Other states are expected to follow though state budget crises in the late 2000s may forestall such efforts.

Child Care

Finding affordable, quality **child care** is a critical concern for most single parents and dual-earner couples with children.[92] In fact, a substantial fraction of such families face this problem shortly after their child's birth, given that 56 percent of all women with infants (and the great majority of fathers) were in the labor force as of 2006.[93] In making their decision about whether to stay in the labor force or leave to spend time raising children, parents must decide how much they value their time spent in the labor market compared to the value of time at home. That is, as we discussed in Chapter 4, they compare the value of market time (w) to the value of home time (w^*). The value of market work includes not only earnings but also nonwage compensation, the nonpecuniary benefits of work, and the impact of working now on career prospects. The value of home time includes not only the value of time with children but also the leisure they would enjoy and the goods and services they would produce if they remain at home.

In the United States most of the costs of raising children are borne by parents, though the federal government does provide some subsidies to assist parents through the tax system, grants, and direct expenditures. As discussed earlier, there are both efficiency and equity motives for the government to play such a role. Nevertheless, there is some opposition to subsidies, particularly to subsidies that directly benefit employed parents who purchase child care. One common argument against such subsidies is that they benefit two-earner families at the expense of those with stay-at-home mothers. In evaluating this argument it is useful to recall from our earlier discussion on taxes that, without such subsidies, the federal tax system heavily favors traditional families because home production is untaxed, and because the tax schedules favor one-earner couples. Thus, child care subsidies may be seen as a way to offset this imbalance. Furthermore, even though these subsidies may encourage some mothers to work outside the home who might not otherwise do so, many are already employed and will

---

[90] Rhode Island, New Jersey, New York, and Hawaii (and the territory of Puerto Rico) had such a program as of 2008.

[91] Steven K. Wisenale, "California's Paid Leave Law: A Model for Other States?" *Marriage & Family Review* 39, no. 1/2 (2006): 177–95. As of 2008, New Jersey had passed legislation to expand its disability insurance programs in this regard and the state of Washington had passed legislation to set up a paid family leave insurance program.

[92] A thorough discussion of these issues is found in Myra H. Strober, "Formal Extrafamily Child Care—Some Economic Observations," in *Sex, Discrimination and the Division of Labor,* edited by Cynthia B. Lloyd (New York: Columbia University Press, 1975); Leibowitz, "Child Care"; and David M. Blau, "Child Care Subsidy Programs," in *Means-Tested Programs,* edited by Robert A. Moffitt (Chicago: University of Chicago Press, 2003), pp. 443–516.

[93] Figure is from U.S. Census Bureau, "Women 15–44 Years Old Who Had a Birth in the Last 12 Months and Their Percentage in the Labor Force," Supplemental Table 5 (August 2008), available at www.census.gov.

remain employed in any case. In fact, as noted earlier, recent changes in welfare rules require that recipients take a job; child care subsidies are needed to make this possible.[94]

There is also some concern that, by reducing parents' costs of raising children, subsidies will encourage people to have more of them. However, as already discussed, providing subsidized day care also encourages mothers to enter the labor market. To the extent that women acquire more—and more market-oriented—education in anticipation of this and accumulate more work experience as a consequence, they will have higher earnings. Hence, the opportunity cost of additional children will also increase. Further, it may be that employed women develop stronger preferences for market goods, and perhaps for having their own income, which gives them a greater feeling of independence. Therefore, it is not possible to determine a priori which set of forces is likely to be stronger.

Another concern frequently voiced by opponents of publicly subsidized day care involves children's well-being. As discussed in Chapter 10, even though some recent studies have found a negative effect of maternal employment on child outcomes, particularly nonparental care in the first year of life, these studies are generally not able to control fully for child care quality, which would be expected to attenuate or even negate any such effects. And, children between ages 2 and 4 tend to do better in center day care both intellectually and socially than children cared for entirely at home. Moreover, as noted earlier, children's development is affected by a host of other factors, most importantly, family characteristics.

One way that the federal government subsidizes purchased child care is through block grants. One example is the **Child Care and Development Block Grant**, which provides states with funds to expand day care services for low-income families, including those on welfare, as well as to improve the overall quality and supply of day care. For instance, states might provide part of these funds to child care providers, who can then allow families to pay for care on a sliding-scale basis, depending on their income. Alternatively states might give vouchers directly to low-income families who would then use them to buy child care from an eligible provider or even from a friend or relative living outside their home. A smaller but important amount of federal support goes to **Head Start**, a program which is explicitly designed to provide early childhood education for low-income preschoolers.[95]

In addition to grants and direct expenditures, the federal government provides a number of tax subsidies for child care. Through the **Dependent Care Tax Credit**, employed parents receive a tax credit in the amount of 35 percent of actual child care expenses up to $3,000 for the care of one child, and $6,000 for the care of two or more children, provided their adjusted income is below $15,000. The credit is gradually reduced to 20 percent of actual expenses for families with adjusted incomes between $15,000 and $43,000 and remains at 20 percent for those with adjusted incomes above $43,000. Since this credit is nonrefundable, low-income families who do not pay taxes do not benefit.[96]

---

[94] See, for instance, Patricia M. Anderson and Philip B. Levine, "Child Care and Mothers' Employment Decisions," in *Finding Good Jobs: Work and Welfare Reform,* edited by David E. Card and Rebecca M. Blank (New York: Russell Sage Foundation, 2000), pp. 420–62; David Blau and Erdal Tekin, "The Determinants and Consequences of Child Care Subsidies for Single Mothers in the USA," *Journal of Population Economics* 20, no. 4 (October 2007): 719–41; and Robert J. Lemke, Robert Witt, and Ann Dryden Witte, "The Transition from Welfare to Work," *Eastern Economic Journal* 33, no. 3 (Summer 2007): 359–73.

[95] For more on federal child care subsidies for low-income families, see Greenberg, "Next Steps for Federal Child Care Policy;" Regarding Head Start, see Blau and Currie, "Preschool, Day Care, and Afterschool Care: Who's Minding the Kids?"

[96] Nicole D. Forry and Elaine A. Anderson, "The Child and Dependent Care Tax Credit: A Policy Analysis," *Marriage and Family Review* 39, no. 1/2 2006): 159–76.

The federal government also indirectly subsidizes child care costs (and other child-related expenses) through tax credits that are determined by the number of children in a family and may be received by families whether or not child care is purchased. In 2008, the **Child Tax Credit** provided up to a $1,000 tax credit for each child under age 17 in the family. For married couples, this credit is phased out when their income reaches $110,000. The credit is partly refundable, so that it is of some benefit to families with lower earnings. Families may also use funds from the EITC for child care. Recall that this program provides a fully refundable tax credit; as of 2008, it provided a maximum of $4,824 to a low-income working family with two or more children.[97]

Another way in which the tax code provides some subsidy for child care expenses is through **flexible spending accounts** provided by some employers. In firms that provide this option, employees may have money deducted from their paychecks for dependent care expenses on a *pretax* basis. Since they do not owe taxes on the money set aside for this purpose, the costs of such care are thereby reduced.

Beyond the various government programs and tax subsidies that we have described, a small but growing number of firms are assisting workers with their child care needs. In 2007, 5 percent of private employees had access to on-site or off-site day care at their firm, 3 percent were able to receive funds from their employers to pay for child care, and 11 percent had access to referral services to assist them in finding child care. These benefits are more often provided by larger establishments and to white-collar workers.[98] On-site day care has both advantages and drawbacks for employees, who typically pay for at least part of the costs. On the one hand, parents do not have to make a separate trip to take children elsewhere, they are nearby in case of emergencies, and the children receive care during whatever hours the parent works.[99] On the other hand, children often are taken out of their own neighborhood, perhaps travel long distances, and must change caregivers when parents change jobs.

Table 11-6 shows the diversity of child care arrangements used by employed mothers of preschool children. In 2005, 24 percent of these mothers had their children in organized child care facilities. While this figure had increased only slightly over the prior decade, it nevertheless reflects a considerable increase from the late 1970s, when just 13 percent of employed mothers used this arrangement (data not shown in the table).[100] This increase is no doubt related to the aforementioned federal subsidies, which serve to lower the price of purchased care, as well as child care subsidies and on-site care provided by employers.[101] Still, as shown in Table 11-6, the largest percentage of families, 43 percent, continue to use child care provided by the child's father or other relatives, either in their own home or in a relative's home. An additional 16 percent used the services of a nonrelative, either in their own home or at the home of the day care provider. The remainder of mothers cared for their children at work or did not have a regular child care arrangement.

---

[97] C. Eugene Steuerle points out that it may make sense to have both policies, because the child credit adjusts for differences in family size, while the child care credit adjusts for the costs of purchased child care in "Systematic Thinking About Subsidies for Child Care, Part Three: Application of Principles" (Washington, DC: Urban Institute, February 1998). For another useful discussion, see Barbara R. Bergmann, "Subsidizing Child Care by Mothers at Home," *Feminist Economics* 6, no. 1 (March 2000): 77–88.

[98] U.S. Bureau of Labor Statistics, "Employee Benefits in Private Industry in the United States, 2007," USDL 07-05 (August 2007).

[99] Many such day care centers are at hospitals, where large numbers of women of childbearing age who have to work nonstandard hours are employed. For more on this arrangement, see Rachel A. Willis, *Kids at Work: The Value of Employee-Sponsored On-Site Child Care Centers* (Kalamazoo, MI: Upjohn Institute, 2004).

[100] U.S. Census Bureau, Historical Time Series, Table A, "Primary Child Care Arrangements Used for Preschoolers by Families with Employers: Selected Years, 1977 to 1994," available at www.census.gov (accessed December 2008).

[101] William Goodman, "Boom in Day Care Industry the Result of Many Social Changes," *Monthly Labor Review* 118, no. 8 (August 1995): 3–12.

TABLE 11-6 Child Care Arrangements Used by Employed Mothers of Preschoolers, Selected Years (Percent Distribution)

	1997	2005
Organized Child Care Facilities	20.4	23.8
Parents	20.8	21.6
Mother cares for child at work	3.2	4.3
Father	17.7	17.2
Other Relatives	24.9	25.8
Grandparent	17.5	19.4
Sibling and other relative	7.4	6.4
Nonrelative Care	20.2	15.6
In child's home	3.8	3.6
In provider's home	16.3	12.0
No Regular Arrangement[a]	13.7	13.2

[a] This category also includes a very small percentage of children who care for themselves or are in kindergarten/grade school.

Source: U.S. Census Bureau, Historical Table, "Primary Child Care Arrangements of Preschoolers with Employed Mothers: Selected Years, 1985 to 2005," available at www.census.gov.

The type of child care arrangement chosen by a family depends, in part, on its financial situation. Poor families are much less likely to use center care and more likely to have their children cared for by relatives at no cost.[102] Among those families that purchase day care, poor families pay less in total because of the type of care they use, whether it is provided at low cost by relatives or through subsidized programs targeted at the low-income population like Head Start. Nonetheless, in 2005, as a *percentage* of their income, poor families with employed mothers who purchased care spent a much greater share on child care than non-poor families; the difference was 30 percent versus 6 percent of monthly income.[103]

Another factor that affects the type of child care chosen is the child's age. A much smaller percentage of infants are in organized group day care as compared to preschool-age children.[104] Parents of infants who can afford to do so may hire a nanny or find some other way to have their children cared for in their own home because there the children generally receive more one-on-one attention and their exposure to infectious diseases is limited. For preschoolers, on the other hand, group care provides the advantages of contact with other children and it teaches them to share and cooperate.[105] For school-age children, the question of after-school care arises. One survey indicated that 2 percent of children ages 5–8 and 10 percent of children ages 9–11 are regularly left

---

[102] Jeffrey Capizzano, Gina Adams, and Freya Sonenstein, "Child Care Arrangements for Children Under Five: Variation Across States," *Assessing the New Federalism*, Series B, No. B-7 (Washington, DC: Urban Institute, March 2000).

[103] U.S. Census Bureau, "Weekly Child Care Costs Paid by Families with Employed Mothers: 1985–2005," Table C2, *Who's Minding the Kids? Child Care Arrangements: Spring 2005*, available at www.census.gov (Accessed October 2008). See also, Dan T. Rosenbaum and Christopher J. Ruhm, "Family Expenditures on Child Care," *B.E. Journal of Economic Analysis and Policy* 7, no. 1 (July 2007): 1–30.

[104] Capizzano, Adams, and Sonenstein, "Child Care Arrangements for Children Under Five."

[105] Jane Waldfogel provides a comprehensive discussion of the benefits of various child care arrangements by child's age in *What Children Need* (Cambridge, MA: Harvard University Press, 2006).

unsupervised.[106] Even though "self-care" can build self-esteem and independence for older children, it is generally viewed as a poor and even a dangerous alternative for younger children. In response to this concern, along with an effort to improve school outcomes, after-school programs that offer supervised educational and recreational activities have received some funding at the federal and state level.[107]

Quality of care, which has important consequences for children's development, varies considerably across different settings—center-based care, family day care (in the home of a nonrelative), and relative care. Quality is typically measured in terms of both the structural characteristics of the child care arrangement and children's experiences in that setting. Structural characteristics include the level of teachers' education and training, group size, and the child–teacher ratio. Criteria for evaluating children's experiences in child care include the way caregivers relate to children, including how much they talk to them, and the continuity of care with the same caregiver. Even though some high-quality child care is available, especially for those who can afford it, much of what is currently available tends to be of poor quality, suggesting considerable room for improvement.[108]

In recent years, access to better child care has become an especially high priority issue for families and society as a greater fraction of women are employed full time, full year, and as more low-income women have moved from welfare to work. A pressing concern is that federal child care funds are insufficient to cover all eligible children and that even funds earmarked for child care in the 2005 federal welfare legislation are not likely to be adequate to close this gap.[109] In addition, as economic activity continues to shift to 24 hours a day, 7 days a week ("24/7"), there is increasing need for care in the very early morning, in the evenings, and on weekends.[110] Another concern is that grants likes the Child Development Block Grant, which provide child care funds to assist low-income workers, focus solely on supporting parents' paid work, not on providing early childhood education like Head Start, though many children in low-income families might benefit from such programs.[111]

Suggested solutions to the child care problem range from sweeping to more modest, and seek to address concerns about affordability, accessibility, quality, or all three. The most ambitious proposal, which is unlikely to be adopted in the United States anytime soon, is universal government-provided child care. Another option would be to increase government subsidies in conjunction with greater regulation to ensure quality.[112] More modest proposals focus on government training for child care workers and expanding information on how to identify high-quality child care. The government might also create financial incentives for families to use and for providers to offer

---

[106] U.S. Census Bureau, *Who's Minding the Kids? Child Care Arrangements: Spring 2005*, Detailed Table 4, at www.census.gov (Accessed October 2008). See also, Sharon Vandivere et al., "Unsupervised Time: Family and Child Factors Associated with Self-Care," Assessing the New Federalism, Occasional Paper No. 71, (Washington, DC: Urban Institute, 2003).

[107] For evidence on the effects of unsupervised care, see Anna Aizer, "Home Alone: Supervision After School and Child Behavior," *Journal of Public Economics* 88, no. 9–10 (August 2004): 1835–48. Regarding after-school options, see contributions in *Organized Activities as Contexts of Development: Extracurricular Activities, After School and Community Programs*, edited by Joseph L. Mahoney, Reed W. Larson, and Jacquelynne S. Eccles (Mahwah, NJ: Lawrence Erlbaum, 2005).

[108] Barbara Wolfe and Deborah Lowe Vandell, "Welfare Reform Depends on Good Child Care," *American Prospect* 13, no. 13 (July 2002): 19–21.

[109] Greenberg, "Next Steps for Federal Child Care Policy."

[110] Harriet S. Presser, *Working in a 24/7 Economy* (New York: Russell Sage Foundation, 2003), Chapter 7.

[111] Ron Haskins and Isabel Sawhill, "The Future of Head Start," *Welfare Reform and Beyond*, Brief No. 27 (Washington, DC: Brookings Institution, July 2003).

[112] Suzanne Helburn and Barbara Bergmann, *America's Child Care Problem: The Way Out* (New York: Palgrave, St. Martin's Press, 2002).

high-quality care. For instance, child care centers that are deemed high-quality might receive government subsidies.[113]

Other Employer Family-Friendly Policies

Many U.S. firms also offer other family-friendly policies, apart from any policies concerning family leave or child care. These include alternative work schedules, such as flextime, nonstandard work schedules, part-time employment, job sharing, and home-based work. Some firms also offer the option of flexible benefits as well as policies specifically crafted to assist couples. As discussed earlier, the number and types of policies offered varies considerably across firms, although larger firms often have greater ability to extend such benefits.

ALTERNATIVE WORK SCHEDULES Alternative work schedules can provide greater flexibility for workers to take care of family responsibilities and to arrange their personal lives more conveniently. A policy often known as **flextime** permits some variation in work schedules at the discretion of the employee, ranging from modest changes in starting and quitting times to varying the number of hours worked per day, week, or pay period. In 2004, an estimated 30 percent of wage and salary workers employed full time had flexible schedules, most often the result of an informal arrangement.[114] Such flexibility can be advantageous, especially for those with young children or other family members who depend on their care.[115] Also, workers on flextime can avoid driving in rush hour, thereby reducing their commuting time. In fact, as more workers take advantage of flextime, even workers who do not have a flexible schedule benefit from less rush-hour traffic. The degree of flexibility offered depends on the nature of the enterprise and the type of work. Some employers may be reluctant to offer this benefit because they need key employees to be present during standard business hours, perhaps to be available to handle customers or to meet work flow demands. Others may be concerned about the potential for abuse.

Other workers have **nonstandard work schedules**, where they are employed on alternating shifts, nights, or weekends. (The term *nonstandard* as used here refers to work schedules, rather than to the type of worker or employment, as in Chapter 9.) These schedules have expanded considerably as economic activity has moved to virtually "24/7."[116] The availability and widespread adoption of technologies such as fax machines, computers, cell phones, and pagers explains part of this change. Another factor is the rise in the number of dual-earner and single-parent families, who must do their shopping on weekends and evenings. According to the most recent comprehensive study of nonstandard work schedules, which was conducted in 1997, only 60 percent of full-time workers over age 18 regularly worked a fixed schedule, say 9 to 5, Monday through Friday. Since then, it is likely that even fewer full-time workers have this schedule. Like flextime, nonstandard work schedules potentially provide some flexibility for workers juggling child care, perhaps schooling, and a job. However, unlike flextime, these schedules are typically set by employers rather than at the discretion of employees. To the extent that workers are not able to choose their schedules, those with

---

[113] For these proposals, among others, see David M. Blau, "Child Care Subsidy Programs"; and Barbara Bergmann, "Thinking About Child Care Policy," in *The Economics of Work and Family*, edited by Jean Kimmel and Emily Hoffman (Kalamazoo, MI: W.E. Upjohn Institute, 2002), pp. 43–70.

[114] Terence M. McMenamin, "A Time to Work: Recent Trends in Shift Work and Flexible Schedules," *Monthly Labor Review* 130, no. 12 (December 2007): 3–15.

[115] This flexibility appears to be so valuable that some workers may be working longer hours in exchange for it. See Lonnie Golden, "Flexible Work Schedules: What Are We Trading Off to Get Them?" *Monthly Labor Review* 124, no. 3 (March 2001): 50–67.

[116] This section and the figure cited are drawn from Harriet B. Presser, "Toward a 24-Hour Economy," *Science* 284 (June 11, 1999): 1778–79; and Presser, *Working in a 24/7 Economy*.

young children may face considerable difficulties finding child care to match their needs, especially on weekends and at night. Also, many people have biological difficulties adjusting to night work. In addition, in two-parent families with such schedules, adults tend to spend less time together, potentially leading to negative consequences for the marriage.

Another alternative is **part-time employment**. This arrangement is especially common among women (as well as young people going to school and older workers retired from their full-time jobs) and does offer some flexibility as compared to a regular full-time job. In 2007, nearly 25 percent of employed women and nearly 11 percent of employed men worked less than full-time (defined as at least 35 hours per week).[117] While part-time work offers a solution to the difficulties of combining work and family responsibilities, as discussed in Chapter 9, it offers few fringe benefits (such as health care and pensions), frequently poor compensation, and few opportunities for promotion.

Some firms may offer the possibility of **job sharing**, where two individuals share one position. For people seeking less than full-time work, this arrangement can be a good way to obtain a more attractive part-time position, while employers may find that this option helps them retain valuable employees. A disadvantage is that people who share jobs, like all part-time workers, may receive only partial benefits or none at all.

Finally, an increasing number of workers are choosing **home-based employment**.[118] It has been estimated that in 2004, 15 percent of all workers did at least some work for their primary job at home. This figure varies dramatically by employment status and occupation. Indeed, about one-third of all self-employed workers conduct at least some work from home, and two-thirds of these workers had businesses exclusively based in their homes.[119] As would be expected, individuals in white-collar occupations such as management, business, and finance were the most likely to work at home for at least 1 hour per week, since much of this work can be done by phone, computer, or fax.

The increase in prevalence of home-based employment is due in part to improvements in computers and communications technology. Additional factors that have contributed include the rise in women's labor force participation, the greater proportion of two-earner couples, and the growing number of small individual- and family-owned businesses. The opportunity for home-based employment likely encourages paid work, especially among women, because the fixed costs associated with this type of employment tend to be lower, and because this arrangement allows workers to be "on call" to meet the needs of young children, teenagers, or infirm parents at home. One recent study suggests that this type of work, which blurs the distinction between paid work and home responsibilities, is likely to have very different implications for women and men.[120] Men in this situation may assume more household responsibilities, a development that might be regarded as a positive outcome for the family. For women, this type of employment may come at a professional cost; because the home has been their traditional sphere, they may be perceived as not having a "real" job. It is important to be realistic about other drawbacks as well as benefits. Inevitably, there is the issue of how much work can be accomplished when

---

[117] U.S. Department of Labor, *Employment and Earnings*, January 2008, Table 8.

[118] The discussion that follows is drawn from William G. Deming, "Work at Home: Data from the Current Population Survey," *Monthly Labor Review* 117, no. 2 (February 1994): 14–20; Linda N. Edwards and Elizabeth Field-Hendry, "Home-Based Workers? Data from the 1990 Census of Population," *Monthly Labor Review* 119, no. 11 (November 1996): 26–34; and Linda N. Edwards and Elizabeth Field-Hendry, "Home-Based Work and Women's Labor Force Decisions," *Journal of Labor Economics* 20, no. 1 (January 2002): 170–200.

[119] U.S. Bureau of Labor Statistics, "Work at Home in 2004," *News*, USDL 05-1768, September 22, 2005.

[120] For an interesting discussion, see Debra Osnowitz, "Managing Time in Domestic Space: Home-Based Contractors and Household Work," *Gender and Society* 19, no. 1 (February 2005): 83–103.

children or an infirm parent are present and require attention. The question of how time is managed and monitored is especially critical for those with an employer based elsewhere. Finally, another possible drawback to home-based work is the isolation the individual may experience without having coworkers in close physical proximity.

FLEXIBLE BENEFITS   As the workforce has become more diverse, with some workers who are members of traditional families, some who have employed spouses, some who are single, and others who live with partners they are not married to, **flexible benefit plans** (often known as *cafeteria plans*) have become increasingly important as an alternative to standard or fixed benefit packages. These plans allow employees to select from an assortment of benefits worth up to a specified amount predetermined by the employer. They increase the value of fringe benefits to workers because workers can choose the benefits that best meet their needs. Thus, such benefits may provide a further inducement to individuals to enter or to remain attached to the labor market and even to the firm.[121] For example, two-earner couples derive no benefit from the double health insurance coverage they receive when one or both are covered under their own employer's health insurance program and under their spouse's. With a cafeteria plan, one of the spouses could instead choose to receive child care benefits or contributions into a pension fund, or any one of the other benefits available.

POLICIES TO ASSIST COUPLES   Dual-earner couples, married or unmarried, whether same-sex or opposite-sex, face particular problems in the workplace. Such couples, especially those with two professionals, must deal with the often daunting task of finding two jobs commensurate with their respective skills in the same location, or having a "commuting relationship," if both are to successfully pursue their careers. As discussed in Chapter 10, many heterosexual couples still give priority to the husband's career, often at the expense of the wife's, although husbands are increasingly making sacrifices too.

Employers can reduce the negative consequences for the "trailing partner" in a number of ways. For example, firms, acting alone or with others, can help partners find employment. Assistance might take the form of sending out a spouse's resume to employers or making use of personal contacts. Many universities as well as some other establishments have set up programs for hiring couples, or offer jobs to partners of employees, whenever suitable positions can be found.[122] Businesses can also reduce difficulties for such couples by not penalizing employees who decline a promotion because they have family responsibilities or decline a transfer to a branch in a different location because their partner might find it difficult to locate a satisfactory job there.

Anti-nepotism rules, once widely used to restrict the hiring or retention of relatives of employees, but most particularly spouses of employees, have virtually disappeared in academia and are less common elsewhere as well. These rules not only prevented couples from being hired, but if two employees married, one—usually the wife—would have to go. Restrictions that still exist today are less severe. Some employers restrict spouses,

---

[121] Federal and state tax policy can encourage the growth of many employer-paid benefits in general by excluding them from taxable employee income, while permitting businesses to treat them as a normal business expense. See Marianne A. Ferber and Brigid O'Farrell, with La Rue Allen, eds., *Work and Family: Policies for a Changing Workforce* (Washington, DC: National Academy Press, 1991).
[122] See, for instance, Lisa Wolf-Wendel, Susan B. Twombly, and Suzanne Rice, *The Two-Body Problem: Dual-Career Couple Hiring Practices in Higher Education* (Baltimore, MD: Johns Hopkins University Press, 2003); and Jane W. Loeb, "Programs for Academic Partners: How Well Can They Work?" in *Academic Couples: Problems and Promises,* edited by Marianne A. Ferber and Jane W. Loeb (Champaign, IL: University of Illinois Press, 1997), pp. 270–98.

unmarried partners, and in some cases even couples with romantic attachments from working in the same department, or at least avoid having one partner directly supervising the other. In these cases, the concern is that a partner who has influence may use it to have the other hired or promoted or that the couple would form a working alliance that may be resented by their coworkers.

Such abuses undoubtedly take place, but there is no evidence that they are more common than among close friends. In fact, couples might be somewhat more circumspect because favoritism would be so obvious. In any case, the risk that such problems may occur must be weighed against the disadvantage of not being able to hire and retain the best-qualified people regardless of their relationships. One problem with even the remnants of anti-nepotism rules is that as long as husbands are most often senior to their wives and in higher positions, it is the woman who will be viewed as more expendable. Further, employment of the partner by a competitor may even create its own problems. For instance, the partners may inadvertently share confidential business information such as trade secrets, putting the firm at risk.

Still, policies that are helpful to married couples, with and without children, raise questions about fairness to those who do not have a family.[123] For instance, such singles are at a disadvantage if employers pay lower wages to all employees as a result of providing benefits such as family leave, on-site day care, or subsidized spousal health care and pensions. Also, singles may be far less interested in flexible schedules and may regret the reduction in "face time" with coworkers. In addition, some single individuals claim that they are often called upon to shoulder extra responsibilities at work when a coworker's child becomes sick, and at times are expected to work weekends, nights, or holidays so that others can spend time with their families. Regarding inequities in benefits, one solution is for firms to offer cafeteria plans, so that workers can choose the benefits they want. Another solution, recently adopted by some larger firms, is to extend benefits to a broader set of household members, including workers' grown children, elderly parents, or unmarried partners, so as to increase the share of their workforce that benefit from the policies.[124] Few would likely benefit from the more radical alternative of scaling back all such benefits, because people's situations change—singles marry, adults have children or adopt, married people get divorced or become widowed, and parents become ill—so that most workers are likely to benefit from even the existing set of policies at some point in their lives.

Also, at present, unmarried couples, whether opposite sex or same sex, still tend to be at a disadvantage relative to married couples because they are generally not eligible for the substantial fringe benefits that are usually available to spouses including dental, health, and life insurance. However, since the early 1980s, a growing number of employers have extended such benefits to unmarried partners as a result of the domestic partnership movement.[125] Further, as discussed previously in Chapters 3 and 10, same-sex marriage, permitted in Massachusetts and Connecticut as of 2008, and civil unions, permitted in Vermont and several other states, extend spousal rights available under state law to same-sex couples. Nevertheless, these couples still do not have the same federal benefits as their opposite-sex married counterparts.

---

[123] See Barbara Bergmann, "Work-Family Policies and Equality Between Women and Men," in *Gender and Family Issues in the Workplace,* edited by Francine D. Blau and Ronald G. Ehrenberg (New York: Russell Sage Foundation, 1997), pp. 277–79; and Michelle Conlin, "Unmarried America," *Business Week,* October 20, 2003, pp. 106–16.

[124] Conlin, "Unmarried America."

[125] "Domestic Partner Benefits: Facts and Background" (Washington, DC: Employee Benefit Research Institute, March 2004).

HOW TO HANDLE A JOB INTERVIEW

How much should you tell a potential employer during a job interview about your current and expected family responsibilities in order to learn about the employer's willingness to accommodate your family concerns?* This question is not easy to answer. On the one hand, mentioning that you plan to marry or have children, that you currently have young children or perhaps other family members who need care, or that you have a spouse who would also need to relocate may reduce your chances of being offered a position for which you are fully qualified. On the other hand, in order for you to be sure that you and the firm will be a good "match," you may need to get sufficient information about issues such as whether the potential employer will make it easier for you to handle possible family emergencies, or whether your progress would be impeded if you were reluctant to move. The question may even arise as to whether you would want to work for an organization that looks askance at anyone who has a life outside the workplace.

At the same time it is likely that because of the high costs of hiring and training workers, employers who interview you are also interested in making a good long-term match and therefore want to learn as much as possible about you. They too, however, face challenges and constraints. On the one hand, employers need to learn about your commitment to the job. On the other hand, they are not allowed by law to ask directly about your family situation, including current or intended pregnancies, whether any family members have disabilities, or even your marital status.** One problem is that some employers may nevertheless ask questions that are illegal, fall into a gray area, or are at least "unwise," depending on how they are asked. Their questions confront you with the difficult decision of how to handle the situation.

Although it is impossible to offer suggestions on precisely what to say and do under all circumstances that may arise, some general recommendations should help you to elicit the information that you need and send the message that you want, while avoiding an explicit discussion about your current or expected family responsibilities. For instance, you might ask your potential employer to describe a "typical day" or a "typical week" for a person who holds this type of job. The answer would give you a sense of whether you would be expected to work late hours during the week or on weekends, without your asking the question directly and thus perhaps giving the appearance that you are not willing to work hard. Also, at a later stage in the interview process, you could ask for materials regarding conditions of employment, which may include information about options for flextime and various fringe benefits, such as on-site child care. In addition, discrete conversations with potential coworkers may serve to answer questions you would be reluctant to raise with the employer directly.

Concerns about family responsibilities remain especially problematic for women because they continue to bear primary responsibility for the family and household. Under these circumstances, employers have the option of hiring men who tend to have fewer family commitments that will interfere with their devotion to their jobs. Even though public policies emphasizing equal opportunity may facilitate change to some extent, it is probably the case that only when women and men more fully share these responsibilities will we see fundamental change.

*This inset is drawn from Sue Shellenbarger, "What You Should Say About Family Duties in a Job Interview," *Wall Street Journal* (April 10, 1996), sec. B1, p. 1; "Advice to Help You Get Ahead from the Experts: Business Newsletters, Magazines and Books; Job Seekers Should Beware," *Atlanta Constitution*, June 20, 1999; Kirsten Downey Grimsley, "Awkward Queries in Interviews," *San Francisco Chronicle*, February 25, 2000, p. B3; and Eileen P. Gunn, "How to Ask About Flexible Hours Without Derailing Your Candidacy," *Wall Street Journal* (February 8, 2007).
**"Advice to Help You Get Ahead from the Experts," p. 1R.

Conclusion

This chapter began by examining the major changes that occurred during the last few years in the U.S. welfare system. This policy, which was implemented at a time of unprecedented economic prosperity, resulted in a considerable decline in welfare caseloads, a rise in the employment of single mothers, and increased earnings and reduced poverty for many, though not all families. Many questions remain, nonetheless, as to the future effects of time limits, and especially how needy families fared during the recession that began in December 2007.

Even though the full effects of welfare changes remain to be sorted out, it is clear that the expansion of the EITC has played an important role in reducing poverty. In addition, child support awards increased for many single-parent families, particularly never-married mothers, as a direct result of changes in federal child support rules. Still, some concern surrounds these policies. For instance, the EITC reduces some married women's incentive to seek employment, may discourage some unmarried couples from marrying, and may encourage some married couples to get divorced. Perhaps most serious, stepping up child support enforcement without sufficient recognition that many noncustodial parents have low incomes themselves may further increase the distance, both geographic and emotional, between them and their children.

This chapter also identified a number of important ways that the federal income taxes and Social Security affect the work and family decisions of individuals. Tax policies often favor families with full-time homemakers as compared to those with two earners, although two-earner couples are now the norm. We also noted that it is critical for policy makers to consider the effects of such policies on incentives for secondary earners to work for pay, especially when evaluating proposals to restructure Social Security or revamp the income tax system.

Next, we looked at how government and some employers have implemented policies to help people meet the dual demands of paid work and family. These policies have received increasing attention as women joined the paid labor force in record numbers and men took on more household responsibilities, including childcare and elder care. Nevertheless, concerns remain. First, many people gain little from the new programs, especially part-time workers and workers in small establishments, as well as the growing numbers of workers who do not have "regular" full-time jobs, as discussed in Chapter 9. In addition, there continues to be a serious shortage of affordable, quality childcare, not just for infants, but also for school-age children and disadvantaged children of all ages. These problems have increased as more low-income women have been leaving welfare for work and as a greater fraction of businesses operate "24/7." It is in the interest of firms that want a focused, committed workforce now and in the future as well as society at large to find solutions to these problems. Increased funding for before- and after-school programs, more flextime, and additional child care subsidies would be useful steps in that direction.

A further issue of growing importance is that *family* is rather narrowly defined as it pertains to various policies. This problem must be addressed because living arrangements other than the traditional family of a husband, wife, and their own biological children residing in the same home are increasingly common. Often members of the same family live in different homes, as parents split up, remarry, or live with other partners, perhaps more than once. In such cases, the question arises as to whose policy covers a given child.[126] The growing number of unmarried couples is one more reason for governments and employers to adjust their policies in this respect as well.

---

[126] Olivia Mitchell, "Work and Family Benefits in the Corporate Setting," in *Gender and Family Issues in the Workplace,* edited by Francine D. Blau and Ronald G. Ehrenberg (New York: Russell Sage Foundation, 1997), pp. 269–76.

Questions for Review and Discussion

1. In what fundamental ways does TANF differ from the former AFDC program?

2. The EITC received bipartisan support, while AFDC was far less widely accepted. What are the key differences in these programs that led one to be popular and the other (now defunct and replaced by TANF) to have received so much less support?

3. Consider a married couple where the husband and the wife each has $75,000 in taxable earnings. Assume they have no children and all income is from earnings. Using the information in Table 11-4:

   a. Compute their tax liability as a married couple.

   b. Compute their tax liability if they live together but are not married.

   c. Assuming they are married, compute their marriage bonus or penalty. Is this outcome what you would have expected based on the discussion in the text? Explain.

   d. Answer the prior questions again, but this time assume that the husband has $150,000 in taxable earnings and the wife has no earnings. Do your findings differ? If so, explain why.

   e. Suppose the wife in part d is deciding whether to enter the labor force. What income tax rate affects this decision? Explain your answer.

4. In recent years, child support enforcement was stepped up considerably. Explain the pros and cons of this policy change.

5. When the Family and Medical Leave Act was passed in the United States in 1993, it was attacked as overly generous by some and as inadequate by others. Discuss the pros and cons of each of these views.

6. Suppose you work for a "singles" lobby group. Point to the various policies that "work against singles." What sort of policies would be useful to families but would be more neutral with respect to family structure?

7. Discuss the pros and cons of taxing each spouse as an individual without regard to marital status.

8. Make the best case you can for:

   a. Parents being entirely responsible for the care of their children.

   b. Employer-financed day care.

   c. Government-financed day care.

9. Discuss the pros and cons of mandating that employers provide relatively long paid parental leaves of, say, one year.

Suggested Readings

Beller, Andrea H., and John W. Graham. "The Economics of Child Support." In *Marriage and the Economy*, edited by Shoshana Grossbard-Schectman. Cambridge: Cambridge University Press, 2003, pp. 153–176.

Bianchi, Suzanne, Lynne M. Casper, and Rosalind Berkowitz King, eds. *Work, Family, Health and Well-Being*. Mahwah, NJ: Lawrence Erlbaum, 2005.

Blank, Rebecca M. *It Takes a Nation: A New Agenda for Fighting Poverty*. Princeton, NJ: Princeton University Press, 1996.

Blau, David M. *The Child Care Problem: An Economic Analysis*. New York: Russell Sage Foundation, 2001.

Blau, Francine D., and Ronald G. Ehrenberg, eds. *Gender and Family Issues in the Workplace*. New York: Russell Sage Foundation, 1997.

Card, David E., and Rebecca M. Blank, eds. *Finding Jobs: Work and Welfare Reform*. New York: Russell Sage Foundation, 2000.

Currie, Janet M. *The Invisible Safety Net: Protecting the Nation's Poor Children and Families*. Princeton, NJ: Princeton University Press, 2008.

Danziger, Sheldon, and Robert Haveman, eds. *Understanding Poverty*. Cambridge, MA: Harvard University Press, and New York: Russell Sage Foundation, 2002.

Grogger, Jeffrey, and Lynn A Karoly. *Welfare Reform: Effects of a Decade of Change*. Cambridge, MA: Harvard University Press, 2005.

Hochschild, Arlie. *The Second Shift*. New York: Viking Press, 1989.

Holzer, Harry J., and Demetra Smith Nightingale, eds. *Reshaping the American Workforce in a Changing Economy*. Washington, DC: Urban Institute Press, 2007.

Jacobs, Jerry A., and Kathleen Gerson. *The Time Divide: Balancing Work and Family in Contemporary Society*. Cambridge, MA: Harvard University Press, 2004.

Leibowitz, Arleen. "Child Care: Private Cost or Public Responsibility?" In *Individual and Social Responsibility: Child Care, Education, Medical Care, and Long-Term Care in America*, edited by Victor R. Fuchs, pp. 33–57. Chicago: University of Chicago Press, 1996.

McCaffery, Edward J. *Taxing Women*. Chicago: University of Chicago Press, 1997.

Moffitt, Robert A., ed. *Means-Tested Transfer Programs in the United States*. Chicago: University of Chicago Press, 2003.

Moynihan, Daniel P., Timothy M. Smeeding, and Lee Rainwater, eds. *The Future of the Family*. New York: Russell Sage Foundation, 2004.

Presser, Harriet B. *Working in a 24/7 Economy*. New York: Russell Sage Foundation, 2003.

Smolensky, Eugene, and Jennifer Appleton Gootman, eds. *Working Families and Growing Kids: Caring for Children and Adolescents*. Washington, DC: National Academies Press, 2003.

Waldfogel, Jane. *What Children Need*. Cambridge, MA: Harvard University Press, 2006.

Key Terms

AFDC *309*
welfare tax rate *311*
welfare guarantee *311*
iron triangle of welfare *311*
break-even level of income *311*
TANF *312*
marriage promotion *315*
Earned Income Tax Credit *316*
Workforce Investment Act *318*
child support enforcement *319*

child support assurance system *320*
federal income tax system *320*
horizontal equity *321*
progressive income tax *321*
marriage penalty *323*
marriage bonus *323*
Social Security system *324*
Supplemental Security Income *326*
externalities *329*
adverse selection *330*

family-friendly policies *332*
Pregnancy Discrimination Act *332*
FMLA *332*
child care *335*
Child Care and Development Block Grant *336*
Head Start *336*
Dependent Care Tax Credit *336*
Child Tax Credit *337*

flexible spending accounts *337*
flextime *340*
nonstandard work schedules *340*
part-time employment *341*
job sharing *341*
home-based employment *341*
flexible benefit plans *342*

CHAPTER 12

Gender Differences in Other Countries

Chapter Highlights

- The Economic Status of the World's Women: Overview
- A Comparison of the United States to Other Economically Advanced Countries
- Challenges Facing Women in Developing Countries
- Countries of the Former Soviet Bloc
- Countries of the Middle East and North Africa

U p to this point we have focused almost entirely on the situation in the United States. Throughout, we have emphasized the influence of economic factors in determining the status of women. This is not, however, to suggest that nothing else matters, but rather that, everything being the same, economic considerations play an important role. Of course, in the real world, everything else is generally not the same. Societies differ in their political systems, economic and social policies, cultures, and religions. In this chapter, we turn to a consideration of women in other countries both to shed light on the causes of the substantial diversity in their status and to see what we can learn about institutions and policies elsewhere that have retarded or enhanced improvements in the position of women.

We begin with a broad description of the economic status of women as compared to men throughout the world, with special attention to women's labor market activity and the forces that influence it. Next, we turn to a more detailed consideration of the economically advanced countries that, in many ways, are most similar to the United States, focusing particularly on Sweden and Japan. These two cases are of particular interest because women have made great progress toward equality along a number of dimensions in Sweden and far less headway in Japan. This is followed by a brief examination of some of the issues of special concern in developing countries, in the countries of the former Soviet bloc, and in the various countries of the Middle East and North Africa.

THE ECONOMIC STATUS OF THE WORLD'S WOMEN: OVERVIEW

A number of measures are, by general agreement, regarded as useful indicators of women's economic status: women's labor force participation, the degree of occupational segregation by sex, the female–male earnings ratio, women's educational attainment as compared to men's, the fertility rate, the allocation of housework, and women's role in government as well as their standing before the law.

These indicators are of interest both because they are themselves direct indicators of women's economic status and because they are causally intertwined with one another. Their importance is underscored by the development goals set forth by the **United Nations Millennium Summit** in 2000, which explicitly include the achievement of gender equality in primary education, increases in women's paid labor market activity, and increases in women's share of political representation as key components of the goal to "promote gender equality and empower women."[1]

Labor Force Participation

Labor force participation is arguably the most important indicator of women's economic status. Although it is true that women perform a great deal of work in all economies, the total amount of time spent on household and paid work and how it is allocated between these activities differs substantially across countries. Paid work is deemed to be particularly important because it provides women with status in their own right, gives them greater power and influence in decision making within the family, and raises the family's standard of living overall.[2] This is true not only in economically advanced countries, but also in many developing countries, even though the burden of women's work in the household is particularly onerous there; water and fuel are often carried for long distances, clothes have to be washed by hand, food must be procured and prepared on a daily basis for lack of refrigeration, and many other goods and services that are generally purchased in economically advanced countries are produced at home.[3]

Table 12-1 provides figures on women's labor force participation rates and other indicators of their labor market activity by world region and level of income, and for selected countries in these regions. The labor force participation rate is the more familiar concept and the one we emphasized in previous chapters and will continue to emphasize here as well. However, for comprehensiveness, we also include two other measures. Each measure has its advantages and disadvantages in international comparisons. International differences in female labor force participation rates reflect differences across countries in women's participation in paid work, but are also influenced by differences across countries in the age range of the population that is included. We have addressed this issue by focusing on the rate for ages 15 to 64 in Table 12-1. However, international differences may still be affected by a number of other factors, including the age distribution of the population, the typical school-leaving and retirement ages, and the prevalence of market work versus family-based activities. Using the share of the labor force that is female largely mitigates these problems. However, the share measure may be influenced by the sex ratio in the general population and also provides less direct information about the extent that women are involved in paid work. The final measure we present is the ratio of women's to men's labor force participation rates; this measure addresses the problems of comparing the female participation rate across countries in much the same way that the female share of the labor force does and it has the advantage of not being affected by the sex ratio. It too has the weakness of giving less direct information about the extent of women's involvement in paid work than does the participation rate measure. The three measures track each other fairly closely and so again we focus our discussion on the labor force participation rate.

---

[1] United Nations, *The Millennium Development Goals Report 2007* (New York: UN, 2007).
[2] The pioneering work on this subject is Ester Boserup, *Women's Role in Economic Development* (New York: St. Martin's Press, 1970). For further discussion, see Esther Duflo, "Gender Equality in Development," MIT Working Paper (December 2005); Anne Mikkola and Carrie A. Miles, "Role of Gender Equality in Development: A Literature Review," Helsinki Center of Economic Research (April 2007); and UNIFEM, *Progress of the World's Women, 2005* (New York: United Nations Development Fund for Women, 2005).
[3] Debra Ann Donahoe, "Measuring Women's Work in Developing Countries," *Population and Development Review* 25, no. 3 (September 1999): 543–76.

TABLE 12-1 Indicators of Women's Economic Status, by World Regions and Selected Countries

	Gross National Income Per Capita 2006	Female Labor Force Participation Rate (age 15–64) 1980	Female Labor Force Participation Rate (age 15–64) 2006
I. WORLD			
Low and Middle Income (average)	$1,997	57.4	56.7
High Income (average)	36,608	53.2	64.1
II. BY WORLD REGION AND INCOME			
Sub-Saharan Africa			
Low and Middle Income (regional average)	829	64.9	62.5
Ethiopia	170	74.1	73.5
Kenya	580	77.5	71.6
Niger	270	70.9	73.1
South Africa	5,390	60.6	49.3
East Asia and Pacific			
Low and Middle Income (regional average)	1,856	72.3	71.2
China	2,000	77.3	75.4
Indonesia	1,420	45.4	53.3
Thailand	3,050	79.8	72.2
High Income			
Australia	35,860	51.9	67.8
Japan	38,630	52.5	60.6
South Korea	17,690	45.5	54.3
South Asia			
Low and Middle Income (regional average)	768	39.7	38.1
Bangladesh	450	66.2	55.0
India	820	37.6	35.9
Pakistan	800	27.9	34.3
Central and Eastern Europe and Central Asia			
Low and Middle Income (regional average)	4,815	69.3	58.0
Moldova[c]	1,080	74.7	63.0
Poland	8,210	67.7	57.3
Russia[c]	5,770	74.8	67.2
Uzbekistan[c]	610	62.3	61.0
High Income			
Czech Republic[c]	12,790	75.2	64.4
Slovenia[c]	18,660	66.9	67.0

Ratio of Female-to-Male Labor Force Participation 2006	Female Share of Labor Force (%) 2006	Adult Illiteracy Rate (%)				Total Fertility Rate[a]	
		Female		Male			
		1980	2006	1980	2006	1970	2006
67.2	39.2	48	28	29	15	5.4	2.7
79.8	43.4	b	b	b	b	2.5	1.7
72.4	42.2	72	47	51	30	6.8	5.2
81.1	44.9	89	77	72	50	6.8	5.3
79.6	44.2	57	30	30	22	8.0	5.0
76.3	42.4	97	85	87	57	8.1	7.0
60.0	37.9	25	19	22	16	5.7	2.7
81.9	43.5	43	13	20	5	5.7	2.0
86.0	44.1	48	13	22	5	5.8	1.8
61.1	37.9	40	13	21	6	5.3	2.2
85.0	46.7	17	9	8	5	5.3	1.8
84.2	44.8	b	b	b	b	2.9	1.8
71.5	40.8	b	b	b	b	2.1	1.3
70.2	40.8	11	b	3	b	4.5	1.1
45.2	29.3	75	55	48	30	5.9	2.8
62.5	36.7	83	59	59	46	6.3	2.9
42.8	28.1	74	52	45	27	5.8	2.5
40.2	27.3	86	64	59	37	7.0	3.9
77.9	44.7	8	4	3	b	2.7	1.6
84.7	46.8	8	b	b	b	2.6	1.2
84.0	45.7	b	b	b	b	2.2	1.3
89.0	48.8	b	b	b	b	2.0	1.3
80.4	44.6	33	b	17	b	5.7	2.4
83.6	44.9	b	b	b	b	1.9	1.3
88.6	46.0	b	b	b	b	2.2	1.3

(*continued*)

TABLE 12-1 Indicators of Women's Economic Status, by World Regions and Selected Countries

	Gross National Income Per Capita 2006	Female Labor Force Participation Rate (age 15–64) 1980	Female Labor Force Participation Rate (age 15–64) 2006
Middle East and North Africa			
Low and Middle Income (regional average)	$2,507	20.3	31.8
Egypt	1,360	17.4	21.6
Iran	2,930	21.2	41.9
Libya	7,290	18.5	36.3
Morocco	2,160	22.4	28.7
High Income			
Israel	20,170	41.2	59.1
Kuwait	30,630	19.3	51.4
Saudi Arabia	13,980	9.2	19.1
Latin America and Caribbean			
Low and Middle Income (regional average)	4,785	35.3	56.7
Brazil	4,710	40.5	61.5
Haiti	430	63.6	58.7
Mexico	7,830	31.1	43.0
Venezuela	6,070	32.3	63.5
High Income			
Trinidad and Tobago	12,500	43.6	51.8
North America and Western Europe			
High Income			
Canada	36,650	57.2	73.2
Germany	36,810	52.0	68.2
Spain	27,340	33.1	57.8
Sweden	43,530	79.0	74.7
United Kingdom	40,560	61.8	69.5
United States	44,710	59.8	70.1

Ratio of Female-to-Male Labor Force Participation 2006	Female Share of Labor Force (%) 2006	Adult Illiteracy Rate (%)				Total Fertility Rate[a]	
		Female		Male			
		1980	2006	1980	2006	1970	2006
40.1	28.0	72	39	44	19	6.8	2.9
28.0	21.7	75	41	47	17	6.1	2.9
55.4	34.3	61	30	38	16	6.6	2.1
43.1	27.8	70	25	29	7	7.5	2.8
34.4	26.1	85	60	58	34	7.0	2.4
90.5	47.0	13	4	5	b	3.8	2.7
59.7	25.7	39	9	26	6	7.1	2.3
23.2	14.2	67	31	33	13	7.3	3.4
68.0	40.8	23	11	18	9	5.3	2.4
73.9	42.9	27	11	23	12	5.0	2.3
69.5	41.3	73	50	66	46	5.8	3.6
51.7	35.2	22	10	14	8	6.6	2.2
73.9	41.3	18	7	14	7	5.3	2.6
62.7	38.9	16	b	7	b	3.6	1.6
88.7	46.1	b	b	b	b	2.3	1.5
85.9	45.1	b	b	b	b	2.0	1.3
71.6	40.6	8	b	3	b	2.8	1.4
94.8	46.6	b	b	b	b	1.9	1.9
85.0	45.4	b	b	b	b	2.4	1.9
86.3	45.9	b	b	b	b	2.5	2.1

Notes: GNI per capita in low and middle-income countries is below $11,116, while GNI per capita exceeds this figure in high income countries.

Figures are for closest year available.

[a] The *total fertility rate* is defined as the number of births that a cohort of 1,000 women would have if they experienced the age-specific birthrates occurring in the current year throughout their childbearing years (see Table 10-3). Here it is divided by 1,000 to measure births per woman.

[b] Figure is 2% or less.

[c] The World Bank provides 1980 data for this country even though it did not officially exist as a separate entity at that time.

Source: World Bank, *World Development Indicators* (various years), published and online database.

Table 12-1 indicates considerable variation in labor force participation rates across regions and selected countries. The income groupings are based on World Bank classifications. Also, following the World Bank, we refer to low- and middle-income countries as **developing countries**. It should be kept in mind that there are large income differences among the countries in this group. Moreover, income is only one dimension of a country's level of economic development.[4] The data show that women's labor force participation rates in developing regions range widely, from just over 70 percent in East Asia and nearly 63 percent in Sub-Saharan Africa to 32 percent in the Middle East and North Africa. Considerable variation is also found within some of these regions. For instance, in East Asia, the female labor force participation rate for China was nearly 75 percent as compared to just 53 percent for Indonesia. And, in Sub-Saharan Africa, the female labor force participation rate was 74 percent in Ethiopia but it was just 49 percent in South Africa.

As may be seen in Table 12-1 and Table 12-2 (which focuses on *trends* in labor force participation rates for selected economically advanced countries), there is also considerable variation in women's participation rates across high income countries. While most of these countries are in Western and Northern Europe and North America, there are a number of exceptions, including some oil exporting countries in the Middle East (e.g. Kuwait and Saudi Arabia), a few countries in Central and Eastern Europe (Czech Republic and Slovenia), Australia and Japan in East Asia and the Pacific, and Trinidad and Tobago in the Caribbean. In these countries, labor force participation figures for 2006 range from just 19 percent in Saudi Arabia, to 51 percent in Italy and Kuwait, to 70 percent in the United States, and to nearly 75 percent or more in the Nordic countries of Denmark, Sweden, and Norway, and in Switzerland. The region of Central and Eastern Europe and Central Asia comprises the countries of the former Soviet bloc and the countries that previously comprised Yugoslavia, which for four decades were dominated to a great extent by a Communist ideology. Countries in this region traditionally had relatively high female labor force participation rates, but as noted later in the chapter, female (and male) participation rates declined following the break up of the Soviet bloc and the transition to market economies. So, for example, female participation rates for the low and middle income countries in the region fell from 69 percent to 58 percent, on average. And, the female participation rate for Russia itself, historically well in excess of those in economically advanced countries, is currently reported to be just 67 percent.[5]

How do we explain this considerable diversity in labor force activity by gender across countries and, more generally, across regions? Part of the explanation is that countries or regions are in various stages of economic development, ranging from agricultural to industrial and postindustrial. As discussed in Chapter 2, one hypothesis that receives some support from the evidence is that the relationship between economic development and women's labor force participation rates tends to be U-shaped. Female labor force participation is high in the stage of subsistence agriculture, when women tend to be heavily involved as family workers, but then declines during the early stages of economic development as the nature of agricultural work changes and the locus of much production moves out of the household and into factories and offices. This stage is effectively the "bottom" of the U. One argument for the much

---

[4] See World Bank, "Country Classifications," Data and Statistics, World Bank web site, www.worldbank.org. Accessed January 2009.
[5] This figure stood at 75 percent in 1980 as shown in Table 12-1. One caution in looking at trends in transition countries is that survey methods may have changed. See UNIFEM, *The Story Behind the Numbers: Women and Employment in Central and Eastern Europe and the Western Commonwealth of Independent States* (New York: UNIFEM, March 2006).

TABLE 12-2 Trends in Labor Force Participation Rates for Women and Men, Age 15–64, Selected Economically Advanced Countries, 1980 and 2006[a]

	Women		Men	
	1980	2006	1980	2006
Australia	52	68	86	80
Austria	50	64	84	77
Belgium	44	58	76	72
Canada	57	73	86	82
Denmark	74	74	86	82
Finland	69	74	79	77
France	55	62	82	73
Germany	52	68	83	79
Greece	40	57	82	79
Ireland	35	63	85	80
Italy	39	51	80	74
Japan	52	61	84	85
Netherlands	48	70	79	84
Norway	62	77	84	83
Portugal	53	68	87	80
South Korea	46	54	77	77
Spain	33	58	86	81
Sweden	79	75	87	79
Switzerland	51	76	90	87
United Kingdom	62	70	88	82
United States	60	70	85	81

Source: The World Bank, *World Development Indicators*, Online Database, at www.worldbank.org.

lower female labor force participation at this stage is that societal norms often work against women performing manual, factory-type work. Then, as countries become more developed and women's education and their opportunities for white-collar employment rise, women's labor force participation once again increases.[6] Consistent with this pattern, we see in Table 12-1 relatively high rates of participation in countries with economies that are predominately agricultural, such as those in Sub-Saharan Africa, but lower rates at the next stage of development, as is true of countries in Latin America. Higher rates are found once again in many of the more economically advanced countries.

As we saw in Chapter 4, the key to women's labor force participation decision is the value of market earnings (w) as compared to the value of time spent in household production (w^*). Our earlier discussion suggests that this comparison may be influenced systematically by the stage of economic development. Differences in women's

---

[6] Claudia Goldin, "The U-Shaped Female Labor Force Function in Economic Development and Economic History," in *Investment in Women's Human Capital*, edited by T. Paul Schultz (Chicago: University of Chicago Press, 1995), pp. 61–90. For additional evidence, see Kristin Mammen and Christina Paxson, "Women's Work and Economic Development," *Journal of Economic Perspectives* 14, no. 4 (Fall 2000): 141–64; and Chinhui Juhn and Manuelita Ureta, "Employment of Married Women and Economic Development: Evidence from Latin American Countries," University of Houston Working Paper (2003).

labor market activity may also be influenced by demand factors (affecting w) and supply factors (affecting w^*) that vary from place to place, as well as over time. The demand for women workers is influenced by such factors as the industrial mix of the economy and relative size of the market and nonmarket sectors, which help to determine the nature of the jobs available in the labor market. The preferences of employers for male versus female workers, perhaps reflecting deep-seated cultural ideas regarding the appropriate role of women, may also play a role. Taken together these factors influence the wages that women can earn in the labor market and the quality of the labor market opportunities available to them. On the supply-side, the value of home time is strongly influenced by fertility rates, the availability of goods and services for purchase in the market, general attitudes toward the appropriate roles for women and men, and tastes for market goods as compared to commodities mainly produced at home.

Social forces such as religion, ideology, and culture also influence women's labor market activity.[7] For instance, women's labor force participation tends to be considerably lower in countries dominated by religious faiths that particularly emphasize women's traditional roles as wives and mothers, such as in Latin America with its predominantly Catholic population and in the Middle East and North Africa, which is largely Muslim. Marxist ideology, which strongly advocates women's entry into the workforce, surely helps to explain why women's participation came to be extremely high in many of the former Soviet bloc countries as well as in China. Similarly, concern for gender equality in the Nordic countries was one of the reasons for the introduction of policies that encouraged female labor force participation such as tax schedules favorable to two-earner couples, family leave, and subsidized day care. Apart from their direct effect, these policies in turn likely influenced attitudes about women's role in the economy.

Women's economic role and status may also be related to other aspects of society, such as the practice of **polygyny** (a husband having multiple wives). Although polygyny is rare elsewhere, it is not unusual in many Sub-Saharan African countries. In fact, in seven Sub-Saharan African countries, more than 40 percent of women have husbands with one or more other wives.[8] Women's status, as measured by a number of factors, including female-to-male illiteracy rates and an index of "gender empowerment" tends to be lower where polgyny is practiced.[9] One explanation for why polygyny has persisted is that in these societies wives perform an important economic function in traditional agricultural production, thus increasing the desirability of having multiple wives. The high demand for wives in these countries also results in a high **brideprice** being paid by the future groom and his family to the bride's father and so the bride's family tends to benefit as well.[10] It seems reasonable to expect that as economic

---

[7] See, for instance, World Bank, "Removing Social Barriers and Building Social Institutions," *World Development Report 2000/2001: Attacking Poverty* (Washington, DC, 2000).

[8] The term *polygamy* is often used synonymously with *polygyny*. However, polygamy includes the case where *either* a husband *or* a wife takes on multiple partners. The practice where a wife has multiple husbands is called *polyandry*, and is much rarer. Polygyny is legal in some Muslim countries as well but is now rarely practiced. Figures are from Michele Tertilt, "Polygyny, Fertility, and Savings," *Journal of Political Economy* 113, no. 6 (December 2005): 1341–68.

[9] Michele Tertilt, "Polygny, Women's Rights, and Development," *Journal of the European Economic Association* 4, no. 2–3 (May 2006): 523–30.

[10] For instance, see Hanan G. Jacoby, "The Economics of Polygyny in Sub-Saharan Africa: Female Productivity and the Demand for Wives in Cote d'Ivoire," *Journal of Political Economy* 103, no. 5 (October 1995): 938–71. See Siwan Anderson, "The Economics of Dowry and Brideprice," *Journal of Economic Perspectives* 21, no. 4 (Fall 2007): 151–74; and Tertilt, "Polygny, Women's Rights, and Development." Shoshana Grossbard-Shectman points to the sex ratio as another factor explaining the practice of polygyny; see *On the Economics of Marriage* (Boulder, CO: Westview Press, 1993), Chap. 11.

development proceeds, including the introduction of modern methods of production, and as women's educational attainment increases, polygyny will decline and women's status in these countries will correspondingly rise.

Occupations

When considering women's economic status, it is interesting to go beyond examining women's participation in the labor market, and also consider what jobs they have. When making comparisons among different countries, there are two serious difficulties. First, many do not provide detailed data on the occupational distribution of men and women, and those that do tend to use various classification schemes. Second, the degree of segregation is affected by the distribution of all workers across occupations. Thus, if, at the extreme, the majority of people in the labor force in one country were employed in a single occupation like agriculture, while in another they are distributed among a considerably larger number of occupations, the indexes of sex segregation would surely differ. The most recent comprehensive study, completed in the mid-1990s, largely overcame the first of these limitations and examined occupational sex segregation for more than 40 countries around the world using data on 75 consistent occupations. Table 12-3 shows the index of occupational segregation for the largest of these countries. As we saw in Chapter 5, the *index* is defined as the percentage of women (or men) who would have to change jobs in order for the occupational distribution of men and women to be the same. Table 12-3 indicates that occupational segregation by sex remains "very extensive in each and every country," but that the extent of segregation varies, particularly across regions.[11] For instance, the index tends to be substantially higher in countries in the Middle East and North Africa, and in "other developing countries," than in the other regions. There is, however, evidence from this study that occupational segregation has declined in recent decades, albeit not in all countries or all regions.

It appears that across all cultures and at all times, occupations have been sex segregated to a greater or lesser extent. One study, which looked at more than 200 cultures over time, found that metal working and hunting were, with few exceptions, exclusively male activities, while activities such as cooking, laundering, and spinning were predominately female. However, with the exception of certain occupations such as these, the more general pattern is that while occupations tend to be sex segregated, they vary as to whether they are dominated by men or women.[12] For instance, while in the United States women are overrepresented in the clerical sector, this is not the case in a number of countries, including Pakistan, Haiti, and Nigeria.[13] This variation suggests that occupational differences cannot be explained simply by inherent differences between women and men or by differences in their preferences or human capital investment decisions alone. Factors such as social norms, traditions, and religious beliefs also appear to play an important role. However, despite this variation, one common feature of women's employment is that it tends to be in lower-paying jobs.

---

[11] The study cited is Richard Anker, *Gender and Jobs: Sex Segregation of Occupations in the World* (Geneva: International Labour Office, 1998). The quote is from p. 407. See especially Chap. 9 (main evidence) and Chap. 16 (summary and conclusion). For other evidence, see Mariko Lin Chang, "Growing Pains: Cross-national Variation in Sex Segregation in Sixteen Developing Countries," *American Sociological Review* 69, no. 1 (February 2004): 114–37.

[12] This conclusion is from Joyce P. Jacobsen, "Sex Segregation at Work: Trends and Predictions," *Social Science Journal* 31, no. 2 (1994): 153–69, based on data from George P. Murdock and Caterina Provost, "Factors in the Division of Labor by Sex: A Cross-Cultural Analysis," in *Ethnology* 12, no. 2 (April 1973): 203–25. See also William Rau and Robert Wazienski, "Industrialization, Female Labor Force Participation, and the Modern Division of Labor by Sex," *Industrial Relations* 38, no. 4 (October 1999): 504–21; and Anker, *Gender and Jobs*, Chaps. 8 and 16.

[13] Anker, *Gender and Jobs*.

TABLE 12-3   Occupational Segregation by Sex, Selected Countries, 1980s/1990s[a]

Region/Country/Area	Occupational Segregation Index	Region/Country/Area	Occupational Segregation Index
North America and Western Europe		**Other Developing Countries**	
Canada	54.1	Angola	65.6
Finland	61.6	Costa Rica	59.8
France	55.6	Ghana	71.0
Germany (West)	52.3	Haiti	66.9
Italy	44.9	Senegal	57.3
Netherlands	56.7		
Norway	57.3		
Spain	56.9		
Sweden	63.0	**Central and Eastern Europe and Central Asia**	
Switzerland	58.1	Bulgaria	54.1
United Kingdom	56.7	Hungary	55.8
United States	46.3	Poland	59.2
Asia/Pacific			
Australia	58.1		
China	36.3	**Middle East and North Africa**	
Hong Kong	49.3	Bahrain	62.7
India	44.6	Egypt	58.7
Japan	50.2	Iran	68.1
Korea	43.2	Jordan	77.6
Malaysia	48.9	Kuwait	73.3
New Zealand	58.2	Tunisia	69.5

[a] Index is computed using 75 similar occupations. Years of data vary, but the majority are from 1985 to 1991.

Source: Richard Anker, *Gender and Jobs: Sex Segregation of Occupations in the World,* 1998, Table 9.1, column 3. Copyright © International Labour Organization 1998. Reprinted by Permission of the International Labour Organization.

Earnings

The available evidence indicates that women everywhere earn less than men, although again large variations occur in the extent to which this is the case. For instance, in 2006, the female–male earnings ratio in selected economically advanced countries ranged from a low of .67 in Japan to a high of .89 in Sweden.[14] We cannot be as specific about developing countries because of problems with data availability and reliability, but considerable variability appears to be the case among these countries as well. A number of factors explain the observed variation, including differences among countries in the extent of occupational segregation, gender differences in educational attainment and labor force attachment, labor market discrimination, and government policies. In addition, general rewards for skills, such as education or labor market experience, or for employment in male-dominated occupations and industries also play a role.

---

[14] Data are presented later in Table 12-4.

Educational Attainment

Women's educational attainment is also important as an indicator of their economic status, in part because it influences their occupations and earnings, which are themselves indicators of women's status. Also, it allows women to make better-informed decisions about affairs in their own household, their community, and their nation. Gender differences in educational attainment are fairly small among economically advanced countries, but vary considerably across all countries, as a result of, and related to, differences in levels of affluence, as well as differences in fertility, social customs, and government policies.

Illiteracy rates provide one useful measure of educational attainment, especially in the developing world. As shown in Table 12-1 and Figure 12-1, female illiteracy rates in 2006 stood at 55 percent in South Asia, 47 percent in Sub-Saharan Africa, and nearly 40 percent in the developing countries of the Middle East and North Africa. The rates for men were also high, but considerably lower than those of women in each region. For example, in South Asia the male illiteracy rate was 30 percent, and in Sub-Saharan Africa and in the developing countries of the Middle East and North Africa, the male rates were 30 and 19 percent, respectively.[15] An important factor that contributes to low levels of educational attainment for both men and women in the poorest countries is that large numbers of children do not even attend school because many of them, especially girls, are helping out at home, while others are employed (see the discussion of child labor later).

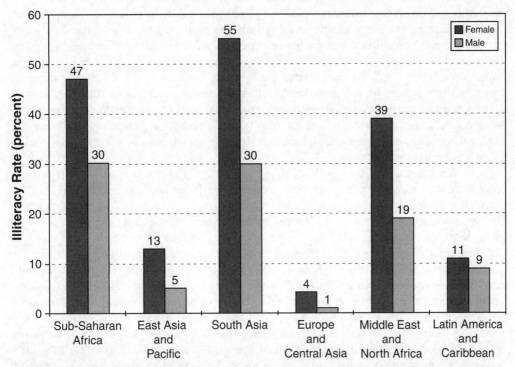

FIGURE 12-1   Illiteracy Rates, Low & Middle Income Economies, World Regions, 2006

---

[15] For data on average years of schooling for women relative to men in 1960 and 2000, see Robert J. Barro and Jong-Wha Lee, "International Data on Educational Attainment: Updates and Implications," *Oxford Economic Papers* 53, no. 3 (July 2001): 541–63.

Although illiteracy rates for both women and men remain high in some regions, Table 12-1 shows that they declined markedly between 1980 and 2006 across all regions and selected countries. In the developing countries of the Middle East and North Africa, female illiteracy rates fell from over 70 percent to just under 40 percent, and from over 70 percent in Sub-Saharan Africa and South Asia to 47 percent in Sub-Saharan Africa and 55 percent in South Asia. Men's rates also declined, so there has been an absolute reduction in illiteracy for both groups. Nevertheless, the gender disparity remains. A key factor behind falling illiteracy rates is the dramatic rise in primary education, across all regions. This trend may have been hastened by the 2000 United Nations Millennium Summit, which placed pressure on nations around the world to work toward the goal of universal primary education for girls and boys by the target date of 2015.

Fertility

There is also a strong relationship between fertility, educational attainment, and labor market activity. Fertility rates are an important indicator of women's economic status because with fewer children, women have greater opportunities to acquire education and engage in production for pay. Conversely, when birthrates are high, women have more difficulty remaining in school and more incentive to remain full-time home-makers. As noted in earlier chapters, however, causation runs in the other direction as well. As women invest more in education and increase their participation in market work, particularly when it is away from the household, the opportunity cost of children rises, thereby providing an incentive to have fewer children. In addition, fertility is at times related to explicit government policies, as well as to religion and ideology. For instance, in recent history, some governments have implemented policies explicitly designed to increase fertility or policies that might be expected to have such an effect. Such policies include relatively generous child allowances, paid parental leaves, and subsidized child care. Some have also introduced laws prohibiting various types of family planning, often justifying them on the grounds of religious strictures. Other countries, however, have sought to control population growth; many have done so by making birth control information available, while China went so far as to impose severe economic penalties for having more than one child. China's policy has, however, been somewhat relaxed since it was first implemented.

Given the various factors that influence fertility, it is not surprising that fertility rates differ dramatically across regions. As shown in Table 12-1 and Figure 12-2, in 2006 fertility rates were as high as 5.2 births per woman in Sub-Saharan Africa, followed by the developing countries of the Middle East and North Africa and the region of South Asia, with rates of just under 3 births per woman. In sharp contrast, the U.S. rate was 2.1, just at the replacement level, and the average rate among all high-income economies was even lower at 1.7. Table 12-1 and Figure 12-2 further show that current fertility rates in all regions are substantially lower than in past decades. Indeed, in light of these trends, Ronald Lee observed: "The question about their fertility transition is no longer 'whether,' but rather 'how far' and 'how fast.'"[16] Sub-Saharan Africa remains the one region where fertility declines are thus far quite modest. In many economically advanced countries, including the Western European nations and Japan, fertility rates have declined to well below replacement level. This trend receives further attention later in this chapter.

---

[16] Ronald Lee, "The Demographic Transition: Three Centuries of Fundamental Change," *Journal of Economics Perspectives* 17, no. 4 (Fall 2003): 167–90. Quote is from p. 175.

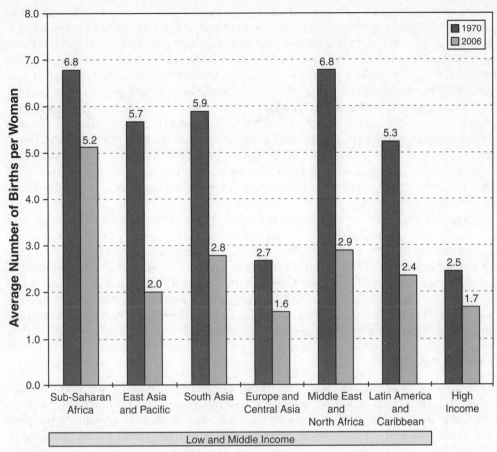

FIGURE 12-2   Total Fertility Rates, World Regions, 1970 and 2006

Housework

As discussed at some length in earlier chapters, the roles of women and men in the labor market are interrelated with their roles in the household. We found that in the United States, although women's participation in the labor market increased rapidly for some time, participation of men in housework began to increase only more recently and still lags substantially behind women's. The continued unequal division of household responsibilities between men and women potentially influences both the amount of leisure time available to them and their achievements on the job. The division of housework is also unequal in other economically advanced countries, as discussed in greater detail later. Further, it is important to recall that women in developing countries, especially in poor rural areas, often do an especially large amount of unpaid work needed for their families' subsistence, including carrying water and firewood, as well as growing agricultural products, in addition to the usual housework.

Women's Role in Government and Their Standing Before the Law

Finally, women's roles in government and their standing before the law have considerable impact on their status. Greater representation of women among public officials is expected to increase the extent to which women's issues receive attention from the government, and greater equality before the law affects, among other things, women's right to inherit and own property, as well as their rights within the family and in case of divorce. Although women today have the right to vote in virtually all countries with representative institutions, they continue to be substantially underrepresented in public positions, especially at high levels. For instance, in 2008, there were eight female presidents and eight female prime ministers out of just under 200 countries in the world.[17] Also as of 2007, women occupied over 40 percent of all parliamentary seats in the Nordic countries, and 17 percent in Asia and Sub-Saharan Africa, but just 9 percent in North Africa and the Middle East.[18] Women remain underrepresented in high-level government positions in the United States as well. In 2008, only 17 percent of representatives and 16 percent of senators were women. They also continue to be underrepresented in U.S. cabinet and cabinet-level appointments, though recent administrations have included substantially more women.[19]

Similarly, women's progress toward equality before the law has been slow and uneven. In some countries, even today only men can inherit or only husbands have the right to dispose of their wives' earnings.[20] On the other hand, as of 2008, 185 countries (over 90 percent of members of the United Nations) had ratified an "international bill of rights for women" known as the Convention for the Elimination of All Forms of Discrimination Against Women (**CEDAW**), though the United States remains one notable exception.[21] At the same time, "even when legal discrimination is removed, it can take generations for practice to catch up with the revised law."[22]

Cultural Factors

The evidence presented here and later in this chapter shows that there is substantial variation in the status of women among different regions and even across countries within the same region, as measured by the indicators discussed, whether it be labor force participation, the female–male earnings ratio, educational attainment, distribution of housework, or women's role in government. This suggests that while economic factors influence the relative status of women and men, the situation is very complex, and that noneconomic factors play an important role as well. The picture is made even more complicated by the fact that women may be doing well in a country in terms of some criteria but not in terms of others.

---

[17] Worldwide Guide to Women in Leadership at www.guide2womenleaders.com. Accessed on September 30, 2008.

[18] Inter-Parliamentary Union, "Women in National Parliaments, Situation as of 30 April 2008," available at http://www.ipu.org, accessed on May 22, 2008. For discussions regarding why women's political participation may matter, see Marianne A. Ferber and Michael Brun, "Does Your Legislator's Sex Matter?" Working Paper, University of Illinois at Urbana-Champaign (2008); and Raghabendra Chattopadhyay, "Women as Policy Makers: Evidence from a Randomized Policy Experiment in India," *Econometrica* 72, no. 5 (September 2005): 1409–43.

[19] For more details, go to the Center for American Women and Politics, Eagleton Institute of Politics, Rutgers University, www.cawp.rutgers.edu. Accessed on January 17, 2009.

[20] Ester Boserup, "Obstacles to Advancement of Women During Development," in *Investments in Women's Human Capital,* edited by T. Paul Schultz (Chicago: University of Chicago Press, 1995), pp. 51–60; and Diane Lee-Smith and Catalina Hinchey Trujillo, "Unequal Rights: Women and Property," in *Women and Gender Equity in Development Theory and Practice,* edited by Jan S. Jacquette and Gale Summerfield (Durham, NC and London: Duke University Press, 2006), pp. 159–72.

[21] United Nations at www.un.org.

[22] United Nations, *Human Development Report 1995,* pp. 42–43. In addition, as Diane Elson points out, legal equality often means little for poor rural women as long as they are concentrated in the informal sector, or in female ghettoes of the formal sector, and intrahousehold distribution is not necessarily affected by these changes. See her "Introduction" in *Male Bias in the Development Process* (Manchester: Manchester University Press, 1991), pp. 1–28.

An example of the importance of noneconomic or cultural factors that affect women's status in a number of countries, including China, India, South Korea, and Taiwan, is the long-standing cultural preference for sons, which has resulted in bias against daughters and women in general. This preference is reflected in the very high **sex ratio**—the ratio of men to women—in these countries as well as by the sizeable estimates of what Nobel laureate Amartya Sen has referred to as **missing women**.[23]

Some evidence indicates that in regions where women work for pay, there is a higher ratio of women to men. For example, in Sub-Saharan Africa the ratio of women's economic activity to men's is high and the ratio of men to women in the population is low while in southern Asia (including India), just the opposite is observed.[24] This pattern of findings suggests that girls are more highly valued and better treated—as reflected by higher survival rates—when girls and women make a substantial economic contribution outside the home. It is likely that girls are more highly valued when they are expected to become economically active, in part because they are viewed as potential providers of financial assistance to parents in old age. In addition, they may be seen as a source of a "bride-price" (where the bride's family receives payment upon marriage) rather than as a financial drain on the family, as in the case where the bride's family must pay a **dowry**.[25]

China is a notable exception to the pattern described earlier, with its high female activity ratio, as shown in Table 12-1, but still a high sex ratio. This situation illustrates that how girls fare relative to boys also likely depends on a number of historical and cultural factors. For instance, in China, it has long been the obligation of sons, not daughters, to support their parents in their old age, which makes sons more valuable.

An interesting line of research also suggests that outcomes for girls improve when mothers have more resources because mothers tend to devote more resources to girls, while fathers tend to favor sons. Further, mounting evidence indicates that mothers tend to spend a larger share of their resources on children, whether boys or girls, than do fathers.[26] Taken together, these findings suggest that advances in women's economic status, as measured by higher rates of labor force participation, better jobs, and greater educational attainment, should benefit children generally, as well as

---

[23] Amartya Sen, "More than 100 Million Women Are Missing," *The New York Review of Books* 37, no. 20 (December 1990): 61–66. For recent evidence, see Stephan Klasen and Claudia Wink, "Missing Women: Revisiting the Debate," *Feminist Economics* 9, no. 2–3 (July–November 2003): 263–99. Even in the United States, some slight preference for sons is evident, as demonstrated by the sex-ratios for third-born children in U.S. families of Chinese, Korean, and Indian descents. See Douglas Almond and Lena Edlund, "Son-Biased Sex Ratios in the 2000 United States Census," *PNAS* 105, no. 15 (April 15, 2008): 5681–82. For further evidence on sex preference in the United States, see Shelly Lundberg, "Sons, Daughters, and Parental Behavior," *Oxford Review of Economic Policy* 21, no. 3 (2005): 340–56.

[24] Jean Dreze and Amartya Sen, *Hunger and Public Action* (Oxford: Clarendon Press, 1989), Chap. 4. See also Mammen and Paxson, "Women's Work and Economic Development"; and Marianne A. Ferber and Helen M. Berg, "Labor Force Participation of Women and the Sex Ratio: A Cross-Country Analysis," *Review of Social Economy* 48, no. 1 (Spring 1991): 2–19; and Klasen and Wink, "Missing Women."

[25] Anderson, "The Economics of Dowry and Brideprice."

[26] For example, see Duncan Thomas, "Intra-Household Resource Allocation: An Inferential Approach," *Journal of Human Resources* 25, no. 4 (Fall 1990): 635–64; Duncan Thomas, "Like Father, Like Son: Like Mother, Like Daughter: Parental Resources and Child Height," *Journal of Human Resources* 29, no. 4 (Fall 1994): 950–88; Shelly J. Lundberg, Robert A. Pollak, and Terence J. Wales, "Do Husbands and Wives Pool Their Resources? Evidence from the U.K. Child Benefit," *Journal of Human Resources* 32, no. 3 (Summer 1997): 463–80; and Bina Agarwal, " 'Bargaining' and Gender Relations: Within and Beyond the Household," *Feminist Economics* 3, no. 1 (March 1997): 1–51. Grandmothers behave similarly to mothers; see Esther Duflo, "Grandmothers and Granddaughters: Old age Pensions and Intra-Household Allocations in South Africa," *World Bank Economic Review* 17, no. 1 (2003): 1–25.

reduce the considerable imbalance in the allocation of resources to girls and boys in countries that have traditionally favored boys.

In spite of wide cultural differences, women from around the world have joined together in recent decades in international efforts to improve women's status. In 1995, women from nearly 190 countries attended the United Nations Fourth World Conference on Women in Beijing and put together a "Plan for Action" that focused on education as a key to women's progress. In addition, they addressed a broad range of other issues, from violence against women to economic development. At follow-up United Nations conferences called "Beijing Plus Five" in 2000 and "Beijing Plus Ten" in 2005, women representatives again came together to take stock of the progress made since 1995, as well as to press for additional rights and to reaffirm each government's commitment to change. Further, in 2000, at the U.N. Millennium Summit, world leaders set forth eight development goals, including the goal of universal primary education, with detailed targets to be accomplished by specified dates. Evidence suggests that these international efforts are having some success in placing pressure on countries to work toward making at least some of the suggested changes, but progress across regions has been uneven.[27]

A COMPARISON OF THE UNITED STATES TO OTHER ECONOMICALLY ADVANCED COUNTRIES

The same trends that have occurred in the United States since the 1970s—women's rising labor force participation, improvements in the female–male wage ratio, a modest reallocation of housework between men and women, declining marriage rates, rising rates of divorce, increased cohabitation, and more births to unmarried mothers—have also occurred in other economically advanced countries, although to varying degrees. Explanations for these trends are similar to those offered for the United States in earlier chapters. However, other factors, including differences in government **family policies** (e.g., the availability and amount of family leave and whether it is with pay, and the availability of publicly funded day care), the design of government tax policy, and variations in wage structures, are particularly important in explaining cross-country differences in outcomes.[28]

This section provides some comparisons of policies relevant to the status of women and the well-being of their families among economically advanced countries. It then goes on to examine labor market outcomes and changes in the division of housework, as well as some demographic trends, in greater detail. Special attention is paid to Sweden and Japan because Sweden, like other Nordic countries, has made notable progress toward greater equality between men and women in the home as well as in the labor market, while Japan has experienced much slower change.

Beginning in the 1960s, Sweden instituted a comprehensive set of policies to achieve the goal of equal treatment of women and men.[29] Efforts were made to discourage

---

[27] World Bank, *Millennium Development Report*. See also Irene Tinker, "Empowerment Just Happened: The Unexpected Expansion of Women's Organizations," in *Women and Gender Equity in Development Theory and Practice*, edited by Jane S. Jacquette and Gale Summerfield (Durham, NC and London: Duke University Press, 2006), pp. 268–302.

[28] For overviews, see OECD, "Female Labour Force Participation: Past Trends and Main Determinants in OECD Countries," *Economic Policy Reforms: Going for Growth* (Paris: OECD, 2005), Chapter 6; Francine D. Blau and Lawrence M. Kahn, "Women's Work and Wages," in *The New Palgrave Dictionary of Economics*, 2nd edition, edited by Steven N. Durlauf and Lawrence E. Blume (Palgrave Macmillan, 2008), pp. 762–72; and European Commission, *Report on Equality Between Women and Men—2008* (Luxembourg: EU, 2008).

[29] See, for instance, Asa Lundqvist and Christine Roman, "Construction of Swedish Family Policy, 1930–2000," *Journal of Family History* 33, no. 2 (2008): 216–36; and Urban Lundberg and Klas Amark, "Social Rights and Social Security: The Swedish Welfare State, 1900–2000," *Scandinavian Journal of History* 26, no. 3 (September 2001): 157–76.

gender-based stereotypes at all levels of the educational system. All gender differences in public aid were removed. Legislation was introduced to make marriage an equal partnership; a husband is no longer required to support his wife. Full participation of women and men in the labor market became the established goal. To encourage married women to enter the labor force, the joint income tax for spouses was eliminated (except for nonwage income) and replaced by a system of individual taxation. As discussed in Chapter 11, a joint income tax can have a considerable negative impact on work incentives, especially for wives, who are often perceived to be secondary workers. This is less true of individual taxation because the applicable marginal tax rate a married woman faces upon entering the labor market is lower than the rate she would have to pay as the second earner.[30]

As discussed in Chapter 7, **antidiscrimination legislation** is also expected to affect labor market outcomes. The United States was a leader in this regard, adopting major antidiscrimination legislation in the early 1960s. Beginning in the 1970s, other economically-advanced countries began to enact similar measures aimed at ensuring women's rights to equal opportunity in employment. Both Sweden and Japan were relative late-comers. Sweden did not pass antidiscrimination laws until 1980 and 1992. Japan did not enact any legislation until 1985 and that legislation, which was extremely weak, was not strengthened until 1997 and 2006.[31] On the other hand, the United States has lagged in mandating **family leave**. Only in 1993 did the United States mandate that firms must provide workers with unpaid family leave of 12 weeks. All other economically advanced countries have for quite some time provided or mandated paid leave for mothers or for both parents. Indeed, Sweden began offering paid maternity leave to all mothers in the mid 1950s and was the first to extend such leave to fathers in 1974.[32] Its policy is among the most generous: It provides 12 months of paid leave that may be taken by either parent at 80 percent replacement pay, and an additional 3 months with a flat-rate payment. Workers are guaranteed their jobs when they return and must be offered the option of working part time (6 hours per day) until the youngest child is age 8. Even Japan's policy is somewhat more generous than that of the United States. Mothers are entitled to 14 weeks leave at 60 percent replacement pay and either parent may take unpaid leave for up to a year.[33]

Many economically advanced countries provide family-friendly policies that extend well beyond parental leave, and the prevalence of such policies has increased considerably in recent years. Such policies include extended part-time work or the option of switching to a flexible schedule after the birth of a child, to care for aged relatives, or to accommodate training and education. For instance, the United Kingdom and New Zealand recently adopted policies whereby parents of pre-school age children have the "right to ask" their employer for flexible or reduced hours. Parents do not have to offer a specific justification such as a child's illness, and employers have the right to say no if the change is not feasible on business grounds. This type of policy provides an

---

[30] See Diane Sainsbury, "Taxation, Family Responsibilities, and Employment," in *Gender and Welfare State Regimes*, edited by Diane Sainsbury (Oxford: Oxford University Press, 1999), pp. 185–210.

[31] Sweden's 1992 Equal Opportunity Act goes further than legislation than in many other countries, however, requiring that employers try to obtain a well-balanced sex distribution in various jobs and must make it easier for workers to combine work and family. For further discussion of policies in Japan and the Nordic countries, see Helina Melkas and Richard Anker, *Towards Gender Equity in Japanese and Nordic Labour Markets: A Tale of Two Paths* (Geneva: ILO, 2003); and Nabanita Datta Gupta, Nina Smith, and Mette Verner, "The Impact of Nordic Countries' Family Friendly Policies on Employment, Wages, and Children," *Review of Economics of the Household* 6, no. 1 (March 2008): 65–89.

[32] The evolution of this policy is described in Britta Hoem and Jan M. Hoem, "Sweden's Family Policies and Roller-Coaster Fertility," *Journal of Population Problems* 52, no. 3–4 (November 1996): 1–22.

[33] Janet C. Gornick and Marcia K. Meyers, *Families That Work* (New York: Russell Sage Foundation, 2003), Chap. 5; and OECD, *Babies and Bosses: Reconciling Work and Family Life, A Synthesis of Findings for OECD Countries* (Paris: OECD, 2007).

intermediate solution between the current situation in the United States, where employees must remain cautious about even asking, and a mandate requiring employers to make accommodations.[34]

As we noted in Chapter 11, policies designed to help workers better balance work and family can be quite important to women in maintaining their attachment to the labor force and to their current firm. Indeed, relatively short leaves have been found to increase women's labor force attachment and wages. However, the situation may be more ambiguous for longer leaves. Such leaves (more than 3 months in one study) were found to have a negative effect on women's wages.[35] Moreover, because leaves tend to be disproportionately taken by mothers, even when available to both parents, they may reinforce traditional gender roles in the family and thus help to perpetuate differences in labor market outcomes between men and women. Related policies, such as the option of part-time work or the opportunity to adopt a more flexible work schedule, pose a similar set of concerns. As discussed in Chapter 9, part-time work frequently provides less opportunity for upward mobility than full-time employment. Consistent with this, it has been suggested that the extensive family policies adopted in Sweden and other Nordic countries may have had the unintended consequence of segmenting women into "female" jobs, thereby creating a "glass ceiling" for women workers.[36]

While only a few countries provide subsidized child care, some of those that do have committed a large amount of resources for this purpose. For instance, in Sweden, heavily subsidized day care is available for nearly half of children ages 1 to 2, and more than four-fifths of children ages 3 to 6. France subsidizes child care even more generously. There, all children ages 3 to 5 are eligible for free preschool, and virtually all of them do attend even if their mother is not employed. In addition, 14 percent of children ages 0 to 2 are in day care. By way of contrast, in Germany, out-of-home care for children ages 0 to 2 is rare, though 90 percent of children ages 3 to 5 are in preschool.[37]

Wage-setting institutions also differ considerably across countries. These differences affect wage structures and, hence, wage inequality and the gender earnings ratio. As discussed in Chapter 8 in our consideration of trends in the gender wage gap, *wage structure* refers to the relative wages paid for various labor market qualifications, such as the proficiency of an experienced worker compared to a new hire, or a college graduate compared to someone who finished only high school. International differences in wage-setting institutions and wage inequality are considerable, especially between the United States and the other economically advanced nations. This makes international differences in wage-setting institutions a particularly important factor in understanding international differences in the gender wage gap. In many of the economically advanced countries, wages are determined in a highly centralized way, with a strong role for unions and government in wage-setting. Wages in the union sector are determined by collective bargaining, and, where unions are strong, collective bargaining agreements are often extended to nonunion workers or may cause nonunion firms to voluntarily imitate

---

[34] For details on these policies, see OECD, *Babies and Bosses*. For comparisons with the United States and recommendations, see Ariane Hegeisch and Janet C. Gornick, *Statutory Routes to Workplace Flexibility in Cross-National Perspective* (Washington, DC: Institute for Women's Policy Research, 2008).

[35] Christopher J. Ruhm, "The Economic Consequences of Parental Leave Mandates: Lessons from Europe," *Quarterly Journal of Economics* 113, no. 1 (1998): 285–317. Another study that looked at 20 advanced economies found that while gender earnings disparities appeared to be less pronounced in countries with developed family policies, this was entirely due to the more compressed wage structures of these "welfare states" rather than to the prevailing family policies; see, Hadas Mandel and Moshe Semyonov, "Family Policies, Wage Structures, and Gender Gaps: Sources of Earnings Inequality in 20 Countries," *American Sociological Review* 70, no. 6 (December 2005): 949–67. The impact of wage structures is considered in greater detail later.

[36] Gupta et al., "The Impact of Nordic Countries' Family Friendly Policies."

[37] OECD, *Starting Strong II: Early Childhood Education and Care* (2006), Tables 4.1 and 4.2.

union pay structures.[38] Unions tend to raise the wages of less-skilled (low-wage) workers and lead to a more compressed wage structure. As a relatively low-wage group in all countries, women disproportionately benefit from wage policies that "bring up the bottom" of the wage distribution. Alternatively, the wage-setting process can be quite decentralized, as in the United States, where only a small proportion of the labor force belongs to labor unions, and wages are largely determined by employers. In 2003, only 14 percent of workers in the United States were covered by collective bargaining agreements as compared with rates of 77 to 95 percent in the Scandinavian countries, which were particularly heavily unionized. Even Britain, one of the least unionized apart from the United States, had a unionization rate of 35 percent. Thus, in the United States, with its more dispersed wage distribution, less-skilled (low-wage) workers tend to receive lower relative pay than in most other economically advanced countries.[39] Moreover, since women are a relatively low-wage group in the United States and do not have their wages boosted by union wage scales, this tends to widen the gender wage gap in the United States relative to other economically advanced countries.

Most economically advanced countries provide child benefits or a child allowance to families based on the number of children, without regard to income. This is not the case in the United States. Nonetheless, the United States does provide child benefits through the tax system via the personal exemption, and tax credits including the Child Tax Credit, Dependent Care Tax Credit, and the Earned Income Tax Credit. The precise amount received by the family depends on the number of children in the family, whether or not the parent or parents are employed, and the family's federal income tax bracket. While the approach in the United States is without doubt more complex, one recent study finds that, all told, the value of the subsidy received by children in the United States is on par with the subsidy provided in Sweden.[40] Finally, unlike the United States, most of the other economically advanced countries offer either national health insurance or a national health care system. Such programs reduce the cost of rearing children and potentially improve the health and, thus, the productivity of present as well as future workers.

Labor Force Participation

Table 12-2 shows that between 1980 and 2006 women's labor force participation increased appreciably, while men's participation decreased somewhat, in all of the economically advanced countries included in the table. Nevertheless, there are substantial cross-country differences, especially in women's participation rates. In 2006 participation rates were highest in Sweden and the other Nordic countries and in Switzerland, with rates of nearly 75 percent or more, followed closely by the United States at 70 percent.[41] Labor force participation rates were somewhat lower in countries such as Japan, Germany, and Austria, and considerably lower in South Korea and in Southern Europe,

---

[38] See, for instance, Francine D. Blau and Lawrence M. Kahn, "International Differences in Male Wage Inequality: Institutions Versus Market Forces," *Journal of Political Economy* 104, no. 4 (August 1996): 791–837.

[39] Figures are from Jelle Visser, "Union Membership Statistics in 24 Countries," *Monthly Labor Review* 129, no. 1 (January 2006): 3–49. For discussion, see Francine D. Blau and Lawrence M. Kahn, *At Home and Abroad: U.S. Labor Market Performance in International Perspective* (New York: Russell Sage Foundation, 2002); and Blau and Kahn, "International Differences in Male Wage Inequality."

[40] Nancy Folbre, *Valuing Children: Rethinking the Economics of the Family* (Cambridge, MA: Harvard University Press, 2007), p. 159.

[41] Interestingly, Sweden was hardly a leader in this respect in earlier days; married women there were not even granted the legal right to enter into work contracts or to control their own earnings until 1920, as discussed in Christina Jonung and Inga Persson, "Combining Market Work and Family," in *Population, Economy and Welfare in Sweden*, edited by Tommy Bengtsson (New York: Springer-Verlag, 1994), pp. 37–64. For further discussion of cross-country differences, see Dora L. Costa, "From Mill Town to Board Room: The Rise of Women's Paid Labor," *Journal of Economic Perspectives* 14, no. 4 (Fall 2000): 101–22.

including Greece, Spain, and especially Italy, where the rate was only 51 percent. Part of the reason for the particularly low rates in Southern Europe may be their emphasis on the traditional family, related to their religious orientation, which would be expected to reduce women's labor force participation.

The high labor force participation rate in Sweden is not surprising in view of all their policies intended to encourage women to enter and remain in the labor force.[42] At the same time, it should be noted that women at home caring for young children, who are covered by Sweden's generous parental leave policies, are considered to be in the labor force. Their inclusion is not unique to Sweden; it is a general reporting practice to include workers on paid leave in labor force statistics. One recent study shows that when the participation rate for Sweden is recalculated excluding these workers, there is a "marked dipping" in women's participation rates during the peak childbearing years.[43] Nonetheless, the official labor force participation rate does provide a useful measure of women's attachment to the labor force because the leave policies give mothers the right to return to their former job and to retain their seniority.

As noted earlier, Japan's female participation rate is about average for the countries included in Table 12-2. Interestingly, one long-standing difference in the nature of employment in Japan relative to the United States and Sweden is quickly disappearing. As recently as 1990, 17 percent of employed women in Japan were unpaid workers in a family enterprise, but that figure steadily decreased to 8 percent by 2007. In contrast, in both 1990 and 2007, fewer than 1 percent of employed women in the United States and Sweden were unpaid family workers.[44] The drawback to this type of employment is that these women earn no independent income that they personally control.

Nevertheless, lifetime participation patterns of women in Japan continue to differ considerably from those of high-participation countries such as Sweden and the United States. As evident in Figure 12-3, the pattern is M-shaped in Japan; labor force participation decreases during the childbearing years but increases to a second peak later. As we saw in Chapter 4, this pattern also prevailed in the United States between World War II and the early 1970s. Today, however, there is an inverted U pattern in the United States and especially in Nordic countries including Sweden; labor force participation rises during the early years as women complete their education, reaches a plateau, and eventually declines as retirement age approaches. This is similar to the male pattern and denotes a higher level of labor force attachment. Some researchers suggest that Japan is merely lagging behind these other countries and will eventually "catch up." It may be, however, that for historical and cultural reasons, the same factors that were operative in the United States and Sweden are not operative in Japan, so that extrapolation based on their experience may be inappropriate.[45] In addition, as we will see, the nature of women's employment in Japan differs in some important respects. Notably, far fewer women have opportunities for career advancement within the firms where they are employed.

---

[42] Finland and Denmark follow similar policies, with correspondingly high rates of labor force participation. For further discussion, see OECD, "Female Labour Force Participation."

[43] The general treatment of paid family leave in labor force statistics, as well as the case of Sweden are discussed in Grant Johnston, "Women's Participation in the Labour Force," New Zealand Treasury Working Paper 05/06 (June 2005).

[44] Data are computed from the International Labour Organization, *Yearbook of Labour Statistics* (Geneva: ILO, 2006). For a discussion of women's labor force participation in Japan, see Yoshi-Fumi Nakata and Ryoji Takehiro, "Employment and Wages of Female Japanese Workers: Past, Present, and Future," *Industrial Relations* 41, no. 4 (October 2002): 521–47; and Sawako Shirahase, "Women's Economic Status and Fertility: Japan in Cross-National Perspective," in *The Political Economy of Low Fertility: Japan in Comparative Perspective*, edited by Frances McCall Rosenbluth (Stanford: Stanford University Press, 2007), Chapter 2.

[45] Mary Brinton, *Women and the Economic Miracle: Gender and Work in Postwar Japan* (Berkeley: University of California Press, 1993), p. 43.

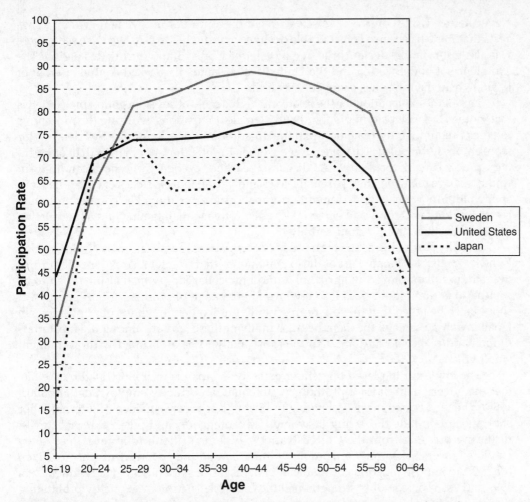

FIGURE 12-3 Labor Force Participation Rates of Women by Age, Selected Countries, 2005

Occupations

As previously noted, Table 12-3 shows that considerable sex segregation by occupation continues in the more economically advanced countries. Although noticeable progress is being made by young college-educated workers, sex segregation appears to be more firmly entrenched for less-educated workers. These findings, which suggest divergent trends in sex segregation by level of education in a number of economically advanced countries, mirror recent trends for the United States described earlier in Chapter 5.[46]

Looking at specific countries, one might expect the index of segregation for Sweden to be relatively low because their policies quite successfully raised not only women's labor force participation but also increased their attachment to the labor force. In fact, Sweden's index is the highest of the economically advanced countries included in the table and higher than that for the United States. Women in Sweden continue to be disproportionately employed in traditionally female clerical and white-collar jobs, most notably in the government sector, and in health care, education, and child care.

---

[46] OECD, "Women at Work: Who Are They and How Are They Faring?" *OECD Employment Outlook* (2002).

Nevertheless, while considerable sex segregation continues in Sweden, evidence suggests that there has been a considerable decline since the 1970s.[47] As we have seen, there was also a substantial decline in segregation in the United States during this period. The experience of both Sweden and the United States stands in marked contrast to that of Japan, where the index has changed very little.

Part of the explanation for the relatively high degree of sex segregation in Sweden is that women are well paid in predominantly female occupations, reducing their incentive to enter predominantly male occupations. In addition, for a long time Sweden put far more emphasis on policies that encourage women to enter the labor market than on opening up new careers for them.[48] As discussed earlier, Sweden and other Scandinavian countries have relatively long parental leaves and permit long stretches of part-time work after childbirth, which tend to reinforce occupational segregation. The counter argument is that working part time is likely to be less disruptive to maintaining and accumulating market skills than dropping out entirely.

Equally surprising as the high index of occupational segregation by sex in Sweden is the low index for Japan. Part of the explanation is that a larger share of the labor force in Japan is still employed in agriculture and blue-collar jobs, which also happen to be occupations that employ a relatively large percentage of women in that country. It should also be noted that the low representation of women in white-collar positions in Japan is a disadvantage for them because many of these jobs are among the most prestigious and well paid and are also the most likely to be associated with permanent employment.[49]

The low priority placed on gender equality in Japan is well illustrated by the fact that the government did not promulgate an equal opportunity employment law until 1985, when it became more acceptable to business as a consequence of internal labor shortages that made the hiring of women advantageous, and when external forces, including pressure from the United Nations, became difficult to ignore. Even then, employers were asked only to comply voluntarily and the government was not given the right to impose sanctions or financial penalties. Legislation passed subsequently in 1997 and 2006 considerably strengthened the earlier legislation by explicitly prohibiting discrimination in hiring, training, and promotion, imposing stricter rules regarding sexual harassment in the workplace, and providing greater protections for women against pregnancy-related discrimination.[50]

Evidence indicates that since the passage of the 1985 legislation a much larger fraction of women are enrolled in college, but these changes are not yet being directly translated into increased gender equality in the workplace.[51] Considerable segregation remains *within* broad occupational categories as women continue to be largely assigned to lower-status, mommy-track type of positions and only rarely offered "core employment," which not only provides job security but also is typically associated with regular wage increases and steady promotions. In fact, one recent Japanese government survey

---

[47] Melkas and Anker, *Towards Gender Equity in Japanese and Nordic Labour Markets.*

[48] See, for instance, Gupta et al., "The Impact of Nordic Countries' Family Friendly Policies."

[49] Anker, *Gender and Jobs,* Chap. 9; Marcus E. Rebick, *The Japanese Employment System: Adapting to a New Economic Environment* (Oxford: Oxford University Press, 2005); and Mary C. Brinton, "Gendered Offices: A Comparative-Historical Examination of Clerical Work in Japan and the U.S.," in *The Political Economy of Low Fertility: Japan in Comparative Perspective,* edited by Frances McCall Rosenbluth (Stanford: Stanford University Press, 2007).

[50] The details of the legislation are described in Hiroya Nakakubo, " 'Phase III' of the Japanese Equal Employment Opportunity Act," *Japanese Labor Review* 4, no. 3 (Summer 2007): 9–19.

[51] Linda N. Edwards and Margaret K. Pasquale, "Women's Higher Education in Japan: Family Background, Economic Factors, and the Equal Employment Opportunity Law," *Journal of the Japanese and International Economies* 17, no. 1 (2003): 1–32.

of more than 200 firms found that women held only a little over 2 percent of all core employment positions.[52]

Some part of the gender inequality in Japan's multiple-track system may be caused by the decision of many women themselves to remain in the less demanding tracks in anticipation of having a family. This choice would be understandable because, in Japan, core employment positions are tailored for men in traditional families, who do extremely little housework. These positions require a degree of commitment that would be hard for women with families to manage. Thus, women are, in effect, faced with the choice of family or career. At the same time, husbands' employment in these positions means that they would find it difficult to share in household tasks and child care, even if they wanted to do so.

Looking toward the future, Japanese firms are likely to experience considerable pressure to modify the multiple-track system, as a result of both the revised EEO law and Japan's low fertility rate. These changes are expected to increase employment opportunities for women workers and to spur the creation and expansion of policies and practices that enable employed women to combine marriage and family. These developments might also alter the long-standing custom that wives of eldest sons are responsible for their in-laws, a duty which adds considerably to their caregiving responsibilities.[53]

The Gender Wage Gap

Table 12-4 shows the ratio of women's to men's earnings in nonagricultural employment for the period from 1970 to 2006 in a number of economically advanced countries. It offers a useful overview, although a number of qualifications must be borne in mind. Some countries provide data for hourly earnings while others provide figures for weekly earnings as in the case of the United States, or monthly earnings as in the case of Japan. Because weekly and monthly earnings are influenced by the number of hours and days worked (even among full-time workers), the gender earnings differential is likely to be larger than if hourly wages were compared. Also, data for the United States are reported for full-time workers, but that is not the case for all countries. The data are also not precisely comparable in other ways. In some cases they are for subgroups of workers such as manufacturing workers in Germany. There are also differences in the definition of wages; they may or may not include income in kind or family allowances and so on. Finally, in the 1990s, some substantial changes were made in several earnings series, notably those for France, Japan, and Switzerland. In such cases, sharp "jumps" in the data are not due to changes in economic behavior, but rather to changes in how the data are measured. As a result, caution must be exercised in interpreting wage *trends* within these countries.

As shown in the table, in all the selected countries women continue to be paid less than men, although the ratio of women's to men's earnings has risen since at least 1970 in all cases. Interestingly, however, the most rapid increases did not occur at the same time, nor did the ratios reach the same level in each of these countries.[54] Instead, there have been a variety of patterns, including intermittent increases, interrupted by periods of stagnation, and even temporary reversals. As we saw in Chapter 5, the ratio of usual

---

[52] Figure is from "Japanese Women Push at the Door of Change," *The Financial Times* (London), April 19, 2002, p. 13. See also, Melkas and Anker, *Towards Gender Equity in Japanese and Nordic Labour Markets;* Joyce Gelb, "The Equal Employment Opportunity Law: A Decade of Change for Japanese Women," *Law and Policy*, 22 no. 3 & 4 (October 2000): 385–407; and Anthony Failola, "Japanese Working Women Still Serve the Tea; Despite Hopes for Change as Their Ranks Have Grown, Discrimination Persists," *Washington Post* (March 2, 2007).

[53] For a discussion of low fertility and late marriage, see Robert D. Retherford, Naohiro Ogawa, and Rikiya Matsukura, "Late Marriage and Less Marriage in Japan," *Population and Development Review* 27, no. 1 (March 2001): 65–102. See also, Rosenbluth, ed. *The Political Economy of Japan's Low Fertility.*

[54] See also, OECD, "Women at Work," pp. 96–100.

TABLE 12-4 Ratio of Women's to Men's Hourly Earnings, Selected Years, 1970–2006

	1970	1980	1990	2000	2006
Australia	0.65	0.86	0.88	0.88	0.86
Finland	0.70	0.75	0.77	0.79	0.80
France	0.78	0.79	0.81	0.74[a]	0.74
Denmark	0.74	0.86	0.85	0.83	0.85
Germany	0.69	0.72	0.73	0.74	0.74
Japan	0.51	0.54	0.50	0.65[a]	0.67
Netherlands	0.71	0.78	0.78	0.78	0.82
New Zealand	0.72	0.77	0.81	0.81	0.82
Norway	0.75	0.82	0.86	0.85	0.87
Sweden	0.82	0.90	0.89	0.88	0.89
Switzerland	0.66	0.68	0.68	0.75[a]	0.76
United Kingdom	0.60	0.70	0.70	0.73	0.76
United States	0.62	0.64	0.72	0.76	0.81

Notes: For Denmark, Finland, Norway, and Sweden, figures for 1990 and before are for the manufacturing sector. For Germany, figures prior to 2000 are for West Germany. Data for Germany for 2000 and on are for the manufacturing sector.

[a] Series is not continuous. A new series starts for France, Japan, and Switzerland in 2000.

Source: Figures are calculated from International Labour Organization, LABORSTA Internet database, http://laborsta.ilo.org. Accessed on September 26, 2008.

median weekly earnings of full-time workers in the United States increased substantially from .64 in 1980 to .77 in 1993. For several years afterwards the ratio fell, but by 1999 it had rebounded to .77 and, by 2006, the ratio climbed to .81.

In the case of Sweden, on the other hand, most of the gains had occurred by the early 1980s, and the ratio has remained virtually unchanged since then at just under .90, which is among the highest for any country. In a number of other countries, including the United Kingdom, the ratio also increased substantially early on, then stagnated for some time, only to show recent evidence of a renewed increase. As may be seen in the table, the gender earnings ratio in the United Kingdom rose from .70 in 1990 to .76 in 2006.

In Australia, the ratio increased sharply from 1970 to 1980, as a result of the introduction of comparable worth (see the inset on Australia), and has fluctuated between .86 and .88 since 1990. The earnings ratio in Japan, historically lower than in other economically advanced countries, actually declined from .54 in 1980 to .50 in 1990 based on a comparable series for those years. However, a newly available series, which cannot be directly compared with the earlier one, indicates that the gender wage ratio in Japan increased from .65 in 2000 to .67 in 2006, suggestive of a recent upward trend.

In sum, there is evidence for the countries examined that women's wages are once again rising relative to those of men. It is difficult to sort out the reasons for the trends in these series, and they need not be the same for all countries. It is, however, likely that changing wage structures within countries, the degree of enforcement of antidiscrimination laws,[55] and changes in the relative qualifications of women workers play a greater or lesser role.

---

[55] An interesting finding in this regard is that the ratification by countries of two International Labor Organization (ILO) conventions supporting equal treatment of men and women has been found to have a strong and significant effect reducing the "unexplained" gender wage gap; see Doris Weichselbaumer and Rudolf Winter-Ebmer, "The Effects of Competition and Equal Treatment Laws on Gender Wage Differentials," *Economic Policy* 22, no. 50 (April 2007): 235–87. For evidence of a "glass ceiling" in 10 European Union countries, see Wiji Arulampalam, Alison L. Booth, and Mark L. Bryan, "Is There a Glass Ceiling over Europe? Exploring the Gender Pay Gap Across the Wages Distribution," *Industrial and Labor Relations Review* 60, no. 2 (November 2006): 163–86.

Another issue that deserves attention is the relationship between the female–male earnings ratio and occupational segregation by sex. On the one hand, for the reasons discussed in Chapter 7, one might expect a negative relationship; the higher the degree of segregation, the lower the female–male earnings ratio. On the other hand, if earnings for women are relatively high in women's fields, they will have less incentive to enter men's occupations so that one could observe both a high degree of segregation and a relatively high earnings ratio. This might occur in countries with strong union policies that serve to compress the overall wage structure, as is the case in Sweden, or where comparable worth policies have been adopted, as is the case in Australia.

It is also worthy of note that the earnings ratio in the United States currently falls in the middle of the selected countries and, in earlier years, lagged considerably behind most of the countries. One might expect the United States to have ranked close to the top throughout this period because the United States was among the first to promulgate antidiscrimination laws, beginning in the early 1960s, and U.S. women tend to have similar, if not higher, levels of human capital relative to men as compared to women in these other countries. The answer to this puzzle lies in the fact that the size of the gender gap is determined not only by differences across countries in women's qualifications and in the extent of discrimination against them but also by international differences in wage structure or the returns that the labor market sets for skills and employment in higher-wage, predominantly-male occupations and industries.[56] Because women tend to have less experience than men, on average, and to be concentrated in low-wage "female" sectors, the gender wage gap will be larger when the return to experience or the reward to employment in higher-wage, predominantly-male occupations and industries is especially large. As we noted earlier in this section, international differences in wage-setting institutions and wage structure are substantial, especially between the United States and the other economically advanced countries.

A comparison with Sweden is particularly instructive. As discussed earlier, the female–male wage ratio is much higher in Sweden than in the United States. One study suggests this is due to differences between the two countries in wage structure, with Sweden's reward structure being considerably more compressed than that in the United States.[57] This compression is largely caused by the role unions play in determining wages in Sweden. With women disproportionately represented among lower-paid workers, wage compression in Sweden raises women's wages relative to men's. In contrast, U.S. wage-setting is highly decentralized and characterized by considerable wage differences between more and less-experienced workers and by occupation and industry. This study suggests that the United States would have as high a gender wage ratio as Sweden if it had the same compressed wage structure. In fact, the high level of U.S. wage inequality raises the gender gap in the United States compared to many other economically advanced countries. In contrast, the even larger gender gap in Japan (which was not included in this study) likely reflects factors specifically related to gender, including the high degree of segregation of women within broad occupational categories there.

---

[56] For a more detailed discussion, see Francine D. Blau and Lawrence M. Kahn, "Gender Differences in Pay," *Journal of Economic Perspectives* 14, no. 4 (Fall 2000): 75–100; and Francine D. Blau and Lawrence M. Kahn, "Wage Structure and Gender Earnings Differentials: An International Comparison," *Economica* 63 (supplement 1996): 29–62. For additional evidence suggesting a role for institutions, see Francine D. Blau and Lawrence M. Kahn, "Understanding International Differences in the Gender Pay Gap" *Journal of Labor Economics* 21, no. 1 (January 2003): 106–44; Blau and Kahn, "Women and Wages"; Mandel and Semyonov, "Family Policies, Wage Structures, and Gender Gaps"; and Anne Daly, Xin Meng, Akira Kawaguchi, and Karen Mumford, "The Gender Wage Gap in Four Countries," *Economic Record* 82, no. 257 (June 2006): 165–76.
[57] Blau and Kahn, "Wage Structure and Gender Earnings Differentials." Another possible explanatory factor, differences in the dispersion of test scores, is explored in Francine D. Blau and Lawrence M. Kahn, "Do Cognitive Test Scores Explain Higher Wage Inequality?" *Review of Economics and Statistics* 87, no. 1 (February 2005): 184–92.

Another factor influencing differences in the gender wage gap across countries is the self-selection of women into employment. We discussed the role of the composition of the female labor force in Chapter 8, when we considered trends over time in the U.S. gender wage gap and now apply it again in examining international differences. As we have seen, female labor force participation rates vary considerably across the economically advanced countries. For example, female participation rates in Southern European countries are quite low. Interestingly, gender wage gaps in these countries also tend to be relatively low in comparison to those in the United States and other European countries with higher labor force participation rates. One study suggests that the reason for the relatively low gender wage gaps in Southern Europe is "probably not . . . more equal pay treatment for women" in these countries, but rather that in these countries, where market work among women is less common, it is concentrated among women who can earn especially high wages when they enter the labor market. This lowers the measured gender wage gap. In countries with higher participation rates, on the other hand, more low-wage women are included in the labor force and the measured gender wage gap is larger.[58]

COMPARABLE WORTH IN AUSTRALIA

Along with the Nordic countries, Australia has the distinction of having one of the highest female-to-male earnings ratios among economically advanced countries. As described here, the implementation of equal pay and, particularly, of comparable worth in Australia in the 1970s played a major role in raising the relative earnings of women.[*]

Australia's wage determination system is markedly different from that in the United States. In Australia, minimum wage rates for occupations are determined by government wage tribunals and unions play a larger role, though the wage system has become somewhat more decentralized in recent years, as discussed shortly.

Up to 1969, the Australian pay structure explicitly discriminated against women. Until 1950, female award rates were set at 54 percent of male rates; that year they were raised to 75 percent. In 1969, the concept of equal pay for equal work was implemented, and the award rate was raised to 100 percent. In 1972, the federal tribunal moved toward **comparable worth** by deciding that the "equal pay for equal work" concept should be expanded to "equal pay for work of equal value" in order to cover employees in predominantly female jobs.

As shown in Table 12-4, the result of the implementation of these policies, particularly of comparable worth, was an increase in the gender earnings ratio from 65 percent in 1970 to 86 percent by 1980. One might expect that if such policies increase the gender earnings ratio, they might result in lower female employment. As expected, female employment grew more slowly than would have been expected if their wages had not risen but the negative effect was nevertheless fairly small. One explanation for the small employment effect is that women and men held very different jobs and so this high degree of occupational segregation may have constituted a substantial barrier to women being replaced by men as their relative wages increased.

Since 1996, Australia's wage determination system has grown more decentralized; individual firms can now negotiate wage agreements, unions possess less bargaining power, and government wage tribunals play a much more modest role in determining wages. These recent changes have prompted concerns about possible negative effects

---

[58] Claudia Olivetti and Barbara Petrongolo, "Unequal Pay or Unequal Employment? A Cross-Country Analysis of Gender Gaps," *Journal of Labor Economics* 26, no. 4 (October 2008): 621–54; quotation is from p. 625.

on women's employment and earnings. In fact, the female–male earnings ratio has fluctuated between .86 and .90 since that time, but there has not been a noticeable decline. Still, it is important to keep in mind that these figures are only broad averages, and, moreover, they reflect only one dimension of what is happening in the labor market.

*This account of comparable worth is based on Robert G. Gregory and Vivian Ho, "Equal Pay and Comparable Worth: What Can the U.S. Learn from the Australian Experience?" The Australian National University, Centre for Economic Policy Research, Discussion Paper No. 123, July 1985; Mark Killingsworth, *The Economics of Comparable Worth* (Kalamazoo, MI: Upjohn Institute for Employment Research, 1990); Glenda Strachan and John Burgess, "Will Deregulating the Labor Market in Australia Improve the Employment Conditions of Women?" *Feminist Economics* 7 no. 2 (July 2001): 53–76; and Francine D. Blau and Lawrence M. Kahn, "Women's Work and Wages," in *The New Palgrave Dictionary of Economics*, 2nd edition, edited by Steven N. Durlauf and Lawrence E. Blume (Palgrave Macmillan, 2008), pp. 762–72.

Demographic Trends

Table 12-5 provides data on trends in various demographic indicators, including fertility, births to unwed mothers, marriage, and divorce for selected economically advanced countries for 1980 through the mid 2000s, though many of these trends started quite a bit earlier. As would be expected in view of the increasing labor force participation rate of women in all these countries, the table shows that fertility rates declined in most of them. With the exception of the United States, fertility rates in these countries are below the replacement rate of 2.1 births per woman, and in several cases they are considerably lower.

A second notable recent pattern is that those economically advanced countries with the highest female labor force participation rates also have the highest fertility rates and vice versa. This is suggested by the data in Table 12-5 and has also been noted by researchers considering a larger number of countries. This positive relationship is surprising in light of the fact that we tend to observe a negative relationship between fertility and female labor force participation when we look across all countries in the world and when we look at these decisions at the individual level as discussed in Chapters 4 and 10. Researchers have pointed to at least three factors behind the positive relationship between female labor force participation and fertility in economically advanced countries: the degree to which family-friendly policies are available, the flexibility of the labor market including the availability of part-time work, and the extent to which child care time is distributed more equally among parents. In the Nordic countries, for instance, fertility rates and female labor force participation are boosted by their strong family-friendly policies of long paid parental leave and subsidized child care combined with the fact that fathers share substantially in child care.[59] In the United States, while the workplace is less family-friendly than in these countries, out-of-home child care is generally available (at least for children over age 2), part-time work is a regular feature of the labor market, and fathers play an important and growing role in

---

[59] For discussion of these factors, see Anne H. Gauthier, "The Impact of Family Policies on Fertility in Industrialized Countries: A Review of the Literature," *Population Research and Policy Review* 26, no. 3 (June 2007): 323–46; Alicia Adsera, "Changing Fertility Rates in Developed Countries: The Impact of Labor Market Institutions, *Journal of Population Economics* 17, no. 1 (February 2004): 17–43; Daniela Del Boca, Silvia Pasqua, and Chiara Pronzato, "Fertility and Employment in Italy, France, and the UK," *Labour* 19 (Special Issue 2005): 51–77; and James Feyrer, Bruce Sacerdote, and Ariel Dora Stern, "Will the Stork Return to Europe and Japan? Understanding Fertility Within Developed Nations," *Journal of Economic Perspectives* 22, no. 3 (Summer 2008): 3–22.

TABLE 12-5   Demographic Trends, Selected Economically Advanced Countries[a]

	Total Fertility Rate[b]		Births to Unmarried Women (as % of all live births)		Marriage Rate per 1,000 Population Age 15–64		Divorce Rate per 1,000 Population Age 15–64		Single-Parent Households (as % of all households with children)[c]	
	1980	2006	1980	2005	1980	2005	1980	2005	1980	2006
Canada	1.7	1.5	12.8	26.0	11.5	6.8	3.7	3.2	12.7	19.3
Denmark	1.5	1.9	33.2	45.7	8.0	10.1	4.1	4.3	13.4	20.5
France	1.9	2.0	11.4	48.4	9.7	7.1	2.4	3.5	11.9	17.1
Germany	1.4	1.3	15.1	29.2	8.2	7.0	2.5	4.0	15.2	20.1
Ireland	3.2	1.9	5.9	32.0	10.9	7.2	^d	1.2	7.2	22.6
Italy	1.6	1.4	4.3	13.8	8.7	6.5	0.3	1.2	n.a.	n.a.
Japan	1.8	1.3	0.8	2.0	9.8	8.4	1.8	3.1	4.9	9.8
Netherlands	1.6	1.7	4.1	34.9	9.6	6.7	2.7	2.9	9.6	15.3
Spain	2.2	1.4	3.9	26.6	9.4	7.0	n.a.	1.7	n.a.	n.a.
Sweden	1.7	1.9	39.7	55.4	7.1	7.5	3.7	3.4	11.2	19.6
United Kingdom	1.9	1.9	11.5	42.9	11.6	8.0	4.1	3.9	13.9	24.1
United States	1.8	2.1	18.4	36.8	15.9	11.2	7.9	5.4	19.5	28.3

[a] Data are for stated year or closest year available.

[b] See footnote a, Table 12-1.

[c] The definition of children differs slightly across countries. See source below.

[d] Divorce not allowed by law prior to 1997.

n.a. Not available.

Source: For all data but fertility rates, U.S. Census Bureau, *U.S. Statistical Abstract* (2007 and 2008). Fertility rates are from World Bank, *World Development Indicators,* Online Database, at www.worldbank.org.

child care, all factors serving to raise aggregate rates of female labor force participation and fertility.

In contrast, as shown in Table 12-5, labor force participation rates and fertility are quite low in the countries of Southern Europe (including Italy and Spain), and Japan. In the case of Southern Europe, high unemployment rates have been identified as one key factor. High unemployment rates deter labor market participation via the discouraged worker effect discussed in Chapter 4, and they raise the cost of children (thereby reducing fertility), by making reentry difficult for employed women who leave the labor force to bear children. The lack of adequate part-time work and adequate out-of-home child care, along with a more traditional division of labor in unpaid work, further deter female labor market participation and fertility in these countries. With the exception of unemployment problems, related explanations have been offered for the co-existence of low female participation and fertility rates in Japan. Low fertility rates there have been attributed to the "inhospitable" nature of the Japanese labor market for women, inadequate government support of families, combined with men's virtual lack of participation in unpaid household work.[60]

---

[60] Frances McCall Rosenbluth, "Conclusion," in *A Political Economy of Japan's Low Fertility,* edited by Frances McCall Rosenbluth (Stanford: Stanford University Press, 2007).

The low fertility rates in much of Europe, as well as Japan, are expected to lead to substantial declines in population in years to come. Governments in these countries are paying close attention to fertility trends because reductions in population size may well reduce their international power and prestige. The declines could be moderated, however, if greater immigration were encouraged, or perhaps if countries were to adopt policies that better enable women to combine employment and childrearing.[61]

Another significant demographic trend is that marriage rates began declining in all of the selected countries in the 1970s and continued their decline through 2005, as shown in Table 12-5. One striking finding is that the marriage rate in the United States remained among the highest in 2005, at 11.2 marriages per 1,000 people age 15 to 64. In Japan, on the other hand, the marriage rate fell considerably from 14 in 1970 (data not shown in table) to 8.4 by 2005.[62] Among the explanations for the trend in Japan is not only the growing economic independence of women, but also the especially low status of married women; husbands spend many hours working for their employers and do very little housework. Further, as noted earlier, wives in Japan have a particularly strong cultural obligation to care for their husbands' elderly parents. Interestingly, Sweden's marriage rate has remained at a low level for a long period of time, perhaps because getting married there continues to offer few tax or other advantages in this highly secular society.[63]

As would be expected, while marriage rates have declined, rates of cohabitation have continued to rise. The increase in cohabitation is a major factor in explaining the dramatic rise in births to unmarried mothers that occurred in the great majority of economically advanced nations, although the degree to which these factors are associated varies considerably across countries.[64] It is estimated that 35 percent of Swedish women ages 20 to 40 are cohabiting as compared with 9 percent of U.S. women.[65] As may be seen in Table 12-5, the proportion of births to unwed mothers in 2005 was as high as 55 percent in Sweden and 37 percent in the United States. Nonetheless, virtually all of the babies born to unmarried mothers in Sweden and 40 percent of babies born to unmarried mothers in the United States were actually brought home to live with cohabiting fathers.[66] The high rates of cohabitation in Sweden, the other Nordic countries, and increasingly elsewhere, suggest that most

---

[61] Paul Demeny, "Population Policy Dilemmas in Europe at the Dawn of the Twenty-First Century," *Population and Development Review* 29, no. 1 (March 2003): 1–28; Lee, "The Demographic Transition"; contributions in Alan Booth and Ann C. Crouter, eds. *The New Population Problem: Why Families in Developing Countries Are Shrinking and What It Means* (Mahwah, NJ: Lawrence Erlbaum, 2005); and Rosenbluth, ed., *A Political Economy of Japan's Low Fertility*, Ch. 9.

[62] The source of the 1970 figure for Japan is from Constance Sorrentino, "The Changing Family in International Perspective," *Monthly Labor Review* 113, no. 3 (March 1990): 41–60.

[63] For a detailed discussion regarding factors affecting Japan, see Hiroshi Ono, "Divorce in Japan: Why It Happens, Why It Doesn't," in *Institutional Change in Japan*, edited by Magnus Blomstrom and Sumner La Croix (London and New York: Routledge, 2006), pp. 221–36. For factors explaining variation across Europe, see Matthijs Kalmijn, "Explaining Cross-National Differences in Marriage, Cohabitation, and Divorce in Europe, 1990–2000," *Population Studies* 61 no. 3 (2007): 243–63.

[64] For instance, Kathleen Kiernan observes that, in the Netherlands and Germany, the rate of unwed births is lower than would be expected based on cohabitation rates, while the reverse is true for the United Kingdom and Ireland in "Cohabitation in Western Europe: Trends, Issues and Implications," in *Just Living Together: Implications of Cohabitation on Families, Children and Social Policy*, edited by Alan Booth and Ann C. Crouter, (Lawrence Erlbaum Assoc., 2002), pp. 3–31.

[65] The figure for Sweden is from OECD, *Society at a Glance 2007*, Table SF8.1. The cohabitation figure for the United States is for ages 15–44 and is from U.S. Department of Health and Human Services, "Fertility, Family Planning and Reproductive Health of U.S. Women: Data from the 2002 National Survey of Family Growth," *Vital and Health Statistics*, series 23, no. 25, Table 47 (December 2005).

[66] The figures for Sweden and the United States, respectively, are from Constance Sorrentino, "The Changing Family in International Perspective," *Monthly Labor Review* 113, no. 3 (March 1990): 41–58; and Larry Bumpass and H.-H. Lu, "Trends in Cohabitation and Implications for Children's Family Context in the United States," *Population Studies* 54, no. 1 (March 2000): 29–41.

men and women continue to choose to live with partners, even as marriage rates decline, albeit without legal (or religious) commitments. Undoubtedly such couples, much like those who do marry, are seeking companionship, but probably also gains from economies of scale as well as from specialization and exchange. Rates of cohabitation for Japan are not known, but are likely to be low, given that births to unwed mothers remain negligible.

Family structure has also changed since the 1970s because of rising divorce rates, though again trends vary considerably across countries. In the United States, the divorce rate increased considerably from the mid-1960s to the early 1980s.[67] Although it has fallen somewhat since then and now stands at 5.4 divorces per 1,000 people age 15 to 64, it remains the highest of the countries shown in Table 12-5. The rates in Denmark, Germany and the United Kingdom are next highest, ranging between 3.9 to 4.3 divorces per 1,000 people age 15 to 64. The divorce rate in Japan, historically quite low, increased from 1.8 in 1980 to 3.1 in 2005. In Italy, the divorce rate has risen to only 1.2, most likely a result of the strong influence of the Vatican against divorce.

Families headed by single parents, generally mothers, are most common in the United States, but have also been increasing in a number of other economically advanced countries. Regrettably, statistics for different countries are not entirely comparable because some include cohabitors with children among married couples while others do not, and age limits for children differ as well. Although women most often become single mothers as a result of divorce or marital separation, the proportion of never-married mothers has been increasing. As shown in Table 12-5, in 2006, single parents maintained 28 percent of households with dependent children in the United States, and rates in the United Kingdom and Ireland, among others, were not all that far behind. In Japan, on the other hand, the rate was just under 10 percent.[68]

In all these countries, single-parent families, especially those headed by women, are among the most economically vulnerable. Policies to assist them vary considerably. On the one hand, in Sweden, single mothers, like all adults, are encouraged to work for pay and are given sufficient support to do so, including parental leave and day care. In addition, Sweden makes available a child support "advance" system, which provides awards to custodial parents when the other parent fails to pay the agreed-upon amount of support. The United States, on the other hand, as we saw in Chapters 10 and 11, provides considerably less assistance. One consequence of these differences, as well as Sweden's more highly compressed wage structure, which leads to a small proportion of single women earning below-poverty wages, is that poverty rates for mother-only families are considerably lower in Sweden than in the United States.[69]

Housework

Comparable international data on gender differences in time spent on housework are limited but a number of sources provide at least some information. As noted earlier, one consistent finding is that men do considerably less housework than women. Time

---

[67] A measure of divorces per 1,000 married persons is preferred, especially in international comparisons, because the measure reported here, divorces per 1,000 population, is influenced by the incidence of marriage—where marriage rates are lower, this rate is also lower. Figures were not available for this measure, however.
[68] The relatively high rate of single parenthood in Sweden is not due to high rates of cohabitation because cohabitors are counted as married couples, not single-parent families. On the other hand, in the United States, some "single-parent" families may be cohabitors with children. See Sorrentino, "The Changing Family in International Perspective."
[69] For policies and evidence, see Karen Christopher, Paula England, Katherin Ross, Timothy Smeeding, and Sara McLanahan, "The Gender Gap in Poverty in Modern Nations: Single Motherhood, the Market, and the State," *Sociological Perspectives* 45, no. 3 (September 2002): 219–42; and Timothy M. Smeeding, "Public Policy, Economic Inequality, and Poverty: The United States in Comparative Perspective," *Social Science Quarterly* 86, S1 (December 2005): 955–83.

use data for 2002 suggests that married women spent around twice as much time on housework as their male counterparts in both Sweden and the United States.[70] This may seem surprising in light of Sweden's more egalitarian social policies, including paid parental leave and women's higher rates of labor force participation. In fact, the aggregate figures mask important differences. For instance, in the United States, wives who earn relatively more than their husbands spend more time in housework than those who earn as much as their husbands, while the opposite is true in Sweden. This finding suggests that relatively high-earning wives in the United States sense a need to exhibit "gender-appropriate" roles in the household while this is not the case for wives in Sweden.[71] Thus, the culture in Sweden does seem more amenable to shifting gender roles in the labor market and household. In Japan, in sharp contrast, women spent 8.6 times as much time on housework as men, consistent with women's more traditional role in Japanese society.[72]

Summary on Economically Advanced Countries

Overall, the available evidence indicates that real progress has been made toward greater economic equality for women in economically advanced countries over the last several decades, but it also highlights the very different experiences in specific countries and the challenges that remain. For instance, in Sweden, with its high rate of labor force participation and high female-to-male earnings ratio, women continue to hold different jobs than men and spend twice as much time than men in housework. In Japan women are entering the labor market, but do not fare as well in other respects, and the gender earnings ratio has only begun to rise in recent years. In the United States, large numbers of single mothers continue to live in poverty. Government policies, along with cultural and historical differences, no doubt help to explain the considerable differences among countries. Much remains to be learned about these factors, and also about ways to ensure the continuation of progress.

CHALLENGES FACING WOMEN IN DEVELOPING COUNTRIES

Women in developing countries merit special attention because they face major challenges and difficulties as a result of the extremely low income levels of these countries.[73] A telling statistic is that the poorest two-fifths of the world's population receives only 3 percent of the income, while the wealthiest 15 percent receives nearly 80 percent.[74] Not surprisingly, then, developing countries are generally characterized by an extremely low standard of living, high rates of infant mortality, short life expectancy, and high rates of illiteracy. In many instances, their high rates of fertility tend to exacerbate some of the other problems. Thus, most people in developing

---

[70] Figures reported in the text are from Makiko Fuwa and Philip N. Cohen, "Housework and Social Policy," *Social Science Research* 36, no. 2 (June 2007): 512–30.
[71] Marie Evertsson and Magnus Nermo, "Dependence Within Families and the Division of Labor: Comparing Sweden and the United States," *Journal of Marriage and the Family* 66, no. 5 (December 2004): 1272–86.
[72] Data are from Fuwa and Cohen, "Housework and Social Policy." See also, Myra H. Strober and Agnes Miling Kaneko Chan, *The Road Winds Uphill All the Way: Gender, Work, and Family in the United States and Japan* (Cambridge, MA: MIT Press, 1999).
[73] A number of useful books and many interesting articles on women in developing countries have been published since Ester Boserup's landmark 1970 volume, *Women's Role in Economic Development*. More recently, see, for instance, Ester Boserup, *Economic and Demographic Relationships in Development* (Baltimore: Johns Hopkins University Press, 1990); T. Paul Schultz, ed., *Investment in Women's Human Capital* (Chicago: University of Chicago Press, 1995) ; and Esther Duflo, "Gender Equality in Development."
[74] Calculated from World Bank, *World Development Indicators*, 2007.

countries live in extremely difficult circumstances. In addition, women most often bear a disproportionate share of the burdens of economic and social deprivation.[75]

It is not possible for us to fully describe the situation of women in developing countries here. Doing so would require a book considerably larger than this one because of the great variation in many respects among the different countries in this category, as shown in Table 12-1 and the accompanying discussion. Some can only euphemistically be called *developing*, while others are soon likely to be reclassified as *economically advanced*. They also differ considerably with respect to religion, customs, geographic location, and economic resource bases, among other factors.[76] Progress within countries may also be very uneven, as is well illustrated by developments in China and India. Both of these countries have recently experienced considerable growth in per capita income along with the creation of modern cities, while their rural populations have been left behind to a great extent.[77]

In this section we focus on four issues that are of great importance in developing countries and are of particular concern to women. The first is education, which enhances prospects for development and also offers the promise of raising women's economic status. The second is the controversial issue of public policies intended to influence fertility, such as those that restrict access to information about means for controlling family size, on the one hand or go so far as to penalize couples to limit the number of children they have on the other. The third is the topic of child labor, which has been receiving considerable attention recently. Finally, we consider the potential role of microcredit in improving women's economic status.

Education as the Pathway to Empowerment

The days when it was widely accepted that it was unnecessary to send daughters to school are coming to an end. Not only in affluent countries but in a growing number of developing countries, virtually all girls and boys attend primary schools, and secondary school attendance is rising as well. Nonetheless, as discussed earlier, in many of the poorest countries, primary education is still not universal and girls continue to receive far less education than boys. Hence, as we have seen, illiteracy rates among women in these countries continue to be substantially higher than among men.

Women's educational attainment has been historically lower than men's for several reasons. From a purely economic standpoint, to the extent that girls do more housework than boys, including caring for siblings, the opportunity cost of sending daughters rather than sons to school is greater. Even more important, sons will become the breadwinners and in most cultures are expected to support their parents in their old age, while girls marry into another family and rarely have independent means to support their parents. In addition, tradition and religion play an important role. In some societies, education, beyond a minimal level, may actually reduce a woman's chance of marrying. In any case, education is likely to postpone marriage, which could defer and possibly reduce the bride-price (still common in many countries) when she does marry.[78] Finally, as discussed in Chapter 6, to the extent that girls receive a smaller return on their educational investments than boys due to a shorter expected work life, it may be that they opt to invest less in it.

In recent years, a very promising development, perhaps hastened by conferences on the status of the world's women as well as the 2000 U.N. Millennium Summit, is a

[75] Allen Tuovi, "Economic Development and the Feminization of Poverty," in *Women's Work in the World Economy*, edited by Nancy Folbre, Barbara Bergmann, Bina Agarwal, and Maria Floro (New York: New York University Press, 1992), pp. 107–19.

[76] Boserup, "Obstacles to Advancement of Women."

[77] United Nations, *Human Development Report 2003*.

[78] Peter Glick, "What Policies Will Reduce Gender Schooling Gaps in Developing Countries: Evidence and Interpretation," *World Development* 36, no. 9 (2008): 1623–46; and M. Anne Hill and Elizabeth M. King, "Women's Education and Economic Well-Being," *Feminist Economics* 1, no. 2 (Summer 1995): 21–46.

greater emphasis on women's education. There is growing awareness that education is not only the key to independence and empowerment for women, but that it gives women both the incentive and ability to reduce their fertility as well as the opportunity to better contribute to their families. There is also growing recognition of the substantial links between women's education and a country's standard of living and general well-being.[79]

Not only does education enhance women's potential for entry into the labor force and increase their potential earnings, it also benefits their families in a number of other important ways. For instance, with education women are better able to read labels and instructions and are thus likely to be better informed about nutrition, proper hygiene, and health care, including birth control. Indeed, one recent study finds that mothers' numeracy and literacy skills improve their children's health outcomes.[80] In addition, parental education significantly positively affects children's schooling levels, with some evidence that a mother's education particularly affects her daughters' schooling.[81] Finally, because the education of women increases the opportunity cost of raising children (due to the increased value of the market time), they are likely to have fewer of them. Smaller families in turn allow parents to devote more of their limited resources to each child.

From a societal perspective, education of women is an effective means of encouraging voluntary family planning that is vastly preferable to government policies such as those in China, that penalize some families for having additional children.[82] Greater literacy may also help to stem the rapid spread of the HIV/AIDS virus, although education is certainly not a panacea for this epidemic. Further, as discussed earlier, women's education and economic empowerment not only shift more resources toward children but also reduce the considerable imbalance between resources devoted to boys as compared to girls. And, evidence suggests that gender equality in education promotes economic growth for the society as a whole.[83] Finally, at the broader societal level, education is necessary for a better informed citizenry, so crucial to the achievement and functioning of a healthy democracy.

Fertility and Population Control

As already noted, fertility and population control in developing countries are critically linked not only to women's economic status but to the economic viability of these countries, especially the poorest among them. The methods developing countries use to control fertility range from encouraging the voluntary use of contraceptives to coercive population control enforced by the government. China, for instance, has combined policies encouraging contraception and sex education, with limits on the number of children couples are permitted to have.[84] In many other developing countries, family planning is entirely voluntary and increasingly common, while in others, family

---

[79] See, for instance, Stephan Klasen, "Low Schooling for Girls, Slow Growth for All? Cross-Country Evidence of the Effect of Gender Inequality in Education on Economic Development, *The World Bank Economic Review* 16, no. 3 (2002): 345–73.

[80] Paul Glewwe, "Why Does Mother's Schooling Raise Child Health in Developing Countries?" *Journal of Human Resources* 34, no. 1 (Winter 1999): 124–59; and Sharada Weir, "An Examination of Some Mechanisms Underlying Externality Benefits of Girls' Schooling," *Journal of Population Economics* 20 (February 2007): 203–22.

[81] Hill and King, "Women's Education and Economic Well-Being"; and Duncan Thomas, "Like Father, Like Son: Like Mother, Like Daughter."

[82] Hill and King, "Women's Education and Economic Well-Being."

[83] For a review of this literature, see Mikkola and Miles, "Role of Gender Equality in Development."

[84] Regarding China, see Judith Banister, "Shortage of Girls in China Today," *Journal of Population Research* 21, no. 1 (2004): 19–45. The policies adopted by India have been less coercive but at times the government's tactics have not been far from compulsion. See Amartya Sen, "Fertility and Coercion," *University of Chicago Law Review* 63, no. 3 (Summer 1996): 1035–61.

planning, including contraceptive use, is quite rare. Among the reasons for this are a lack of adequate information, lack of availability or high cost of contraceptives, concerns about their side effects, or, in some cases, religious strictures that specifically discourage their use. Expanding women's education is an exceptionally promising solution to controlling population growth because it enhances women's economic status while also reducing fertility, without using any form of compulsion.

The data in Table 12-1 and Figure 12-2 provide evidence that considerable strides have been made in reducing fertility in much of the developing world over the last 30 years. Nonetheless, the very high rates that persist in Sub-Saharan Africa and a few countries in the Middle East and North Africa are a matter of serious concern, especially because most of these countries are very poor.[85]

A second concern is that in a handful of countries efforts to control fertility, whether voluntary or coercive, appear to have substantially increased the ratio of men to women in the population. The increase in this ratio is especially pronounced in countries in East and South Asia, including not only China and India but also South Korea and Taiwan, where there is a strong preference for boys over girls. This preference is evident in their historically lopsided sex ratios in the population, particularly in China and India, which indicate the presence of considerably more men than women, as compared to what would be expected based on normal rates of infant mortality and subsequent survival rates.[86] Although about 105 to 106 boys would normally be expected to be born for every 100 girls, recent estimates put this figure at 111 to 112 for China and India, and in some Indian provinces the figure is considerably higher. The figures are slightly lower at 108 to 109 boys for every 100 girls in South Korea and Taiwan.[87]

In the past, in some cases imbalanced sex ratios were the result of outright infanticide and, in other cases, of girls being given less food and medical care than boys, amounting to what has been termed *passive infanticide,* so that the family would have more resources for present or future sons. In recent years, the major factor leading to the high sex ratios in these countries is the availability of pre-natal sex-determination tests and use of sex-selective abortion as a form of birth control. In China, and perhaps elsewhere as well, another contributing factor is that births of girls are underreported. Moreover, these high sex ratios prevail despite the fact that sex-determination tests were officially banned in all these countries in the 1990s, with the exception of Taiwan. The impact appears especially pronounced in second- and higher-order births, suggesting that if a couple already has a girl, they are much less willing to accept another. The bias is also much more pronounced in rural areas, where sons, according to custom, must support parents in old age.[88] Urban couples are more likely to receive pensions, lessening the importance of having a son.

One promising trend is that while the sex ratio in South Korea is still higher than would be expected, as shown by the figures earlier, it has declined in recent years. As an explanation, one recent study points to a considerable reduction in son preference as measured by wives' reports regarding whether they "must" have a son. In fact, changing social norms across the population at large, not just among those who are highly educated, appear to be behind this trend. What remains to be seen is whether the strong

---

[85] In the Middle East and North Africa, fertility rates are nearly 5 or higher in Yemen and in the West Bank and Gaza.

[86] Banister, "Shortage of Girls in China Today"; and V. Bhaskar and Bishnupriya Gupta, "India's Missing Girls: Biology, Customs, and Economic Development," *Oxford Review of Economic Policy* 23, no. 2 (Summer 2007): 221–38.

[87] CIA, *The World Factbook* (2008), available at www.cia.gov.

[88] Banister, "Shortage of Girls in China Today."

preference for sons in other countries, including China and India, will similarly lessen in coming years.[89]

Fewer baby girls translate into a shortage of marriageable women—a phenomenon already observed in China, for example. Ironically, the declining supply of women, which resulted from a bias against women, may eventually increase their value in the "marriage market" and girls who are the only children in their families may benefit from greater parental investments than would have been the case if they grew up with brothers.[90] This policy may result in larger social consequences as well. Among the dire predictions, the large numbers of unmarried men may substantially increase crime rates, the kidnapping and trafficking of women, and perhaps even foment social unrest.[91]

It is particularly interesting to take a closer look at China, with just over 20 percent of the world's population, and thus the distinction of being the most populous country in the world. Around 1980, it instituted a particularly rigid **one-child policy** for urban residents unless the first child was incapacitated or died. In rural areas, couples were allowed to have a second child if their first child was a daughter. The one-child policy was pursued through political and social pressure, as well as by creating powerful economic incentives. Couples with a single child were entitled to such perks as cash bonuses, longer maternity leave, better child care, and preferential housing. However, couples who had more than the number allowed, particularly in the city, could face steep fines or the loss of their jobs or other benefits.[92]

This policy was rigorously administered until 1983, when it became clear that it was not accepted by the public and was thus eased somewhat. Greater emphasis was placed on other ways of reducing fertility such as later marriage and education about contraception. Also, more control was given to autonomous regions and provinces in setting their own policies, including exemptions for minority groups. Since the late 1990s, the one-child policy has been eased further. For instance, married men and women living in large urban areas who are both "only" children are permitted to have two children. And, in some instances, wealthier couples are able to pay the required fines and have a larger family. China's easing of its policy was likely prompted not only by social pressures, but also by rising incomes and economic growth, and the fact that the current fertility rate in China is now just below the replacement level.[93] In March 2008, a senior Chinese official nonetheless announced that the one-child policy would continue for the coming decade.[94] Recent history suggests, however, that further easing is likely, even if the official policy remains in name.

---

[89] Woojin Chung and Monica Das Gupta, "Why Is Son Preference Declining in South Korea? The Role of Development and Public Policy, and the Implications for China and India," World Bank Working Paper, No. 4373 (2007); and Choe Sang-Hun, "Where Boys Were Kings, a Shift Toward Baby Girls," *New York Times* (December 23, 2007).

[90] Vanessa L. Fong, "China's One-Child Policy and the Empowerment of Urban Daughters," *American Anthropologist* 104, no. 4 (2002): 1098–109; and Ming Tsui and Lynne Rich, "The Only Child and Educational Opportunity for Girls in Urban China," *Gender & Society* 16, no. 1 (February 2002): 74–92. It is also argued that another possible effect of parents' preference for sons, along with a preference for children who eventually marry, is that it may lead to a society in which upper-class families have boys because they have a good chance in life and a good chance to marry, while lower-income parents tend to choose daughters, who would have a good chance to marry men who are as well or better off than they are. See Lena Edlund, "Son Preference, Sex Ratios, and Marriage Patterns," *Journal of Political Economy* 107, no. 6, pt. 1 (December 1999): 1275–304.

[91] Valerie M. Hudson and Andrea M. den Boer, *Bare Branches: Security Implications of Asia's Surplus Male Population* (Cambridge, MA: MIT Press, 2004); and Esther Duflo, "Too Many Boys...," *Vox* (August 18 2008), available online at www.voxeu.org.

[92] For a detailed study of this policy, see Judith Bannister, *China's Changing Population* (Stanford: Stanford University Press, 1987).

[93] Therese Hesketh, Li Lu, and Zhu Wei Xing, "The Effect of China's One-Child Family Policy After 25 Years"; *New England Journal of Medicine* 353, no. 11 (15 September 2005): 1171–76; and Judith Banister, "Shortage of Girls in China Today," *Journal of Population Research* 21, no. 1 (May 2004): 19–45.

[94] Jim Yardley, "China Says One-Child Policy Will Stay for At Least Another Decade," *New York Times* (March 11, 2008).

Table 12-1 shows that family planning policies in China reduced fertility substantially from 5.7 children per woman in 1970 to 2.0 by 2006. The greatest decline occurred in urban areas, presumably because of tighter government control and greater penalties. Fertility rates declined much less in rural areas, where the majority of the population lives, in part because families there are more economically dependent on their children, particularly their sons, as is generally the case in traditional societies. In addition, unlike most urban residents, they are not entitled to old-age pensions or heavily subsidized housing.

Even though the one-child policy in China probably increased discrimination against girls at least in the short run, and women are far from achieving equality either in the household or the public sphere, some progress toward gender equality is evident. Women's labor force participation in China is relatively high compared with that of countries such as India and Japan, and women's educational attainment has risen considerably. Despite these gains, recent research suggests that the growing private sector in China has been accompanied by an increase in gender discrimination, as well as an increase in the gender earnings gap.[95]

Child Labor

As discussed earlier, girls often face particular challenges in developing countries because of gender bias in parental investments in education, and, in some cases, even in the nutrition and health care they receive. Compounding these difficulties, many girls as well as boys in developing countries are engaged in **child labor**. While definitions vary somewhat, child labor goes beyond performing tasks after school for the family business or farm, doing chores for one's own household, or for children age 12 to 14, doing some "light work" such as working for pay after school. Rather, child labor typically refers to work that prevents children from going to school or that involves potential physical or mental harm. Using this definition, the International Labour Organization (ILO) estimates that in 2004 166 million boys and girls ages 5 to 14 were child laborers. Two-fifths of these children (74 million) were employed in hazardous work such as mining and construction. For a slightly earlier year, 2000, it is estimated that 8.4 million children were subject to the **worst forms of child labor**: these include forced labor conditions or bondage; child trafficking; forced prostitution, pornography or other illegal activities; and recruitment into armed conflict.[96] More often than not, children end up in these situations because their families are in a dire economic situation, not because their parents are indifferent or seek to exploit them.

The problems faced by girl child laborers have raised a particular set of concerns because many girls are employed as domestic workers in other people's homes, and are hence "invisible." For this reason they may well be undercounted in official statistics. In many cases, these arrangements are "akin to slavery"; the girls often work long hours, are at the mercy of the family for whom they work, and may receive no compensation apart from room and board. Helping them is a difficult task because the prevailing norm is that domestic work is female work, regardless of the working

---

[95] For a fuller assessment of women's status, see Elaine Zukerman, *China: Country Gender Review* Washington, DC: World Bank, 2000); Junsen Zhang, Jun Han, Pak-Wai Liu, and Yaohui Zhao, "Trends in the Gender Earnings Differential in Urban China, 1988–2004," *Industrial and Labor Relations Review* 61, no. 2 (January 2008): 224–43; and Gunseli Berik, Xiao-yuan Dong, and Gale Summerfield, "China's Transition and Feminist Economics," *Feminist Economics* 13, no. 3–4 (July–October 2007): 1–33.

[96] For 2004 figures, see International Labour Organization, *The End of Child Labour: Within Reach* (Geneva: ILO 2006). For detailed definitions and the 2000 figure on children involved in the worst forms of child labor, see International Labour Organization, *Every Child Counts: New Global Estimates on Child Labour* (Geneva: ILO, 2002).

conditions or the individual's age.[97] Nevertheless, some efforts are underway to inform these girls of their rights and raise awareness about abuse, as well as provide various forms of assistance.[98]

Concerning the larger issue of child labor, proposed solutions abound, but in order for them to be successfully implemented, alternative ways for solving the problem of dire poverty must be found and each country's specific cultural and economic conditions must also be considered. For instance, proposals to ban imports to the United States of goods produced in countries using child labor may merely cause children's employment to shift to other sectors where conditions may be even more harmful. In one instance, just the anticipation of such policies caused many girls in Bangladesh to be forced out of work stitching carpets and into prostitution.[99] Another possibility is for the countries themselves to ban all forms of child labor and seriously enforce the policy. However, any one country may well be reluctant to adopt such a ban if others do not take similar actions, because doing so unilaterally would likely make its producers less competitive and hurt the economy. Further, such a policy ignores the harsh reality that, more often than not, children are employed out of economic necessity.

Another option is the establishment of a set of minimal labor standards, such as ensuring safe working conditions and the right to organize, that would be universally adopted by all countries.[100] However, this type of policy faces considerable opposition in many developing countries because of concern it would lead to a decline in their exports. Concern also centers on the questions of who would enforce such standards and what sort of punitive measures would be taken if they were violated, as well as fear that their adoption might leave children and their families in developing countries worse off.[101]

Policies that encourage a combination of school and work, or those that encourage schooling by providing economic incentives such as free lunches or a payment to the student's family, may help families to survive and end the cycle of poverty that results from lack of education. However, for such approaches to be successful, schools need to be accessible and of sufficient quality, obstacles that must be overcome in many parts of the developing world. Another complementary policy is to improve access to credit so that families can weather difficult economic times without their children's help. Finally, government policies that improve the adult labor market or increase families' incomes would be expected to reduce their dependence on child labor.[102]

As may be seen by this discussion of the problem of child labor and the possible policies to address it, no simple solution is readily available. The issue is of particular concern

---

[97] Regarding girl domestic workers, see International Labour Organization, "The Girl Child Labourer: ILO-IPEC's Response," Unit 2: Gender Issues in the World of Work, ILO/SEAPAT's OnLine Gender Learning & Information Module, at www.ilo.org; and International Labour Organization, *IPEC Action Against Child Labour: Achievements, Lessons Learned and Indications for the Future 1998–1999* (Geneva: ILO, 1999); and International Labour Organization, *Helping Hands or Shackled Lives? Understanding Child Domestic Labour and Responses to It* (Geneva: ILO, 2004).

[98] International Labour Organization, *Helping Hands or Shackled Lives?*

[99] Kaushik Basu, "International Labor Standards and Child Labor," *Challenge* 42, no. 5 (September–October 1999): 80–93; and Miriam Wasserman, "Eliminating Child Labor," *Regional Review* 10, no. 2 (Second Quarter 2000): 8–17.

[100] Druscilla K. Brown, "Labor Standards: Where Do They Belong on the International Trade Agenda?" *Journal of Economic Perspectives* 15, no. 3 (Summer 2001): 89–112.

[101] For a discussion of the issues, see Kaushik Basu, "Child Labor: Cause, Consequence, and Cure, with Remarks on International Labor Standards," *Journal of Economic Literature* 37, no. 3 (September 1999): 1083–119.

[102] Kaushik Basu and Zafiris Tzannatos, "The Global Child Labor Problem: What Do We Know and What Can We Do?" *The World Bank Economic Review* 17, no. 2 (2003): 147–73; Basu, "Child Labor"; and Eric V. Edmonds and Nina Pavcnik, "Child Labor in the Global Economy, "*Journal of Economic Perspectives* 19, no. 1 (Winter 2005): 199–220.

for girls because employment as domestic workers is far less visible, a circumstance that makes these girls particularly vulnerable to exploitation. While child labor remains a serious problem in developing countries, it is at least encouraging that ongoing international efforts appear to be helping to reduce the worst forms of child labor.[103]

Microcredit for Women: Lifeline or Mirage?

Most people are well aware that in a modern economy, businesses, large and small, are heavily dependent on credit. Funds are needed to get an enterprise started, to keep it going, and often even more so to expand it to an efficient scale. In developing countries the amounts needed are often rather small, but have nonetheless been beyond the reach of millions of poor people, particularly poor women, who tend to lack contacts with potential lenders, have no collateral, and are generally regarded as poor credit risks. At the same time, demand for labor in large-scale agriculture continues to decline as a result of mechanization, and demand in the emerging modern sectors is frequently inadequate to absorb rapidly growing populations. Therefore it is not surprising that interest in self-employment has been growing as one solution to this problem, and in the role credit can play in facilitating it. In recent years, both governments and non-governmental organizations have recognized the contribution that the extension of even small loans could make toward increasing the earnings and raising the standard of living of the poor.[104]

Microcredit loans started with the Grameen Bank of Bangladesh in 1976. Subsequently similar institutions were founded in other developing countries, including Indonesia, India, and Peru.[105] In 2006, the founder of the Grameen Bank, Muhammad Yunus, along with the bank itself, received the Nobel Peace Prize in recognition of their efforts to improve the lives of poor women. Such programs now even operate in depressed areas of economically advanced countries, including the United States, as discussed in Chapter 11. Here, our focus is on the role of such programs in developing countries.

One of the distinctive features of microcredit institutions is that they mainly extend credit to women. While the proportion of women among those obtaining loans from commercial banks is rarely above 20 percent, it is about 70 percent among those who borrow from the poverty-centered development banks, and some of them make loans only to women. Local groups of borrowers guarantee one another's loans, and no one receives a second loan until all the first loans are repaid. This arrangement has led to high repayment rates, often an astonishing 90 percent, which have enabled these banks not only to continue but to expand.[106] In recent years, there has been a push for international agencies to channel funds to some of the "poorest of the poor" in these countries, those living on less than $1 per day. Since 2000, one-half of U.S. funds for international microenterprise programs have been mandated to be spent on this group. As of 2006, however, only 30 percent of such funds reached the very poor, thereby falling quite a bit short of the target.[107]

---

[103] For recent trends, see International Labour Organization, *The End of Child Labour.*

[104] Interestingly, there are historic precedents in nineteenth-century Europe of similar organizations that lasted for many decades. Aidan Hollis and Arthur Sweetman found that organizations that obtained funds from depositors, especially if they were also able to adjust interest rates, were more long lasting than those that relied on charity in "Microcredit: What Can We Learn from the Past?" *World Development* 26, no. 10 (October 1998): 1875–89.

[105] For an excellent review of the research on microcredit, see Beatriz Armendariz de Aghion and Jonathan Morduch, *The Economics of Microfinance* (Cambridge, MA: MIT Press, 2005).

[106] Figures are from Rosintan D. M. Panjaitan-Driodisuryo and Kathleen Cloud, "Gender, Self-Employment and Microcredit Programs: An Indonesian Case Study," *The Quarterly Review of Economics and Finance* 39 (Special Issue, 1999): 769–79; See also, Sengupta and Aubuchon, "The Microfinance Revolution."

[107] US AID, *Microenterprise Results Reporting*, Annual Report to Congress, Fiscal Year 2006 (June 2007).

Microcredit institutions provide loans for activities ranging from the processing and sale of food, the brewing of beer, and the production of a variety of crafts, to petty trade in other items and the provision of services to affluent households as well as larger businesses. Many of the credit institutions provide other useful services as well, such as providing technical information and offering workshops on what kind of business to start and how to run it, as well as some on broader topics related to improving literacy and health. Participants in such programs have an opportunity to share information and learn from one another.[108]

Studies on the impact of microcredit provide substantial evidence that the income of the women who were able to borrow these meager amounts rose perceptibly, and recent evidence further points to positive returns to the accompanying technical and social support assistance as well.[109] Among other encouraging effects, wives' participation in such programs has the added benefit of increasing their bargaining power in the family, and perhaps most important, leading to higher aspirations for their children's education.[110]

Even so, it would be a mistake to exaggerate the favorable effects of these programs or to ignore the reservations of critics. One of these points out that "most studies of microfinance programs have drawn their conclusions exclusively from successful borrowers in large, mature, and successful programs."[111] Also, a surprisingly large proportion of eligible women do not choose to participate in such programs. Further, some observers question whether shifting a part of the microcredit funds toward the poorest is the best allocation of limited resources because members of this group are likely to have greater difficulties in starting a successful enterprise than those in "near" poverty. Finally, the same group pressures that have been so successful in assuring high repayment rates can create serious hardships for women who have difficulty meeting these obligations.[112] Therefore, microcredit should not be viewed as a panacea for either poverty or women's inferior status. At the same time, any program that succeeds in mitigating the dire destitution and powerlessness of many women and helps to give their children a start toward a better life should not be heedlessly discarded, but should rather be seen as a useful first step toward solving these serious problems.

GENITAL MUTILATION AND PATRIARCHAL TRADITIONS

For some years, a rising tide of condemnation of the age-old practice of genital cutting of women has echoed from the podiums of United Nations assemblies in Vienna, Cairo, and Beijing. A host of individual countries, including the United States, have also condemned this practice. Genital cutting is frequently referred to as *female circumcision*, but is in fact far more drastic than that term implies. It dates back about

---

[108] Signe-Mary McKernan, "The Impact of Microcredit Programs on Self-Employment Profits: Do Noncredit Program Aspects Matter?" *The Review of Economics and Statistics* 84, no. 1 (February 2002): 93–115.

[109] For discussions of impacts, see, for instance, Amendariz de Aghion and Morduch, *The Economics of Microfinance;* and McKernan, "The Impact of Microcredit Programs."

[110] Simeen Mahmud, "Actually How Empowering Is Microcredit?" *Development and Change* 34, no. 4 (September 2003): 577–605; and Panjaitan-Driodisuryo and Cloud, "Gender, Self-Employment and Microcredit Programs."

[111] Michael J. V. Woolcock, "What Unsuccessful Cases Tell Us About How Group-Based Programs Work," *American Journal of Economics and Sociology* 58, no. 1 (January 1999): 17–42. Quote is from p. 36.

[112] These various criticisms are raised in Timothy G. Evans, Alayne M. Adams, Rafi Mohammed, and Alison H. Norris, "Demystifying Nonparticipation in Microcredit: A Population-Based Analysis," *World Development* 27, no. 2 (February 1999): 419–30; McKernan, "The Impact of Microcredit Programs on Self-Employment"; Celia W. Dugger, "Debate Stirs over Tiny Loans for World's Poorest," *New York Times*, April 29, 2004; and Aminur Rahman, "Microcredit Initiatives for Equitable and Sustainable Development: Who Pays?" *World Development* 27, no. 1 (January 1999): 67–82.

2,000 years and continues to be widespread in some parts of the world. It is, undoubtedly, one more indication of the strength of patriarchal tradition and of women's subservient status in the 28 countries where it is practiced.* It is most prevalent among Muslims but is also common among Christians and followers of traditional African religions; it most generally occurs among the illiterate, but it is by no means unknown among those with some education, nor among emigrants from countries where cutting was traditionally practiced. The proportion of women subjected to cutting ranges from 6 in 1,000 in Uganda to over 90 out of 100 women in six countries, including Egypt, Mali, and Somalia. In these countries, the practice is deeply entrenched and even accepted by a substantial number of women. At the same time, there is increasing awareness that women who are cut suffer excruciating pain, because the operation is usually performed without any kind of anesthetic and that they are deprived of normal sexual pleasure for the remainder of their lives. There are also reports that suggest that they frequently experience complicated deliveries, and even that some die as a result of this procedure.

Public interest in the United States was first aroused by the story of Fauzija Kassindja, who arrived in this country on December 17, 1994, after fleeing her native Togo to avoid forced genital cutting.** As it turned out, she spent more than a year in prison before a precedent-setting decision by the highest administrative tribunal in the immigration system reversed the decision of an immigration judge who had dismissed her story because he did not believe it and considered it irrational. As a result of publicity about this case and growing social awareness of the problem, support for action on this matter grew, and in 1995 the Immigration and Naturalization Service (INS) introduced guidelines that advise asylum officers that gender-based persecution is a valid ground for asylum. Further, in 1996 Congress outlawed the practice of genital cutting in the United States. Still, this issue is not fully resolved. Advocates for refugees and some members of Congress remain adamant that current INS guidelines for those seeking asylum in the United States are insufficient because judges continue to have discretion over whether to grant asylum.

One particularly vocal opponent of genital cutting is former supermodel Waris Dirie, who spent her early life as a nomad in Somalia and was herself subjected to genital mutilation. In addition to serving as a Special U.N. Ambassador on this issue, she coauthored a book titled *Desert Flower: The Extraordinary Journey of a Desert Nomad* that tells of her horrifying experience. Indeed, a growing awareness that genital mutilation is a form of violence against women led half of the 28 countries where it was widely practiced to take action to ban this practice, though it remains to be seen whether these governmental actions will substantially reduce the practice. Another critical step is for economically advanced countries to follow suit and impose a ban so that this practice is not further perpetuated by migrants from these countries. Such countries where genital mutilation is banned include the United States, Canada, Australia, and New Zealand, as well as many, though not all, countries in Western Europe.***

*The figures in this inset are from the World Health Organization, *Eliminating Gender Mutilation: An Interagency Statement* (Geneva: WHO, 2008). For more details regarding this practice, see Tina Rosenberg, "Mutilating Africa's Daughters: Laws Unenforced, Practices Unchanged," *New York Times,* July 5, 2004; Waris Dirie and Catherine Miller, *Desert Flower: The Extraordinary Journey of a Desert Nomad* (New York: William Morrow & Co, 1998); and Sara Corbett, "A Cutting Tradition: Inside a Female-Circumcision Ceremony for Young Muslim Girls, *New York Times Magazine,* January 20, 2008, pp. 45–52.

**Celia W. Dugger, "A Refugee's Body Is Intact but Her Family Is Torn," *New York Times,* September 11, 1996, pp. A1, B6–B7; and Celia W. Dugger, "Woman Betrayed by Loved Ones Mourns a Double Loss," *New York Times,* September 11, 1996, p. B7.

***World Health Organization, "Female Genital Mutiliation—New Knowledge Spurs Optimism," in *Progress in Sexual and Reproductive Health Research,* no. 72 (2006).

Summary on Women and Economic Development

Women in developing countries continue to face tremendous challenges, but at the same time it would be a mistake to overlook the tremendous progress made over the last several decades. As we emphasized, the gender gap in schooling continues to decline with the growing recognition, both by individual governments and international organizations, that resources devoted to the advancement of women have a greater payoff than many other types of investments, and that economic growth is more rapid when gender inequality is reduced. Therefore, the emphasis of development policies may be expected to further shift in this direction. Further, women have been gaining greater control over their own fertility. Looking forward, it is important to keep in mind that women's empowerment depends not only on policies that directly facilitate women's entry into the labor market but also on policies that encourage overall economic development.

COUNTRIES OF THE FORMER SOVIET BLOC

The economies of the countries that were formerly part of the Union of Soviet Socialist Republics (USSR) and the countries in Central and Eastern Europe (CEE) that were part of the "Soviet bloc" have undergone a major transition in the last 20 years.[113] The transition began with Lech Walesa and his union movement in Poland in the middle of the 1980s, followed by the "Velvet Revolution" in Czechoslovakia, the fall of the Berlin Wall in 1989, and finally the dissolution of the USSR shortly thereafter. These countries shifted from an economic system of central planning and public ownership of resources, to a market system with largely private ownership. Perhaps not surprisingly, the speed and manner of these changes varied considerably.[114] Today, these **transition economies** continue to face challenges that are more or less unique to them, much as developing countries did many years after colonialism ended.

During the time of the dominance of the USSR, its government and those of its satellites officially subscribed to Marxist ideology, including Marxist views concerning the role of women. The leaders of the Communist revolution in Russia at the end of World War I, whose ideas initially dominated the USSR, espoused the notion that the abolition of private property and class structure is both necessary and sufficient for achieving equality between women and men. Consistent with these views, they initially struck down all legal discrimination against women, mandated equal treatment of men and women in the educational system and in the labor market, introduced family laws that made the marriage contract egalitarian, and not only legalized abortion, but made it readily available. Although legislation concerning abortion was later modified,[115] in other respects the dominant ideology of the Soviet bloc remained unchanged as long as the USSR lasted.

Because, for the most part, there was not only full employment but often a labor shortage, doctrinal belief in labor force participation of women was reinforced by the

---

[113] In addition to Russia, the USSR included Armenia, Azerbaijan, Belarus, Estonia, Georgia, Kazakhstan, Kyrgyzstan, Latvia, Lithuania, Moldova, Tajikistan, Turkmenistan, Ukraine, and Uzbekistan. The Soviet Bloc included the USSR, Bulgaria, Czechoslovakia (now the Czech Republic and Slovakia), Hungary, the German Democratic Republic (now part of Germany), Poland, Romania, and for some time, Albania. The former Yugoslavia was also a communist state in this region, though not officially part of the Soviet Bloc.

[114] For more information on the economic transition in the various countries, see Jan Svejnar, "Transition Economies: Performance and Challenges," *Journal of Economic Perspectives* 16, no. 1 (Winter 2002): 3–28; and Andrei Shleifer and Daniel Treisman, "A Normal Country: Russia After Communism," *Journal of Economic Perspectives* 19, no. 1 (Winter 2005): 151–74.

[115] During the Stalinist period abortions were made illegal, and later, when there was concern about the low birth rate, pronatalist policies were introduced.

need for them in order to achieve the rapid industrialization that was the main goal of the regime. For the same reason, however, little progress was made in "socializing housework," although, as mentioned in the brief discussion of Marxist views of the family in Chapter 3, this was the solution the Soviets proposed for women's "double burden."

In practice, however, much housework still needed to be done. Although good child care was provided, at least for children 3 years of age and older,[116] housekeeping was, for the most part, more demanding than in capitalist countries. There were frequently long lines in stores where necessities had to be purchased, and many of the appliances middle-class households in economically advanced countries have long taken for granted were often not available. Women were told that these problems would be taken care of as soon as higher-priority goals had been achieved but that day never came. Thus, housekeeping continued to be a major burden, and one that rested squarely on the shoulders of women. Although women were now expected to be workers as well as homemakers, there was no equivalent recognition that men could be homemakers as well as workers, and sharing of household responsibilities was never part of the official ideology. Data from the 1980s, the last decade of the Soviet Union, show that despite women's high rates of labor market activity, women still spent 2.3 times as much time on housework as men, a figure slightly higher than that for the United States during the same period.[117]

The results of this mixed situation were, inevitably, also mixed. On the one hand, the status of women was clearly better than it had been in earlier days, and in some respects it compared favorably with that of women in the economically advanced countries in the West. For instance, women's labor force participation rate of nearly 80 percent was well in excess of the rates in most economically advanced countries.[118] Also, occupational segregation declined, and both the amount and the kind of education women received more nearly approximated that of men. On the other hand, women still continued to be concentrated in low-status, low-paying occupations, as well as in lower levels of the hierarchies within occupations, and the earnings gap appeared to be within the same range as that in market economies.[119] Nor did women succeed in penetrating the top echelons of the powerful government hierarchy.

Thus, the Marxist solution to "the woman question" left something to be desired, even in principle, and was far from satisfactory in practice. Consequently, most women in the Soviet orbit came to see their greater participation in paid work not as a right but rather as an obligation dictated by an oppressive regime and, in the satellite countries, one that was imposed by a foreign power. By the same token, many women came to have an idealized view of the family as a refuge from the harsh realities of a world that was not of their own making.

The cataclysmic events that culminated in the end of Soviet domination in Central and Eastern Europe and then subsequently the dissolution of the Soviet Union ushered in a new political and economic era. It was widely assumed that many women would retreat to their more traditional roles as homemakers and that women's labor force participation would decline substantially, all the more so because of higher unemployment rates, cuts in public child care, and in many cases, the failure of governments to enforce

---

[116] For further information see Tatyana Teplova, "Welfare State Transformation, Childcare, and Women's Work in Russia," *Social Politics* 14, no. 3 (Fall 2007): 284–322.

[117] Figures are from Thomas Juster and Frank P. Stafford, "The Allocation of Time: Empirical Findings, Behavioral Models, and Problems of Measurement," *Journal of Economic Literature* 29 (June 1991): 477.

[118] Elizabeth Brainerd, "Women in Transition: Changes in Gender Wage Differentials in Eastern Europe and the Former Soviet Union," *Industrial and Labor Relations Review* 54, no. 1 (October 2000): 138–62.

[119] For a comparison of women's earnings and labor market activity before and shortly after the economic transition, see UNICEF, "Women in Transition," Chaps. 2 and 3. For evidence from earlier years, see Jacob Mincer, "Inter-Country Comparisons of Labor Force Trends and of Related Developments: An Overview," in *Trends in Women's Work, Education, and Family Building*, edited by Richard Layard and Jacob Mincer, *Journal of Labor Economics* 3, no. 1, pt. 2 (January 1985).

women's right to have their jobs held open during maternity and child care leaves. In fact, data from 1990 (around the start of the transition) through 2004 indicate that although women's labor force participation rates declined somewhat more than men's in some of these countries, no "tectonic shift" occurred in the gender ratio in participation rates.[120]

Many families in the transition economies also face new challenges trying to balancing paid work and family because of the shift from public enterprises to private firms. In Russia, for instance, there has been a "practical collapse" in the number of public child care centers, combined with very little privately provided child care.[121] Further some private firms are hiring women using "informal contracts" to avoid the costs of social benefit programs, while others may be avoiding hiring women altogether.[122] At least partly related to the changing economic structure and instability, and also perhaps due to changes in family policies, fertility rates have fallen well below the replacement-rate level in virtually of all the countries of the former Soviet bloc.[123] Another notable demographic change is the fall in life expectancy for women and men in Russia, along with some of the other countries in this region. In this regard, men have borne a disproportionate negative impact, largely attributed to rising rates of alcoholism and the consequences of stress.[124]

The effect of economic restructuring on the gender wage ratio has varied widely in the countries of the former Soviet bloc. Women in Russia and the Ukraine experienced a decline in their wages relative to men's, largely as a result of widening wage inequality in these countries while women in Central and East European countries (e.g., the Czech Republic, Hungary, and Poland) fared considerably better. Wage inequality also widened in these countries, but it appears that the gender earnings ratio increased because of the rise in the return to women's labor market skills.[125] In East Germany, however, the increase in the gender earnings ratio came at the expense of women's reduced employment.[126] In sum, this varied evidence suggests that it would be a mistake to try to generalize about how women are faring over the course of the economic transition.

For a long time, feminist movements fared poorly in these countries mainly because they shared the goal of equality in the labor market with the Communist regimes. Increasingly, however, women in the countries of the former Soviet bloc, particularly highly educated professional women, are coming to recognize to what extent they share the same problems that feminists struggle with in the rest of the world, and particularly in economically advanced countries.[127] This process has been hastened by the entry of nine

---

[120] Quoted phrase is from UNICEF, "Women in Transition," p. 26 regarding the period of 1990 through the late 1990s. Data for a longer period, 1990 to 2004 yield a similar conclusion. See UNIFEM, "The Story Behind the Numbers." See also Marni Lazreg, ed., *Making the Transition Work for Women in Europe and Central Asia* (Washington, DC: World Bank, 2000); and Pierella Paci, *Gender in Transition* (Washington, DC: World Bank, 2002).

[121] Quoted material is from Teplova, "Welfare State Transformation," p. 292. The particularly serious difficulties of single mothers are discussed in Judith Record McKinney, "Lone Mothers in Russia: Soviet and Post-Soviet Policy," *Feminist Economics* 10, no. 2 (July 2004): 37–60.

[122] Tatyana Teplova and Frances Woolley, "Balancing Work and Care in the Post-Soviet Russian Labor Market," Carleton University Working Paper (April 2005).

[123] Exceptions are a few Central Asian nations, including Turkmenistan, Azerbaijan, and Kyrgyzstan.

[124] World Bank, *Millennium Development Goals: Progress and Prospects in Europe and Central Asia* (Washington, DC: World Bank, 2005); and Elizabeth Brainerd and David M. Cutler, "Autopsy on an Empire: Understanding Mortality in Russia and the Former Soviet Union," *Journal of Economic Perspectives* 19, no. 1 (Winter 2005): 107–30. For trends, see World Bank, *World Bank Indicators*.

[125] Brainerd, "Women in Transition: Changes in Gender Wage Differentials." For evidence on changes in the gender gap unadjusted for human capital and other factors, see UNIFEM, "The Story Behind the Numbers."

[126] Jennifer Hunt, "The Transition in East Germany: When Is a Ten-Point Fall in the Gender Wage Gap Bad News?" *Journal of Labor Economics* 20, no. 1 (January 2002): 148–68.

[127] See articles on "Feminist and Economic Inquiry in Central and Easter Europe," edited by Marianne A. Ferber and Edith Kuiper, *Feminist Economics* 10, no. 3 (November 2004): 81–118.

countries of the former Soviet bloc into the European Union (EU), further linking the interests of women who formerly lived under different regimes.[128] Notably, many women's groups in the countries of the former Soviet bloc have been agitating against restrictions on the right to abortions and have been putting up stiff resistance against the elimination of such family-friendly policies as child care and generous paid maternity leave.[129]

COUNTRIES OF THE MIDDLE EAST AND NORTH AFRICA

The countries of the Middle East and North Africa vary considerably as a consequence of their diverse history and experiences as well as due to differences in their natural resources, culture, government, and religion.[130] Thus, it is to be expected that the status of women and economic opportunities for women and men within this region differ as well. Therefore, care must be taken when making sweeping generalizations about patterns in this region.

Some of the countries in the region have colonial legacies while others do not. For instance, Syria and Lebanon were previously under French control and Iraq, Jordan, and Egypt have a British legacy. Turkey, on other hand, remained independent. Some have a history of hereditary rulers, such as the Saudi royal family, while others have experienced a variety of political regimes, notably Iran, including monarchy and most recently an Islamic Republic.

Similarly, resources vary considerably among these countries. Many, though not all of the nations in this region, have considerable reserves of oil and gas as well as other natural resources. Oil has made some of them among the richest nations in the world, such as Saudi Arabia and the Gulf states, including the United Arab Emirates, Oman, and Kuwait. However, economic growth of these countries has, for the most part, been unbalanced with a primary focus on extractive industries. Other countries, among the most populous in the region, such as Egypt, Jordan, Morocco, and Tunisia lack such natural resources.[131] Israel, a Jewish state, also located in this region, is a high-income country with a highly diversified economy. It is fairly similar to other economically advanced countries in other regions of the world. Thus, here we focus on the other countries in the Middle East and North Africa.

---

[128] These countries are Bulgaria, Czech Republic, Estonia, Hungary, Latvia, Lithuania, Poland, Romania, and Slovakia. Countries joining the EU are expected to "harmonize" their policies, including those regarding gender equality. See Nicholas Barr, ed. *Labor Markets and Social Policy: The Accession and Beyond* (Washington, DC: World Bank, 2005).

[129] See Marianne A. Ferber and Edith Kuiper, "Introduction" and other contributions, in "Exploration in Feminist and Economic Inquiry in Central and Easter Europe," edited by Marianne A. Ferber and Edith Kuiper, *Feminist Economics* 10, no. 3 (November 2004): 81–118.

[130] The Middle East is typically defined to include Algeria, Bahrain, Egypt, Jordan, Iran, Iraq, Israel, Kuwait, Lebanon, Libya, Morocco, Oman, Qatar, Saudi Arabia, Syria, Tunisia, Turkey, United Arab Emirates, West Bank and Gaza, and Yemen. See, for instance, World Bank, *World Development Indicators* (2007); and Farzaneh Roudi-Fahimi and Mary Mederios Kent, "Challenges and Opportunities—The Population of the Middle East and North Africa," *Population Bulletin* 62, no 2 (June 2007). Jennifer Olmsted suggests that the term *Middle East* is a legacy of the colonialist period and that "Southwest Asia" would be better. See Olmsted, "Economic History, Middle East and North Africa," in *The Elgar Companion to Feminist Economics*, edited by Janice Peterson and Margaret Lewis (Cheltenham, UK and Northhampton, MA, USA: Edward Elgar, 1999), pp. 219–26. This section draws on Nikki R. Keddie, *Women in the Middle East: Past and Present* (Princeton and Oxford: Princeton University Press, 2007); and Roudi-Fahimi and Kent, "Challenges and Opportunities."

[131] Karen Pfeifer and Marsha P. Posusney, "Arab Economies and Globalization: An Overview," in *Women and Globalization in the Arab Middle East*, edited by Eleanor A. Doumato and Marsha P. Posusney (Boulder and London: Lynne Rienner Publishers, 2003), pp. 25–54. See also Tarik M. Yousef, "Development, Growth and Policy Reform in the Middle East and North Africa," *Journal of Economic Perspectives* 18, no. 3 (Summer 2004): 91–116.

The countries in the Middle East and North Africa are predominantly Islamic (with the obvious exception of Israel), although religion in the region is not entirely monolithic, not even among people who classify themselves as Arabs.[132] Some Islamic countries are predominantly Shia, while others are Sunni, and in Lebanon about 40 percent of the population is Christian. One common feature of virtually all of the countries in the region is the growth in political Islam since the 1970s. This development is generally attributed to their history as colonies of Western countries, and more recently also to their high rates of unemployment and a lack of economic opportunities, as well as to "growing hostility to the West and to Israel."[133] Most notably, Iran became an Islamic Republic in 1979 after the overthrow of the Shah, and recently, Hamas, an Islamic group, won a majority in the 2006 election in Gaza.

In most of the predominately Muslim countries, laws governing marriage, divorce, child custody, and inheritance follow Islamic law to a greater or lesser extent. These laws, like orthdox Jewish and fundamentalist Christian laws, restrict women's rights. Turkey, Tunisia, and since 2004, Morocco, are important exceptions, and have family (personal status) laws that are much more favorable to women.[134] Regarding the recent legal changes in Morocco, Valentine Moghadam and Farzaneh Roudi-Fahimi write: "The Moroccan case is a striking example of how women's rights advocates can build coalitions to generate social dialogue, affect key policy debates, help reform laws, and change public policy."[135] They also note another positive sign in this regard, namely that a majority of the countries in the Middle East and North Africa regions have now ratified the United Nations CEDAW. Nevertheless, most of these countries signed with reservations that limit its potential to change women's status.

Given this considerable diversity, it is not surprising that women's economic progress in the region is mixed. Female illiteracy rates remain high as compared to many regions of the world, not only compared to the economically advanced countries where rates are generally less than 2 percent, but also compared to all but the poorest developing countries in the rest of the world. Nevertheless, rates have fallen considerably since 1980. For instance, in the developing countries of the Middle East and North Africa region, the female illiteracy rate declined from 72 to 39 percent between 1980 and 2006. Generally, female illiteracy rates in the region are lower in the higher-income countries, including Israel and Kuwait, though a notable exception is Saudi Arabia, where the rate stands at 31 percent.[136] Fertility has also substantially decreased in virtually all Middle East countries, partly related to increases in women's educational attainment, but perhaps even more because of increased access to health care and birth control.[137] A few of these countries even have a fertility rate below or near replacement level.

---

[132] Further not all of the countries in the Middle East and North Africa region, excluding Israel, are members of the League of Arab States. Neither Iran nor Turkey is a member. On the other hand, Sudan and Mauritania are examples of countries that are members of the Arab League but are not included in the Middle East and North Africa region. See http://www.britannica.com.

[133] See Keddie, "Women in the Middle East," p. 106 and pp. 160–165. See also, Suha Sabbagh, ed. "Introduction: The Debate on Arab Women," in *Arab Women: Between Defiance and Restraint* (New York: Olive Branch Press, 1996).

[134] Valentine M. Moghadam and Farzaneh Roudi-Fahimi, "Reforming Family Laws to Promote Progress in the Middle East and North Africa," *MENA Policy Brief* (Washington, DC: Population Reference Bureau), December 2005.

[135] Moghadam and Roudi-Fahimi, "Reforming Family Laws," p. 6.

[136] Marianne A. Ferber and Michael Brun, "Men's and Women's Literacy Rates in Developing Countries," Working Paper, University of Illinois at Urbana-Champaign (2008). See also Jennifer Olmsted, "Gender, Aging and the Evolving Arab Patriarchal Contract," *Feminist Economics* 11, no. 2 (July 2005): 53–78.

[137] World Bank, "Gender in Mena," *Sector Brief* (Washington, DC: World Bank), 2007; and Frazaneh Roudi-Fahimi, "Islam and Family Planning," *MENA Policy Brief* (Washington, DC: Population Reference Bureau), 2004.

However, women's labor force participation in the countries of this region is still lagging, although it has increased in some instances. Although the religion of Islam and the generally patriarchal nature of the society in many of these countries (the prohibition in Saudi Arabia against women driving provides a notable example) are among the reasons typically cited,[138] they are likely not the sole causes. For one, there are other countries with large Islamic populations, such as Indonesia, with substantially higher rates of female labor force participation than in most countries in the Middle East and North Africa. As shown in Table 12-1, women's labor force participation rate stood at 53 percent in Indonesia, as compared with the average for the developing countries in the Middle East and North Africa of 32 percent.[139] Another explanation that has been proffered is the often unbalanced nature of the economic growth occurring in the region. Extractive industries, such as oil, minerals and gas, which dominate many of the economies of the Middle East, tend to offer women fewer employment opportunities than are provided by countries with a more balanced economic structure. Also, men's higher incomes in the oil-rich countries reduce the economic incentive for women's employment.[140]

Even for those women who are in the labor force, employment in sectors other than agriculture remains quite low compared to that in other regions.[141] Moreover, those women who find employment outside of agriculture tend to be in jobs in the public sector. Thus, gender segregation by industry and occupation remains substantial.[142] Women, especially those with higher education, must also confront unemployment rates that considerably exceed those of men.[143] This lack of progress in employment represents lost economic opportunity because this valuable resource is not being put to its best use.[144] Women's participation in the political arena is also very low compared to other regions.

In sum, the evidence indicates that women's economic status in the Middle East and North Africa tends to lag behind women's progress in other regions. This generalization should not, however, lead us to overlook such progress that has occurred. For instance, family law has been liberalized in Morocco, and there are now even nonfamily arrangements to care for the elderly in some of these countries.[145] Also, women's educational attainment has risen, along with more modest increases in women's participation rates, though levels remain low, and fertility has been declining at least somewhat in most countries in the region.

---

[138] Olmsted, "Gender, Aging, and the Evolving Arab Patriarchal Contract."

[139] Jennifer Olmsted, "Reexamining the Fertility Puzzle in MENA," in *Women and Globalization in the Arab Middle East*, edited by Eleanor A. Doumato and Marsha P. Posusney (Boulder and London: Lynne Rienner Publishers, 2003), pp. 25–54.

[140] Olmsted, "Gender, Aging and the Evolving Arab Patriarchal Contract." In a related paper, Michael Ross argues that the oil-centered economies of the Middle East, which largely employ men, also inhibit progress toward equality for women because women's greater labor force participation would help to change their self-identity and ultimately lead to increased political power. See "Oil, Islam and Women," *American Political Science Review* 102, no. 1 (February 2008): 107–23.

[141] World Bank, "Gender in MENA," p. 107.

[142] Yousef, "Development, Growth and Policy Reform"; Valentine M. Moghadam, "Women, Work, and Economic Restructuring: A Regional Overview," in *The Economics of Women and Work in the Middle East and North Africa, Research in Middle East Economics*, vol. 4, edited by E. Mine Cinar (Amsterdam, New York and London: Elsevier Science, JAI, 2001); and Zafiris Tzannatos and Iqbal Kaur, "Women in the MENA Labor Market," in *Women and Globalization in the Arab Middle East*, edited by Eleanor A. Doumato and Marsha P. Posusney (Boulder and London: Lynne Rienner Publishers, 2003), pp. 55–72.

[143] World Bank, "Gender in MENA"; and Yousef, "Development, Growth and Policy Reform," p. 103.

[144] UNDP, *The Arab Human Development Report*, 2005: *Toward the Rise of Women in the Arab World*; and "Saudi King's Daughter Urges Including Women in Decisionmaking," *BBC Monitoring*, March 20, 2007.

[145] Olmsted, "Gender, Aging, and the Evolving Arab Patriarchal Contract."

Conclusion

In this chapter, we found that, outside the economically advanced countries and most of the countries of the former Soviet bloc, women generally have lower educational attainment than men. The gender difference is largest in many of the poorest developing countries and the countries of the Middle East and North Africa. Women also tend to earn less, are generally segregated into different occupations, and hold fewer government positions. International differences in these outcomes are the result of a variety of economic factors, as well as government policies, social custom, ideology, and religion. Women's status continues to be particularly precarious in many of the developing countries, but almost everywhere there has been some improvement.

We also discussed how government can play a crucial role in promoting education and women's participation in the labor market. In many of the developing countries, governments are making efforts to expand educational opportunity for women. In a number of economically advanced countries, notably the Nordic countries and particularly Sweden, governments have, with considerable success, used a variety of policies to encourage women's labor force participation, while also making it possible for them to take care of their families. Even there, the situation is still far from perfect, mainly because occupational segregation remains high and housework continues to be divided quite unequally. Nonetheless, our review leads us to be cautiously optimistic about the outlook for women throughout the world, and specifically about the possibility of government playing a constructive role in advancing their status.

Questions for Review and Discussion

1. To what extent are comparisons of women's labor force participation among various countries a reliable indicator of women's contributions to the standard of living in those countries?

2. As seen in Table 12-2, women's labor force participation rates in economically advanced countries vary considerably. What economic and noneconomic factors might help to explain this disparity?

3. What are some specific policies that might improve women's well-being in the poorest countries? What are the difficulties and challenges entailed in undertaking them?

4. How does the experience of women living in the United States, Sweden, and Japan compare in terms of the following?

   a. Labor force participation
   b. Occupational segregation
   c. Gender wage ratio
   d. Housework

5. Occupational segregation by sex in Sweden is very high, and yet it has the smallest gender earnings gap of any economically advanced country in the world. "This proves that occupational segregation does not reduce women's earnings relative to the earnings of men." Evaluate the validity of this statement.

6. A number of countries have policies intended to encourage people to have larger families, while others offer inducements to reduce family size. Would you favor either policy for the United States? Why or why not?

7. It is widely believed that government investments in women's education result in societal as well as private benefits. Discuss each. Such investments are particularly important in developing countries. Why?

8. Some occupations are predominantly female in some countries and predominantly male in others. What factors might help to explain these differences?

9. Apart from religion, what other factors affect women's experiences and opportunities in the Middle East and North Africa?

Suggested Readings

Banerjee, Abhijit V., and Esther Duflo, "The Economic Lives of the Poor." *Journal of Economic Perspectives* 21, no. 1 (Winter 2007): 141–67.

Blau, Francine D., and Lawrence M. Kahn, "Gender Differences in Pay." *Journal of Economic Perspectives* 14, no. 4 (Fall 2000): 75–100.

Blau, Francine D., and Lawrence M. Kahn, "Women and Wages." In *New Palgrave Dictionary of Economics*, 2nd edition. (2008).

Boserup, Ester. *Women's Role in Economic Development.* New York: St. Martin's Press, 1970.

Brainerd, Elizabeth. "Women in Transition: Changes in Gender Wage Differentials in Eastern Europe and the Former Soviet Union." *Industrial and Labor Relations Review* 54, no. 1 (October 2000): 138–62.

Duflo, Esther. "Gender Equality in Development." MIT Working Paper (December 2005).

Einhorn, Barbara. *Citizenship in an Enlarging Europe.* Palgrave Macmillan, 2006.

Gornick, Janet C., and Marcia K. Meyers. *Families That Work: Policies for Reconciling Parenthood and Employment.* New York: Russell Sage Foundation, 2003.

Gregory, Mary. "Gender and Economic Inequality." In *Oxford Handbook on Economic Inequality*, edited by Wiemer Salverda, Brian Nolan, and Timothy M. Smeeding. Oxford: Oxford University Press, 2009.

Jacquette, Jane S., and Gale Summerfield, eds. *Women and Gender Equity: Development Theory and Practice.* Durham, NC and London: Duke University Press, 2006.

Keddie, Nikki R. *Women in the Middle East: Past and Present.* Princeton, NJ: Princeton University Press, 2007.

Mammen, Kristin, and Christina Paxson. "Women's Work and Economic Development." *Journal of Economic Perspectives* 14, no. 4 (Fall 2000): 141–64.

Melkas, Helina, and Richard Anker. *Towards Gender Equity in Japanese and Nordic Labour Markets: A Tale of Two Paths.* Geneva: International Labour Organization, 2003.

Rosenbluth, Frances McCall, ed. *The Political Economy of Japan's Low Fertility.* Stanford, CA: Stanford University Press, 2007.

Sainsbury, Diane, ed. *Gender and Welfare State Regimes.* Oxford: Oxford University Press, 1999.

Schultz, T. Paul, ed. *Investment in Women's Human Capital.* Chicago: University of Chicago Press, 1995.

Strober, Myra H., and Agnes Miling Kaneko Chan. *The Road Winds Uphill All the Way: Gender, Work, and Family in the United States and Japan.* Cambridge, MA: MIT Press, 1999.

Key Terms

United Nations Millennium Summit 349

developing countries 354

polygyny 356

brideprice 356

CEDAW 362

sex ratio 363

missing women 363

dowry 363

family policies 364

antidiscrimination legislation 365

family leave 365

wage-setting institutions 366

comparable worth 374

one-child policy 383

child labor 384

worst forms of child labor 384

transition economies 389

AUTHOR INDEX

SUBJECT INDEX